Volkswagen

Dasher

Service Manual
1974/1975/1976/1977/1978/1979
Including Diesel

Complete Service Manuals Published by Robert Bentley, Inc.

Volkswagen Beetle and Karmann Ghia Official Service Manual Type 1: 1966–1969. Volkswagen of America

Volkswagen Super Beetle, Beetle and Karmann Ghia Official Service Manual Type 1: 1970–1979. Volkswagen of America

Volkswagen Station Wagon/Bus Official Service Manual Type 2: 1968–1979. Volkswagen of America

Volkswagen Fastback and Squareback Official Service Manual Type 3: 1968–1973. Volkswagen of America

Volkswagen Dasher Service Manual: 1974–1979. Robert Bentley

Volkswagen Rabbit/Scirocco Service Manual: 1975–1979, Gasoline Models. Robert Bentley

Volkswagen Rabbit/Scirocco Service Manual: 1980, Gasoline Models. Robert Bentley

Volkswagen Rabbit Diesel Service Manual: 1977–1980. Robert Bentley

Audi Fox Service Manual: 1973–1979. Robert Bentley

Capri Complete Service Manual: 1970–1975. Robert Bentley

Toyota Corolla 1600 Service Manual: 1975–1979. Robert Bentley

Complete Official Triumph TR2 & TR3: 1953–1961. Includes Driver's Instruction Book and Service Instruction Manual. British Leyland Motors

Complete Official Triumph TR4 & TR4A: 1961–1968. Includes Driver's Handbook, Workshop Manual, Competition Preparation Manual. British Leyland Motors

Complete Official Triumph GT6, GT6+ & GT6 Mk III: 1967–1973. Includes Driver's Handbook and Workshop Manual. British Leyland Motors

Complete Official Triumph TR6 & TR250: 1967–1976. Includes Driver's Handbook and Workshop Manual. British Leyland Motors

Complete Official Triumph Spitfire Mk III, Mk IV & 1500: 1968–1974. Includes Driver's Handbook and Workshop Manual. British Leyland Motors

Complete Official Triumph Spitfire 1500: 1975–1979. Includes Driver's Handbook and Workshop Manual. British Leyland Motors

Complete Official Triumph TR7: 1975–1979. Includes Driver's Handbook and Workshop Manual. British Leyland Motors

Complete Official Austin-Healey 100-Six and 3000: 1956–1968. British Leyland Motors

MG Workshop Manual: Complete Tuning and Maintenance for All Models from "M"-Type to TF 1500. W.E. Blower

Complete Official MGB: 1962–1974. Includes Driver's Handbook, Workshop Manual, Special Tuning Manual. British Leyland Motors

Complete Official MGB: 1975–1979. Includes Driver's Handbook and Workshop Manual. British Leyland Motors

Complete Official Jaguar "E." Includes Driver's Handbook, Workshop Manual, Special Tuning Manual. British Leyland Motors

Complete Official 948cc & 1098cc Sprite/Midget. Includes Driver's Handbook, Workshop Manual, Special Tuning Manual. British Leyland Motors

Complete Official 1275cc Sprite/Midget: 1967–1974. Includes Driver's Handbook, Workshop Manual, Emission Control Supplement. British Leyland Motors

Complete Official MG Midget 1500: 1975–1979. Includes Driver's Handbook and Workshop Manual. British Leyland Motors

Volkswagen Dasher

Service Manual
1974/1975/1976/1977/1978/1979
Including Diesel

Robert Bentley
Cambridge, Massachusetts

Published and distributed by

Robert Bentley, Inc.
872 Massachusetts Avenue
Cambridge, Massachusetts 02139

Copies of this Manual may be purchased from authorized Volkswagen dealers, from selected booksellers and automotive accessories and parts dealers, or directly from the publisher by mail.

Readers' and users' comments have been a valuable aid in the preparation and revision of this and other service manuals. The publisher encourages and invites readers and users to send in their criticisms and suggestions for use in future manuals and revisions.

All information in this Manual is based on the latest product information available from Volkswagen at the time of printing. Volkswagen has not reviewed and does not vouch for the accuracy of the technical specifications and procedures described and given. The publisher has made every effort to present accurate instructions and specifications but cannot be responsible for any errors in the Manual.

Library of Congress Catalog Card No. 79-53188
ISBN 0-8376-0086-3
Third Revised Edition
10 9 8 7 6 5 4 3 2 1

LPV 997 333

Manufactured in the United States of America

FOREWORD

The Volkswagen Dasher is a thoroughly modern automobile that has set new standards worldwide for outstanding economy and performance. Though its exceptional style and handling have made the Dasher a great favorite with automobile enthusiasts, its sportiness has been achieved without a sacrifice of dignity. This same air of dignity and refinement, together with luxurious appointments and ample interior room, has also brought the Dasher broad acceptance among everyday drivers who are interested primarily in practical and efficient transportation.

This VW Dasher Service Manual covers the Dasher two-door sedans, four-door sedans, and station wagons sold in the United States and Canada for the Model Years 1974, 1975, 1976, 1977, 1978, and 1979—including those with diesel engines. The chassis numbers assigned to VW Dasher two-door sedans, four-door sedans, and station wagons during these model years are:

Two-door Sedan/Four-door Sedan	Station Wagon
1974: 324 2000 001 to 324 2500 000	1974: 334 2070 237 to 334 2300 000
1975: 325 2000 001 to 325 2300 000	1975: 335 2000 001 to 335 2300 000
1976: 326 2000 001 to 326 2300 000	1976: 336 2000 001 to 336 2300 000
1977: 327 2000 001 to 327 2300 000	1977: 337 2000 001 to 337 2300 000
1978: 328 2000 001 to 328 2300 000	1978: 338 2000 001 to 338 2300 000
1979: 329 2000 001 to 329 2300 000	1979: 339 2000 001 to 339 2300 000

The chassis number of your VW is found in two places: on the panel at the rear of the engine compartment, just above the fluid reservoir for the windshield washer, and on the left-hand windshield pillar. This Manual is organized so that changes from model year to model year are noted, and if a change within one model year is made, the chassis number of the first Volkswagen Dasher with this change is given. Very often, the first two digits of the chassis number will be omitted and indicated by blanks. For example, the chassis number __6 2007 654 is used when a change can apply either to Chassis No. 326 2007 654 (a sedan) or to Chassis No. 336 2007 654 (a wagon).

For the VW owner with mechanical skills and for independent garages, this Manual gives all the specifications that are available in a VW workshop. In addition, a VW owner who has no intention of working on his or her car will find that reading and owning this Manual will make it possible to discuss repairs intelligently with a professional mechanic.

The aim throughout has been simplicity, clarity, and completeness, with step-by-step procedures and accurate specifications. Every human effort has been made to ensure the highest degree of accuracy possible. When the vast array of data presented in this Manual is taken into account, however, no claim to infallibility can be made. We therefore cannot be responsible for the result of any errors in the text.

Readers' and users' comments have been a valuable aid in the preparation of this and other service manuals. The publisher encourages and invites readers and users to send in their criticisms and suggestions for use in future manuals and revisions.

The VW owner intending to do maintenance and repairs should have a set of metric wrenches, a torque wrench, screwdrivers, and feeler gauges, since these basic hand tools will be used in accomplishing a majority of the repairs described in this Manual. Usually there will be a caution in the text when a repair requires special tools or special skills.

If you are a professional mechanic already working on imported cars, you may have some VW special tools that are shown in some of the illustrations in this Manual. If you have previously worked only on American-manufactured cars, you will not have to replace your expensive micrometers, vernier calipers, and other precision tools because specifications are given both in millimeters and in inches, except when special VW metric tools are indispensable (and then measurements are given in millimeters only).

Volkswagens are constantly being improved and sometimes changes—in both parts and specifications—are made applicable to older VWs. Thus, a replacement part to be used on an older VW may not be the same as the part used in the original installation. Such changes are noted in this Manual. If a specification given in this Manual differs from one in an earlier source, disregard the earlier specification. The specifications in this Volkswagen Service Manual are accurate as of the publication date of this Manual.

Volkswagen offers an extensive warranty. Therefore, before deciding to repair a VW that is covered by the new-car warranty, consult your Authorized VW Dealer. You may find that he can make the repair either free or at minimum cost. Should any repair ever be needed that you feel is too difficult to do yourself, a trained VW mechanic is ready to do the job for you.

Robert Bentley

NOTES, CAUTIONS, AND WARNINGS

Throughout this Manual you will find many NOTES, CAUTIONS, and WARNINGS. A NOTE gives information that will help you do the work correctly. A CAUTION points out incorrect work practices that could damage either the car or your tools. A WARNING describes dangerous working procedures that could cause physical injury either to you or to those who may later use the car.

Please read these general cautions and warnings before you proceed with maintenance and repair work

CAUTION ——

● If you lack the skills, tools and equipment, or a suitable workshop for any procedure described in this Manual, we suggest you leave such repairs to an Authorized Dealer or other qualified shop. We especially urge you to consult your Authorized Dealer before attempting any repairs on a car still covered by the new-car warranty.

● Before starting a job, make certain that you have all necessary tools and parts on hand. Read all instructions thoroughly; do not attempt shortcuts. Use tools appropriate to the work and use only replacement parts meeting Volkswagen Dasher specifications. Makeshift tools parts, and procedures will not make good repairs.

● Use pneumatic and electric tools only to loosen threaded parts and fasteners. Never use these tools to tighten fasteners, especially on light alloy parts.

● Be mindful of the environment and ecology. Before you drain the crankcase, find out the proper way to dispose of the oil. Do not pour oil onto the ground, down a drain, or into a stream, pond or lake. Consult local ordinances that govern the disposal of wastes.

WARNING ——

● Never work under a lifted car unless it is solidly supported on stands intended for the purpose. Do not support a car on cinder blocks, hollow tiles, or other props that may crumble under continuous load. Do not work under a car that is supported solely by a jack.

● If you are going to work under a car on the ground, make sure that the ground is level. Block the wheels to keep the car from rolling. Disconnect the battery ground strap to prevent others from starting the car while you are under it.

● Never run the engine unless the work area is well ventilated. Carbon monoxide kills.

● Tie long hair behind your head. Do not wear a necktie, scarf, loose clothing, or necklace when you work near machine tools or running engines. If your hair, clothing, or jewelry were to get caught in the machinery, severe injury could result.

● Disconnect the battery ground strap whenever you work on the fuel system or the electrical system. When you work around fuel, do not smoke or work near heaters or other fire hazards. Keep an approved fire extinguisher handy.

● Illuminate your work area adequately but safely. Use a portable safety light for working inside or under the car. Make sure its bulb is enclosed by a wire cage. The hot filament of an accidentally broken bulb can ignite spilled fuel or oil.

● Catch draining fuel, oil, or brake fluid in suitable containers. Do not use food or beverage containers that might mislead someone into drinking from them. Store flammable fluids away from fire hazards. Wipe up spills at once, but do not store the oily rags, which can ignite and burn spontaneously.

● Finger rings should be removed so that they cannot cause electrical shorts, get caught in running machinery, or be crushed by heavy parts.

● Keep sparks, lighted matches, and open flame away from the top of the battery. If hydrogen gas escaping from the cap vents is ignited, it will ignite gas trapped in the cells and cause the battery to explode.

● Always observe good workshop practices. Wear goggles when you operate machine tools or work with battery acid. Gloves or other protective clothing should be worn whenever the job requires it.

Using Torque Wrenches

In adopting the SI *(Systeme International)* units of measure, which constitute the Modernized Metric System, tool manufacturers are beginning to introduce torque wrenches that are calibrated in newton meters. As metrification proceeds, torque specifications given in foot pounds (ft. lb.) and meter kilograms (mkg) will eventually be replaced by torque specifications given in newton meters (N· m or Nm).

At present, there are in use too few torque wrenches calibrated in newton meters to justify the inclusion of newton meter torque specifications in this manual. Nevertheless, if you purchase a new torque wrench, we recommend that you try to obtain one that is calibrated in newton meters. Such a tool can easily be used with this manual by converting the meter kilogram specifications to newton meters.

To convert meter kilograms (mkg) to newton meters, simply disregard the decimal point. For example, 3.5 mkg would become 35 Nm. To convert centimeter kilograms (cmkg) to newton meters, point-off the one place with a decimal. For example, 50 cmkg would become 5.0 Nm. These conversions are not mathematically precise (3.5 mkg actually equals 34.3 Nm) but they are adequate for normal workshop purposes.

BODY AND INTERIOR

Contents

Body and Interior

The cars covered by this manual have unit construction steel bodies that are exceptionally strong and light. Their lightness contributes greatly to the outstanding performance and fuel economy that these cars deliver. Because very few screws and bolts are used in assembling the body, there is little opportunity for annoying rattles to develop. A quiet ride is further ensured by the application of plastic-impregnated sound-dampening material to the floor plates and the body panels.

The bottom of the body is made up of three subassemblies called the front floor plate, the rear floor plate, and the rear wall. The upper part of the body is made up of seven subassemblies called the front end, the inner side panels (2), the outer side panels (2), the roof, and the tail end. During manufacture, these ten subassemblies, plus a number of smaller pressed steel panels, are joined by electric welding into a durable, integrated structure.

The front fenders and the grille are bolted to the main body structure so that they can be easily and economically replaced in the event of collision damage. The hood, the doors, and the tailgate or trunk lid are also readily removable. To simplify front body repairs further, the engine and transaxle are removable as a unit together with the front suspension and the front suspension/engine-mounting subframe. This work is described in **SUSPENSION AND STEERING.** The engine can be removed separately as described in **ENGINE AND CLUTCH** or **DIESEL ENGINE**; the transaxle can be removed separately as described in **MANUAL TRANSMISSION** or **AUTOMATIC TRANSMISSION.**

Though all body panels are available as replacement parts, replacement panels must be butt welded to the undamaged parts of the body after the damaged panels have been cut away. This work should be undertaken only by an experienced body repair technician. If you lack the skills, special equipment, or a suitable workshop for extensive body repairs, we suggest that you leave such work to your Authorized Dealer or other qualified shop. We especially urge you to consult your Authorized Dealer before attempting repairs on a car still covered by the new-car warranty.

Also covered in this section of the Manual are the seats, the ventilation and heating system, and the removal of the dashboard and other interior trim. Repairs related to the gauges and the instrument cluster are covered in **ELECTRICAL SYSTEM.** For information on the care and maintenance of carpeting, seat upholstery, and other interior appointments, we suggest that you refer to **LUBRICATION AND MAINTE-NANCE** or to the Owner's Manual, which is supplied with the car.

1. GENERAL DESCRIPTION

Because the engine, the transaxle, and the driving wheels are all located at the front of the car, the longitudinal hump in the front floor panel is not used to accomodate a driveshaft. The hump has been designed to serve as a stengthening member and as a housing for the exhaust system, the parking brake cables, and the hydraulic brake lines.

Doors and Windows

The front passenger doors are attached to the front body pillars by concealed hinges. On four-door models, similar hinges are used to attach the rear passenger doors to the center body pillars. Only the front passenger doors are equipped with lock cylinders but all passenger doors have press-down locking buttons. Except for the driver's door, the buttons can be used to lock the doors from outside the car without a key.

Curved glass is used for the side windows as well as for the windshield and the rear window. The passenger windows may be raised and lowered. Except on basic models, an electrically heated rear window is installed to conveniently prevent fogging.

Hood, Trunk Lid, and Tailgate

The engine hood is equipped with a lock which must be released from inside the car before the hood can be opened. The lock control lever is located beneath the left-hand end of the dashboard. The engine hood opens on hinges mounted beneath the front cowl panel.

The station wagon's tailgate is mounted on hidden upward-opening hinges suspended from the roof reinforcing members. Similar hinges are used on the trunk lids of sedans. The tailgate or the trunk lid is equipped with a lock.

Fenders and Trim

The front fenders are bolted onto the main body structure so that they can be readily replaced in the event of collision damage. The rear fenders are integral with the body outer side panels. Replacement of the rear fenders requires cutting and welding.

The bumpers, the door handles, the outside mirror(s) and other functional brightwork are chrome plated. For maximum corrosion resistance, most of the decorative bright trim pieces are either stainless steel or anodized aluminum. However, the model-identification markings and emblems are plated.

Seats and Interior

The front seats are individually mounted and can be moved forward or backward. The angle of the seat backs is also adjustable. Locks built into the seat backs keep them upright even during hard braking. Fully reclining front seat backrests are available as optional equipment.

The rear seat backrest is mounted on the body rear wall. The rear seat cushion is readily removable for access to the rear seat belt mountings and the electrical wiring for the rear of the car.

The portions of the floor plate that are within the passenger compartment are soundproofed with thermoplastic damping material. This material also acts as an insulator against road heat. The floor and front side panels are carpeted. The upholstery is easily cleaned vinyl, perforated for improved air circulation.

Ventilation and Heating

The flow-through ventilation system admits air to the car interior through a grille in the engine hood. Air from the car's interior is exhausted through vents in the rear roof pillars. Controlled amounts of incoming air can be admitted to the passenger compartment through four vents in the face of the dashboard, two side air nozzles on top of the dashboard ends, a full-length slot along the lower inside edge of the windshield, and a through vent beneath the dashboard.

A two-speed fan can be used to create a flow through the ventilation system while the car is moving slowly or standing still. Also, the ventilating air can be heated to warm the car interior. Except for the outboard vents in the face of the dashboard, which are for unheated air only, heated air is available through all of the ventilation vents listed above.

Sliding Roof

A sliding steel roof (sun roof) is supplied as an optional accessory. Opening the sliding roof creates a clear space above the driver and front passenger seats. A hand crank controls the roof, which can be adjusted to any position from fully open to fully closed. For safety, the crank should be folded into its recess when not in use.

2. MAINTENANCE

Only one maintenance operation, lubrication of the door hinges and the door checks, is required at regular mileage intervals. During routine servicing, the operation of the heater valve should be checked. These procedures are covered in **LUBRICATION AND MAINTENANCE.** Care of the body, trim, upholstery, and windows is also described briefly in **LUBRICATION AND MAINTENANCE.**

3. REMOVING AND INSTALLING BUMPERS

The front and the rear bumpers are bolted to reinforcements on the car body. The spring-loaded damping elements used on 1974 and later models are fastened to the car in the same way as the bumper brackets used on 1973 models. If only part of the bumper assembly needs to be replaced, it is best to first remove the bumper assembly as a unit and then disassemble it for repairs.

To remove:

1. In removing a front bumper, disconnect the battery ground strap. Then disconnect the wires for the bumper-mounted parking lights.

2. Working under the fenders, remove the bolts that hold the bumper brackets or the damping elements on the car body.

3. Remove the bumper assembly together with the rubber grommets that seal the bumper mounting openings in the body.

4. In order to separate the bumper assembly into its individual components, take out the bolts and screws which are accessible from the rear of the bumper.

Fig. 4-1. Front fender and lower body trim strip removed from car.

Installation is the reverse of removal. Replace the rubber grommets if they are weathered or damaged. Lubricate the threads on the nuts and bolts before you install them.

When installing the bumper assembly on the car, install the mounting bolts but do not tighten them. Then adjust the bumper to a uniform gap with the body before you tighten the mounting bolts.

4. REMOVING AND INSTALLING FRONT FENDER

The front fenders are bolted onto the body and can be removed and installed using common hand tools. The rear fenders are welded onto the body and can be replaced only by an experienced body repair technician. Front fender removal is illustrated in Fig. 4-1.

To remove:

1. Disconnect the battery ground strap. Then disconnect the wires for the sidemarker light.

2. Remove the radiator grille. To do this, take out the screws, which are visible through the front of the grille.

3. Remove the front bumper as described in **3. Removing and Installing Bumpers.**

4. Using a wooden or plastic wedge, carefully pry off the lower body trim strip.

5. Open the front door. Then remove the bolt that holds the upper rear corner of the front fender to the body.

6. Working under the fender, remove the other bolts that hold the rear edge of the fender to the body.

7. Remove the bolts that hold the front of the fender to the body.

8. Loosen, but do not remove, the bolts that hold the top of the fender to the body. Then, to break away the undercoating, pull out on the lower edge of the fender until it is 13 to 25 mm (½ to 1 in.) away from the body.

> **CAUTION ——**
> *If the fender does not pull away with a moderate amount of effort, check to see that you have not overlooked one or more of the mounting bolts. Excessive force will damage the fender.*

9. After you have broken the undercoating, support the fender so that it does not bend of its own

weight as the remaining mounting bolts are removed. Then take out the bolts that hold the top of the fender to the body and take off the fender.

Installation is the reverse of removal. Torque the mounting bolts to 1.5 mkg (11 ft. lb.). Fully undercoat new fenders. If the original fender is reinstalled, renew the undercoating along the joint between the wheel housing and the body front pillar, over the heads of the mounting bolts, and wherever else the original undercoating was chipped or scratched during removal.

5. HOOD, TRUNK LIDS, AND TAILGATE

When you remove and install the hood or the trunk lid (or the tailgate on a station wagon), it is important that the hood, lid, or tailgate be properly aligned during installation. If misaligned, they may rattle or leak.

5.1 Removing and Installing Hood

Usually, the hood must be removed before you can remove the engine. It is unnecessary, however, to remove the hinges from the body. In the event that the hinges must be unbolted from the body, use a procedure similar to that described in **5.3 Removing and Installing Tailgate or Trunk Lid.**

To remove hood:

1. Open the hood. If the hood is not being replaced, carefully mark the locations of the hinges on the hood so that you can reinstall the hood in its exact original position.

2. Remove the two hood bolts from one of the hinges.

3. While someone holds the unbolted side, remove the two hood bolts from the other hinge.

4. Working together, lift the hood up and off toward the front of the car.

To install:

1. Before installing the hood, check the condition of the rubber weatherstrip which is on the dividing panel at the rear of the engine compartment. If necessary, reglue or replace the weatherstrip.

> **NOTE ——**
> Remove all old trim cement with solvent so that the new weatherstrip will adhere properly.

2. Using all four bolts, loosely install the hood on its hinges. Move the hood in the elongated bolt holes

until the hinges are in the positions you marked for them prior to removal. If a new hood is being installed, align it with the body so that the gap is even all around and the hood locks engage properly. Then tighten the bolts.

3. Check the lock operation by opening and closing the hood several times. If necessary, adjust the positions of the lock plates and the rubber stops on the hood.

5.2 Removing and Installing Engine Hood Locks and Lock Cable

There are two hood locks, one at each side of the hood's front edge. Both locks are cable-operated by a lever that is below the left-hand side of the dashboard.

To remove locks:

1. Remove the radiator grille. To do this on a 1973 through 1977 car, open the hood and pry off the clips, then remove the screws that are visible through the front of the grille. On 1978 and later cars, open the hood, pry off the two clips at the ends of the grille, then lift up the plastic tabs for the four grille retaining clips (these are integral with the grille), pulling outward on the grille at the same time.

2. Remove the connecting rod guide sleeve from the reinforcement bracket. To do this, squeeze together the clips, as indicated by the arrows in Fig. 5-1. Then press the sleeve out toward the radiator.

Fig. 5-1. Connecting rod guide sleeve being removed. Squeeze clips together as indicated by the arrows.

3. Remove the bolts that hold the left lock and the right lock (Fig. 5-2). Unhook the cable from the lever on the left lock. Then remove the locks and the connecting rod from the car.

Installation is the reverse of removal. Be careful not to damage the connecting rod guide sleeve as you press the clips into the reinforcement bracket.

Fig. 5-2. Bolts (arrows) that hold right-hand hood lock. Two similar bolts hold the left lock.

Replacing Hood Lock Cable

To replace the hood lock cable, first remove the radiator grille. To do this, remove the screws that are visible through the front of the grille. Open the hood. If the cable has broken, you can release the hood locks by pulling the connecting rod toward the left-hand side of the car. Unbolt the left hood lock (Fig. 5-3). Then unhook the cable from the lever. Pull the front end of the cable out into the engine compartment.

Fig. 5-3. Bolts (arrows) that hold the left-hand hood lock.

Working inside the car, remove the driver's glove shelf. Then remove the screws indicated in Fig. 5-4. Remove the clip (**A** in Fig. 5-4) and pull the lever off the shaft. Unhook the cable from the lever and then pull the cable out into the engine compartment.

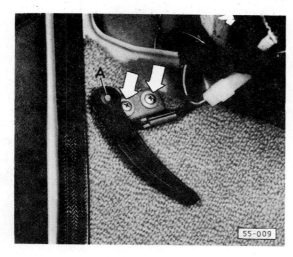

Fig. 5-4. Screws (arrows) and clip **(A)** that hold lever and cable under left side of dashboard.

Installation is the reverse of removal. Insert the cable from the engine compartment and connect it to the lever. Make sure that the rubber grommet and the water trap plate are correctly installed in the panel at the rear of the engine compartment before you install the cable at the front of the car.

5.3 Removing and Installing Tailgate or Trunk Lid

Fig. 5-5 is an exploded view of the hinge and the torsion bars for the station wagon's tailgate. The hinge and torsion bars for the sedan's lid are similar, though the parts are not interchangeable with those for the wagon. The removal procedure given here applies both to trunk lids and to tailgates.

To remove tailgate or lid:

1. Disconnect the battery ground strap. Open the tailgate or lid. Where applicable, disconnect the wire for the license plate light.

2. If the tailgate or lid is not being replaced, carefully mark the locations of the hinges so that you can reinstall them in their exact original positions.

3. Remove the two mounting bolts from one of the hinges.

4. While someone holds the unbolted side of the tailgate or lid, remove the two mounting bolts from the other hinge.

5. Working together, lift the tailgate or lid up and off toward the rear of the car.

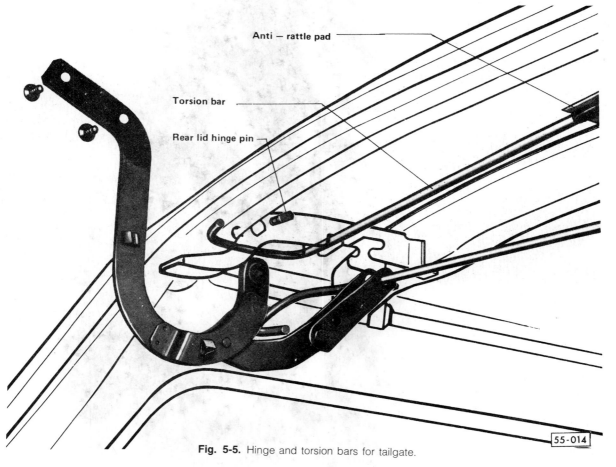

Fig. 5-5. Hinge and torsion bars for tailgate.

To install:

1. Before installing the tailgate or lid, check the condition of the rubber weatherstrip. If necessary, reglue or replace the weatherstrip.

    NOTE ——
    Remove all old trim cement with solvent so that the new weatherstrip will adhere properly.

2. Using all four bolts, loosely install the tailgate or lid on its hinges so that it contacts the weatherstrip evenly all around and the hinges are in the positions you marked for them prior to removal. If a new tailgate or lid is being installed, align it with the body so that the gap is even all around and the lock engages properly. Then tighten the bolts.

3. Check the lock operation by opening and closing the tailgate or lid several times. If necessary, adjust the position of the lock plate that is on the body.

4. Reconnect the license plate light wire and the battery ground strap.

To remove hinge:

1. On station wagons only, partially remove the rear interior roof trim.

2. Remove the tailgate or trunk lid. Pull down the hinge, then use a hammer handle to block the linkage as shown in Fig. 5-6. Remove the circlip and the hinge pin.

    NOTE ——
    Some trunk lids have coil springs rather than torsion bars. On those cars, unhook the spring at the bottom.

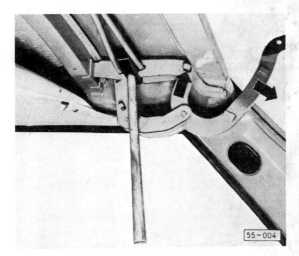

Fig. 5-6. Hinge pin being removed. Pin and circlip are at left arrow. Hinge has been pulled down as indicated by right arrow. A hammer handle is inserted in the linkage so that there is no tension on the hinge pin.

3. Using a hook-shaped tool as indicated in Fig. 5-7, pry the torsion bar out of the mounting channel. Then remove the hinge.

Installation is the reverse of removal. If the hinge operates stiffly or if it squeaks, lubricate the pivot points with multipurpose grease. To prevent rattles, make sure that the anti-rattle pad is firmly glued to the torsion bar. If necessary, reglue or replace the pad.

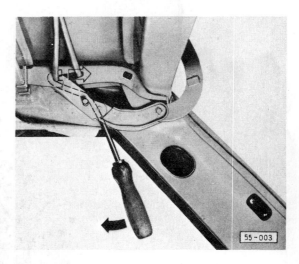

Fig. 5-7. Torsion bar being pried out of the mounting channel.

Replacing Lock Cylinder

Fig. 5-8 illustrates the removal of the tailgate/trunk lid lock cylinder. To prevent the tumblers and the tumbler springs from falling out, insert the key before you remove the cylinder. Prior to installation, clean the lock cylinder. Then lubricate it with special lock lubricant only.

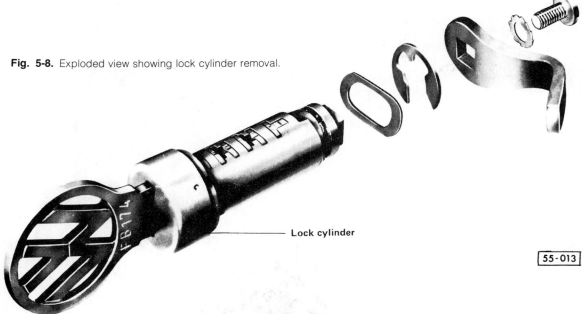

Fig. 5-8. Exploded view showing lock cylinder removal.

Lock cylinder

55-013

6. DOORS AND DOOR LOCKS

Despite detail variations, the rear doors on four-door models share the same basic design as the front doors which are illustrated here. However, the lock for the driver's door is different from the locks used on other doors in that it cannot be locked from outside the car without using the key.

6.1 Removing and Installing Door Handle, Lock Cylinder, and Door Lock

Fig. 6-1 illustrates the removal of the lock cylinder and the construction of the door handle. You must remove the handle in order to remove the lock cylinder. On four-door models, only the front doors have lock cylinders.

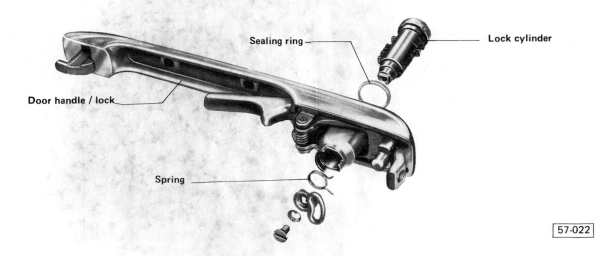

Sealing ring

Lock cylinder

Door handle / lock

Spring

57-022

Fig. 6-1. Rear view of door handle with lock cylinder removed.

To remove the door handle, pry off the plastic cap that is in the edge of the door. Then remove the screw that holds the door handle in the door. Pull the handle free of the door and unhook the handle at its forward edge.

When installing, clean the lock and the door release trigger, then apply door and lock lubricant. Make sure the gaskets are in good condition and that they seat properly when you mount the handle on the door.

If you remove the lock cylinder from the door handle, do so only with the key inserted in the cylinder. Otherwise the tumblers and the tumbler springs will fall out. During lock cylinder installation, replace the sealing ring if it is hard, cracked, or broken. The hairpin spring that is beneath the lock operating cam must be installed so that it is under tension.

Removing and Installing Door Lock

Since October of 1976, a new kind of door lock has been installed on the 1977 and later models. This new lock (Fig. 6-2) is installed on the outside of the door, making it possible to remove the lock without removing the door trim panel. The components of the new-type lock are identified in Fig. 6-3.

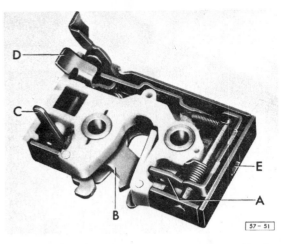

A. Remote control lever   D. Locking lever No. 2
B. Rotary latch   E. Access hole
C. Locking lever No. 1

Fig. 6-3. Components of new-type lock.

To remove new-type lock:

1. Using the locking knob or the key, lock the door lock with the door open.

2. Remove both of the screws that hold the lock to the door. Then pull the lock about 10 to 12 mm (or ⅜ to ½ in.) away from the door.

3. Hold the remote control lever in its turned-out position with a screwdriver, as indicated in Fig. 6-4. Fig. 6-5 shows how the screwdriver should be positioned inside the lock.

Fig. 6-2. New-type lock (circled) installed on outside of door.

Fig. 6-4. Remote control lever (**A**) being held in its turned-out position with screwdriver inserted through access hole (**E**).

Fig. 6-7. Adaptor plate (**A**) installed with Phillips head screws (arrows **B**) in standard replacement door.

Fig. 6-5. Position of screwdriver inserted through access hole (**E**) to hold remote control lever (**A**) in turned-out position.

4. Detach the remote control lever from its pullrod; withdraw locking lever No. 1 from the sleeve. See Fig. 6-6.

2. Close the rotary latch and lock it with one or the other of the locking levers (Fig. 6-8).

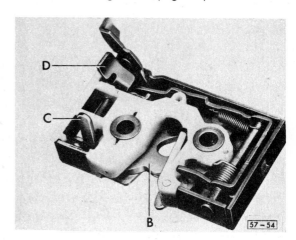

Fig. 6-8. Rotary latch (**B**) in closed position. Lock rotary latch in place by pressing locking lever No. 1 (**C**) or locking lever No. 2 (**D**).

3. Pull the remote control lever into its turned-out position and keep it in that position with a screwdriver exactly as shown previously in Fig. 6-5.

Fig. 6-6. Lock being removed. Remote control lever (**A**) has been detached from pullrod (**G**). Locking lever No. 1 (**C**) should be pulled out of sleeve (**H**).

To install:

1. If a new door is being installed, it will have a large hole in the edge that will accept the old-type lock. To install the new-type lock, first install adaptor plate Part No. 171 831 349 (right door) or 171 831 350 (left door), as shown in Fig. 6-7.

4. Reattach the lock to the locking knob sleeve and to the pullrod, as indicated in Fig. 6-9.

5. Remove the screwdriver from the access hole in the lock, then mount the lock on the door with the two screws.

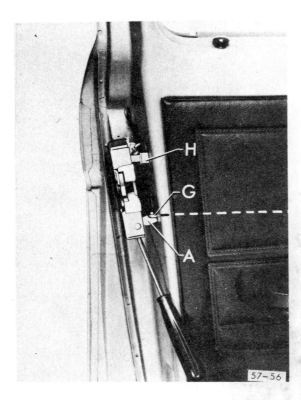

Fig. 6-9. Locking lever No. 1 reattached to sleeve (**H**) and remote control lever (**A**) reattached to pullrod (**G**).

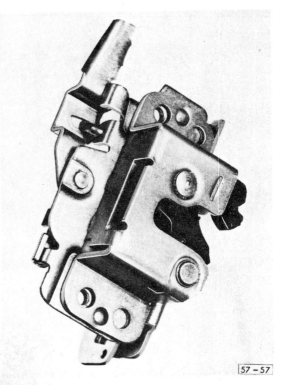

Fig. 6-10. Old-type lock used through September 1976. This component remains available as a replacement part.

To remove the old-type lock (Fig. 6-10), you must first remove the door window handle, the door's interior handle, the armrest, and the door opening lever. Pry off the door trim panel—working all around its periphery with a thin wooden wedge so that the panel's clips are pulled gently from their holes in the door. Carefully peel back the protective foil weatherseal sheet in the area of the lock.

With the lock mounting screws removed (Fig. 6-11), you can detach the lock from the control rods and remove the lock through the access opening in the door. Installation is the reverse of removal.

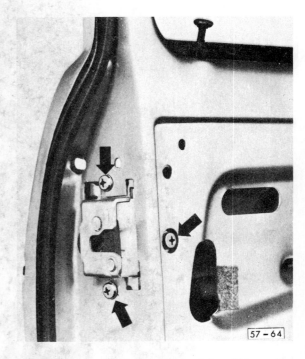

Fig. 6-11. Mounting screws (arrows) for old-type door lock.

6.2 Removing and Installing Door

The door hinges are welded to the body. The doors are held on the hinges by screws. If it is necessary to remove a door, carefully mark the positions of the hinges on the door so that you can easily align the door during installation.

To remove a door, take out the screws that hold the door check strap on the body. Use an impact driver to loosen the screws that hold the door on the hinges. Support the door, then remove the screws and take off the door.

CAUTION ——

If you fail to support the door as you remove the screws from the first hinge, the second hinge may be bent or broken.

During installation, check the weatherseal. If it is cracked, torn, or otherwise damaged, replace it.

NOTE ——

Before installing a new weatherseal, clean away all the old adhesive with solvent. Install the new seal with trim cement.

Using the marks made prior to removal, install the door on the hinges. If a replacement door is being installed, install it so that the door contacts the weatherseal evenly all around and the lock works smoothly. Set the hinge screws firmly with the impact driver.

6.3 Removing and Installing Door Lock, Door Windows, Window Lifter, and Moldings

Fig. 6-12 and Fig. 6-13 show the lock assembly, the door windows, the window lifter, the moldings, and other parts that are attached to the door. The door need not be removed from the car to replace any of the parts shown. However, the arm rest and door trim panel must be removed for access to the door's interior.

To remove the arm rest, take out the Phillips head screws. Then slide the arm rest forward and off the door release lever. Pry the plastic cover off the window crank, remove the crank-mounting screw, then remove the crank. Using a wooden wedge, pry off the trim panel all around the door. Then remove the trim panel.

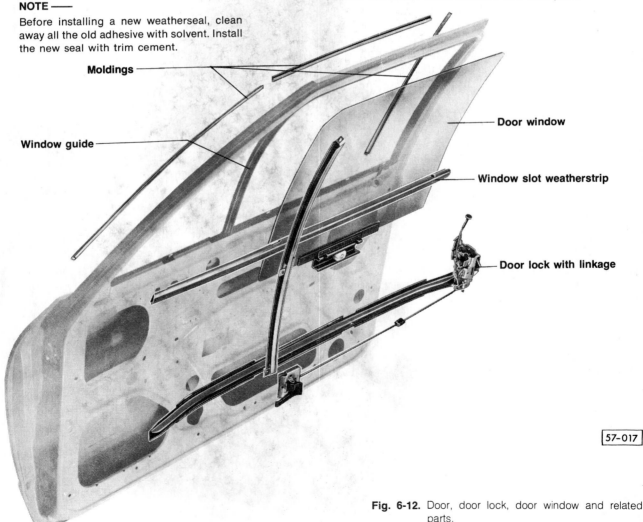

Fig. 6-12. Door, door lock, door window and related parts.

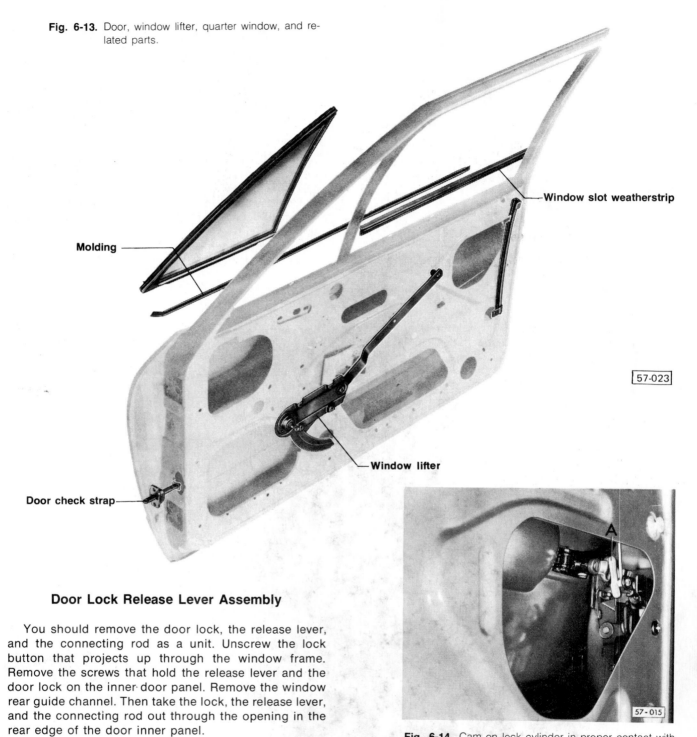

Fig. 6-13. Door, window lifter, quarter window, and related parts.

Window slot weatherstrip

Molding

Window lifter

Door check strap

57-023

57-015

Fig. 6-14. Cam on lock cylinder in proper contact with lock lever (**A**).

Door Lock Release Lever Assembly

You should remove the door lock, the release lever, and the connecting rod as a unit. Unscrew the lock button that projects up through the window frame. Remove the screws that hold the release lever and the door lock on the inner door panel. Remove the window rear guide channel. Then take the lock, the release lever, and the connecting rod out through the opening in the rear edge of the door inner panel.

Installation is the reverse of removal. Clean all parts and grease them with door and lock lubricant prior to installation. Make sure that the seal for the lock is in good condition and properly positioned. The lock lever should contact the cam on the lock cylinder as shown in Fig. 6-14. The anti-rattle pad should be glued in position on the center of the connecting rod. Check the operation of the lock before you install the door trim panel and the arm rest.

Door Window, Window Lifter, and Guide Channels

The window lifter need not be removed in order to remove the window. The window glass is taken out through the top of the door. The window guide channels and the window slot weather strips must be removed before the glass can be taken out.

To remove window lifter:

1. Remove the door trim panel. Then install the window lifter handle loosely on its shaft.

2. Remove the four lifter-mounting bolts. Press the lifter inward and lower the window until you can disengage the locating spring from the lifter channel that holds the window glass.

3. Lower the window carefully by hand until it rests inside the door. Then remove the lifter handle and remove the lifter from the door.

To install:

1. Grease the moving parts of the lifter.

2. Hook the locating spring into the window lifter channel and install the window lifter in the door.

> **NOTE** ——
>
> There have been important changes in the designs of the window lifters (Fig. 6-15). Only the newer kinds of window lifters are available as replacement parts. If you install the new kind of lifter in an earlier car, you must also replace the window lifter channel on the glass, as described in the next procedure. Additionally, the door inner panel must be modified as indicated in Fig. 6-16.

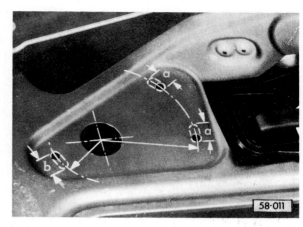

Fig. 6-16. Early door inner panel being modified to accept late-type window lifter. Elongate holes as shown. Dimension **a** is 15 mm ($^{19}/_{32}$ in.); dimension **b** is 12 mm ($\frac{1}{2}$ in.).

3. Loosely install the window lifter crank on its shaft. Then turn the crank one way or the other until the mounting bolt holes in the lifter are aligned with the holes in the door inner panel.

Early type front door window lifter
(up to Chassis No. _ _ 5 2054 499)

Early type rear door window lifter
(up to Chassis No. _ _ 2054 499)

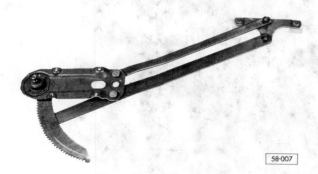

Late type front door window lifter
(from Chassis No. _ _ 2054 500)

Late type rear door window lifter
(from Chassis No. _ _ 5 2054 500)

Fig. 6-15. Early and late type window lifters.

4. Install the mounting bolts. If you have modified the door inner panel as previously shown in Fig. 6-16, use flat washers (Part No. N 11 666.5) in addition to the spring washers and install the bolts with Loctite®.

5. Install the trim panel and the window lifter handle.

To replace door window:

1. Lower the window. Disengage the locating spring from the lifter channel on the window glass.

2. Remove the front and the rear window guides.

3. Remove the window slot weatherstrips. The inner strip is held by 3 clips; the outer strip is held by 5 clips. The trim molding along the edge of the outer weatherstrip should be carefully pried off its 7 clips. The weatherstrip clips are removed and installed as shown in Fig. 6-17.

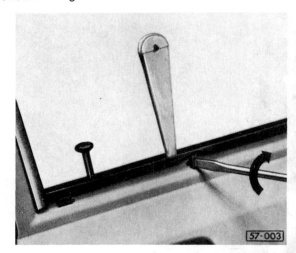

Fig. 6-17. Clip for weatherstrip being removed or installed. Wedge prevents weatherstrip from slipping out of door under pressure from the screwdriver. Turn the screwdriver as indicated by the arrow to engage the clips. Turn it in the opposite direction to disengage the clips.

4. Lift the window upward and out of the door together with its attached lifter channel.

5. If the glass must be replaced, knock the window lifter channel off the old glass with a rubber hammer and a wooden or plastic block. Inspect the rubber channel in the lifter channel. Replace the rubber channel if it is loose-fitting or otherwise faulty.

NOTE ——

If you have installed the late-type window lifter in an early-type door, as described in the preceding procedure, you must also replace the early-type lifter channel with the late-type channel.

6. On front door windows, install the lifter channel in the exact center of the lower edge of the glass. See Fig. 6-18.

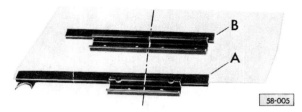

Fig. 6-18. Front door window lifter channel being installed. Channel **A** is the type installed through Chassis No. _ _5 2054 499; channel **B** is the type installed from Chassis No. _ _5 2054 500.

7. On rear door windows, install the lifter channel so that the front end of the channel is just slightly back from the angled lower front corner of the glass. See Fig. 6-19.

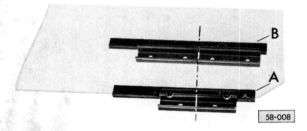

Fig. 6-19. Rear door window lifter channel being installed. Channel **A** is the type installed through Chassis No. _ _5 2054 499; channel **B** is the type installed from Chassis No. _ _5 2054 500.

Installation is the reverse of removal. Replace the weatherstrips and the guide channels if they are worn or otherwise faulty. Lubricate the guide channels with silicone spray. Then check to see that the window operates smoothly before you install the trim panel. If necessary, slightly reposition the guide channels.

Quarter Window

To replace the quarter window, you must first remove the door window. Pull the window guide mount out of the window frame. Then pull the quarter window and its rubber gasket out of the window frame. Installation is the reverse of removal. Use a wooden wedge to press the window guide mount into the frame against the quarter window's rubber gasket.

Moldings

The trim moldings around the window opening in the outer door panel are snapped on over clips on the door.

Use a thin wooden or plastic wedge to pry off the moldings. To avoid bending the moldings, work as near each clip as possible.

Remove first the bottom molding, then the rear molding, the front molding, and finally the top molding. Install the moldings in reverse order so that they overlap properly where they meet one another.

Repairing Door Check Strap Bracket

On some four-door models, the rear door check strap brackets may become loose or break off. This can be repaired without replacing the entire door.

To repair:

1. Remove the door.

2. Remove the interior trim and other inflammable components that are near the check strap bracket location.

3. Remove the door check strap from its bracket, and repair any associated damage to the door itself.

4. Drill four 6-mm (or ¼-in.) holes in the door's inner panel, locating them as indicated in Fig. 6-20.

a = 70 mm (2¾ in.)   d = 33 mm (1⁵/₁₆ in.)
b = 80 mm (3⅛ in.)   e = 55 mm (2³/₁₆ in.)
c = 50 mm (2 in.)   f = 25 mm (1 in.)

Fig. 6-20. Dimensions for locating holes and door check strap bracket in door inner panel prior to welding.

5. Install and position the door check strap bracket to dimension **a**, as previously given in Fig. 6-20. Then clamp it in place.

6. Using MIG (metal inert gas) welding equipment, plug-weld the holes to secure the bracket to the door.

7. Grind down the welds, then refinish the door as required.

8. Install the door check strap, with a new rubber sleeve, Part No. 823 837 323 (indicated in Fig. 6-21).

9. Reinstall the other door components, then reinstall the door on the car.

Fig. 6-21. Rubber sleeve for door check (**B**).

7. BODY INTERIOR

The removal and installation procedures described here can be used to replace damaged interior trim and equipment. Many of the procedures must also be carried out in order to gain access to certain electrical or mechanical components that are covered elsewhere in this Manual.

7.1 Removing and Installing Dashboard Panels and Glove Compartment Lid

The dashboard panels must be removed for access to the ventilation ducts, the instrument panel, the ventilation and heating controls, the steering column mountings, and the pedal cluster. You can select which parts of the following procedure you need to use in order to accomplish the repairs you are undertaking.

To remove dashboard:

1. Disconnect the battery ground strap (necessary only if you will be disconnecting electrical wires).

2. Remove the center under-dash panel by taking out the four Phillips head screws indicated in Fig. 7-1. Lower the panel, then disconnect the cigarette lighter.

Fig. 7-1. Screws (arrows) that hold center under-dash panel.

3. To remove the right-hand under-dash panel, take out the Phillips head screw indicated in Fig. 7-2.

Fig. 7-2. Screw (arrow) that holds right-hand under-dash panel.

4. To remove the glove compartment lid, take off the two nuts indicated in Fig. 7-3.

5. To remove the left-hand under-dash panel and the driver's glove shelf, remove the Phillips head screws indicated in Fig. 7-4.

6. Remove the left-hand dashboard mounting screw (Fig. 7-5).

Fig. 7-3. Nuts that hold glove compartment lid hinges to car body. Lid must be open for access.

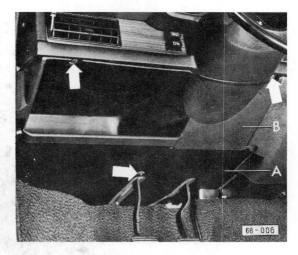

Fig. 7-4. Screws (arrows) that hold left-hand under-dash panel (A) and driver's glove shelf (B).

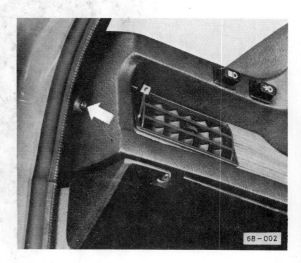

Fig. 7-5. Left-hand dashboard mounting screw (arrow).

7. Remove the right-hand dashboard mounting screw and the screw under the dashboard that is indicated in Fig. 7-6.

Fig. 7-6. Screws (arrows) that hold right-hand end of dashboard.

8. Remove the two dashboard mounting nuts that are below the cowl panel water trap.

9. Remove the ventilation duct hoses from the left and right dashboard vents.

10. Unscrew the ferrule nut that holds the speedometer cable to the speedometer head. Then disconnect the cable from the speedometer.

11. Pull the dashboard forward slightly so that you can reach behind it. One by one, disconnect the electrical wires from the rear of the dashboard. Attach identifying tags to each wire as you remove it so that you will easily be able to install the wires in their original locations.

12. Remove the dashboard from the car.

Installation is the reverse of removal. Make sure that the dashboard is properly hooked onto the support bracket and that the air ducts all fit properly.

7.2 Removing and Installing Front Seat

Fig. 7-7 shows a front seat and its controls. Before you remove a front seat, place paper in the rear footwell to protect the carpet from grease stains.

Fig. 7-7. Seat and seat controls. Backrest release lever is at **A**, the backrest angle adjuster lever is at **B**, and the backward/forward adjusting lever is at **C**.

To remove:

1. Unplug the extensible wire for the seat belt warning system.

2. Raise the backward/forward adjusting lever. Then push back the seat to the next to last position.

3. Pry the covers (Fig. 7-8) off the side runners.

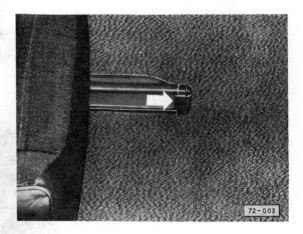

Fig. 7-8. Cover (arrow) on rear of inboard seat runner.

4. Using a screwdriver inserted into the central bracket from the front (Fig. 7-9), press down the leaf-spring stop.

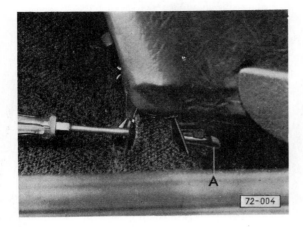

Fig. 7-9. Leaf-spring stop on central bracket being pressed down.

5. Raise the backward/forward adjusting lever. Then, with the lever up and the leaf-spring stop depressed, push the seat out of its runners to the rear.

To install:

1. Check the friction pads (Fig. 7-10) on the seat mounts. Also check the two spring clips pressed into the upper friction pads.

> **NOTE ——**
> If the clips are faulty, missing, or not pressed in, the seat will rattle.

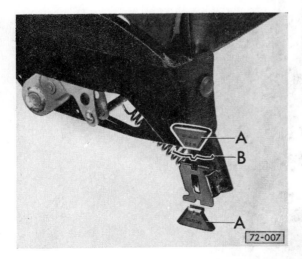

Fig. 7-10. Friction pads **(A)** and spring clip **(B).** There are similar parts at the opposite side of the seat.

2. Insert the seat into the side runners from the rear.

3. Pull back the backward/forward seat adjusting lever and slide the seat forward and into the central bracket.

4. Press each cover into the rear of its side runner. Then reconnect the extensible wire for the seat belt warning system.

7.3 Removing and Installing Front Seat Backrest and Backrest Adjuster

In order to remove the backrest or to remove or repair the backrest angle adjuster mechanism, it is best if you first remove the front seat from the car.

To remove backrest and adjuster:

1. Pull off the knob on the backrest angle adjuster lever. Carefully pry out the plastic caps. Then remove the Phillips head screws and washers that hold the trim on the side of the seat. Remove the trim. See Fig. 7-11.

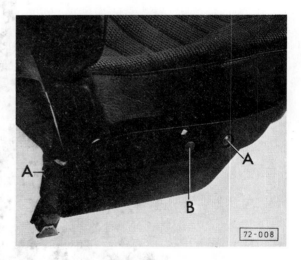

Fig. 7-11. Removing seat side trim. Plastic caps are at **A.** Knob that must be pulled off the backrest angle adjuster lever is at **B.**

2. Remove the trim from the opposite side of the seat. On models with the fully reclining backrest, you must first pull the knob off the fully reclining backrest adjuster.

3. Unhook the springs from both sides of the backrest angle adjuster mechanism. Remove the bolt and the washer from the outboard side only (Fig. 7-12).

4. Raise the backrest release lever. Remove the backrest from its mounting.

5. If necessary, remove the adjuster mechanism from the seat.

1

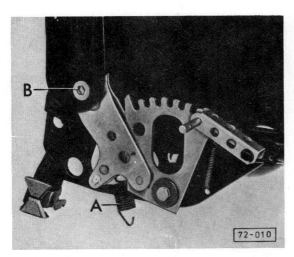

Fig. 7-12. Spring **(A)** and bolt **(B)**. The bolt is secured with Loctite®. Use a properly fitting tool to snap it loose.

Installation is the reverse of removal. To install the adjuster mechanism on the seat, bolt the adjuster quadrant on so that its base is parallel with the square-section connecting tube. See Fig. 7-13. You must raise the backrest release lever in order to install the backrest on its mountings. Secure the mounting bolt with Loctite®.

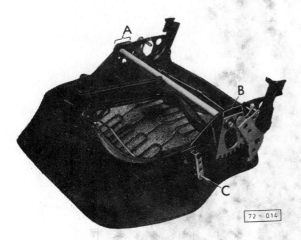

Fig. 7-13. Backrest adjuster installation on seat. Edge of lever **(A)** and quadrant **(B)** must be parallel with square-section seat tubes. Check the operation of the backrest adjuster lever **(C)** before you install the backrest.

7.4 Removing and Installing Front Seat Backrest Release Cables

In order to remove the front seat backrest release cables, you must first remove the backrest from the adjuster mechanism as described in **7.3 Removing and**

Installing Front Seat Backrest and Backrest Adjuster. Though the upholstery has been removed from the backrest illustrated here, it has been done solely for clarity. You need not remove the upholstery in order to replace the cable.

To remove cable:

1. Disconnect the spring that is at **A** in Fig. 7-14. Disconnect the cables from the release lever.

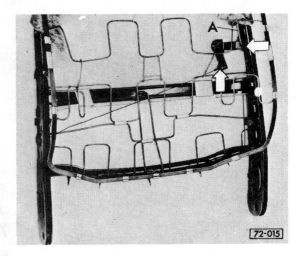

Fig. 7-14. Cables being disconnected from release lever. Spring is at **A.** Arrows indicate points at which cables are attached.

2. Remove the Phillips head screws from the latching hooks (Fig. 7-15). Then pull out the cables.

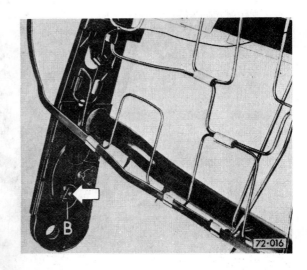

Fig. 7-15. Cable-retaining screw (arrow) on latching hook **(B).**

To install cables:

1. Install first the short cable and then the long cable. To prevent rattles, route the long cable under the spring core as shown in Fig. 7-16.

2. So that both latching hooks will unlatch together, select whichever one of the three holes in the release lever that will equally tension the long and the short cables.

Fig. 7-17. Sedan rear seat removal and installation. Lift out as indicated by arrow. Securing eyes are at letters **A.**

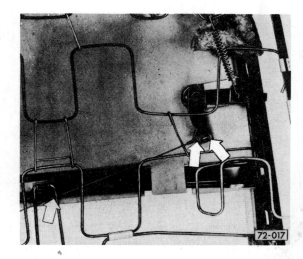

Fig. 7-16. Long cable installation. Route cable underneath spring core at left arrow. Right arrows indicate two alternative holes into which the long cable can be hooked.

3. Hook the spring onto the release lever. Then test the operation of the latches before you reinstall the backrest on the seat.

7.5 Removing and Installing Rear Seat and Backrest

The rear seat of the sedan and the rear seat of the station wagon are different. Each will be covered separately.

Sedan

To remove the rear seat, push the seat slightly rearward and then lift it up and out of the car as indicated by the arrow in Fig. 7-17. During installation, the securing eyes must enter the openings in the body cross member.

To remove the rear seat backrest, bend open the securing tabs that are indicated in Fig. 7-18. Pull out on the bottom of the backrest, then push the backrest slightly downward in order to unhook it from the body. Remove the backrest, lower edge first, from the car. After reinstalling the backrest on the three eyes welded to the rear wall, bend over the securing tabs to keep the backrest in place.

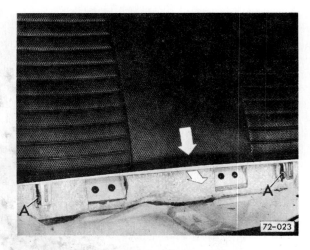

Fig. 7-18. Sedan rear seat backrest removal. Securing tabs are at **A.** To remove the backrest, pull the bottom outward and then down as indicated by the two arrows.

Station Wagon

To remove the rear seat, tip it up, then remove the Phillips head screws indicated in Fig. 7-19. Lift out the seat. Installation is the reverse of removal.

To remove the rear seat backrest, first tip up the rear seat. Release the rear seat backrest and tip it forward. Remove the bolts (Fig. 7-20). Then remove the backrest from the car. Installation is the reverse of removal.

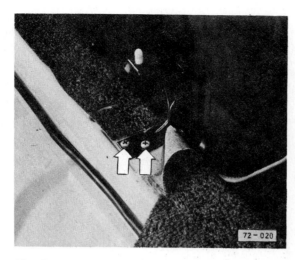

Fig. 7-19. Station wagon rear seat removal and installation. Arrows indicate the mounting screws.

Fig. 7-20. Station wagon rear seat backrest removal and installation. One mounting bolt is indicated by the arrow. A similar bolt is at the opposite end of the backrest.

7.6 Seat Belts and Retractors

For safety while driving, the seat belts should be maintained in good condition at all times. Never clean the belts with anything other than mild soap and water. Solvents and other cleaning agents may weaken the webbing. Replace frayed or cut belts and belts that have been in use during an accident.

If the retractors bind, first make sure that the belts are not frayed or deformed. If nothing is wrong with the belt material, check that the belt is not rubbing the retractor sides. If the retractor spool is sticking, clean it and then lightly lubricate the spindle bearings with oil. On two-door cars, the operation of the retractors can sometimes be improved through the addition of a belt guide (Part No. 323 857 827).

Removing and Installing Front Seat Belts

Do not attempt to repair faulty seat belt retractors. Doing this may prevent them from locking correctly in the event of a collision. Always replace faulty retractors as a complete unit.

To remove belt and retractor:

1. On two-door cars, remove the belt guiding cover from the shoulder belt retractor by taking out the Phillips head screw. Then, on all models, take out the bolt that holds the retractor to the door's lock pillar. Pull the retractor off the body.

2. Carefully pry off the bolt head plastic cap, then remove the bolt that holds the lap belt to the outside edge of the floorboard. Be careful not to lose any of the washers or spacers.

3. Carefully pry the plastic cap off the relay bracket mounting for the shoulder belt. Then unbolt the relay bracket from the lock pillar and remove the belts.

4. If necessary, carefully pry off the plastic cap, then unbolt the press-button buckle assembly from the body's central tunnel. Where applicable, disconnect the wire for the seat belt warning system.

To install:

1. If previously removed, install the press-button buckle assembly as shown in Fig. 7-21. Torque the bolt to 3.6 to 4.8 mkg (26 to 35 ft. lb.). Press on the plastic cap. Where applicable, reconnect the wire for the seat belt warning system.

2. Install the relay bracket on the door's lock pillar as shown in Fig. 7-22. Torque the mounting bolt to 3.6 to 4.8 mkg (26 to 35 ft. lb.).

3. On four-door and station wagon models, install the lap belt and the retractor on the body as indicated in Fig. 7-23. Torque the mounting bolts to 3.6 to 4.8 mkg (26 to 35 ft. lb.). Install the bolt head plastic cap on the lap belt mounting bolt.

NOTE ——

When correctly installed, the belts should lie flat without twists when they are worn by the vehicle occupants. Also be sure that the retractor housing is not at all tilted either vertically or horizontally and that the belt does not rub the edges of the retractor housing.

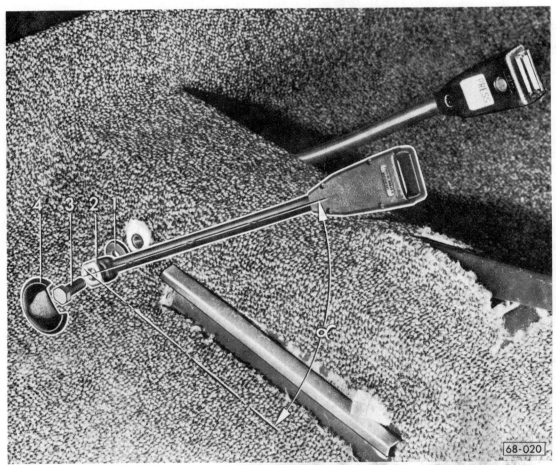

1. Seal
2. Buckle assembly
3. Bolt
4. Plastic cap
a Installation angle: 45° ±5°

68-020

Fig. 7-21. Press-button buckle installation.

1

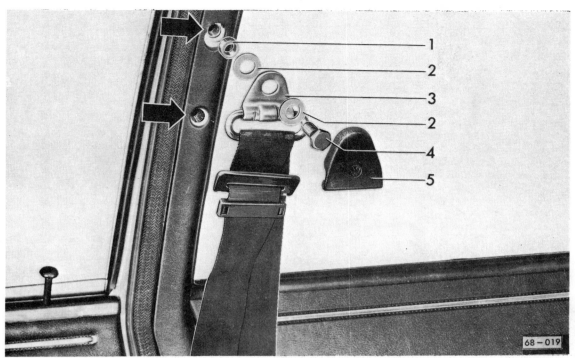

1. 8.5-mm ($^{21}/_{64}$-in.)
   spacer
2. Plastic washer
3. Relay bracket
4. Bolt
5. Plastic cap

Fig. 7-22. Relay bracket installation. Depending on the size of the belt user, the relay bracket bolt should be installed either in the upper or the lower hole (arrows).

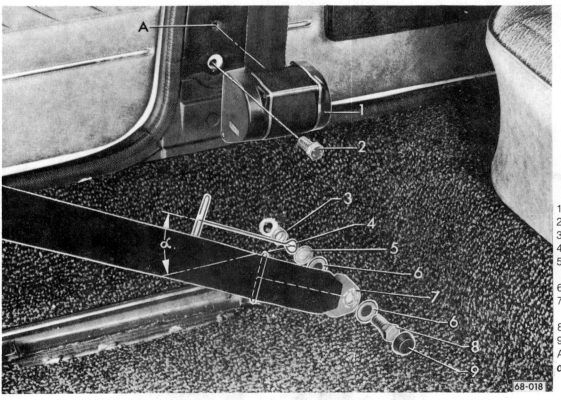

1. Retractor
2. Bolt
3. Spacer
4. Belt guide
5. Washer
   (Part No. N 11 511.1)
6. Plastic washer
7. Belt end with
   swivel plate
8. Bolt
9. Bolt head plastic cap
A. Hole for locating pin
α Installation angle:
   50° ± 10°

Fig. 7-23. Retractor and lap belt installation (four door and station wagon).

4. On two-door cars, install the lap belt and the retractor on the body as indicated in Fig. 7-24. Torque the mounting bolts to 3.6 to 4.8 mkg (26 to 35 ft. lb.).

> **NOTE**
>
> When correctly installed, the belts should lie flat without twists when they are worn by the vehicle occupants. Before you install the belt guiding cover, be sure that the retractor housing is not at all tilted either vertically or horizontally and that the belt does not rub the edges of the retractor housing.

5. On two-door cars, install the belt guiding cover. Make sure that it is carefully aligned and does not rub against the belt in such a way that the belt binds. Especially if the cover is new, it may be necessary to rework or deburr the guide slot (Fig. 7-25).

Fig. 7-25. Belt guiding cover installed. If necessary, rework or deburr the ends of the guide slots in the dimension indicated by the arrows.

1. Plastic dust seal	8. Seal
2. Washer (Part No. N 11 511.1)	9. 5-mm ($^{13}/_{64}$-in.) spacer
3. Retractor	10. Plastic washer
4. Bolt	11. Belt end with swivel plate
5. Belt guiding cover	12. Bolt
6. Washer	13. Bolt head plastic cap
7. Phillips head screw	

Fig. 7-24. Retractor and lap belt installation (two door).

Removing and Installing Rear Seat Belts

Before you can remove or install the rear seat belts, the rear seat must be removed as described in **7.5 Removing and Installing Rear Seat and Backrest.**

To remove the rear seat belts, simply take out the bolts that hold the belt ends to the body. The bolts for the outer belts are covered by a bolt head plastic cap that must be pried off.

To install:

1. Install the center seating position belts as indicated in Fig. 7-26. Torque the mounting bolts to 3.6 to 4.8 mkg (26 to 35 ft. lb.).

2. Install the outer seating position belts as indicated in Fig. 7-27. Torque the mounting bolts to 3.6 to 4.8 mkg (26 to 35 ft. lb.).

3. Install the bolt head plastic cap. Then reinstall the back seat as described in **7.5 Removing and Installing Rear Seat and Backrest.**

1. Seal	4. Seal
2. Belt with tongue	5. Belt with buckle
3. Bolt	6. Bolt

Fig. 7-26. Rear center seating position seat belt installation.

1. Seal
2. 8.5-mm ($^{21}/_{64}$-in.) spacer
3. Belt with retractor
4. Bolt
5. Bolt head plastic cap
6. Seal
7. Belt with buckle
8. Bolt

Fig. 7-27. Rear outer seating position seat belt installation.

8. VENTILATION AND HEATING

Fig. 8-1 is an exploded view of the ventilation and heating system used on 1973 through 1976 cars. It has a two-speed fan motor that is accessible after the heater cover and the cutoff flap have been removed. (You

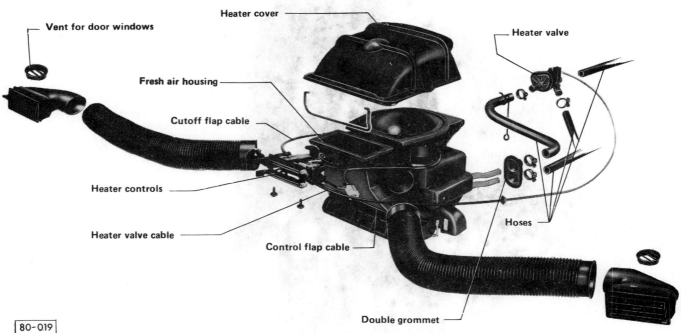

Fig. 8-1. Exploded view of ventilation and heating system.

remove the cover and the flap by working under the engine hood.) If the motor is faulty, the motor and fan should be replaced as a unit.

Fig. 8-2 shows the heater/ventilation unit used on 1977 and later cars. Instructions for disassembly are given in the illustration. If the motor is faulty, the motor and the fresh air blower should be replaced as a unit. The blower has three speeds.

In removing the heater valve, it is unnecessary to drain the coolant. Simply remove and plug the hoses. If the heater valve is binding or is hard to operate, replace it. If the entire heater must be removed, drain the coolant beforehand as described in **ENGINE AND CLUTCH.** Before you can disconnect the hoses from the heater, you must remove the windshield washer container and the ignition coil for access.

8.1 Removing, Adjusting, and Installing Ventilation and Heating Controls

The procedure given here can also be used to check and repair the flaps that are mounted inside the fresh air housing.

To remove controls:

1. Disconnect the battery ground strap. Pull the knobs off the ventilation and heating controls, which are in the center of the dashboard.

2. Using the procedures described in **7.1 Removing and Installing Dashboard Panels and Glove Compartment Lid,** remove the center under-dash panel, the left-hand under-dash panel, and the driver's glove shelf. Open the glove compartment lid.

3. If the car has a radio, remove the radio and the radio bracket.

4. Disconnect the wiring from the fan or blower motor.

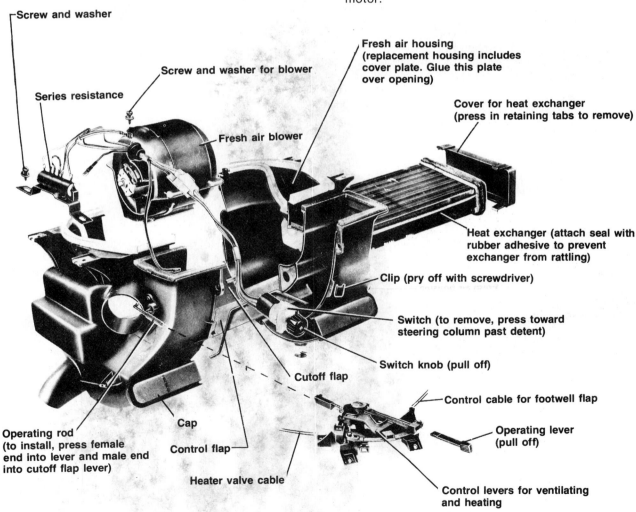

Fig. 8-2. Exploded view of three-speed heater/ ventilation unit used on 1977 and later cars.

5. On 1973 through 1976 cars, disconnect the heater valve cable from the heater control rotary knob. Remove the screws that hold the heater controls as shown in Fig. 8-3, then pry off the spring clip that holds the fresh air housing. You can then remove the heater controls, the cables, and the fresh air housing as a unit.

6. On 1977 and later cars, disconnect the heater valve cable and the control cable for the footwell flap. Remove the screws that hold the heater controls as shown in Fig. 8-3. Then remove the heater controls, detaching the cutoff flap control lever from the operating rod.

Fig. 8-3. Ventilation and heating controls being removed.

To install and adjust (1973 through 1976):

1. Inspect the cutoff flap cable, the control flap cable, and the heater valve cable. Replace faulty cables.

2. To install and adjust the cutoff flap cable, hand-press the cutoff flap located in the water drain box into its closed position. Hook the cable onto the volume control (upper) lever. Push the lever to the left until gap **a**, indicated in Fig. 8-4, is 2.00 mm (.080 in.). Then secure the cable housing on the control quadrant with the clamp.

3. To install and adjust the control flap cable, hook the cable onto the distribution control (lower) lever. Push the lever fully to the left and hold it there while you push the cable housing as far as it will go to the right. (See Fig. 8-4.) Then secure the cable housing on the control quadrant with the clamp.

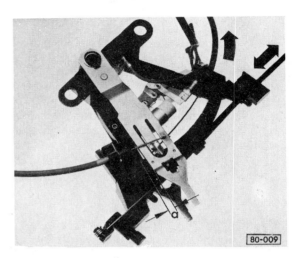

Fig. 8-4. Cable adjustments. Adjust cutoff flap cable so that dimension **a** is 2.00 mm (.080 in.); adjust control flap cable by pulling its housing to the right as indicated by the curved arrow; adjust the heater valve cable by moving its housing back and forth as indicated by the double arrow.

4. To install and adjust the heater valve cable, open the engine hood and then disconnect the cable from the lever on the valve. Move the lever as far as possible toward the cable securing clamp location. Then secure the cable housing on the valve as shown in Fig. 8-5. Working beneath the dashboard, move the cable housing back and forth until the heater control rotary knob points upward. Then secure the cable housing on the control quadrant with the clamp.

5. The remainder of installation is the reverse of removal. Check that the controls operate properly before you reinstall the under-dash panels.

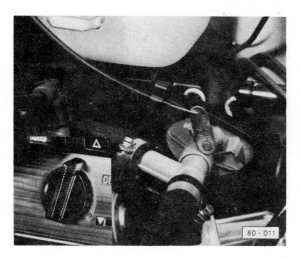

Fig. 8-5. Cable installed on heater valve with valve lever positioned as far as possible toward the cable securing clip. Inset at lower left shows position of rotary knob.

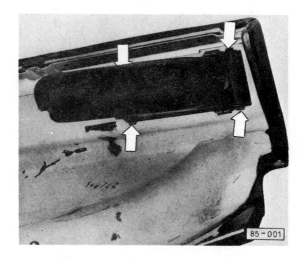

Fig. 8-6. Lugs (arrows) that hold vent in dashboard (dashboard removed for clarity).

To install and adjust (1977 and later):

1. Inspect the heater valve cable and the control cable for the footwell flap. Replace faulty cables.

2. Install the controls beneath the dashboard, pressing the female end of the cutoff lever connection onto the operating rod. (If you removed the connection from the control lever, press the male end into the hole in the control lever.)

   NOTE ——
   The control lever should be in its "off" position and the cutoff flap closed.

3. Reconnect the cables. Either release the clamps that hold the cable conduits to the control quadrant or do not install the clamps.

4. Fully close the heater valve; fully close the footwell flap. With the control levers in their "off" positions, before you install the clamps.

5. The remainder of installation is the reverse of removal. Check that the controls operate properly before you reinstall the under-dash panels.

To remove an air outlet grille from the body, carefully pry off the grille with a wooden or plastic wedge. If the plastic grommets are damaged or loose-fitting, replace them before you install the grille. See Fig. 8-7.

Fig. 8-7. Air outlet grille removed from body. Notice the plastic grommets (removed) that hold the grille in place.

8.2 Removing and Installing Dashboard Vents and Body Outlet Grilles

To remove the fresh air vents from the rear of the dashboard, first remove the under-dash panels, the driver's glove shelf, and the glove compartment's lid as described in **7.1 Removing and Installing Dashboard Panels and Glove Compartment Lid.** Then squeeze the vent so that the securing lugs, indicated in Fig. 8-6, are disengaged from the dashboard. Installation is the reverse of removal.

MANUAL TRANSMISSION

2 ▊

Contents

TABLES

2

Manual Transmission

The four-speed manual transmission, standard equipment on the cars covered by this Manual, is fully synchronized in all forward gears. Both the transmission and the final drive are housed in a single lightweight alloy case. Taken as a unit, the transmission, final drive, and case are called the transaxle.

The transaxle with four-speed manual transmission operates on entirely different principles from the optional transaxle with automatic transmission. However, the constant velocity joint repairs described in this section of the Manual apply to both the standard and the optional transaxles. See **AUTOMATIC TRANSMISSION** for all other repairs related to the transaxle with automatic transmission.

Though much of the repair data given in this section of the Manual may prove practical only to professional mechanics, a general knowledge of the transaxle's operation can often be helpful when troubleshooting. Such knowledge can also lead to better understanding between you and your service advisor or mechanic. But if you lack the skills, tools, or a clean workshop for transaxle repairs, we suggest that you leave such work to your Authorized Dealer or other qualified shop. We especially urge you to consult an Authorized Dealer before attempting any repairs on a car still covered by the new-car warranty.

Though the home mechanic often lacks the tools and experience necessary actually to repair his car's transaxle, he may be perfectly capable of removing and installing the unit. If so, he should deliver the transaxle to an Authorized Dealer or other qualified repair shop after giving the case a thorough exterior cleaning but without doing any disassembly work. A partially disassembled transmission in a box or a basket is a mechanic's nightmare, so the car owner is not likely to be greeted with sympathy after trying a job which is over his head and then giving up. Also, precision measurements must be made on the transaxle before you disassemble it in order to reassemble it correctly.

Cleanliness and a careful approach are imperative when repairing either the transmission or the final drive. If necessary, mark the parts to show their proper assembly order. Also make sure that you have the necessary tools—particularly for procedures given only with metric specifications. Work that is designated by the lack of U.S. equivalents can be carried out correctly only with metric tools and instruments.

1. GENERAL DESCRIPTION

A cross section of the transaxle with manual transmission is shown in Fig. 1-1. The gears on the two labeled shafts are called the transmission gear train. The pinion gear, the ring gear, and the differential gears—all of which carry driving torque from the transmission gear train to the front wheel driveshafts—are called the final drive. Throughout this section of the manual, we will use the term transmission gear train when we are speaking of the gears that are used to select the four forward speeds and reverse. The term final drive will be used for the gears that drive the front axle driveshafts. The term transaxle will be used to designate the transmission gear train, the final drive gears, and the transaxle case when these three main components are handled as a unit.

Transaxle Case

The transaxle case, which contains the transmission gear train and the final drive gears, is die cast in magnesium alloy. A cast-in partition divides the transmission housing from the final drive housing. A second cast-in partition divides the final drive housing from the flywheel bellhousing. All repairs related to the flywheel and the clutch are covered in **ENGINE AND CLUTCH.**

The flanged shafts that carry driving torque to the front wheels extend from two openings at either side of the final drive portion of the transaxle case. A removable final drive cover on the left-hand side of the case provides access to the final drive gears.

Transmission Gear Train

The transmission gears are of the constant-mesh type with balk ring synchronizers. The 3rd and 4th gear synchronizers are on the mainshaft; the 1st and 2nd gear synchronizers are on the pinion shaft. The sliding reverse idler gear is at the rear of the gear train where it can be moved into engagement with the teeth on the outer surface of the 1st gear/2nd gear clutch gear assembly.

Final Drive Gears

The ring and pinion gearset has a hypoid offset that elevates the axis of the pinion gear above that of the ring gear. The differential gearset, which consists of the two differential side gears and the two differential pinions, allows the front wheels to turn at different speeds, as is necessary when making turns (the outside wheel must travel farther than the inside wheel in the same amount of time).

Driveshafts and Constant Velocity Joints

The front wheels are driven by driveshafts which have a constant velocity joint at each end. The repairs described in this section also apply to the driveshafts and constant velocity joints used with the optional transaxle with automatic transmission.

2. MAINTENANCE

Only two items, checking the constant velocity joint screws and boots and checking and correcting the transaxle oil level, are required at a prescribed mileage. These jobs are described in **LUBRICATION AND MAINTENANCE.**

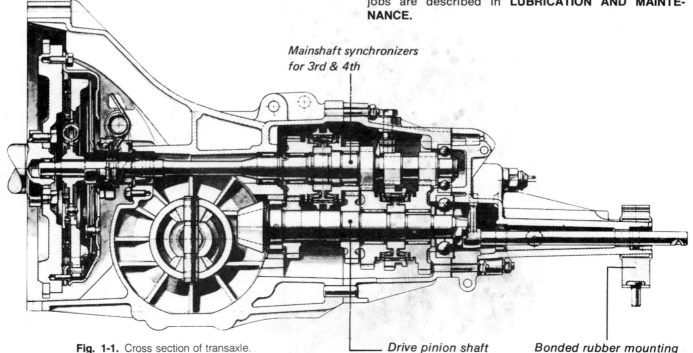

Mainshaft synchronizers
for 3rd & 4th

Fig. 1-1. Cross section of transaxle.

Drive pinion shaft   Bonded rubber mounting

Fig. 3-1. Exploded views of early-type gearshift levers and linkages. Inset shows earlist type. Lever in large illustration was used on VW cars only.

3. REMOVING AND INSTALLING GEARSHIFT LEVER AND SHIFT LINKAGE

Three different gearshift levers and shift linkages have been used on the cars covered by this Manual. Fig. 3-1 shows the two early versions. Fig. 3-2 shows the latest kind of shift lever and linkage, which was introduced on the 1975 models. Repair procedures for the three types of levers and linkages will be given separately.

2

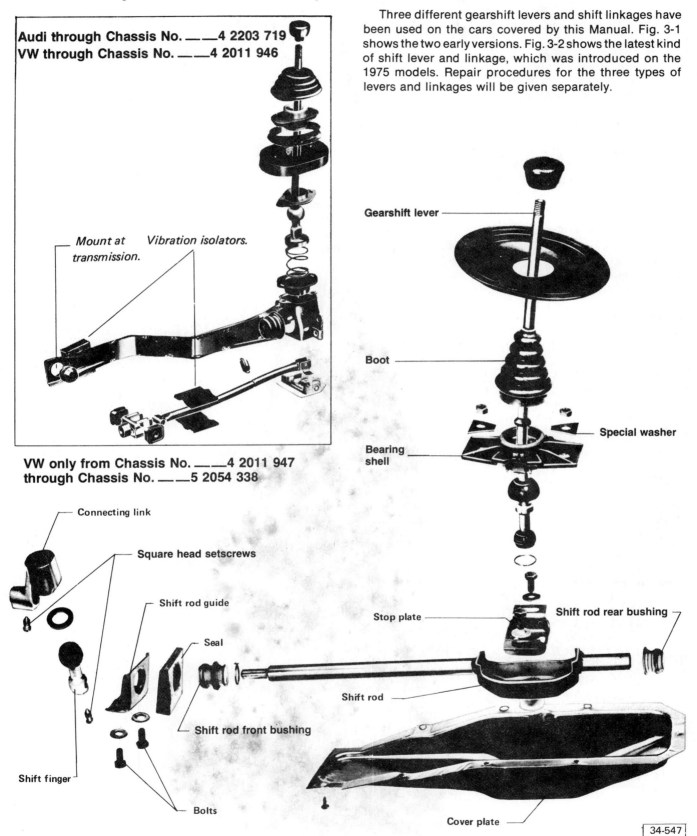

Audi through Chassis No. ___ 4 2203 719
VW through Chassis No. ___ 4 2011 946

Mount at transmission.   *Vibration isolators.*

VW only from Chassis No. ___ 4 2011 947
through Chassis No. ___ 5 2054 338

Connecting link

Square head setscrews

Shift rod guide

Seal

Shift rod front bushing

Shift finger

Bolts

Gearshift lever

Boot

Special washer

Bearing shell

Stop plate

Shift rod rear bushing

Shift rod

Cover plate

34-547

To remove earliest-type lever and linkage:

1. Unscrew the shift knob. Remove the boot and the rubber cover parts upward.

2. Working under the car, unhook the exhaust system rubber support rings that are located behind the front muffler. Then lower the exhaust system.

3. Cut the locking wire for the square head setscrew that holds the shift rod coupling on the transmission's inner shift rod. Then remove the setscrew.

4. Remove the bolts that hold the transaxle carrier to the body. Remove the bolt that holds the shift linkage strut to the transmission (Fig. 3-3).

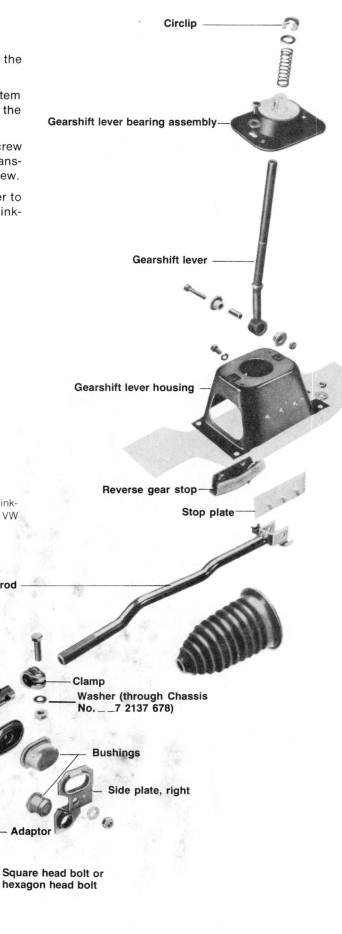

Circlip

Gearshift lever bearing assembly

Gearshift lever

Gearshift lever housing

Reverse gear stop

Stop plate

Shift rod

Fig. 3-2. Exploded view of late gearshift lever and linkage (Audi from Chassis No. 8__5 2000 009, VW from Chassis No. 3__5 2054 339).

From Chassis No. __7 2137 679

Shift finger

Clamp

Washer (through Chassis No. __7 2137 678)

Side plate, left

Support

Bushings

Side plate, right

Adaptor

Square head bolt or hexagon head bolt

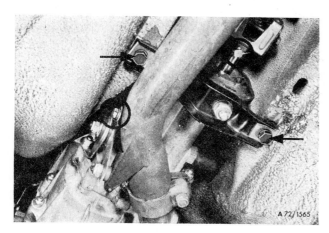

Fig. 3-3. Bolts to be removed at rear of transaxle. Arrows indicate transaxle carrier bolts. Setscrew, removed in step 3, is in right circle; bolt for shift linkage strut is in left circle.

5. Remove the bolts indicated in Fig. 3-4. Pry the shift linkage strut off the pin on the transaxle. Then remove the lever and the linkage as a unit, pulling the lever down through the car's floor.

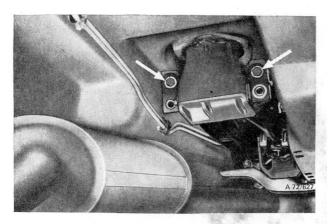

Fig. 3-4. Bolts (arrows) that hold the lever/linkage assembly to the car body.

6. Further disassembly should be carried out, if necessary, with the parts on the workbench.

No adjustment is required following assembly and installation. However, the square head setscrew must enter the recess in the transmission's inner shift lever. Secure the setscrew with a new locking wire.

Installation is the reverse of removal. Inspect the vibration isolators, the boots, and other non-metallic parts. Replace all worn or damaged parts. If you have removed the lever from the linkage, lubricate the moving parts with white multipurpose grease and apply Molykote® to the selector gate. Torque the bolt that holds the shift linkage strut to the transaxle to 2.0 mkg (14 ft. lb.).

To remove VW-only lever and linkage:

2

1. Unscrew the shift knob. Carefully pry the plastic cover out of the floor. Take the cover and the boot off upward.

2. Remove the nuts and the special washers that hold the bearing shell to the floor. Lift the bearing shell up and off the lever. Then remove the bolts that hold the stop plate.

3. Lift out the gearshift lever and the stop plate.

4. Working under the car, remove the cover plate that is beneath the gearshift linkage. Cut the locking wire for the square head setscrew that is in the shift finger. Then remove the setscrew.

5. To remove the shift finger from the shift rod, hand-pull the shift rod to the rear so that it slides out of the shift finger. Pull the shift finger out of the connecting link.

6. Remove the bolts and the washers that hold the shift rod guide on the car. Lower the front of the shift rod slightly, then hand-pull the rod toward the front of the car until it is out of the shift rod rear bushing.

7. If necessary, remove the connecting link from the transmission's inner shift lever. Any further disassembly should be carried out with the parts on the workbench.

To install and adjust VW-only lever and linkage:

1. Inspect the seal, the shift rod bushings, the shift finger and the gearshift lever for wear. Replace worn or damaged parts. The shoulders of the shift rod bushings should be toward the center of the shift rod. Use weatherproof cement to stick the seal onto the shift rod guide.

2. Install the shift rod without the shift finger. Install, but do not fully tighten, the bolts that hold the shift rod guide to the car.

3. If previously removed, reinstall the connecting link on the transmission's inner shift lever. Tighten the setscrew, then secure it with a new locking wire.

4. Slide the shift rod forward until it contacts the connecting link. Then adjust the lateral position of the shift rod guide so that the end of the shift rod is aligned laterally with the inner shift lever bore in the connecting link. See Fig. 3-5.

NOTE ——

In a vertical plane, the shift rod must be no more than 2.00 mm (⅛ in.) above or below the inner shift lever bore in the connecting link.

Fig. 3-5. Shift rod aligned laterally with inner shift lever bore (arrow) in connecting link.

5. When you have correctly aligned the shift rod, tighten the bolts that hold the shift rod guide to the car.

6. Hand-pull the shift rod to the rear. Lubricate the shift finger and the connecting link with molybdenum grease. Then install the shift finger. Tighten the setscrew and secure it with a new locking wire.

7. Install the cover.

8. Working inside the passenger compartment, loosely install the stop plate so that the side of the plate that has the longer shoulder is on the right.

9. Loosely install the gearshift lever and the bearing shell. Engage neutral. Move the bearing shell forward and backward, as indicated in Fig. 3-6, until the lever inclines approximately 5° to the rear. Then tighten the nuts.

10. Engage 2nd gear. Adjust the stop plate, as indicated in Fig. 3-7, until there are approximately 10 to 15 mm (⅜ to ⅝ in.) of lateral play at the knob-end of the gearshift lever. To increase lateral play, move the plate to the right; to decrease lateral play, move the plate to the left. When the play is within the specified range, tighten the bolts.

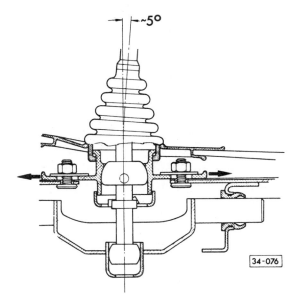

Fig. 3-6. Gearshift lever angle being adjusted. Move bearing shell as indicated by arrows.

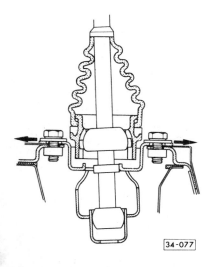

Fig. 3-7. Gearshift lever lateral play being adjusted. Move the stop plate as indicated by the arrows.

11. Check whether the gears engage easily. Especially check the operation of reverse. If necessary, repeat the adjustment steps to obtain good operation.

12. When the gearshift is working correctly, install the boot, the plastic cover, and the shift knob.

To remove latest-type lever and linkage:

1. Remove the gearshift knob. Remove the screws that hold the center console to the floorboard, then remove the console and gearshift lever boot as a unit, raising the assembly up and off of the gearshift lever.

2. Remove the circlip, the washer, and the spring that are on the gearshift lever.

3. Remove the two bolts and washers that hold the gearshift lever bearing assembly to the top of the gearshift lever housing. Then lift the bearing assembly up and off of the gearshift lever.

4. Remove the nuts and the washers that hold the gearshift lever housing to the floorboards. Then remove the gearshift lever housing.

5. Remove the nut, the bolt, and the bushings that hold the lower end of the gearshift lever to the shift rod. Remove the gearshift lever.

6. Working beneath the car, remove the bolt indicated in Fig. 3-8. Push the shift rod slightly rearward into the passenger compartment. Remove the rubber boot and then remove the shift rod.

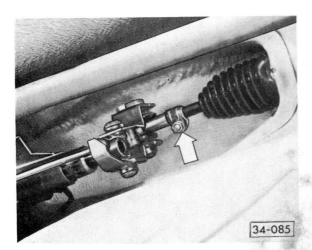

Fig. 3-8. Clamp bolt that holds shift rod to shift finger of shift rod coupling assembly.

7. Remove the nut and bolt that hold the support to the lug on the bottom of the transaxle's shift housing. If necessary, refer to Fig. 3-2 given earlier.

8. Cut the locking wire for the setscrew that holds the shift rod coupling assembly to the transmission's inner shift lever. Then remove the setscrew (Fig. 3-9).

> **NOTE**
>
> Until the early part of 1975, a square-head setscrew was installed. After that, a setscrew with a hexagon head was used. If the setscrew of the car you are working on has a square head, discard the setscrew and obtain a new setscrew with a hexagon head (Part No. 823 711 833) for use during installation.

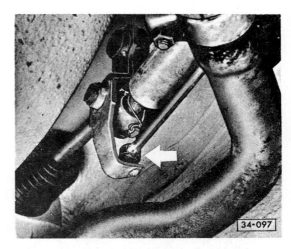

Fig. 3-9. Setscrew for shift rod coupling assembly (arrow).

9. Remove the shift rod coupling assembly from the transaxle as a unit. If necessary, disassemble the shift rod coupling assembly on a workbench, using as a guide Fig. 3-2 which was given earlier.

To install and adjust latest-type lever and linkage:

1. If it was previously disassembled, reassemble the shift rod coupling assembly using as a guide Fig. 3-2 which was given earlier.

2. Install the shift rod coupling assembly on the transmission's inner shift lever, making sure that the setscrew hole in the coupling assembly's adapter is correctly aligned with the recess in the inner shift lever.

3. Install a new hexagon head setscrew to a torque of 1.5 mkg (11 ft. lb.). Then secure the setscrew in place with a new locking wire.

4. Install the clamp on the shift rod coupling assembly's shift finger. Install the shift rod and the rubber boot so that the shift rod fits loosely inside the shift rod coupling assembly's shift finger.

5. Working inside the car, install the gearshift lever on the shift rod using the bolt, the bushings, and the nut. The bend in the gearshift lever should incline the lever to the left.

6. Install the gearshift lever housing. Torque the nuts to 1.5 mkg (11 ft. lb.).

7. Install the gearshift lever bearing assembly, the spring, the washer, and the circlip on the gearshift lever. Align the centering holes in the bearing as-

sembly with those in the gearshift lever housing. See Fig. 3-10. Then install the bolts and torque them to 1.5 mkg (11 ft. lb.).

Fig. 3-10. Centering holes (arrows) in bearing assembly that must be aligned with centering holes in housing. The adjusting jig, Tool 3009, is used to hold the gearshift lever in its neutral position.

8. Install the adjusting jig, Tool 3009, so that its locating pin is at the front. To eliminate play in the bearing assembly, lift up on the gearshift lever and push down on the jig. Then, while holding the lever and the jig in position, clamp the jig to the lever by tightening the knurled thumbscrew that is on the top of the jig.

9. Working beneath the car, move the shift rod coupling assembly so that the transmission gears are in neutral. The shift rod should then be correctly positioned in the coupling assembly's shift finger. Correctly align the clamp, then torque the clamp bolt to 1.5 mkg (11 ft. lb.).

10. Remove the adjusting jig. Then check that all the gears can be engaged without difficulty or jamming. Correct difficult shifting by altering slightly the position of the gearshift lever bearing assembly on the gearshift lever housing.

Disassembling and Lubricating Gearshift Lever Bearing Assembly

Individual internal parts are not available for the gearshift lever bearing assembly. However, the bearing assembly can be disassembled for cleaning and relubricating. Fig. 3-11 is an exploded view of the gearshift lever bearing assembly.

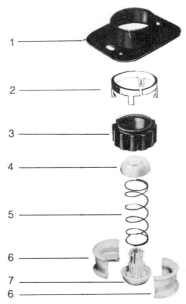

1. Bearing mounting
2. Retaining ring (late models only)
3. Guide
4. Upper ball half
5. Spring
6. Shell (2)
7. Lower ball half

Fig. 3-11. Exploded view of gearshift lever bearing assembly. Item **2** should be service-installed on earlier cars.

To disassemble the gearshift lever bearing assembly, hand-press the guide out of the bearing mounting. Remove the ball halves and the spring from the guide, then carefully pry the shells out of the guide. After the parts have been cleaned, you should lubricate them with multipurpose grease as you reassemble them.

To assemble:

1. Place the shells in the guide.

2. Hold the guide so that its shoulder is uppermost. Then push the lower ball half into the shells.

3. Insert the spring and the upper ball half from the top, pushing the shells apart so that the upper ball half will enter them.

4. Place the retaining ring around the guide, then hand-press the guide and the bearing parts into the bearing mounting.

4. DRIVESHAFTS

The driveshafts used on cars with manual transmissions are not the same length as either of the two driveshafts used on cars with automatic transmissions. When you buy replacement parts for a transaxle with manual transmission, dimension **a** indicated in Fig. 4-1

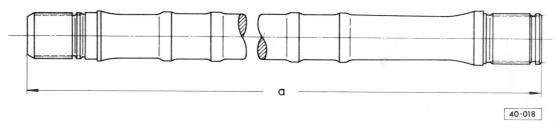

40-018

Fig. 4-1. Driveshaft length measurement **(a).**

2

must be 506.00 mm (19.92 in. or 19 $^{59}/_{64}$ in.). On transaxles with automatic transmissions, the left driveshaft should be 531.00 mm (20.90 in. or 20 $^{29}/_{32}$ in.) long and the right driveshaft should be 437. 00 mm (17.20 in. or 17 $^{13}/_{64}$ in.) long.

4.1 Removing and Installing Driveshaft

Because the inboard constant velocity joints are different from the outboard constant velocity joints, the procedure for disconnecting the driveshaft inner ends differs from the procedure for disconnecting driveshaft outer ends. To avoid difficulty, follow the sequence given here.

To remove:

1. Pry off the dust cap that is pressed into the center of the front wheel hub. Then loosen, but do not remove, the axle shaft nut.

> **WARNING ——**
>
> *Loosen axle shaft nuts with the car on the ground. The leverage needed for this job is enough to topple a car off the lift.*

2. Raise the car on a lift. If you intend to remove a right-side driveshaft, unbolt the exhaust pipe from the engine's exhaust manifold and from the bracket on the rear of the transaxle.

3. If you intend to remove a left-side driveshaft from a car with an automatic transmission, scribe or otherwise mark the position of the left suspension ball joint on the track control arm. (By doing this, you will simplify—or eliminate—the job of adjusting the front wheel camber since the ball joint can easily be installed in its original location.) Then unbolt the ball joint as shown in Fig. 4-2.

4. Remove the six socket head bolts (Fig. 4-3) that hold the inboard constant velocity joint to the transaxle's flanged shaft.

5. Lower the inboard end of the driveshaft. Pull the axle shaft out of the wheel hub and remove the driveshaft from the car.

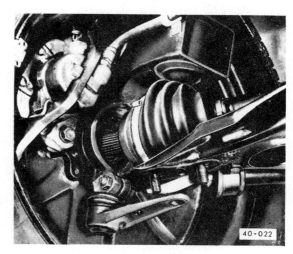

40-022

Fig. 4-2. Left-side suspension ball joint unbolted from track control arm (automatic transmission only). Push wheel outward and off axle shaft as shown.

40-020

Fig. 4-3. One of six socket head bolts (arrow).

To install:

1. Inspect the boots. If they are torn or otherwise damaged, replace them. If the constant velocity joints are difficult to move by hand or feel gritty, remove and disassemble the joints so that they can be inspected and, if necessary, replaced or cleaned and lubricated. See **4.2 Removing and Installing Constant Velocity Joints.**

2. Insert the axle shaft in the wheel hub. Raise the inboard end of the driveshaft and install the constant velocity joint on the flanged shaft. Torque the socket head bolts to 3.5 mkg (25 ft. lb.).

3. Reconnect the exhaust system and the front suspension ball joint if either of these parts were disconnected during driveshaft removal. Torque the ball joint nuts to 6.5 mkg (47 ft. lb.). Loosely install the axle shaft nut.

4. Lower the car to the ground. Then torque the axle shaft nut to 25 to 30 mkg (180 to 216 ft. lb.).

> *WARNING ——*
>
> *Torque axle shaft nuts with the car on the ground. The leverage needed for this job is enough to topple a car off the lift.*

4.2 Removing and Installing Constant Velocity Joints

Fig. 4-4 is an exploded view of a driveshaft and its two constant velocity joints. Notice the ridges that are forged into the shaft for the purpose of holding the rubber boots in place.

To remove an outboard constant velocity joint, first cut off the clamp for the rubber boot. Then turn the boot inside out over the driveshaft. Clamp the driveshaft in a vise.

Working through the opening indicated at arrow **A** in Fig. 4-5, fully expand the circlip into the groove in the constant velocity joint's ball hub. With the circlip expanded, grasp the axle shaft (arrow **B** in Fig. 4-5) and pull the axle shaft and the constant velocity joint off the driveshaft. If necessary, use a rubber or plastic hammer to drive off the axle shaft and joint.

Fig. 4-4. Exploded view of driveshaft and constant velocity joints.

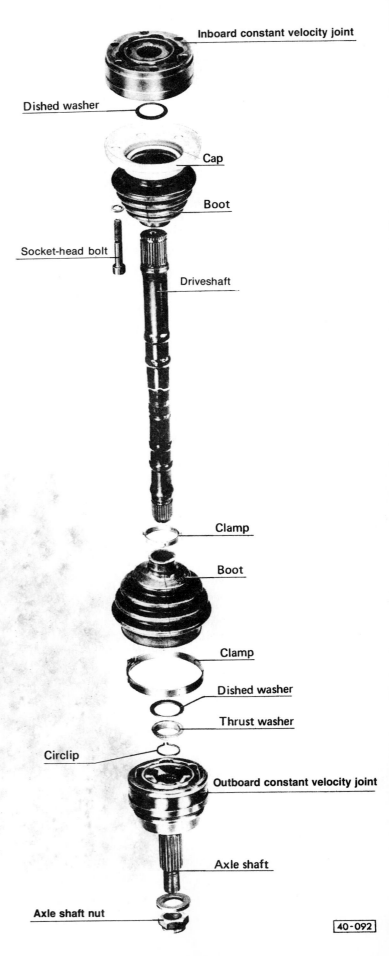

40-092

Fig. 4-5. Outboard constant velocity joint removal. Circlip is at arrow **A**; axle shaft is at arrow **B**.

If the rubber boot is torn or otherwise damaged, be sure to replace it before you install the constant velocity joint. When installing a rubber boot, either use a plastic guide sleeve or cover the driveshaft splines with tape in order to protect the boot's sealing surface as you slide the boot onto the driveshaft.

Install the dished washer and the thrust washer on the driveshaft in the positions shown in Fig. 4-6. Install a new circlip in the groove inside the constant velocity joint's ball hub. Using circlip pliers, fully expand the circlip while you start the constant velocity joint on the driveshaft splines. Then, using a rubber or plastic hammer, drive the axle shaft and the constant velocity joint onto the driveshaft until the circlip snaps firmly into the groove on the driveshaft.

If the constant velocity joint has not been disassembled, cleaned, and lubricated as described in **4.3 Servicing Constant Velocity Joints,** add just enough molybdenum grease to make up for any that was lost during removal and installation of the joint. Using a new clamp, secure the boot to the constant velocity joint as shown in Fig. 4-7. If the boot has been replaced, position its small end between the ridges on the driveshaft so that the boot is not twisted. Then secure it with a new clamp.

NOTE ——

In installing a new large clamp, be sure to position it so that its locking projection will not interfere with the installation of any of the socket head screws.

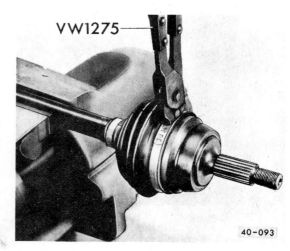

Fig. 4-7. Special pliers being used to tighten and lock the clamp for the rubber boot.

Fig. 4-6. Proper positions for washers and circlip. Circlip **(1)** is seated in groove in driveshaft; convex side of thrust washer **(2)** is toward constant velocity joint; convex side of dished washer **(3)** is against shoulder on driveshaft.

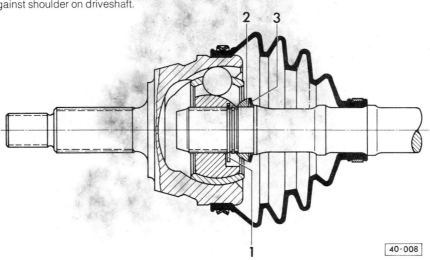

To remove an inboard constant velocity joint, remove the circlip as shown in Fig. 4-8. Then, using a drift and a hammer, drive the cap off the outer side of the joint and turn the boot inside out over the driveshaft.

Fig. 4-8. Circlip being removed.

CAUTION ——

After you have removed the cap and boot, do not tilt the ball hub more than 20° in the joint outer rings. If you do, the balls may fall out.

Slide the joint outer ring as far as possible toward the end of the driveshaft. Then, with the ball hub supported, press the driveshaft out of the ball hub as shown in Fig. 4-9. Remove the dished washer from the driveshaft.

Fig. 4-9. Driveshaft being pressed out of constant velocity joint. Notice that only the ball hub is supported, so that no stress is placed on the balls or the outer ring.

If the rubber boot is torn or otherwise damaged, be sure to replace it before you install the constant velocity joint. When installing a rubber boot, either use a plastic guide sleeve or cover the driveshaft splines with tape in order to protect the boot's sealing surface as you slide the boot onto the driveshaft.

Install the dished washer with its convex side against the shoulder on the driveshaft. Then, with the driveshaft supported in a collet clamp, as shown in Fig. 4-10, press the constant velocity joint onto the driveshaft. While using the press to hold the ball hub down against the tension of the dished washer, install the circlip. After you have raised the press tool, use pliers to squeeze the circlip around its periphery until the circlip is completely seated in the groove.

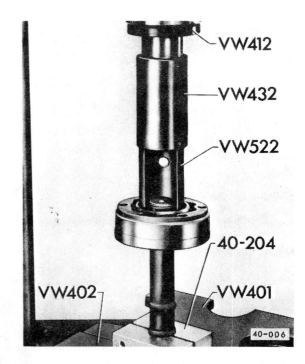

Fig. 4-10. Constant velocity joint being pressed onto the driveshaft. Notice the collet clamp that is positioned below the ridge on the driveshaft.

If the constant velocity joint has not been disassembled, cleaned, and lubricated as described in **4.3 Servicing Constant Velocity Joints,** add just enough molybdenum grease to make up for any that was lost during removal and installation of the joint. Then install the cap and boot on the joint's outer surface. If the boot has been replaced, position its small end between the ridges on the driveshaft so that the boot is not twisted.

4.3 Servicing Constant Velocity Joints

It is not possible to repair the constant velocity joints. The components of each joint are factory-matched and cannot be replaced individually. The joints can, however, be disassembled for cleaning, inspection, and repacking with molybdenum grease. Because the outboard and the inboard constant velocity joints are constructed differently, separate procedures are given for servicing each kind.

To disassemble outboard joint:

1. Remove the constant velocity joint from the driveshaft as described in **4.2 Removing and Installing Constant Velocity Joints.**

2. Using a waterproof felt-tip marker, mark the relative positions of the ball hub, the ball cage, and the outer ring. Then tilt the ball cage and the hub as shown in Fig. 4-11 and remove the balls.

> **CAUTION** ——
>
> *The ball cage, the outer ring, and the balls themselves are selected for matching tolerances. When disassembling more than one joint, be sure not to intermix the parts. If you do, the joints may seize, make noise, or wear rapidly.*

Fig. 4-11. Balls being removed from outboard constant velocity joint. Notice the mark that has been made on the outer ring. Similar marks should be made on the ball hub and the ball cage.

3. Turn the ball cage and the ball hub so that the two large rectangular openings are positioned as shown in Fig. 4-12. Then remove the cage and the hub from the outer ring.

4. To remove the ball hub from the ball cage, turn the hub so that one ridge is in line with one of the large rectangular openings in the cage (Fig. 4-13). The ball hub now has sufficient clearance to be tipped out of the ball cage.

Fig. 4-12. Large rectangular opening (arrow) in position for cage and hub removal.

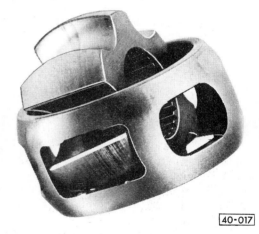

Fig. 4-13. Ball hub being removed or installed in the ball cage. Notice how the large rectangular opening in the cage just accommodates the ridge on the hub.

To assemble outboard joint:

1. Clean and inspect all parts. If any is worn or damaged, replace the entire joint.

> **NOTE** ——
>
> In addition to galling, pitting, and other obvious wear, replace joints that have excessive radial clearance or excessive play when changes of load direction take place. Do not replace a joint merely because the parts appear polished or the ball track is clearly visible.

2. Thoroughly coat all parts with molybdenum grease. Then install the ball hub in the ball cage as illustrated earlier in Fig. 4-13.

3. Install the balls in the ball cage and ball hub. If necessary, use additional molybdenum grease as an adhesive to hold the balls in place.

4. Insert the ball hub together with the balls and ball cage into the outer ring, making sure that the marks made prior to disassembly are properly aligned. Also make sure that the circlip-access groove in the ball hub is visible following assembly.

5. Repack the joint with 90 g (3.2 oz.) of molybdenum grease. Force about two-thirds of the grease into the joint and use the remaining third to pack the open side of the joint.

6. Install the constant velocity joint on the driveshaft.

To disassemble inboard joint:

1. Remove the inboard constant velocity joint from the driveshaft as described in **4.2 Removing and Installing Constant Velocity Joints.**

2. Using hand pressure, push the ball hub and ball cage out of the outer ring as shown in Fig. 4-14.

40-009

Fig. 4-14. Ball cage and ball hub being separated from outer ring. Position the ball hub and ball cage perpendicular to the outer ring, then push in the direction indicated by the arrow.

3. Lift the six steel balls out of the ball cage, taking care not to drop them.

CAUTION ——

The ball cage, the outer ring, and the balls themselves are selected for matching tolerances. When disassembling more than one joint, be sure not to intermix the parts. If you do, the joints may seize, make noise, or wear rapidly.

4. Rotate the ball hub into the position shown in Fig. 4-15. The groove in the ball hub must be in line with the outer edge of the ball cage. The ball hub now has sufficient clearance to be tipped out of the ball cage.

40-010

Fig. 4-15. Ball hub being removed from or installed in the ball cage. Arrows indicate the alignment of the ball hub groove with the ball cage edge.

To assemble inboard joint:

1. Clean and inspect all parts. If any is worn or damaged, replace the entire joint.

2. Thoroughly coat all parts with molybdenum grease. Then install the ball hub in the ball cage as illustrated earlier in Fig. 4-15.

3. Install the balls in the ball cage and ball hub. If necessary, use additional molybdenum grease as an adhesive to hold the balls in place.

4. Insert the ball hub together with the balls and ball cage into the outer ring. The chamfer on the splines and the larger diameter portion of the outer ring must be on the same side of the joint.

NOTE ——

Insert the ball and hub assembly in the outer ring at a 90° angle, as shown in Fig. 4-16. The narrow ball hub grooves **b** and the wide outer ring grooves **a** must be positioned as illustrated.

5. Hold the ball and hub assembly steady and push it in the direction indicated in Fig. 4-17 (left arrow). This will align the balls with their respective grooves (right arrows) in the outer ring.

6. When the balls are aligned with their grooves in the outer ring, firmly press the ball cage, as indicated in Fig. 4-18, until it swings fully into place. Heavy pressure should not be required.

2

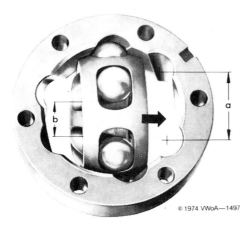

Fig. 4-16. Ball and hub assembly positioned in the outer ring. Arrow indicates the direction in which the ball and hub assembly must be turned to complete the installation.

© 1974 VWoA—1499

Fig. 4-18. Balls being engaged in the grooves of the outer ring. Apply hand pressure at the point indicated by the arrow.

joint and the cap. Use the remaining third to pack the open side of the joint.

9. Install the constant velocity joint on the driveshaft as described in **4.2 Removing and Installing Constant Velocity Joints.** Then hand-squeeze the boot tightly so that grease will be forced into the joint from the rear.

Replacing Flanged Shaft Oil Seal

With the driveshaft removed, you can replace a leaky flanged shaft oil seal without removing the transaxle from the car. Remove the flanged shaft bolt as shown in Fig. 4-19.

© 1974 VWoA—1498

Fig. 4-17. Balls being aligned with the grooves of the outer ring. Apply finger pressure in the direction indicated by the left arrow.

CAUTION ——
Excessive force will result in improper joint assembly. Double-check the previous steps if the joint does not go together readily. An improperly assembled joint will lock solidly and render the unit unserviceable.

7. Check the operation of the joint. The ball hub should be able to turn smoothly throughout the entire range of travel.

8. Repack the joint with 90 g (3.2 oz.) of molybdenum grease. Pack two-thirds of the grease between the

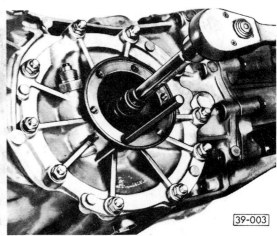

39-003

Fig. 4-19. Flanged shaft bolt being removed. Notice the drift that has been inserted through one of the bolt holes in the flanged shaft in order to keep the shaft from turning.

Pull the flanged shaft out of the transaxle. Then use a large screwdriver to pry the faulty seal out of its recess in either the transaxle case or the final drive cover. Pack the open side of the new seal with multipurpose grease before you install the seal as shown in Fig. 4-20.

NOTE——

The left and the right seals are different and must not be interchanged. Seals for the right side have an unbroken groove on their side; Seals for the left side have a broken groove. On early Audi models the left-side seal is identified by right angle corners on the face side.

Fig. 4-20. New seal being driven in (arrow) with seal driving mandrel.

Inspect the flanged shaft before you install it. Replace the shaft if it has a groove worn into it at the point where it is contacted by the oil seal. Thoroughly clean the threads of the flanged shaft bolt, then coat the threads with VW locking compound D6 or a similar product. Install the bolt to a torque of 2.0 mkg (14 ft. lb.). Then install the driveshaft.

NOTE——

Partway through the 1976 model year, the number of splines on the flanged shafts and the differential side gears was increased from 31 to 33. If you must obtain a new flanged shaft, compare the new part to the old part in order to make sure that you obtain the correct replacement. Additional information is given in **8.3 Disassembling and Assembling Differential.**

5. REMOVING AND INSTALLING TRANSAXLE

You can remove the transaxle, the engine, the front suspension, and the front suspension/engine-mounting subframe as a unit. This procedure is described in **SUSPENSION AND STEERING.** The transaxle can also be removed separately, as described in the following procedure, leaving the engine and suspension in the car. If only

the transaxle requires repair, it is usually best to remove it separately.

Fig. 5-1 shows the locations of components that must be either removed or disconnected preparatory to transaxle removal. Each numbered location in the illustration corresponds to the number for the step in the following procedure wherein the removal or disconnecting of the component is described.

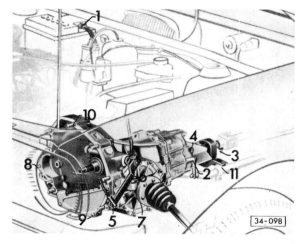

Fig. 5-1. Locations of components that must be removed or disconnected preparatory to transaxle removal.

To remove transaxle:

1. Disconnect the battery ground strap.

2. Disconnect the exhaust pipe from the engine's exhaust manifold. Then unbolt the exhaust pipe bracket from the rear of the transaxle.

3. Cut the locking wire. Then remove the setscrew that holds the shift linkage to the transmission's inner shift lever. If necessary, refer to **3. Removing and Installing Gearshift Lever and Shift Linkage.**

4. Disconnect the wires from the back-up light switch. Also remove the bolt that, on some models, holds the gearshift linkage to the transaxle. (See **3. Removing and Installing Gearshift Lever and Shift Linkage.**)

5. Loosen the clutch cable adjusting nuts and disengage the clutch cable housing from the left-side engine mount. Then unhook the clutch cable from the clutch operating lever.

6. Disconnect the speedometer cable from the transaxle's final drive cover.

7. Unbolt the inboard ends of the front wheel driveshafts from the flanged shafts on the transaxle. Then use wire hooks to suspend the disconnected shafts from the car body.

8. Remove the starter as described in **ELECTRICAL SYSTEM.**

9. Remove the bellhousing front cover plate.

10. Remove the bolts that hold the transaxle to the engine.

   NOTE ——

   In order to support the transaxle while you carry out the following step, either position a floor jack with a transaxle adapter beneath the transaxle or have at least one person to help you hold the transaxle. If a jack is not used, it requires no fewer than two people to remove and lower the transaxle from the car.

   WARNING ——

   If you are not confident of your ability to hand-remove the transaxle, either recruit additional helpers or use a jack. The transaxle will be damaged if it falls and, in falling, could injure you or your helper.

11. Unbolt the transaxle carrier from the car body. Pull the transaxle to the rear until the mainshaft is clear of the clutch assembly. Then carefully lower the transaxle to the floor.

To install:

1. Position the transaxle on the engine.

   NOTE ——

   In order to mesh the splines on the mainshaft with those inside the hub of the clutch driven plate, either rotate the transaxle about its longitudinal axis or, if the transaxle is on a jack, hand-turn the engine's crankshaft.

2. Fully install, but do not tighten, the bolts that hold the transaxle carrier to the car body. Two kinds of carriers have been used, as shown in Fig. 5-2 and Fig. 5-3.

Fig. 5-2. Transaxle carrier used until early in 1975.

Fig. 5-3. Transaxle carrier introduced on early 1975 cars.

3. Install the bolts that hold the transaxle to the engine. Torque the bolts to 5.5 mkg (40 ft. lb.).

4. Install the bellhousing front cover plate.

5. Install the starter as described in **ELECTRICAL SYSTEM.** Torque the bolts to 2.0 mkg (14 ft. lb.).

6. Install the driveshafts as described in **4.1 Removing and Installing Driveshaft.** Torque the socket head bolts to 3.5 mkg (25 ft. lb.).

7. Reconnect the speedometer cable.

8. Reconnect the clutch cable. Then adjust the clutch pedal freeplay as described in **ENGINE AND CLUTCH.**

9. Connect the wires to the back-up light switch. On cars that are so equipped, bolt the shift linkage support or shift linkage strut to the transaxle case.

10. Connect the shift linkage to the transmission's inner shift lever. If the car originally had a square-head setscrew, replace it with a new hexagon head setscrew, Part No. 823 711 833. Torque the setscrew to 1.5 mkg (11 ft. lb.), then secure the setscrew with a new locking wire.

11. Install the exhaust pipe on the engine's exhaust manifold and on the bracket at the rear of the transaxle. Torque the manifold flange bolts to 2.5 mkg (18 ft. lb.); torque the exhaust pipe bracket bolt to 2.0 mkg (14 ft. lb.).

12. Reconnect the battery ground strap.

13. Lower the car so that it is resting on its wheels. Then align the engine/transaxle assembly so that the bonded rubber mountings are not under tension as described in one of the next two steps.

14. On cars with the early-type transaxle carrier, shift the carrier on the car body so that the engine mounts are not twisted. Then torque the bolts that

hold the carrier to 2.5 mkg (18 ft. lb.). Check that the bonded rubber mounting is positioned so that its rubber core is not in contact with the outer ring. Then torque the nut that holds the bonded rubber mounting to the transaxle carrier to 4.0 mkg (29 ft. lb.).

15. On cars with the late-type transaxle carrier, which is located on the left side of the transaxle, shift the carrier on the center bolt of the bonded rubber mounting so that the engine mounts are not twisted. Then torque the nut that holds the carrier to the bonded rubber mounting to 4.0 mkg (29 ft. lb.). Make sure that the bonded rubber mounting is not twisted, then torque the bolt that holds the bonded rubber mounting to the car body to 3.0 mkg (22 ft. lb.).

6. TRANSMISSION

Fig. 6-1 shows the shift housing removed from the transmission gear carrier and the transmission gear carrier and transmission gear train removed from the part of the transaxle case that contains the final drive. The thicknesses of the gasket and the shim that go between the shift housing and the transmission gear carrier must be selected with the help of precision measurements.

NOTE ——
Please read **9.1 Locating and Adjusting Drive Pinion Position** before you begin to disassemble the transaxle.

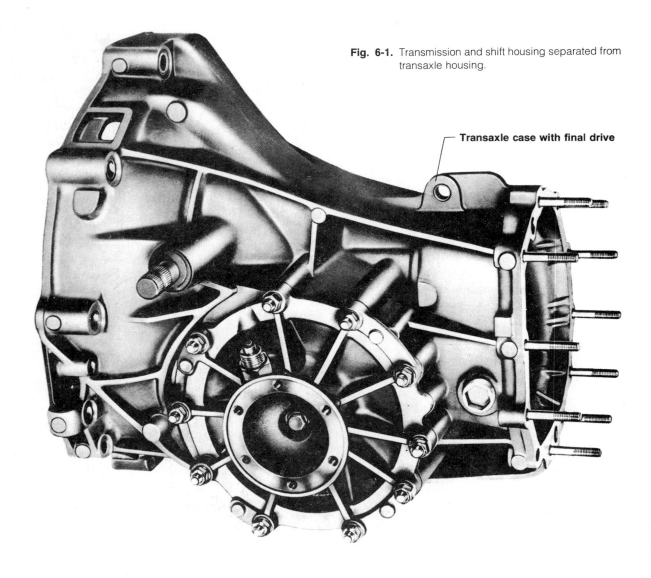

Fig. 6-1. Transmission and shift housing separated from transaxle housing.

— **Transaxle case with final drive**

6.1 Removing and Installing Shift Housing

Thoroughly clean the outside of the transaxle case before you remove the shift housing. On transaxles built before the middle of the 1974 model year, the shift housing is held to the transaxle by nuts on studs. Later transaxles have bolts instead of studs and nuts. Shift housing removal requires only that you remove the nuts or the bolts that hold the shift housing to the transmission gear carrier.

If you replace the mainshaft ball bearing, the drive pinion ball bearing, the gear carrier, or the shift housing, you must make precision measurements before you reinstall the shift housing. These measurements are necessary in order to determine the thicknesses of the shim and the gasket that determine the position of the shift housing on the gear carrier. If the position of the shift housing on the gear carrier is incorrect, either there will be excessive axial play in the transmission's mainshaft and drive pinion or there will be oil leaks between the shift housing and the gear carrier. Excessive axial play in the drive pinion will cause the final drive gears to make noise and wear rapidly.

NOTE ——
Please read **9.1 Locating and Adjusting Drive Pinion Position** before you begin to disassemble the transaxle.

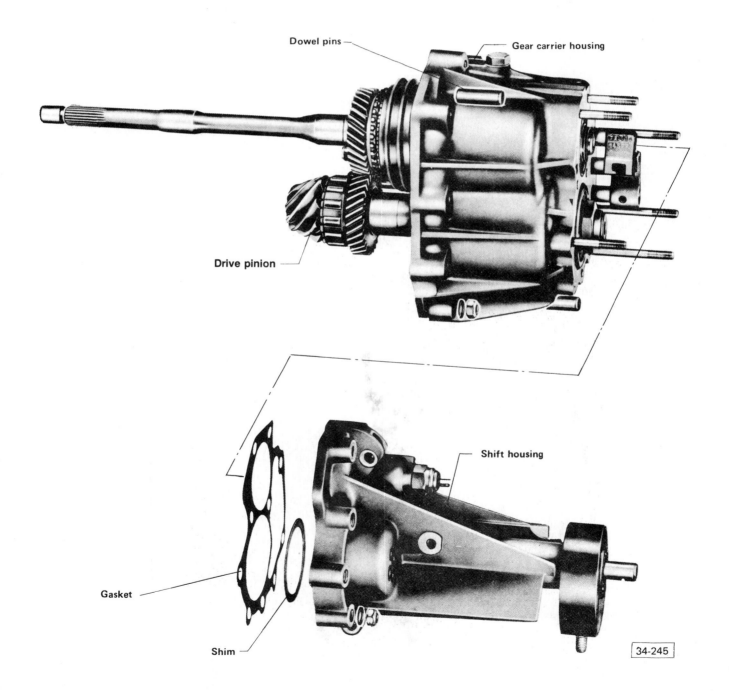

34-245

To install shift housing:

1. If you have not replaced the mainshaft ball bearing, the drive pinion ball bearing, the gear carrier, or the shift housing, simply install the shift housing with the original shim and a new gasket that has the same part number as the original gasket. (Only two different gasket thicknesses are used.) Make sure that the inner shift lever is correctly engaged with the selector shafts. Working diagonally, gradually torque the nuts or the bolts to 2.0 mkg (14 ft. lb.).

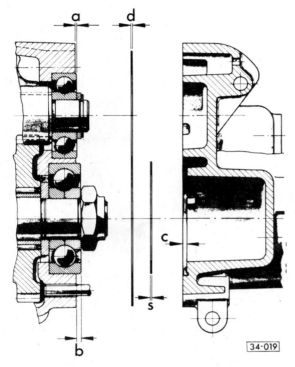

a. Height of mainshaft ball bearing above surface of gear carrier
b. Height of drive pinion ball bearing above surface of gear carrier
c. Depth of drive pinion ball bearing recess in shift housing
d. Thickness of gasket
s. Thickness of shim

Fig. 6-2. Dimensions that determine position of shift housing on gear carrier.

NOTE ——

On late transaxles that have the shift housing held to the gear carrier by bolts, it is helpful to use home-made locating pins to guide the shift housing into position. You can make such pins by grinding the heads off of two M8 × 1.25 bolts that are each 75 mm long. Hacksaw a slot in each bolt shank so that you can remove or install the pins with a screwdriver. Install the locating pins in two of the bolt holes. Then install the shift housing with all but two of the bolts. Finally, remove the locating pins and install the last two bolts.

2. If you have replaced the mainshaft ball bearing, the drive pinion ball bearing, the gear carrier, or the shift housing, you must make precision measurements in order to determine the dimensions listed in Fig. 6-2.

3. Install a dial indicator on a measuring bridge so that there is a 3.00-mm preload when the bridge is placed on a steel gauge block, as shown in Fig. 6-3. Then zero the dial indicator.

Fig. 6-3. Dial indicator and measuring bridge zeroed on steel gauge block.

4. Make certain that both the drive pinion ball bearing and the mainshaft ball bearing are seated fully in the gear carrier. Then, using the dial indicator as shown in Fig. 6-4, measure the heights of the ball bearings above the surface of the gear carrier (dimensions **a** and **b,** given earlier in Fig. 6-2). Write down the measurements.

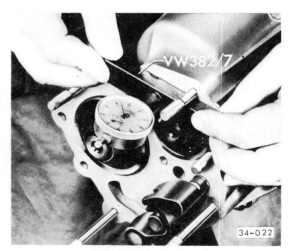

Fig. 6-4. Height of mainshaft ball bearing (dimension **a**) being measured. Use a similar procedure to measure the height of the drive pinion ball bearing (dimension **b**).

5. Using the dial indicator as shown in Fig. 6-5, measure the depth of the drive pinion ball bearing in the shift housing (dimension **c,** given earlier in Fig. 6-2). Write down the measurement.

Fig. 6-5. Depth of drive pinion ball bearing recess in shift housing (dimension **c**) being measured.

NOTE ———

Please be sure that you read the correct scale on the dial indicator. Since you will be measuring depths, the needle will move counterclockwise on the dial. On most dial indicators, the depth scale is indicated by red numerals and graduations. However, if your dial indicator has only one scale, read the number of graduations counterclockwise from zero in determining the correct figure for depth measurements.

6. To determine the thickness of the shim (dimension **s** given earlier in Fig. 6-2), add dimension **a** and dimension **c.** From the sum of **a** plus **c,** subtract dimension **b.** Use the remainder (the answer from your subtraction) to select the proper shim (dimension **s**) from **Table a.**

Table a. Shift Housing Shim Dimensions

Remainder (a + c − b)	Shim thickness "s" (mm)	Part No.
0.44–0.48	0.45	014 311 390
0.49–0.53	0.50	014 311 391
0.54–0.58	0.55	014 311 392
0.59–0.63	0.60	014 311 393
0.64–0.68	0.65	014 311 394
0.69–0.73	0.70	014 311 395
0.74–0.78	0.75	014 311 396

7. Use the height of the mainshaft ball bearing (dimension **a** given earlier in Fig. 6-2) to select the proper gasket thickness (dimension **d**) from **Table b.**

Table b. Shift Housing Gasket Dimensions

bearing height "a"	gasket "d" (mm)	Part No.
0.20–0.26	0.30	014 301 235
0.27–0.32	0.40	014 301 237

8. Making sure that the inner shift lever correctly engages the selector shafts, install the shift housing together with the correct shim and a new gasket of the proper thickness. Working diagonally, gradually torque the nuts or the bolts to 2.0 mkg (14 ft. lb.).

NOTE ———

On late transaxles that have the shift housing held to the gear carrier by bolts, it is helpful to use the home-made locating pins that were described in the NOTE that follows the first step of this procedure.

6.2 Disassembling and Assembling Shift Housing

Fig. 6-6 is an exploded view of the shift housing. The bonded rubber mounting can be replaced without removing the shift housing from the transaxle. If you replace the shift housing, you must make precision measurements, as described in **6.1 Removing and Installing Shift Housing,** in order to select a new shim of the correct thickness.

NOTE

Please read **9.1 Locating and Adjusting Drive Pinion Position** before you begin to disassemble the transaxle.

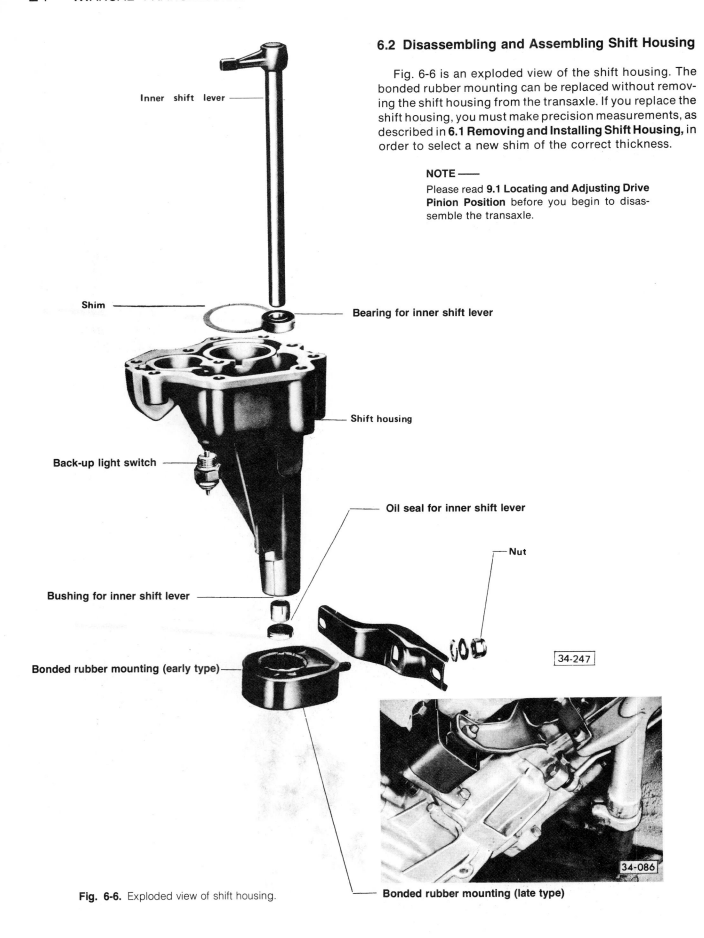

Inner shift lever

Shim

Bearing for inner shift lever

Shift housing

Back-up light switch

Oil seal for inner shift lever

Nut

Bushing for inner shift lever

34-247

Bonded rubber mounting (early type)

34-086

Fig. 6-6. Exploded view of shift housing.

Bonded rubber mounting (late type)

On cars manufactured up to the early part of the 1975 model year, you can remove the inner shift lever from the shift housing merely by sliding the lever out of the housing. On later models, remove the spring shown in Fig. 6-7 before you slide the inner shift lever out of the shift housing. During assembly, install the spring in the position shown so that the gearshift lever will be spring loaded in the direction of 3rd and 4th gears.

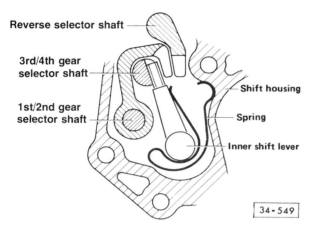

Reverse selector shaft

3rd/4th gear selector shaft

1st/2nd gear selector shaft

Shift housing

Spring

Inner shift lever

34-549

Fig. 6-7. Spring installed in late-type shift housing.

To replace the early-type bonded rubber mounting with the shift housing removed from the transaxle, first press the housing out of the mounting as shown in Fig. 6-8. Then press on a new bonded rubber mounting as shown in Fig. 6-9. The stud on the mounting must be exactly in line with the bottom of the housing.

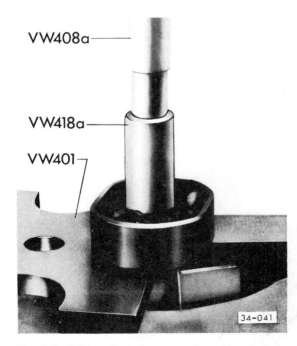

VW408a

VW418a

VW401

34-041

Fig. 6-8. Shift housing being pressed out of bonded rubber mounting.

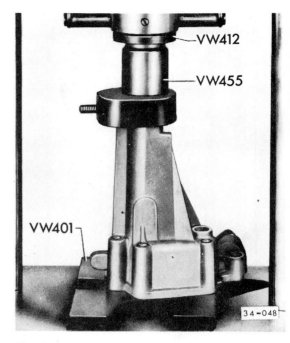

VW412

VW455

VW401

34-048

Fig. 6-9. New bonded rubber mounting being pressed onto shift housing. Sleeve-type press tool must exert pressure only on innermost part of mounting.

To replace the early-type bonded rubber mounting with the transaxle installed in the car, unbolt the transaxle carrier from the car body. Then remove the nut that holds the carrier on the bonded rubber mounting and remove the carrier. Working carefully with a sharp knife, cut off the bonded rubber mounting outer ring as indicated in Fig. 6-10.

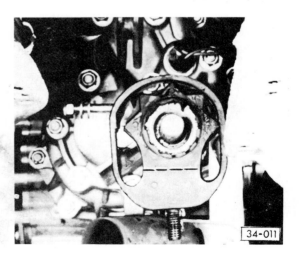

34-011

Fig. 6-10. Dashed line indicating where bonded rubber mounting should be cut. Pull down the rear of the transaxle for working clearance.

2

Being careful not to damage the shifthousing, use a power-driven abrasive disk to cut the bonded rubber mounting inner ring off the shift housing. Then, using a hammer and a drift, drive off the inner ring as indicated in Fig. 6-11.

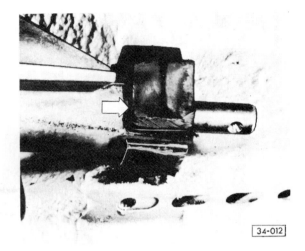

Fig. 6-11. Inner ring removal. Drive off as indicated by arrow. Notice where ring has been ground through.

Install the new bonded rubber mounting as shown in Fig. 6-12. Screw the special tool's central guide sleeve into the shift housing. Then press the bonded rubber mounting onto the shift housing by tightening the nut of the special tool.

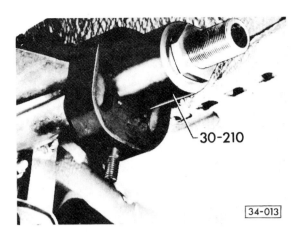

Fig. 6-12. Bonded rubber mounting being pressed on with a special tool.

To replace oil seal, bushing, and bearing:

1. Remove the shift housing. Remove the inner shift lever from the housing. Pry out the oil seal as shown in Fig. 6-13.

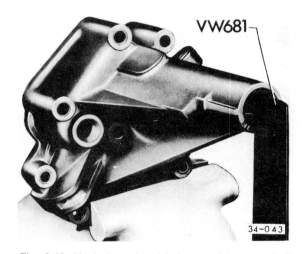

Fig. 6-13. Hook-shaped tool being used to pry out oil seal.

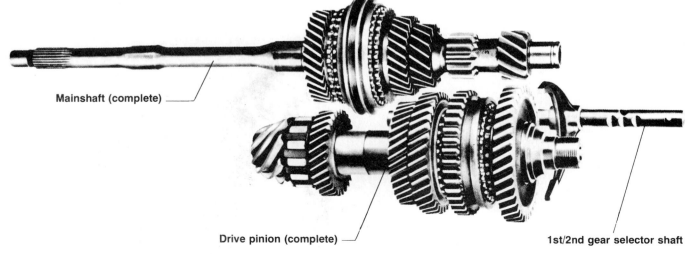

Mainshaft (complete)

Drive pinion (complete)

1st/2nd gear selector shaft

2

2. Using a long drift, drive out the bearing for the inner shift lever as indicated in Fig. 6-14.

34-042

Fig. 6-14. Bearing for inner shift lever being removed. Drive out in direction indicated by arrow.

3. Using the new bushing as a guide, select a bushing driver or press tool that is no larger in diameter than the outside diameter of the bushing. Then use the tool to drive or press out the bushing for the inner shift lever.

4. Press in the new bushing until its outer edge is flush with the bushing boss that is inside the shift housing. Then press in a new oil seal, open side inward, until it is past the threads that are inside the shift housing.

5. Press in the new bearing for the inner shift lever, closed side first, as shown in Fig. 6-15.

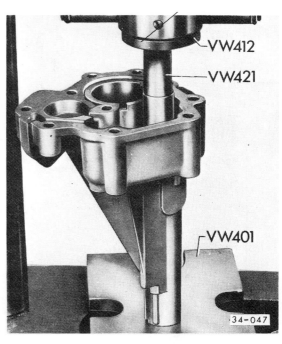

VW412
VW421
VW401

34-047

Fig. 6-15. Bearing for inner shift lever being pressed into shift housing.

6.3 Removing and Installing Transmission Gear Train

Fig. 6-16 is an exploded view that illustrates the removal of the transmission gear train from the gear carrier. The mainshaft and the drive pinion shaft must be removed as described here before either can be disassembled.

NOTE ——

Please read **9.1 Locating and Adjusting Drive Pinion Position** before you begin to disassemble the transaxle.

Fig. 6-16. Transmission gear train removed from transmission gear carrier.

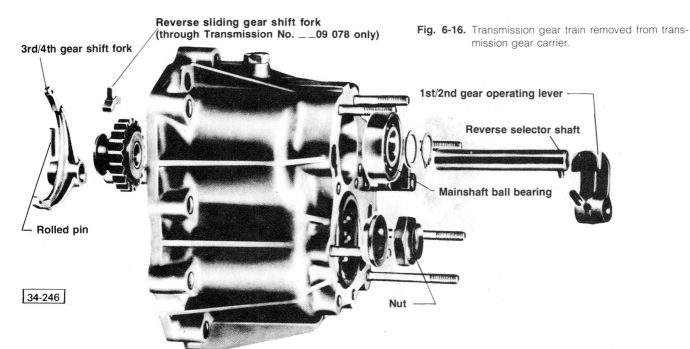

3rd/4th gear shift fork

Reverse sliding gear shift fork
(through Transmission No. __09 078 only)

1st/2nd gear operating lever

Reverse selector shaft

Mainshaft ball bearing

Rolled pin

Nut

34-246

To remove:

1. Install the transaxle on a work stand. Thoroughly clean the outside of the transaxle case. Do not remove the shift housing.

2. If necessary, determine the drive pinion location as described in **9.1 Locating and Adjusting Drive Pinion Position.**

3. Remove the nuts from the ten studs that hold the transmission gear carrier to the transaxle case.

4. Using a rubber or plastic hammer, tap the clutch end of the mainshaft until the sealer between the gear carrier and the transaxle case is broken. Then pull the gear carrier and gear train out of the transaxle case.

> *CAUTION ——*
>
> *Never insert any tools between the gear carrier and the transaxle case. Prior to Transmission No. XZ 14055, built during the early part of the 1976 model year, there is no gasket used and the slightest scratch can produce an oil leak. The gasket, used on late models, can be installed in earlier transaxles. However, the final drive pinion adjustment must be changed to compensate for the thickness of the gasket. See* **9.1 Locating and Adjusting Drive Pinion Position.**

5. Remove the shift housing as described in **6.1 Removing and Installing Shift Housing.**

6. Using a drift, drive out the rolled pin that holds the 3rd/4th gear shift fork on the selector shaft (Fig. 6-17).

Fig. 6-17. Rolled pin being driven (arrow) out of 3rd/4th gear shift fork.

7. To keep the 3rd/4th gear selector shaft from moving, engage reverse by pulling out on the reverse selector shaft as indicated by the black arrow in Fig. 6-18. Then engage 3rd gear by moving the 3rd/4th shift fork on its selector rod as indicated by the white arrow.

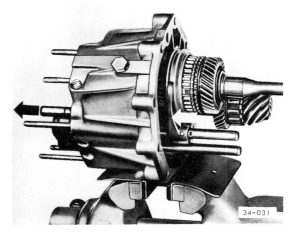

Fig. 6-18. 3rd gear being engaged by moving shift fork in direction shown by white arrow. Move reverse selector shaft as shown by black arrow so that 3rd/4th gear selector rod cannot move.

8. With both 3rd gear and reverse engaged, in order to prevent the rotation of the drive pinion shaft, loosely reinstall the gear carrier and the gear train on the transaxle case. (Use at least half of the nuts.) Then remove the nut from the end of the drive pinion as shown in Fig. 6-19.

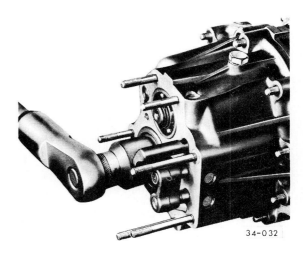

Fig. 6-19. Nut being removed from drive pinion.

9. Install a support bar against the clutch end of the mainshaft as shown in Fig. 6-20. It is necessary to do this in order to remove the mainshaft ball bearing from the gear carrier.

Fig. 6-20. Support bar against clutch end of mainshaft. Tighten the bolt until it firmly contacts the shaft.

10. Remove the circlip and the washer from the end of the mainshaft. Then install a bearing puller on the mainshaft ball bearing as shown in Fig. 6-21. Use a puller to remove simultaneously the ball bearing from both the mainshaft and the gear carrier.

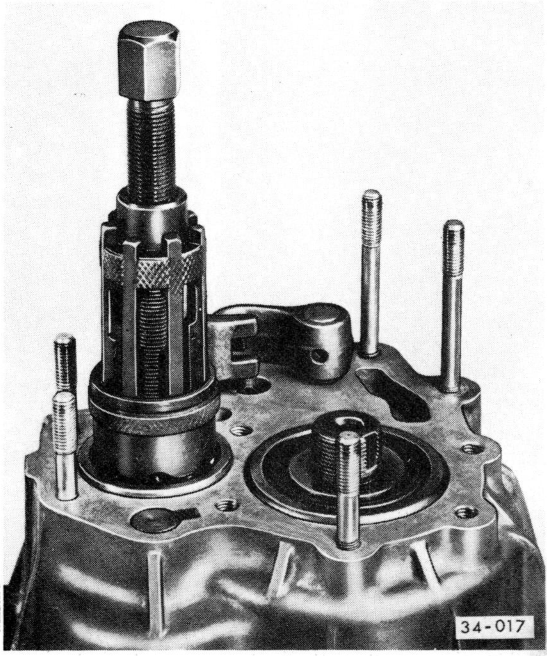

Fig. 6-21. Mainshaft ball bearing being pulled simultaneously off mainshaft and out of gear carrier.

11. Being careful that the mainshaft does not fall suddenly and damage the gears, remove the gear carrier and the gear train from the transaxle case. Remove the mainshaft and the 3rd/4th gear shift fork.

12. Drive out the reverse gear shaft as indicated in Fig. 6-22 and remove the reverse sliding gear and, where applicable, its shift fork.

Fig. 6-22. Reverse gear being removed. Drive out shaft as indicated by arrow.

13. Remove the rolled pin (Fig. 6-23) that holds the 1st/2nd gear operating lever on the 1st/2nd gear selector rod. Remove the operating lever.

Fig. 6-23. Rolled pin (arrow) that holds the operating lever on the 1st/2nd gear selector rod.

14. Using the setup shown in Fig. 6-24, press the drive pinion out of the pinion ball bearing. Advance the press ram slowly, keeping constant watch to see that the 1st/2nd gear selector rod does not jam. The selector rod must come out of the gear carrier along with the pinion shaft. If necessary, use a rubber or plastic hammer to tap the end of the selector shaft so that it slides out without jamming.

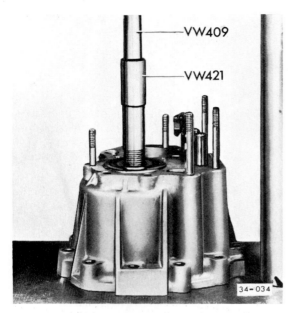

Fig. 6-24. Drive pinion being pressed out of ball bearing. The 1st/2nd gear shift fork and selector rod must come out of the gear carrier simultaneously with the pinion shaft.

15. If necessary, remove the selector rods, the drive pinion ball bearing, and the reverse-gear selector lever as described in **6.4 Disassembling and Assembling Gear Carrier.**

To install:

1. If you have replaced the transaxle case, the gear carrier, the drive pinion ball bearing, the 1st gear needle bearing, or the ring and pinion gearset—or if you intend to install a gasket between the gear carrier and the transaxle case on a transaxle that did not originally have this gasket—select a new S_3 shim as described in **9.1 Locating and Adjusting Drive Pinion Position.**

2. Engage the 1st/2nd gear shift fork in its groove in the 1st/2nd gear clutch gear assembly. Then, using the setup shown in Fig. 6-25, press the gear carrier and pinion ball bearing inner races down onto the pinion shaft and the 1st/2nd gear selector shaft. Use a press tool that will apply pressure only to the outer half of the pinion ball bearing's inner race.

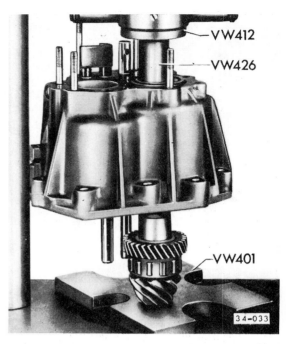

Fig. 6-25. Drive pinion and 1st/2nd gear selector shaft being installed in gear carrier.

3. Install the reverse sliding gear and, where applicable, the reverse gear shift fork. Drive in the reverse gear shaft.

4. Engage the 3rd/4th gear shift fork in the groove on the 3rd/4th gear clutch gear assembly. Without a mainshaft ball bearing, loosely install the mainshaft and the 3rd/4th gear shift fork in the gear carrier.

5. Engage both reverse gear and 3rd gear so that the drive pinion cannot turn. (If necessary, refer to step 6 of the removal procedure.) Then install the gear carrier and the gear train in the transaxle housing.

6. Install the support bar against the clutch end of the mainshaft as shown earlier in Fig. 6-20. Then drive the mainshaft ball bearing into the gear carrier and onto the mainshaft as shown in Fig. 6-26.

NOTE ——

If you install a new mainshaft ball bearing, you must select a new shim and a new gasket as described in **6.1 Removing and Installing Shift Housing.**

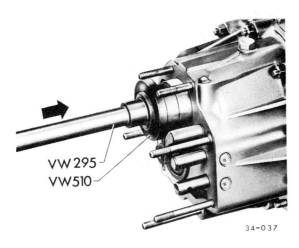

VW 295
VW 510

34-037

Fig. 6-26. Mainshaft ball bearing being driven (arrow) into gear carrier and onto mainshaft. The special driving tool exerts equal pressure on the ball bearing inner and outer races.

7. Install the washer and the circlip on the end of the mainshaft.

8. Install the nut and, if not previously installed, the outer half of the inner race for the drive pinion ball bearing. Torque the nut to 10 mkg (72 ft. lb.).

9. Using the rolled pin, install the 1st/2nd gear operating lever on the 1st/2nd gear selector rod. Use a new rolled pin if the original pin does not fit tightly.

10. Remove the gear carrier and gear train from the transaxle case. Using the rolled pin, install the 3rd/4th gear shift fork on the 3rd/4th gear selector shaft.

11. Check to see that the shift forks are properly engaged and that the selector rods work correctly.

   NOTE ——

   In order to move one selector rod, the other two rods must be in their natural positions.

12. Inspect the mainshaft oil seal which is in the final drive portion of the transaxle case. Replace the seal if it is worn, cracked, or otherwise damaged.

13. Wipe clean the mating surfaces of the transaxle case and the gear carrier. Make sure that the alignment dowels are in place and tight-fitting.

14. On transaxles that do not have a gasket between the gear carrier and the transaxle case, evenly coat the mounting flange of the gear carrier with a good quality oil resistant sealing compound. Then

install the transmission gear carrier and transmission gear train in the transaxle case. Torque the nuts to 2.0 mkg (14 ft. lb.).

   CAUTION ——

   If you install a gasket in a transaxle that did not originally have a gasket between the gear carrier and the transaxle case, you must adjust the pinion position to compensate for the thickness of the gasket. See **9.1 Locating and Adjusting Drive Pinion Position.** *If you do not adjust the pinion, the final drive will make noise and wear rapidly.*

15. On transaxles that have a gasket between the gear carrier and the transaxle case, install a new gasket without sealer. Then install the transmission gear carrier and transmission gear train in the transaxle case. Torque the nuts to 2.0 mkg (14 ft. lb.).

16. Using a shim and a gasket of the correct thickness, install the shift housing as described in **6.1 Removing and Installing Shift Housing.**

2

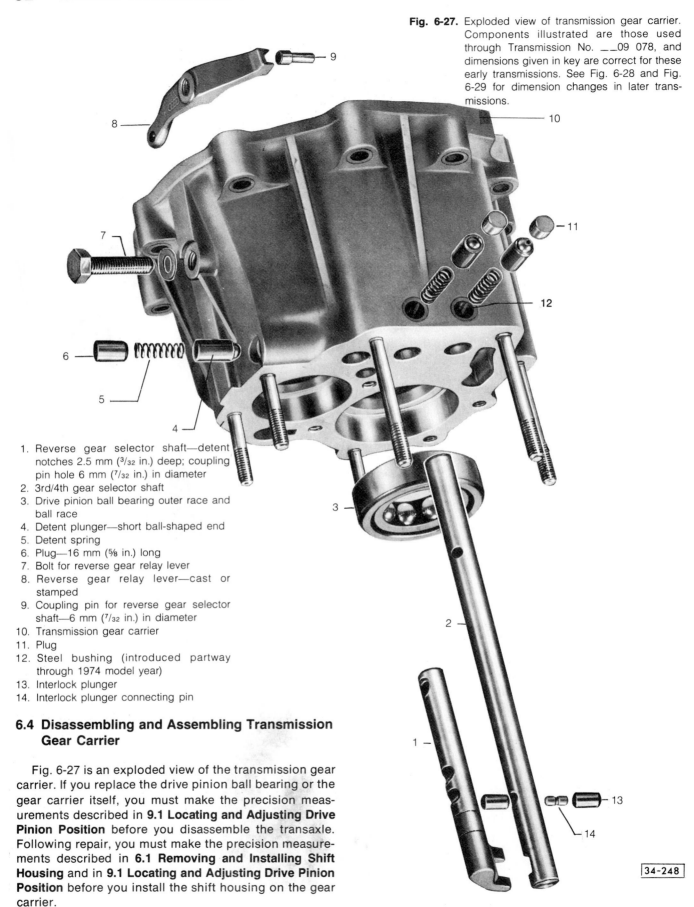

Fig. 6-27. Exploded view of transmission gear carrier. Components illustrated are those used through Transmission No. __09 078, and dimensions given in key are correct for these early transmissions. See Fig. 6-28 and Fig. 6-29 for dimension changes in later transmissions.

1. Reverse gear selector shaft—detent notches 2.5 mm (³/₃₂ in.) deep; coupling pin hole 6 mm (⁷/₃₂ in.) in diameter
2. 3rd/4th gear selector shaft
3. Drive pinion ball bearing outer race and ball race
4. Detent plunger—short ball-shaped end
5. Detent spring
6. Plug—16 mm (⅝ in.) long
7. Bolt for reverse gear relay lever
8. Reverse gear relay lever—cast or stamped
9. Coupling pin for reverse gear selector shaft—6 mm (⁷/₃₂ in.) in diameter
10. Transmission gear carrier
11. Plug
12. Steel bushing (introduced partway through 1974 model year)
13. Interlock plunger
14. Interlock plunger connecting pin

6.4 Disassembling and Assembling Transmission Gear Carrier

Fig. 6-27 is an exploded view of the transmission gear carrier. If you replace the drive pinion ball bearing or the gear carrier itself, you must make the precision measurements described in **9.1 Locating and Adjusting Drive Pinion Position** before you disassemble the transaxle. Following repair, you must make the precision measurements described in **6.1 Removing and Installing Shift Housing** and in **9.1 Locating and Adjusting Drive Pinion Position** before you install the shift housing on the gear carrier.

34-248

Fig. 6-28 shows the modified components installed in the gear carrier from Transmission No. __10 078 through Transmission No. __17 098. If, owing to wear, it becomes difficult to engage reverse, you can modify these transmissions to the configuration given in Fig. 6-29, using the modification procedure given under the first of the unnumbered headings that follow.

1. Reverse gear selector shaft—detent notches 5.5 mm ($^5/_{32}$ in.) deep; coupling pin hole 7.5 mm ($^9/_{32}$ in.) in diameter
2. Plug—12.8 mm (½ in.) long
3. Phillips head bolt
4. Detent plunger—long ball-shaped end
5. Transmission gear carrier—with larger clearance for reverse gear relay lever
6. Reverse gear relay lever—stamped, with jaw instead of shift fork
7. Reverse sliding gear—with no groove for shift fork
8. Coupling pin—7.5 mm ($^9/_{32}$ in.) in diameter

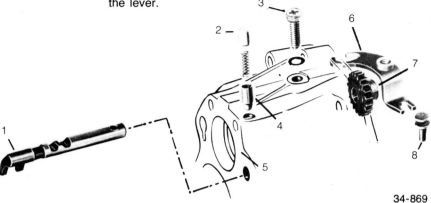

34-869

Fig. 6-28. Modified components used from Transmission No. __10 078 through Transmission No. __17 098.

Regardless of the components installed, the procedures for removing and installing the reverse gear linkage or the detents and interlocks are essentially the same. The adjustment procedure given under the unnumbered heading **Reverse Gear Linkage** applies to all transmissions, and should be carried out during installation of the reverse gear relay lever. No adjustment is required except during installation of the lever.

1. Reverse gear selector shaft—detent notches 2.5 mm ($^3/_{32}$ in.) deep; coupling pin hole 7.5 mm ($^9/_{32}$ in.) in diameter
2. Plug—16 mm (⅝ in.) long
3. Phillips head bolt
4. Detent plunger—with short ball-shaped end
5. Transmission gear carrier—with larger clearance for reverse gear relay lever
6. Reverse gear relay lever—stamped, with jaw instead of shift fork
7. Reverse sliding gear—with no groove for shift fork
8. Coupling pin—7.5 mm ($^9/_{32}$ in.) in diameter

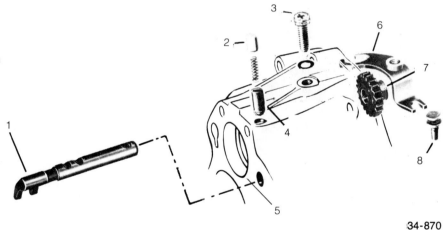

34-870

Fig. 6-29. Modified components used from Transmission No. __18 098.

Modifying Early Gear Carriers

If the earliest kind of gear carrier housing, installed through Transmission No. __09 078, is faulty, a replacement may no longer be available. So you should install the latest kind of gear carrier instead. The necessary parts for this conversion are given in **Table c**. The reverse gear linkage and the detents and plungers used from Transmission No. __10 078 through Transmission No. __17 098 should also be modified to the latest specification if it becomes difficult or impossible to engage reverse. The procedure for this modification is given here.

To modify:

1. Remove the transaxle. Then remove the transmission gear carrier as described in **6.3 Removing and Installing Transmission Gear Train,** but do not remove either the complete mainshaft or the complete drive pinion from the gear carrier.

2. Drill and tap a 6-mm or 8-mm (or a ¼-in. or ³/₁₆-in.) threaded hole in the plug for the reverse selector shaft detent. Then screw in a bolt and use it to pull out the plug. If necessary consult Fig. 6-31, which appears later.

3. Remove the detent spring and the detent plunger.

4. Make sure that the gears are in neutral. Then remove the Phillips head bolt that holds the reverse gear relay lever.

5. Remove the coupling pin for the reverse gear selector

shaft, which is a light press fit in the selector shaft.

6. Remove the reverse gear selector shaft.

7. Obtain a new reverse gear selector shaft, Part No. 014 311 577 D, a new detent plunger, Part No. 014 301 119, and a new 16-mm (⅝-in.) plug, Part No. 014 301 119. Consult **Table c.**

8. Lubricate all components that are to be installed with SAE 80W or SAE 80W/90 gear oil.

9. Install the new reverse gear selector shaft so that the side with the two detent notches is toward the hole for the reverse gear detent plunger.

10. Install the new detent plunger. Then install the spring. Drive in the new plug until it is flush with the bottom of the chamfer that surrounds the hole. If necessary, consult Fig. 6-33, which appears later.

11. Loosely position the reverse gear relay lever inside the transmission gear carrier, so that the jaw of the lever grips the reverse sliding gear.

NOTE ——

You may need to use long-nosed pliers for this job if the gear train is installed in the gear carrier.

12. Adjust the reverse gear linkage as described under the next unnumbered heading.

13. Install the transmission gear carrier and the transmission gear train as described in **6.3 Removing and Installing Transmission Gear Train.** Then install the transaxle in the car.

Table c. Parts Used for Reverse Sliding Gear Repairs and Modifications

Replacement part name	Replacement part numbers for three versions of reverse gear linkage		
	Through Trans. No. __09 078	From Trans. No. __10 078 through Trans. No. __17 098	From Trans. No. __18 098
Transmission gear carrier	014 301 211 G	014 301 211 J	
Reverse gear relay lever	014 301 583	014 311 573	
Bolt for reverse gear relay lever	014 311 589 (M8 × 40 thread)	084 311 589 B (M 10 × 32 thread)	
Reverse sliding gear	014 311 529 A	020 311 501	
Coupling pin for reverse gear selector shaft	014 311 587	084 311 593	
Reverse gear selector shaft	014 311 577 A	014 311 577 C	014 311 577 D
Detent plunger	014 311 621 A	084 311 621 D	014 311 621 A
Detent spring		014 311 641 A	
Plug	014 301 119	014 301 119 A	014 301 119

Reverse Gear Linkage

To remove the reverse gear relay lever, remove the bolt for the reverse gear relay lever from the gear carrier. Then slide the relay lever off the coupling pin. (The pin is a light press fit in the reverse gear selector shaft.) To remove the reverse gear selector shaft, use pliers to pull out the coupling pin. Then, with the 3rd/4th gear selector shaft in its neutral position, withdraw the reverse gear selector shaft from the gear carrier.

During installation of the reverse gear relay lever and the reverse gear selector shaft, you must adjust the reverse gear linkage.

To adjust:

1. Install the reverse gear selector shaft, the coupling pin, the reverse sliding gear, the reverse sliding gear shift fork (where applicable), and the reverse gear shaft.

2. Loosely install the bolt and the washer for the reverse gear relay lever in the gear carrier. Screw in the bolt until it just emerges inside the carrier.

3. Loosely install the reverse gear relay lever without screwing the bolt into it. Hand-press the relay lever in the direction indicated by the arrow in Fig. 6-30. Then screw in the bolt until it just contacts the relay lever.

4. Align the bolt hole in the relay lever with the bolt end. With the lever hand-pressed against the bolt end, carefully turn the bolt counterclockwise until you hear and feel the bolt's threads drop into engagement with the threads in the lever.

5. Turn the bolt clockwise to start its threads into those of the lever. Then torque the bolt to 3.5 mkg (25 ft. lb.).

6. Check to see that the relay lever moves easily throughout the full range of the reverse sliding gear's travel. If the lever does not, repeat the adjustment. If the lever moves easily, remove the reverse sliding gear, the reverse gear shift fork (where applicable), and the reverse gear shaft in preparation for transmission gear train installation.

Detents and Interlocks

In order to remove the detent plungers, the detent springs, and the interlock plungers, you must first remove the plugs. To remove the plug for the reverse gear selector shaft detent, drill and tap a 6-mm or 8-mm (or a ¼-in. or 5/16-in.) threaded hole in the plug. Then screw in a bolt and use it to pull out the plug as indicated in Fig. 6-31.

To remove the plugs for the 1st/2nd gear and the 3rd/4th gear detent plungers, use a drift as indicated in Fig. 6-32. Drive the plug into the gear carrier until you can remove the plug through the selector shaft bore.

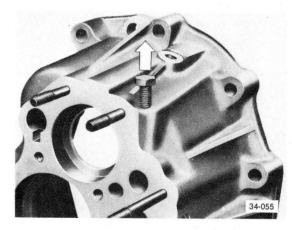

Fig. 6-31. Plug for reverse selector shaft detent being removed.

Fig. 6-30. Reverse relay lever being adjusted. Hand-press lever in direction shown by arrow so that the shift fork firmly contacts the reverse sliding gear.

Fig. 6-32. 3rd/4th gear selector shaft detent being removed. Drive plug down as indicated by top arrow, take out plug as indicated by lower arrow.

Install the detent springs, the detent plungers, the selector shafts, and related parts in the sequence given in Fig. 6-33. In order to install the selector shafts, you must insert a small screwdriver in the opposite end of the bore and press down the detent. Always place previously-installed shafts in their neutral positions before you attempt to install another shaft. The 1st/2nd gear selector shaft should not be installed until you are ready to install the transmission gear train in the transmission gear carrier.

Drive Pinion Ball Bearing

If necessary, you can remove the drive pinion ball bearing outer race and ball race as shown in Fig. 6-34. If you install a new drive pinion ball bearing, you must select a new S_3 shim as described in **9.1 Locating and Adjusting Drive Pinion Position** and a new shift housing shim and gasket as described in **6.1 Removing and Installing Shift Housing.**

Fig. 6-34. Pinion ball bearing outer race and ball race being driven out of transmission gear carrier.

Press in the drive pinion ball bearing outer race and ball race as shown in Fig. 6-35. The press tool must apply pressure to the outer race only.

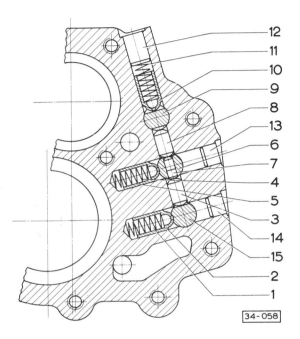

1. Spring for 1st/2nd gear selector shaft detent
2. 1st/2nd gear selector shaft detent plunger
3. Lower interlock plunger
4. Spring for 3rd/4th gear selector shaft detent
5. 3rd/4th gear selector shaft detent plunger
6. 3rd/4th gear selector shaft
7. Interlock plunger connecting pin
8. Upper interlock plunger
9. Reverse gear selector shaft
10. Reverse gear selector shaft detent plunger
11. Spring for reverse gear selector shaft detent
12. Long plug
13. Upper short plug
14. Lower short plug
15. 1st/2nd gear selector shaft

Fig. 6-33. Detent and interlock installation sequence.

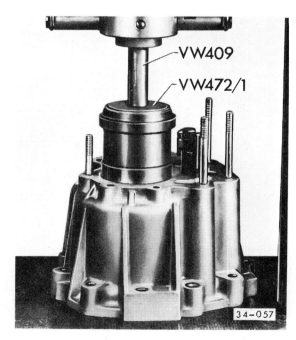

Fig. 6-35. Drive pinion ball bearing outer race and ball race being pressed into transmission gear carrier.

35-033

6.5 Disassembling and Assembling Mainshaft

Fig. 6-36 gives an exploded view of the transmission's mainshaft. The 1st gear, 2nd gear, and reverse gear driving gears are integral with the shaft itself.

1. 3rd gear and 4th gear synchronizing rings
2. 4th gear thrust washer
3. Rolled pin (discontinued early in 1976 model year)
4. 3rd gear needle bearing
5. 3rd gear
6. 3rd/4th gear clutch gear assembly
7. Snap ring
8. 4th gear
9. 4th gear needle bearing
10. Circlip

Fig. 6-36. Exploded view of mainshaft.

To disassemble:

1. Remove the mainshaft from the gear carrier as described in **6.3 Removing and Installing Transmission Gear Train.**

2. Remove the circlip, the 4th gear thrust washer and, where applicable, the rolled pin.

3. Remove 4th gear, its needle bearing, and the 4th gear synchronizing ring.

4. Remove the snap ring as shown in Fig. 6-37.

35-008

Fig. 6-37. Snap ring being removed. Notice the kind of pliers being used.

5. Using the setup shown in Fig. 6-38, simultaneously press off 3rd gear, the 3rd gear synchronizing ring, and the 3rd/4th gear clutch gear assembly. Then remove the 3rd gear needle bearing.

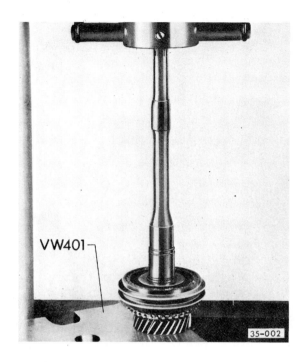

Fig. 6-38. 3rd gear, its synchronizing ring, and the clutch gear assembly being pressed off mainshaft.

6. If necessary, remove the spring rings from the clutch gear assembly and separate the synchronizer hub from its operating sleeve as shown in Fig. 6-39.

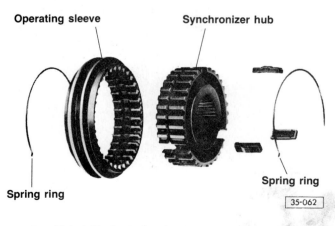

Fig. 6-39. Exploded view of clutch gear assembly.

To assemble:

1. Inspect all parts. Replace any that is worn or damaged.

   NOTE ——

   There have been some changes in gear designs and tooth ratios. If you must replace a gear, first consult the Gear Application table in **10. Manual Transmission Technical Data**.

2. Hand-press the synchronizing rings into the gears as illustrated in Fig. 6-40. Measure clearance **a** with a feeler gauge. The wear limit is 0.60 mm (.023 in.). With new parts dimension **a** should be between 1.35 and 1.90 mm (.053 and .075 in.).

Fig. 6-40. Clearance measurement **a**.

NOTE ——

Early in the 1976 model year, a new kind of synchronizing ring was introduced. The new ring has two additional pockets, as indicated in Fig. 6-41. This ring, Part No. 014 311 295 D, is the standard replacement ring for all four gears. If you install it in a transaxle built prior to Transmission No. XK 29 096, you must also install either a new, slightly shorter, spring ring (Part No. 014 311 311 B) or the most recent spring ring (Part No. 014 311 311 C). The obsolete spring ring will interfere with the movement of the current-type synchronizer rings.

3. If the clutch gear assembly was taken apart, align the flattened tooth in the operating sleeve with the recess in the synchronizer hub (Fig. 6-42). Then assemble the clutch gear assembly. Another kind of alignment mark is indicated in Fig. 6-43.

   NOTE ——

   The spring rings on opposite sides of the clutch gear assembly must be installed 120° apart as indicated in Fig. 6-43.

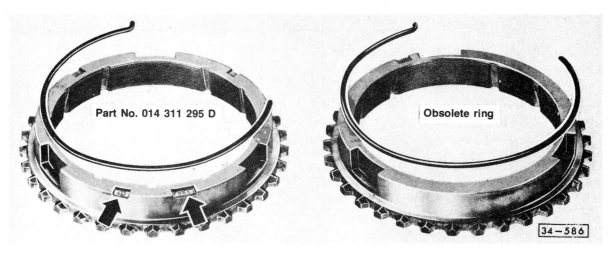

Fig. 6-41. New-style synchronizer ring with two additional pockets (arrows). Old-style ring is at right.

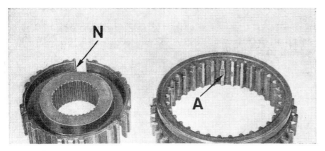

Fig. 6-42. Alignment mark for clutch gear assembly. Flattened tooth is at **A**. Recess in sychronizer hub is at **N**.

4. Install the 3rd gear needle bearing on the mainshaft.

5. Place the clutch gear assembly, the 3rd gear synchronizing ring, and 3rd gear in their correct relationship atop one another. The chamfered splines in the synchronizer hub of the clutch gear assembly must be toward 3rd gear. The notches in the 3rd gear synchronizing ring must engage the three synchronizer keys in the clutch gear assembly.

6. Press the mainshaft into the clutch gear, 3rd gear, and its synchronizing ring as shown in Fig. 6-44.

Fig. 6-43. Positions for the spring rings. Make sure the spring ring ends hook inside the hollow synchronizer keys. Arrow indicates alignment marks.

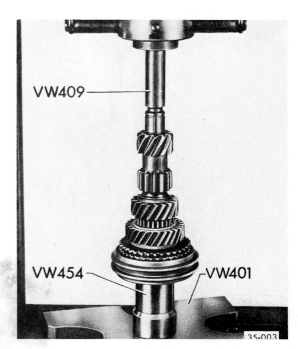

Fig. 6-44. Mainshaft being pressed into clutch gear splines. Align splines carefully.

7. Install the snap ring.

8. If necessary, use the repair press to move 3rd gear and the clutch gear assembly toward the snap ring until the synchronizer hub of the clutch gear assembly is in firm contact with the snap ring. Do not exceed a pressure of 2000 kg (4400 lb.).

9. Install the 4th gear synchronizing ring in the 4th-gear side of the clutch gear assembly. The notches in the ring must engage the three synchronizer keys in the clutch gear assembly.

10. Where applicable, install the rolled pin in the mainshaft. Then install the 4th gear thrust washer as shown in Fig. 6-45. Install the circlip.

11. Using feeler gauges of various thicknesses, as shown in Fig. 6-46, determine the clearance between the 4th gear thrust washer and the 4th gear. This measurement cannot be made accurately unless the clutch gear assembly has been positioned as described previously in step 8.

12. If the clearance measured in step 11 is not between 0.10 and 0.40 mm (.004 and .016 in.), install a thicker or thinner 4th gear thrust washer. Washers for use with the rolled pin are available in thicknesses of 3.50 mm (.138 in.), in 3.60 mm (.142 in.), and 3.70 mm (.146 in.). Washers for use with a flat on the mainshaft are available in thicknesses of 3.45 mm (.136 in.), 3.55 mm (.140 in.), and 3.65 mm (.144 in.). Adjust the clearance to as near 0.10 mm (.004 in.) as possible without reducing it below that minimum.

Fig. 6-46. Clearance being measured between 4th gear and 4th gear thrust washer.

6.6 Disassembling and Assembling Drive Pinion Shaft

Fig. 6-47 gives an exploded view of the transmission's drive pinion shaft. The final drive pinion gear is integral with the shaft itself.

NOTE ——

If you replace the drive pinion ball bearing, the ring and pinion gearset, or the 1st gear needle bearing, you must select a new S_3 shim as described in **9.1 Locating and Adjusting Drive Pinion Position.** You must also select a new shim and gasket for the shift housing as described in **6.1 Removing and Installing Shift Housing.**

Fig. 6-45. 4th gear thrust washer installation. Late-type shim engages a flat on the mainshaft (arrow). Early-type shim engages the rolled pin as shown at right.

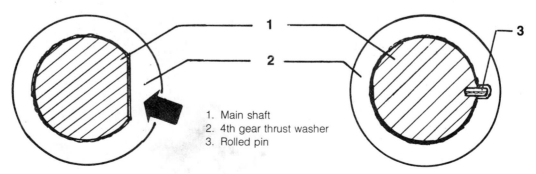

1. Main shaft
2. 4th gear thrust washer
3. Rolled pin

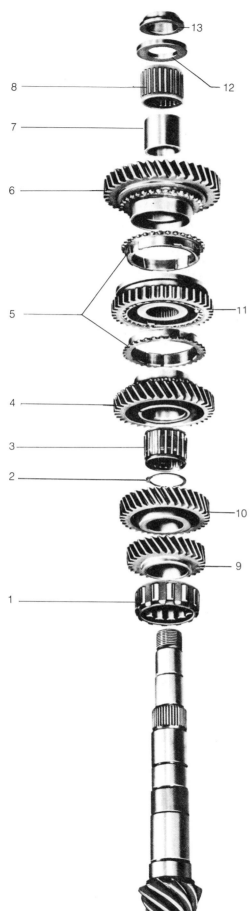

35-034

Fig. 6-47. Exploded view of drive pinion shaft.

1. Drive pinion roller bearing
2. Circlip
3. 2nd gear needle bearing
4. 2nd gear
5. 1st and 2nd gear synchronizing rings
6. 1st gear
7. 1st gear needle bearing inner race
8. 1st gear needle bearing
9. 4th gear
10. 3rd gear
11. 1st/2nd gear clutch gear assembly
12. S_3 shim
13. Inner half of drive pinion ball bearing inner race

2

To disassemble:

1. With 1st gear supported as shown in Fig. 6-48, press the pinion shaft out of the 1st gear, S_3 shim, and the inner half of the drive pinion ball bearing inner race.

CAUTION ——

Be ready to catch the drive pinion shaft as it is pressed free of the ball bearing inner race. Otherwise, the drive pinion may fall and be damaged.

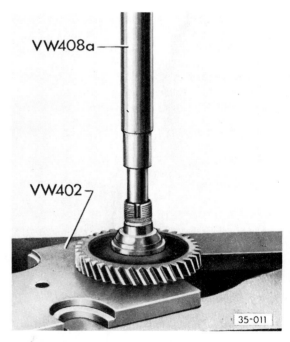

Fig. 6-48. Drive pinion shaft being pressed out of inner half of drive pinion ball bearing inner race.

2. Remove 1st gear and its synchronizing ring. Remove the 1st gear needle bearing and the 1st gear needle bearing inner race.

NOTE ——

If the 1st gear needle bearing inner race is tight-fitting, heat it slightly before driving it off the drive pinion shaft.

3. Using the setup shown in Fig. 6-49, simultaneously press off 2nd gear, the 2nd gear synchronizing ring, and the 1st/2nd gear clutch gear assembly. Then remove the 2nd gear needle bearing.

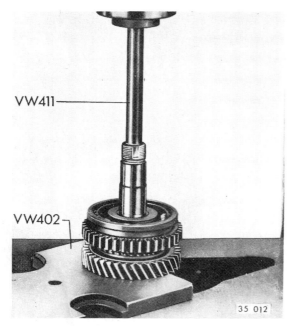

Fig. 6-49. 2nd gear, its synchronizing ring, and the 1st/2nd gear clutch gear assembly being pressed off drive pinion shaft.

4. Remove the circlip. Using the setup shown in Fig. 6-50, press off 3rd gear. With 3rd gear removed, repeat the operation in order to press off 4th gear.

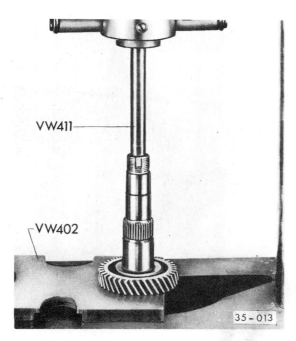

Fig. 6-50. Setup used in order to press off 3rd gear and 4th gear individually.

5. Remove the drive pinion roller bearing from the drive pinion shaft.

6. If necessary, remove the spring rings from the clutch gear assembly and separate the synchronizer hub from its operating sleeve as shown in Fig. 6-51.

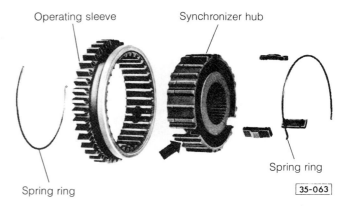

Fig. 6-51. Exploded view of clutch gear assembly. Arrow indicates alignment recess.

To assemble:

1. Inspect all parts. Replace any that is worn or damaged.

NOTE ——

There have been some changes in gear designs and tooth ratios. If you must replace a gear, first consult the Gear Application table in **10. Manual Transmission Technical Data.**

2. Hand-press the synchronizing rings into the gears as illustrated in Fig. 6-52. Measure clearance **a** with feeler gauge. The wear limit is 0.60 mm (.023 in.). With new parts, dimension **a** should be between 1.10 and 1.70 (.042 and .066 in.).

Fig. 6-52. Clearance measurement **a**.

NOTE ——

Early in the 1976 model year, a new kind of synchronizing ring was introduced. The new ring has two additional pockets, as indicated in Fig. 6-53. This ring, Part No. 014 311 295 D, is the standard replacement ring for all four gears. If you install it in a transaxle built prior to Transmission No. XK 29 096, you must also install either a new, slightly shorter, spring

ring (Part No. 014 311 311 B) or the most recent spring ring (Part No. 014 311 311 C). The obsolete spring ring will interfere with the movement of the current-type synchronizer rings. Beginning with Transmission No. XK 27 017, the 1st gear synchronizing ring has a different angle to the tooth points. This new part is not available as a replacement part and should be replaced if worn or damaged by the standard ring, Part No. 014 311 295 D.

2

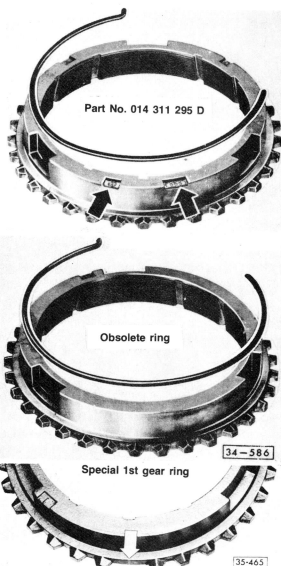

Fig. 6-54. Alignment marks for clutch gear assembly. Flattened tooth is at **A**, recess in synchronizer hub is at **N**. Groove at black arrow (current parts) or groove at white arrow (early parts) identifies end of hub that should be toward 1st gear.

NOTE ──

The spring rings on opposite sides of the clutch assembly must be installed 120° apart as indicated in Fig. 6-55.

Fig. 6-53. New-style synchronizer ring (top) with two additional pockets (black arrows). Old-style ring is in middle. Special 1st gear ring (bottom) with 110° (instead of 120°) tooth points can be identified by missing teeth (white arrow) at three points on its periphery.

3. If the clutch gear assembly was taken apart, align the flattened tooth in the operating sleeve with the recess in the synchronizer hub (Fig. 6-54). Then assemble the clutch gear assembly. Another kind of alignment mark is indicated in Fig. 6-55.

Fig. 6-55. Positions for the spring rings. Make sure the spring ring ends hook inside the hollow synchronizer keys. Arrow indicates alignment mark.

4. Install the drive pinion roller bearing on the drive pinion shaft. The wide shoulder on the bearing must be toward the pinion gear. Then press the drive pinion shaft into the 4th gear as shown in Fig. 6-56.

NOTE——

Both the drive pinion and 4th gear must be absolutely grease-free. 3rd gear must also be grease-free when you install it.

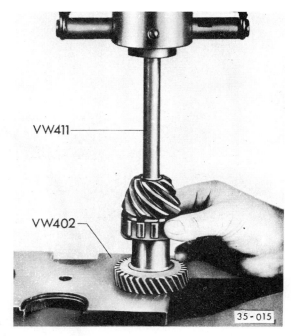

Fig. 6-56. Drive pinion roller bearing being held while drive pinion shaft is pressed into 4th gear. Shoulder on 4th gear goes toward the bearing.

5. Using a procedure identical to that described for installing 4th gear, press 3rd gear onto the pinion shaft. Then, using feeler gauges of various thicknesses, determine the distance between the face of 3rd gear and the further edge of the circlip groove. See Fig. 6-57.

6. If the space measured in step 5 is less than 1.60 mm (.063 in.), install a new circlip that is 1.50 mm (.060 in. thick); if the space is greater than 1.60 mm (.063 in.), install a new circlip that is 1.60 mm (.063 in.) thick.

7. Install the 2nd gear needle bearing. Place the clutch gear assembly, the 2nd gear synchronizing ring, and 2nd gear in their correct relationship atop one another. The groove on the splines of the synchronizer hub of the clutch gear assembly must be toward 1st gear. The notches in the 2nd gear synchronizing ring must engage the three synchronizer keys in the clutch gear assembly.

Fig. 6-57. Available space for circlip being measured.

8. Press 2nd gear, its synchronizing ring, and the clutch gear assembly onto the pinion shaft as shown in Fig. 6-58.

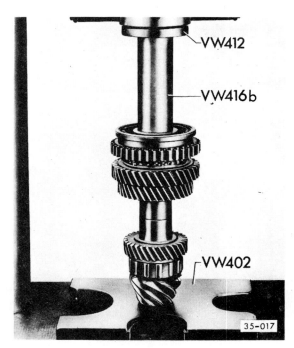

Fig. 6-58. Clutch gear assembly being pressed into pinion shaft. Align splines carefully.

9. Install the 1st gear synchronizing ring in the 1st gear side of the clutch gear assembly. The

notches in the ring must engage the three synchronizer keys in the clutch gear assembly.

10. Install the 1st gear needle bearing inner race, the 1st gear needle bearing, and 1st gear.

> **NOTE ——**
>
> If the 1st gear needle bearing inner race is a tight fit, heat the inner race to about 212°F (100°C) in a pan of oil placed in a larger pan of boiling water before you install the inner race on the pinion shaft.

11. If you have replaced the transaxle case, the ring and pinion gearset, the drive pinion ball bearing, the gear carrier, or the 1st gear needle bearing, select a new S_3 shim as described in **9.1 Locating and Adjusting Drive Pinion Position.** You must also select a new shift housing shim and gasket as described in **6.1 Removing and Installing Shift Housing.**

12. Install the correct S_3 shim. Then install the inner half of the drive pinion ball bearing inner race as shown in Fig. 6-59.

> **NOTE ——**
>
> If the drive pinion ball bearing inner race is a tight fit, heat the inner race to about 212°F (100°C) in a pan of oil placed in a larger pan of boiling water before you install the inner race on the drive pinion shaft.

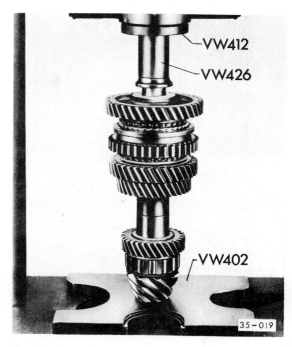

Fig. 6-59. Inner half of drive pinion ball bearing inner race being installed on drive pinion shaft.

7. TRANSAXLE CASE

Fig. 7-1 shows the parts that remain in the transaxle case after the transmission gear train and the final drive gearset have been removed. You must remove the differential in order to replace the drive pinion roller bearing's outer race, the mainshaft needle bearing, or the mainshaft support sleeve.

Clutch Release Bearing, Shaft, and Related Parts

To remove the clutch release bearing, use a screwdriver to pry off the spring clips and retainers that hold the release bearing to the arms of the clutch operating shaft. Then slide the release bearing off the release bearing guide sleeve.

Fig. 7-1. Exploded view of transaxle case. Plastic guide sleeve with steel nut plate was introduced at Transmission No. XH 16 105.

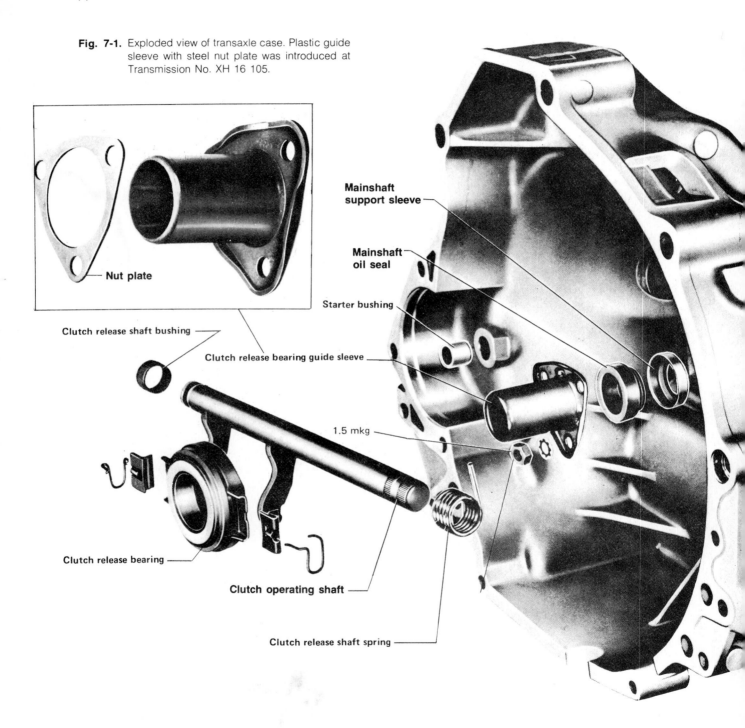

Never wash the clutch release bearing in solvent. Doing this will remove the factory-installed lubricant.

Before installing the clutch release bearing, lightly lubricate steel release bearing guide sleeves with molybdenum grease. Plastic guide sleeves should not be lubricated. Also rub a small amount of molybdenum grease into the facing on the release bearing that will contact the release levers of the clutch pressure plate assembly.

Install the release bearing on the guide sleeve. Then, using the spring clips and retainers, attach the bearing to the arms of the clutch operating shaft. Replace loose-fitting spring clips.

To remove the clutch release shaft, remove the nut for the clamp bolt that holds the clutch operating lever on the clutch operating shaft. Remove the lever and the circlip. Then carefully pry out the clutch operating shaft bearing.

Pull the operating shaft out of its bushing in the starter side of the transaxle case. Then take the operating shaft out through the mouth of the bellhousing.

2

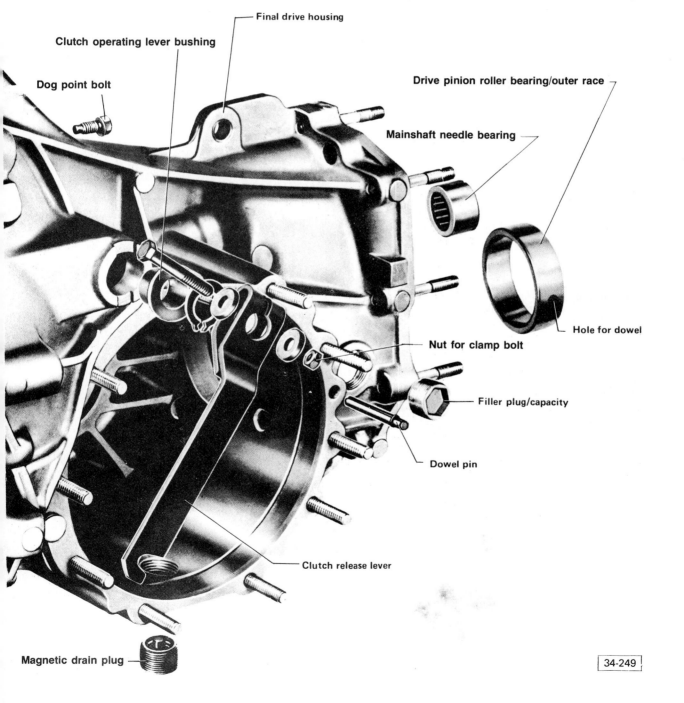

Final drive housing

Clutch operating lever bushing

Dog point bolt

Drive pinion roller bearing/outer race

Mainshaft needle bearing

Hole for dowel

Nut for clamp bolt

Filler plug/capacity

Dowel pin

Clutch release lever

Magnetic drain plug

34-249

To remove the clutch operating shaft bushing, take out the dog point bolt. Then, using an extractor and a slide hammer, pull out the bushing in the direction indicated in Fig. 7-2.

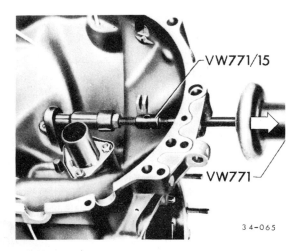

Fig. 7-2. Clutch operating shaft bushing being removed. Pull out in direction indicated by arrow.

Install the new clutch operating shaft bushing so that the hole in the side will be in line with the hole for the dog point bolt. Then drive in the bushing as indicated in Fig. 7-3 until the holes align. Install the dog point bolt and torque it to 1.5 mkg (11 ft. lb.).

Fig. 7-3. Clutch operating shaft bushing being driven (arrow) into transaxle case.

Lubricate the clutch operating shaft bushing with molybdenum grease. Then, using a reverse of the removal procedure, install the operating shaft in the transaxle case. Lubricate the operating shaft bearing with molybdenum grease and install the bearing so that its lugs engage the recesses in the transaxle case. Install the circlip. Then install the clutch operating lever so that,

when the release bearing is fully retracted, the tip of the lever will be in the position shown in Fig. 7-4. Torque the nut for the clamp bolt to 2.0 mkg (14 ft. lb.).

Fig. 7-4. Clutch operating lever installed so that its tip is in line (dashes) with lug on transaxle case bellhousing.

Mainshaft Oil Seal

In order to replace the mainshaft oil seal, you must first remove the clutch release bearing and the clutch release bearing guide sleeve. Use a hook-shaped tool (Fig. 7-5) to pry out the mainshaft oil seal. If necessary, you can pry out the seal with the mainshaft installed. However, you should be careful not to scratch the sealing surface on the mainshaft.

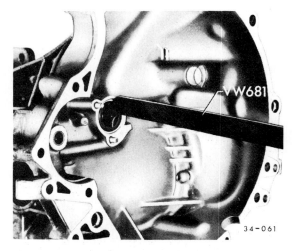

Fig. 7-5. Mainshaft oil seal being pried out with a hook-shaped tool.

Using an appropriate mandrel, as shown in Fig. 7-6, drive in the new seal until its outer surface is flush with the surface of the transaxle case. The seal lip must point into the final drive housing. In installing the clutch release bearing guide sleeve, torque the nuts to 1.5 mkg (11 ft. lb.).

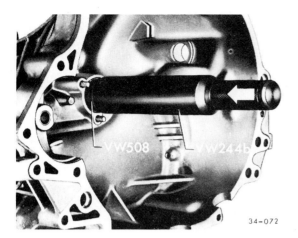

Fig. 7-6. Mainshaft oil seal being installed.

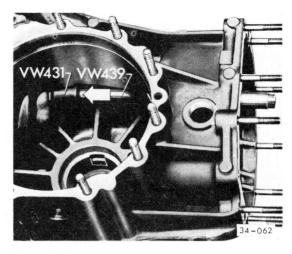

Fig. 7-8. Mainshaft support sleeve being driven (arrow) out of transaxle case.

Mainshaft Needle Bearing and Mainshaft Support Sleeve

Before you remove either the mainshaft needle bearing or the mainshaft support sleeve, you must remove the clutch release bearing, the clutch release bearing guide sleeve, and the mainshaft oil seal. Drive out the mainshaft needle bearing in the direction indicated in Fig. 7-7; drive out the mainshaft support sleeve in the direction indicated in Fig. 7-8.

Drive in the new needle bearing, as shown in Fig. 7-9, until the bearing is flush with the surface of the transaxle case. Working through the bellhousing, drive in the new mainshaft support sleeve until it bottoms in the recess (Fig. 7-10). In installing the clutch release bearing guide sleeve, torque the nuts to 1.5 mkg (11 ft. lb.).

Fig. 7-9. Mainshaft needle bearing being driven (arrow) into transaxle case.

Fig. 7-7. Mainshaft needle bearing being driven (arrow) out of transaxle case.

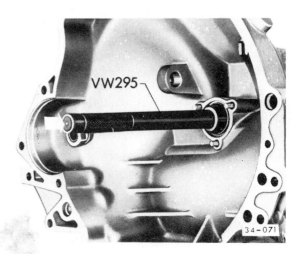

Fig. 7-10. Mainshaft support sleeve being driven (arrow) into transaxle case. Open side of support sleeve must be toward the engine.

Drive Pinion Roller Bearing Outer Race

In order to remove the drive pinion roller bearing outer race you must first pull out the dowel pin with a pair of pliers. See Fig. 7-11.

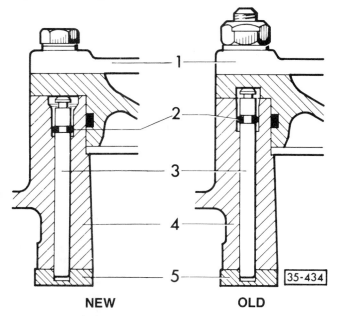

NEW   **OLD**

1. Final drive cover
2. Seal
3. Dowel pin

4. Transaxle case
5. Drive pinion roller bearing outer race

Fig. 7-11. Dowel pin removal or installation. Beginning with the 1976 models, the pin is shorter and does not project above the surface of the transaxle case.

The procedure for driving the drive pinion roller bearing race out of—or into—the transaxle case is shown in Fig. 7-12. During installation, the hole in the bearing race must be aligned with the dowel pin hole in the case. The grooved side of the bearing race goes toward the transmission gear train. On 1973 through 1975 transaxles, drive in the dowel pin until it projects approximately 3 mm (1/8 in.) from the final drive cover mounting flange. On 1976 and later transaxles, drive in the pin until it is flush with the mounting flange. See Fig. 7-11, given earlier.

Starter Bushing

To remove the starter bushing from the transaxle case, use an extractor as shown in Fig. 7-13. Drive in the new bushing (Fig. 7-14.) until the bushing is flush with the surface of the case. Lubricate the bushing with multipurpose grease.

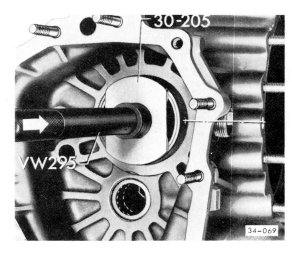

Fig. 7-12. Pinion roller bearing outer race being removed or installed (arrow). Notice the alignment of the hole in the bearing race with the dowel hole in the transaxle case. Groove on bearing race is also visible.

Fig. 7-13. Starter bushing being removed from transaxle case.

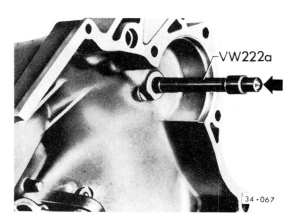

Fig. 7-14. Starter bushing being driven (arrow) into transaxle case.

8. Differential

Fig. 8-1 is an exploded view that illustrates the removal of the differential and its related parts. If you intend to replace the transaxle case, the final drive cover, one or both of the tapered-roller bearings, the differential housing, or the ring and pinion gearset, please read **9. Adjusting Final Drive** before you undertake any disassembly.

2

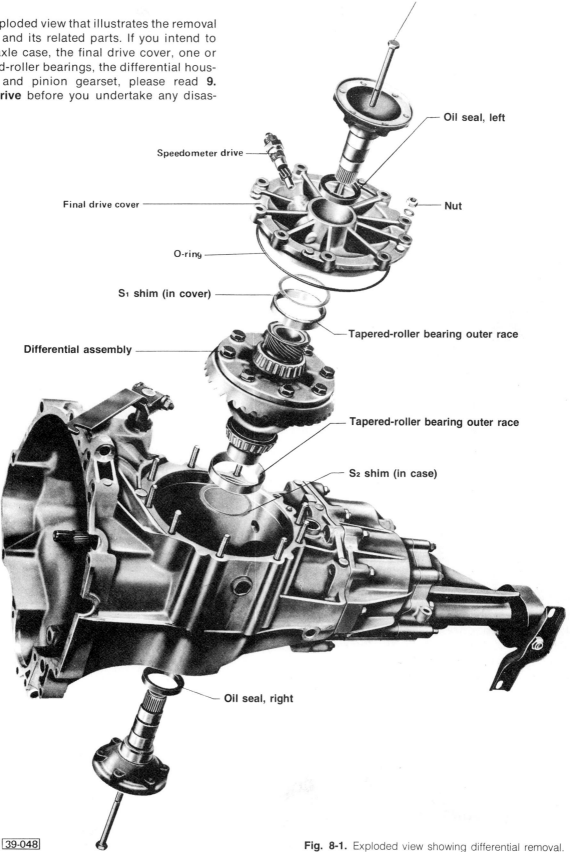

Bolt

Oil seal, left

Speedometer drive

Final drive cover

Nut

O-ring

S_1 shim (in cover)

Tapered-roller bearing outer race

Differential assembly

Tapered-roller bearing outer race

S_2 shim (in case)

Oil seal, right

39-048

Fig. 8-1. Exploded view showing differential removal.

8.1 Removing and Installing Differential

Remove the transaxle from the car before you remove the differential. Though the differential can be removed with the transaxle installed, installation is awkward and could lead to accidental damage of the tapered-roller bearings. Also, there is a risk that road dirt from the car underbody will enter the transaxle case. You cannot adjust the final drive with the transaxle installed.

To remove:

1. Take out the bolts for both flanged shafts as shown in Fig. 8-2. Then remove the flanged shafts.

   NOTE ——

   If the flanged shafts or the flanged shaft oil seals are worn, cracked, or otherwise damaged, replace them as described in **4.3 Servicing Constant Velocity Joints.**

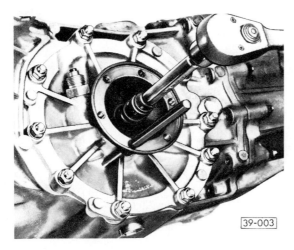

Fig. 8-2. Bolt for flanged shaft being removed. Notice the drift which has been inserted through one of the bolt holes in the flanged shaft to prevent the shaft from turning.

2. Remove the speedometer drive.

3. Remove the ten nuts or bolts that hold the final drive cover on the transaxle case. Then carefully pry off the cover as shown in Fig. 8-3.

4. Remove the differential from the transaxle case.

To install:

1. If you have replaced the transaxle case, the transmission gear carrier, the final drive cover, the tapered-roller bearings, the differential housing, or the ring and pinion gearset, select and install new shims as described in **9. Adjusting Final Drive.**

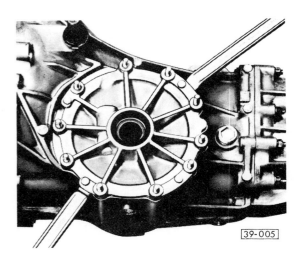

Fig. 8-3. Final drive cover being removed with two levers. Position the transaxle so that the cover is on top before you remove the cover.

2. Lubricate the tapered-roller bearings, the differential gearset, and the ring and pinion gearset with hypoid oil. With the transaxle positioned left side up, carefully lower the differential into the case until the tapered roller bearing rests in its outer race and the ring gear meshes with the pinion gear.

3. Using a new O-ring, install the final drive cover. Install the ten nuts or bolts and washers. Working diagonally, gradually torque the ten nuts or bolts to 2.5 mkg (18 ft. lb.).

4. Install the speedometer drive with a torque of 2.5 mkg (18 ft. lb.). Install the flanged shafts and the flanged shaft bolts. Torque the bolts to 2.0 mkg (14 ft. lb.).

   NOTE ——

   Before you install the flanged shaft bolts, thoroughly clean their threads. Then coat the threads with VW locking compound D6 or a similar product.

8.2 Removing and Installing Tapered-roller Bearings

Remove the tapered-roller bearing races only if the bearings must be replaced. Replace bearings that are noisy, obviously worn, rough, galled, flattened, or heat-blued. It is unnecessary to remove the tapered-roller bearing inner races in order to disassemble the differential.

To remove the tapered-roller bearing outer race and the S_1 shim from the final drive cover, pry out the oil seal. Then use a drift to drive out the bearing race as indicated in Fig. 8-4. Use a similar procedure to remove the tapered-roller bearing outer race and the S₂ shim from the transaxle case. If you intend to reuse either the bearings or the shims, mark them for correct reinstallation.

Fig. 8-4. Drift in position for driving out a tapered-roller bearing outer race.

If you have replaced the transaxle case, the final drive cover, the differential housing, the ring and pinion gearset, or the tapered-roller bearings, install the tapered roller bearing outer race in the final drive housing without any S₁ shim; install the tapered-roller bearing in the transaxle case with a temporary S₂ adjusting shim that is 1.20 mm thick. Then select new S₁ and S₂ shims as described in **9. Adjusting Final Drive** before you make a final installation of the bearing outer races. Drive in the tapered-roller bearing outer races as shown in Fig. 8-5 and Fig. 8-6. Then install new flanged shaft oil seals.

Fig. 8-5. Tapered-roller bearing outer race being driven into final drive cover.

Fig. 8-6. Tapered-roller bearing outer race being driven into transaxle case.

To remove the tapered-roller bearing inner races from the differential, use a puller as shown in Fig. 8-7. On the ring gear side of the differential, simultaneously remove the speedometer drivegear.

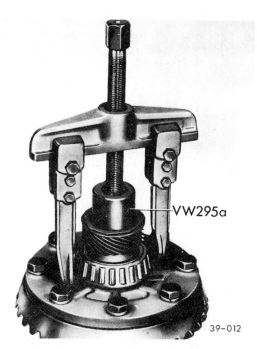

Fig. 8-7. Tapered-roller bearing inner race being removed from differential. Notice the central support that has been installed in the differential's flanged shaft opening.

To install the tapered-roller bearing inner races, heat them to approximately 212°F (100°C) in a pan of oil placed in a larger pan of boiling water. Then press the bearing races onto the differential as shown in Fig. 8-8.

NOTE ——

If you must adjust the ring gear as described in **9.2 Adjusting Ring Gear Position,** do so before you install the speedomter drivegear.

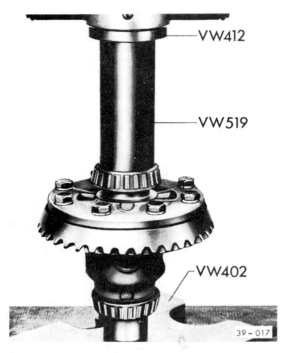

Fig. 8-8. Tapered-roller bearing inner race being pressed onto differential. On the ring gear side, install the speedometer drivegear in a separate operation following the installation of the bearing.

To install the speedometer drivegear, start the gear on the differential. Install a new octagonal-flanged speedometer drivegear bushing atop the gear. Insert a 1.80-mm thick shim plate (Part No. N 11 9581) in the bushing as shown in Fig. 8-9. Then press on the bushing and the drivegear as a unit. Remove the shim plate.

NOTE ——

The shim plate assures correct alignment of the gear and the bushing as they are pressed on.

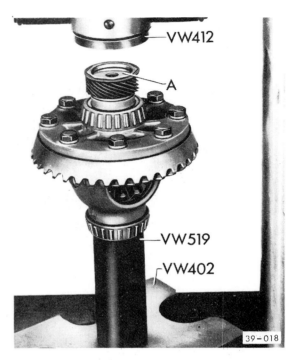

Fig. 8-9. Shim plate **(A)** inserted in gear and bushing.

8.3 Disassembling and Assembling Differential

Fig. 8-10 is an exploded view of the differential. The tapered-roller bearing inner races and the speedometer drivegear need only be removed if they require replacement. See **8.2 Removing and Installing Tapered-roller Bearings.** If you replace the bearings, the differential housing, or the ring and pinion gearset, you must adjust the final drive as described in **9. Adjusting Final Drive** before you reinstall the repaired differential.

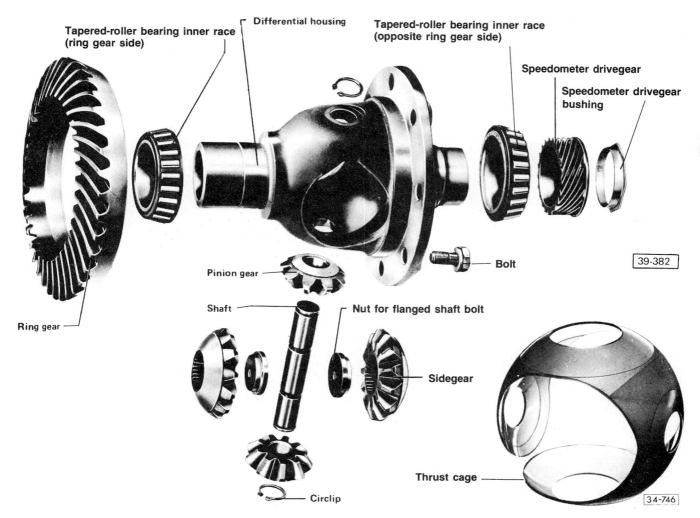

Fig. 8-10. Exploded view of differential. Thrust cage for sidegears and pinions is used on 1977 and later cars. Previous units have no thrust cage or thrust washers.

To disassemble:

1. Remove the eight bolts, then drive off the ring gear as shown in Fig. 8-11.

   CAUTION —

   When removing the ring gear, be careful not to let it fall against the vise. Doing so could damage the ring gear teeth. A pad of rags placed beneath the ring gear is a worthwhile precaution.

2. Using circlip pliers, remove one of the circlips from the differential pinion shaft. Then drive the shaft out of the differential housing and differential pinion gears.

Fig. 8-11. A drift being used to drive off the ring gear. Work alternately on both sides of the differential housing, going all around the ring of bolt holes until the gear is free.

3. Temporarily install the flanged shaft bolts. Then, using the procedure illustrated in Fig. 8-12, rotate the differential gearset until the differential pinions can be removed through the openings in the differential housing.

Fig. 8-12. Differential gearset being rotated in housing. Keep housing and lower flanged shaft stationary; hand-turn the upper flanged shaft as indicated by the arrow.

4. Remove the flanged shaft bolts and the flanged shafts. Then remove the differential sidegears and the nuts for the flanged shaft bolts.

To assemble:

1. Install the differential sidegears and the nuts for the flanged shaft bolts. Then temporarily install the flanged shafts and their bolts.

   NOTE ——

   Part way through the 1976 model year, the number of splines on the flanged shafts and the side gears was increased from 31 splines to 33 splines. At the same time, different nuts for the flanged shaft bolts were introduced. If any of the parts shown in Fig. 8-13 must be replaced, compare the new part to the old part in order to make sure that it is the correct replacement.

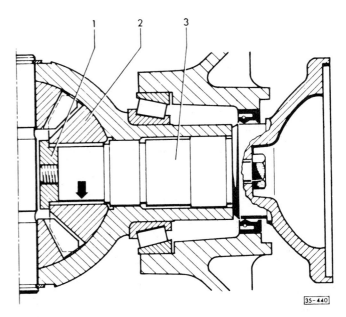

Fig. 8-13. Flanged shaft components changed part way through 1976 model year. Nut is at **1**, sidegear at **2**, and flanged shaft at **3**.

2. Install the differential pinions in the openings in the differential housing so that they mesh with the sidegears. Then, repeating the procedure illustrated previously in Fig. 8-12, rotate the differential gearset until the pinions are aligned with the holes for the differential pinion shaft.

3. Insert the differential pinion shaft, with one circlip installed, as shown in Fig. 8-14. The shaft should slide in easily if the pinions are correctly aligned with the holes in the housing.

4. Install the second circlip on the differential pinion shaft.

5. Heat the ring gear to approximately 212°F (100°C) in a pan of oil placed in a larger pan of boiling water. Then, making sure that the bolt holes in the ring gear are aligned with those in the differential housing, install the gear on the housing as shown in Fig. 8-15. If it is necessary to align the bolt holes more precisely after the gear is in place, use a brass drift and a hammer to rotate the ring gear slightly on the housing.

6. Install the eight bolts that hold the ring gear to the differential housing. If the bolts have spring-type lockwashers, as used on early cars, torque the bolts to 5.5 mkg (40 ft. lb.). If the later bolts with serrated washer surfaces are used, torque the bolts to 7.0 mkg (50 ft. lb.).

   CAUTION ——

   Do not use spring washers with the later bolts. Doing this will result in poor ring gear mounting.

39-014

Fig. 8-14. Differential pinion shaft being installed in differential housing and differential pinions.

39-015

Fig. 8-15. Ring gear being installed on differential housing. Use a pad of rags, as shown, to protect your hands from the heated ring gear.

9. ADJUSTING FINAL DRIVE

Beginning with Transmission No. XK 26 076, at the start of 1977 production, the final drive housing is longer than formerly, the ring gear is larger, and the drive pinion is longer. Therefore, variations in the adjusting procedures are noted at several points in the course of the instructions given under this and later headings. The

late-type parts, which include the bearings and a number of other components, cannot be installed in earlier transaxles.

Careful adjustment of the mesh between the ring gear and drive pinion is essential to ensure long service and quiet operation. The adjustments described here are necessary to the life of the gearset, the differential bearings, and drive pinion ball bearing. The final drive gearset requires adjustments only when parts directly affecting the adjustment have been replaced or when careless disassembly has resulted in the loss of the original shims.

Table d lists what adjustments must be made when certain parts are replaced. Shift housing adjustment, to determine shim and gasket thicknesses, is described in **6.1 Removing and Installing Shift Housing.**

NOTE ——

In addition to the part replacements listed in **Table c**, you must also adjust the drive pinion if you install a gasket between the gear carrier and the transaxle case of a transaxle that did not originally have a gasket in this location. If you are adjusting the pinion for some other reason, it is a good idea to add the gasket at the same time. The gasket is factory-installed beginning with Transmission No. XZ 14055, manufactured early in the 1976 model year. It is unnecessary to adjust the pinion if you simply replace the gasket on one of these late transaxles.

Table d. Necessary Adjustments for Replaced Parts

Part replaced	Parts to be adjusted		
	Drive pinion	Ring gear	Shift housing
Transaxle case	X	X	
Final drive cover		X	
Differential tapered-roller bearings		X	
1st gear needle bearing inner race	X		
Drive pinion ball bearing	X		X
Ring and pinion gearset	X	X	
Differential housing		X	
Transmission gear carrier	X		X
Mainshaft ball bearing			X
Shift housing			X

The ring gear and pinion are run on special testing machines during transmission manufacture to check the tooth contact pattern and silent running under both drive and coast conditions. When the optimum relationship of the two gears is found, they are installed in the transmission using S_3, S_1, and S_2 shims that will duplicate the gearset's position in the testing machine. The purpose of all subsequent adjustments is to restore the gearset to this position following repair.

If the drive pinion position must be adjusted, do so before adjusting either the ring gear position or the shift housing. Dimension **r**, given in Fig. 9-1, is the deviation of the pinion gear's pinion gear's position from a standard dimension called R_0. (R_0 is the length of the master gauge that is used in the factory testing machine.) The deviation **r** is not marked on the ring and pinion gearset during manufacture. Therefore, if adjustments are necessary following parts replacement, you must measure deviation **r** before you remove the transmission gear train. Replacement ring and pinion gearsets have the deviation **r** marked on them. During the installation of such gearsets, you must adjust the pinion to the deviation **r** that is marked on the gearset.

CAUTION —

The ring gear and the pinion should only be replaced as a factory-matched gearset. Mixing the ring gear from one gearset with a drive pinion of another gearset will almost certainly result in rapid wear and noisy operation.

Table e defines the terms and symbols that are used in making final drive adjustments. For accurate adjustment, you must have metric measuring tools and special tools such as those illustrated in the work procedures.

Table e. Symbols Used in Final Drive Adjustments

Symbol	Description	Dimension
S_1	Shim thickness on ring gear side of differential	measured in 1/100 mm
S_2	Shim thickness on side of differential opposite the ring gear	measured in 1/100 mm
S_3	Shim thickness between drive pinion ball bearing and 1st gear needle bearing inner race	measured in 1/100 mm
r	Deviation of drive pinion position from length of master gauge	measured in 1/100 mm marked on replacement gearsets (25 = 0.25 mm)
R_0	Length of master gauge used in factory testing machine	1973-76: 48.70 mm 1977 on: 50.70 mm
e	Measured position of drive pinion with a 4.00-mm measuring shim installed in place of the S_3 shim	measured in 1/100 mm ($e = r + 4.00$ mm)
x	Actual measured thickness of the 4.00-mm measuring shim	thickness in 1/100 mm when measured with a micrometer
S_{total}	Combined thickness of the S_1 and S_2 shims	measured in 1/100 mm

CAUTION —

If you lack the skills, special measuring tools, or a clean workshop for adjusting the final drive, we suggest you leave such repairs to an Authorized Dealer or other qualified and properly equipped shop. We especially urge you to consult your Authorized Dealer before attempting repairs on a vehicle covered by a new-car warranty.

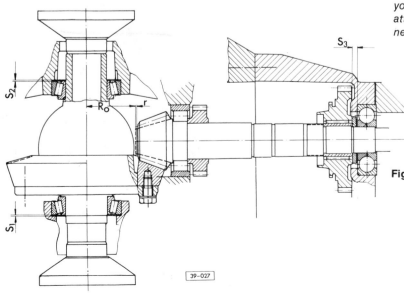

Fig. 9-1. Final drive adjustments. R_0 is the length of the factory master gauge. Dimension **r** is the pinion position's deviation from the standard dimension, R_0. Pinion position is controlled by the S_3 shim which is installed between the drive pinion ball bearing and the 1st gear needle bearing's inner race. The S_1 and S_2 shims control ring gear position and the preload of the differential tapered-roller bearings.

9.1 Locating and Adjusting Drive Pinion Position

If there is a possibility that you will replace any of the parts that affect drive pinion position, you must make precision measurements before you remove the transmission gear train. In doing so, you will accurately locate the drive pinion's original position so that you can return it to the same position following repair. If you install a new ring and pinion gearset, you need not measure the drive pinion position before disassembly. However, you will need to locate the drive pinion's position during pinion installation so that you can determine the thickness of the S_3 shim which must be used during final assembly.

To locate drive pinion position:

1. If not previously removed, remove the differential and flanged shaft oil seals.

2. Adjust the clamp ring on the universal measuring bar (Tool VW 385/1). Dimension **a** shown in Fig. 9-2 is approximately 50 mm.

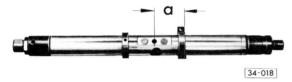

Fig. 9-2. Clamp ring adjustment.

3. Slide the centering discs (VW 395/1) onto the bar until they contact the clamp ring and the setting ring. Then attach measuring pin VW 385/13 with extension VW 385/15 (VW 385/16 beginning with Transmission No. XK 26 076) to the gauge pin hole in the center of the bar. Install a dial indicator with a 3-mm or a 5-mm range (early transaxles) or with a 5-mm range (1977 and later transaxles). Zero the dial indicator with a 2-mm preload (4-mm preload beginning with Transmission No. XK 26 076).

    NOTE

    The 4-mm preload is necessary with late transaxles because setting block VW 385/23 is designed for an R_0 of 48.70 mm, whereas 1977 and later gearsets have an R_0 of 50.70 mm. The 4-mm preload will become 2-mm when the measuring bar is installed in the final drive housing. This should cause no concern.

4. If you are locating the drive pinion position prior to gear train removal, proceed with step 8. If you are making a preliminary measurement for the installation of a new ring and pinion gearset, install the drive pinion in the gear carrier with a 4.00-mm temporary S_3 shim. If you are making a preliminary measurement after replacing parts

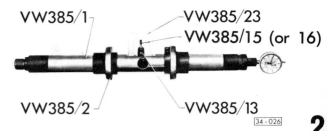

Fig. 9-3. Measuring bar ready for use. Notice how the setting block VW 385/23 has been placed over the measuring pin extension. Insert the dial indicator into the bar until it reads 2 mm (or 4 mm on 1977 and later transaxles). Then zero the dial with the gauge in that position.

2

other than the ring and pinion gearset, install the drive pinion in the gear carrier with the original S_3 shim. See Fig. 9-4.

NOTE

Check the thickness of the 4.00-mm measuring shim (Part No. 014 311 400) with a micrometer to make sure that you know its actual thickness. Any variation of 1/100 mm or more must be taken into account during computation of the permanent S_3 shim's thickness.

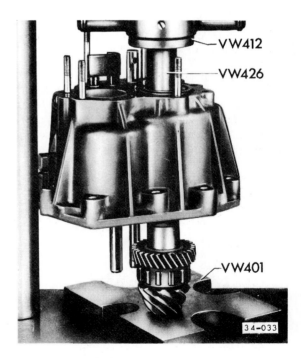

Fig. 9-4. Drive pinion with original S_3 shim, or with the 4.00-mm measuring shim, being installed in gear carrier. Only the drive pinion roller bearing, 4th gear, 1st gear, the 1st gear needle bearing, the 1st gear needle bearing inner race, the shim, and the drive pinion ball bearing inner race need be installed on the drive pinion shaft during preliminary measurement.

5. With 4th gear clamped in a vice that has soft jaws, install the nut for the drive pinion ball bearing as shown in Fig. 9-5. Then torque the nut to approximately 2 to 3 mkg (14 to 22 ft lb.)—not to the final assembly torque which is 10.0 mkg (72 ft. lb.).

Fig. 9-6. Pinion locked with a 36-mm socket and tensioner VW 297/8.

Fig. 9-5. Nut being installed on drive pinion.

6. Using at least four of the nuts, install the drive pinion and the transmission gear carrier on the transaxle case. Do not use sealer.

> **NOTE** ──
> If the transaxle had a gasket between the gear carrier and the transaxle case, install a new gasket at this time. If the transaxle did not have a gasket, it is advisable to add the gasket at this time. If you intend to use a gasket, the gasket must be in place during the measuring and adjustment of the drive pinion position.

7. To keep the drive pinion from turning while you make measurements, leave the 36-mm socket in place on the pinion nut. Then install tensioner VW 297/8 as shown in Fig. 9-6. Tighten the knurled knob until the screw locks the socket in place.

8. Place the magnetic measuring plate VW 385/17 on the drive pinion face as shown in Fig. 9-7. Then insert the measuring bar.

9. Hand-press the final drive cover down over the measuring bar so that it is in firm contact with the transaxle case. Do not strike the cover with a rubber or plastic hammer, since doing this could upset the setting of the dial indicator.

Fig. 9-7. Magnetic measuring plate and measuring bar installed in transaxle.

10. Install the nuts and torque them to 2.5 mkg (18 ft. lb.).

11. By turning the knurled knob on the end of the measuring bar that is opposite the dial indicator, move the lower setting ring and centering disk outward until it is just barely possible to hand-turn the measuring bar.

12. Hand-turn the measuring bar until the measuring pin extension rests against the measuring plate on the drive pinion face. See Fig. 9-8.

13. Rotate the bar back and forth over center. (Fig. 9-9). The maximum dial indicator reading should be observed and written down.

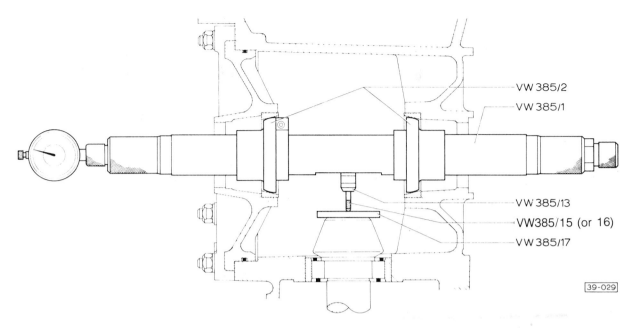

Fig. 9-8. Arrangement of measuring tools inside the final drive portion of the transaxle case.

Fig. 9-9. Measuring bar being rotated (arrow) back and forth over center.

14. If you are locating the original drive pinion position prior to gear train removal, the reading that you have obtained in step 12 is **r**. If you are making a preliminary measurement with a new ring and pinion gearset, the reading that you have obtained in step 12 is **e**. Use **r** or **e** as described under one of the two following headings in order to select the correct permanent S_3 shim.

Selecting S_3 Shim(s)
(original ring and pinion retained)

To correct the drive pinion position following the installation of a new transaxle case, 1st gear needle bearing inner race, drive pinion ball bearing, or transmission gear carrier, compare the **r** measurement you obtained prior to gear train removal with the measurement that you obtained following repairs with the original S_3 shim installed. If the drive pinion location measurement obtained following repairs is less that the **r** measurement obtained prior to gear train removal, you must install a thinner S_3 shim. If the drive pinion location measurement obtained following repairs is greater than the **r** measurement obtained prior to gear train removal, you must install a thicker S_3 shim.

CAUTION ——

Every number or setting in the following example is imaginary. Using them as specifications for a car could cause serious damage.

Example:

Measurement before disassembly (**r**)	0.45 mm
Measurement after replacing parts	0.36 mm
Difference	0.09 mm

Because the second measurement is smaller, an S_3 shim that is 0.09 mm thinner must be used in final assembly.

Example:

Original S_3 shim thickness	4.60 mm
Difference shown in previous example	0.09 mm
New S_3 shim thickness required	4.51 mm

Select the required shim from **Table f.** Because S_3 shims have a manufacturing tolerance range of several hundredths mm, you can use a micrometer to select shims which will equal any required S_3 thickness. If you use the 0.15-mm shim in combination with another shim, always install the 0.15-mm shim between the thick shim and the drive pinion ball bearing inner race. After you have installed the correct S_3 shim(s), again check the deviation of the pinion to see that the drive pinion is in its original location

Table f. Available S_3 Shims

Part No.	Nominal thickness (mm)
019 311 391	0.15
014 311 398	3.80
014 311 399	3.90
014 311 400	4.00
014 311 401	4.10
014 311 402	4.20
014 311 403	4.30
014 311 404	4.40
014 311 405	4.50
014 311 406	4.60
014 311 407	4.70
014 311 408	4.80
014 311 409	4.90
014 311 410	5.00
014 311 411	5.10
014 311 412	5.20

Selecting S_3 Shim(s)
(new ring and pinion gearset installed)

To find the thickness(es) of the S_3 shim(s) required to adjust a new pinion to the **r** dimension stamped on the replacement gearset, you use the simple formula $S_3 = e - r + x$.

e is the preliminary measurement obtained with the 4.00-mm measuring shim installed.

r is the deviation **r** stamped on the replacement gearset.

x is the actual measured thickness of the 4.00-mm measuring shim.

CAUTION ——

Every number or setting in the following example is imaginary. Using them as specifications for a car could cause serious damage.

Example:

$e = 0.90$ mm

$r = 0.45$ mm

$x = 4.00$ mm

$0.90 - 0.45 + 4.00 = 4.45$ mm

Two shims—one that is 4.30 mm thick and another 0.15 mm thick—would be required to equal the 4.45-mm S_3 dimension. If you use the 0.15-mm shim in combination with another shim, always install the 0.15-mm shim between the thick shim and the drive pinion ball bearing inner race. Select the necessary shims from **Table f** which is given earlier. After you have installed the correct S_3 shim(s), again check the deviation **r** of the pinion to see that it is the same as the **r** dimension stamped on the replacement pinion.

9.2 Adjusting Ring Gear Position

If you have replaced the ring and pinion gearset, the differential housing, one or both of the differential tapered-roller bearings, the transaxle case, or the final drive cover, you must make precision measurements in order to select new S_1 and S_2 shims.

To adjust ring gear:

1. Remove the differential. Remove the flanged shaft oil seals. Drive out the differential tapered-roller bearing outer races and remove the S_1 and the S_2 shims. See **8.1 Removing and Installing Differential** and **8.2 Removing and Installing Tapered-roller Bearings.**

2. Using a temporary S_2 shim that is 1.20 mm thick (Part No. 113 517 202 A), install the tapered-roller bearing outer race in the transaxle housing.

3. Install the tapered-roller bearing outer race in the final drive cover without any S_1 shim.

4. If not previously removed, remove the transmission gear carrier and the transmission gear train.

5. Without the speedometer drivegear, install the differential—ring gear side up—in the transaxle case. Do not lubricate the bearings or rotate the differential in the bearings.

6. Using all the nuts or bolts and washers, install the final drive cover. Working diagonally, gradually torque the nuts or bolts to 2.5 mkg (18 ft. lb.).

7. Install the magnetic measuring plate VW 385/17 on the differential housing. Then install a dial indicator with a 3.00-mm range as shown in Fig. 9-10. Zero the gauge against the measuring plate with a 1.00-mm preload.

8. Install locking sleeve VW 521/4 together with sleeve VW 521/8 on the lower end of the differential (opposite the ring gear). See Fig. 9-11.

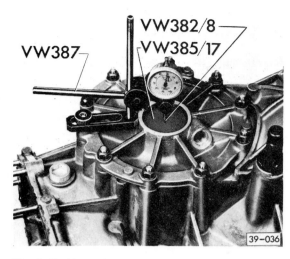

Fig. 9-10. Magnetic measuring plate and dial indicator installed.

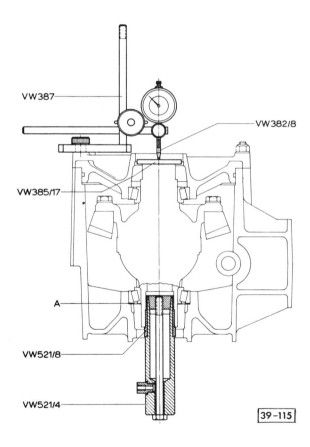

Fig. 9-11. Setup for measuring differential axial play in preparation for temporary S_1 shim selection.

9. By grasping locking sleeve VW 521/4, move the differential up and down as indicated in Fig. 9-12. Write down the maximum dial indicator reading.

2 ■

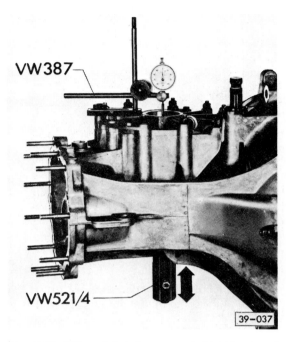

Fig. 9-12. Differential being moved (double arrow) throughout its available range of axial play.

10. Add the reading you obtained in step 8 ($^1/_{100}$mm) to the standard value 0.40 mm. The sum is the thickness of the temporary S_1 shim(s) that you will need to install in order to proceed with the next phase of adjustment. (The standard value 0.40 mm represents the combined depth to which the tapered-roller bearings will settle when you turn the differential.)

NOTE ——

The available shims are given later in **Table f.**

11. To the thickness of the temporary S_1 shim(s), obtained in step 10, add the 1.20-mm thickness of the temporary S_2 shim that you have already installed in the transaxle case. Write down the sum, which is the S_{total}.

Example:

Axial play measured in step 8	0.30 mm
Standard value for bearing settling	+ 0.40 mm
Thickness of temporary S_1 shim(s)	0.70 mm
Thickness of temporary S_2 shim	+ 1.20 mm
The S_{total}	1.90 mm

12. Remove the final drive cover. Drive the tapered-roller bearing outer race out of the cover. Then install the temporary S_1 shim(s) that you selected in step 10. Press in the bearing outer race.

13. Lubricate both differential tapered-roller bearings with hypoid oil. Then install the final drive cover. Working diagonally, gradually torque the nuts or bolts to 2.5 mkg (18 ft. lb.).

   NOTE ——

   Use only hypoid oil as a lubricant. The test results will be inaccurate if the turning torque is checked with the bearings dry or lubricated with another kind of oil.

14. If you have installed new tapered-roller bearings, install a torque gauge on the locking sleeve as shown in Fig. 9-13. Using the handle of the torque gauge, spin the differential 15 or 20 turns in each direction. Then while continuing to spin the differential, note the reading on the torque gauge. It should be at least 25 cmkg (22 in. lb.).

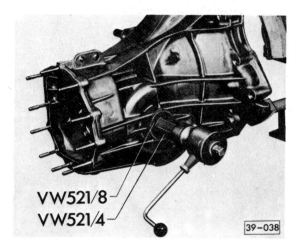

Fig. 9-13. Torque gauge installed on differential.

   NOTE ——

   If the tapered-roller bearings have been in service for 30 mi. (50 km) or more, it is not necessary to check the turning torque. If the turning torque of new bearings is less than 25 cmkg (22 in. lb.) or significantly greater than 25 cmkg (22 in. lb.), either the bearings are faulty or you have made an error in selecting the temporary S_1 shim(s).

15. If turning torque is correct, install the trans-

mission gear carrier and the gear train (or partially-assembled drive pinion instead of the gear train). To prevent the drive pinion from turning, install a 36-mm socket and Tensioner VW 297/8 as illustrated earlier in Fig. 9-6.

16. Install measuring bar VW 388 on the locking sleeve as shown in Fig. 9-14. Then position a dial indicator against the measuring bar. This is the setup you will use in measuring ring gear backlash.

Fig. 9-14. Measuring bar and dial indicator installed. Adjust the measuring bar so that dimension **a** is 68 mm on 1973 through 1976 cars or 71 mm on 1977 and later cars. The angle indicated between the measuring bar and the dial indicator's gauge pin must be approximately 90°.

17. By grasping the locking sleeve, turn the measuring bar as far as it will go away from the dial indicator before differential rotation is stopped by the locked drive pinion. Then zero the dial indicator. Turn the differential in the opposite direction until it is stopped by the pinion and write down the dial reading indicator. This is the ring gear's backlash.

18. Loosen the locking bolt on the locking sleeve. Reposition the measuring bar in a location that is 90° from its previous location. Tighten the locking bolt.

19. Loosen the knurled knob on the tensioner that is holding the drive pinion. Then turn the differential until the measuring bar is again positioned against the gauge pin of the dial indicator. Lock the pinion.

20. Again measure the backlash and write down the reading. Make two more backlash measurements so that you have four readings taken at four points 90° apart around the circumference of the ring gear.

NOTE ——

The difference between the four readings must not exceed 0.05 mm; if it is greater, something is wrong with the gearset or its installation. Left in this condition, the final drive will be noisy and wear rapidly.

21. Add the four measurements, then divide the sum by four. The quotient is the average backlash for the ring and pinion gearset.

22. To determine the thickness(es) of the permanet S_2 shim(s) that you must install during final assembly, subtract the average backlash from the thickness of the 1.20-mm temporary S_2 shim. To the remainder (the answer from your subtraction), add the standard value of 0.15 mm. The sum is the thickness(es) for the permanent S_2 shim(s). (The standard value 0.15 mm represents the nominal gear lift that occurs when the ring and pinion gearset are in operation.).

CAUTION ——

The average backlash and S_{total} given in the following examples are imaginary. In making actual repairs, you could seriously damage the final drive by using the S_1 and S_3 shim thicknesses derived from these imaginary numbers.

Example:

Thickness of temporary S_2 shim	1.20 mm
Average backlash found in step 21	− 0.41 mm
	0.79 mm
Standard value for gear lift	+ 0.15 mm
Thickness of permanent S_2 shim(s)	0.94 mm

23. To determine the thickness(es) of the permanent S_1 shim(s) that you must install during final assembly, subtract the thickness computed for the permanent S_2 shim in step 22 from the S_{total} computed in step 11. The remainder is the thickness(es) of the permanent S_1 shim(s).

Example:

The S_{total}	1.90 mm
Thickness of permanent S_2 shim(s)	− 0.94 mm
Thickness of permanent S_1 shim(s)	0.96 mm

Select the required permanent S_1 and S_2 shims from **Table g.** Because shims have a manufacturing tolerance range of several hundredths mm, you can use a micrometer to select shims that will equal any required thickness. If you use the 0.15-mm shim in combination with another shim, always installk the 0.15-mm shim between the thick shim and the tapered roller bearing outer race.

After you have installed the correct permanent S_1 and S_2 shims, again measure the backlash four times around the circumference of the ring gear. The average backlash should be between 0.10 mm and 0.20 mm and individual measurements should not differ from one another by more than 0.05 mm. If backlash is not within specifications either something is wrong with the gearset or its installation or you have made an error in selecting the permanent S_1 and S_2 shims.

Table g. Available S_1/S_2 Shims

Part No.	Nominal Thickness (mm)
113 517 201 A	0.15
113 517 202 A	0.20
113 517 203 A	0.30
113 517 204 A	0.40
113 517 205 A	0.50
113 517 206 A	0.60
113 517 207 A	0.70
113 517 208 A	0.80
113 517 209 A	0.90
113 517 210 A	1.00
113 517 211 A	1.20

10. MANUAL TRANSMISSION TECHNICAL DATA

I. Basic Data for Transaxle with Manual Transmission

Designation	Specification
1. Transaxle identification code	1973 Audi only: ZV 1974 models: ZS 1975 models: YZ Early 1976 models: YZ Later 1976 models: XH 1977 and 1978 models: XK 1977 through 1979 models (except diesel): XK 1979 diesel: YT or 1T
2. Oil capacity—initial filling	4.2 U.S. pints (2.0 liters, 3.5 Imperial pints)
3. Oil capacity—at change	3.4 U.S. pints (1.6 liters, 2.8 Imperial pints)
4. Hypoid oil	SAE 80 or SAE 80/90 that meets specification MIL-L-2105 (sulphur-phosphorus additive)

II. Gear Ratios

Gears	No. of teeth	Primary ratio	Overall ratio
1st gear	11:38	3.454	14.202
2nd gear—through July 1974	18:37	2.055	8.450
2nd gear—from August 1974	19:37	1.947	8.015
2nd gear—from October 1974	18:35	1.944	7.995
3rd gear—ZV, ZS, YZ	27:37	1.370	5.633
3rd gear—XH, XK, YT, 1T	28:36	1.286	5.284
4th gear—ZV, ZS	32:31	0.968	3.983
4th gear—YZ	33:31	0.939	3.860
4th gear—XH, XK, YT, 1T	34:30	0.882	3.626

2

III. Tightening Torques

Location	Designation	mkg	ft. lb.
Inboard constant velocity joint to flanged shaft	socket head bolt	3.5	25
Front suspension ball joint to track control arm	nut and bolt	6.5	47
Front wheel hub to axle shaft of outboard constant velocity joint	nut	25.0–30.0	180–216
Flanged shaft to differential	bolt	2.0	14
Transaxle to engine	bolt	5.5	40
Shift housing to transmission gear carrier	nut	2.0	14
Back-up light switch in shift housing	switch	2.0	14
Seat belt warning switch in shift housing	switch	2.0	14
Shift linkage strut or support to transaxle (where applicable)	bolt	2.0	14
Pinion ball bearing to drive pinion shaft	nut	10.0	72
Transmission gear carrier to transaxle case	nut	2.0	14
Bolt for reverse relay lever in transmission gear carrier	bolt	3.5	25
Clutch operating shaft bushing in transaxle case	dog point bolt	1.5	11
Clutch operating lever to clutch operating shaft	clamp bolt and nut	2.0	14
Clutch release bearing guide sleeve to transaxle case	nut	1.5	11
Final drive cover to transaxle case	nut	2.5	18
Ring gear to differential housing	bolt with spring washer	5.5	40
	bolt with serrated washer surface	7.0	50
Speedometer drive in final drive cover	threaded sleeve	2.5	18
Oil filler plug/magetic drain plug in transaxle case	socket head plug	2.5	18
Bonded rubber mounting to transaxle carrier	nut	4.0	29
Transaxle carrier to car body	bolt	2.5	18
Starter to bellhousing	bolt	2.0	14
Shift linkage to transmission inner shift lever	bolt	1.5	11
Exhaust pipe to exhaust manifold	nut	2.5	18
Exhaust pipe bracket to transmission rear mounting	bolt	2.0	14

IV. Tolerances, Wear Limits, and Settings

Designation	New installation mm (in.)	Wear limit mm (in.)
1. Synchronizing rings (measured between coupling teeth on ring and coupling teeth on gear)		
1st/2nd gears ....clearance	1.10–1.70 (.043–.066)	0.60 (.023)
3rd/4th gears ....clearance	1.35–1.90 (.053–.075)	0.60 (.023)
2. 4th gear/4th gear thrust washer ....clearance	0.10–0.40 (.004–.016)	—
3. Front wheel driveshafts		
Manual transmission transaxle ....length of both driveshafts	506.00 (19.92)	—
Automatic transmission transaxle......................length of left driveshaft	531.00 (20.90)	—
Automatic transmission transaxle ....length of right driveshaft	437.00 (17.20)	—
4. Gearshift lever ....lateral play	10–15 (⅜–⅝)	—
5. Preload on differential tapered-roller bearings ....turning torque	25 cmkg (22 in. lb.).	—
6. Molybdenum grease for constant velocity joint ....quantity	90 g (3.2 oz.)	—

V. Gear Applications

Gear	Model	Location	No. of teeth	Identifying marks on gear	Spare part number
1st 1st	1973–1979 1973–1979	mainshaft pinion shaft	11 38	none none	integral with mainshaft 014 311 257
2nd 2nd	1973–1974 early 1975 1975 from Oct. '74 through 1979 1973–1974 early 1975 1975 from Oct. '74 through 1979	mainshaft mainshaft mainshaft pinion shaft pinion shaft pinion shaft	18 19 18 37 37 35	none one groove two grooves none two grooves two grooves	014 311 105 014 311 105 D 014 311 105 E 014 311 271 014 311 271 D 014 311 271 E
3rd 3rd	1973–early 1976 late 1976–1979 1973–early 1976 late 1976–1979	mainshaft mainshaft pinion shaft pinion shaft	27 28 37 36	none none none none	014 311 285 A* 014 311 285 E* 014 311 131* 014 311 131 B*
4th 4th	1973–1974 early 1975 1975 from Oct. '74 through early 1976 late 1976–1979 1973–1974 early 1975 1975 from Oct. '74 through early 1976 late 1976–1979	mainshaft mainshaft mainshaft mainshaft pinion shaft pinion shaft pinion shaft pinion shaft	32 33 33 34 31 31 31 30	none one groove two grooves three grooves none one groove two grooves three grooves	014 311 351 A 014 311 351 B* 014 311 351 C* 014 311 351 H* 014 311 149 014 311 149 A* 014 311 149 B* 014 311 149 C*
Reverse	1973–1974 1975–1979	— —	— —	none one groove	014 311 529 014 311 529 A

*Mainshaft and pinion shaft gears now available individually instead of as a matched set only.

2

ENGINE AND CLUTCH

3

Contents

Engine and Clutch

3

The four cylinder inline engine is front mounted and water cooled. It has inline valves that are operated by a belt-driven single overhead camshaft. The piston displacement of engines with carburetors is 1471 cc (89.7 cu. in.); the piston displacement of engines with fuel injection is 1588 cc (96.9 cu. in.). Basic simplicity, proven mechanical concepts, and a highly accessible arrangement of external components make the engine exceptionally easy to service and maintain.

The engine is bolted to a bellhousing on the front of the transaxle and is inclined 30° toward the right-hand side of the car—thereby permitting a lower hood line than would be practical with the engine fully upright. (A low, flat front body profile improves forward visibility and makes the car less sensitive to strong or gusty crosswinds.) The radiator is mounted left of center. Its position, together with the canted engine, improves access to the drive belts, water pump, and alternator.

The engine's placement ahead of the front axle makes possible a roomier passenger compartment and concentrates weight over the (front) driving wheels, where it will improve traction in mud or snow. Despite a slight forward weight bias when the car is empty, total vehicle weight is distributed about equally on the front and rear wheels when the car is loaded. Equal weight distribution increases vehicle stability and assures precise handling.

The early cars covered by this Manual are equipped with a network of test wiring for the Computer Analysis system. On the engine, there is a sensor in the high tension cable leading to the No. 1 cylinder (for obtaining spark timing data) and a battery-testing wire attached to the starter solenoid. Another timing sensor is installed in the flywheel bellhousing. All sensor wires must remain properly attached if the Computer Analysis system is to work as designed. Never connect any device other than the test plug of the Computer Analysis system to the test network central socket in the engine compartment. Incorrect equipment could damage the plug connectors, the test sensors, or the components that contain sensors.

The information in this section of the Manual is intended to serve as a guide to both car owners and professional mechanics. Some of the operations may require special equipment and experience that only a trained mechanic will normally have. If you lack the skills, tools, or a suitable workshop for servicing the engine, we suggest you leave these repairs to an Authorized Dealer or other qualified shop. We especially urge you to consult your Authorized Dealer before attempting any repairs on a car still covered by the new-car warranty.

1. GENERAL DESCRIPTION

A cutaway view of the water-cooled, overhead camshaft engine appears in Fig. 1-1. Notice the drive belt, the camshaft, and the intermediate shaft that drives the oil pump, the distributor, and the fuel pump.

Engine Mounting

The engine is supported by three bonded rubber mountings. One mounting is at the front, and there is one at each side. Four bolts join the rear of the engine to the bellhousing of the transaxle.

Engine Block

The engine block is made of cast iron. For extra strength, the sides of the crankcase extend well below the main bearing centerline. The cylinders are integral with the block and completely exposed on all sides to the coolant that circulates through the water jacket.

Crankshaft and Bearings

The fully-counterweighted crankshaft revolves in five split-shell main bearings. The center bearing shells are flanged to take crankshaft end thrust. Seals, pressed into lightweight alloy seal carriers, are used at both ends of the crankshaft to prevent oil leakage.

Valve Train

The single overhead camshaft is driven by the crankshaft via a toothed, steel-reinforced belt. The cam lobes operate on hardened steel valve adjusting disks that are placed in recesses atop the bucket-type cam followers. Dual valve springs are used on both the intake valves and the exhaust valves.

Cylinder Head

The cylinder head is an aluminum alloy casting with integral bearing surfaces for the overhead camshaft. Pressed-in valve guides are used, but the bores for the cam followers are machined directly into the cylinder head material.

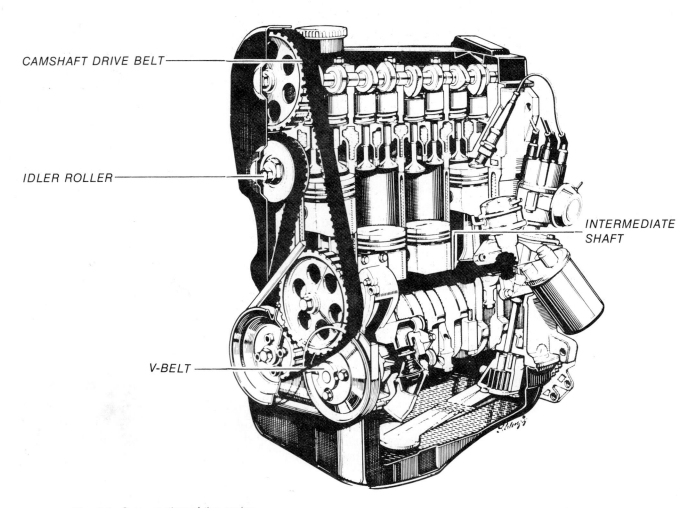

CAMSHAFT DRIVE BELT

IDLER ROLLER

V-BELT

INTERMEDIATE SHAFT

Fig. 1-1. Cutaway view of the engine.

Connecting Rods and Pistons

The connecting rods are steel forgings. Split-shell bearings are used at the crankshaft end and lead-bronze coated steel bushings at the piston pin end. The pistons are of the three-ring type with full-floating pins secured by circlips.

Flywheel and Drive Plate

The flywheel, used on cars with manual transmissions, is mounted on the crankshaft with six steel bolts. Instead of a flywheel, engines used with automatic transmissions have a similarly mounted drive plate to which the torque converter is bolted. Both the flywheel and the drive plate are equipped with a ring gear for the starter drive.

Cooling System

Coolant is circulated through the radiator and the engine by a centrifugal-type water pump. The pump is crankshaft-driven by the same V-belt that drives the alternator. The radiator cooling fan is powered by an electric motor and begins to operate only at coolant temperatures of 90°C (194°F) or above. The coolant, warmed by the engine, is used to heat the car interior, the intake manifold, and, except on fuel injection cars, the carburetor's automatic choke.

Emission Controls

Exhaust emissions are controlled by engine modifications, exhaust gas recirculation (EGR), and—on cars sold in California—air injection (AI). The closed positive crankcase ventilation (PCV) system, which eliminates crankcase emissions, contains no PCV valve that would require periodic servicing or replacement. Some 1975 and later models have a catalytic converter built into the exhaust system.

Ignition System

The ignition is a conventional coil and battery system. The distributor, which has both vacuum and centrifugal advance mechanisms, is driven by the intermediate shaft.

Lubrication System

A gear-type oil pump, driven by the distributor shaft, draws oil through a strainer in the bottom of the oil pan and forces it through a cartridge-type filter and into the engine's oil passages. A pressure relief valve limits the pressure in the system and a filter bypass valve assures lubrication even if the filter is plugged.

Clutch

The engines used with manual transmissions have a dry, single-plate clutch. The pressure plate assembly, which has a diaphragm spring, and the driven plate

remain on the flywheel when the engine is removed. The clutch release bearing and the clutch release shaft remain in the bellhousing of the transaxle. The operating lever on the clutch release shaft is operated by a cable that is attached to the clutch pedal.

2. MAINTENANCE

The following routine maintenance steps are covered briefly in **LUBRICATION AND MAINTENANCE**. Additional instructions can be found in this section under the headings listed after some of the items.

1. Changing engine oil and checking the oil level
2. Servicing and replacing spark plugs. **3.5**
3. Checking distributor and the ignition timing. **3.2**
4. Checking valve clearance. **5.2**
5. Checking compression
6. Servicing the air cleaner
7. Checking the exhaust system
8. Checking clutch pedal freeplay. **9.3**
9. Checking V-belt adjustment
10. Checking and adjusting idle. (Described in detail in **FUEL AND EXHAUST SYSTEMS**.)
11. Checking the cooling system. **4.**

3. IGNITION SYSTEM

The VW ignition is a conventional coil and battery system. On 1974 models, the ignition is wired to an interlock system that is coupled to the front safety belts. The engine cannot be started until the driver's seat is occupied and the safety belts are fastened both for the driver's seat and, if it is occupied, for the front passenger seat. For a period of approximately three minutes after the engine has stalled or the ignition has been switched off, the engine can be restarted without fastening the belts. Unfastening the belts while driving or while the engine is idling does not cause the engine to stop.

3.1 Coil

By the process of electrical induction, the coil steps up the primary circuit's 12-volt battery current to as much as 20,000 volts. This high voltage is required to ionize the air in the spark plug gaps so that a spark can jump across them. Despite the painful electrical shock that spark current can produce, its low amperage (current flow) renders it harmless. When you test the spark, you can avoid getting shocks either by wearing rubber gloves or by holding the high tension cable with a spring-type clothespin. A cable with sound insulation, however, is safe to handle.

When removing and installing the coil, please be sure you connect the wire from the ignition switch to terminal 15 and the wire from the distributor to terminal 1. Reversing the coil wires will change the polarity of the spark current from positive to negative. Such reversed polarity limits the ability of the spark voltage to ionize the air in the spark plug gaps, causing misfiring at high speeds or during hard acceleration.

Keep the coil tower clean and dry and make sure that the rubber boot surrounding the high tension cable is tight-fitting and waterproof. Otherwise, spark current may begin arcing from terminal 4 to ground. Such a short can prevent the engine from running well or even from running at all. The arcing may also burn irreparable carbon tracks into the coil tower.

Ignition coils seldom produce trouble. However, if all the other ignition components are sound and the car still misses or is hard to start, check the coil. First test the battery as described in **ELECTRICAL SYSTEM** to make sure it is not run down. Then disconnect the high tension cable from the center terminal of the distributor cap and hold it about 10 mm (⅜ in.) from the engine block. Have someone run the starter while you observe the spark produced. If the spark is weak and yellowish, fires only when the cable is moved close to the engine block, or fails to fire at all, the coil is probably weak and should be replaced.

Since faulty wiring between the ignition switch and coil, distributor faults, or a weak condenser can produce similar symptoms, it is best to have the coil tested before investing in a new one. If the coil proves satisfactory, use a voltmeter to check the voltage between coil terminals 15 and 1. The distributor points must be closed and the ignition key on. If the voltage at the coil is below 9.6 volts, check for poor distributor point contact, a shorted condenser, high resistance in the ignition switch or the wire that connects the switch to coil terminal 15 or, on 1974 cars, trouble in the ignition switch/safety belt interlock system. The circuit for the interlock system is shown in the wiring diagram given in **ELECTRICAL SYSTEM.**

NOTE ——

Some of the cars covered by this manual have a ballast resistor installed in the wire that connects the ignition switch with terminal 15 of the coil. Instead of a ballast resistor, the latest cars have a resistance wire that connects fuse box terminal C15 with terminal 15 of the coil. Use an ohmmeter to test either a ballast resistor or a resistance wire. The resistance should be between 0.85 and 0.95 ohms. The resistance wire insulation is clear

with violet stripes. Replacement wires, Part No. N 900 120 01, are 1280 mm (50⅜ in.) long and have a conductor diameter of 0.75 mm (.030 in.). The ballast resistor can be tested in the same way, after disconnecting all wires from the resistor.

3.2 Distributor

Servicing the distributor includes checking, replacing, and adjusting the breaker points, checking and possibly replacing the rotor and cap, checking the spark advance mechanism, and adjusting the ignition timing. The condenser should not be replaced routinely but only when electrical testing proves it defective.

Removing and Installing Distributor

You should remove the distributor to protect it during engine disassembly. Many experienced mechanics also prefer to remove the distributor from the engine before servicing the breaker points or other distributor parts.

To remove distributor:

1. Remove the distributor cap. Using a wrench on the bolt that is in the center of the crankshaft pulley, handturn the crankshaft clockwise until the distributor rotor tip points to the No. 1 cylinder mark on the distributor body (Fig. 3-1).

Fig. 3-1. Distributor rotor aligned with the No. 1 cylinder mark on the distributor body.

2. If not previously removed, disconnect all hoses and wiring from the distributor.

3. Remove the distributor hold-down bolt and the hold-down clamp. Then lift out the distributor.

4. Lift off the washer that surrounds the distributor shaft opening in the engine block. Cover the opening to keep out dirt.

To install:

1. Check to see that the lug on the oil pump drive gearshaft is in the position shown in Fig. 3-2. If it is not, use a screwdriver to reposition it.

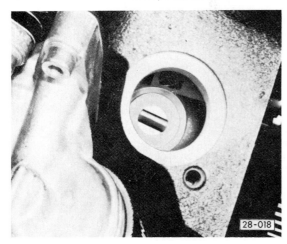

Fig. 3-2. Lug on oil pump drive gearshaft. The lug must be parallel to the engine's crankshaft.

2. If the crankshaft was turned while the distributor was out of the engine, hand-turn the crankshaft until the No. 1 cylinder is in position to fire and the top dead center (TDC) mark is next to the pointer on the flywheel bellhousing (Fig. 3-3).

> **NOTE ——**
>
> To check the position of the No. 1 cylinder, look through the oil filler and see whether both cam lobes for the No. 1 cylinder are pointing upward. If the lobes are not up, hand-turn the crankshaft one full revolution to realign the TDC mark.

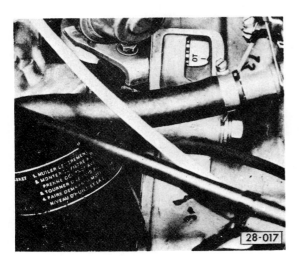

Fig. 3-3. TDC mark aligned with pointer in window on bellhousing. TDC is designated by the numeral zero and the letter T (0T).

3. Place the large washer in the recess that surrounds the distributor shaft opening in the engine block.

4. Before you install the distributor, hand-turn the distributor shaft until the rotor tip points to a position approximately 18° clockwise from the No. 1 cylinder mark on the distributor housing.

5. Insert the distributor into the engine. As the helical gears mesh, the rotor should turn counterclockwise 18° and the lug on the oil pump drive gearshaft should engage the slot in the lower end of the distributor shaft.

6. Make sure that the distributor housing's mounting flange and washer are firmly seated against the engine block and that the rotor tip is aligned with the No. 1 cylinder mark on the distributor housing.

7. Loosely install the hold-down clamp and the hold-down bolt.

8. Install the distributor cap. Then adjust the ignition timing as described in **3.3 Adjusting Timing** before you torque the hold-down bolt to 2.0 mkg (14 ft. lb.).

3

Disassembling and Assembling Distributor

A screwdriver is the only tool required for disassembling the distributor. Though it is possible to disassemble the breaker plate, the centrifugal advance mechanism, and the distributor shaft for cleaning and inspection, only the components shown in Fig. 3-4 are available as replacement parts. Prior to 1975, two kinds of rotors and shield plates were installed. Rotors of one kind must not be used with shield plates of the other kind.

The distributor cap, rotor, and shield plate must be removed for access to the breaker points. A single fillister head screw holds the one-piece breaker point assembly on the breaker plate. The same screw locks the breaker points in adjustment. A slip-on terminal connects the point wire with the primary wire from the coil. In removing the vacuum advance unit, you must pry off the E-clip that holds the vacuum advance unit's pull rod on the pin on the breaker plate.

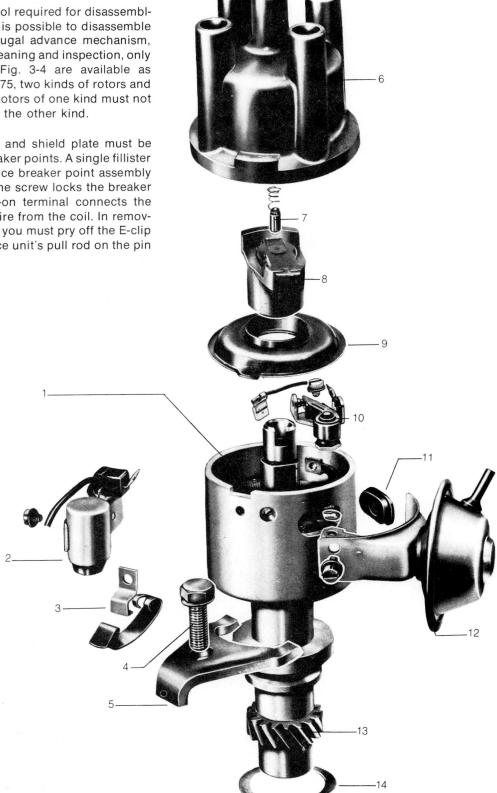

1. Distributor housing assembly
2. Condenser
3. Spring clip and bracket
4. Hold-down bolt
5. Hold-down clamp
6. Distributor cap
7. Carbon brush and spring
8. Rotor
9. Shield plate
10. Breaker point assembly
11. Rubber seal
12. Vacuum advance unit
13. Drive gear
14. Washer

Fig. 3-4. Exploded view of the distributor. The condenser is integral with the primary wire and the point wire terminal.

28-059

The distributor's breaker points should be replaced and adjusted every 10,000 mi. (16,000 km). Remove the old point assembly, then wipe clean the inside of the distributor. Make sure that the contacts of the new point assembly meet squarely. If the contacts do not meet squarely, carefully bend the stationary contact to align the points. Never bend the movable contact arm since doing this will impair its strength.

Lubricate the distributor as indicated in Fig. 3-5. Wipe off any excess lubricants so that they will not be thrown onto the point contacts, then adjust the breaker points.

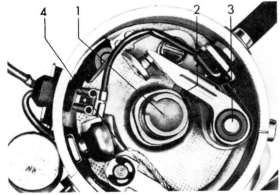

© 1973 VWoA—1167

Fig. 3-5. Distributor lubrication. Saturate felt wick (1) with engine oil. Apply a small amount of multipurpose grease to the distributor cam and point rubbing block (2), one drop of engine oil to the breaker point pivot (3), and a small amount of multipurpose grease to the breaker plate ball (4).

Adjusting Points

The breaker points must be adjusted after you have installed them. The adjustment can be made either with a feeler gauge or with a dwell meter.

To adjust with feeler gauge:

1. Remove the distributor cap and rotor.

2. Using a wrench on the bolt that is in the center of the crankshaft pulley, hand-turn the crankshaft clockwise until the breaker point rubbing block is on a high point on the distributor cam (points wide open).

   NOTE ——
   If you are doing a complete tune-up, adjust the points while the spark plugs are out. Doing this will make it easier to turn the crankshaft to the correct position.

3. To determine whether the points are gapped correctly, insert a 0.40-mm (.016-in.) feeler gauge in the point gap. The points are gapped correctly if

the feeler gauge just slips into the gap without forcing the contacts apart. (Fig. 3-6).

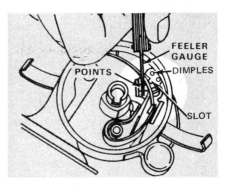

Fig. 3-6. Feeler gauge inserted between points. To adjust the point gap, engage a screwdriver in the slot in the breaker point assembly and between the dimples on the breaker plate.

4. If necessary, loosen the breaker point assembly mounting screw. Then, using the tip of a screwdriver as shown in Fig. 3-7, move the fixed contact one way or the other until you get the specified breaker point gap.

Fig. 3-7. Breaker point gap being adjusted.

5. Tighten the breaker point assembly mounting screw, then recheck the gap. If the gap is incorrect, repeat the adjustment. If the gap is correct, install the shield plate, the distributor rotor, and the cap. Then adjust the ignition timing as described in **3.3 Adjusting Timing.**

To adjust with dwell meter:

1. If the points have not already been gapped with a feeler gauge, do so to make sure that the engine will start. The adjustment can be approximate.

2. Connect the dwell meter. The black clip should be attached to ground on any bare metal part and the colored clip attached to terminal 1 at the coil.

3. Switch the dwell meter to the tachometer position. Start the engine and run it at 1000 rpm.

4. Switch the meter to measure dwell. Read the dwell.

NOTE ——

The dwell angle for distributor 056 905 205 C, used on 1974 carburetor-engined cars sold in California, should be between 47° and 53°. The dwell angle for distributor 055 905 205 used on other carburetor-engined cars and distributor 049 905 205 A used on fuel injection cars should be between 44° and 50°. Points that have been in service for less than 10,000 mi. (16,000 km) on 1973 and 1974 cars or less than 15,000 mi. (24,000 km) on 1975 and later cars can be retained without adjustment so long as dwell is within the specified range.

5. If necessary, remove the distributor cap, the rotor, and the shield plate. Then adjust the dwell. To adjust dwell, loosen the breaker point assembly mounting screw. Using the tip of a screwdriver, as shown previously in Fig. 3-7, move the stationary contact either to widen the gap and decrease dwell, or to narrow the gap and increase dwell.

NOTE ——

Run the engine with the starter to check the dwell during adjustment but always make the final check with the engine running.

6. Fully tighten the breaker point assembly mounting screw. Then install the distributor rotor and cap. Check the dwell at 1000 rpm to make sure that it is within the specified range.

7. Run the engine at about 2000 rpm. The dwell should not vary more than ±1° from the reading obtained at 1000 rpm. Larger deviations indicate a worn distributor, which should be replaced.

8. After you have adjusted the dwell to specifications, adjust the ignition timing as described in **3.3 Adjusting Timing.**

Abnormal Point Wear

Moderate contact pitting and build-up with bright contact surfaces can be considered normal breaker point wear. When properly installed, aligned, and lubricated, the breaker point assembly should provide reliable service without further attention until the mileage specified for point replacement is reached.

Vehicle operating symptoms that suggest abnormal point wear include engine missing at high speeds or

Table a. Abnormal Point Condition Diagnosis

Abnormal Condition	Probable Cause	Remedy
1. Blued point contacts	Weak spark owing to defective coil or condenser	Test coil and condenser. Replace either if it is faulty. See **3.1, 3.2.**
2. Gray point surfaces	a. Point gap adjusted too narrow b. Point gap narrowed by rapid rubbing block wear c. Point spring weak	a. Readjust points. See **3.2.** b. Replace points. Lubricate distributor cam and rubbing block with multipurpose grease. See **3.2.** c. Use a spring scale to measure spring tension. Replace points if tension is below 400 to 600 g (14⅛ to 21⅛ oz.). See **3.2.**
3. Point contacts have yellow or black markings. A smudgy line may appear directly under the contacts	a. Oil or grease on point contacts owing to excessive distributor lubrication b. Oil on points owing to dirty feeler gauge c. Points fouled by engine oil that has been forced up around the distributor shaft by excessive crankcase pressure	a. Replace points. Lubricate to specifications, then wipe away excess lubricants. See **3.2.** b. Replace points. Clean feeler gauge with solvent before adjusting points. See **3.2.** c. Replace points. Clean distributor. Locate and remove restrictions in the crankcase ventilation system. See **3.2** and **FUEL SYSTEM.**
4. One point contact pitted, metal transferred to other point	a. Misaligned points b. Electrical system voltage excessive owing to a faulty regulator c. Condenser faulty d. Extended engine operation outside normal speed range	a. Replace points. Make sure that new point contacts squarely. See **3.2.** b. Test charging system. Replace regulator, if faulty. Replace points if build-up exceeds 0.05 mm (.002 in.); if it is less, adjust points with dwell meter. See **3.2** and **ELECTRICAL SYSTEM.** c. Test condenser and replace if faulty. Replace points if build-up exceeds 0.05 mm (.002 in.); if it is less, adjust points with dwell meter. See **3.2.** d. Replace points if build-up exceeds 0.05 mm (.002 in.); if it is less, adjust points with dwell meter. See **3.2.**

during acceleration, rough idling, hard starting, or the failure to start. You will often be able to find the cause of such trouble by using **Table a** to diagnose the abnormal point condition that accompanies the operating symptom.

If the abnormal condition is severe, it may be necessary to replace or adjust the breaker point assembly before the normal replacement mileage. Filing or honing the point contacts to correct abnormal pitting or build-up or to remove hard deposits is not recommended.

3.3 Adjusting Timing

Adjust the timing after you install or adjust the breaker points, or whenever you reinstall the distributor. A change of only 0.10 mm (.004 in.) in the point gap will alter ignition timing about 3°.

To adjust timing:

1. Following the instrument manufacturer's instructions, install a tachometer and a stroboscopic timing light.

2. Start the engine and allow it to warm up until the idle stabilizes at 850 to 1000 rpm. Do not disconnect the vacuum hoses from the distributor.

3. Aim the timing light at the window in the flywheel bellhousing. The 3° ATDC (after top dead center) timing mark should appear in line with the pointer in the window, as shown in Fig. 3-8.

   NOTE ———
   The window in the bellhousing is to the right and slightly below the distributor, as shown previously in Fig. 3-3.

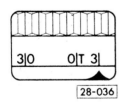

28-036

Fig. 3-8. The 3° ATDC mark in line with the pointer in the window in the flywheel bellhousing.

4. If the 3° ATDC timing mark is not aligned with the pointer, loosen the distributor hold-down bolt. Then, with the engine idling at 850 to 1000 rpm, hand-turn the distributor housing clockwise or counter-clockwise until the 3° ATDC mark, illuminated by the timing light, is aligned with the pointer.

5. While you hold the distributor in the correct position, tighten the hold-down bolt.

6. Torque the hold-down bolt to 2.0 mkg (14 ft. lb.). Then recheck the timing. Repeat the adjustment procedure given in step 4 if the timing is incorrect.

3

The throttle valve must close adequately for accurate timing adjustments. To check, disconnect the green (retard) hose from the distributor with the engine idling. The timing should shift so that the 30° BTDC (before top dead center) timing mark is near the pointer. If timing does not shift, the throttle valve is not closing adequately and the throttle valve gap must be adjusted as described in **FUEL AND EXHAUST SYSTEMS**. Readjust the timing after adjusting the throttle valve gap.

Checking Spark Advance Mechanism

The distributor has both vacuum and centrifugal spark advance mechanisms. Special timing lights are available that incorporate a built-in meter you can use to measure spark advance. The instructions supplied with such timing lights tell you how to use the device to check the centrifugal advance mechanisms. By using the special timing light in conjunction with a vacuum gauge (attached to T-fittings inserted in the two hoses that are connected to the distributor), you can also check the vacuum advance mechanism.

Table b lists the rpm and vacuum levels where critical changes in the spark advance curve take place. Comparing actual distributor operation to the data in the table will help you locate dirty, binding advance mechanisms or mechanical faults in the distributor. The distributor number is stamped on the distributor itself.

If testing reveals irregularities in the spark advance curve, first clean and lubricate the moving parts of the distributor. If the vacuum advance still fails to conform to specifications, install a new vacuum unit. If retesting reveals discrepancies in the centrifugal advance curve, it indicates worn internal parts. In that case you should replace the distributor body and internal parts as a unit.

Though you may not have a special timing light for checking the spark advance curve, you can still quick-check the spark advance mechanisms without running the engine. To check the vacuum advance, hand-turn the breaker plate counterclockwise. It should move without grittiness and spring back solidly to its original position when released. To check the vacuum unit for leaks, disconnect the vacuum hoses. Turn the breaker plate as far as it will go counterclockwise, cover the hose connections on the vacuum unit with your fingers, then release the breaker plate. Vacuum should keep the breaker plate from returning fully to its original position until you uncover the hose connections. If the breaker plate returns fully, there is a leak in the diaphragm or vacuum unit housing.

To quick-check the centrifugal advance, hand-turn the distributor rotor clockwise. When you release it, the rotor should return automatically to its original position. If it does not, either the mechanism is dirty or the distributor body and internal parts are faulty and should be replaced as a unit.

Cleaning Spark Advance Mechanism

Clean the distributor if dirt or hardened grease is causing the spark advance mechanism to jam, or if the interior of the distributor has become oil soaked. First remove and disassemble the distributor as described in **3.2 Distributor**. Then wash the distributor body assembly thoroughly in clean solvent. Blow the distributor body assembly dry with compressed air.

Table b. Spark Advance Curves

Distributor	Centrifugal Advance Range						
	Begin ⟶ End						
	rpm	rpm	degrees	rpm	degrees	rpm	degrees
055 905 205 055 905 205 C	1050–1350	2200–2300	16–20	3000	19–23	5000	26–30
056 905 205 C	1100–1400	2100–2200	15–20	3000	19–23	5000	26–30
049 905 205 A	1120–1400	2000–2400	11–21	4800	25–29	5200	26–30

	Vacuum Advance Range			Timing direction
	Begin ⟶ End			
	mbar (mm/Hg, in./Hg)	mbar (mm/Hg, in./Hg)	degrees	
055 905 205	280–327 (210–245, 8.4–9.8)	447–467 (335–350, 13.4–14.0)	—	advance
055 905 205 C	213–239 (160–220, 6.4–8.8)	327–393 (245–295, 9.8–11.8)	—	retard
056 905 205 C	267–327 (200–245, 8.0–9.8)	467 (350, 14.0)	—	advance
	200–293 (150–220, 6.0–8.8)	333–400 (250–300, 10.0–12.0)	—	retard
049 905 205 A	267–333 (200–250, 8.0–10.0)	360–386 (270–290, 10.5–11.5)	4°–8° max.	advance
	133–267 (100–200, 4.0–8.0)	280–373 (210–280, 8.25–11.0)	8°–10° max.	retard

CAUTION —

Be careful not to direct a strong blast of air into the housing at close range. Doing this could damage the calibrated springs in the centrifugal advance mechanism.

Thoroughly lubricate the distribution shaft and bearings with engine oil by applying the oil to the space between the drive gear and the distributor body. With the distributor body inverted, hand-turn the shaft until the oil has worked its way all along the shaft. The shaft should turn smoothly without binding. Apply one drop of engine oil to each pivot point in the centrifugal advance mechanism and to the breaker plate bearing. If necessary, you can remove the breaker plate to gain access to the centrifugal advance.

3.4 Secondary Circuit

The secondary circuit of the ignition system consists of the distributor rotor, the distribution cap, the spark plug cables, and the high tension cable that links the coil with the distributor cap. Secondary circuit resistance, for radio suppression and to reduce spark plug gap erosion, is built into the distributor rotor and spark plug connectors. This resistance allows the use of metallic conductor ignition cables.

You can check the rotor resistor with an ohmmeter as shown in Fig. 3-9. You can test individual plug connectors the same way. Rotor resistance should not exceed 10,000 ohms; plug connector resistance should range from 5000 to 10,000 ohms.

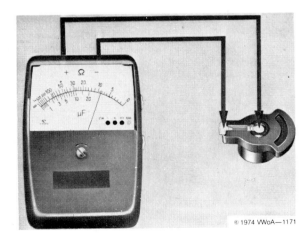

Fig. 3-9. Rotor resistance being measured.

To prevent spark flashover, which could cause irreparable carbon tracks on the distributor cap and rotor, keep the cap and rotor clean and dry. Also keep the ignition cables clean and replace them when the insula-

tion shows signs of cracking or deterioration. The rubber boots at the coil nose, distributor cap towers, and plug connectors must be sound and tight fitting if the secondary circuit is to remain waterproof.

3.5 Spark Plugs

Replace the spark plugs each 10,000 mi. (16,000 km) on 1973 and 1974 cars or each 15,000 mi. (24,000 km) on 1975 and later cars. After this distance, the electrodes will have worn to the point that ionization of the spark plug gap is discouraged. The color of the deposits on the firing tip of the used plugs may vary, indicating the following combustion chamber conditions:

1. Gray or light tan deposits indicate good combustion, proper fuel mixtures, and consistently good spark plug performance.

2. Light gray or chalky-white deposits indicate too lean a fuel/air mixture or an overhead spark plug.

3. Soft, fluffy, black deposits indicate a plug that is misfiring or too rich a fuel/air mixture.

4. A spark plug fouled by oil indicates severe oil leakage past the piston rings or valve guides or a spark plug that is no longer firing.

Replacement spark plugs must be of the correct heat range and physical dimensions. The plug reach (the length of the threaded portion of the shell) should be ¾ in.; the thread diameter should be 14 mm. Suitable spark plugs are listed in **12. Engine and Clutch Technical Data.** Before you install the spark plugs, measure their gaps as illustrated in Fig. 3-10.

If the spark plug gap is too wide or too narrow, adjust the gap by bending the side electrode only. Never attempt to bend the center electrode. Doing this will

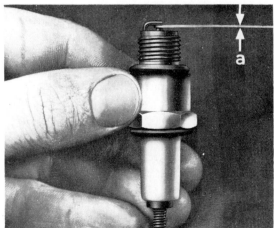

Fig. 3-10. Spark plug gap being measured. Dimension **a** should be 0.60 to 0.70 mm (.024 to .028 in.).

break the insulator and render the spark plug unserviceable. If the old spark plugs were difficult to remove, the spark plug holes in the cylinder head should be cleaned with a thread chaser made especially for the job.

During installation, lightly coat the spark plug threads with anti-seize compound or multipurpose grease. Such lubricants will prevent corrosion damage and stuck spark plugs. If nothing else is available, lubricate the spark plug threads with engine oil.

> **CAUTION ——**
>
> *Most anti-seize compounds contain graphite, which must not contact the plug electrodes or insulator. If it does, the graphite could short out the spark plug.*

Start the plug in the cylinder head with your fingertips or by hand-holding the spark plug socket. This will give improved fuel and help prevent accidental cross-threading. Turn the spark plug in until you feel the gasket contact the cylinder head. Then install a torque wrench on the spark plug socket and torque the plug to 2.5 to 3.0 mkg (18 to 22 ft. lb.).

4. COOLING SYSTEM

To maintain the anti-corrosion properties of the coolant, you should use a permanent-type anti-freeze year-round. If coolant must be added, use the same proportion of water to anti-freeze that is already in the cooling system. Typical proportions are given in **Table c.**

> **CAUTION ——**
>
> *Never add cold water or coolant while the engine is hot or overheated. Doing this could crack the engine block or cylinder head.*

The cooling system is shown in Fig. 4-1. The system is unusual in that the thermostat is mounted in the

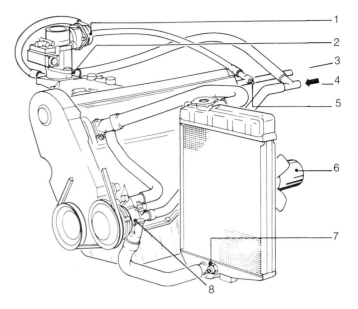

1. Water-heated automatic choke
2. Water-heated intake manifold
3. Pipe to heater
4. Pipe from heater
5. Temperature guage
   sending unit
6. Electric fan
7. Thermo switch for fan
8. Water pump and thermostat

Fig. 4-1. Cooling system.

external-type water pump and the cooling fan is powered by an electric motor. The cooling fan does not operate constantly, but only after the coolant has reached a temperature of 90° to 95°C (194° to 203°F) and above on 1973 through 1978 cars or 93° to 98°C (200° to 208°F) and above on 1979 and later cars. The advantages of this system are fast warm-up, stable operating temperature, low noise level while driving, fast heater reaction, and more available power from the engine. The thermo switch turns the fan off when the coolant temperature falls to between 85° and 90°C (185° and 194°F) or below on 1973 through 1978 cars or between 88° and 93°C (190° and 200°F) on 1979 or later cars.

Table c. Anti-Freeze-to-Water Proportions

For outside temperatures down to	Anti-freeze			Water		
	Quarts	Imp. Quarts	Liters	Quarts	Imp. Quarts	Liters
−4°F	2.5	2.1	2.4	4.4	3.65	4.2
−13°F	2.8	2.3	2.6	4.1	3.4	3.9
−22°F	3.1	2.6	2.9	3.8	3.1	3.6
−31°F	3.5	2.9	3.3	3.4	2.8	3.2
−40°F	3.6	3.0	3.4	3.3	2.7	3.1

4.1 Replacing Hoses

To prevent hose failure and overheating, you should periodically inspect the heater and radiator hoses. Replace hoses that are hard and cracked, spongy, rotted, or that have a tendency to collapse.

To replace:

1. Remove the radiator cap. Place a receptacle beneath the radiator for catching the draining coolant. Then remove the drain plug (Fig. 4-2) and allow the coolant to drain from the radiator.

CAUTION ——

Never drain the coolant while the engine is hot. Doing this could warp the engine block or the cylinder head.

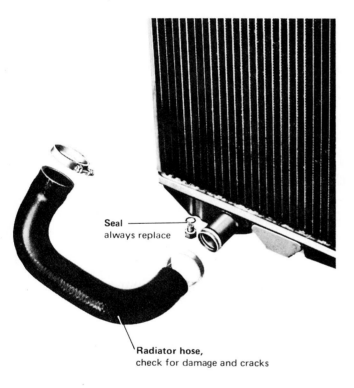

Seal
always replace

Radiator hose,
check for damage and cracks

Fig. 4-2. Drain plug and drain plug seal removed from bottom of radiator. The lower hose, shown removed, connects the radiator with the thermostat housing on the bottom of the water pump.

2. Using a screwdriver, loosen the hose clamps at each end of the hose you must remove. Then slide the clamps toward the center of the hose.

3. Pull the hose off its connections.

CAUTION ——

If a radiator hose is stuck to the radiator connection by sealer, it is best to cut the old hose off the connection. Prying the hose loose can damage the brass connection or the radiator.

4. Clean bits of old hose and sealer off the connections. Lightly coat the connections with water resistant sealer.

5. Slip the hose clamps onto the hose. Then slide the hose onto its connections.

6. Position the hose clamps so that they are past the bead on the connection, but no nearer than 2.5 mm (⅛ in.) to the end of the hose. Then tighten the hose clamps just enough to compress the hose firmly around the connections.

CAUTION ——

Overtightening the clamps will cause them to cut into the hose material, damage that may eventually lead to hose failure.

7. Install the radiator drain plug together with a new seal. Then fill the radiator with the mixture of water and permanent-type anti-freeze that is recommended in **Table c,** given earlier. Do not fill above the mark indicated in Fig. 4-3.

Fig. 4-3. Full mark (arrow) in radiator.

4.2 Cooling System Troubleshooting

Most cooling system malfunctions not caused by leaks can be traced to a faulty thermostat, a restricted hose, a faulty radiator cap, or a clogged radiator. Clogged radiators and heater cores should be repaired only by an Authorized Dealer of a qualified radiator repair shop.

Virtually all clogged cooling systems are caused by neglect or the addition of substances to the coolant that are not recommended by the car manufacturer. Because radiator repairs are expensive, it is not wise economically to neglect the cooling system in an attempt to save the few dollars that proper maintenance will cost. You will never have to worry about a clogged radiator or heater core if you observe the following precautions:

1. To prevent the formation of rust and scale, keep the cooling system filled with at least 40% solution of an approved-quality, permanent-type anti-freeze. Change the anti-freeze solution as recommended by the manufacturer or when a chemical test shows the old solution lacking in anti-corrosion protection.

2. Never add more than one can of leak sealer to the cooling system as a precaution against leaks. Doing this is especially likely to clog rust-filled, neglected cooling systems.

3. Never fill the radiator from a roadside ditch, a stream, or other water sources that may contain silt and organic material.

4. Do not add engine oil to the coolant as a rust preventative. Doing this will encourage the formation of oil sludge in the cooling system and will damage the heater and radiator hoses.

Table d lists possible overheating and underheating symptoms, their probable causes, and suggested repairs. The boldface numbers in the suggested repair column refer to the numbered headings in this section where the suggested repairs are described.

Testing Thermostat

To test the thermostat, first remove it from the water pump as described in **4.4 Disassembling and Assembling Water Pump.** You should also test new thermostats before you install them in the car.

Measure the thermostat to determine dimension **a** given in Fig. 4-4. If it exceeds 31 mm (1.220 in. or $1^7/_{32}$ in.), the thermostat is not closing fully and should be replaced. If dimension **a** is correct, place the thermostat in a pan of cool water together with a thermometer for measuring the water temperature. Heat the water. On 1973 through 1978 cars the thermostat should begin to open at approximately 80°C (176°F), and on 1979 or later cars the thermostat should begin to open at approximately 85°C (185°F). At 94°C (201°F), dimension **b**, given in Fig. 4-4, should be at least 38 mm (1.496 in. or 1½ in.). If not, replace the thermostat.

Table d. Cooling System Troubleshooting

Symptom	Probable cause	Suggested repair
Inadequate heater output, temperature gauge reads normal	a. Installed position of heater hoses reversed b. Heater hose restricted c. Heater core clogged d. Heater control out of adjustment	a. Install hoses as previously indicated in Fig. 4-1. See **4, 4.1.** b. Replace hose. See **4.1.** c. Replace heater core or have core cleaned. See **4.5.** d. Adjust control cables. See **BODY AND INTERIOR.**
Inadequate heater output, temperature gauge reads low	a. Faulty thermostat b. Electric fan not switching off	a. Remove and test thermostat. See **4.2, 4.3.** b. Replace thermo switch for fan. See **4.5.**
Temperature gauge reads low, heater output normal	Faulty temperature gauge or sending unit	Test temperature gauge and sending unit. Replace faulty part. See **4.2.**
Engine overheats	a. Low coolant level b. Burst hose c. Radiator hose restricted (lower hose may collapse only at highway speeds) d. V-belt loose or broken e. Faulty thermostat f. Electric fan not switching on g. Faulty radiator cap h. Clogged radiator i. Incorrect ignition timing or valve timing j. Radiator blocked internally by electrodeposits	a. Fill radiator to Full mark. Check cooling system for leaks with pressure tester. See **4.2.** b. Replace hose. Refill radiator to Full mark. See **4.1.** c. Replace hose. See **4.1.** d. Adjust or replace V-belt. See **4.3.** e. Remove and test thermostat. Replace if necessary. See **4.2, 4.3.** f. Test thermo switch and fan. Replace faulty part. See **4.2, 4.5.** g. Test pressure relief valve in cap. Replace faulty caps. See **4.2.** h. Replace radiator or have core cleaned. See **4.2, 4.5.** i. Check camshaft drive belt installation. Adjust ignition timing and check spark advance. See **3.3, 5.1.** j. Test fan for electrical leakage; inspect thermo switch. See **4.2.**

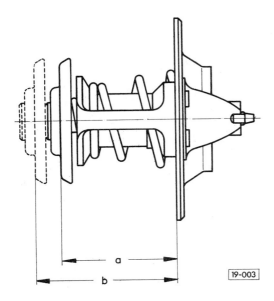

Fig. 4-4. Thermostat test dimensions. Dimension **a** is the closed (cold) length; dimension **b** is the open (hot) length.

Pressure Testing Radiator Cap and Cooling System

Various kinds of cooling system pressure testers are available. In carrying out pressure tests, follow the instructions supplied by the tester's manufacturer and use a procedure that is suitable to the tester's design.

The pressure relief valve in the radiator cap should maintain a seal up to a pressure of 0.88 to 1.02 atu (13 to 15 psi) on 1973 through 1978 cars or 1.20 to 1.35 atu (17 to 19 psi) on 1979 and later cars. Replace radiator caps that do not test within this range.

To pressure test the cooling system, pump the pressure up to approximately 0.95 atu (14 psi) on 1973 through 1978 cars or approximately 1.25 atu (18 psi) on 1979 and later cars. Observe the gauge on the pressure tester pump. The gauge should not indicate a pressure loss during a two-minute waiting period. If it does, there are leaks in the system that should be shown by the seepage of coolant.

CAUTION ———

Never pump the pressure above 1.02 atu (15 psi) on 1973 through 1978 cars or above 1.35 atu (19 psi) on 1979 or later cars—the maximum pressures permitted by the radiator caps' relief valves. Exceeding these pressures could burst the radiator.

Testing Thermo Switch and Cooling Fan

A faulty fan motor that has an electrical leak to ground through its motor housing can cause the formation of electrodeposits in the radiator. These deposits may eventually cause overheating by clogging the water passages. To test the motor, disconnect the wires from the thermo switch. Then connect a voltmeter as indicated in Fig. 4-5. If a positive (+) voltage greater than 0 volts is measured, the fan motor is faulty and should be replaced. You can detect the presence of electrodeposits by removing the thermo switch and inspecting it. If the thermo switch has a greenish-blue coating, you should replace both the radiator and the thermo switch.

If the electric cooling fan fails to operate, check the coolant temperature. If a defective thermostat is not allowing the coolant to warm up to the switch's cut-in temperature, the fan will not be switched on by the thermo switch. The cut-in temperature is 90° to 95°C (194° to 203°F) on 1973 through 1978 cars or 93° to 98°C (200° to 208°F) on 1979 and later cars.

If the coolant is reaching the thermo switch's cut-in temperature, bridge the terminals on the thermo switch. If the fan operates, the thermo switch is defective and should be replaced. If the fan still does not operate, use a

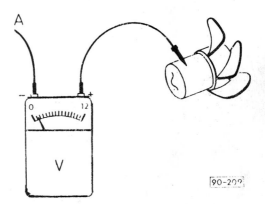

Fig. 4-5. Fan motor switch being checked for ground leak. Connect voltmeter's negative probe to battery negative post (**A**). Touch positive probe to motor housing. There should be no voltage reading. (It is normal for the voltmeter needle to move slightly toward the negative range.) Also test newly installed replacement motors to make sure that they are not faulty.

voltmeter to test the fan circuit. Five different wiring systems have been used (Fig. 4-6). Fig. 4-7 shows the location of the fan relay used in wiring system V.

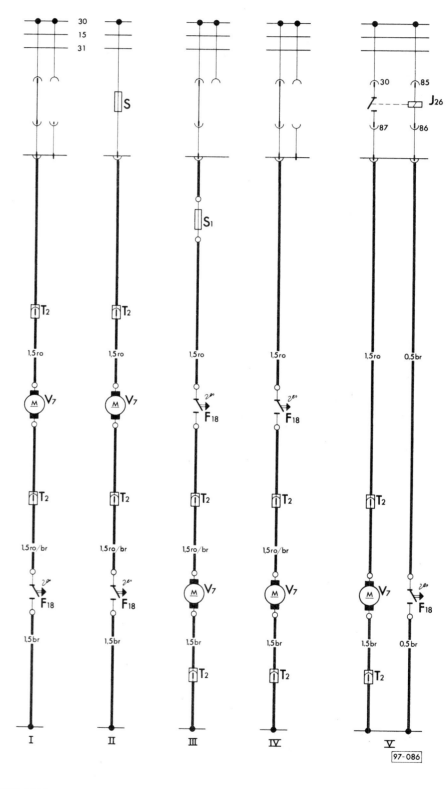

I. Activated through ground wire
II. Activated through ground wire via fuse (S) in fuse box
III. Activated through positive wire via single fuse (S₁)
IV. Activated through positive wire
V. Activated by relay (J₂₆)
F_{18} Thermo switch for radiator fan
J_{26} Radiator cooling fan relay
S Fuse in fuse box
S_1 Single fuse
V_7 Radiator cooling fan

Color codes
ro — red
br — brown

Fig. 4-6. Cooling fan circuits that have been used.

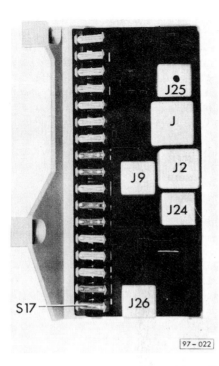

Fig. 4-7. Locations in fuse box of fuse (S17) and relay (J26) for radiator cooling fan.

Testing Temperature Gauge and Sending Unit

If the temperature gauge needle remains at its rest position even though the engine has been operating for some time, turn on the heater so that you can judge the temperature of the coolant. If the heater delivers little or no heat, the thermostat is probably defective. If the heater delivers adequate heat, the trouble is in the gauge or the sending unit.

Should the preceding check indicate that the coolant is reaching normal operating temperatures but the gauge does not indicate heat, turn on the ignition. Then pull the gauge wire off of the sending unit that is screwed into the heater hose connection at the rear of the cylinder head. Ground the wire on some clean, unpainted metal part of the car. If the gauge needle moves upward, the sending unit is faulty and should be replaced. If the needle does not move, the wire or the gauge is faulty.

You can make another similar test if the temperature gauge needle advances to the high end of the dial whenever the ignition is switched on. Should the needle fall when you disconnect the wire from the sending unit, the sending unit is faulty. If the needle does not fall to a lower reading, the wire leading to the gauge is probably grounded. If the gauge itself is stuck or has an internal short circuit to ground, replace the gauge.

4.3 Removing and Installing Water Pump

The front part of the water pump, which contains the shaft, the seals, the bearing, and the impeller, can be replaced separately. However, you can avoid removing the camshaft drive belt and sprockets by removing the water pump as a unit before you disassemble it.

To remove:

1. Drain the coolant as described in **4.1 Replacing Hoses.** Loosen the upper and lower alternator mounting bolts. Loosen the bolt that holds the alternator belt adjusting bracket to the cylinder head.

2. Push the alternator as far as possible toward the engine. Then take the V-belt off the alternator and water pump pulleys.

   NOTE ——

   Unless you are going to remove the water pump by working under the car, you may wish to remove the alternator completely for better access to the water pump mounting bolts. If you want to remove the alternator/water pump V-belt completely from certain cars sold in California, you must first remove the belt for the air injection pump. To do so, loosen the air pump mounting bolts. Push the air pump as far as possible toward the engine, then remove the air pump V-belt.

3. Remove the nut from the T-head bolt that holds the camshaft drive belt cover to the water pump. Then remove the T-head bolt from the water pump. The two spacer washers and the rubber grommet can remain in the drive belt cover.

4. Disconnect both hoses from the rear of the water pump. See **4.1 Replacing Hoses.**

5. Take out the four bolts that hold the water pump to the engine block. Two short bolts are at the top of the pump, one long bolt is at about the center of the pump, and one long bolt is between the two hose connections. Remove the pump as you take out the last bolt.

To install:

1. Install a new O-ring in the recess that surrounds the water outlet in the pump's mounting flange. Clean the surface of the engine block where it will be contacted by the pump and the O-ring.

   NOTE ——

   Do not use sealer between the water pump mounting flange and the engine block.

2. Using all four mounting bolts, loosely install the water pump on the engine. Then, tightening each bolt a little at a time, torque the mounting bolts to 2.0 mkg (14 ft. lb.).

3. Install the V-belt on the crankshaft pulley, the water pump pulley, and the alternator pulley.

4. By pulling the alternator away from the engine block, adjust the V-belt tension so that you can depress the V-belt 10 to 15 mm (3/8 to 9/16 in.) at the point indicated in Fig. 4-8.

Fig. 4-8. Point at which V-belt should be depressed. Dimension **a** should be 10 to 15 mm (3/8 to 9/16 in.).

5. When the V-belt tension is correct, torque the lower alternator mounting bolts to 2.5 mkg (18 ft. lb.) and the bolts that hold the adjusting bracket on the alternator and the cylinder head to 2.0 mkg (14 ft. lb.). On California cars that are so equipped, install the air pump V-belt and adjust it using the same procedure used to adjust the alternator/water pump belt.

> **CAUTION ——**
>
> *Do not tension the V-belts too tightly. Doing this may cause the alternator bearings, water pump bearings, or air pump bearings to fail after only a short period of service.*

6. Install the hoses as described in **4.1 Replacing Hoses.** Install the T-head drive belt cover bolt and tighten the nut just enough to compress slightly the rubber grommet that is in the drive belt cover. Fill the cooling system (See **4. Cooling System**).

4.4 Disassembling and Assembling Water Pump

By working under the car, you can easily remove the thermostat housing and thermostat with the water pump installed on the engine. Once you have removed the thermostat, you can test it as described in **4.2 Cooling System Troubleshooting.** The mechanical (front) part of the water pump can also be removed from the water pump housing with the pump installed but it is usually more convenient to remove the water pump first.

To disassemble:

1. Remove the three bolts and washers that hold the pulley on the water pump shaft.

   > **NOTE ——**
   >
   > Though it is not absolutely necessary to remove the pulley, removing it will improve access to the bolts that hold the water pump together.

2. Remove the seven bolts and washers that hold the front part of the pump to the housing. Then remove the front part of the pump and the gasket.

3. Remove the two bolts and washers that hold the thermostat housing to the water pump housing. Then remove the thermostat housing, the O-ring, and the thermostat as shown in Fig. 4-9.

Assembly is the reverse of disassembly. Use a new O-ring between the thermostat housing and the water pump housing and a new gasket between the housing and the front part of the pump. Tighten each of the seven bolts a little at a time until all are torqued to 1.0 mkg (7 ft. lb.) Torque the bolts that hold the pulley to the water pump hub to 2.0 mkg (14 ft. lb.).

4.5 Removing and Installing Radiator, Cooling Fan, and Air Ducts

The cooling fan is mounted on the radiator. It can be removed from the radiator while the radiator is installed in the car, or the radiator and the cooling fan can be removed together as a unit.

To remove:

1. Remove the radiator cap. Place a receptacle beneath the radiator for catching the draining coolant. Then remove the drain plug from the bottom of the radiator and allow the coolant to drain.

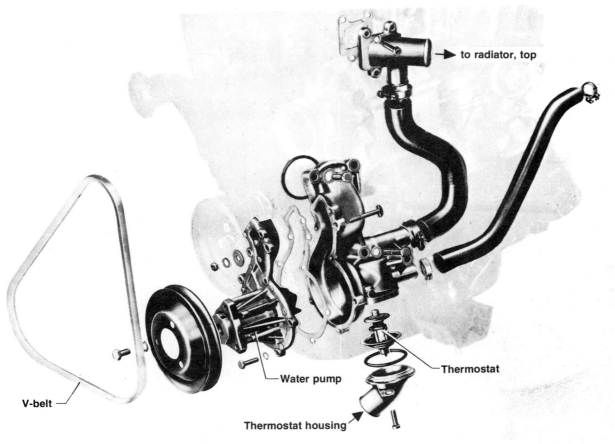

Fig. 4-9. Exploded view of the water pump and related parts.

V-belt

Water pump

Thermostat housing

Thermostat

to radiator, top

CAUTION ——

Never drain the coolant while the engine is hot. Doing this could warp the engine block or the cylinder head.

2. Remove the upper and lower radiator hoses from the radiator. See **4.1 Replacing Hoses.**

3. Disconnect the battery ground strap. Then disconnect the wires from the thermo switch that is on the bottom tank of the radiator and from the connector that is on the fan motor. On early cars, dismount the fuse box for working clearance.

4. Remove the clips, indicated by arrows in Fig. 4-10, then remove the air ducts.

Fig. 4-10. Clips that hold air ducts (arrows), lower radiator mounting nut (**1**), side radiator mounting nut (**2**), and mounting bracket bolt (**3**).

5. Remove the lower radiator mounting nut and the side radiator mounting nut, but leave the bonded rubber mountings (Fig. 4-11) attached to the radiator. Remove the mounting bracket bolt.

6. Move the radiator slightly to the left and tilt it toward the engine. Then lift the radiator out upward, complete with the fan and air duct.

7. Remove the air duct from the radiator. If necessary, unbolt the fan and fan duct from the radiator.

NOTE ——

To remove the cooling fan with the radiator installed, disconnect the battery ground strap and the wire to the fan. Unbolt the fan duct from the radiator and remove the duct and motor. Then unbolt the fan motor from the fan duct.

Installation is the reverse of removal. Align the radiator in a vertical position by sliding the mounting bracket on its elongated bolt hole. Install the hoses as described in **4.1 Replacing Hoses.** Fill the cooling system with clear water and run the engine for about two minutes. Then completely drain the cooling system and refill it with the correct mixture of water and anti-freeze, as given earlier in **Table c.**

Radiator

Thermo switch for fan

Drain plug and seal

Bonded rubber mounting

Fig. 4-11. The radiator, cooling fan, and related parts.

5. VALVES, CAMSHAFT, AND CYLINDER HEAD

The camshaft drive belt, camshaft, and cylinder head can be removed from the engine without first removing the engine from the car. You do not need to replace the camshaft drive belt unless inspection shows it to be faulty.

1. Camshaft sprocket
2. Drive belt tensioner
3. Tension adjuster locknut
4. Camshaft drive belt
5. V-belt
6. Crankshaft sprocket retaining bolt
7. Socket head screw for crankshaft pulley
8. Bolt for water pump pulley
9. Intermediate shaft sprocket retaining bolt
10. Crankshaft sprocket
11. Intermediate shaft sprocket

5.1 Removing, Installing, and Adjusting Camshaft Drive Belt

The removal of the camshaft drive belt and related parts is illustrated in Fig. 5-1. In replacing the drive belt, you need not remove the drive belt sprockets.

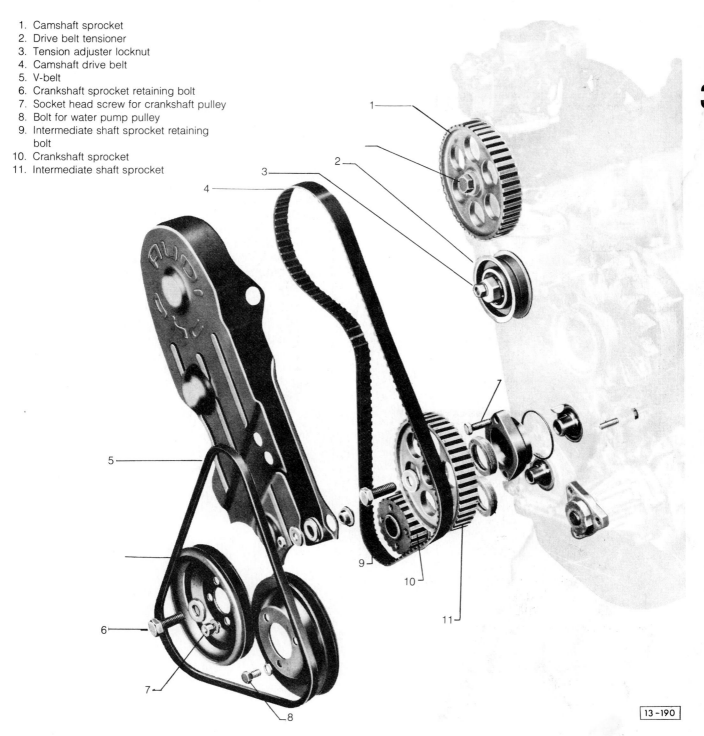

13-190

Fig. 5-1. Camshaft drive belt removal.

To remove camshaft drive belt:

1. Only on certain cars sold in California, remove the V-belt for the air injection pump. To do this, loosen the air pump mounting bolts, push the pump toward the engine, then remove the air pump V-belt.

2. Loosen the upper and lower alternator mounting bolts. Loosen the bolt that holds the alternator belt adjusting bracket to the cylinder head. Push the alternator toward the engine, then remove the alternator V-belt.

3. Take out the three bolts that hold the water pump pulley on the water pump and remove the pulley. Remove the nuts and the bolts that hold the camshaft drive belt cover on the water pump and on the front of the engine. Then remove the cover.

4. Loosen the camshaft drive belt tension adjuster locknut. Using a wrench on the tension adjuster, turn the adjuster counterclockwise so that tension is removed from the drive belt. Then remove the drive belt. (Work it off the sprockets toward the front of the car.).

To install and adjust drive belt:

1. Hand-turn the camshaft sprocket until the centerpunch mark indicated in Fig. 5-2 is exactly in line with the upper surface of the cylinder head cover's mounting flange.

Fig. 5-2. Centerpunch mark (arrow) on camshaft sprocket aligned with the upper surface of the cylinder head cover mounting flange. Align the mark with the flange on the left-hand (spark plug) side of the engine and never with the flange on the opposite (carburetor) side of the engine.

2. Hand-turn the crankshaft and the intermediate shaft until the centerpunch mark on the intermediate shaft sprocket is positioned in the V-notch on the crankshaft pulley (Fig. 5-3).

Fig. 5-3. Centerpunch mark (arrow) on intermediate shaft sprocket positioned within the V-notch on the crankshaft pulley.

3. Being careful not to move any of the sprockets, install the camshaft drive belt first at the bottom and then at the top so that there is no slack between the crankshaft and intermediate shaft sprockets or between the intermediate shaft and camshaft sprockets.

4. Using a wrench to turn the tension adjuster clockwise, tighten the belt until it can just be finger-twisted 90° at a point halfway between the camshaft and intermediate shaft sprockets (Fig. 5-4). Then torque the locknut to 4.5 mkg (33 ft. lb.). If the timing marks have moved from their setting positions, repeat the installation and adjustment procedure.

The remainder of installation is the reverse of removal. Adjust the V-belt tension as shown in Fig. 5-5. You should just be able to depress the V-belt 10 to 15 mm (3/8 to 9/16 in.).

Fig. 5-4. Drive belt being adjusted.

Make the adjustment by pulling the alternator away from the engine. When the V-belt tension is correct, torque the lower alternator mounting bolts to 2.5 mkg (18 ft. lb.) and the bolts that hold the adjusting bracket to the alternator and the cylinder head to 2.0 mkg (14 ft. lb.). Use the same procedure to adjust the air pump V-belt tension on California cars that are so equipped.

> **CAUTION** —
> *Do not tension the V-belts too tightly. Doing this may cause the alternator bearings, water pump bearings, or air pump bearings to fail after only a short period of service.*

5.2 Adjusting Valves

The clearance between the heel of the cam lobe and the bucket-type cam follower is adjustable by means of replaceable adjusting disks (shims), as shown in Fig. 5-6.

Fig. 5-5. Point at which V-belt should be depressed. Dimension **a** should be 10 to 15 mm (⅜ to 9/16 in.).

3

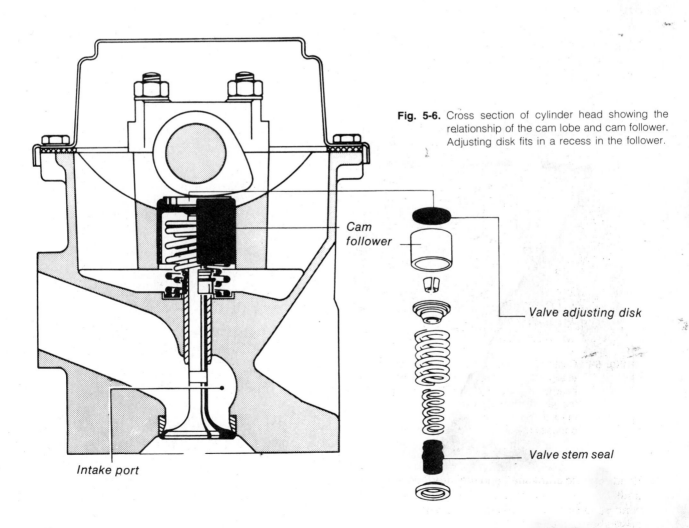

Fig. 5-6. Cross section of cylinder head showing the relationship of the cam lobe and cam follower. Adjusting disk fits in a recess in the follower.

Cam follower

Valve adjusting disk

Valve stem seal

Intake port

The adjusting disks are available in twenty-six different thicknesses from 3.00 to 4.25 mm (.1181 to .1673 in.). The disks most frequently required in making adjustments fall in the thickness range of 3.55 to 3.80 mm (.1397 to .1496 in.). **Table e** lists the available disks by thickness and part number. The thickness of each disk is etched on its underside.

Table e. Adjusting Disk Thicknesses and Part Numbers

Thickness	Part No.	Thickness	Part No.
3.00	056 109 555	3.65	056 109 568
3.05	056 109 556	3.70	056 109 569
3.10	056 109 557	3.75	056 109 570
3.15	056 109 558	3.80	056 109 571
3.20	056 109 559	3.85	056 109 572
3.25	056 109 560	3.90	056 109 573
3.30	056 109 561	3.95	056 109 574
3.35	056 109 562	4.00	056 109 575
3.40	056 109 563	4.05	056 109 576
3.45	056 109 564	4.10	056 109 577
3.50	056 109 565	4.15	056 109 578
3.55	056 109 566	4.20	056 109 579
3.60	056 109 567	4.25	056 109 580

You can adjust the valves with the engine hot—coolant temperature approximately 35°C (95°F)—or with the engine cold. However, the clearance will be different depending on whether the engine is hot or cold.

To adjust valve clearance:

1. Remove the eight bolts and cylinder head cover retaining plates. Then carefully lift off the cylinder head cover and its gasket. If the gasket is stuck to the cylinder head, use a dull knife to separate the gasket from the head.

2. Using a wrench on the bolt that is in the center of the crankshaft pulley, hand-turn the crankshaft clockwise until both cam lobes for the No. 1 (front) cylinder are pointing upward. Then, to determine the valve clearance, insert feeler gauges of various thicknesses between the cam lobes and the adjusting disks (Fig. 5-7).

> **NOTE** ——
>
> With the engine hot, the intake valve clearance should be between 0.20 and 0.30 mm (.008 and .012 in.); exhaust valve clearance should be between 0.40 and 0.50 mm (.016 and .020 in.). With the engine cold, the intake valve clearance should be between 0.15 and 0.25 mm (.006 and .010 in.); exhaust valve clearance should be between 0.35 and 0.45 mm (.014 and .018 in.).

Fig. 5-7. Valve clearance being measured. Notice that both cam lobes for No. 1 cylinder are pointing up, away from the cam followers. The feeler gauge is inserted between the cam lobe and the adjusting disk that is on top of the cam follower.

3. If either the intake or exhaust valve clearance is incorrect, write down the actual clearance that you have measured. Then depress the cam followers with special tool VW 546 and lift out the adjusting disk(s) with special pliers (Fig. 5-8).

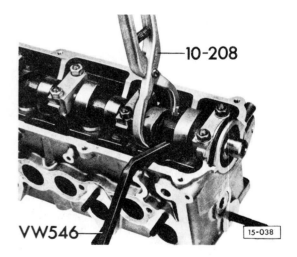

Fig. 5-8. Adjusting disk being removed. The special tool depresses both cam followers simultaneously. Special pliers (tool 10-208) are used to remove the disk from the cam follower.

4. Read the thickness that is etched on the underside of the removed disk. (If the number has worn off, check the disk thickness with a micrometer.) Then

determine the thickness of the required replacement disk as described in one of the next two steps.

5. If the measured clearance was less than the specified clearance range for the valve, subtract the measured clearance from the specified maximum clearance. Then subtract the difference from the thickness of the original disk to determine the thickness of the required replacement disk. If the computed thickness comes out equal to a standard disk thickness, or if the computed thickness is less than a standard disk thickness, use the next thicker disk.

6. If the measured clearance was greater than the specified clearance range for the valve, subtract the specified maximum clearance from the measured clearance. Then add the difference to the thickness of the original disk to determine the thickness of the required replacement disk. If the computed thickness comes out equal to a standard disk thickness, or if the computed thickness is less than a standard disk thickness, use the next thicker disk.

7. Install the required replacement disk(s) with the etched numbers toward the cam follower. Remove the special cam follower depressing tool. Then re-check the clearance to make sure that it is within the specified range.

8. Using a wrench on the bolt that is in the center of the crankshaft, hand-turn the crankshaft 180° clockwise and repeat steps 1 through 7 on the No. 3 cylinder. Hand-turn the crankshaft another 180° and adjust the valves of the No. 4 cylinder and, finally, 180° farther to adjust the valves of the No. 2 cylinder.

9. Install the cylinder head cover. Torque the bolts to 1.0 mkg (7 ft. lb.)

5.3 Removing and Installing Cylinder Head and Manifolds

The cylinder head can be removed without removing the engine from the car and without removing the camshaft or other valve gear prior to cylinder head removal.

To remove cylinder head and manifolds:

1. Remove the radiator cap. Place a receptacle beneath the radiator for catching the draining coolant. Then remove the drain plug from the bottom of the radiator and allow the coolant to drain.

   CAUTION ——

   Never drain the coolant while the engine is hot. Doing this could warp the engine block or the cylinder head.

2. Remove the camshaft drive belt as described in **5.1 Removing, Installing, and Adjusting Camshaft Drive Belt.**

3. Remove the air cleaner as described in **LUBRICATION AND MAINTENANCE.** Then disconnect all of the hoses, cables, and wires that are connected to the carburetor and the intake manifold. Only on certain cars sold in California, disconnect the air lines from the air injection connections on the exhaust manifold.

   NOTE ——

   On cars with fuel injection, remove the intake air distributor as described in **FUEL AND EXHAUST SYSTEMS.**

4. Remove the four nuts that hold the exhaust pipe to the exhaust manifold (Fig. 5-9). Then remove the nuts and the bolts that hold the intake and exhaust manifolds on the cylinder head and remove the manifolds from the cylinder head as a unit.

Fig. 5-9. The four nuts that hold the exhaust pipe onto the exhaust manifold. Nuts, bolts, and metal brakets join together the intake and exhaust manifolds.

5. Remove the upper alternator mounting bolt. Then unbolt the alternator V-belt adjusting bracket from the cylinder head and remove the bracket.

6. Disconnect all coolant hoses from the cylinder head. Disconnect the wire for the temperature gauge.

7. Disconnect the spark plug cables from the spark plugs. Disconnect the high tension cable from the coil at terminal 4. Then remove the distributor cap complete with the spark plug cables and the high tension cable.

8. Remove the spark plugs.

9. Remove the eight bolts and cylinder head cover retaining plates. Then carefully lift off the cylinder head cover and its gasket. If the gasket is stuck to the cylinder head, use a dull knife to separate the gasket from the head.

10. Beginning at the outer ends of the cylinder head and working toward the center from both directions, use a hex-shaped driver to remove the eight socket head cylinder head bolts.

11. Lift the cylinder head off the engine block. If the head is stuck, insert two wooden hammer handles in the outermost exhaust ports. Then, using a tilting motion, pull the head free.

To install:

1. Thoroughly clean the cylinder head.

> **CAUTION** ——
>
> *Do not use a metal scraper or a power-driven wire brush to clean the combustion chambers or gasket sealing surface. Doing this can gouge the aluminum, which could cause the head gasket to leak, or leave scratches in the combustion chambers that could become "hot spots." Instead, use solvent to soften combustion chamber deposits, dried sealer, and material torn from the old head gasket. Then remove this foreign matter with a wooden or plastic scraper.*

2. Thoroughly clean the gasket sealing surface of the cylinder block. Then clean the threads in the head bolt holes.

> **NOTE** ——
>
> To keep out dirt, stuff clean rags into the cylinder bores and seal all water and oil passages with tape. After you have cleaned the sealing surface of the block, use a thread-cutting tap or thread chaser to clean the bolt holes. It is extremely important that all debris be removed from the bottoms of the holes after you have cleaned the threads.

3. Check the cylinder head for warping. To do this, lay a straightedge lengthwise across the sealing surface of the head as shown in Fig. 5-10. You should not be able to insert a 0.13-mm (.005-in.) feeler gauge between the sealing surface and the straightedge at any point. Repeat the check with the straightedge placed diagonally across the surface in both directions.

> **NOTE** ——
>
> If a 0.13-mm (.005-in.) feeler gauge can be inserted at any point, either replace the cylinder head or take it to an automotive machine shop where the head can be milled to obtain a true surface.

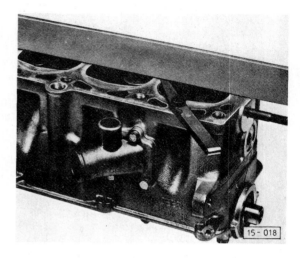

Fig. 5-10. A 0.10-mm (.004-in.) feeler gauge inserted between the straightedge and cylinder head sealing surface. 0.10 mm (.004 in.) is the maximum allowable distortion. So if a 0.13-mm (.005-in.) feeler gauge can be inserted, the head must be replaced or milled to a true surface.

4. Using the procedure you used for the head, check the engine block for warping. Warped blocks can also be milled but the engine must be removed and completely disassembled beforehand.

5. Using a thread-cutting die, clean the cylinder head bolt threads. Do not use a power-driven wire brush, which could distort the threads. Replace damaged or distorted bolts. Then coat the bolt threads and head bolt washers with anti-seize compound.

6. Install a new cylinder head gasket as shown in Fig. 5-11. Place two 200-mm long, 9-mm diameter (8-in. long, ⅜-in. diameter) wooden dowels in two of the outermost head bolt holes to hold the gasket on the engine block and to serve as guides when you install the cylinder head.

> **CAUTION** ——
>
> *Never reinstall a cylinder head gasket that has previously been compressed by tightening the cylinder head bolts. Once compressed, such gaskets lose their resilience and will not produce a reliable seal if reused.*

Fig. 5-11. Cylinder head gasket installed on block. The word OBEN (top) identifies the top surface of the gasket, which must be upward.

7. Using the two dowels as a guide, carefully lower the cylinder head onto the new cylinder head gasket and the engine block. Then immediately install, but do not tighten, several head bolts and washers. With the cylinder head thus supported, remove the dowels and loosely install the remaining head bolts and washers.

8. On engines with hexagon-socket socket-head cylinder head bolts—as originally installed on the 1973 through 1977 models—torque the head bolts to 3.0 mkg (22 ft. lb.) in the sequence given in Fig. 5-12. Go over the sequence a second time, torquing the bolts to 6.0 mkg (43 ft. lb.), then a third time, torquing the bolts to 7.5 mkg (54 ft. lb.).

9. On engines with 12-point polygon socket-head cylinder head bolts—introduced on the 1978 models—torque the head bolts to 3.0 mkg (22 ft. lb.) in the sequence given in Fig. 5-12. Go over the sequence a second time, torquing the bolts to 6.0 mkg (43 ft. lb.), then a third time, torquing the bolts to 7.5 mkg (54 ft. lb.). Go over the sequence one more time, tightening each bolt by precisely one-quarter (¼) turn.

NOTE ——

The new-type cylinder head bolts, with 11-mm 12-point sockets in their heads, can be installed in place of the 10-mm hexagon-socket bolts used in early models—if all ten bolts are replaced. The new-type bolts, Part No. 049 103 385, make it unnecessary to retorque the bolts after 1000 mi. (1500 km) or at any other servicing interval.

10. Install the remaining engine parts. See **5.1 Removing, Installing, and Adjusting Camshaft Drive Belt** and **4.1 Replacing Hoses.** Use a new gasket when you install the cylinder head cover and torque the bolts to 1.0 mkg (7 ft. lb.). Install new gaskets for the manifolds, then install the manifolds and torque the nuts and bolts to 2.5 mkg (18 ft. lb.).

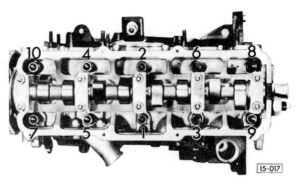

Fig. 5-12. Head bolt tightening sequence.

Reconnect the hoses, cables, and wires to the induction system as described in **FUEL AND EXHAUST SYSTEMS.** Fill the cooling system as described in **4. Cooling System.**

11. Start the engine. When it has warmed up to the specified temperature, adjust the idle speed to 850 to 1000 rpm as described in **FUEL AND EXHAUST SYSTEMS.**

12. After the car has been driven for approximately 1000 mi. (1500 km), remove the cylinder head cover with the engine stopped. On engines with the old-type hexagon-socket cylinder head bolts, loosen each bolt by turning it approximately 30° counterclockwise—following the reverse of the sequence given earlier in Fig. 5-12. Then, following the sequence given in Fig. 5-12, torque each cylinder head bolt to 7.5 mkg (54 ft. lb.) if the engine is cold or to 8.5 mkg (61 ft. lb.) if the engine is warm (coolant temperature 35°C (95°F) or above).

CAUTION ——

Do not loosen or retorque the new-type 12-point socket-head cylinder head bolts at 1000 mi. (1500 km) or at any other time following installation. Doing this is unnecessary and could disturb the sealing of the cylinder head gasket.

13. On all engines, check the valve clearances and, if necessary, adjust the clearances as described in **5.2 Adjusting Valves.**

14. Install the cylinder head cover. Use a new gasket if the old gasket is hardened or damaged.

5.4 Disassembling and Assembling Cylinder Head

You should not completely disassemble the cylinder head in one continuous operation. Instead, disassemble the head in stages, following the sequence given here, so that you can make various checks and measurements at each stage of disassembly. By doing this, you will be able to determine which parts can be reused and which parts require reconditioning or replacement.

Camshaft and Cam Followers

To check the condition of the camshaft and its bearings, you must first relieve the pressure that is exerted on the cam lobes by the valve springs. Relieving the pressure requires only that the camshaft be removed, the cam followers lifted out, and the camshaft reinstalled. The valves and valve springs need not be removed.

The camshaft is held to the cylinder head by five bearing caps. Each cap is held by two nuts that thread onto studs. The bearing caps and the nuts are shown in Fig. 5-13. Notice that each camshaft bearing cap is numbered, beginning at the camshaft drive end of the cylinder head, to simplify correct installation. Because the factory has not always marked the numbers on the same ends of the caps, the numbered ends will not necessarily be toward the manifold side of the head as shown. During bearing cap installation, observe the off-center bearing position.

To remove the camshaft, remove the nuts and washers from bearing caps 5, 1, and 3 in that order. Then, loosening each of the four nuts a little at a time so that the valve spring tension is relieved evenly, simultaneously remove bearing caps 2 and 4. If this procedure is not followed, the camshaft may tilt in its bearings, which could damage the bearings or bend the camshaft.

To check camshaft axial play, remove the camshaft and lift out the cam followers. Number each cam follower as you remove it so that the followers can be reinstalled in their original bores. Install the camshaft using only bearing caps 1 and 5. Install a dial indicator as shown in Fig. 5-14. Move the camshaft forward and backward while you observe the dial indicator. Axial play should not exceed 0.15 mm (.006 in.). If the play is greater, the head or the camshaft is worn and must be replaced.

Fig. 5-14. Dial indicator being used to measure camshaft axial play.

Fig. 5-13. Camshaft bearing caps and bearing cap nuts. There is a flat washer under each nut. It is important that the bearing caps be removed in the correct sequence.

To check the camshaft for bending and runout, install the camshaft between centers as shown in Fig. 5-15. Mount a dial indicator so that its gauge pin is against the center bearing journal on the camshaft. Then rotate the camshaft and observe the runout range shown by the dial indicator. If runout exceeds 0.01 mm (.0004 in.), replace the camshaft.

Fig. 5-15. Dial indicator being used to measure camshaft runout.

To measure camshaft bearing clearance, either install one bearing cap at a time and measure the camshaft's radial play with a dial indicator, or use Plastigage®. Plastigage is available from automotive supply stores. Further information on its use can be found in **10.1 Removing, Checking, and Installing Pistons, Piston Rings, Connecting Rods, and Connecting Rod Bearings.** Camshaft bearing clearance should be between 0.02 and 0.05 mm (.0008 and .002 in.).

Inspect the camshaft lobes for wear (Fig. 5-16). Worn cam lobes are caused by a lack of lubrication. So always lubricate the cam lobes and the adjusting disks on the cam followers during assembly and make certain that the engine's oil passages are clear. Replace worn camshafts and worn adjusting disks.

3

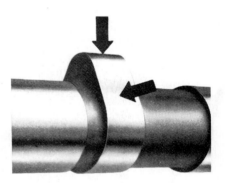

© 1974 VWoA—1242

Fig. 5-16. Cam lobe. Toe of the cam (top arrow) should not be scored or worn unevenly. There should be no sign of wear at the second arrow. If there is wear at the second arrow, check for incorrect valve clearances, abrasive substances in the oil, or inadequate lubrication.

Inspect the cam followers for galling and signs of seizure—conditions that indicate a lack of lubrication. If aluminum from the cylinder head is found adhering to a cam follower, replace the cam follower. The cylinder head should be replaced if any of the cam follower bores is rough, gouged, worn or otherwise damaged.

To install the cam followers and the camshaft, first clean all the parts to remove sludge and abrasive dirt. Lightly lubricate the cam follower bores with assembly lubricant (available from automotive supply stores), or with a thin coat of multipurpose grease. Then, with reference to the numbers marked on the cam followers during removal, install each cam follower in its original bore. If undamaged, install the original adjusting disks so that the valve clearance can be measured after you have installed the camshaft.

Coat the tops of the adjusting disks, the camshaft bearing surfaces, and the cam lobes with assembly lubricant or with a thin coating of multipurpose grease. Then position the camshaft on the cylinder head. Loosely install bearing caps 2 and 4. Gradually tighten all four bearing cap nuts until the camshaft is drawn down fully and evenly into the bearing saddles. Then install bearing caps 5 and 3. Finally, install a new oil seal on the front of the camshaft and install bearing cap 1. See Fig. 5-17. Torque the bearing cap nuts to 2.0 mkg (14 ft. lb.). Install the end plug at the rear of the cylinder head. Obtain a new plug if the original is damaged or does not fit tightly.

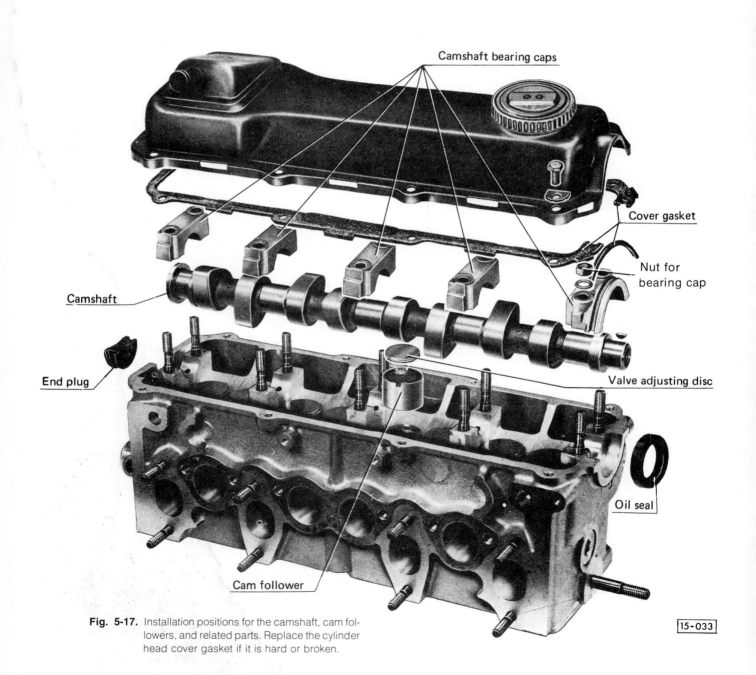

Camshaft bearing caps

Cover gasket

Nut for bearing cap

Camshaft

Valve adjusting disc

End plug

Oil seal

Cam follower

Fig. 5-17. Installation positions for the camshaft, cam followers, and related parts. Replace the cylinder head cover gasket if it is hard or broken.

15-033

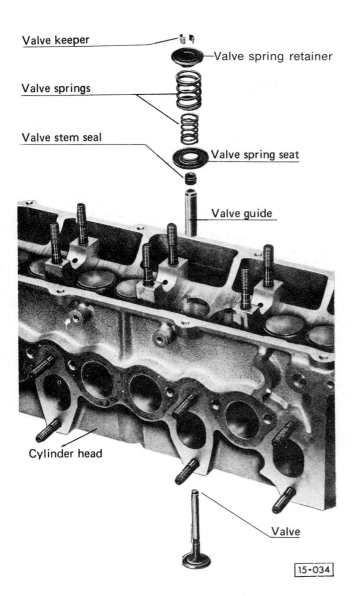

Fig. 5-18. Components of a valve assembly. The valve guides are a press fit in the cylinder head.

If previously removed, install the drive belt sprocket on the camshaft. Then, gripping the sprocket, hand-turn the camshaft to the required positions so that you can adjust the valve clearances as described in **5.2 Adjusting Valves.**

NOTE ——

If the cylinder head is not installed on the engine block, you can delay the valve adjustment until after the cylinder head has been installed. By doing so, your adjustments will take into account minor clearance changes that may result from the torquing of the cylinder head bolts.

Valves and Valve Guides

You must remove the camshaft and the cam followers before you can remove the valves. Do not remove the valve guides unless they are worn badly enough to require replacement. The components of a valve assembly are shown disassembled in Fig. 5-18.

To remove valves:

1. With the camshaft and cam followers removed and the cylinder head removed from the engine, compress the valve springs as shown in Fig. 5-19. Doing this should press the valve spring retainer down the valve stem so that the split valve keeper is uncovered.

2. Remove the split keeper halves from the valve stem. Release the compressing tool. Then take off the spring retainer and the valve springs.

Fig. 5-19. Lever tool that is used to press down the valve spring retainer and compress the valve springs. The plate, placed beneath the cylinder head, has projections on it that support the valve heads.

3. Using long-nose pliers, remove the valve spring seat and the valve stem seal.

4. When all eight valve assemblies have been disassembled, install a dial indicator as shown in Fig. 5-20 so that you can check the valve guides for wear.

CAUTION ——

If the keeper grooves in the valve stems are burred, file them smooth before proceeding. If the burred stems are forced into the valve guides, the guides will be ruined.

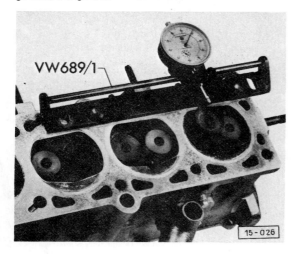

Fig. 5-20. Dial indicator being used to measure the rock of the valves in their guides.

5. One at a time, lift each valve off its seat until the tip of the valve stem is flush with the top of the valve guide. Position the dial indicator's gauge pin against the valve head. Then rock the valve from side to side in its guide while you observe the play range shown by the dial indicator.

NOTE ——

If the rocking play of an intake valve exceeds 1.00 mm (.039 in.), or the rocking play of an exhaust valve exceeds 1.30 mm (.051 in.)— even when a new valve is used—the guides are excessively worn. The inside diameter of valve guides should be between 8.013 and 8.035 mm (.315 and .316 in.).

CAUTION ——

Before you decide to replace the valve guides, determine whether new guides and the proper installation equipment are available. If guides and tools are unavailable, replace the entire cylinder head. Do not replace the valve guides routinely; replace them only if they are worn. To replace valve guides, follow the procedure given below.

6. Remove the dial indicator. Remove the valves, numbering each one so that you can reinstall the valves in their original locations.

7. To determine whether the original valve springs can be reused, check them with a valve spring tester as shown in Fig. 5-21. The outer valve spring should indicate a load of 43.5 to 48.0 kg (96 to 106 lb.) when compressed to a length of 22.3 mm (⁷⁄₈ in.). The inner valve spring should indicate a load of 21.0 to 23.0 kg (46 to 51 lb.) when compressed to a length of 18.3 mm (²³⁄₃₂ in.). Replace weak springs.

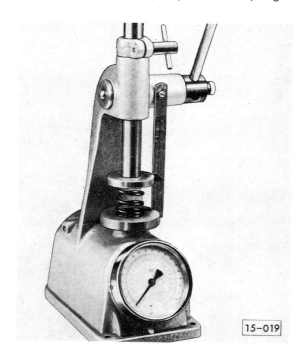

Fig. 5-21. Valve spring tester with spring in place.

NOTE ——

If you do not have a spring tester, have the springs tested by your Authorized Dealer or by a qualified automotive machine shop.

8. To check the keepers, oil them and then install them on a removed valve. Hold the keeper halves together while you turn the valve. The valve stem should rotate freely in the assembled keeper. If the keeper is a loose fit, you can grind the mating surfaces to make it fit tighter.

9. Inspect the valve seats and the valve facings as described in **5.5 Reconditioning Valves and Valve Seats.** If necessary, recondition (grind) the seats and the facings.

CAUTION ——

The exhaust valves must not be machine-ground. If their facing is too deeply worn or pitted to be restored by lapping, replace the valve.

To replace valve guides:

1. Clean and carefully inspect the cylinder head. Do not replace the valve guides in a cylinder head that is cracked or warped. Do not replace the valve guides if the valve seats are too badly worn to be refaced.

2. Using a repair press, press out the worn guides from the combustion chamber side, as shown in Fig. 5-22.

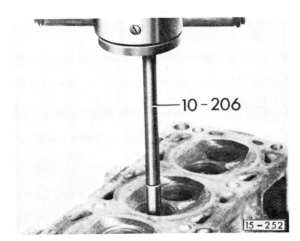

Fig. 5-22. Valve guide being pressed out.

3. Coat the new valve guides with engine oil. Then press the new guides into the cold cylinder head from the camshaft side until the shoulder on the guide firmly contacts the top of the cylinder head. The correct replacement guide, with the shoulder, is Part No. 056 103 419A.

CAUTION —

Once the shoulder on the guide is seated against the head, do not use more than 1 ton pressure or the shoulder may break.

4. Ream the guides to obtain a uniform inside diameter of from 8.013 to 8.035 mm (.315 to .316 in.). See Fig. 5-23. Lubricate the reamer with cutting oil during the reaming operation.

NOTE —

The correct tool for checking the guide bore is a "go/no-go" bore gauge that has a "go" diameter of 8.013 mm (or .315 in.) and a "no-go" diameter of 8.035 mm (or .316 in.). The 8.013-mm (.315-in.) end of the gauge should enter the guide easily but it should be impossible for the 8.035-mm (.316-in.) part of the gauge to enter the guide bore.

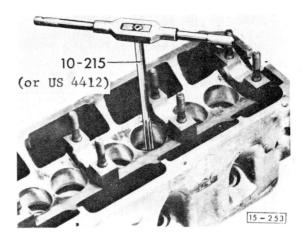

Fig. 5-23. New valve guide being reamed.

5. To ensure that the valve seats are concentric with the new valve guides, reface the seats as described in **5.5 Reconditioning Valves and Valve Seats.**

To install valves:

1. Lubricate the valve stems with engine oil. Then, with reference to the numbers marked on the valves during removal, install the valves in their original locations.

2. Place the cylinder head upright atop the plate for the valve removal tool. Install all eight valve spring seats. Then install plastic caps over the valve stem ends (Fig. 5-24).

Fig. 5-24. Plastic protective cap **(A)**, new valve stem seal **(B)**, and installing tool—part 10-204.

CAUTION —

If you do not have the plastic protective cap, wrap the valve stem ends with smooth plastic tape. If you force the new valve stem seals over the bare valve stems, the keeper grooves will damage the seals and the engine will use excessive oil.

3. Using the installing tool shown in Fig. 5-24, or a plastic tube of suitable diameter, press the new valve stem seals down over the valve stems and onto the tops of the valve guides.

4. Install the valve springs so that the closely spaced coils of the outer springs are against the spring seats.

5. Install the spring retainers. Then compress the springs with the valve spring compressing tool and install the keepers.

Removing and Installing Valve Springs and Seals
(cylinder head installed)

A worn valve stem seal, broken valve spring, damaged keeper, or damaged spring retainer can be replaced without removing the cylinder head. To replace these parts, use the procedure that follows.

To remove spring:

1. Remove the spark plug, cylinder head cover, camshaft drive belt, camshaft, and cam follower. Install air hose adapter VW 653/2 in the spark plug hole. Install the valve spring compressing tool as shown in Fig. 5-25.

2. Hand-turn the crankshaft until the piston of the cylinder you are working on is at bottom dead center (BDC). Then apply a constant air pressure of at least 85 psi (6 kg/cm²) to the cylinder.

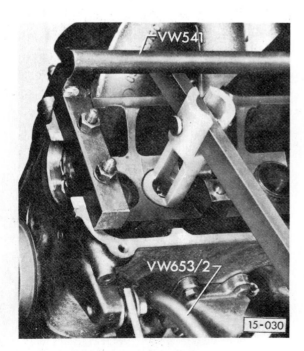

Fig. 5-25. Spring compressing tool and air hose adapter installed.

3. Compress the valve spring retainer and the valve springs. Then remove the keeper.

4. Replace the worn or damaged parts. Then reassemble the valve assembly using a reverse of the disassembly procedure.

5.5 Reconditioning Valves and Valve Seats

Carefully inspect used valves to determine whether they are suitable for reuse. You can reface intake valves, but not exhaust valves, by machine-grinding. In doing this, follow a procedure suitable to the valve refacing machine that you have. Alternatively, have worn intake valves refaced by an Authorized Dealer or a qualified automotive machine shop.

To inspect and recondition used valves:

1. Discard any valve with damaged keeper grooves or with a stem that has been warped or galled by seizure.

2. Using a motor-driven wire brush, remove the combustion chamber deposits from the valves.

3. Examine the part of the valve facing that contacts the valve seat for pits, burns, and other signs of wear. If the damage to an intake valve is too extensive to be corrected by machine-grinding, replace the valve. Replace any exhaust valve that has pitting or wear that is too extensive to be corrected by lightly hand-lapping the valve into its seat.

> **NOTE ——**
> Because of the extreme conditions under which exhaust valves operate, many experienced mechanics routinely replace any exhaust valves that have been in service for 25,000 mi. (40,000 km) or more.

4. After you have refaced the intake valves by machine-grinding, the remaining margin must not be less than the minimum specified in Fig. 5-26. Discard any intake valve that has an irregular margin after machine-grinding—a condition that indicates a warped valve.

> *CAUTION ——*
> *Do not machine-grind exhaust valves. Doing this will shorten their service life. Exhaust valves should be hand-lapped only.*

To inspect and reface valve seats:

1. If any valve seat is cracked or so badly gas-cut that it cannot be refaced to the specified dimensions, replace the cylinder head.

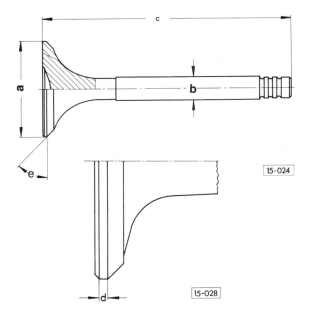

15-024

15-028

Dimension **a**, valve head diameter	Intake: 34.00 mm (1.338 in.) Exhaust: 31.00 mm (1.220 in.)
Dimension **b**, valve stem diameter	Intake: 7.97 mm (.314 in.) Exhaust: 7.95 mm (.313 in.)
Dimension **c**. valve length	Intake: 98.70 mm (3.886 in.) Exhaust: 98.50 mm (3.878 in.)
Dimension **d**, valve head margin	Intake: 0.50 mm (.020 in.) minimum Exhaust: Do not machine-grind
Dimension **e**, facing angle	Intake: 45° Exhaust: 45°

Fig. 5-26. Dimensions for reusable valves.

2. If inspection has shown that the valve guides are no longer serviceable (see **5.4 Disassembling and Assembling Cylinder Head**), either replace the guides or replace the cylinder head. If the proper replacement guides and replacement tools are available, replace the guides before you reface the valve seats.

3. Whether you use a hand-operated seat cutter or a power-driven seat grinder, make sure that the tool pilot fits the valve guides with little or no play.

4. Select a 45° seat cutter or a 45° seat grinding stone. Cutter blades should be straight and not chipped; grinding stones should be freshly dressed to the prescribed 45° angle.

5. Cut or grind to 45° the contact areas of the intake and the exhaust valve seats. See Fig. 5-27 for the finished dimensions of the intake valve seats; see Fig. 5-28 for the finished dimensions of the exhaust valve seats. Remove no more metal than is necessary to erase wear and pitting—the less metal removed the better.

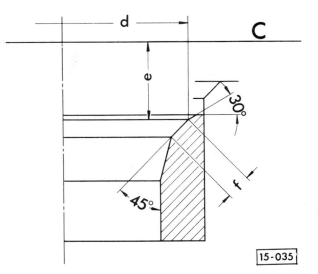

15-035

C. Gasket sealing surface of cylinder head
d. Diameter: 33.20 mm (1.307 in.)
e. Depth: 9.00 mm (3.54 in.)
f. Seat contact area width:
   2.00 mm (.079 in.)
30°. Angle of correction chamfer
45°. Angle of valve seat contact area

Fig. 5-27. Dimensions for finished intake valve seat.

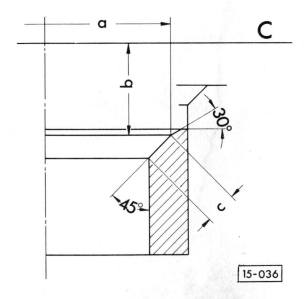

15-036

C. Gasket sealing surface of cylinder head
a. Diameter: 30.80 mm (1.212 in.)
b. Depth: 9.60 mm (.378 in.)
c. Seat contact area width:
   2.40 mm (.094 in.)
30°. Angle of correction chamfer
45°. Angle of valve seat contact area

Fig. 5-28. Dimensions for finished exhaust valve seat.

6. Using a 30° hand seat cutter or a 30° grinding stone, chamfer the seats so that the contact areas are narrowed to the widths specified in Fig. 5-27 or Fig. 5-28.

CAUTION ——

Do not neglect narrowing the valve seats to specifications. Overly wide seats produced by using only a 45° cutter or stone tend to trap carbon particles and other deposits.

To hand-lap valves and seats:

1. Lubricate the valve stem with engine oil. Coat the valve seat contact area with a small amount of valve grinding compound (available from automotive supply stores).

2. Using a suction cup tool as shown in Fig. 5-29, turn the valve clockwise and counterclockwise against the seat. Lift the valve off the seat every few turns to avoid cutting concentric grooves into the seat.

Fig. 5-29. Suction cup tool used to turn valve against seat, as indicated by the curved double arrow.

3. Clean away every trace of grinding compound. Inspect the valve and the seat. There should be a uniform dull-gray band completely around the valve facing and the seat contact area.

4. To check the valve seating, lightly coat the valve facing with Prussian blue. Then install the valve. While applying light pressure to the valve, rotate the valve about a quarter turn against its seat.

5. Remove the valve and examine the contact pattern. If the seating is correct, the valve will leave an even coating of Prussian blue on the seat. If it does not, either the valve is warped and must be replaced or the seat must be reconditioned with greater care.

6. LUBRICATION SYSTEM

Oil pressure for the lubrication system is supplied by a gear-type oil pump that is located inside the engine's crank case. The oil from the pump passes through a full-flow oil filter before it reaches the moving parts of the engine. Instructions for replacing the oil filter are given in **LUBRICATION AND MAINTENANCE.**

Fig. 6-1 is a schematic view of the lubrication system. In the event that the filter becomes plugged, the filter bypass valve permits oil to bypass the filter and reach the engine's bearings until a new filter can be installed. Whenever the pressure in the system exceeds a predetermined level, the pressure relief valve opens to return oil to the crankcase. By doing so, the pressure relief valve prevents over-pressurization of the system, which could increase oil consumption or burst the filter. To ensure that pressure indications accurately reflect the pressure of the entire system, the oil pressure switch is installed in the part of the system that is most remote from the pump. The switch closes when oil pressure falls below a predetermined level, thereby causing the oil warning light in the instrument panel to light up.

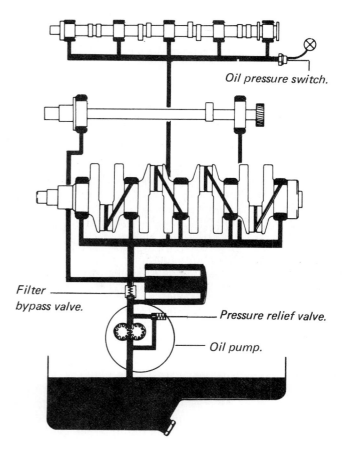

Fig. 6-1. Schematic view of the lubrication system. Pressure relief valve is integral with pump.

6.1 Testing and Replacing Oil Pressure Switch

The oil pressure switch is located at the rear of the cylinder head. If the oil pressure warning light in the instrument panel fails to light when the ignition is turned on (engine not running), check the bulb for the warning light and replace it if necessary. If the bulb is not burned out, turn on the ignition. Then remove the wire from the oil pressure switch and ground the wire against a clean, unpainted metal part of the engine. If the warning light comes on, the pressure switch is defective and must be replaced. If the light fails to come on, the wiring is faulty. Troubleshoot faulty wiring using the wiring diagrams given in **ELECTRICAL SYSTEM.**

If the oil pressure warning light comes on while the engine is operating, and if the oil level in the crankcase is correct, test the accuracy of the oil pressure switch before you assume that there is trouble in the lubrication system.

To test the oil pressure switch, remove the switch from the cylinder head. Then install a pressure gauge (Fig. 6-2) that has a T-fitting or other provision for the installation of the switch. Ground the switch housing and connect the warning light wire to the terminal on the switch. The warning light should come on when the ignition is turned on (engine not running).

Fig. 6-2. Pressure gauge installed in place of oil pressure switch. The switch has been installed in the base of the gauge. Wire **A** goes to warning light; wire **B** goes to ground.

Start the engine; if there is no pressure, immediately stop the engine. On cars built prior to VW Chassis No. _ _6 2074 222 and Audi Chasis No. _ _6 2050 000, the warning light should go out when the gauge indicates a

pressure of 0.3 to 0.6 kg/cm² (4.3 to 8.5 psi)—or more. On cars with these or later Chassis Nos., the warning light should go out when the gauge indicates a pressure of 0.15 to 0.45 kg/cm² (2.1 to 6.4 psi)—or more.

If the light stays on despite adequate oil pressure, replace the switch. Torque the switch to 1.0 mkg (7 ft. lb.). With SAE 10W oil at an oil temperature of 60°C (140°F), the minimum permissible pressure at 2000 rpm is 2.0 atu (28 psi). If the pressure is less, remove and inspect the oil pump.

6.2 Removing, Checking, and Installing Oil Pump

Because the oil pump is housed inside the crankcase, you must remove the oil pan before you can remove the pump. Also, the subframe for the front suspension must be partially removed so that the oil pan can be lowered from the engine.

To remove and check oil pump:

1. To support the engine while the subframe is off, install a support on the lug at the rear of the cylinder head as shown in Fig. 6-3. Then remove the two nuts that hold the side engine mounts on the subframe and the four bolts that hold the subframe on the body. If necessary, consult **SUSPENSION AND STEERING.**

Fig. 6-3. Support bar installed across engine compartment. A threaded rod attaches the support bar to the lug on the cylinder head.

2. Pull the subframe downward, disengaging it from the side engine mounts and the car body.

NOTE——

The stabilizer bar for the front suspension and the front suspension track control arms remain attached to the subframe and will support the subframe while it is unbolted from the engine and the body.

3. Place a receptacle of at least one gallon (or four liters or one Imperial gallon) capacity beneath the engine. Then remove the oil drain plug and allow the engine oil to drain into the receptacle. If necessary, consult **LUBRICATION AND MAINTENANCE.**

4. Using a 5-mm hex driver on a 175 or 200-mm (7 or 8-in.) extension, remove the socket head pan screws and their washers as shown in Fig. 6-4.

Fig. 6-4. Oil pan screws being removed.

5. Remove the oil pan from the engine. If the pan is stuck in place with sealer, tap the sides of the pan with a rubber mallet to break the pan free with a tilting motion.

6. Remove the two socket head pump-mounting bolts. Then remove the oil pump from the engine, leaving the oil pump's pickup tube attached.

7. With the oil pump on the workbench, remove the pickup tube from the pump body.

8. Using feeler gauges of various thicknesses, determine the backlash clearance between the pump gears as shown in Fig. 6-5. The clearance should be between 0.05 and 0.20 mm (.002 and .008 in.). If the clearance is greater, replace the gears or replace the pump.

9. Using a machinist's square and feeler gauges of various thicknesses, determine the axial play of the oil pump gears as shown in Fig. 6-6. If the play exceeds 0.15 mm (.006 in.), replace the pump.

Fig. 6-5. Feeler gauges being used to determine backlash.

Fig. 6-6. Gear axial play being measured.

To install oil pump:

1. Assemble the pump (Fig. 6-7). Torque the bolts that hold the pickup tube to the housing to 1.0 mkg (7 ft. lb.).

2. Thoroughly clean the mating surfaces of the oil pump and the engine block. Turn the drive gearshaft until it is positioned to engage the distributor drive gear. Then install the pump and torque the socket head mounting bolts to 2.0 mkg (14 ft. lb.).

3. Clean the mating surfaces of the engine block and the oil pan. Then, using a new gasket, install the oil pan on the engine block. Torque the socket head screws to 1.0 mkg (7 ft. lb.). Wait several minutes for the gasket to compress, then re-torque to the same specification.

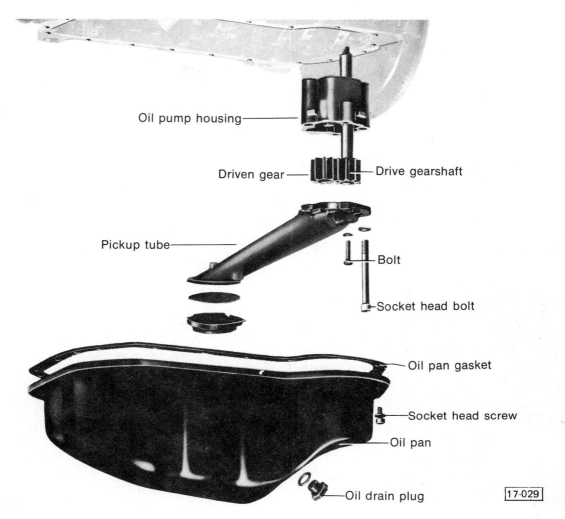

Oil pump housing

Driven gear — Drive gearshaft

Pickup tube

Bolt

Socket head bolt

Oil pan gasket

Socket head screw

Oil pan

Oil drain plug

17-029

Fig. 6-7. Relative positions of parts in oil pump.

3

4. Install the subframe. Torque the four bolts to 7.0 mkg (50 ft. lb.). Torque the engine mount nuts to 4.0 mkg (29 ft. lb.). Then check and, if necessary, adjust the front wheel alignment as described in **SUSPENSION AND STEERING**.

7. REMOVING AND INSTALLING ENGINE

Though it is possible to remove the oil pan and the cylinder head so that the pistons and connecting rods can be removed and installed with the engine in the car, more extensive engine reconditioning should be performed only with the engine removed. The engine can be removed separately, as described here, or the engine and the transmission can be removed as a unit together with the front suspension subframe as described in **SUSPENSION AND STEERING**. Fig. 7-1 shows the locations of components that must be either removed or disconnected preparatory to engine removal. Each numbered location in the illustration corresponds to the numbered step in the following procedure wherein the removal or disconnecting of the component is described.

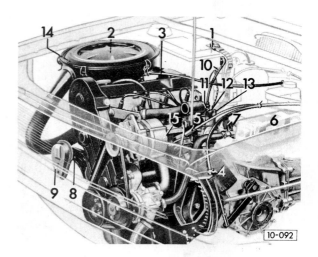

Fig. 7-1. Locations of components that must be removed or disconnected preparatory to engine removal.

To remove engine:

1. Disconnect the battery ground strap. Drain the oil. On 1978 and later cars with air conditioning, remove the battery.

2. Pull the intake air preheating duct and the crankcase ventilation hose off the air cleaner. Release the five clips, then remove the air cleaner cover and filter. Remove the nut from the air cleaner mounting bolt and remove the air cleaner. Air cleaner servicing is covered in **LUBRICATION AND MAINTENANCE.**

3. Pull off the spring clip, then disconnect the accelerator cable from the carburetor or the throttle valve housing.

4. Loosen the upper clutch cable adjusting nut. Then pull the cable down and unhook it from the clutch operating lever. Disengage the cable housing from the bracket on the engine mount.

5. Disconnect the fuel hose that connects the engine with the tank. Use a punch, pencil, or golf tee to plug the hose so that gasoline does not drain out.

WARNING ——

Do not smoke or work near heaters or other fire hazards. Have a fire extinguisher handy.

6. Remove the fuse box mounting screws and then bend open the clip for the wiring harness. Tie the fuse box, clutch cable, and fuel hose up and out of the way in the rear of the engine compartment.

7. Pull off the spring clip, then disconnect the heater control cable from the water valve lever.

8. Completely remove the front engine mount.

9. Completely remove the front engine mount support.

NOTE ——

As you disconnect each of the following wires, attach a tag or numbered piece of tape to the wire so that the wire can be returned to the correct terminal during engine installation.

10. At the ignition coil, disconnect the high tension cable from terminal 4 and the wires from terminals 1 and 15.

11. Disconnect the wire from the oil pressure switch.

12. Disconnect the wires from the ignition distributor. Where applicable, disconnect the computer analysis wire that is attached to the No. 1 cylinder's spark plug cable.

13. Disconnect the wire from the temperature gauge sending unit.

14. Disconnect the wire from the electromagnetic cutoff valve that is on the carburetor.

15. By pulling out the multiple connector plug, disconnect the wires from the alternator. On 1978 and later cars with air conditioning, fully remove the alternator.

16. Disconnect the wires (not indicated in Fig. 7-1) from the radiator cooling fan motor and the thermo switch on the radiator. On fuel injection cars, disconnect the wires from all fuel injection components mounted on the engine.

17. Remove the radiator cap. Place one receptacle for catching the draining coolant beneath the radiator and another receptacle beneath the engine, just ahead of the starter. Remove the radiator drain plug and the drain plug indicated in Fig. 7-2. Allow the coolant to drain from the engine and the radiator.

CAUTION ——

Never drain the coolant while the engine is hot. Doing this could warp the engine block or the cylinder head.

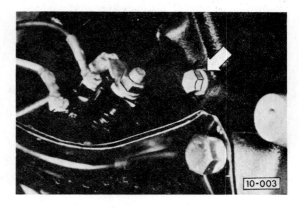

Fig. 7-2. Engine block drain plug (arrow), located just ahead of the starter. Torque to 3.5 mkg (25 ft. lb.) during installation.

18. On carburetor engined cars with air conditioning only, remove the horn, the air conditioner compressor, and the condensers, and disconnect the vacuum hoses. Move the air conditioner components out of the way as shown in Fig. 7-3. On cars with fuel injection, carry out the work described in Fig. 7-4, Fig. 7-5, or Fig. 7-6.

CAUTION ——

Do not disconnect any of the refrigerant lines. Disconnecting the lines will result in a loss of refrigerant and will make necessary extensive servicing of the air conditioning system.

Fig. 7-3. Air conditioning components partially removed from carburetor engine. Compressor is at **K**, condensers are at **C**.

Fig. 7-4. Air conditioning components partially removed from 1975-1977 fuel injection engine (first step). Remove intake air duct from injection system, dismount condenser (**C**) and store in a safe place. Then remove radiator with electric fan.

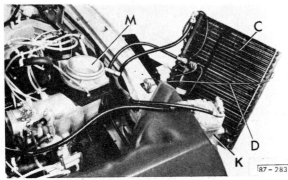

Fig. 7-5. Air conditioning components partially removed from 1975-1977 fuel injection engine (second step). Remove air cleaner, intake air distributor, and fuel metering unit (**M**); store them in a safe place. Remove EGR valve and horn. Then dismount compressor (**K**). Move compressor and condenser (**C**) out of way, suspending condenser with wire (**D**).

3

Fig. 7-6. Air conditioning components partially removed from 1978 or later fuel injection engine. Remove clamp that holds compressor-to-evaporator refrigerant hose, then temporarily route hose around intake air distributor. Unbolt compressor together with mounting bracket; unbolt condensers. Move compressor and condensers aside and tie in out-of-way positions as shown.

NOTE ——

The fuel metering unit and the intake air distributor may be located differently on your car. For further information about removing fuel injection components, please consult **FUEL AND EXHAUST SYSTEMS.**

19. Remove the radiator hoses and the heater hoses as described in **4.1 Replacing Hoses.** Remove the radiator, fan, and related parts as described in **4.5 Removing and Installing Radiator, Cooling Fan, and Air Ducts.**

20. If it is necessary to accommodate the hoist you will use to lift out the engine, remove the hood as described in **BODY AND INTERIOR.**

21. Working under the car, disconnect the wires and the battery cable from the starter solenoid. Then unbolt the starter and remove it.

22. Remove the four nuts that hold the exhaust pipe on the exhaust manifold (Fig. 7-7). During installation, torque these nuts to 2.5 mkg (18 ft. lb.).

Fig. 7-7. Nuts that hold exhaust pipe on manifold.

23. Remove the nuts indicated in Fig. 7-8. During installation, torque these nuts to 4.0 mkg (29 ft. lb.).

Fig. 7-8. Nuts (arrows) that hold the left side and right side engine mounts to the front suspension subframe.

24. On cars with automatic transmissions only, hand-turn the crankshaft so that the bolts that hold the torque converter on the drive plate are accessible, one at a time, through the starter hole in the bellhousing. Then remove all three bolts. During installation, torque these bolts to 3.0 mkg (22 ft. lb.).

25. Loosen the upper bolts that mount the engine on the transmission. Completely remove the lower bolts that hold the engine on the transmission.

26. Install a support bar beneath the bellhousing on the transmission case (Fig. 7-9). The transmission must be thus supported when you later remove the upper bolts that hold the engine on the transmission.

Fig. 7-9. Support bar in place beneath transmission.

27. With the car standing on its wheels, attach a chain sling to the engine as shown in Fig. 7-10. Hook the sling onto the hoist that you will use to lift out the engine.

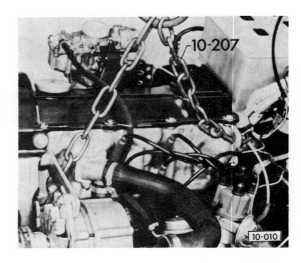

Fig. 7-10. Chain sling attached to lugs on head and block.

28. Raise the engine and transmission assembly until the transmission contacts the steering rack housing. Use the threaded adjustment on the support bar to support the transmission in this position. Then remove the upper bolts that hold the engine on the transmission.

29. Carefully pry the engine loose from the transmission. Then remove the intermediate plate.

30. On cars with manual transmission, pull the engine straight forward until the transmission mainshaft is out of the clutch driven disk. On all models, rotate the front of the engine toward the left side of the car. Then, being careful not to damage any body or mechanical parts, lift out the engine as shown in Fig. 7-11.

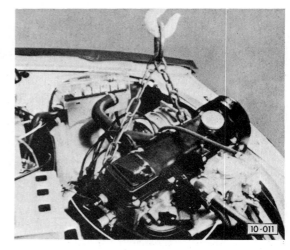

Fig. 7-11. Engine being lifted out of car.

31. On cars with automatic transmission, immediately install a metal strap across the bellhousing to keep the torque converter from falling out.

Before you install the engine in a car with an automatic transmission, make certain that the torque converter has not slipped off its support inside the bellhousing (Fig. 7-12). On cars with manual transmissions, you should check and lubricate the clutch as described in **9. Clutch and Flywheel** before you install the engine.

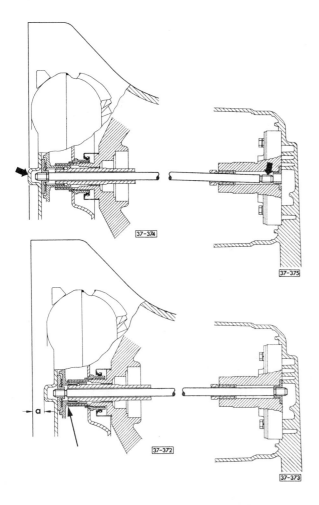

Fig. 7-12. Torque converter positions. Top: converter slipped off support; pilot projects at left arrow, pump driveshaft may be disengaged as at right arrow. Bottom: converter correctly positioned on support (arrow); dimension **a** should be 30 mm (1³/₁₆ in.).

Engine installation is the reverse of removal. Check the dowels that align the engine with the transaxle. Replace damaged dowels. Stick the intermediate plate to the engine with grease so that the plate will not fall off the dowels. Then install the engine. On cars with manual transmissions, hand-turn the crankshaft to mesh the clutch with the transmission's mainshaft.

NOTE

During installation, align the front engine mount and support (Fig. 7-13) so that the rubber buffer has a clearance of approximately 1 mm (or ¹/₃₂ in.) and does not touch the sides of the housing. Also check the alignment of the transmission rear mount as described in **MANUAL TRANSMISSION** or **AUTOMATIC TRANSMISSION**. If necessary, you can reposition the engine on its side mountings by loosening the nuts and moving the side mountings in the elongated holes in the subframe.

Fig. 7-13. Correct installation of front engine mount and support.

Torque the bolts that hold the engine to the transmission to 5.5 mkg (40 ft. lb.). Torque the side engine mount nuts to 4.0 mkg (29 ft. lb.) and the front engine mount bolts to 2.5 mkg (18 ft. lb.). Install the radiator and heater hoses as described in **4.1 Replacing Hoses.** Adjust clutch pedal freeplay to 15 mm (⅝ in.) as described in **9.3 Servicing and Repairing Clutch.**

On 1973 through 1978 cars with air conditioning, torque the bolts and the nuts that hold the compressor bracket to the engine to 3.0 mkg (22 ft. lb.). The 1978 cars have a belt tension adjusting bolt (Fig. 7-14), and the 1979 cars have belt tension adjusting shims (Fig. 7-15). On 1979 cars, use the torque specifications given in Fig. 7-15. On 1979 models, adjust the V-belt tension until thumb pressure deflects the belt by 5 to 10 mm (¼ to ⅜ in.); on earlier models, the deflection is specified at about 10 mm (⅜ in.).

In tightening the belt of a 1979 model, place any shim removed from between the pulley halves at the storage point indicated in Fig. 7-15. By doing this you will keep all of the shims supplied with the car available for future use. (Shims must be moved from the storage point to a position between the pulley halves to reduce belt tension, as may be necessary later when a new V-belt is installed.)

Fill the radiator and the crankcase as specified in **LUBRICATION AND MAINTENANCE**. Adjust the ignition timing as described in **3.3 Adjusting Timing**. Then adjust the idle mixture and rpm as described in **FUEL AND EXHAUST SYSTEMS**.

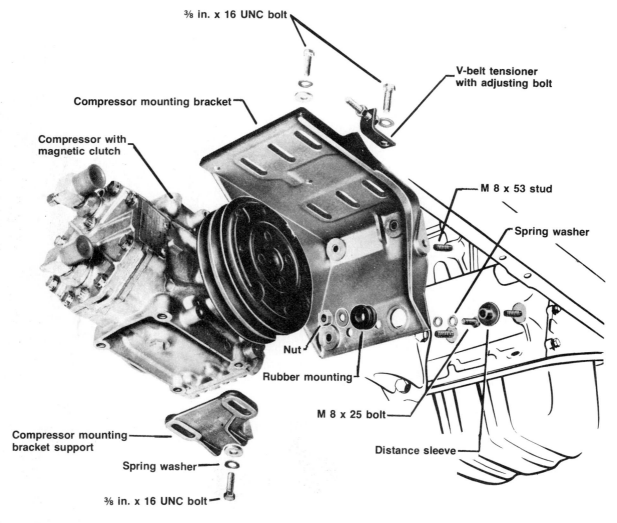

Fig. 7-14. Exploded view of air conditioning compressor installation on 1978 car. Torque all bolts and nuts to 3.0 mkg (22 ft. lb.).

87-498

3

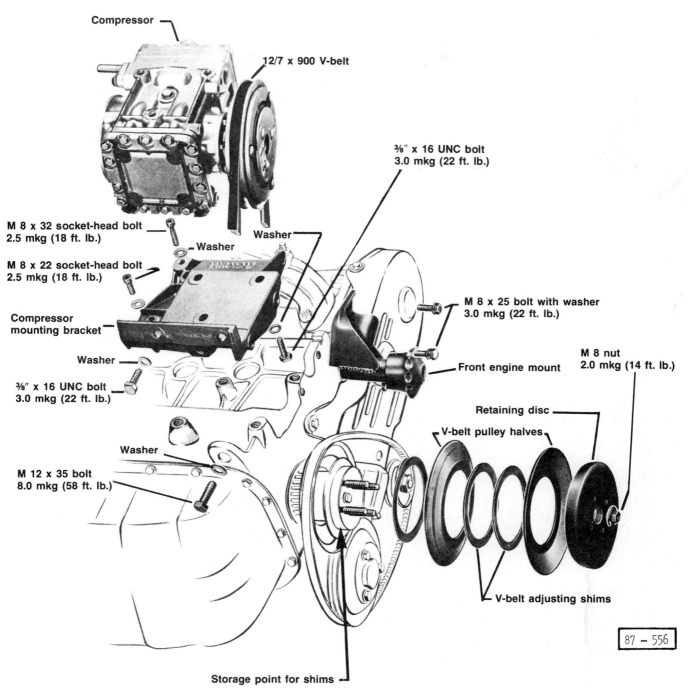

Compressor

12/7 x 900 V-belt

⅜″ x 16 UNC bolt
3.0 mkg (22 ft. lb.)

M 8 x 32 socket-head bolt
2.5 mkg (18 ft. lb.)

Washer

Washer

M 8 x 22 socket-head bolt
2.5 mkg (18 ft. lb.)

Compressor
mounting bracket

M 8 x 25 bolt with washer
3.0 mkg (22 ft. lb.)

Washer

M 8 nut
2.0 mkg (14 ft. lb.)

⅜″ x 16 UNC bolt
3.0 mkg (22 ft. lb.)

Front engine mount

Retaining disc

V-belt pulley halves

Washer

M 12 x 35 bolt
8.0 mkg (58 ft. lb.)

V-belt adjusting shims

87 – 556

Storage point for shims

Fig. 7-15. Exploded view of air conditioning compressor
installation on 1979 cars. Bolt torques are
given in illustration.

8. TORQUE CONVERTER AND DRIVE PLATE

Cars equipped with automatic transmissions have a torque converter instead of a clutch, and a drive plate rather than a conventional flywheel. The converter is held to the drive plate by three bolts that are taken out when the engine is removed. Torque converter repair and replacement is covered in **AUTOMATIC TRANSMISSION.**

8.1 Removing and Installing Drive Plate

When you must disassemble the engine, remove the drive plate before you remove the crankshaft. The drive plate can also be removed and installed with the transmission removed and the engine in the car. Two kinds of drive plates have been used, as shown in Fig. 8-1. The new kind of drive plate can be installed on earlier engines if you also replace the engine's rear oil seal carrier and the drive plate washer.

Previous torque converter drive plate

New torque converter drive plate

13-195

Fig. 8-1. New and previous drive plates.

To remove:

1. Mark the drive plate so that you can install it in the exact original position on the crankshaft.

2. Install a drive plate holding fixture—a dog that engages the starter ring gear teeth—on the engine. Alternatively, use coat hanger wire to bind a bolt hole in the drive plate to a bolt hole in the engine block's transmission mounting flange.

3. Remove the six bolts and the washer that hold the drive plate to the crankshaft. Then remove the drive plate.

To install:

1. If the crankshaft oil seal is leaking, replace the seal as described in **11.1 Replacing Crankshaft and Intermediate Shaft Oil Seals.**

2. With reference to the marks made prior to removal, install the drive plate on the crankshaft. Install the washer and two of the six bolts, then check dimension **a** as shown in Fig. 8-2.

3. If dimension **a,** measured in step 2, is less than 31.30 mm ± 0.80 mm (1.232 in. ± .031 in.), install a shim or shims between the drive plate and the crankshaft to bring dimension **a** within tolerance. See Fig. 8-3. If dimension **a** exceeds the specified range, and there are no shims that can be removed from between the drive plate and the crankshaft, check the drive plate and replace it if there is excessive runout or other distortion.

13-042

Fig. 8-2. Dimension **a** being measured with a depth gauge.

Fig. 8-3. Drive plate installation. Washer is at **1**; shim is at **2**.

4. Clean and dry all six drive plate mounting bolts and mounting bolt holes.

5. With the drive plate holding fixture in place, apply an even coating of Loctite⑪ 270 or 271 to the bolt threads. Then install all six drive plate mounting bolts and torque them to 7.5 mkg (54 ft. lb.).

6. Remove the drive plate holding fixture.

9. CLUTCH AND FLYWHEEL

The pressure plate assembly and driven plate remain on the flywheel when you remove the engine. The clutch release bearing and related parts stay in the transmission.

9.1 Removing, Checking, and Installing Clutch Plates

When you must disassemble the engine, remove the clutch and flywheel before you remove the crankshaft. The clutch and flywheel can also be removed and installed with the transmission removed and the engine in the car.

3

To remove:

1. To ensure proper reinstallation, mark the flywheel and pressure plate assembly as shown in Fig. 9-1.

Fig. 9-1. Marks on flywheel and pressure plate. The flywheel is held with locking fixture 10-201.

2. Loosen the pressure plate mounting bolts (Fig. 9-2) a quarter turn at a time. Work around the flywheel until the pressure is relieved, then remove the bolts completely.

3. Remove the pressure plate assembly from the dowels on the flywheel. As you do so, catch the driven plate and remove it also.

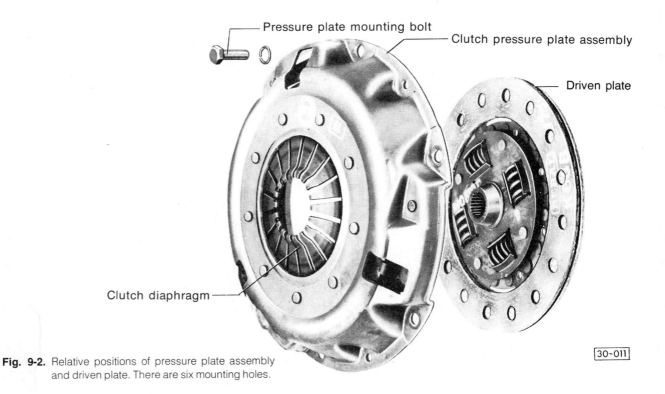

Pressure plate mounting bolt

Clutch pressure plate assembly

Driven plate

Clutch diaphragm

30-011

Fig. 9-2. Relative positions of pressure plate assembly and driven plate. There are six mounting holes.

To check and install:

1. Inspect the levers on the diaphragm spring (Fig. 9-3). If they are out of line with one another, or scored deeper than 0.30 mm (0.12 in.), replace the pressure plate assembly.

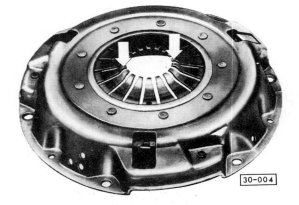

30-004

Fig. 9-3. Levers (arrows) on diaphragm spring.

2. Thoroughly clean the pressure plate assembly. Then inspect the straps that connect the pressure plate with the pressure plate assembly cover. If any strap is cracked or broken, or if any rivet (arrows in Fig. 9-4) is loose or missing, replace the pressure plate assembly.

Fig. 9-4. Rivets (arrows) that hold together the main parts of the pressure plate assembly.

3. Clean the friction surface on the flywheel and inspect it for wear, cracks, and grooves. Maximum permissible runout, measured at the center of the friction suface, is 0.08 mm (.003 in.). Minor defects may be correctable by grinding at a specialty shop. If the flywheel is unserviceable, replace it.

4. Inspect the pressure plate friction surface for wear, cracks, grooves, and burned (blued) areas. Alternately bright and dull areas indicate a warped plate. Shake the pressure plate assembly. The diaphragm spring should be under tension and should not rattle loosely. Lay a straightedge across the friction surface as shown in Fig. 9-5. Using feeler gauges of various thicknesses, determine the amount of inward taper on the surface. If inward taper exceeds 0.30 mm (.012 in.), replace the pressure plate assembly.

Fig. 9-5. Pressure plate being checked for inward taper.

5. Check the driven plate for wear. There should be at least 2.00 mm (about $^1/_{16}$ in.) of friction material remaining above the rivet heads. When checked at a diameter of 175 mm (6 $^7/_8$ in.), as shown in Fig. 9-6, runout should not exceed 0.40 mm (.016 in.).

Fig. 9-6. Dial indicator being used to measure driven plate runout. Rotate plate, note gauge movement.

6. Inspect the splines in the driven plate and on the transmission's mainshaft. The splines must not be broken or distorted. Lubricate the splines with molybdenum disulfide powder. Then see that the driven plate slides freely on the mainshaft without undue radial play. If the driven plate is in any way unserviceable, replace it.

7. Clean, inspect, and lubricate the pilot bearing, which is in the center of the crankshaft, as described in **9.2 Removing and Installing Flywheel.**

8. Inspect the clutch release bearing. If it feels gritty when you turn it, or if it has been making noise, replace it. Never wash the bearing in solvent since doing this will remove the factory-installed lubricant. If the release bearing is unserviceable, replace it as described in **9.3 Servicing and Repairing Clutch.**

9. Using a centering tool (Fig. 9-7) or a spare transmission mainshaft, install the driven plate against the flywheel. Then, aligning the marks you made on the flywheel and pressure plate assembly prior to removal, loosely install the pressure plate assembly on the flywheel using all six bolts.

NOTE ——

On some replacement pressure plate assemblies a white paint spot is used as a balance mark. This should be positioned 180° from the 5-mm (³/₁₆-in.) countersunk hole or from the white paint balance mark on the flywheel.

10. Working diagonally, tighten the pressure plate mounting bolts a turn or two at a time until the pressure plate assembly cover contacts the flywheel. Then torque the bolts to 2.5 mkg (18 ft. lb.).

Fig. 9-7. Centering tool used to align driven plate with pilot bearing. Alignment marks, made prior to clutch plate removal, are circled.

9.2 Removing and Installing Flywheel

The clutch pressure plate assembly and the clutch driven plate must be removed before you can remove the flywheel. See **9.1 Removing, Checking, and Installing Clutch Plates.**

To remove flywheel:

1. Mark the flywheel so that you can install it in its exact original position on the crankshaft.

2. Install a flywheel-holding fixture—a dog that engages the starter ring gear teeth, shown earlier in Fig. 9-1—on the engine. Alternatively, use coat hanger wire to bind a partially-installed clutch pressure plate mounting bolt to a bolt hole in the engine block's transmission mounting flange.

3. Remove the six bolts that hold the flywheel to the crankshaft. Then remove the flywheel.

To install:

1. If you are installing a replacement flywheel, it may have only a TDC (top dead center) mark (**0**). If so, measure off 7 mm (⁹/₃₂ in.) as shown in Fig. 9-8, then cut a 3° BTDC (before top dead center) ignition timing mark into the new flywheel.

Fig. 9-8. Cutting timing mark on replacement flywheel. Dimension **a** is 7 mm (⁹/₃₂ in.). Cut the timing mark with a sharp cold chisel.

2. If the crankshaft oil seal is leaking, replace the seal as described in **11.1 Replacing Crankshaft and Intermediate Shaft Oil Seals.**

3. Using solvent, clean the pilot bearing that is in the center of the crankshaft. Check to see that the needles are not flattened by wear. If the bearing is undamaged, pack the needles with 1 gram ($1/_{32}$ oz.) of multipurpose grease (just enough to coat all needles lightly). If the bearing is damaged, remove it as shown in Fig. 9-9. Using an appropriate bushing driver, drive in a new bearing, lettered end outward, until it is seated as indicated in Fig. 9-10. Then lubricate the new bearing as just described.

Fig. 9-9. Pilot bearing being removed with puller 10-202.

Fig. 9-10. Needle bearing correctly installed so it is recessed in crankshaft. Dimension **a** is 1.5 mm ($1/_{16}$ in.).

4. Clean and dry all six flywheel mounting bolts and mounting bolt holes.

5. With reference to the marks that you made prior to removal, install the flywheel on the crankshaft.

6. Install the flywheel holding fixture as shown previously in Fig. 9-1. Alternatively, use coat hanger wire to bind a partially-installed pressure plate mounting bolt on the flywheel to a bolt hole in the engine block's transmission mounting flange.

7. Apply an even coating of Loctite® 270 or 271 to the bolt threads. Then install all six flywheel mounting bolts and torque them to 7.5 mkg (54 ft. lb.).

8. Remove the flywheel holding fixture.

9.3 Servicing and Repairing Clutch

Clutch servicing and repair is limited to adjustment and to the replacement of faulty parts. Replacement parts are not available for rebuilding the pressure plate assembly or the driven plate. Used properly and kept in adjustment, the clutch should give reliable service for the life of the car.

Adjusting Clutch Pedal Freeplay

As the clutch linings wear, the clearance between the release bearing and the release levers is reduced. If this condition progresses until there is no clearance at all, clutch pressure will decrease and permit slippage that can lead to burned linings. When checking for the proper clearance, you should be able to depress the clutch pedal about 15 mm (⅝ in.) before you encounter working resistance. If not, adjust the clutch cable to obtain the prescribed amount of freeplay.

3

To adjust the cable, raise the hood and locate the adjusting nuts (Fig. 9-11) that are just ahead of the oil filter. To increase clutch pedal freeplay, loosen the adjusting nut that is on top of the bracket, then tighten the nut that is beneath the bracket. To reduce clutch pedal freeplay, loosen the nut that is beneath the bracket, then tighten the nut that is on top of the bracket. Make the adjustment by turning each nut two or three turns at a time. Then recheck the freeplay at the clutch pedal and make further adjustments as required. When you have

Fig. 9-11. Clutch cable adjusting nuts. Adjust to obtain pedal freeplay of 15 mm (⅝ in.).

obtained the correct 15-mm (⅝-in.) freeplay at the pedal, tighten the nut that is on top of the bracket so that the washers grip the bracket firmly.

Replacing Clutch Cable

To replace the clutch cable, loosen the adjusting nuts so that you can disengage the clutch cable housing from the bracket that is on the engine mount. With the housing disengaged from the bracket, unhook the cable end from the clutch operating lever that is on the side of the transmission bellhousing. The relative position of these parts is shown in Fig. 9-12. Working beneath the dashboard, unhook the cable end from the clutch pedal. Then pull the cable and its housing out of the firewall and into the passenger compartment. After you have installed a replacement cable, following the reverse of the removal procedure, adjust the clutch pedal freeplay to 15 mm (⅝ in.) as previously described. If you have installed a new cable, again check the clutch pedal freeplay after 300 mi. (500 km) of driving and, if necessary, correct the freeplay.

Replacing Clutch Release Bearing

The clutch release bearing is a maintenance-free part. However, it can be damaged by inadequate clutch pedal freeplay, careless driving, or improper cleaning.

CAUTION ——
Never wash the clutch release bearing in solvent. Doing so will remove the factory-installed lubricant.

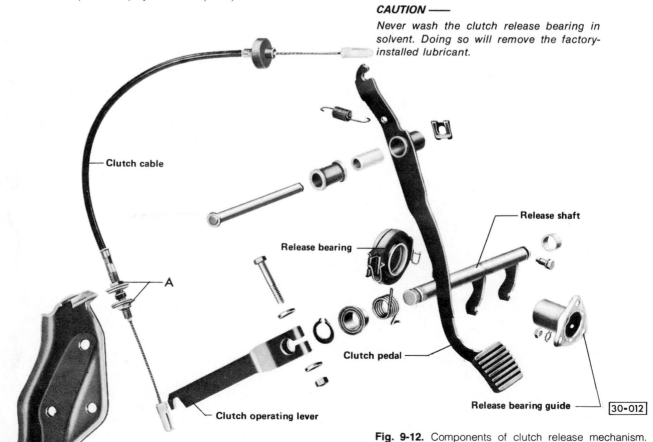

- Clutch cable
- A
- Clutch operating lever
- Release bearing
- Clutch pedal
- Release shaft
- Release bearing guide
- 30-012

Fig. 9-12. Components of clutch release mechanism. Cable adjustment is indicated at **A**.

If the release bearing is noisy, replace it. In doing so, either the engine or the transmission must be removed from the car. See **7. Removing and Installing Engine** or **MANUAL TRANSMISSION.** Then, using a screwdriver, pry off the spring clips that hold the clutch release bearing on the arms of the clutch operating shaft. Slide the release bearing off the release bearing guide sleeve.

NOTE ——

The clutch operating shaft is located in the transmission bellhousing. Removal, installation, and repair of the operating shaft and its bearings are covered in **MANUAL TRANS-MISSION.**

Wipe clean the release bearing, the operating shaft, and other parts in the bellhousing. Do not wash the parts with solvent. Lightly lubricate the operating shaft bushings with multipurpose grease. If the transaxle has a steel guide sleeve, lubricate it with molybdenum grease. Also rub a small amount of molybdenum grease onto the facing on the release bearing that will contact the release levers of the clutch pressure plate assembly. If the transaxle has the plastic guide sleeve introduced with Transmission No. __ 16 10 5, do not lubricate the sleeve.

Install the release bearing on the guide sleeve. Then, using the spring clips, attach the bearing to the arms of the clutch operating shaft. Replace loose-fitting spring clips. After you have installed the engine or the transmission, adjust the clutch pedal freeplay.

Clutch Troubleshooting

Road testing is an important part of troubleshooting the clutch because it lets you base your diagnosis on first-hand information. For example, trouble described as "lack of power" might be caused by a slipping clutch and not inadequate engine output. Similarly, a complaint that "it's hard to shift gears" may mean a dragging clutch, not transmission trouble. **Table f** lists the most common clutch complaints, their probable causes, and suggested repairs. The numbers in bold type in the Suggested Repair column refer to the headings in this section where the repairs are described.

3

Table f. Clutch Troubleshooting

Problem	Probable Cause	Suggested Repair
1. Clutch noise	a. Pilot bearing worn	a. Replace pilot bearing; lubricate with 1 gram (1/32 oz.) multipurpose grease. See **9.2.**
	b. Driven plate fouling pressure plate	b. Replace driven plate. See **9.1.**
	c. Diaphragm spring weak or tension uneven	c. Replace pressure plate assembly. See **9.1.**
	d. Release bearing defective	d. Replace release bearing. See **9.3.**
2. Clutch grabbing	a. Engine or transmission mountings loose	a. Tighten mounting bolts and nuts. See **7.** and **MANUAL TRANSMISSION.**
	b. Pressure plate contacting unevenly	b. Replace pressure plate assembly. See **9.1.**
	c. Driven plate spring segments deformed	c. Replace driven plate. See **9.1.**
3. Clutch dragging	a. Excessive pedal freeplay	a. Adjust pedal freeplay to 15 mm (⅝ in.). See **9.3.**
	b. Driven plate not running true	b. Replace driven plate. See **9.1.**
	c. Driven plate spring segments deformed	c. Replace driven plate. See **9.1.**
	d. Driven plate linings broken	d. Replace driven plate. See **9.1.**
	e. Mainshaft not running true with pilot bearing	e. Remove engine or transmission. Check the steel alignment dowels. Replace deformed dowels or repair holes. See **7.**
	f. Pilot bearing defective or insufficiently greased	f. Replace pilot bearing or lubricate bearing with 1 gram (1/32 oz.) of multipurpose grease. See **9.2.**
	g. Splines on mainshaft or clutch driven plate dirty or burred	g. Clean splines. Remove burrs. See **9.1.**
	h. Sticky clutch linings (lining dust)	h. Replace driven plate. See **9.1.**
	i. Stiffness in pedal bearing, clutch cable, or operating shaft	i. Grease the parts thoroughly with multipurpose grease. See **BRAKES AND WHEELS, MANUAL TRANSMISSION.**
4. Clutch slipping	a. Insufficient pedal freeplay	a. Adjust pedal freeplay to 15 mm (⅝ in.). See **9.3.**
	b. Linings worn out	b. Replace driven plate. See **9.1.**
	c. Oily linings	c. Replace driven plate. If necessary, replace engine oil seal or transmission oil seal. See **9.1, 11.1, MANUAL TRANSMISSION.**
	d. Pressure plate has lost tension	d. Replace pressure plate assembly. See **9.1.**

10. PISTONS, PISTON RINGS, AND CONNECTING RODS

Though it is possible to remove the cylinder head and the oil pan so that the connecting rods and pistons can be removed and installed with the engine in the car, such a procedure is advisable mainly for the purpose of inspecting the piston rings and connecting rod bearings. Any work that requires grinding or machining—such as removing the top-cylinder ridge or honing the cylinder bores—should be done with the engine removed and disassembled. Otherwise, abrasive dirt and metal particles will remain in the engine, causing bearing damage and rapid wear.

The components of the piston/connecting rod assembly for one cylinder of the engine are shown in Fig. 10-1.

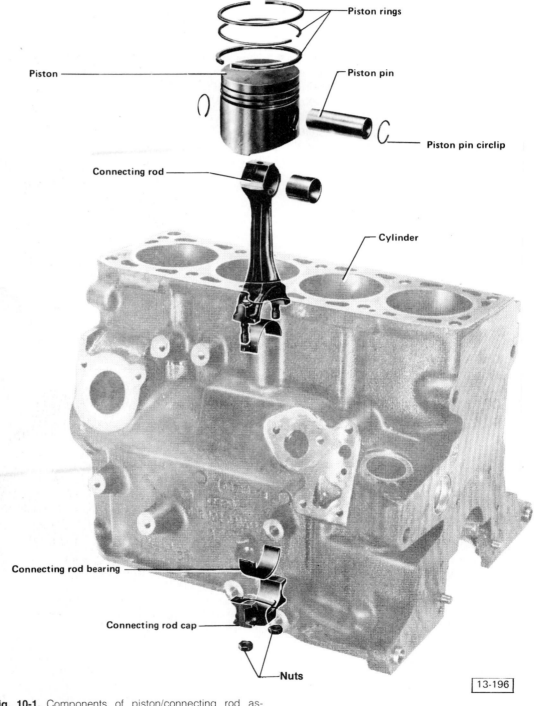

Fig. 10-1. Components of piston/connecting rod assembly.

10.1 Removing, Checking, and Installing Pistons, Piston Rings, Connecting Rods, and Connecting Rod Bearings

Because the pistons, connecting rods, and many of their related parts must be reinstalled in their original locations and positions, you should mark the parts as you remove them. Replacement parts must be selected with careful reference to the cylinder bore, the original part, and to the other parts in the piston/connecting rod assembly.

To remove, check, and install:

1. Unless you are replacing connecting rod bearings only, or are removing the piston and connecting rod for inspection purposes only, remove the engine as described in **7. Removing and Installing Engine.**

2. Remove the cylinder head as described in **5.3 Removing and Installing Cylinder Head and Manifolds.** Remove the oil pan and the oil pump as described in **6.2 Removing, Checking, and Installing Oil Pump.**

3. Mark the cylinder number on the crown of each piston. If necessary, mark arrows on the piston crowns to indicate which side of each piston is toward the front of the engine block. See Fig. 10-2.

Fig. 10-2. Cylinder numbers and forward-pointing arrows marked on piston crowns.

4. Remove the connecting rod nuts. Remove the connecting rod cap from the connecting rod bolts. Then, using a wooden hammer handle, push the piston/connecting rod assembly away

from the crankshaft and out through the top of the cylinder.

CAUTION ——

If the engine block has pronounced top-cylinder ridges, remove them with a cylinder ridge reamer before you remove the pistons. Otherwise, the piston rings and pistons may be damaged during removal. A top-cylinder ridge is a band of unworn cylinder wall that remains above the part of the cylinder that has been worn to a larger diameter by contact with the piston rings.

5. As soon as you remove each piston/connecting rod assembly, mark the cylinder number on both the rod cap and connecting rod as shown in Fig. 10-3.

Fig. 10-3. Numerals **1** (arrows) marked on the connecting rod and the rod cap for No. 1 cylinder.

6. Using needle-nosed pliers or a punch, as shown in Fig. 10-4, remove the piston pin circlips from both ends of each piston pin. Then press out the piston pin and remove the piston from the rod.

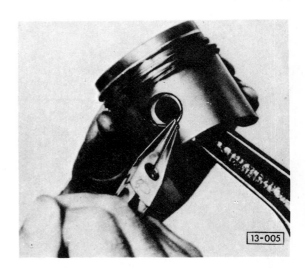

Fig. 10-4. Circlip being removed. Notice the notch in the piston where the pliers have been inserted.

7. Check each piston for wear as shown in Fig. 10-5. Measure the piston at right angles to the piston pin at a point approximately 15 mm (⅝ in.) from the lower edge of the piston skirt.

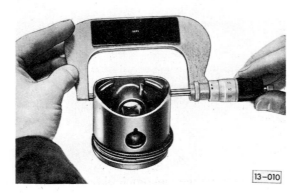

Fig. 10-5. Piston diameter being measured.

8. Compare the measurement obtained in step 7 with the nominal piston diameter that is marked on the piston crown (Fig. 10-6). This comparison will give an indication of the extent to which the piston is worn. However, you can determine whether the piston is suitable for reuse only after measuring the cylinder bore as described in step 9 of this procedure.

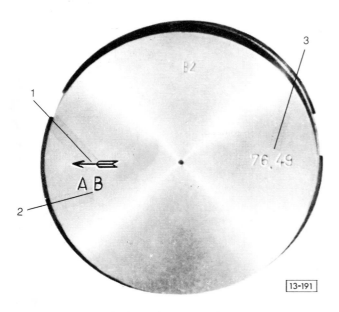

1. Arrow that must point to front of engine
2. Weight class
3. Nominal diameter in mm

Fig. 10-6. Markings on piston crown.

9. Using a dial indicator device, as shown in Fig. 10-7, determine the cylinder diameter and the degree of wear.

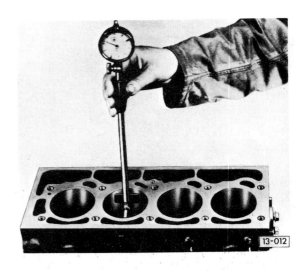

Fig. 10-7. Cylinder bore being measured with a special dial indicator.

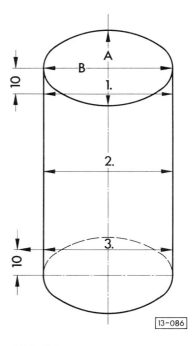

Fig. 10-8. Cylinder bore measuring points. Measurement **1** should be made 10 mm (⅜ in.) from the top of the cylinder, measurement **2** should be made in the middle of the cylinder, and measurement **3** should be made 10 mm (⅜ in.) from the bottom of the cylinder. Make each measurement first in direction **A** and then in direction **B.**

NOTE——

When checking the cylinder bores, make your measurements at three points throughout each cylinder and at right angles to one another (Fig. 10-8). Minor variations in cylinder diameter can be corrected by honing, as described in later steps of this procedure. If, however, there are variations of 0.05 mm (.002 in.) or more among the measurements made in any one cylinder, the cylinder must be rebored to accept an oversize piston.

10. Write down the largest bore diameter measurement you obtain for each of the cylinders.

11. Compare the measurements written down in step 10 with the honing group that is marked on the engine block (Fig. 10-9). This comparison will give an indication of the extent to which the cylinder is worn.

NOTE ——

If the measured bore diameter of any cylinder exceeds the largest cylinder diameter listed for the basic dimension or repair stage (as given in **Table g**) by 0.04 mm (.0015 in.) or more, all the cylinders must be rebored and honed to accept new pistons from the next larger repair stage. If the original bore diameter was at the lower limit of the basic dimension or repair group tolerance range, you can hone the cylinders to accept a larger piston from the same basic dimension or repair stage. However, your goal should always be to obtain a clearance of 0.03 mm (.001) between the pistons and the cylinders of a repaired or rebuilt engine.

Fig. 10-9. Honing group code stamped on the engine block. This number is derived from the diameter of the original cylinder bore. For example, code 653 indicates that, when manufactured, the cylinders were honed to a diameter of 76.53 mm.

3

12. Compute the clearance between the original pistons and their cylinders. To do so, subtract the measurements obtained in step 7 from the measurements that you obtained in step 9. With new parts, the clearance should be 0.03 mm (.0011 to .0012 in.). The wear limit is 0.07 mm (.0025 in.).

13. If the piston clearance exceeds the wear limit, but the cylinders are not worn to a diameter more than 0.04 mm (.0015 in.) greater than their original honing group, you can correct the clearance by

Table g. Piston and Cylinder Diameters

Engine	Repair stage	Piston diameter mm (in.)	Cylinder bore mm (in.)	Honing group
	Basic dimension	76.48 (3.0110)	76.51 (3.0122)	651
		76.49 (3.0114)	76.52 (3.0126)	652
		76.50 (3.0118)	76.53 (3.0130)	653
	Repair stage 1	76.73 (3.0209)	76.76 (3.0221)	676
		76.74 (3.0213)	76.77 (3.0224)	677
		76.75 (3.0217)	76.78 (3.0228)	678
1471 cc (89.7 cu. in.)	Repair stage 2	76.98 (3.0307)	77.01 (3.0319)	701
		76.99 (3.0311)	77.02 (3.0323)	702
		77.00 (3.0315)	77.03 (3.0327)	703
	Repair stage 3	77.48 (3.0504)	77.51 (3.0516)	751
		77.49 (3.0508)	77.52 (3.0520)	752
		77.50 (3.0512)	77.53 (3.0524)	753
	Basic dimension	79.48 (3.1291)	79.51 (3.1303)	951
		79.49 (3.1295)	79.52 (3.1307)	952
		79.50 (3.1299)	79.53 (3.1311)	953
	Repair stage 1	79.73 (3.1390)	79.76 (3.1402)	976
		79.74 (3.1394)	79.77 (3.1406)	977
		79.75 (3.1398)	79.78 (3.1409)	978
1588 cc (96.9 cu. in.)	Repair stage 2	79.98 (3.1488)	80.01 (3.1500)	001
		79.99 (3.1492)	80.02 (3.1504)	002
		80.00 (3.1496)	80.03 (3.1508)	003
	Repair stage 3	80.48 (3.1685)	80.51 (3.1697)	051
		80.49 (3.1689)	80.52 (3.1701)	052
		80.50 (3.1693)	80.53 (3.1705)	053

installing new pistons of the original diameter for the cylinder honing group, or by honing the cylinders to the next larger diameter in the same basic dimension or repair stage and then installing new pistons to match the new honing group.

14. If the piston clearance exceeds the wear limit because of cylinder wear, then the cylinders must be rebored and honed to accept new pistons from the next larger repair stage. This work can be done by your Authorized Dealer or by a qualified automotive machine shop.

15. Using feeler gauges of various sizes, determine the side clearance of all the piston rings as shown in Fig. 10-10.

NOTE ——

The piston ring side clearance should be from 0.02 to 0.05 mm (.0008 to .002 in.) with new parts. If you install new piston rings, make certain that side clearance is not less than 0.02 mm (.0008 in.). If there is too little clearance, either replace the piston or have the grooves reconditioned by your Authorized Dealer or a qualified automotive machine shop.

Fig. 10-10. Piston ring side clearance being measured. Insert the feeler gauge between the piston ring and one of the piston lands. Then move the gauge completely around the piston. The clearance must not be outside the specified range at any point.

16. Using a tool such as the one shown in Fig. 10-11, remove the piston rings from the pistons.

CAUTION ——

If you intend to install new rings, it is of no consequence if you break the rings during removal. However, if you intend to reuse the rings, you must work carefully to prevent

accidental breakage. It is imperative that used rings be reinstalled in their original grooves and on their original pistons. Otherwise, poor sealing will result—which may cause excessive oil consumption or lost power.

Fig. 10-11. Piston ring being removed from piston.

17. Push each ring about 15 mm (⅝ in.) into the bottom of its cylinder. Then measure the ring gap as shown in Fig. 10-12.

NOTE ——

Replacement rings for engines with oversize pistons must be the correct size for the oversize cylinder honing group. If you are

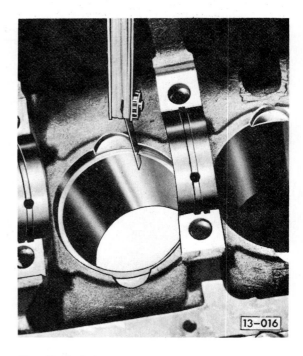

Fig. 10-12. Ring gap being measured with feeler gauge.

checking the end gaps of new rings, which you should always do, the gap should be 0.30 to 0.45 mm (.012 to .018 in.) for the upper and lower compression rings or 0.25 to 0.40 mm (.010 to .016 in.) for the oil scraper ring. If the gap is too narrow, enlarge it with a file or an oil stone. If you are checking used piston rings, the measurement obtained in step 17 must not exceed 1.00 mm (.039 in.)—which is the wear limit. Replace worn-out rings.

18. Check the piston pin fit in each piston. The pin must be a light push fit with the piston heated to approximately 60°C (140°F) in an oil bath. If not, replace both the piston and the pin.

19. Check the piston pin fit in each connecting rod. If the clearance exceeds 0.04 mm (.0015 in.), the wear limit, either replace the rod and pin or fit a new pin and a new rod bushing. Hone the new bushing to obtain a clearance of 0.01 to 0.02 mm (.0004 to .0008 in.), then check the rod's alignment. This work can be done by your Authorized Dealer or by a qualified automotive machine shop.

NOTE ——

If for any reason you replace pistons or connecting rods, all four must be of the same weight class. Connecting rod weight classes are designated by a number on the rod cap. Unmarked replacement pistons must be within 10 grams of the weight of the other pistons in the engine. Beginning early in 1975, the factory stopped supplying individual connecting rods that were marked according to weight groups. Present factory replacement rods are available only as sets of four rods of the same weight group.

20. Using the tool shown in Fig. 10-11, install the piston rings as indicated in Fig. 10-13.

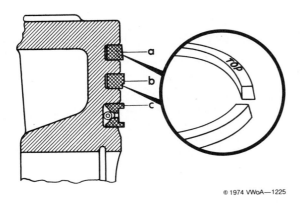

© 1974 VWoA—1225

a. Upper compression ring
b. Lower compression ring
c. Oil scraper ring

Fig. 10-13. Proper ring installation. Word TOP must be toward piston crown.

21. Install one circlip only in one end of the piston pin bore of each piston. Then heat all of the pistons to approximately 60°C (140°F) in an oil bath.

22. With reference to the cylinder numbers you marked on the pistons and connecting rods during removal, install the pistons on their original connecting rods so that, when the arrow marked on the piston crown is pointing toward the front of the engine, the marks indicated in Fig. 10-14 will be toward the engine's intermediate shaft.

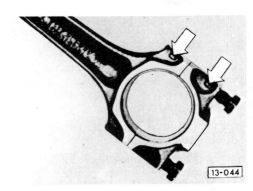

13-044

Fig. 10-14. Forged marks (arrows) that must be toward the engine's intermediate shaft with the connecting rod and piston installed in the engine.

23. Working quickly, so that the pistons do not have an opportunity to cool, hand-press the piston pins into position as shown in Fig. 10-15. Seat the pin against the circlip that you have already installed in the piston, then install the other circlip. Make sure that all circlips are firmly engaged in the grooves in the pistons.

24. If the cylinders have not been rebored, but you have installed new piston rings, inspect the cylinders to see whether there are top-cylinder ridges.

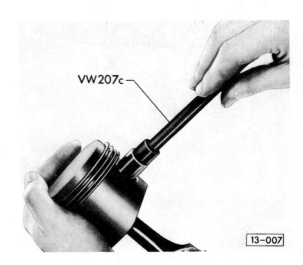

VW 207c

13-007

Fig. 10-15. Special drift being used to press piston pin into piston and connecting rod.

Remove top-cylinder ridges with a cylinder ridge reamer. Then—whether there were ridges or not—lightly hone the cylinder bores with a hone that has fine 220-grit stones. Move the spinning hone smoothly in and out of the bore to produce a fine cross-hatch pattern on the cylinder walls.

NOTE——

A top-cylinder ridge is a band of unworn cylinder wall that remains above the part of the cylinder that has been worn to a larger diameter by contact with the piston rings. If the ridge is not removed, the new upper compression ring will strike the ridge, breaking the ring and damaging the piston. The object of honing the cylinder is to remove "glaze" that could keep the new rings from seating. In breaking the glaze, remove as little metal as possible.

25. Thoroughly clean the engine block to remove metal particles and abrasive dust. Then install the crankshaft, the intermediate shaft, and their bearings and oil seals. See **11. Crankshaft and Intermediate Shaft.** Hand-turn the crankshaft to place the connecting rod journal for No. 1 cylinder at bottom dead center (BDC).

26. Thoroughly lubricate the cylinder bores and the piston rings with engine oil only. Stagger the ring gaps so that the oil scraper ring's gap will be toward the front or the rear of the engine and the other two ring's gaps will be offset 120° to each side of the scraper ring's gap. Then install a piston ring compressor on the piston for No.1 cylinder and fully compress the rings (Fig. 10-16).

Fig. 10-16. Piston ring compressor installed on piston. Rings must be pressed into their grooves so that piston can be pushed into the cylinder.

27. If previously removed, install the connecting rod bearing shells in the connecting rod and the connecting rod cap. Make sure that the anti-rotation tabs on the bearing shells engage the notches in the rod and the cap. Do not install the cap on the rod.

28. Install the piston/connecting rod assembly in the No. 1 cylinder until the piston ring compressor band contacts the engine block.

29. Being careful to guide the connecting rod bolts over opposite sides of the crankshaft journal, use a wooden hammer handle to tap the piston out of the ring compressor and into the cylinder. Then use the hammer handle to press the piston down in the cylinder until the connecting rod bearing is seated squarely on the crankshaft journal.

CAUTION——

Check the progress of the connecting rod as you press the piston toward the crankshaft. The rod bearing or the crankshaft will be damaged if you drive them together at an angle.

30. Loosely install the connecting rod cap. Using the same procedure you used on the No. 1 cylinder, install the piston/connecting rod assembly of the No. 4 cylinder. Then hand-turn the crankshaft 180° and install the piston/connecting rod assemblies of the No. 2 and No.3 cylinders.

31. One at a time, remove the connecting rod caps. Then place a piece of Plastigage (available at automotive supply stores) on the crankshaft journal. Do not lay the Plastigage across the oil hole in the crankshaft journal.

NOTE——

In checking the clearance of new bearings, you can use green Plastigage, which measures clearances from 0.025 to 0.076 mm (.001 to .003 in.) In checking used bearings or new bearings installed in high-mileage engines use red Plastigage, which measures clearances from 0.050 to 0.150 mm (.002 to .006 in.).

32. Install the connecting rod cap. Torque the nuts to 3.5 mkg (25 ft. lb.), then remove the nuts and the connecting rod cap.

NOTE——

Torquing the nuts will compress and flatten the Plastigage, which you will measure to determine the connecting rod bearing clearance. Do not turn the crankshaft as you compress the Plastigage. Doing this will spread the Plastigage and cause inaccurate measurement.

33. To determine the bearing clearance, compare the flattened Plastigage to the scale that is printed on the edge of the Plastigage package. Read the clearance printed adjacent to the scale band that has the same width as the flattened Plastigage strip (Fig. 10-17).

Fig. 10-17. Flattened Plastigage being measured to determine connecting rod bearing clearance.

NOTE ——

Used bearings must be installed in their original positions in their original connecting rod. New bearings must be installed so that their anti-rotation tabs engage the notches in the connecting rod and rod cap. With new parts, the connecting rod bearing clearance should be from 0.028 to 0.088 mm (.0011 to .0035 in.). If clearance is at or near the 0.12-mm (.0047-in.) wear limit, check the crankshaft as described in **11.2 Removing, Checking, and Installing Crankshaft and Main Bearings.** Then replace the bearings.

CAUTION ——

Use solvent to remove the flattened Plastigage. Scraping off the Plastigage could damage the connecting rod bearings.

34. If bearing clearance is correct, lightly coat the connecting rod bearing shells and the crankshaft journals with assembly lubricant.

   NOTE ——

   If assembly lubricant is not available from your automotive supply store, use a light coating of multipurpose grease instead.

35. Install the connecting rod caps. Torque the connecting rod nuts to 4.5 mkg (33 ft. lb.)

36. Using feeler gauges of various thicknesses, determine the connecting rod bearing axial play. To do this, push each connecting rod as far as possible toward one side of the crankshaft journal. If you can insert an 0.25-mm (.010-in.) feeler gauge between the opposite side of the journal the connecting rod (Fig. 10-18), the clearance is excessive. Excessive clearance can be corrected by installing new bearings, a new crankshaft, a

new connecting rod, or all three—depending on the extent to which any of these parts is worn.

37. Install the oil pump and the oil pan as described in **6.2 Removing, Checking, and Installing Oil Pump.** Install the cylinder head as described in **5.3 Removing and Installing Cylinder Head and Manifolds.** Then install the engine, if previously removed, as described in **7. Removing and Installing Engine.**

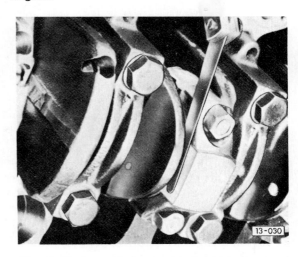

Fig. 10-18. Connecting rod axial play (side clearance) being measured with a feeler gauge.

11. CRANKSHAFT AND INTERMEDIATE SHAFT

You must remove the engine if you intend to remove the crankshaft or the intermediate shaft from the engine block. The front oil seals for both shafts can be replaced with the engine installed. However, you can replace the crankshaft's rear oil seal only after you have removed the transmission or the engine. See **MANUAL TRANSMISSION** or **AUTOMATIC TRANSMISSION.**

The crankshaft revolves in five split-shell main bearings. The center (no. 3) main bearing shells are flanged. The flanges control crankshaft axial play. The intermediate shaft runs in two ring-type bearings that are driven into bores in the front and the rear of the engine block.

11.1 Replacing Crankshaft and Intermediate Shaft Oil Seals

The oil seals used at the front ends of the crankshaft, the intermediate shaft, and the camshaft are identical. See **5.4 Disassembling and Assembling Cylinder Head** for information on the replacement of the camshaft oil seal.

To replace crankshaft front oil seal:

1. Remove the camshaft drive belt as described in **5.1 Removing, Installing, and Adjusting Camshaft**

Drive Belt. Then remove the crankshaft sprocket.

2. Being careful not to damage the light alloy seal carrier, pry out the old oil seal (Fig. 11-1).

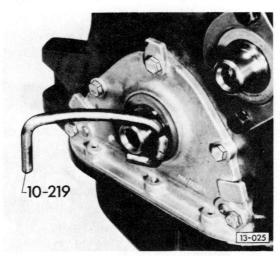

Fig. 11-1. Crankshaft front oil seal being removed. Special tool hooks under inner edge of seal.

3. Using the tool shown in Fig. 11-2, press in the new seal until it is flush with the front of the seal carrier.

Fig. 11-2. Seal being pressed in. Turn bolt (threaded into crankshaft) as indicated by arrow.

4. Remove the seal-installing tool. Then, so that it does not get stuck in the seal recess, remove the steel driving sleeve from the tool. Using the aluminum part of the tool only, press in the seal until it is recessed 2 mm (.080 in.) from the front of the seal carrier. Then remove the tool and install the sprocket and the camshaft drive belt.

NOTE ——
You can mark the outer surface of the seal-installing tool at a point 2 mm (.080 in.) from the end of the tool that contacts the seal. Press in the seal until the mark on the tool is flush with the seal carrier.

To replace crankshaft rear oil seal:

1. Remove either the engine or the transmission. Remove the flywheel as described in **9.2 Removing and Installing Flywheel** or remove the drive plate as described in **8.1 Removing and Installing Drive Plate.**

2. Carefully insert a large screwdriver between the crankshaft's flywheel flange and the inner edge of the old oil seal. Then, bracing the screwdriver against the flange, pry out the oil seal.

3. Install the seal guide sleeve tool over the crankshaft flange as shown in Fig. 11-3 or Fig. 11-4. Then hand-start the new oil seal into the seal recess in the oil seal carrier.

Fig. 11-3. Crankshaft rear oil seal being started in recess (1973 and 1974 cars with 82-mm (3 $\frac{15}{64}$-in.) flywheel mounting flanges). Press in as indicated by arrows.

Fig. 11-4. Crankshaft rear oil seal being started in recess (1975 and later cars with 85-mm (3 $\frac{11}{32}$-in.) flywheel mounting flanges).

4. Remove the guide sleeve. Then, using the driving plate shown in Fig. 11-5 or Fig. 11-6, press in the seal by alternately tightening the two flywheel or

Fig. 11-5. Seal driving plate and two flywheel mounting bolts being used to press in rear oil seal (1973 and 1974 cars with 82-mm (3 $^{15}/_{64}$-in.) flywheel mounting flanges).

Fig. 11-6. Seal driving plate and two flywheel mounting bolts being used to press in rear oil seal (1975 and later cars with 85-mm (3 $^{11}/_{32}$-in.) flywheel mounting flanges).

drive plate mounting bolts so that the plate advances evenly toward the seal carrier. When the seal is flush with the carrier, remove the plate and the bolts, install the flywheel or drive plate, then install the transmission or the engine.

To replace intermediate shaft oil seal:

1. Remove the camshaft drive belt as described in **5.1 Removing, Installing, and Adjusting Camshaft Drive Belt.** Remove the intermediate shaft sprocket. Use the tools and procedure given for replacing the crankshaft front oil seal, but press the seal in only until it is flush with the seal carrier. Alternatively, remove the two bolts and take off the intermediate shaft oil seal carrier.

2. Press the old oil seal out of the carrier. Then press in the new seal as shown in Fig. 11-7.

3. Using a new O-ring, install the seal carrier and seal. Torque the two bolts to 2.0 mkg (14 ft. lb.). Then install the sprocket and the camshaft drive belt.

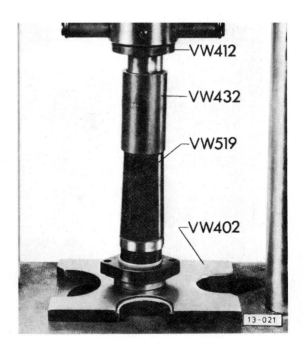

Fig. 11-7. Oil seal being pressed in until it is flush with front of seal carrier.

11.2 Removing, Checking, and Installing Crankshaft and Main Bearings

Fig. 11-8 illustrates the removal of the crankshaft, crankshaft bearings, and intermediate shaft. In removing the crankshaft, both crankshaft oil seal carriers must be removed from the engine block.

Though the bearing shells for main bearings 1, 2, 4, and 5 are identical, you must always reinstall used bearing shells in their original locations. Similarly, the main bearing caps must always be reinstalled on their original bearing saddles.

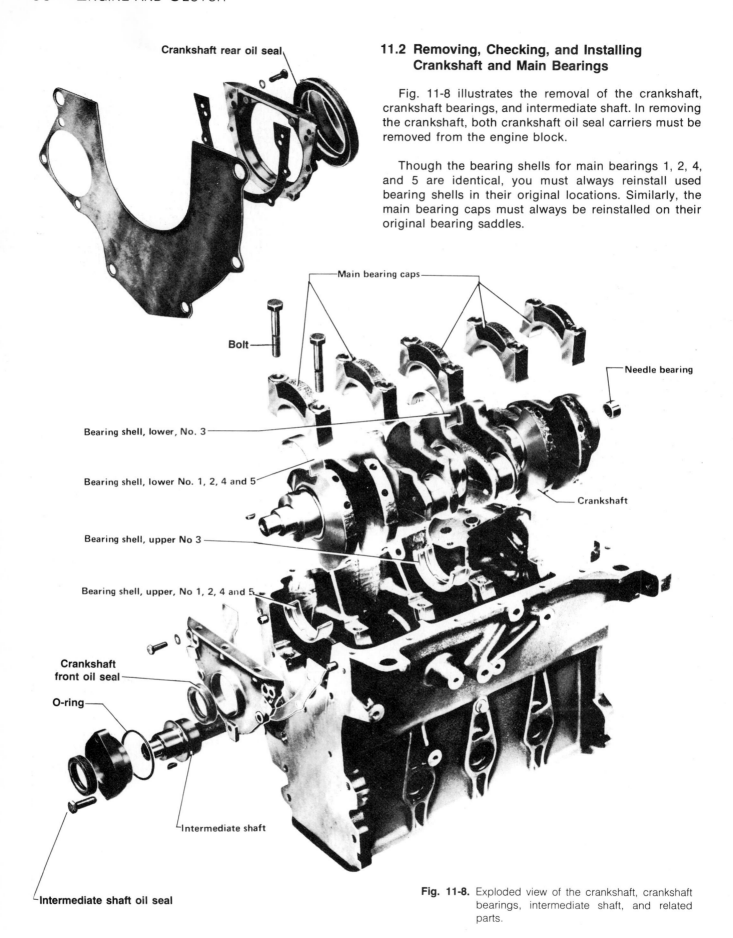

Fig. 11-8. Exploded view of the crankshaft, crankshaft bearings, intermediate shaft, and related parts.

To remove, check, and install:

1. Remove the engine. Remove the pistons and connecting rods as described in **10.1 Removing, Checking and Installing Pistons, Piston Rings, Connecting Rods, and Connecting Rod Bearings.** Remove the flywheel or the drive plate.

2. With the engine block inverted on an engine repair stand or clamped upside down on a workbench, remove the crankshaft oil seal carriers. Remove the bolts from the main bearing caps, remove the caps and bearings, then lift out the crankshaft.

   NOTE ——

   The main bearing caps are factory-numbered to ensure correct installation. However, if you intend to reuse the bearings, mark the bearing numbers on the backs of the bearing shells as you remove them from the caps and the main bearing saddles.

3. Using a micrometer, measure the crankshaft's main bearing and connecting rod journals. Then compare the measurements with the dimensions given in **Table h.** So that you can be certain the journals are not worn to a taper, duplicate each measurement at opposite sides of each journal. To determine eccentricity, make a second pair of measurements at a point 90° from the initial measurements. Alternatively, check the eccentricity out-of-round of the main bearing journals by placing main bearing journals 1 and 5 on V-blocks, and then rotating the crankshaft against a dial indicator gauge pin positioned, one journal at a time, against main bearing journals 2, 3, and 4.

   NOTE ——

   If the journals are rough or scored, tapered, exceed the limit for maximum out-of-round, or have worn to such a degree that the

Fig. 11-9. Upper main bearing shells, identified by oil groove (lower arrow). Oil holes (upper arrow) must align with oil holes in engine block.

connecting rod or the main bearing clearances exceed the wear limit even with new bearings, the crankshaft must be either replaced or reconditioned. You can exchange your worn crankshaft for a new crankshaft or for an undersize reconditioned crankshaft at your Authorized Dealer's parts department. Alernatively, a specialty shop can recondition your worn crankshaft to one of the undersizes listed in **Table h.**

4. Using the original bearings, original-size replacement bearings, or undersize main bearings—depending on the condition of the crankshaft, as determined in step 3—install the upper main bearing shells (with oil holes and lubrication grooves) in the bearing saddles of the engine block (Fig. 11-9). Make certain that the bearing saddles are clean and

Table h. Crankshaft Journal Sizes

Sizes	Crankshaft main bearing journal		Crankshaft connecting rod journal	
	diameter in mm (in.)	Maximum out-of-round mm (in.)	diameter in mm (in.)	maximum out-of-round mm (in.)
Original grade 1 grade 2	54.00 −0.04 (2.126 −.0015) 54.00 −0.06 (2.126 −0.002)	0.03 (.0012) 0.03 (.0012)	46.00 −0.04 (1.811 −.0015) 46.00 −0.06 (1.811 −.002)	0.03 (.0012) 0.03 (.0012)
Undersize I grade 1 grade 2	53.75 −0.04 (2.1161 −.0015) 53.75 −0.06 (2.1161 −.002)	0.03 (.0012) 0.03 (.0012)	45.75 −0.04 (1.8012 −.0015) 45.75 −0.06 (1.8012 −.002)	0.03 (.0012) 0.03 (.0012)
Undersize II grade 1 grade 2	53.50 −0.04 (2.1063 −.0015) 53.50 −0.06 (2.1063 −.002)	0.03 (.0012) C.03 (.0012)	45.50 −0.04 (1.7913 −.0015) 45.50 −0.06 (1.7913 −.002)	0.03 (.0012) 0.03 (.0012)
Undersize III grade 1 grade 2	53.25 −0.04 (2.0965 −.0015) 53.25 −0.06 (2.0965 −.002)	0.03 (.0012) 0.03 (.0012)	45.25 −0.04 (1.7815 −.0015) 45.25 −0.06 (1.7815 −.002)	0.03 (.0012) 0.03 (.0012)

that the anti-rotation tabs engage the notches in the saddles.

5. Place the crankshaft in the engine block. Install the lower main bearing shells in the bearing caps. Then, making sure you install the caps as shown in Fig. 11-10, use Plastigage® to check the bearing clearance with the bolts torqued to 3.5 mkg (25 ft. lb.). Plastigage measurement is described in **10.1 Removing, Checking, and Installing Pistons, Piston Rings, Connecting Rods, and Connecting Rod Bearings.**

Fig. 11-10. Main bearing cap numbers. Number **1** is at front of engine. All numbers must be toward the right (manifold) side of the engine.

6. With new bearings, the bearing clearance (measured with Plastigage) should be between 0.03 and 0.08 mm (.0012 and .003 in.). If the clearance with used bearings exceeds the wear limit—0.17 mm (.007 in.), replace the bearings. If the clearance exceeds the wear limit even with new bearings, the crankshaft must be replaced or reconditioned to accept bearings for one of the three undersize ranges.

7. Remove the flattened Plastigage® strips. Then lift out the crankshaft.

CAUTION ——

Use solvent to remove the flattened Plastigage. Scraping off the Plastigage could damage the main bearings.

8. Lightly coat the main bearing shells and the main bearing journals with assembly lubricant.

NOTE ——

If assembly lubricant is not available from your automotive supply store, use a light coating of multipurpose grease instead.

9. Place the crankshaft in the engine block, install the bearing caps as shown earlier in Fig. 11-10, then torque the bolts to 6.5 mkg (47 ft. lb.).

10. Using feeler gauges of various thicknesses, determine the crankshaft's axial play. To do this, push the crankshaft as far as it will go toward the rear of the engine. Then insert the feeler gauge between the crank throw for No. 2 cylinder and the front flange of the No. 3 main bearing, as shown in Fig. 11-11.

Fig. 11-11. Crankshaft axial play being measured.

NOTE ——

With new parts, axial play should be between 0.07 and 0.17 mm (.0025 and .0065 in.). If you can insert a 0.25 mm (.010-in.) feeler gauge between the bearing and the crank throw, the clearance is excessive. Excessive clearance can usually be corrected by replacing the No. 3 main bearing.

11. Using new gaskets, install the crankshaft oil seal carriers. Install the flywheel or the drive plate. Install the pistons and connecting rods as described in **10.1 Removing, Checking, and Installing Pistons, Piston Rings, Connecting Rods, and Connecting Rod Bearings.** Then install the engine.

11.3 Removing and Installing Intermediate Shaft

The intermediate shaft and its bearings are subject to very little wear. Nevertheless, remove the shaft during engine rebuilding so that abrasive particles and other foreign matter can be thoroughly cleaned off the bearings and out of the oil passages.

To remove the intermediate shaft, first remove the engine as described in **7. Removing and Installing Engine.** Then remove the distributor as described in **3.2 Distributor** and remove the fuel pump from engines with carburetors as described in **FUEL AND EXHAUST SYSTEMS.** Remove the camshaft drive belt as described in **5.1 Removing, Installing, and Adjusting Camshaft Drive Belt.**

Remove the two bolts, then remove the intermediate shaft oil seal carrier. Being careful not to damage the bearings, the gear that drives the distributor, or the eccentric for the fuel pump, withdraw the intermediate shaft from the engine block.

Installation is the reverse of removal. If the oil seal is cracked or worn, replace it as described in **11.1 Replacing Crankshaft and Intermediate Shaft Oil Seals.** If the bearings are worn so that their copper backing shows through the silvery bearing surfaces, drive out the old bearings. Then, being careful to align the oil holes in the new bearings with the oil holes in the engine block, drive in first the rear bearing and then the front bearing. You must use a bearing driver that accurately fits the inside of the bearings and the oil holes must align with the bearings installed.

Coat the bearings with assembly lubricant or multipurpose grease before you install the shaft. Also apply assembly lubricant or multipurpose grease to the eccentric for the fuel pump and the gear that drives the distributor. Torque the two bolts for the intermediate shaft oil seal carrier to 2.0 mkg (14 ft. lb.).

> **NOTE ——**
> The specifications for 1976 models given in the tables in **12. Engine and Clutch Technical Data** apply to the 1977 models also.

12. ENGINE AND CLUTCH TECHNICAL DATA

The horsepower figures given in Table III are taken from the VW and Audi parts lists, and do not match the advertised horsepowers for the cars. The purpose of these ratings is to help you identify the correct replacement parts and replacement engine for your car. The torque figures given in Table III are the advertised figures for the most recent Audi model equipped with an engine having a particular code letter. These figures are somewhat higher than the figures advertised for VW cars.

However, the engines are the same and the Audi torque is obtained at a slightly higher rpm than are the advertised torque figures for VW cars.

I. Basic Tune-Up Specifications

Coolant capacity	12.7 pints (10.5 Imperial pints, 6.0 liters)
Oil capacity	With filter change: 3.7 quarts (3.2 Imperial quarts, 3.5 liters) Without filter change: 3.1 quarts (2.7 Imperial quarts, 3.0 liters)
Firing order	1–3–4–2
Cylinder location	No. 1 at front of car, cylinders numbered consecutively from front to rear
Valve clearance	Intake (cold): 0.15–0.25 mm (.006–.010 in.) Intake (hot): 0.20–0.30 mm (.008–.012 in.) Exhaust (cold): 0.35–0.45 mm (.014–.018 in.) Exhaust (hot): 0.40–0.50 mm (.016–.020 in.)
Electrical system	12-volt, negative ground
Spark plug type	1973–1974 VW and Audi: Champion N-8Y Bosch W 175 T30 or W 175 T2 Beru 175/14/3A or 175/14/3 1975 VW: Champion N-8Y Bosch W 200 T30 Beru 200/14/3A1 1975 Audi: Champion N-8Y Bosch W 175 T30 Beru 175/14/3A 1975 and later VW and Audi: Champion N-8Y Bosch W 175 T30 Beru 175/14/3A (or plugs with similar specifications from other manufacturers)
Spark plug gap	0.60 to 0.70 mm (.024 to .028 in.)
Plug connector resistance	5000 to 10,000 ohms
Distributor rotor resistance	10,000 ohms maximum
Point gap	0.40 mm (.016 in.)
Dwell angle	44° to 50° (unless otherwise specified on the engine's emission decal)
Ignition timing	3° after TDC at 850 to 1000 rpm with vacuum hose(s) connected
Idle speed	850 to 1000 rpm
CO content	1973–1974 (with air injection): 1.0 volume % 1973–1974 (without air injection): 0.4–1.6 volume % 1975 (with carburetor): 1.5–2.5 volume % 1976 and later (with manual transmission): 1.5 volume % max. 1976 and later (with automatic transmission): 1.0 volume % max. 1976 and later (California only): 0.5 volume % max. (or as listed on the engine's emission decal)

3

II. Tightening Torques

Location	Designation	mkg	ft. lb.
Distributor hold-down to engine block	bolt	2.0	14
Spark plug in cylinder head	spark plug	2.5–3.0	10–22
Temperature gauge sensor in heater hose connection	sensor	0.7	5 (60 in. lb.)
Hose connections to engine block and cylinder head	bolt	1.0	7
Water pump to engine block	bolt	2.0	14
Alternator adjusting bracket to head and alternator	bolt/socket-head bolt	2.0	14
Alternator to mounting bracket	nut	2.5	18
Alternator mounting bracket to engine block	bolt	3.3	24
Air conditioning compressor and brackets (1973 through 1978)	nut or bolt	3.0	22
Air conditioning compressor bracket to engine (1979)	bolt	2.5	18
Air conditioning compressor to bracket (1979)	bolt	3.0	22
Air conditioning compressor and brackets	nut or bolt	3.0	22
Water pump front part to water pump housing	bolt	1.0	7
Camshaft drive belt tensioner	locknut	4.5	33
Camshaft drive belt cover to engine	nut	1.0	7
Camshaft drive belt sprockets to camshaft, crankshaft, and intermediate shaft	bolt	8.0	58
Camshaft bearing caps to cylinder head	nut	2.0	14
Cylinder head to engine block (engine cold)	hex. socket-head bolt	7.5	54
Cylinder head to engine block (engine hot)	hex. socket-head bolt	8.5	61
Cylinder head to engine block (engine cold)	12-point socket-head bolt	7.5, then ¼-turn tighter	54, then ¼-turn tighter
Coolant drain plug in engine block	hex-head plug	3.5	25
Manifolds to cylinder head	nut or bolt	2.5	18
Guard to exhaust manifold	nut	2.0	14
Exhaust pipe to exhaust manifold	nut	2.5	18
Intake manifold support to intake manifold	bolt	2.0	14
Intake manifold support to intake manifold	bolt	2.5	18
Core plug in front of cylinder head	socket-head plug	6.0	43
Cylinder head cover to cylinder head	bolt	1.0	7
V-belt pulleys to water pump hub, air pump hub, or crankshaft sprocket	bolt	2.0	14
Oil filter mounting flange to engine block	socket-head bolt	1.0	7
Fuel pump to engine block	socket-head bolt	2.0	14
Oil pressure warning light switch in cylinder head	sensor	1.0	7
Oil pickup tube to oil pump housing	bolt	1.0	7
Oil pump to engine block	socket-head bolt	2.0	14
Oil pan to engine block	socket-head screw	1.0	7
Oil drain plug in oil pan	hex-head plug	3.0	22
Front suspension subframe to body	bolt	7.0	50
Side engine mounts to subframe or engine	nut	4.0	29
Torque converter to drive plate	bolt	3.0	22
Engine to transmission bellhousing	nut	5.5	40
Front engine mount and support	nut	2.5	18
Flywheel or drive plate to crankshaft (use Loctite® 270 or 271)	bolt	7.5	54
Clutch pressure plate assembly on flywheel	bolt	2.5	18
Connecting rod cap to connecting rod	nut	4.5	33
Crankshaft and intermediate shaft oil seal carriers to engine block	bolt	2.0	14
Main bearing cap to engine block	bolt	6.5	47

III. General Engine Data

Engine code letter	Manual transmission— 1973 (carburetor): ZD 1974 (carburetor, California only): XZ 1974 (carburetor, U.S. except Calif.): XW 1975 (carburetor): XS 1975 (fuel injection): YG 1976 and later (fuel injection): YG 1976 (fuel injection, no EGR): YK	Number of cylinders	4
		Cylinder layout	Inline
		Valve operation	Belt-driven single overhead camshaft
		Cylinder bore	Carburetor: 76.50 mm (3.012 in.) Fuel injection: 79.50 mm (3.130 in.)
		Piston stroke	80.00 mm (3.150 in.)
		Piston displacement	Carburetor: 1471 cc (89.7 cu. in.) Fuel injection: 1588 cc (96.9 cu. in.)
	Automatic transmission— 1973 (carburetor): ZE 1974 (carburetor, California only): XY 1974 (carburetor, U.S. except Calif.): XV 1975 (carburetor): XR 1975 (fuel injection): YH 1976 and later (fuel injection): YH	Compression ratio	1973–1974: 8.5:1 1975–early 1976: 8.2:1 late 1976 through 1978: 8.0:1
		Fuel requirement	91 octane RON—lead-free only for cars with catalytic converters

continued on next page

III. General Engine Data (continued)

Horsepower	Code letters ZD, ZE, XZ, XW, XY, XV: 78 DIN (57 kw) @ 5800 rpm 75 SAE net @ 5800 rpm Code letters XS, XR: 78 DIN (57 kw) @ 5800 rpm 75 SAE net @ 5800 rpm Code letters YG, YH, YK: 83 DIN (61 kw) @ 5800 rpm 81 SAE net @ 5800 rpm (California models slightly less)	Torque	Code letters ZD, ZE, XZ, XW, XY, XV: 11.2 mkg DIN @ 4000 rpm 81 ft. lb. SAE @ 4000 rpm Code letters XS, XR: 11.0 mkg DIN @ 4000 rpm 80 ft. lb. SAE @ 4000 rpm Code letters YG, YH, YK: 11.5 mkg DIN @ 3200 rpm 83 ft. lb. SAE @ 3200 rpm (California models slightly less)

IV. Tolerances, Wear Limits, and Settings

3

Designation	New parts on installation	Wear limit mm (in.)
A. Crankshaft		
1. Journal dimensions		
a. Main journals.................................grade 1, diameter	54.00–0.04 (2.126–.0015)	—
....grade 2, diameter	54.00–0.06 (2.126–.002)	—
b. Connecting rod journals...................grade 1, diameter	46.00–0.04 (1.811–.0015)	—
....grade 2, diameter	46.00–0.06 (1.811–.002)	—
c. Three undersizes of 0.25 mm (.010 in.) each		—
2. Main journals.................................out-of-round	—	0.03 (.0012)
3. Connecting rod journal.........................out-of-round	—	0.03 (.0012)
4. Main bearing/main journal............................clearance	0.03–0.08 (.0012–.003)	0.17 (.007)
5. Connecting rod bearing/rod journal ....clearance	0.028–0.088 (.0011–.0035)	0.12 (.0047)
6. Crankshaft/main bearing No. 3 ....axial play	0.07–0.17 (.0025–.0065)	0.25 (.010)
B. Connecting Rods		
a. Piston pin/connecting rod bushing......................clearance	0.01–0.02 (.0004–.0008)	0.04 (.0015)
b. Connecting rod/crankshaft......................side clearance	—	0.25 (.010)
C. Pistons and Cylinders		
1. Piston and cylinder sizes		
a. Pistons, 1471-cc (89.7-cu. in.) engine............grade 1, diameter	76.48 (3.0110)	—
...........grade 2, diameter	76.49 (3.0114)	—
...........grade 3, diameter	76.50 (3.0118)	—
b. Three oversizes of 0.25 mm (.010 in.) each	—	
c. Cylinders, 1471-cc (89.7-cu. in.) engine.......grade 1, diameter	76.51 (3.0122)	76.55 (3.0138)
.......grade 2, diameter	76.52 (3.0126)	76.56 (3.0141)
.......grade 3, diameter	76.53 (3.0130)	76.57 (3.0146)
d. Three oversizes of 0.25 mm (.010 in.) each	—	
e. Pistons, 1588-cc (96.9-cu. in.) engine...........grade 1, diameter	79.48 (3.1291)	—
...........grade 2, diameter	79.49 (3.1295)	—
...........grade 3, diameter	79.50 (3.1299)	—
f. Three oversizes of 0.25 mm (.010 in.) each	—	
g. Cylinders, 1588-cc (96.9-cu. in.) engine.......grade 1, diameter	79.51 (3.1303)	79.55 (3.1319)
.......grade 2, diameter	79.52 (3.1307)	79.56 (3.1323)
.......grade 3, diameter	79.53 (3.1311)	79.57 (3.1327)
h. Three oversizes of 0.25 mm (.010 in.) each	—	
2. Cylinders.....................maximum taper or out-of-round	—	0.05 (.002)
3. Piston/cylinder.....................................clearance	0.03 (.001)	0.07 (.0025)
4. Piston ring/piston.............................side clearance	0.02–0.05 (.0008–.002)	—
5. Ring gap (with ring installed in cylinder)		
a. Compression rings ....end gap	0.30–0.45 (.012–.017)	1.00 (.039)
b. Oil scraper rings ....end gap	0.25–0.40 (.010–.016)	1.00 (.039)
D. Camshaft, Valves, and Cylinder Head		
1. Camshaft ....axial play	—	0.15 (.006)
2. Camshaft (measured at center bearing, bearings 1 and 5 on V-blocks).................................runout	—	0.01 (.0004)
3. Camshaft/camshaft bearings ....clearance	0.02–0.05 (.0008–.002)	—
4. Valve spring tensions		
a. Outer spring at loaded length of 22.3 mm (⅞ in.)..............load	43.5–48.0 kg (96–106 lb.)	—
b. Inner spring at loaded length of 18.3 mm (²³/₃₂ in.)............load	21.0–23.0 kg (46–51 lb.)	—
5. Valve seats		
a. Contact area facing.....................................angle	45°	—
b. Intake ....width of 45° facing	2.00 (.079)	—
c. Intake.........................outside diameter of 45° facing	33.20 (1.307)	—
d. Intake ....distance from head gasket surface on head to outer edge of 45° facing	9.00 (.354)	—

continued on next page

IV. Tolerances, Wear Limits, and Settings (continued)

Designation	New parts on installation	Weat limit mm (in.)
e. Exhaust ....width of 45° facing	2.40 (.094)	—
f. Exhaust ....outside diameter of 45° facing	30.80 (1.212)	—
g. Exhaust..distance from head gasket surface on head to outer edge of 45° facing	9.60 (.378)	—
h. Seat width correction chamfer..angle	30°	—
6. Valve guides		
a. Valve guide/intake valve stem ....rock	—	1.00 (.039)
b. Valve guide/exhaust valve stem..rock	—	1.30 (.051)
c. Valve guide..inside diameter	8.013–8.035 (.315–.316)	—
d. Tops of valve guides below cover gasket surface on cylinder head ....distance	56.00 ± 0.50 (2.204 ± .020)	—
7. Valve stem		
a. Intake..diameter	7.97 (.314)	—
b. Exhaust..diameter	7.95 (.313)	—
c. Intake..overall valve length	98.70 (3.886)	—
d. Exhaust..overall valve length	98.50 (3.878)	—
8. Valve head		
a. Intake..diameter	34.00 (1.338)	—
b. Exhaust..diameter	31.00 (1.220)	—
c. Intake ....margin	—	0.50 (.020) min.
d. Exhaust ....margin	—	Do not machine-grind
9. Valve clearance		
a. Intake (cold) ....setting	0.15–0.25 (.006–.010)	—
b. Intake (hot—coolant temp. approx. 35°C (95°F)).............setting	0.20–0.30 (.008–.012)	—
c. Exhaust (cold) ....setting	0.35–0.45 (.014–.018)	—
d. Exhaust (hot—coolant temp. approx. 35°C (95°F))...........setting	0.40–0.50 (.016–.020)	—
10. Cylinder head		
a. Cylinder head warp ....twist or arch	—	0.10 (.004)
b. Engine block deck warp ....twist or arch	—	0.10 (.004)
E. Cooling system		
1. Radiator cap .... 1973 through 1978 relief pressure	0.88–1.02 atu (13–15 psi)	—
1979 and later relief pressure	1.20–1.35 atu (17–19 psi)	—
2. Thermostat		
a. Begins opening .... 1973 through 1978 temperature	80°C (176°F)	—
1979 and later temperature	85°C (185°F)	—
b. Fully open .... temperature	94°C (210°F)	—
3. Radiator fan thermo switch		
a. Fan goes on .... 1973 through 1978 temperature	90°–95°C (194°–203°F) and above	—
1979 and later temperature	93°–98°C (200°–208°F) and above	—
b. Fan goes off .... 1973 through 1978 temperature	85°–90°C (185°–194°F) and below	—
1979 and later temperature	88°–93°C (190°–200°F) and below	—
4. V-belt tension—deflection under thumb pressure at a point midway between the alternator pulley or water pump pulley and crankshaft pulley	10–15 (3/8–9/16)	—
5. V-belt tension—deflection under thumb pressure at a point midway between the air conditioner pulley and the crankshaft pulley	5–10 (¼–⅜)	—
F. Lubrication System		
1. Oil pressure		
a. Warning light goes out		
through VW Chassis No. __6 2074 222 ....pressure	0.30–0.60 kg/cm² (4.3–8.5 psi)	—
through Audi Chassis No. __6 2050 000 ....pressure	0.30–0.60 kg/cm² (4.3–8.5 psi)	—
from VW Chassis No. __6 2074 223 ....pressure	0.15–0.45 kg/cm² (2.1–6.4 psi)	—
from Audi Chassis No. __6 2050 001 ....pressure	0.15–0.45 kg/cm² (2.1–6.4 psi)	—
b. Normal oil pressure (@ 2000 rpm with SAE 10W oil at 60°C (140°F))..minimum	—	2.0 kg/cm² (28 psi)
2. Oil pump		
a. Oil pump gears ....backlash clearance	0.05–0.20 (.002–.008)	—
b. Oil pump gears........................axial play	—	0.15 (.006)
G. Drive Plate or Flywheel and Clutch		
1. Rear surface of drive plate—distance from rear surface of engine block..	31.30 ± 0.80 (1.232 ± .031)	—
2. Diaphragm spring levers on clutch pressure plate assembly........................depth of wear or scoring	—	0.30 (.012)
3. Flywheel........................runout at center of friction surface	—	0.08 (.003)
4. Clutch pressure plate ....inward taper of friction surface	—	0.30 (.012)
5. Clutch driven plate ....runout at a diameter of 175 mm (6⅞ in.)	—	0.40 (.016)
6. Clutch freeplay measured at pedal........................distance	15 (⅝)	—

ELECTRICAL SYSTEM

4

Contents

TABLES

Electrical System

4

The electrical system is basically an efficient means for transmitting power from the engine to remote parts of the car. It does this with the help of an alternator that converts some of the engine's mechanical energy into electrical energy. The electrical energy is carried over wires to motors that convert it back into mechanical energy or to bulbs that convert it into heat and light. The battery in the system supplies electrical power mainly when the engine is not running.

Every terminal in the electrical system is numbered. The terminal numbers for all major electrical connections are given in the wiring diagrams that appear at the end of this section. The terminal number is usually stamped on the component itself as an aid to proper installation.

Though most of the electrical terminal numbers are used only once to denote a particular terminal on a particular component, there are several numbers that do not designate specific terminals and that appear in numerous locations throughout the electrical system. These numbers identify main sources of electrical current. All terminals numbered 15 originate at the ignition switch and supply current only when the ignition switch is in its on position. Terminals numbered 30 supply positive polarity current directly from the battery with no intervening switch that can be used to turn it off. Terminals numbered 31 are ground connections and the ground wires connected to them are always brown. Terminals identified by the number 50 receive current only when the ignition switch is in its start position. A letter suffix is sometimes added to the terminal number to distinguish separate parts of the same circuit or to prevent the confusion of two circuits that have similar functions.

All electrical circuits other than those required for starting and operating the engine are protected by fuses. To prevent accidental shorts that might blow a fuse, or damage wires and electrical components that are not protected by fuses, you should always disconnect the ground strap from the negative pole of the battery before working on the electrical system of your car. If you lack the skills or the equipment needed for testing and repairing the electrical system we suggest that you leave such work to an Authorized Dealer or other qualified shop. We especially urge you to consult your Authorized Dealer before attempting repairs on a car still covered by the new-car warranty.

1. GENERAL DESCRIPTION

The components of the electrical system are discussed in detail in later parts of this section. However, a brief description of the principal components is presented here for purposes of familiarization.

System Voltage and Polarity

The cars covered by this Manual have a 12-volt, negative-ground electrical system. In other words, the voltage regulator keeps voltage in the system at approximately the 12-volt rating of the battery and the negative pole of the battery is connected directly to the car's chassis.

Battery

The six-cell, 12-volt lead-acid battery is located in the right-hand side of the engine compartment. The battery is rated at 54 ampere-hours on most of the models covered in this Manual. The 1973 models without air conditioning have a battery rated at 45 ampere-hours.

Starting System

The 0.7-horsepower starter is series-wound and has an overrunning clutch. The starter and its attached solenoid are located on the left-hand side of the engine. Three nuts and bolts hold the starter to the flywheel bellhousing; a fourth bolt holds the starter to the engine block.

Charging System

The charging system consists of a belt-driven alternator and a regulator. The regulator is integral with the alternator brush holder and is readily removable for brush inspection or replacement. Two different alternators are used on cars covered by this Manual. One is rated at 35 ampers and the other—used in conjunction with the 54 ampere-hour battery—is rated at 55 amperes. There is also a 65-ampere alternator introduced in 1977 on cars with factory air conditioning.

Ignition System

The ignition is a conventional coil and battery, distributor-controlled system. Ignition troubleshooting and repair are covered in ENGINE AND CLUTCH. Radio suppression is by resistance built into the spark plug connectors and distributor rotor.

Wiring

All components of the electrical system (except for the heavy battery cables) have push-on connectors. A system of fuses prevents short circuits or excessive current from damaging the electrical system and wiring.

Lights

The lighting system includes the parking lights, side marker lights, turn signals, back-up lights, interior lighting, and sealed beam headlights. The headlight beams are dimmed or raised by pulling the turn signal lever toward the steering wheel. Actual switching is carried out by a dimmer relay mounted on the fuse box.

Computer Analysis

Some of the early cars covered by this Manual are equipped with a network of wiring that serves the Computer Analysis system. A central socket in the engine compartment receives the individual wires that are connected to various measuring points on the car. These connections are identified by encircled numbers in the wiring diagrams that appear at the end of this section.

Although they are not vital to car operation, all such connections must be kept intact if the Computer Analysis system is to work properly. Never connect any device other than the test plug of the Computer Analysis system to the test network central socket in the engine compartment. Incorrect equipment could damage the plug connectors, the test sensors, or the vehicle components that contain sensors.

Heating and Ventilation Fan

The heating and ventilation system includes a two-speed fan. The fan, which is used primarily to assist heating and ventilation while the car is being driven slowly or standing still, is controlled by a dashboard-mounted switch. Removal and installation of the fan is covered in BODY AND INTERIOR.

Windshield Wipers

The blades of the two-speed windshield wiper system automatically return to their parked position when they are switched off. The wiper switch includes a windshield washer control. The washers are supplied with fluid by a motor-driven pump.

Instruments

The gauge cluster contains warning lights, an electric fuel gauge, and an electric water temperature gauge. Except on the Basic Two Door, there is an electric clock mounted between the speedometer and the gauge cluster. The speedometer is operated by a flexible cable that is driven by a gear in the transmission.

2. MAINTENANCE

No routine lubrication of the generator, starter, or other motors is required. However, the following checks are included in **LUBRICATION AND MAINTENANCE.**

1. Checking the lights and switches

2. Checking the windshield wipers and washers

3. Checking the battery

4. Testing the charging and starting systems.

3. BATTERY

Each of the six battery cells contains a set of brown lead oxide positive plates and gray sponge lead negative plates. The cells are connected in series by heavy lead bars and are enclosed in a plastic case having six compartments. The battery case also serves as a tank for the electrolyte—a solution of sulfuric acid diluted with water to a specific gravity of 1.285, which means that the electrolyte weighs 1.285 times as much as an equal volume of water. The battery plates that make up the cells are completely immersed in the electrolyte.

The terminal posts are labeled + and − and are further identified by having a positive post that is the thicker of the two. A ground strap connects the negative (−) post to the chassis of the car. Two cables are attached to the positive (+) post; one cable connects the battery to the starter solenoid and the other (thinner) cable connects the battery to the fuse box and the rest of the electrical system. Some batteries also have an additional central terminal with a small-gauge wire attached to it. This is the Computer Analysis connection used to check the electrolyte level.

Discharging

The battery does not store electricity. Rather, it produces electrical current by means of a reversible electrochemical reaction. When a circuit is completed between the two battery posts, sulfuric acid from the electrolyte combines with the lead in the plates to produce lead sulfate, releasing a great many electrons in the process.

Charging

The electrochemical reaction by which the battery produces electrical current is reversed when direct current is sent back into the cells. The charging system of the car supplies this current. When the discharged battery plates are charged with direct current from an outside source, the lead sulfate in the plates is converted back to it original state, returning sulfuric acid to the solution in the electrolyte.

A battery can never be charged to a voltage level in excess of the voltage it is capable of producing electrochemically. As charging proceeds, the battery's voltage builds to a peak called terminal voltage. If charging is continued beyond the terminal voltage, the water in the electrolyte begins to decompose into hydrogen and oxygen. This condition is called gassing.

Temperature Effects

Temperature changes modify the efficiency of the battery as well as alter the specific gravity of its electrolyte. Low outside temperatures can create slow starting by thickening the engine and transmission oils and simultaneously reducing the battery power available for running the starter motor. The current producing capacity of a battery chilled to −15°C (5°F) is only half its capacity at 20°C (68°F).

In addition, there is danger of partly-discharged batteries freezing in cold weather owing to the higher proportion of water in their electrolyte. A frozen battery will produce no current, but can usually be restored to service if thawed out slowly. The following list shows the safe low temperature limits for batteries in various states of charge.

Specific gravity	Freezing point
1.285	−68°C (−90°F)
1.200	−27°C (−17°F)
1.120	−11°C (12° F)

3.1 Servicing and Testing Battery

The level of the electrolyte should never be allowed to fall below the tops of the plates in any cell. As water is lost through evaporation and electrolysis, fresh water must be added to maintain the electrolyte's level at the bottoms of the indicator tubes that are built into the battery filler openings. Use only distilled water to replenish the electrolyte. Water that is not chemically pure may have an adverse effect on battery life and efficiency.

The battery will lose more water in summer than in winter. In very hot weather it may be necessary to check the electrolyte level as often as once a week. Never overfill the cells. This could cause the electrolyte to boil over during a long daylight drive when the load on the electrical system is light and the generator output is high.

Battery terminals must be tight-fitting and free of corrosion and acid salts. If you notice even a trace of corrosion, remove the positive cable and ground strap from the battery posts and clean the posts and terminal clamps with a battery terminal cleaning tool. After the terminals have been cleaned and the positive cable and ground strap tightly installed on the battery posts, the terminals and posts should be coated lightly with petroleum jelly or sprayed with a commercial battery terminal corrosion inhibitor.

WARNING

Keep sparks and open flame away from the top of the battery. Hydrogen gas from the battery could explode violently.

The top of the battery should always be kept clean. Even a thin layer of dust containing conductive acid salts can cause the battery to discharge. Corrosion and acid salt accumulations should be washed away with baking soda solution. Be extremely careful that none of this solution enters the cells through the vent holes. Even a drop or two will seriously impair the efficiency of the battery.

Periodic battery tests should be made to help keep track of battery condition. Such tests can also be made to help pinpoint the source of suspected battery trouble.

WARNING

Wear goggles when you work with battery electrolyte and do not allow the liquid to contact your skin or clothing. Electrolyte is corrosive and can cause severe burns. If it should spill onto your skin, flush the area of contact immediately with large quantities of water. Spilled electrolyte can be neutralized with a strong baking soda solution.

Hydrometer Testing

The simplest tool for testing the battery is a hydrometer. It consists of a glass cylinder with a freely moving float inside. When electrolyte is drawn into the cylinder by squeezing and releasing a rubber bulb, the level to which the float sinks indicates the specific gravity of the electrolyte. A specific gravity scale on the float is read at the point where it intersects the surface of the electrolyte. The more dense the concentration of sulfuric acid in the electrolyte, the less the float will sink and the higher the reading. Specific gravity values for different states of charge are as follows:

State of charge	Specific gravity
Fully discharged	1.120
Half discharged	1.200
Fully discharged	1.285

Voltage Testing

Total battery voltage can be tested with a special voltmeter. The tester should consist of a voltmeter connected in parallel with a test load of approximately

110 amps. The minimum voltage indicated should not be less than 9.6 volts. If total voltage drops below this value during the 5- to 10-second test, the battery is either discharged or sulfated. A sulfated battery is one in which the plates are covered by a layer of lead sulfate that is difficult to reconvert. Sulfating is visible as a gray coating on the plates.

CAUTION

A discharged battery should be recharged immediately. Otherwise, sulfating will lead to the loss of active plate materials and to reduced battery capacity.

The voltage of an individual cell should not vary from the others by more than 0.2 volts. This can be determined by applying one prong of the tester to the negative battery post, then dipping the other prong into the electrolyte of successive cells, and finally applying it to the positive post (Fig. 3-1). The readings should be 2, 4, 6, 8, 10, and 12 volts. This test should last for no more than 10 seconds.

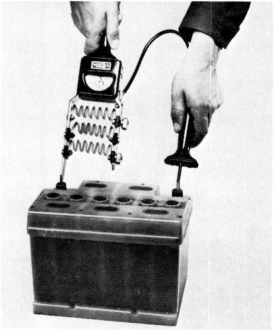

© 1974 VWoA—1329

Fig. 3-1. Using voltmeter to test total voltage of battery.

3.2 Removing and Installing Battery

The battery is fastened in position by a bolt and hold-down plate (Fig. 3-2). Before removing the bolt, disconnect first the ground strap and then the positive cable from the battery posts. Where applicable, remove the wire from the center terminal that serves the Computer Analysis system.

Remove the hold-down plate bolt and then remove the battery. On some models, a double-ended insulator bolt with a bonded rubber center is used in this location to mount a fuel system component. If you do not have a crow's-foot wrench that will grip only the lower hex of the insulator bolt, the rubber part will probably break. Therefore, you may wish to obtain a replacement insulator bolt beforehand.

Fig. 3-2. Battery installed, showing correct hold-down plate position.

When installing the battery, clean and install the terminals as described earlier in **3.1 Servicing and Testing Battery.** The battery must be mounted firmly to the body during installation to prevent road shocks and vibration from damaging the plates. On VW diesel models, the positive cable and wires must be routed as indicated in Fig. 3-3. Be especially careful that the wiring is not jammed between the battery and the suspension strut mounting because this will almost

Fig. 3-3. Positive wiring correctly installed on VW diesel model. Cable (1) should pass through plastic clip (arrow). Wires to alternator and fusebox (2) should pass through opening between battery, firewall, and suspension strut mounting.

certainly lead to damaged insulation and electrical short circuits.

3.3 Charging

Normally, a battery should be charged at no more than 10 percent of its rated capacity. For example, a charging current of 5.4 amperes would be used on a battery having 54 Ah (ampere-hours) capacity. However, a current as low as 5 percent of the rated capacity (2.7 amps for a 54 Ah battery) can be used in normal charging and should always be used the first time a new battery is charged.

In normal charging, the battery is considered fully charged when it is gassing freely and the voltage of the individual cells has risen to 2.5 to 2.7 volts each (about 15 volts for the battery). An hour or so after you have switched off the charging current, use the voltmeter/tester to determine the rest voltage of the battery. This should be 2.1 to 2.2 volts per cell, or approximately 12.5 to 13.0 volts for the battery.

Quick-Charging

To save time in an emergency, a higher current can be used to charge batteries in good condition. Only sound batteries that are already in service are suitable for quick-charging. Neither factory-new nor sulfated batteries should ever be quick-charged.

WARNING ——

Do not boost a sulfated battery at a high charging rate. Doing this could cause the battery to explode.

To quick-charge:

1. Remove the battery caps, then connect a battery charger and voltmeter to the battery. Quick-charge 45-Ah batteries at 36 to 40 amperes for three minutes. Quick-charge 54-Ah batteries at 44 to 48 amperes for three minutes.

2. Observe the voltmeter reading during charging. If total battery voltage exceeds 15.5 volts, the battery plates are sulfated or worn out and the battery should be replaced.

3. If the total voltage is less than 15.5 volts, test the individual cell voltages. If cell voltages vary by more than 0.1 volt, the battery plates are worn out and the battery should be replaced. If cell voltages are within 0.1 volt, measure the specific gravity and continue quick-charging at 44 to 48 amperes for 54-Ah batteries or 36 to 40 amperes for 45-Ah batteries (80 to 90% of total battery capacity).

4

Use the following times:

Specific gravity	Period of charge
1.150 or less	1 hour
1.150 to 1.175	45 minutes
1.175 to 1.225	15 minutes
Above 1.225	Slow charge only

WARNING ——

Smoking and open flames should not be permitted in a room where batteries are charged. Charging causes excess water in the electrolyte to decompose into hydrogen and oxygen, a dangerously explosive combination of gases.

CAUTION ——

Do not store precision tools in a room where batteries are charged. The corrosive fumes generated during charging can severely damage these tools.

Storing a Battery

A battery that is not in use will gradually discharge itself. At room temperature it will lose about one percent of its remaining capacity each day. The rate of discharge increases with higher temperatures. If the battery is allowed to remain in a partly or fully discharged condition for long periods, it will become badly sulfated and may never be serviceable again. The following procedure is recommended to prevent self-discharge and sulfating in a battery that is to be stored either in or out of the car.

To store battery:

1. Charge the battery. Check the electrolyte level and the specific gravity. If necessary, add distilled water to the electrolyte.

2. Store the battery in a cool, dry place.

3. Every 6 to 8 weeks, discharge the battery and recharge it.

4. Before returning the battery to service, charge it with a very low current (not over 3 amps).

4. STARTING SYSTEM

Two slightly different starters, manufactured by Bosch, are used in the cars covered by this Manual. Early cars have starter 056 911 023 A. Cars built after VW Chassis No. _ _ 5 2159 522 and Audi Chassis No. _ _ 5 1039 371 have starter 056 911 023 B. Both starters are of the multipolar series wound variety with four brushes and aluminum field coils. A solenoid is used to engage the starter's drive pinion with the starter ring gear on the engine's flywheel or drive plate.

To minimize wear and stress on the starter's drive pinion and the starter ring gear, the solenoid is designed so that it does not switch starting current to the starter motor until the drive pinion has fully engaged the ring gear. Also, the drive pinion is mounted on an overrunning clutch so that, in the event that the driver does not immediately release the ignition key as soon as the engine has started, the starter motor will not sustain over-speed damage in being driven by the engine.

4.1 Starting System Troubleshooting

Troubleshooting procedures that are applicable to the starting system appear in **Table a.** The bold numbers in the Remedy column refer to the headings in this section under which the prescribed service and repair procedures are described. If more than one test or probable cause is listed, check them one by one in the order in which they appear.

The 1974 seatbelt interlock system can be tested with the help of the wiring diagrams given in **12. Wiring, Fuses, and Relays.** Current and continuity tests should be made using an ohmmeter and a voltmeter only. There are solid-state electronic circuits in the seatbelt interlock relay that can be damaged if you attempt to test the circuits by "sparking" (intentionally shorting wires, thereby making sparks to indicate the presence of electrical current).

Table a. Starting System Troubleshooting

Problem	Test and Probable Cause	Remedy
1. Starter does not operate when ignition is turned to start position (1974 seat belt interlock bypassed or in good working order)	Turn lights on for test: a. Lights are out. Loose battery connections or battery run down b. Lights go out when key is moved to starting position. Insufficient current owing to loose battery connections or corroded terminals c. Lights become dim when key is moved to starting position. Battery run down d. Lights stay bright, solenoid operates (clicks). Connect jumper cable from starter terminal 30 to solenoid's starter connector strap terminal. Solenoid contacts are faulty if starter runs e. Lights stay bright, solenoid does not operate (car with automatic transmission). Connect jumper cable between terminals on neutral safety switch. If starter can be operated normally, neutral safety switch is defective f. Lights stay bright, solenoid does not operate, neutral safety switch not defective. Connect a jumper cable between starter terminals 30 and 50. If starter runs, wire from terminal 30 of main lighting switch to terminal 30 of ignition switch is faulty, the seatbelt interlock relay is faulty, or there is an open circuit in wire 50 between the ignition switch and the relay or between the relay and the solenoid	a. Check battery cable terminals. Test battery. Charge if necessary. See **3.1, 3.3.** b. Clean and tighten all battery cable connections. See **3.1, 3.2.** c. Charge battery. See **3.3.** d. Replace solenoid. See **4.3.** e. Replace neutral safety switch. See **AUTOMATIC TRANSMISSION.** f. Eliminate open circuits. Replace defective parts. At least 7 volts must be available at terminal 50 for the solenoid to operate. See **8.3, 12.**
2. Starter does not operate when battery cable is directly connected with terminal stud of connector strip	a. Brushes sticking b. Brushes worn c. Weak spring tension. Brushes do not make contact d. Commutator dirty e. Commutator rough, pitted, or burned f. Armature or field coils defective	a. Clean brushes and guides of brush holders. See **4.3.** b. Replace brushes. See **4.3.** c. Replace springs. See **4.3.** d. Clean commutator. See **4.3.** e. Recondition or replace starter motor. See **4.2, 4.3.** f. Recondition or replace starter motor. See **4.2, 4.3.**
3. Starter turns too slowly or fails to turn the engine over	a. Battery run down b. Insufficient current flowing to loose or corroded connections c. Brushes sticking d. Brushes worn e. Commutator dirty f. Commutator rough, pitted, or burned g. Armature or field coils defective	a. Charge battery. See **3.3** b. Clean battery terminals and cable clamps, tighten connections. See **3.1, 3.2.** c. Clean brushes and guides of brush holders. See **4.3.** d. Replace brushes. See **4.3.** e. Clean commutator. See **4.3.** f. Recondition or replace starter motor. See **4.2, 4.3.** g. Recondition or replace starter motor. See **4.2, 4.3.**
4. Starter makes unusual sounds, cranks engine erratically, or fails to crank	a. Drive pinion defective b. Flywheel or drive plate ring gear defective	a. Replace drive pinion. See **4.3.** b. Replace flywheel or drive plate. See **ENGINE AND CLUTCH.**
5. Drive pinion does not disengage	a. Drive pinion or armature shaft dirty or damaged b. Solenoid switch defective	a. Recondition or replace starter motor. See **4.2, 4.3.** b. Replace solenoid switch. See **4.3.**

4

4.2 Removing and Installing Starter

Because the starter is located on the same side of the engine as the intake and exhaust manifolds, you should remove the starter by working under the car. The starter used on VW diesel models is different, and its removal and installation are covered separately.

Removing and Installing Starter for Spark-ignition Engine

In addition to being bolted to the flywheel bellhousing, the starter is held to the side of the engine block by a support bracket. Be sure that you have a suitable wrench for the socket head bolt that holds this bracket to the engine.

To remove:

1. Disconnect the ground strap from the negative post of the battery.

2. Support the engine either from above or with a jack placed beneath its right-hand side. This will keep the engine from settling to the right when you remove the right side engine mount.

3. If the car has a splash shield beneath the right-hand side of the engine or beneath the transaxle, remove the splash shield(s). Then disconnect the wires indicated in Fig. 4-1.

Fig. 4-1. Wires on solenoid. Terminal 50 (**A**) receives the wire from the seatbelt interlock relay or from the ignition/start switch. Terminal 16 (**B**) receives the wire from terminal 15 on the ignition coil. Terminal 30 (**C**) receives the cable from the positive battery pole.

4. Remove the right side engine mount. To do this, first remove the nut that holds the mount's bonded rubber part to the subframe, and then remove the bolts that hold the mount to the engine block.

5. Remove the three nuts indicated in Fig. 4-2.

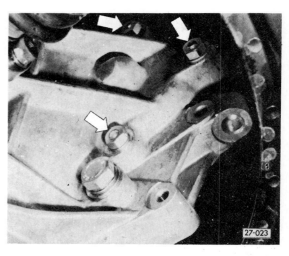

Fig. 4-2. Nuts for bolts that hold starter on bellhousing.

6. Remove the socket-head bolt that holds the support bracket to the engine block. The support bracket is located at the front of the starter motor.

7. The three bolts that hold the starter to the bellhousing should be removed now, if they were not removed previously. Then withdraw the starter from the bellhousing and remove the starter from the car.

To install:

1. Inspect the starter bushing that is pressed into the transmission case, inside the bellhousing. If the bushing is worn or damaged, replace it as described in **MANUAL TRANSMISSION** or in **AUTOMATIC TRANSMISSION.**

2. Lubricate the starter bushing with multipurpose grease. Then apply a good sealing compound around the starter's mounting flange.

3. Insert the starter in the bellhousing and loosely install the three mounting bolts and nuts.

4. Working alternately, gradually torque all three fasteners to 2.0 mkg (14 ft. lb.). Then install the socket head bolt that holds the support bracket on the engine block and torque the bolt to 2.0 mkg (14 ft. lb.).

CAUTION ——
A new support bracket is used on late cars that have starters 056 911 023 B or 056 911 023 C. If you replace a bracket, the new bracket must be the correct one for the starter. Using the wrong bracket can damage the starter.

5. Clean the wires and terminals. Tightly install the two wires and the cable on the solenoid. If necessary, refer to Fig. 4-1 to determine the correct

terminals for the wires. The black wire should go on terminal 16.

6. If necessary, raise the engine slightly, and then reinstall the right side engine mount. Torque the nut and the bolts that hold the mount to the engine and to the subframe to 4.0 mkg (29 ft. lb.).

7. If necessary, reinstall the splash shield(s) beneath the engine/transaxle assembly. Remove the jack or overhead support from the engine. Reconnect the battery's ground strap.

Removing and Installing Starter for VW Diesel Engine

A different starter, Part No. 068 911 023, is used with the VW diesel engine. There is no support bracket to hold the front end of the starter to the engine block as on spark-ignition engines.

To remove:

1. Disconnect the ground strap from the negative post of the battery.

2. Support the engine either from above or with a jack placed beneath its right-hand side to keep the engine from settling to the right when you remove the right side engine mount.

3. If the car has a splash shield beneath the right-hand side of the engine or beneath the transaxle, remove the splash shield(s).

4. Remove the right side engine mount by removing first the nut and then the bolts indicated in Fig. 4-3.

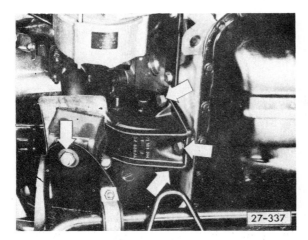

Fig. 4-3. Nut and bolts that hold right side engine mount. Nut (left arrow) holds mount to subframe. Three bolts (right arrows) hold mount to engine block.

5. Detach the wires from the starter solenoid.

6. Working at the rear of the bellhousing, remove the nuts that hold the starter bolts. If necessary, consult Fig. 4-3 which is given earlier.

7. If they were not removed previously, remove the three bolts that hold the starter to the bellhousing. Then withdraw the starter from the bellhousing and remove the starter from the car.

To install:

1. Inspect the starter bushing that is pressed into the transmission case, inside the bellhousing. If the bushing is worn or damaged, replace it as described in **MANUAL TRANSMISSION.**

2. Lubricate the starter bushing with multipurpose grease. Then apply a good sealing compound around the starter's mounting flange.

3. Insert the starter in the bellhousing and loosely install the three mounting bolts and nuts. Then, working alternately, gradually torque all three fasteners to 2.0 mkg (14 ft. lb.).

4. Clean the wires and terminals. Tightly install the wires and the cable on the starter solenoid, making sure that they are correctly routed through the plastic clip indicated in Fig. 4-4.

Fig. 4-4. Plastic clip (arrow) that holds starter wiring away from exhaust manifold. (Manifolds have been removed here for clarity.)

5. If necessary, raise the engine slightly, and then reinstall the right side engine mount. Torque the nuts and the bolts that hold the mount to the engine and to the subframe to 4.0 mkg (29 ft. lb.).

6. If necessary, reinstall the splash shield(s) beneath the engine/transaxle assembly. Remove the jack or overhead support from the engine. Reconnect the battery's ground strap.

4.3 Disassembling and Assembling Starter

If a faulty starter proves to have a number of defects, it is often best economically to replace it with a new or rebuilt starter rather than to attempt repairs. Some tasks, such as removing the pole shoes and the field windings, may require special tools.

> *CAUTION ——*
>
> *If you lack the skills, tools, or test equipment needed to repair the starter, we suggest you leave such repairs to an Authorized Dealer or a qualified automotive electrical shop. We especially urge you to consult your Authorized Dealer before attempting repairs on a car still covered by the new-car warranty.*

Removing and Installing Solenoid

If troubleshooting has shown the solenoid to be faulty, it can be replaced separately. New and rebuilt starters are delivered with solenoids installed. The removal of the solenoid, as well as complete disassembly of the starter motor and starter drive, is illustrated in Fig. 4-5. The starter connector strap is shown attached to the field coils.

To remove solenoid:

1. Remove the starter from the car.

2. Remove the nut and the starter connector strap from the starter connector terminal on the solenoid. Then remove the two screws that hold the solenoid to the starter drive housing.

3. Lift the solenoid plunger's pull rod upward and off the engaging fork. (It will be easier to do this if you pull the pinion clockwise and outward at the same time.)

4. Withdraw the solenoid.

To install:

1. Make sure that the seal and disk are tight and correctly positioned in the starter drive housing. Also check the rubber seal for the starter connector strap.

2. Place a thin strip of plastic sealing compound around the outer edge of the solenoid end face.

3. Withdraw the drive pinion as far as possible. Then hook the solenoid plunger's pull rod over the engaging fork. The spring and spring cup on the pull rod should be compressed toward the plunger.

4. Position the solenoid against the starter drive housing. Then allow the drive pinion to return to its disengaged position.

5. Apply sealer to the screw heads. Then install the two screws that hold the solenoid on the starter drive housing.

6. Install the starter connector strap and the nut on the solenoid's connector strap terminal.

Disassembling and Assembling Starter Motor and Starter Drive

You must disassemble the starter motor in order to inspect, repair, or replace the starter drive or replace the brushes.

To disassemble:

1. Remove the starter. Then remove the solenoid.

2. Remove the nuts and washers from the through bolts. Take off the support bracket.

3. Remove the end cap screws. Remove the end cap and its gasket. Then pry the C-clip off the end of the armature shaft and remove the two spacer

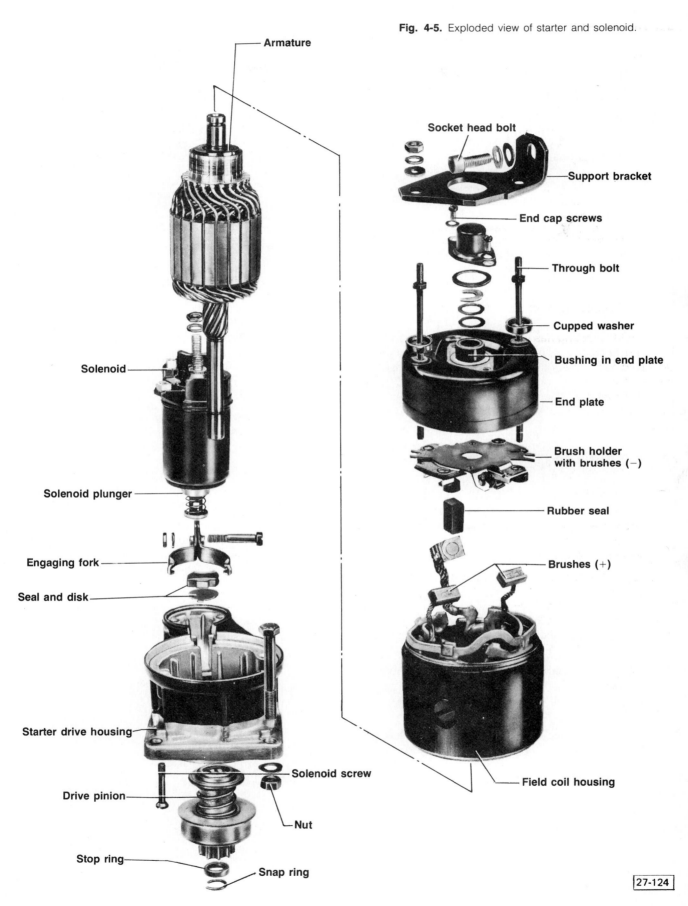

Fig. 4-5. Exploded view of starter and solenoid.

- Armature
- Socket head bolt
- Support bracket
- End cap screws
- Through bolt
- Cupped washer
- Solenoid
- Bushing in end plate
- End plate
- Brush holder with brushes (−)
- Solenoid plunger
- Rubber seal
- Engaging fork
- Brushes (+)
- Seal and disk
- Starter drive housing
- Solenoid screw
- Drive pinion
- Nut
- Field coil housing
- Stop ring
- Snap ring

4

washers. If there are burrs beside the C-clip groove in the armature shaft, remove them with a file.

4. Remove the small nuts and cupped washers from the through bolts. Remove the end plate from the motor.

5. Lift aside the brush springs. Remove the positive (+) brushes from the brush holder. Then remove the brush holder.

6. Lift the field coil housing off the armature.

7. Using a tool such as the one shown in Fig. 4-6, press the stop ring off of the snap ring. (The snap ring is concealed beneath the stop ring in a groove in the armature shaft.)

Fig. 4-6. Stop ring being pressed off of snap ring toward drive pinion.

8. Using circlip pliers, remove the snap ring from the armature shaft. Remove the stop ring.

9. If there are burrs beside the snap ring groove in the armature shaft, remove them with a file. Then remove the armature.

10. Remove the bolt, nut, and washer that hold the engaging fork in the starter drive housing. Remove the seal, the disk, and then the engaging fork from the housing.

11. If the field coils must be replaced, loosen the pole shoe screws as shown in Fig. 4-7. If the screws cannot be loosened in this manner, take the field coil housing to your Authorized Dealer or to a qualified automotive machine shop where special tools are available for removing pole shoe screws.

To inspect and assemble:

1. Wipe clean all of the parts for the starter motor and starter drive.

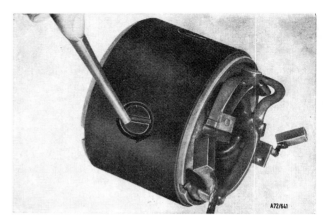

Fig. 4-7. Punch being used to loosen pole shoe screw. Strike punch with hammer to turn screw counterclockwise. After removing screw, you can take out pole shoe and field coil.

CAUTION ——

Do not wash the armature, the field coils, the self-oiling end plate bushing, or the drive pinion assembly in solvent. Doing this may damage the insulation of the armature or field coils and will destroy the factory-installed lubricants in the bushing and in the drive pinion's overrunning clutch.

2. If there has been trouble in the starter, make the electrical tests described under the next heading. If necessary, replace the armature, the field coils, or the entire starter.

3. Inspect the bushing in the end plate. If the bushing is worn or damaged, press it out. Then press in a new bushing as shown in Fig. 4-8.

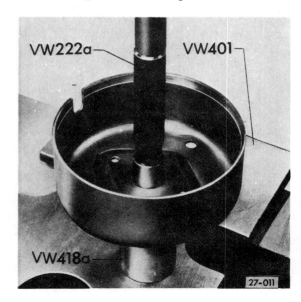

Fig. 4-8. New bushing being pressed into end plate.

4. Inspect the brushes. If the brushes have worn to a length of less than 13 mm (½ in.), replace the brushes.

5. To replace the negative (–) brushes, replace the entire brush holder. Alternatively, check whether new brushes are available. If so, unsolder the brush wires from the brush holder. Then install the new brushes, soldering on their wires in place of the original wires.

6. To replace the positive (+) brushes, replace the field coils with new field coils that have brushes attached. Alternatively, check whether new brushes are available. If so, crush the old brushes in a vise, then solder the new brushes onto the original brush wires. Because the field coils are aluminum, the brush wires are welded to the field coils and cannot be detached.

7. Inspect the commutator for taper and uneven wear. (The commutator is a ring of brass bars permanently affixed to the armature.) To check the commutator for out of round, place the armature shaft on V-blocks and hand-turn the commutator against a machinist's square that has been positioned beside the commutator. If there is more than 0.03 mm (.001 in.) of taper, uneven wear, or out-of-round, the commutator must be machined.

NOTE ———

The commutator should be machined by an Authorized Dealer or by a qualified automotive machine shop. The commutator diameter must not be reduced to less than 34.50 mm (1.358 in.). After the commutator has been turned on a lathe, the insulation strips between the commutator bars must be undercut by about 0.50 mm (.020 in.) below the surfaces of the bars.

8. Inspect the drive pinion for chipped and burred teeth. Make sure that the overrunning clutch operates smoothly without noise or binding. If any of these faults is found, replace the drive pinion assembly.

9. To prevent damage to the bushing in the end plate or to the interior of the drive pinion, remove any burrs from the snap ring and C-clip grooves in the armature shaft.

10. Install the armature in the starter drive housing. Then install the drive pinion.

CAUTION ———

Do not grease the drive pinion or the armature shaft. Doing this may cause the starter drive to jam in cold weather.

11. Install the stop ring on the armature shaft. Then install a new snap ring as shown in Fig. 4-9.

Fig. 4-9. Stop ring and snap ring installed on armature shaft.

12. With the stop ring supported on the press bed, press down the armature shaft as shown in Fig. 4-10 until the snap ring is seated inside the stop ring.

Fig. 4-10. Snap ring being seated inside the stop ring.

13. With the exception of the end cap and the support bracket, assemble the remaining parts of the starter and starter drive. During assembly, all

points indicated in Fig. 4-11 should be made weatherproof with a good sealer.

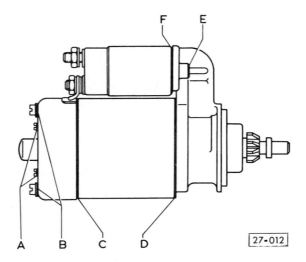

27-012

A. Holes for end cap screws
B. Holes for through bolts
C. Joint between field coil housing and end plate
D. Joint between field coil housing and starter drive housing
E. Holes for solenoid mounting screws
F. Surface between solenoid and starter drive housing

Fig. 4-11. Sealing locations on starter. Do not install end cap and screws until you have checked the armature's axial play.

14. After you have installed the spacer washers and the C-clip on the armature shaft, use feeler gauges of various thicknesses to determine the clearance between the C-clip and the washers. By doing this you will be measuring the armature's axial play. Axial play should be between 0.10 and 0.30 mm (.004 and .012 in.). If it is not, either add or remove spacer washers in order to obtain armature axial play that is within the prescribed range.

15. Using sealer on the screw heads, install the end cap. Then install the support bracket.

Testing Disassembled Starter

If the troubleshooting checks given in **4.1 Starting System Troubleshooting** indicate trouble in the armature or in the field coils, further tests can be made after you have removed and disassembled the starter. Several of these tests can be made with a simple battery-powered test light, although an ohmmeter is preferable.

Short circuits in the armature occur when the insulation between the windings breaks down. An armature tester called a growler is used to test for shorts. Growlers are available at most automotve supply stores that offer

machine shop service. The shop will test an armature for you at low cost. If the armature is shorted, it must be replaced.

Armature grounds occur when insulation breaks down and allows the windings to come into electrical contact with the armature laminations or the shaft. It is easy to detect this condition with a battery-powered test light or with an ohmmeter as shown in Fig. 4-12.

Fig. 4-12. Armature ground test. The windings are grounded if testing for continuity between the commutator and the armature body, or shaft, produces an ohmmeter reading (or causes a battery-powered test lamp to light).

Occasionally, carbon dust from the brushes will short an armature. If arcing current has not permanently damaged the insulation, cleaning with trichloroethylene or a similar solvent will usually cure such shorts.

To check the armature for open circuits, inspect the commutator bars. Burn marks between the bars indicate that there is an open circuit in the winding coil that is connected to one of the bars. You can also test for open circuits by applying the test probes of an ohmmeter or a battery-powered test light to adjacent bars all around the commutator. There should be electrical continuity among all of the bars. If not, there is an open circuit and the armature must be replaced.

A minimum of 7 volts must be available at terminal 50 in order to operate a removed solenoid. A minimum of 8 volts must be available at terminal 50 for the solenoid to hold the pinion in engagement under load. Sometimes, though the voltage at terminal 50 is adequate, an installed solenoid will fail to work properly. In this case it is necessary to distinguish trouble caused by a binding starter drive from trouble caused by faulty solenoid windings.

To test the solenoid windings, connect a switch and a fully charged 12-volt automobile battery as indicated in

Fig. 4-13. Close the switch (**S**). Normally, the solenoid plunger will pull in. However, on some removed solenoids it may be necessary to start the plunger into the solenoid housing by hand. Immediately after the plunger pulls in, open the switch (**S**). The plunger must drop out of the housing at once. If it does not, the windings are unserviceable and the solenoid must be replaced.

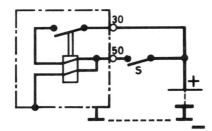

Fig. 4-13. Solenoid test hookup. The switch (**S**) goes between the battery's positive pole and terminal 50 on the solenoid. The solenoid housing is connected to the battery's negative pole.

Because of the high conductivity of the aluminum field coils and the relatively few windings in each coil, it is not practical to test the coils for shorts by comparing the relative resistance or the relative current flow through the coils. However, you can test the field coils to determine whether they are short-circuited to the starter's field coil housing. To locate this kind of trouble, test for continuity between the field coils and the housing. Make certain that neither positive (+) brush is touching the housing when this test is made. If there is continuity between the coil windings and the housing, replace the field coils.

To test the field coils for open circuits, apply one test probe of an ohmmeter or a battery-powered test light to the starter connector strap and the other test probe alternately to each of the positive (+) brushes. If there is no electrical continuity, there is an open circuit and the field coils must be replaced.

Testing Assembled Starter

A battery, or several batteries wired in parallel, with a rated capacity of 135 ampere hours, should be available for starter bench tests. This will ensure that decreasing battery power does not influence the test readings. Automotive electrical shops that have starter motor test stands will find the data given here useful in determining how closely starters conform to factory specifications. Testing should be carried out in the following sequence:

No-load test—starter motor running freely:

The starter should run at 6000 to 8000 rpm, the voltage should read 11.5, and the current draw should be between 35 and 55 amps.

If the rpm is below 6000 rpm and the current is above 55 amps, either mechanical parts are binding or there are shorts in the armature or the field coils. If the rpm is below 6000 rpm and the current draw is below 35 amps, inadequate voltage is reaching all or part of the starter. Check for worn-out solenoid contacts, unsoldered connections between the armature windings and the commutator bars, or poor contact between the brushes and the commutator. Severe brush sparking indicates an out-of-round commutator, protruding commutator insulation strips, or armature windings that are open-circuited or unsoldered from the commutator bars.

Load test—starter braked to approximately 1000 rpm:

This is a simple functional test that must last no longer than 10 seconds. Look for severe brush sparking.

If the commutator is not out-of-round and the commutator insulation strips are properly undercut, severe brush sparking indicates that the armature or field coil windings are shorted or that the armature windings are open-circuited or unsoldered frm the commutator bars.

Stall test—starter braked to a standstill under load:

This test must last no longer than 1 or 2 seconds. At a voltage of 8.5, the current draw should be 340 to 430 amps. At a voltage of 7.5, the current draw should be 290 to 380 amps. Not less than 8 volts must be available at terminal 50 on the solenoid.

If the current draw is above 430 amps at 8.5 volts or above 380 amps at 7.5 volts, there are either internal short circuits or a short circuit to ground. If the current draw is below 340 amps at 8.5 volts or below 290 amps at 7.5 volts, check for poor contact between the brushes and the commutator, open-circuited armature windings, or armature windings that are unsoldered from the commutator bars. If none of these faults is found, there is an open circuit in the field coils.

5. CHARGING SYSTEM

Some early cars have 35-ampere Bosch alternators, but most have Bosch or Motorola 55-ampere units. Many later cars, particularly those with air conditioning, have Bosch or Motorola alternators rated at 65 amperes.

The alternator is belt-driven by the same V-belt that drives the water pump. The regulator, which is transistorized, is mounted on the end of the alternator housing. To prevent damage to the alternator and the regulator when you are making tests and repairs, please observe the following precautions:

1. If you connect a battery charger or a booster battery to the battery in the car, make certain that

you connect the negative cable to the battery's negative (−) pole and the positive cable to the battery's positive (+) pole. Otherwise, the diodes (transistors) will be damaged—even by momentary reversed polarity.

2. In installing a battery in the car, make certain that the ground strap is connected to the battery's negative (−) pole and that the cable that goes to terminal 30 on the starter solenoid is connected to the battery's positive (+) pole.

3. In installing the alternator or a replacement alternator on the car, never attempt to polarize the alternator. This practice is required by the DC (direct current) generators used on some cars, but is unnecessary on alternators and will damage the alternator used on the cars covered by this Manual.

4. Never operate the alternator while the battery cables are disconnected. Also, never operate the alternator with its output terminal (B+) disconnected and the other terminals connected.

5. Never short, bridge, or ground any terminals of the charging system except as specifically described in **5.1 Charging System Troubleshooting.**

6. Do not test the alternator diodes with an outside power source of more than 1.5 volts.

5.1 Charging System Troubleshooting

Charging system trouble is indicated by an alternator warning light that does not function normally, an undercharged battery, or an overcharged battery. Before you proceed with any testing, however, make sure that the alternator V-belt is correctly adjusted as described in **5.3 Removing and Installing Alternator.** Visually-inspect all electrical connections. The terminals and connectors must be clean and tight-fitting; the alternator must be properly grounded (by a ground strap from terminal 31 on the alternator to a bolt on the engine). Replace wires that have cracked or broken insulation.

In addition to alerting the driver to charging system malfunctions, the warning light has another important function. In order to explain this other function, it is necessary to describe briefly the operation of the alternator.

The alternator generates electrical power by means of electrical induction. That is, a magnetic field is placed in motion so that its invisible magnetic lines of force sweep over many stationary coils of wire. When they do this, the magnetic lines of force produce electrical current in the coils. The alternator's rotor is the electromagnet that produces this magnetic field. When the field is set into motion by the turning of the rotor, electrical power is generated in the windings of the alternator's stator. (The stator consists of overlapping coils of wire mounted on a soft iron core inside the alternator housing.)

Once the alternator has started to convert mechanical energy from the engine into electrical current in the stator coils, some of that current is used to magnetize the rotor. However, battery current must be used to magnetize the rotor until the alternator is generating enough electricity to become self-sufficient (or, to use the correct technical terminology, self-exciting).

The necessary battery current is supplied to the rotor through the filament of the alternator warning light bulb. As soon as the alternator's output has risen to a level that is equal to the battery's voltage, the current through the warning light bulb reaches a state of equilibrium and the light goes out.

Normally, the warning light should be off when the ignition is off and the engine is stopped. The light should be on with the ignition turned on and the engine stopped. The light should be off with the ignition turned on and the engine running. If the light does not function as described, carry out the tests and checks given in **Table b.**

If charging system trouble seems to be indicated by an undercharged or overcharged battery, but the warning light operates in the normal way, you should carry out the tests described in **5.2 In-car Testing of Alternator and Regulator.** Suspect overcharging if you frequently need to add large quantities of distilled water to the battery electrolyte. Since a worn out battery will also exhibit greater-than-normal need for water, make sure that the battery is fully charged and in good condition before assuming that there is trouble in the charging system.

An undercharged battery is usually associated with starting trouble. Again, make sure that the battery is in good condition and capable of accepting a full charge before you assume that there is charging system trouble. Other causes of a run down (undercharged) battery are the simultaneous use of a great many electrical accessories for long periods of time, leaving accessories or lights in operation with the engine stopped, frequent long periods of starter useage, and frequent short-trip driving that does not provide adequate time for the battery to recharge after operation of the starter. Broken or frayed charging system wiring and worn, corroded, or loose battery cable connections will also prevent adequate charging or increase the time required for the battery to become fully recharged.

Table b. Warning Light Troubleshooting

Symptom	Test and Probable Cause	Remedy
1. Ignition off, engine not running. Warning light glowing or on	**(TEST)** Disconnect connector plug from alternator: a. Light goes out. Shorted diode carrier or faulty positive (+) diode in diode carrier b. Light does not go out. Short in wiring harness or in connector plug	a. Replace diodes and diode carrier as a unit. See **5.4**. b. Repair or replace faulty wiring. See **12**.
2. Ignition on, engine not running. Warning light off	a. Battery discharged **(TEST)** Remove and test warning light bulb: b. Bulbs burned out **(TEST**—bulb not burned out) Disconnect connector plug from alternator. Using a voltmeter, test between the plug terminal for the red wires and ground: c. No voltage. Open circuit between connector plug and battery positive (+) pole **(TEST**—bulb not burned out, battery voltage reaching connector plug) Disconnect the connector plug from the alternator. With the ignition on, ground the plug terminal for the blue wire against a clean, unpainted metal part of the engine: d. Light does not come on. Faulty bulb socket, open circuit in blue wire, or open circuit in wire between socket and terminal 15 on the ignition switch e. Light comes on. Loose connection between regulator and alternator or loose connection between brushes and regulator f. Light comes on, regulator properly connected. Worn out brushes, dirty slip rings (on rotor), or both g. Light comes on, regulator properly connected. Brushes not excessively worn and slip rings clean. Burned-out field winding in rotor h. Light comes on, regulator properly connected; brushes, slip rings, and rotor not defective. Faulty regulator	a. Charge battery. See **3.3**. b. Replace bulb. See **11.3**. c. Repair wire or connections. See **12.2**. d. Replace faulty socket. Repair wires or connections. See **11.3, 12.2**. e. Correct loose connections. See **5.4**. f. Clean slip rings. Measure brushes. Replace brushes that have worn to a length of 5 mm ($^7/_{32}$ in.) or less See **5.4**. g. Using an ohmmeter or a battery-powered test light, test for continuity between slip rings. If there is no continuity, replace the rotor. See **5.4**. h. Replace regulator. See **5.4**.
3. Ignition on, engine running. Engine can be accelerated to 2000 rpm or more but warning light stays on	a. Loose or broken alternator V-belt b. Exciter diodes burned out c. Faulty regulator or faulty alternator windings	a. Replace or adjust V-belt. See **5.3**. b. Test diodes. If diodes are faulty, replace the diodes and the diode carrier as a unit. See **5.4**. c. Test charging system with engine running. Replace faulty regulator, alternator, or both. See **5.2, 5.4**.

4

5.2 In-car Testing of Alternator and Regulator

Fig. 5-1 shows the hook-up for testing alternator output. The positive battery cable must be disconnected and a battery cutout switch installed as shown, with the cable reconnected to the cutout switch.

CAUTION ——

An alternator must never be run with the battery disconnected. Doing this will severely damage the alternator, the regulator, or both.

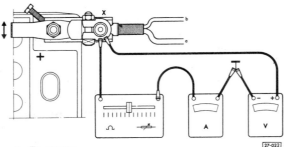

a. To starter
b. To fuse box terminal 30
X. Battery cutout switch (SUN electric No. 7052–003 or similar equipment)

Fig. 5-1. Alternator charging system test. Variable resistance, ammeter, and voltmeter are connected in series as shown. Note that the ammeter lead and the negative voltmeter lead connected to it are both grounded to the chassis. The double arrow at the left indicates switch operation.

To test:

1. With the engine stopped (alternator stationary), remove the battery ground strap. Then make the test connections and connect the battery ground strap. Close the cutout switch as shown in Fig. 5-2, then start the engine.

2. In testing a 55-ampere alternator, run the engine at 2500 to 3000 rpm and adjust the variable resistance so that the ammeter gives a reading between 20 and 30 amps. In testing a 65-ampere alternator, run the engine at 3000 rpm and adjust the variable resistance to 44 amps.

   NOTE ——

   If there is no charging system output, and earlier troubleshooting has uncovered no open circuits, loose connections, or trouble in the brushes or the rotor, the trouble is in the alternator. Test the diodes as described in **5.6 Testing Alternator Components.** If open diodes are found, replace the diodes and the diode carrier as a unit. If the diodes

are not faulty, there are open circuits in the stator coil windings and the entire alternator should be replaced if a new stator is not available.

Fig. 5-2. Battery cutout switch in closed position. Notice the test connections.

3. Move the cutout switch as shown in Fig. 5-3 in order to cut the battery out of the test circuit. The load current is now determined by the variable resistance.

Fig. 5-3. Battery cutout switch in open position.

4. Readjust the variable resistance, if necessary, so that the ammeter reading is 25 amps with the engine at 2500 to 3000 rpm—or 44 amps at 3000 rpm if you are testing a 65-ampere alternator.

5. Read the voltage indicated on the voltmeter. It should be between 12.5 and 14.5 volts.

If charging system output is above the prescribed range (overcharging), the trouble is probably a faulty regulator. However, test the diodes as described in **5.6 Testing Alternator Components** before you replace the regulator. If any diodes are open-circuited, replace the diodes and the diode carrier as a unit. If there is still an overcharge, or if the diodes are not faulty, replace the regulator.

If the charging system output is below the prescribed range (undercharging), test the diodes as described in **5.6 Testing Alternator Components.** If any diodes are shorted, replace the diodes and the diode carrier as a unit. If the diodes are not faulty, test the stator for grounded coil windings as described in **5.6 Testing Alternator Components.** If there are grounded windings, replace the entire alternator if a new stator is not available. If neither the diodes nor the stator windings are faulty, the trouble is in the regulator, which should be replaced. Instructions for replacing stators, diode carriers, and regulators can be found either in **5.4 Disassembling and Assembling Bosch Alternator** or in **5.5 Disassembling and Assembling Motorola Alternator.**

Noisy Alternator

Alternator noises are usually mechanical in origin but a continuous high, soft whistling sound may be produced by an alternator that is overcharging because of a faulty regulator or an open diode. The same sound may be heard if there is a shorted diode that is placing abnormal electrical strain on the alternator. The sound may also be heard for short periods of time soon after starting the engine, when the alternator is operating normally at maximum output. No trouble is indicated if the noise goes away after several minutes of operation.

Alternator mechnical noises are usually the result of misalignment between the V-belt and the pulley, a loose or broken pulley, worn bearings, or a bent rotor shaft. If any such faults are found, either replace the faulty parts as described in **5.4 Disassembling and Assembling Alternator** or replace the entire alternator.

5.3 Removing and Installing Alternator

Fig 5-4 and Fig. 5-5 are exploded views of the alternator and its mountings. These illustrations can be used as guides if it is necessary to remove or replace any of the alternator mounting components. During installation, the bolts that hold the alternator mounting brackets to the engine block should be torqued to 3.0 mkg (22 ft. lb.) on spark-ignition engines or to 2.0 mkg (14 ft. lb.) on VW diesel engines. These specifications apply equally to the bolt that holds the alternator's ground strap or ground wire to the bracket on the engine block.

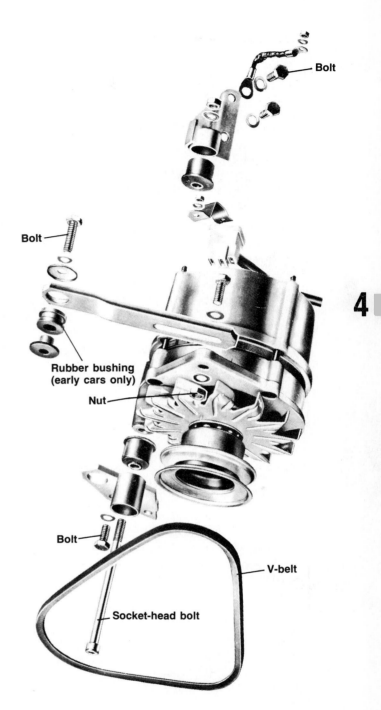

4

Fig. 5-4. Alternator and mountings for spark-ignition engines.

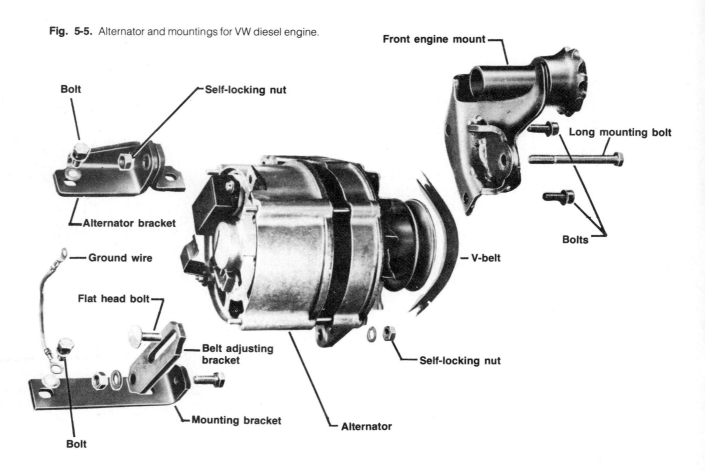

Fig. 5-5. Alternator and mountings for VW diesel engine.

To remove alternator:

1. Disconnect the battery ground strap.

2. Detach the alternator's wiring harness from the alternator housing by taking off the clamp and the plastic clip (Bosch alternators) or the plastic cable binder (Motorola alternators).

3. Remove the connector plug(s) from the alternator. Take off the nut, and then disconnect the ground strap or wire (which goes to the alternator mounting bracket on the engine block) from the alternator housing. See Fig. 5-6 and Fig. 5-7.

NOTE ——

On 65-ampere alternators, the wire to the B+ terminal is attached with a nut, as shown in Fig. 5-6. Fig. 5-7 shows the Motorola alternator's terminals, which are not marked on the housing.

Fig. 5-6. Terminal locations on 65-ampere alternator introduced on 1977 cars with factory air conditioning.

1. B+ terminal
2. D+ terminal for warning light wire
3. B+ terminal for connecting suppression condenser
4. Terminal for ground strap to engine

Fig. 5-7. Terminals of Motorola alternator.

4. On spark-ignition engines, loosen the alternator's upper and lower mounting bolts and also the bolt that holds the alternator's belt adjusting bracket to the cylinder head. Then push the alternator as far as possible toward the engine so that you can take the V-belt off the alternator and water pump pulleys. See Fig. 5-8.

   NOTE ——

   If you want to remove the alternator V-belt completely from certain cars sold in California, you must first remove the belt for the air injection pump. To do this, loosen the air pump mounting bolts. Push the air pump as far as possible toward the engine, and then remove the air pump V-belt.

Fig. 5-8. Socket-head lower mounting bolt for alternator of spark-ignition being loosened. Use socket wrench to hold nut at opposite end.

5. On VW diesel engines, loosen the bolts that are at each end of the alternator's belt adjusting bracket. Then loosen the alternator's upper mounting bolt, which passes through a bracket on the front engine mount. Push the alternator as far as possible downward toward the engine so that you can take the V-belt off the alternator pulley.

6. On spark-ignition engines, pull the lower mounting bolt (the socket-head bolt) out only as far as is necessary to disengage it from the alternator. Then remove the alternator from the car.

7. On VW diesel engines, completely remove the upper mounting bolt. Then remove the alternator from the car.

To install:

1. Position the alternator on its mounting brackets. Then, to hold the alternator in place, push the long mounting bolt through the alternator's mounting flange and the rear mounting bracket. Loosely install the nut and the washer for the long bolt.

2. Loosely install the mounting bolt that holds the alternator to the belt adjusting bracket. Push the alternator as far as it will go toward the engine. Then install the V-belt on the pulley(s).

3. By pulling the alternator away from the engine block, adjust the V-belt tension so that you can depress the V-belt 10 to 15 mm (⅜ to ⁹/₁₆ in.) at the point indicated in Fig. 5-9. Then torque the mounting bolts and nuts to 2.0 mkg (14 ft. lb.) on spark-ignition engines or to 2.5 mkg (18 ft. lb.) on VW diesel engines.

   NOTE ——

   On VW diesel engines, which have the alternator mounted on the side opposite to the alternator location of spark-ignition engines, depress the V-belt at a point midway between the crankshaft pulley and the alternator pulley.

Fig. 5-9. Point at which V-belt should be depressed (spark-ignition engine shown). Dimension **a** should be 10 to 15 mm (⅜ to ⁹/₁₆ in.).

4. On spark-ignition engines sold in California, install the air pump V-belt and adjust it using the same procedure used to adjust the alternator belt.

   CAUTION ——

   Do not tension the V-belts too tightly. Doing this may cause the alternator bearings, the water pump bearings, or the air pump bearings to fail after only a short period of service.

5. Reconnect the wiring to the alternator. If necessary, consult Fig. 5-6 and Fig. 5-7, which were given earlier in this procedure.

6. Reattach the alternator's wiring harness to the end of the alternator housing as indicated in Fig. 5-10, Fig. 5-11, Fig. 5-12, or Fig. 5-13.

Fig. 5-10. Wiring harness correctly attached to alternator of VW diesel engine. Clamp is at **1**, plastic clip at **2**.

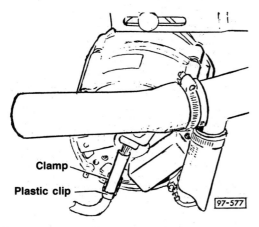

Fig. 5-11. Wiring harness correctly attached to Bosch alternator of spark-ignition engine.

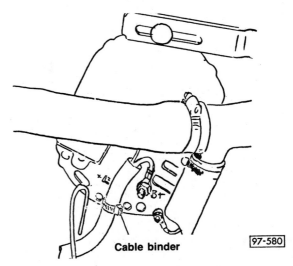

Fig. 5-13. Wiring harness correctly attached to 65-amp Motorola alternator of spark-ignition engine.

4

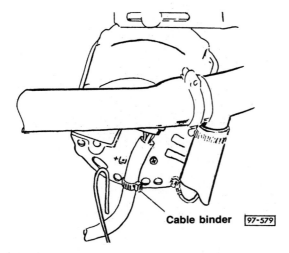

Fig. 5-12. Wiring harness correctly attached to 55-amp Motorola alternator of spark-ignition engine.

5.4 Disassembling and Assembling Bosch Alternator

A Bosch alternator is shown separated into its replaceable components in Fig. 5-14. The ball bearing races are a press fit on the rotor shaft. Do not reuse bearings that have been pressed off the shaft. In installing new bearings, use a press tool that will apply pressure to the inner bearing race only.

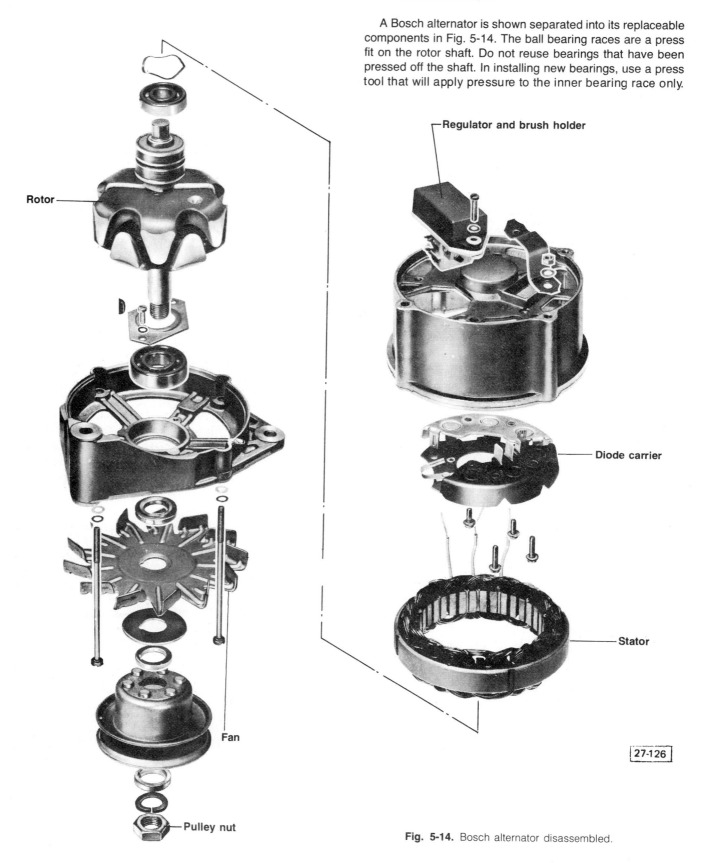

Fig. 5-14. Bosch alternator disassembled.

27-126

The diodes and diode carrier must be replaced as a unit. If either the diode carrier or the stator is replaced, the stator wires must be unsoldered from the diode carrier and the connections resoldered after the faulty component has been replaced. In using the soldering iron, be careful not to overheat the diodes. Overheating will cause the diodes to open-circuit or short. Before applying the soldering iron to the connection, grip the diode wire near the diode with a pair of needle-nose pliers. Alternatively, install a special heat sink on the diode lead wire. By absorbing heat from the lead wire, the heat sink or pliers will prevent excessive heat from reaching the diode itself.

You can press the rotor out of the front half of the alternator housing as shown in Fig. 5-15. Once the rotor is removed, you can remove the bearings as shown in Fig. 5-16. If you must replace a rotor, always replace the bearings also.

Fig. 5-16. Puller being used to remove ball bearing race from Bosch rotor shaft. Press on new bearings using a sleeve-type driver that will contact the inner bearing race only.

Brushes and Regulator

You can remove the regulator and brush holder from the Bosch alternator by taking out the two screws indicated in Fig. 5-17. If the brushes are worn to less than 5 mm ($^7/_{32}$ in.), replace the brushes. See Fig. 5-18.

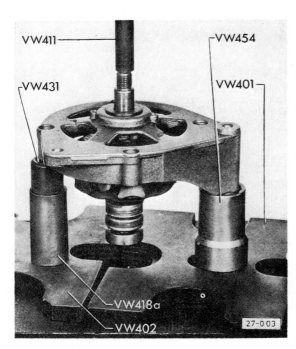

Fig. 5-15. Rotor being pressed out of Bosch alternator's pulley-end housing.

Fig. 5-17. Screws (arrows) that hold regulator and brush holder to Bosch alternator.

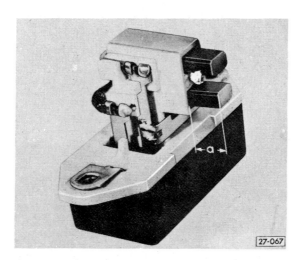

Fig. 5-18. Brush length being checked. Length (dimension **a**) of new brushes is 10 mm (⅜ in.). Replace brushes that have worn to 5 mm (⁷/₃₂ in.) or less.

5.5 Disassembling and Assembling Motorola Alternator

A Motorola alternator is shown separated into its main components in Fig. 5-19. Replacement parts for some of the components may not be available, so check that the parts needed for repair are sold as standard replacement parts before you decide to rebuild a faulty alternator.

CAUTION ——

If you lack the skills or tools required to repair the alternator, we suggest you leave these repairs to an Authorized Dealer or other qualified shop. Alternatively, you can replace a faulty alternator with a new or rebuilt alternator. We especially urge you to consult your Authorized Dealer before attempting repairs on a car still covered by the new-car warranty.

The diodes and diode carrier must be replaced as a unit. If either the diode carrier or the stator is replaced, the stator wires must be unsoldered from the diode carrier and the connections resoldered after the faulty component has been replaced. In using the soldering iron, you must be careful not to overheat the diodes. Overheating will cause the diodes to open-circuit or short. Before applying the soldering iron to the connection, grip the diode wire near the diode with a pair of needle-nose pliers. Alternatively, install a special heat sink on the diode lead wire. By absorbing heat from the lead wire, the heat sink or pliers will prevent excessive heat from reaching the diode itself.

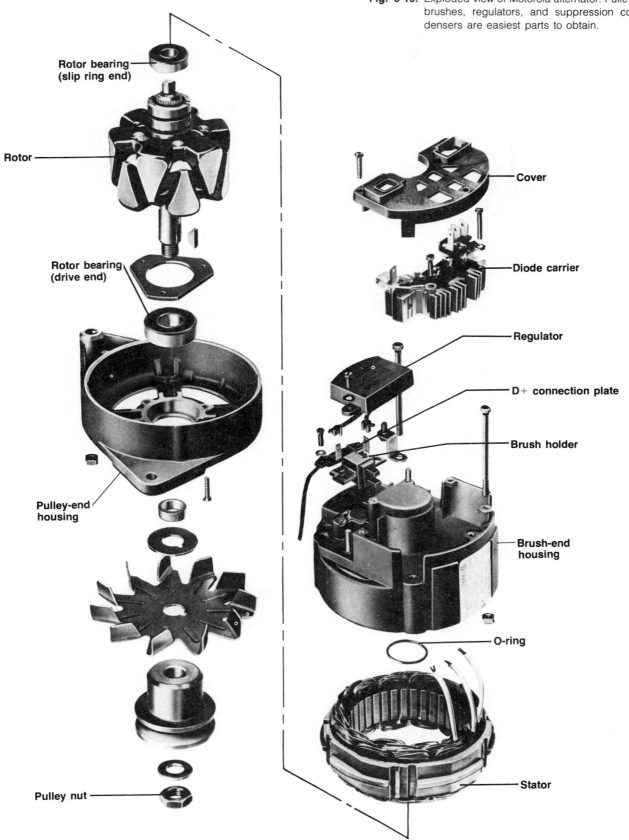

Fig. 5-19. Exploded view of Motorola alternator. Pulleys, brushes, regulators, and suppression condensers are easiest parts to obtain.

Rotor bearing (slip ring end)

Rotor

Rotor bearing (drive end)

Pulley-end housing

Pulley nut

Cover

Diode carrier

Regulator

D+ connection plate

Brush holder

Brush-end housing

O-ring

Stator

4

27-109

You can remove the rotor from the pulley-end housing after the screws for the bearing retaining plate have been removed. The bearings can be removed from the rotor shaft as shown in Fig. 5-20. The ball bearing races are a press fit on the rotor shaft and should not be reused once they have been pulled off. In installing new bearings, use a press tool that will apply pressure to the inner bearing race only.

1. Green wire to terminal DF
2. Red wire to terminal D+

Fig. 5-21. Regulator connections on Motorola alternator.

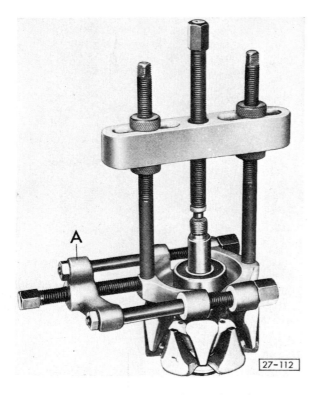

Fig. 5-20. Bearing being pulled off rotor shaft. Never pull off the slip rings.

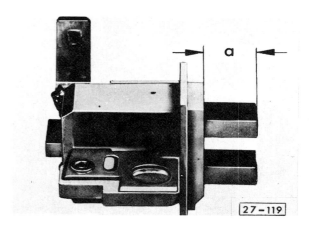

Fig. 5-22. Brush length being checked. Length (dimension **a**) of new brushes is 9 mm ($^{11}/_{32}$ in.). Replace brushes that have worn to 5 mm ($^{7}/_{32}$ in.) or less.

Brushes and Regulator

You can remove the regulator from the Motorola alternator by taking out the two screws that hold it to the brush-end housing. Then lift off the regulator and disconnect its wires from the terminals in the alternator. During installation, connect the wires of the regulator as indicated in Fig. 5-21.

With the regulator removed, you can take out the screws that hold the D+ connection plate and the brush holder to the alternator. The brush holder can then be removed for inspection or replacement. If the brushes are worn to less than 5 mm ($^{7}/_{32}$ in.), replace the brushes. See Fig. 5-22.

5.6 Testing Alternator Components

A diode is a kind of transistor that has the unique property of permitting electrical current to flow through it in only one direction. To test the diodes in the alternator's diode carrier, first unsolder the connections for the stator wires. You will notice that there are three diode groups of three diodes each in the diode carrier. Unsolder the connections that join the three groups. This will isolate each group from the other two.

Using an ohmmeter or a 1.5-volt battery-powered test light, apply one test probe to the diode's lead wire and the other test probe to the diode's case. Then reverse the positions of the two test probes. The ammeter should show a reading (or the test light should light) with the test probes in one position but not in the other. If no reading (or light) is obtained in either position, the diode (or diode group) is open-circuited and the diodes and the diode carrier should be replaced as a unit.

You should also replace the diode carrier if the ammeter produces a reading (or the test light comes on) with the test probes in both positions. This is an indication that one or more of the diodes are shorted.

If all three diode groups show continuity in one test probe position but not in the other, it is still possible that an individual diode is faulty. Unsolder each diode lead from its connection with the other diodes, then test the diodes individually. If one or more diodes show no continuity in either position, replace the diodes and the diode carrier as a unit.

NOTE ──

Voltage surges in the car's electrical system may damage the alternator diodes. When you replace the diodes, install a suppression condenser (Part No. 059 035 271) if the alternator did not originally have this condenser. The condenser, shown installed on a Bosch alternator in Fig. 5-23, should prevent a recurrence of the trouble. The same condenser is also suitable for use with the Motorola alternator.

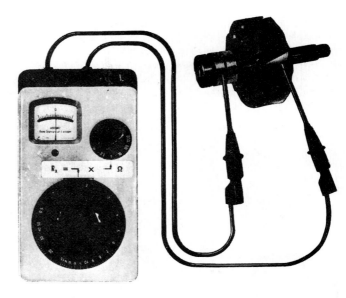

Fig. 5-24. Ohmmeter being used to test rotor for grounded field coil. The poles and the shaft should not be in electrical contact with the slip rings.

Using an ohmmeter, you can measure the resistance between the slip rings as shown in Fig. 5-25. If the resistance is significantly less than 3.40 to 3.74 ohms, the field coil is shorted (this specification is valid for 55-ampere Bosch alternators only). A battery-powered test light should be dim when the test probes are applied to the slip rings. If there is no continuity, the field coil is burned out.

Fig. 5-23. Suppression condenser (Part No. 059 035 271) installed on alternator.

You can use an ohmmeter or a battery-powered test light to test the rotor's field coil. There should be no electrical continuity when the test probes are applied to the slip rings and to the rotor shaft or the poles (Fig. 5-24). If there is continuity, the field coil is grounded and the rotor must be replaced.

Fig. 5-25. Ohmmeter being used to measure the resistance between the two slip rings. Resistance is created by the field coil, through which the test current must flow.

There should be no electrical continuity between any of the stator coil winding leads and the stator's laminated iron frame (Fig. 5-26). If there is continuity, the windings are grounded and the stator must be replaced.

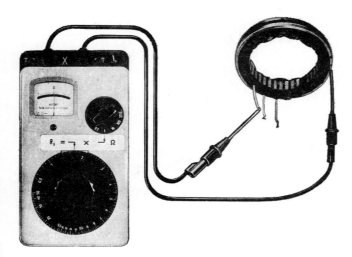

Fig. 5-26. Ohmmeter being used to test stator for grounded coil windings. You can also use a battery-powered test light for this test.

If there is no electrical continuity between any two of the stator coil winding leads when checked as shown in Fig. 5-27, there is an open circuit in the windings. If the resistance between any two leads of a 55-amp alternator is significantly more or less than 0.14 to 0.15 ohms, the windings are shorted. Replace stators that have open or shorted windings.

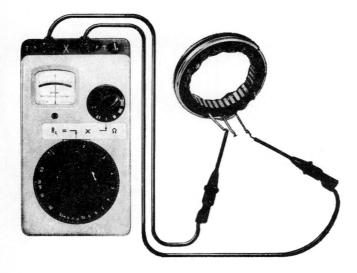

Fig. 5-27. Ohmmeter being used to check continuity and resistance through stator coil windings. A battery-powered test light can be used in testing continuity only.

6. TURN SIGNALS AND EMERGENCY FLASHERS

The turn signal switch and relay are often mistakenly blamed for troubles caused by dirty, corroded, or loose-fitting turn signal bulb contacts. Before starting to troubleshoot either the turn signal switch or the turn signal/emergency flasher relay, be sure that all bulb contacts are clean and tight.

6.1 Turn Signal and Emergency Flasher Troubleshooting

The turn signals and the emergency flashers share the same flasher relay. The flasher relay is labeled J[2] in the wiring diagrams that appear at the end of this section of the Manual. On some cars, current to the flasher relay comes from a relay that is designated as the windshield wiper relay on the transparent cover for the fuse box.

The turn signals operate only with the ignition turned on. The emergency flashers operate whether the ignition is on or off. If the emergency flashers work but the turn signals do not, you can be certain that neither the flasher relay or the windshield wiper relay is faulty. The same is true if the turn signals work but the emergency flashers do not. However, if neither system operates you should not conclude that either of the relays is faulty without further troubleshooting.

Table c should be used in conjunction with the wiring diagrams given at the end of this section of the Manual. The bold numbers in the table's Remedy column refer to headings in this section where the suggested repairs are described. Before you begin, make sure that the battery is not run down and that the bulbs and their contacts are in good condition.

NOTE ——

If one bulb is burned out, the other bulbs may come on without flashing or may flash very slowly.

Testing Switches after Removal

After they have been removed, the turn signal switch and the emergency flasher switch can be tested independently of the car's electrical system. See **6.2 Removing and Installing Steering Column Switches** or **8.3 Removing and Installing Switches in Dashboard.**

To test the turn signal switch, you will need either an ohmmeter or a battery-powered test light. Apply one test probe of the ohmmeter or test light to terminal 54 on the switch. With the switch turned to the position used in signaling a right turn, there should be electrical continuity to terminal R; with the switch turned to the

Table c. Turn Signal and Emergency Flasher Troubleshooting

Symptom	Additional symptoms and probable cause	Remedy
1. Turn signals do not work (ignition on) but emergency flashers work. Rear window defogger does not work	a. Gauges and warning lights not working: Fuse 5 burned out b. Connector plug (located behind instrument panel) for red/black wire faulty or disconnected c. Loose connection at terminal 54 on turn signal switch d. Red/black wire or red/white wire broken between fuse box and emergency flasher switch e. No voltage at terminal 49d on emergency flasher switch with ignition and emergency flasher switches on: Emergency flasher switch faulty	a. Replace fuse 5. If fuse again burns out, look for shorts in the circuits served by fuse 5. See **12.**, **12.2.** b. Clean and tighten connector terminals. Reconnect connector. See **12.2.** c. Clean and tighten loose connection. See **6.2.** d. Test wires for continuity. Replace faulty wires. See **12.2.** e. Replace emergency flasher switch. See **8.4.**
2. Turn signals work (ignition on) but emergency flashers do not work	a. Loose connections or broken red wire between fuse box and terminal 30 on emergency flasher switch b. Loose connection at terminal 49a or at terminals L and R on emergency flasher switch c. No voltage at terminal 49d on emergency flasher switch with ignition off and emergency flasher switch on—or no voltage at terminal L or R with emergency flasher switch on and voltage present at terminal 49a on emergency flasher switch: Faulty emergency flasher switch	a. Clean and tighten loose connections. Replace faulty wire. See **12.2.** b. Clean and tighten loose connections. See **8.4.** c. Replace emergency flasher switch. See **8.4.**
3. Neither the turn signals nor the emergency flashers work—or the correct bulbs light up but fail to flash	a. Windshield washers (or wipers) work (ignition on): Fuse 7 burned out b. Windshield washers (or wipers) work (ignition on), fuse 7 not burned out: Red/black wire disconnected from terminal fuse box—or red/black wire broken between fuse box and turn signal switch c. Windshield washers (or wipers) work (ignition on). Fuse 7 not burned out. Wire from fuse box to turn signal switch not broken or disconnected: Faulty flasher relay d. Windshield washers (or wipers) do not work (ignition on): Faulty windshield wiper relay	a. Replace fuse 7. If fuse again burns out, look for shorts in the circuits served by fuse 7. See **12.**, **12.2.** b. Clean and tighten loose connections. Replace faulty wire. See **12.2.** c. Replace flasher relay. See **12.** d. Replace windshield wiper relay. See **12.**
4. Bulbs and bulb terminals not faulty but only some of the bulbs light up	a. Loose connections or broken wires between turn signal switch and fuse box or between fuse box and bulbs or between emergency flasher switch and bulbs	a. Clean and tighten loose connections. Replace faulty wires. See **12.2.**

4

position used in signaling a left turn, there should be electrical continuity to terminal L. If there is no continuity to one or both of the terminals, replace the switch.

To test the emergency flasher switch, first apply one test probe of the ohmmeter or test light to terminal 49d. With the switch turned off there should be electrical continuity to terminal 15; with the switch turned on there should be electrical continuity to terminal 30. If there is no continuity to one of the terminals, replace the switch. If there is continuity to the terminals, remove the test probe from terminal 49d and place the probe on terminal 49a. With the switch turned on, there should be electrical continuity to terminals R and L and to the positive

contact in the emergency flasher warning light bulb socket. If there is no continuity to one of these three locations, replace the switch.

6.2 Removing and Installing Steering Column Switches

Two switches—the turn signal switch and the windshield wiper/washer switch—are mounted on the steering column. On 1973 through 1977 cars, the switches are separate components. On 1978 and later cars the two switches are assembled by screws into a single unit with the ignition/steering lock.

Removing and Installing
1973 through 1977 Switches

To remove the turn signal switch and the windshield wiper/washer switches on 1973 through 1977 cars, first remove the steering wheel as described in **SUSPENSION AND STEERING.** Then remove the four Phillips head screws that hold the switch housing on the steering column (Fig. 6-1). The Phillips head screws that are visible through the switch control handle opening hold the turn signal switch in the switch housing.

Fig. 6-1. Screws (arrows) that hold switch housing on steering column.

Once the switches and the switch housing have been withdrawn from the steering column trim (Fig. 6-2), you can remove the multiple connector plugs from the backs of the turn signal and windshield wiper/washer switches.

Fig. 6-2. Switch housing pulled away from steering column and steering column trim.

To remove the switches from the switch housing, remove the two phillips head screws that hold each switch to the mounting plate inside the switch housing.

Then slide the mounting plates out of the grooves in the housing and withdraw the switches from the housing. See Fig. 6-3.

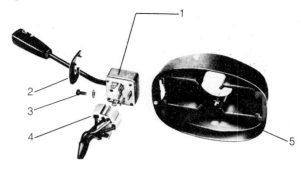

1. Switch
2. Mounting plate
3. Phillips head screw (2)
4. Multiple connector
5. Switch housing

Fig. 6-3. Removal of switch from switch housing.

Installation is the reverse of removal. Before you install the switches and the switch housing on the steering column, make sure that the turn signal switch is in its centered (neutral) position. Otherwise, you may damage the canceling lug on the turn signal switch as the mounting screws are tightened.

Removing and Installing 1978 and Later Switches

Fig. 6-4 shows the steering column switches introduced on 1978 models. Switches of this kind are not interchangeable with those of earlier cars.

To remove the steering column switches, first disconnect the battery ground strap. Then carefully pry off the padded cover (Fig. 6-5) using your fingertips only. Remove the nut and the washer so that you can pull the steering wheel off the steering column. (Normally, it is not necessary to use any kind of tool for this.)

Remove the two fillister head screws that hold the lower part of the switch housing to the upper part. Remove the bottom half of the housing. Disconnect the wiring plugs from the switches, then remove the three screws that hold the turn signal and windshield wiper/washer switches to the mounting for the ignition/steering lock. See Fig. 6-4. Remove the switches from the steering column.

If it is also necessary to remove the ignition/steering lock, remove the socket-head screw that holds the lock mounting to the steering column tube. Push the housing as far as possible toward the dashboard, then remove the spacer sleeve and disconnect the wiring from the ignition switch. Pull the ignition/steering lock assembly upward off the steering column and the steering column tube. It is also possible to remove the ignition/steering lock assembly with the turn signal and windshield wiper/washer switches still attached.

4 ■

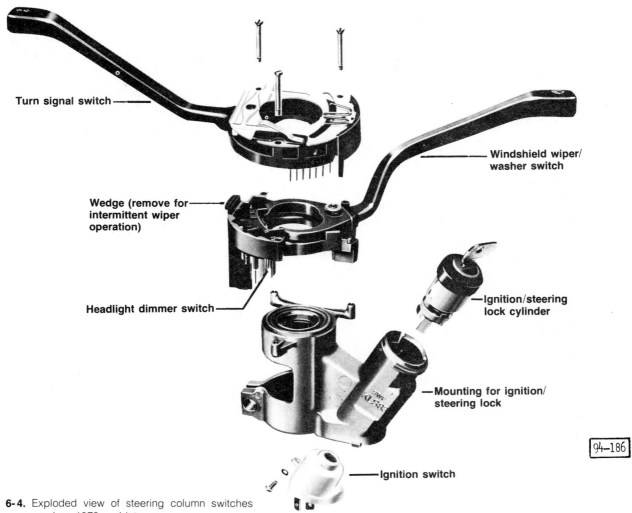

Fig. 6-4. Exploded view of steering column switches used on 1978 and later cars.

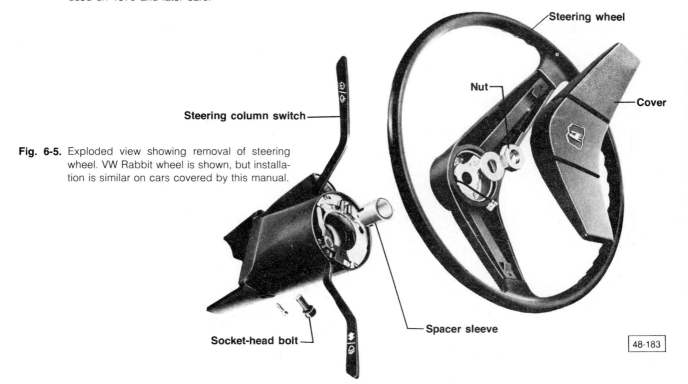

Fig. 6-5. Exploded view showing removal of steering wheel. VW Rabbit wheel is shown, but installation is similar on cars covered by this manual.

Installation is the reverse of removal. After you have installed the switches, drive on the spacer sleeve until its upper end is flush with the bevel on the steering column. (If the spacer sleeve is damaged or loose-fitting, replace it.) Reconnect the wiring, but for the moment do not tighten the socket-head bolt that holds the ignition/steering lock mounting. (You need not loosen the bolt, however, if you have not removed the ignition/steering lock.)

Before you install the steering wheel, make certain that the steering is centered (front wheels pointed straight ahead). Then install the steering wheel so that its spokes are horizontal and the lug for the turn signal canceling mechanism is pointed toward the left-hand side of the car. Install the washer, then install the nut and torque it to 5.0 mkg (36 ft. lb.). If necessary, pull the column switch assembly upward until it contacts the spacer sleeve. Then torque the socket-head bolt to 1.0 mkg (7 ft. lb.). Install the lower half of the housing using the two Phillips head screws. Reinstall the pad on the horn control. Reconnect the battery ground strap.

Removing and Installing Ignition Switch and Ignition/Steering Lock Cylinder

(1978 and later models)

The following instructions apply specifically to 1978 and later cars. On earlier cars, the ignition/steering lock is not an integral part of the steering column switch assembly. Removal of the early-type ignition/steering lock is covered in conjunction with steering column removal in **SUSPENSION AND STEERING.** Removal of the early-type ignition/starter switch is covered in **8.2 Removing and Installing 1973 through 1977 Ignition/Starter Switch.**

To remove the ignition/steering lock cylinder from a 1978 or later model, you must drill a 3-mm (⅜-in.) hole at the point indicated in Fig. 6-6. Then insert a pin through the hole in order to press down the spring that holds the lock cylinder in the mounting. If necessary, you can insert the key to help pull out the cylinder. To install the cylinder, simply press it in without the key until it snaps into place.

To remove the ignition switch, remove the screw indicated in Fig. 6-7. The terminals identified in the illustration may not match those of cars covered by this Manual. Installation is the reverse of removal.

Fig. 6-6. Hole being located in mounting for ignition/steering lock. Dimension **a** is 12 mm (¹⁵/₃₂ in.); dimension **b** is 10 mm (⅜ in.).

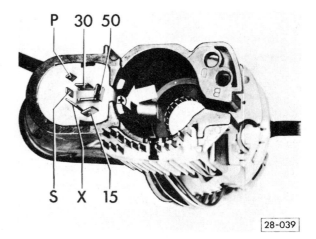

Fig. 6-7. Screw (arrow) that holds ignition switch in housing. Switches shown are not for a car covered by this Manual.

Testing Steering Column Switches

(1978 and later models)

Fig. 6-8, Fig. 6-9, and Fig. 6-10 identify the terminals of the steering column switches used on 1978 and later cars. These illustrations will help in testing and troubleshooting the switches, and should be used in conjunction with the wiring diagrams at the end of this section of the Manual.

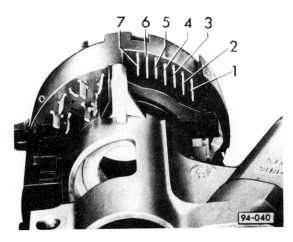

1. Terminal R
2. Terminal 49a
3. Terminal L
4. Terminal PR
5. Terminal 71
6. Terminal P
7. Terminal PL

Fig. 6-8. Identification of turn signal switch terminals

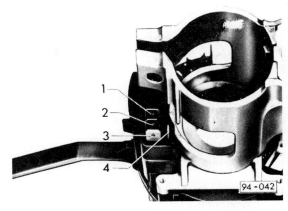

1. Terminal 56a
2. Terminal 56b
3. Terminal 56
4. Terminal 30

Fig. 6-10. Identification of headlight dimmer switch terminals.

4

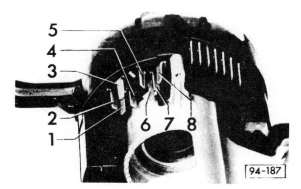

1. Terminal 53e
2. Terminal 53
3. Terminal 53a
4. Terminal J
5. Terminal 53b
6. Terminal L
7. Terminal T
8. Terminal 31

Fig. 6-9. Identification of wiper/washer switch terminals.

7. WINDSHIELD WIPERS and WASHER

The operation of the two-speed windshield wipers and the windshield washer is controlled by a lever on the steering column. The wiper blades park automatically when turned off. The windshield washers are supplied with water by a motor-driven pump.

7.1 Windshield Wiper Motor Troubleshooting

Table d is designed to help you quickly determine the cause and remedy for malfunctions in the windshield wiper motor and drive linkage. The bold numbers in the Remedy column refer to headings in this section where the suggested repairs are described.

7.2 Removing, Servicing, and Installing Wiper Blades and Arms

Before removing a wiper blade, first fold the wiper arm away from the windshield. Turn the blade as shown in Fig. 7-1.

NOTE ——
The pivot joint in the wiper arm has a built-in stop that prevents the blade from swinging to an excessive angle when the arm is folded away from the windshield.

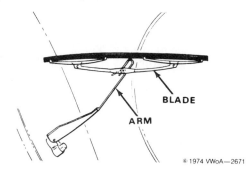

© 1974 VWoA—2671

Fig. 7-1. Wiper blade turned to an angle with the wiper arm.

With the blade angled until it is against the stop, lift the retaining spring and slide the blade down the wiper arm until the hook of the arm is off the pivot pin. You may then lift the blade off upward. The sequence is illustrated in Fig. 7-2.

Table d. Windshield Wiper Motor Troubleshooting

Symptom	Probable Cause	Remedy
1. Windshield wipers do not work, operate too slowly, cut out, or come to a standstill on the glass	a. Shorted wiring or wiper motor overloaded. Fuse 11, fuse 12, or both burned out b. Battery down c. Faulty windshield wiper relay or fuse 5 burned out owing to a short or overload in one of the accessories served by fuse 5 d. Moving joints of windshield wiper linkage dry or jammed e. Wiper/washer switch faulty or wires loose f. Faulty wiper motor and drive	a. Replace faulty fuses. Find and repair shorts or eliminate cause of overload on wiper motor. See **12.** b. Charge battery. Check battery cables and connections. See **3.1, 3.2.** c. Turn on emergency flashers. If flashers do not work, windshield wiper relay is faulty. If flashers work, turn on wipers while flashers are operating. If wipers work, fuse 5 is burned out. Replace faulty fuses and relays; eliminate shorts or overloads. See **12.** d. Thoroughly lubricate all moving parts with multipurpose grease. Eliminate cause of jamming. See **7.3.** e. Replace switch. Repair faulty connections. See **6.2, 12.2.** f. Replace wiper motor assembly. See **7.3.**
2. Windshield wiper motor continues to run or fails to return blades to parking position after manual switch has been turned off	a. Wire to terminal 53a on wiper motor assembly broken or disconnected b. Drive crank installed at wrong angle on wiper motor drive gearshaft c. No continuity between terminals 53 and S (31b) on wiper switch with switch turned off d. Faulty wiper motor and drive	a. Clean and tighten loose connections. Replace faulty wire. See **12.2.** b. Adjust drive crank angle. See **7.3.** c. Replace switch. See **6.3.** d. Replace wiper motor assembly. See **7.3.**
3. Wiper linkage squeaks. Motor operates slowly. Motor overheats or emits an odor of overheated electrical equipment	a. Moving joints of windshield wiper linkage dry or jammed b. Drive housing not seated squarely on motor c. Dry bearings in wiper motor drive d. Faulty wiper motor and drive	a. Thoroughly lubricate all moving parts with multipurpose grease. Eliminate cause of jamming. See **7.3.** b. Install drive housing correctly. See **7.3.** c. Lubricate drive parts with molybdenum grease. See **7.3.** d. Replace wiper motor assembly. See **7.3.**

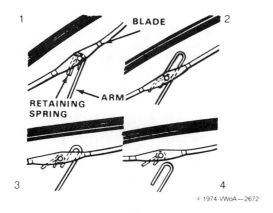

Fig. 7-2. Blade removal sequence.

To install wiper blade:

1. Position the new blade on the arm. The arm must enter through the hole in the blade frame on the side opposite the retaining spring.

2. Slide the blade down the arm until you can slip the hook on the arm over the pivot pin.

3. Pull the blade upward until the retaining spring is fully enclosed in the hook, then place the wiper against the windshield. This installation procedure is the reverse of the sequence given in Fig. 10-6.

The rubber filler can be replaced without replacing the entire wiper blade. See Fig. 7-3.

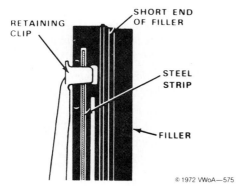

Fig. 7-3. Components of wiper blade filler assembly.

To replace filler:

1. Remove the wiper blade from the wiper arm.

2. Tightly compress the short end of the filler between your thumb and finger, then twist one side of the filler out of the retaining clip.

3. With the free side of the retaining clip resting in the groove with the steel strip, repeat the preceding step to free the other side of the filler from the retaining clip.

4. Slide the short end of the filler toward the center of the blade until the short end is completely free of the retaining clip.

5. Shift the filler sideways and unhook the steel strips from the retaining clip as indicated in Fig. 7-4. Then slide the filler out of the other retaining clips.

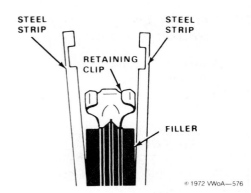

Fig. 7-4. Steel strips unhooked from retaining clip.

6. Place both steel strips in the grooves of the new filler. Make sure the notches in the steel strips face the filler and engage the projections in the filler grooves.

7. Hold the filler so that the strips are kept in the grooves. Starting at the open end of the filler, carefully slide the filler and the steel strips into the retaining clips.

8. When the closed end of the filler has reached the end retaining clip, compress the filler until the retaining clip rides over the raised edge next to the retaining clip recess in the end of the filler.

9. Make sure the retaining clip completely engages the recess in the filler. Then install the wiper blade on the wiper arm.

Removing, Installing, and Adjusting Wiper Arms

The wiper arm is held on the wiper shaft by a concealed M 6 hexagon nut. On 1973 through 1977 cars, the nut is covered by a hinged cap. To lift up the cap for access to the mounting nut, first lift the wiper arm fully away from the windshield, then lower the wiper back against the glass while at the same time prying the cap upward (Fig. 7-5).

Fig. 7-5. Hinged cap being lifted up and wiper arm lowered (arrows).

On 1978 and later cars, the mounting nut is covered by a pressed-on cap. In removing the wiper arm, it is necessary to pry out the cap carefully in order to gain access to the nut. See Fig. 7-6.

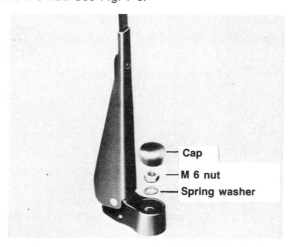

Fig. 7-6. Exploded view showing cap that covers wiper arm mounting nut.

The wiper arms must be installed at the correct angle after they have been removed for replacement or repairs. Proper wiper operation under all weather conditions is possible only when the arms are adjusted accurately to specifications. The adjustment of the wipers on the wiper arm shafts is measured at the two points indicated in Fig.

7-7. Dimension **a** must be 35 mm ($1\frac{3}{8}$ in.). Proper installation requires that the spring washer be seated under the nut. After you have adjusted the angle of the wiper arms to specifications, torque the nuts to 0.7 mkg or 70 cmkg (60 in. lb.).

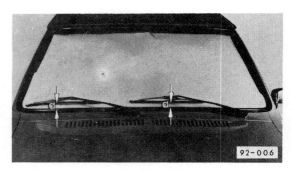

Fig. 7-7. Points where wiper arm adjustment is measured. Dimension **a** is 35 mm ($1\frac{3}{8}$ in.).

7.3 Removing, Repairing, and Installing Wiper Motor and Frame

The wiper motor and frame are mounted inside the ventilation compartment that is immediately to the rear of the engine compartment. Removal can be carried out with the hood fully raised. (The hood need not be removed from the car.)

To remove:

1. Disconnect the battery ground strap.

2. Remove the wiper arms from the wiper shaft as described in **7.2 Removing, Servicing, and Installing Wiper Blades and Arms.**

3. Remove the nuts, washers, and seals that hold the wiper bearings in the cowl panel.

4. Disconnect the multiple connector from the wiper motor. Then remove the single sheet metal bolt that holds the wiper frame mounting bracket on the car body.

5. Pull the wiper bearings downward through the holes in the cowl panel, then lower the frame until it can be removed from the car with the wiper motor still attached.

Installation is the reverse of removal. Make sure that the wiper shafts are perpendicular to the surface of the windshield and that the bearing washers and seals are installed in the proper order. See Fig. 7-8.

Fig. 7-8. Exploded view of wiper motor and frame.

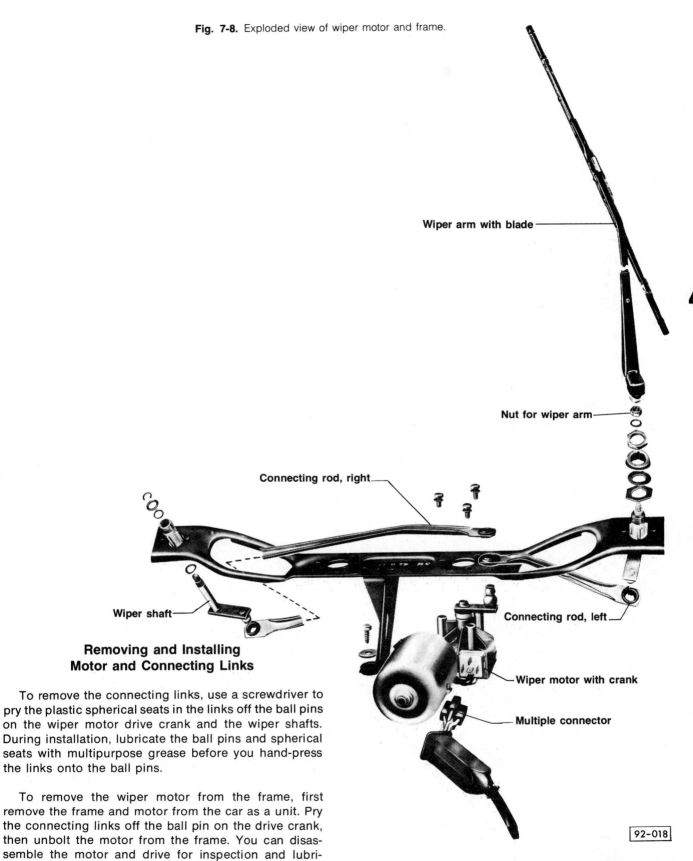

Wiper arm with blade

Nut for wiper arm

Connecting rod, right

Connecting rod, left

Wiper shaft

Wiper motor with crank

Multiple connector

92-018

Removing and Installing Motor and Connecting Links

To remove the connecting links, use a screwdriver to pry the plastic spherical seats in the links off the ball pins on the wiper motor drive crank and the wiper shafts. During installation, lubricate the ball pins and spherical seats with multipurpose grease before you hand-press the links onto the ball pins.

To remove the wiper motor from the frame, first remove the frame and motor from the car as a unit. Pry the connecting links off the ball pin on the drive crank, then unbolt the motor from the frame. You can disassemble the motor and drive for inspection and lubrication. However, individual parts are not available and, if faulty, the motor and drive assembly should be replaced as a unit.

If you disassemble the drive for the purpose of lubricating the gears and bearings with molybdenum grease, or if you install a different wiper motor and drive assembly, check the adjustment of the drive crank before you install the connecting links. To check, temporarily install the multiple connector plug on the motor and reconnect the battery ground strap. It is unnecessary to ground the motor housing. Turn on the ignition. Then turn on the windshield wiper switch and allow the motor to run for about 15 seconds. Turn off the windshield wiper switch. The motor should stop in its correct parking position. If the drive crank is not at the angle indicated in Fig. 7-9, loosen the nut at the center of the drive crank, position the drive crank properly on the drive gearshaft, then tighten the nut. Recheck the adjustment and, if necessary, correct it.

Fig. 7-9. Angle of drive crank with motor at correct parking position. Crank should stop 90° to one side of the motor's axis.

Removing and Installing Wiper Shafts

In the event that the wiper shafts require lubrication, you can remove the shafts from their bearings after the windshield wiper frame has been removed from the car. Using a screwdriver, pry the connecting links off the ball pins on the wiper shafts. Carefully remove the circlip and washers from the outward end of the wiper shaft. Then withdraw the shafts from their bearings.

Installation is the reverse of removal. Lubricate the shafts and bearings with multipurpose grease and make sure that the circlips snap solidly into the grooves in the wiper shafts. If the shafts or bearings are badly worn, replace them. New rivets are available for the installation of the bearings.

7.4 Removing, Testing, and Installing Windshield Wiper/Washer Switch

Removal of the windshield wiper/washer switch is described in **6.2 Removing and Installing Steering Column Switches.** To test the switch after it has been

removed, apply one test probe of an ohmmeter or a battery-powered test light to terminal 53. With the switch turned off, there should be electrical continuity both to terminal 53b and to terminal S (31b). With the wiper switch turned on, there should be continuity between terminals 53a and 53b. With the windshield washer switch turned on, there should be continuity between terminals 86 and 31. Faulty switches cannot be repaired and should be replaced as a unit.

7.5 Windshield Washers

On 1973 through early 1977 cars, the electric motor-powered windshield washer pump is mounted on the side of the windshield washer fluid reservoir as shown in Fig. 7-10. Early in 1977, the fluid pick-up line was eliminated and the pump pick-up on subsequent cars is inserted directly into the fluid reservoir as shown in Fig. 7-11.

Fig. 7-10. Early-type windshield washer pump, reservoir, and connections.

If the pump fails to operate when the windshield wiper/washer switch is pulled toward the steering wheel (ignition on), check the fuses (No. 12 and No. 5, for example) that the wiring diagrams show to be in control of washer operation. Additional troubleshooting can be carried out with the help of the wiring diagrams, using a voltmeter or a test light.

To clean a windshield washer jet, insert a fine steel wire into its orifice. If the spray does not strike the windshield at a satisfactory angle, adjust the jets as shown in Fig. 7-12.

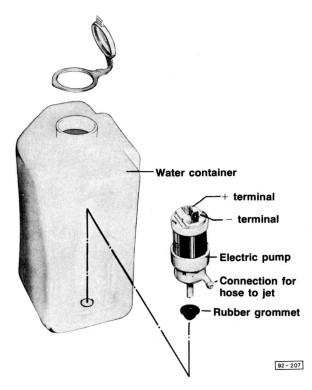

Water container

— **+ terminal**

— **– terminal**

— **Electric pump**

— **Connection for hose to jet**

— **Rubber grommet**

92 - 207

Fig. 7-11. Redesigned reservoir and pump introduced early in 1977.

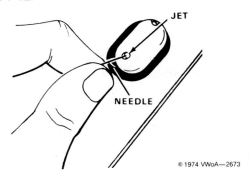

© 1974 VWoA—2673

Fig. 7-12. Ball-shaped windshield washer jet being pivoted in its socket. A sewing needle inserted into the orifice is a satisfactory tool.

To remove the early-type pump from the reservoir, simply detach the wires and the hoses, then pull the pump off the plastic lugs of the windshield washer fluid reservoir. The late-type pump can be pulled out of the rubber grommet.

7.6 Troubleshooting Windshield Wipers

Table e lists the probable causes and suggested remedies for windshield wiping problems. The numbers in bold type in the Remedy column refer to the numbered headings in this section where repairs are described.

Table e. Windshield Wiping System Troubleshooting

Problem	Probable Cause	Remedy
1. Smearing	a. Blade dirty	a. Clean blade with hard nylon brush and soap solution or alcohol.
	b. Blade lips frayed; rubber damaged or worn out	b. Install new rubber fillers. See **7.2**.
	c. Blades old, blade surface cracked	c. Install new rubber fillers. See **7.2**.
2. Traces of water on windshield form small beads	Window soiled by paint, polish, oil, or diesel exhaust deposits	Clean windshield with clean cloth and grease/oil/silicone remover.
3. Blade misses parts of windshield	a. Filler torn out of retainer	a. Reinstall filler carefully. See **7.2**.
	b. Blade not in uniform contact with glass; spring or retainer distorted	b. Install new blade. See **7.2**.
	c. Insufficient wiper pressure	c. Lightly lubricate arm linkage and spring or install new arm. See **7.2**.
4. Blade wipes well in one direction but badly in other, shudders	a. Filler distorted, no longer flips	a. Clean blade with hard nylon brush and soap solution or alcohol, or install new filler.
	b. Wiper arm distorted; blade not perpendicular to the windshield	b. Carefully twist wiper arm until it is perpendicular to the windshield.

8. LIGHTS AND SWITCHES

For safety reasons, it is important that all lights on the vehicle are working properly at all times. Aside from the instrument panel light bulbs, the replacement of which is described in **11.3 Removing and Installing Instruments,** all light bulbs on the car are available as standard U.S. replacement numbers.

8.1 Removing and Installing Sealed Beam Units and Aiming Headlights

On 1973 through 1977 cars, the radiator grille must be removed before you can replace a sealed beam unit. This is done by removing the clips and taking out the Phillips head screws that are visible through the front of the grille. On 1978 VW cars you must also remove the grille. Open the hood, then carefully pry off the two metal clips and release the plastic catches that are integral with the grille. On 1978 Audi models, remove the headlight trim. See Fig. 8-1.

Once the grille or the headlight trim has been removed, you can remove the sealed beam unit and its retaining ring by taking out the three short screws that hold the retaining ring to the support ring. Then pull the sealed beam unit forward and remove the electrical wire connector from the terminals.

> CAUTION ─
>
> *Do not alter the position of the long head-light adjustment screws. If you do, you will have to readjust the headlights.*

When you install a sealed beam unit, be sure that its three glass lugs correctly engage the support ring. Install the retaining ring and then the grille. It should not be necessary to aim the headlights after changing a sealed beam unit. If you are in doubt, however, the aim should be checked.

Each headlight has two adjusting screws. Adjust vertical aim with the top screw; adjust lateral aim with the screw at the left side of the support ring.

> NOTE ─
>
> Check your state laws to determine whether adjustments must be made by a licensed shop. Your state may also have laws specifying aiming different from that described here.

To adjust:

1. Position the car on a level surface 7.62 m (25 ft.) from a vertical wall. Have the fuel tank about half-filled and make certain that the tire pressures are correct.

2. Roll the car back and forth a few yards to settle the suspension. Then load the driver's seat with one person or a weight of 70 kg (154 lb.).

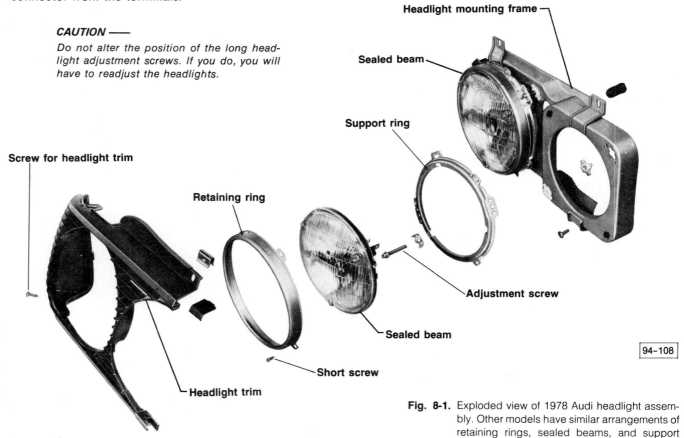

Screw for headlight trim

Retaining ring

Headlight mounting frame

Sealed beam

Support ring

Adjustment screw

Sealed beam

Short screw

Headlight trim

94-108

Fig. 8-1. Exploded view of 1978 Audi headlight assembly. Other models have similar arrangements of retaining rings, sealed beams, and support rings.

3. On 1973 through 1977 cars, remove the headlight grille. On 1978 and later models, the headlight aim adjusting screws are accessible through cutouts in the grille or the headlight trim.

4. Turn on the headlights and, if necessary, switch them to low beam. Cover one headlight at a time. The uncovered light's upper and left edges of high intensity should be in the positions shown in Fig. 8-2. If not, adjust the light's position using the adjustment screws.

5. Repeat step 4 on the opposite headlight and adjust as necessary. The high beams of the two sealed beam units adjusted on low beam will automatically be in adjustment once the low beams are aimed to the proper specifications.

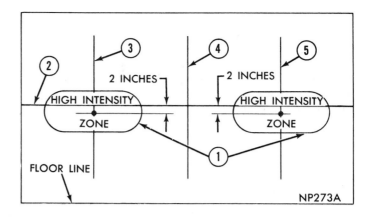

Fig. 8-3. High beam aiming target. Numbers represent the same factors given in Fig. 8-2.

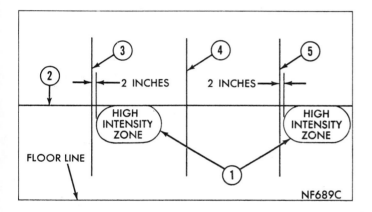

Fig. 8-2. Low beam aiming target on vertical wall. Light intensity areas are at 1. Line 2 is at the height of the headlight centers. Vertical lines 3 and 5 are spaced equally on each side of line 4 and are exactly as far from one another as the centers of the (outermost) sealed beam units.

6. On 1978 and later models (dual headlights), switch the headlights to high beam. Check the aim of each headlight with the other three headlights covered. The high intensity zones of all four lights should fall on the target as shown in Fig. 8-3.

NOTE——

It is unnecessary to adjust the headlights of 1973 through 1977 models on high beam. Nor do the outermost headlights of 1978 and later cars need to be adjusted on high beam if the low beam positions are correct. If there is any discrepancy, adjust the low beams correctly.

Replacing Side Marker, License Plate, and Front Turn Signal/Parking Light Bulbs

To replace a bulb in the side marker lights, the license plate lights, or the front turn signal/parking lights, remove the screw at each side of the lens (Fig. 8-4). Remove the lens. Press the bulb gently into its holder, turn the bulb counterclockwise, then take out the bulb. Install the new bulb by pressing it into the socket and turning the bulb clockwise. The double-filament bulbs used for the turn signal/parking lights have an asymmetrical pin arrangement that prevents the bulbs from being installed backward. In installing the lens, tighten the screws evenly but do not overtighten them, since overtightening may crack the lens.

Fig. 8-4. Screws (arrows) that hold turn signal/parking light lens (shown) or side marker light lens.

Replacing Rear Turn Signal, Stop/Tail Light, or Back-up Light Bulb

The rear turn signal, stop/tail light, and back-up light bulbs are accessible from inside the luggage compartment. To replace a bulb, unscrew the knurled screw, then remove the tail light inner cover. Squeeze the bulb housing slightly in the middle and pull out the bulb holder (Fig. 8-5). Press the faulty bulb gently into its holder, turn the bulb counterclockwise, then take out the bulb. Install the new bulb by pressing it into the socket and turning the bulb clockwise. In installing the tail light inner cover, do not overtighten the knurled screw.

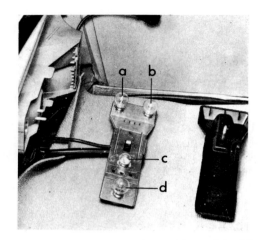

Fig. 8-5. Rear light bulb positions; (**a**) stop light, (**b**) turn signal, (**c**) tail light, and (**d**) back-up light.

Interior Light Bulb

To replace the tubular bulb (U.S. replacement number 211) in the interior light, you must pry the light assembly out of the roof headliner. To do this, insert a screwdriver into the cut-out on the switch end of the interior light assembly. Then carefully pry the assembly out until it is possible to remove it with your fingers. Install the new bulb, then hand-press the light assembly back into the headliner.

8.2 Removing and Installing 1973 through 1977 Ignition/Starter Switch

A faulty ignition/starter switch can be replaced without removing the lock cylinder or the steering column lock assembly from the car. Though it is unnecessary to remove the steering column lock in order to remove the ignition/starter switch, a removed lock is illustrated in the interest of clarity. For access to the installed switch and steering column lock, the left and center under-dash panels and the driver's glove shelf must be removed as described in **BODY AND INTERIOR**. To replace the switch, remove the setscrew indicated in Fig. 8-6. Then

withdraw the switch from the lock as shown. In installing the replacement switch, the setscrew must engage the recess in the switch. Removal, repair, and installation of the steering column lock are described in **SUSPENSION AND STEERING**.

Fig. 8-6. Ignition/starter switch removal. Setscrew is at left arrow, recess in switch is at right arrow.

8.3 Removing and Installing Switches in Dashboard

Press-type switches are used for headlights, the parking lights, the emergency flashers and the heated rear window. A headlight switch, typical of these press-type switches, is shown in Fig. 8-7.

If the indicator bulb inside of the switch is burned out, you can replace the bulb after you have removed the switch cap. Squeeze the cap together at the sides and then pull it off of the spring plates of the switch. Pull the bulb straight out without turning it.

To remove the switch, disconnect the battery ground strap. Then wrap a strong piece of string around the switch so that the string slips between the dashboard padding and the flange on the outer end of the switch body. Tie the string tightly, then use it to pull the switch out of the dashboard. Unplug the switch from the multiple connector, then anchor the connector in some way so that it does not slip through the switch opening and become inaccessible behind the dashboard. To install the switch, attach the multiple connector, then hand-press the switch into the opening in the dashboard.

The rheostat that controls the brightness of the instrument panel lights cannot be removed through the front of the dashboard. To remove the rheostat, disconnect the battery ground strap. Then take off the left under-dashboard cover panel and the driver's glove shelf

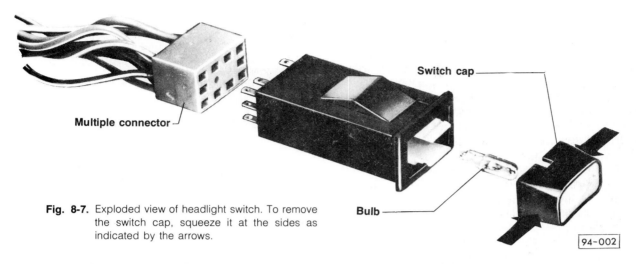

Fig. 8-7. Exploded view of headlight switch. To remove the switch cap, squeeze it at the sides as indicated by the arrows.

as described in **BODY AND INTERIOR.** Unscrew the knob from the rheostat and, using a special wrench, remove the escutcheon (the threaded ring that holds the rheostat in the dashboard). Reach behind the dashboard and pull the rheostat out toward the front of the car. Then detach the rheostat from the multiple connector. Installation is the reverse of removal.

9. HORN AND BUZZERS

Fig. 9-1 is an exploded view that shows the steering wheel in relation to the horn circuit. The horn is located under the front of the car, at the right side. The horn circuit is controlled directly by the horn control on the steering wheel, there being no horn relay.

Fig. 9-1. Steering wheel horn control and horn operating circuit.

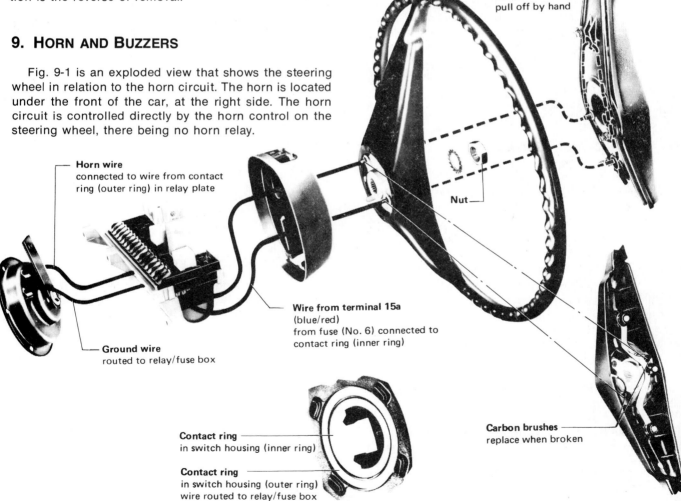

Horn Troubleshooting

The best way to troubleshoot the horn circuit is with a voltmeter. Using Fig. 9-1 and the wiring diagrams that appear at the end of this section as your guides, you can test whether battery voltage is reaching the horns, the fuse box, and other parts of the circuit. Once you have isolated the faulty wire or component, you can take steps to repair it.

In particular, check for loose, dirty terminals and worn electrical contacts. If ground (negative (−) polarity) is weak either at the brown wire to the horn or to the three-wire multiple connector in the engine compartment, the horn will not operate satisfactorily despite undamaged components elsewhere throughout the circuit. If the horn fails to operate when connected directly to the battery posts with jumper cables, the horn is faulty and must be replaced.

Warning Buzzer

All cars covered by this Manual are equipped with an ignition key warning buzzer that sounds if the ignition key is in the lock when the driver's door is opened. The same buzzer serves the seat belt warning system. The buzzer is an integral part of the seat belt warning system relay, which is located under the dashboard at the left side of the car. If the buzzer is faulty, the entire seat belt warning system relay must be replaced.

10. HEATING AND VENTILATION

The heater motor and heater controls are covered in **BODY AND INTERIOR.** Faulty heater motors cannot be repaired and must be replaced as a unit.

Heated Rear Window

A relay located in the fuse box controls the temperature of the heated rear window. Disconnect the battery ground strap before you disconnect any of the wires related to the system. In removing the rear window, disconnect the two wires from the terminals that are at the edge of the glass. Removal and installation of the heated rear window are the same as for any other rear window. However, they should only be attempted by someone familiar with automotive glass work who has the special tools required.

If only the conductive grid is damaged, it is unnecessary to replace the window. Repair material is available at Authorized Dealers to patch broken circuits.

To repair:

1. Apply a strip of masking tape along each edge of the broken conductor.

2. Apply the repair material evenly over the break.

3. Allow the repair to dry for one hour at room temperature. Then remove the tape and test the heating effect.

11. INSTRUMENTS

The instrument cluster includes a speedometer, a gauge cluster and—except on basic models—an electric clock. In addition to a fuel gauge and a coolant temperature gauge, the gauge cluster contains warning lights for the oil pressure, the alternator, and the brakes as well as indicator lights for the turn signals and high beams.

11.1 Replacing Speedometer Cable

The speedometer is driven off the transaxle via a flexible cable. Fig. 11-1 shows the cable and cable-installing components in relation to the instrument cluster.

To replace cable:

1. Remove the left under-dashboard cover panel and the driver's glove shelf as described in **BODY AND INTERIOR.**

2. Reach behind the dashboard and unscrew the knurled ferrule nut that holds the speedometer cable on the speedometer head.

3. Using pliers or a special wrench that will engage the notches in the union, unscrew the cable union from the pinion seat on the transmission (Fig. 11-2).

4. Inside the engine compartment, remove the plastic retainer that binds the speedometer cable to the fuel line.

5. Hand-press the rubber grommet out of the instrument panel carrier toward the front of the car; hand-press the rubber grommet out of the front cross panel toward the front of the car. Pull the cable forward, then hand-press the rear rubber grommet through the hole in the front cross panel and remove the cable toward the front of the car.

Fig. 11-1. Speedometer cable and related parts.

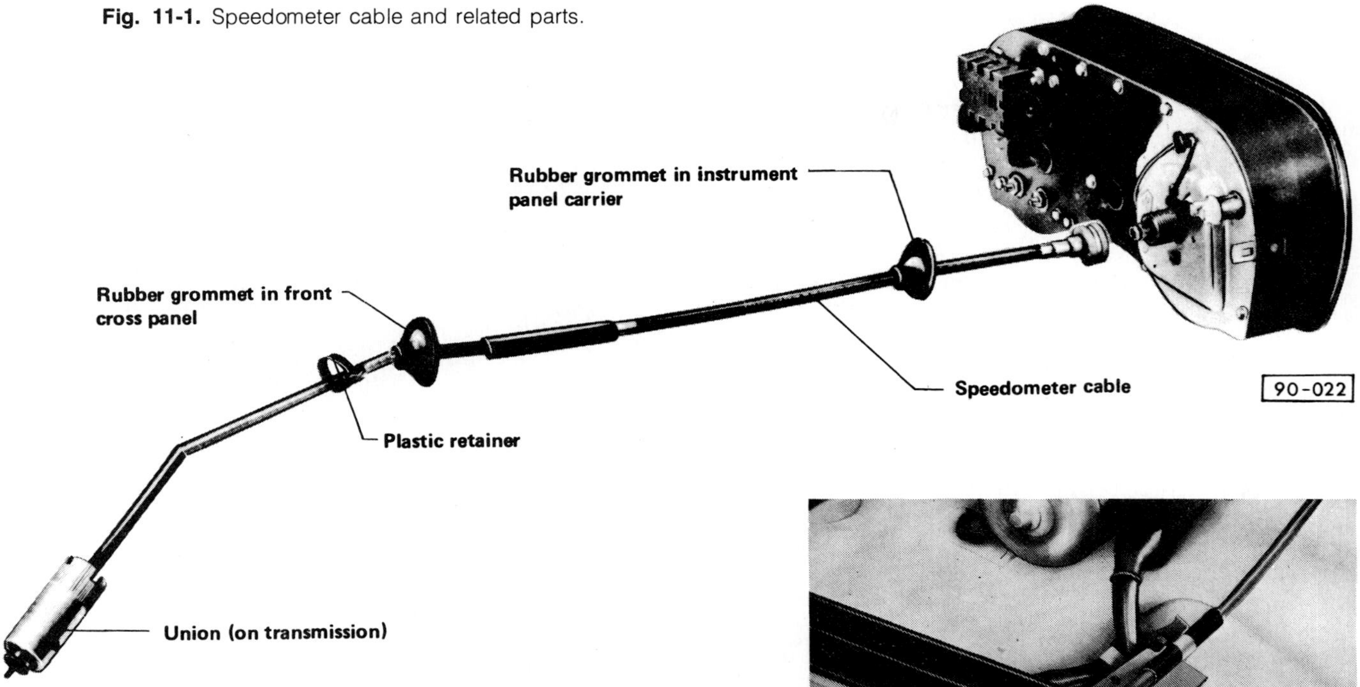

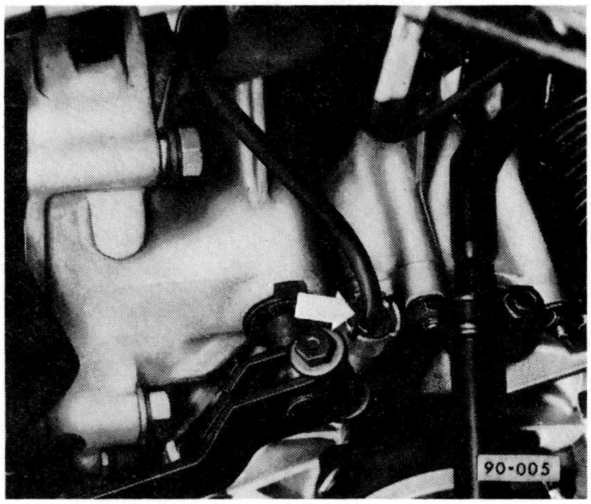

Rubber grommet in instrument panel carrier

Rubber grommet in front cross panel

Speedometer cable

90-022

Plastic retainer

Union (on transmission)

4

90-005

Fig. 11-2. Position of union (arrow) on speedometer pinion seat of manual transmission. Installation is similar on automatic transmissions.

Installation is the reverse of removal. Inspect the replacement cable to see that it has not been kinked or flattened; see that the ferrule nut has not been dented or deformed. Do not lubricate the cable prior to installation. Make sure that the rubber grommets fully engage the holes in the panels (Fig. 11-3) and that the cable contains no sharp bends.

CAUTION ——

The radius of any bend must be at least 150 mm (6 in.). Otherwise the cable will soon break at the bend.

90-023

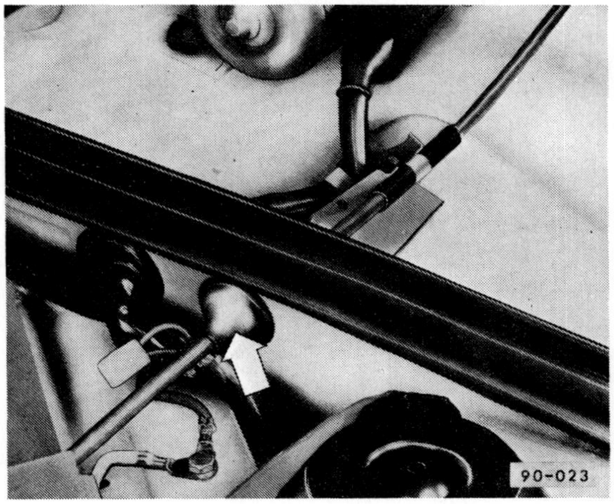

Fig. 11-3. Rubber grommet (arrow) properly installed in cross panel.

11.2 Fuel Gauge Troubleshooting

The fuel gauge is controlled by an electromechanical sending unit in the fuel tank. Inaccurate fuel gauges must be replaced or returned to their manufacturer for calibration (VDO Instruments Ltd., 116 Victor Ave., Detroit, Michigan 48203).

A fuel gauge that never moves from the $1/1$ position has a grounded control circuit. Disconnect the violet and black striped control wire from the sending unit on top of the fuel tank. If the gauge falls from the $1/1$ mark, the trouble is in the sending unit. If it does not, the control wire is grounded somewhere between the sending unit and the gauge.

If the gauge fails to register at all, remove the gauge wire from the sending unit and ground it against a clean, unpainted part of the car. If the gauge moves up to $1/1$, the sending unit is faulty or not properly grounded via the brown wire. If the gauge still fails to move, the gauge or the wire is faulty.

Removing, Testing, and Installing Fuel Gauge Sending Unit

If an ohmmeter indicates infinite ohms when it is connected between the two terminals on the sending unit, the sending unit is burned out and must be replaced.

NOTE ——

The latest fuel injection models have a sending unit that is connected to the wiring harness with a two-prong flat connector (Fig. 11-4).

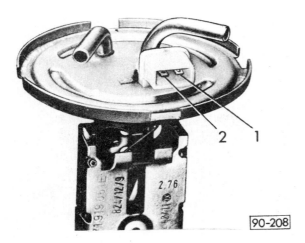

Fig. 11-4. Latest type sending unit. Wire to gauge is connected at **1**; ground wire is connected at **2**.

To remove sending unit:

1. Disconnect the battery ground strap.

2. Remove the liner from the trunk floor. Remove the three Phillips head screws and take off the access cover and its gasket.

3. Disconnect the wires from the terminals on the sending unit. Then remove the fuel hose(s) and quickly plug each disconnected hose with a punch, a pencil, or a golf tee.

WARNING ——

Do not smoke or work near heaters or other fire hazards. Have a fire extinguisher handy.

4. Using universal pliers, turn the sending unit's bayonet fitting (Fig. 11-5) counterclockwise to release the sending unit/fuel pickup from the bayonet socket in the tank. Then lift out the sending unit.

The sending unit can be tested by connecting a battery and voltmeter in series between the ground terminal and the gauge wire terminal.

WARNING ——

Do not make tests near the fuel tank. An electrical spark could cause an explosion.

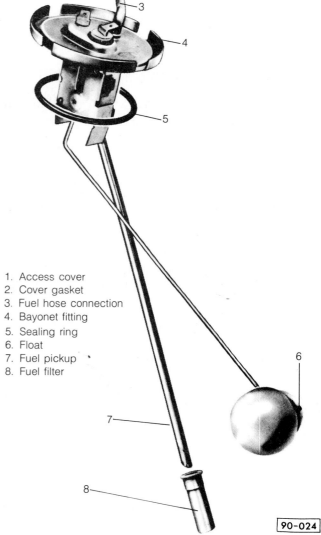

1. Access cover
2. Cover gasket
3. Fuel hose connection
4. Bayonet fitting
5. Sealing ring
6. Float
7. Fuel pickup
8. Fuel filter

Fig. 11-5. Access cover, seal, and fuel gauge sending unit/fuel pickup. Note the notches in bayonet fitting that forms the top of the unit.

Observe whether the voltmeter reading changes continuously as the sending unit's float is moved by hand through its full range. If the voltmeter needle does not move, or does not move smoothly, the sending unit is defective and should be replaced.

Installation is the reverse of removal. Inspect the sealing ring and the fuel filter. Replace hard or cracked sealing rings; replace clogged or torn filters. Lubricate the sealing ring with glycerine so that it will not be twisted or deformed as the bayonet fitting is pressed down and turned clockwise. Fig. 11-6 shows the correct installation of the hose and wires.

1. Ground wire (brown)
2. Control wire for gauge (violet/black)
3. Fuel hose clamp.

Fig. 11-6. Wire and hose connections. Always use a new hose clamp when you install the hose.

4

- Voltage stabilizer
- Bulb (quantity max. 9)
- Printed circuit board
- Washer (conical)
- Blanking cover
- Trim plate
- Fuel gauge
- Coolant temperature gauge
- Instrument cluster housing

Fig. 11-7. Exploded view of instrument cluster.

11.3 Removing and Installing 1973 through 1977 Instruments

The instrument cluster is shown removed and disassembled in Fig. 11-7. Except on basic models, the blanking cover shown in the illustration is replaced by an electrically-wound clock. A tachometer can also be installed in this location as optional equipment.

To remove instrument cluster:

1. Disconnect the battery ground strap.

2. Remove the left under-dashboard cover panel and the driver's glove shelf as described in **BODY AND INTERIOR.**

3. Reach behind the dashboard and unscrew the knurled ferrule nut that holds the speedometer cable on the speedometer head.

4. Using long-nosed pliers, unhook the left and right securing springs from the instrument cluster (Fig. 11-8).

Fig. 11-8. Springs that hold instrument cluster in dashboard (steering column and wiring harness removed for clarity). The speedometer head is at arrow **A,** the securing springs are at arrows **B.**

5. Tilt the instrument cluster outward at the top as shown in Fig. 11-9. Then disconnect the multiple connector plug from the prongs on the printed circuit board. One at a time, disconnect all other wires from the rear of the cluster, labeling each wire so that you can reinstall it in its original location.

6. Remove the instrument cluster.

Fig. 11-9. Instrument cluster being removed from the front of the dashboard.

Installation is the reverse of removal. Reconnect all wires in their original locations before you connect the battery ground strap. Do not lubricate the speedometer cable or speedometer head when you connect the speedometer cable.

Replacing Instrument Light Bulbs

It is unnecessary to remove the instrument cluster to replace instrument light bulbs. Remove the left under-dashboard cover panel and the driver's glove shelf as described in **BODY AND INTERIOR.** Then reach behind the dashboard and remove the appropriate bulb holder from the rear of the instrument cluster. To do this, turn the bulb holder until its lugs can be slipped out through the notches in the cluster. Replace the faulty bulb, then insert the bulb holder and turn it so that its lugs engage the back of the instrument cluster.

Disassembling, Checking, and Assembling Instrument Cluster

In troubleshooting the fuel and temperature gauges, take into consideration whether both gauges or only one gauge reads inaccurately. If both gauges are inaccurate, the trouble is likely to be a faulty voltage stabilizer or a poor connection for the voltage stabilizer. If only one gauge is inaccurate, the stabilizer is not faulty.

To disassemble the instrument cluster into the components shown earlier in Fig. 11-7, first pull the voltage stabilizer off the terminals on the printed circuit board. Remove the self-tapping bolts that hold the instruments and the printed circuit board to the instrument cluster housing. Then remove the bolts and nuts indicated in Fig. 11-10.

If you must replace the voltage stabilizer on a 1973 through 1977 model, be sure to install the correct kind. (The voltage stabilizer is called a "vibrator" in the VW parts list.) Cars with factory-installed radios have a solid-state voltage stabilizer to prevent radio noise. See Fig. 11-11, Fig. 11-12, and Fig. 11-13.

CAUTION ——

After replacing the voltage stabilizer or the fuel gauge, insulate the studs and nuts that hold the fuel gauge, either with tape or with plastic caps. This will prevent the voltage stabilizer terminals from shorting against the studs.

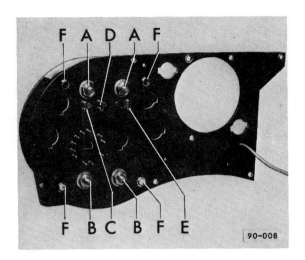

A. Nuts that hold fuel gauge
B. Nuts that hold temperature gauge
C. Voltage stabilizer ground (terminal 31)
D. Voltage stabilizer connection to gauges (terminal J)
E. Voltage stabilizer positive (+) connection (terminal 15)
F. Bolts that hold trim plate

Fig. 11-10. Voltage stabilizer connections and gauge cluster mounting fasteners.

Fig. 11-12. New-type solid state voltage stabilizer for use on cars with factory-installed radios.

4

Fig. 11-13. Standard voltage stabilizer for cars without radios.

Fig. 11-11. Old-type voltage stabilizer that is no longer used or available.

Assembly is the reverse of disassembly. If there have been electrical problems, check the tightness of the various electrical connections and carefully inspect the printed circuit board for breaks in the conductive strips. Either repair broken conductive strips or replace the printed circuit board. Fig. 11-14 can be used to troubleshoot open circuits in the instrument cluster or multiple connector plug. In installing the printed circuit board, make sure that the plastic lugs on the gauge cluster trim plate correctly engage the holes in the printed circuit board before you tighten the trim plate mounting bolts.

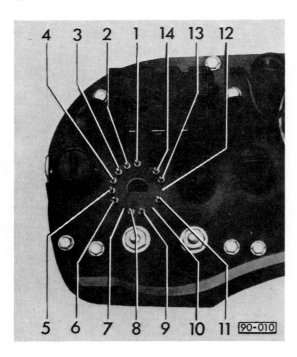

1. Turn signal warning light (49a)
2. Ground for instrument cluster (31)
3. Fuel gauge sending unit
4. Alternator warning light (15)
5. Alternator warning light (D+)
6. Oil pressure warning light switch
7. Vacant
8. Positive (+) wire (15)
9. Temperature gauge sending unit
10. Vacant
11. Positive wire for clock (30)
12. Brake warning light
13. Instrument lights positive (+) wire (from 58)
14. High beam warning light positive (+) wire (from 56a)

Fig. 11-14. Designations of multiple connector points on printed circuit board. Terminal numbers, where applicable, appear in parentheses in the key.

Be especially careful to ensure that the terminals for the voltage stabilizer fit tightly. A faulty voltage stabilizer or a faulty voltage stabilizer ground connection may permit full battery current to reach the gauges, driving their needles above the maximum reading on the dial. This condition may so damage the gauges that they will be inaccurate even after the voltage stabilizer fault has been corrected. Inaccurate gauges and speedometers must be either replaced or returned to their manufacturer for calibration (VDO Instruments, Ltd., 116 Victor Ave., Detroit, Michigan 48203).

Tachometer or Clock Installation

When a tachometer or clock is installed in a vehicle not originally so equipped, or if a new printed circuit board must be installed on a vehicle that has a clock or tachometer, it is necessary to solder in an additional instrument light connection that will link the opening for the clock/tachometer light with the connection for the speedometer light (Fig. 11-15).

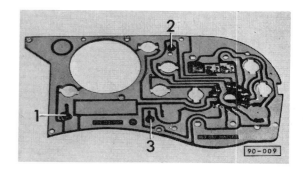

Fig. 11-15. Connections for tachometer or clock. Connection for speedometer lighting is at **1**, connection for terminal 15 of tachometer is at **2**, and connection for terminal 30 of clock is at **3**.

The connections for the tachometer are shown in Fig. 11-16. The red/black wire that links ignition coil terminal 1 with the tachometer is already in the wiring harness and need only be connected to the tachometer. See **12.2 Wiring Diagrams.**

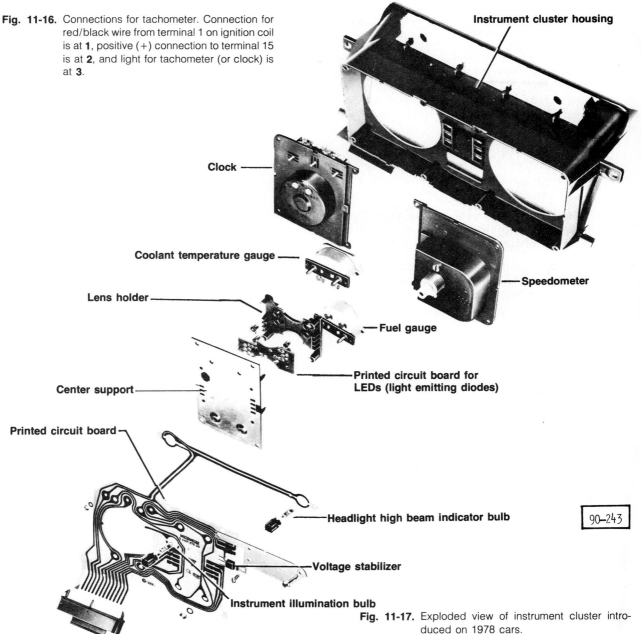

Fig. 11-16. Connections for tachometer. Connection for red/black wire from terminal 1 on ignition coil is at **1**, positive (+) connection to terminal 15 is at **2**, and light for tachometer (or clock) is at **3**.

11.4 Removing and Installing 1978 and Later Instruments

The instrument cluster introduced in 1978 cars is shown removed and disassembled in Fig. 11-17. On some models, a tachometer may be installed in place of the clock.

To remove instrument cluster:

1. Disconnect the battery ground strap.

2. Remove the radio (if fitted) or the shelf.

3. Pull the knobs off the heater/ventilation controls and the blower switch. Then remove the heater/ventilation control panel trim.

Instrument cluster housing

Clock

Coolant temperature gauge

Lens holder

Center support

Printed circuit board

Speedometer

Fuel gauge

Printed circuit board for LEDs (light emitting diodes)

Headlight high beam indicator bulb

Voltage stabilizer

Instrument illumination bulb

Fig. 11-17. Exploded view of instrument cluster introduced on 1978 cars.

4. Remove the screws indicated in Fig. 11-18. Then partially withdraw the instrument panel from the dashboard's padded surround.

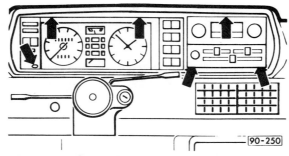

Fig. 11-18. Screws (arrows) that hold instrument panel to dashboard structure.

5. Snap out the switches for the lighting, the emergency flashers, and the rear window defogger. This is done by reaching behind the instrument panel and squeezing together the plastic spring clips on the sides of each switch. The switch can then be pulled out of the panel and the wires disconnected from it.

6. Disconnect the multiple connector from the heater/ventilation blower switch. Then remove the instrument panel, leaving the instrument cluster in the dashboard.

7. Remove the two screws—one at the left and the other at the right—that hold the instrument cluster to the dashboard structure.

8. Reach behind the cluster and unscrew the knurled ferrule nut that holds the speedometer cable to the speedometer head. Then detach the cable from the speedometer.

9. Tilt the instrument cluster outward at the top. Remove the bulb holders by turning and withdrawing them.

10. Disconnect the multiple connector plug from the prongs on the printed circuit board, then remove the instrument cluster.

Installation is the reverse of removal. Reconnect all wires in their original locations before you connect the battery ground strap. Do not lubricate the speedometer cable or the speedometer head when you connect the speedometer cable.

Replacing Instrument Light Bulbs

It is unnecessary to remove the instrument cluster to replace instrument light bulbs. Remove the left glove compartment and its upper part. Then reach behind the dashboard and remove the appropriate bulb holder from the rear of the instrument cluster. To do this, turn the bulb holder until its lugs can be slipped out through the

notches in the cluster. Replace the faulty bulb with a new 12-volt, 1.2 watt bulb. Then insert the bulb holder and turn it so that its lugs engage the back of the instrument cluster.

Troubleshooting Gauges

In troubleshooting the fuel and temperature gauges, take into consideration whether both gauges or only one gauge reads inaccurately. If both gauges are inaccurate, the trouble is likely to be a faulty voltage stabilizer or a poor ground connection for the voltage stabilizer. If only one gauge is inaccurate, the stabilizer is not faulty.

> **NOTE** ——
> Complete disassembly of the instrument cluster is not necessary in order to replace the voltage stabilizer. Simply take out the screw that holds the voltage stabilizer to the cluster, then disconnect the stabilizer's leads. The correct installation of the new voltage stabilizer is indicated in Fig. 11-19.

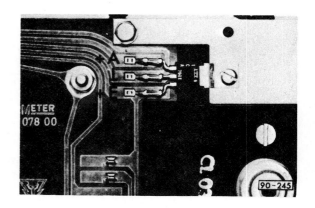

Fig. 11-19. Voltage stabilizer installation. Terminal +E is voltage input, terminal ⊥ is ground, and terminal +A is voltage output.

To test the voltage stabilizer, partially remove the instrument cluster, leaving the multiple connector attached to the printed circuit board. Turn on the ignition with the battery ground strap connected—making sure that no disconnected wire is in electrical contact with the car's body. Connect a voltmeter to stabilizer terminals ⊥ and +A. The voltage should be approximately 10 volts and, if it is above 10.5 volts or below 9.5 volts, the voltage stabilizer is faulty and should be replaced.

> **NOTE** ——
> For accurate testing, the voltmeter must have an internal resistance of at least 1000 ohms/volt and the battery must be charged and in good condition.

The individual gauges can be tested while they are installed with a variable resistance tester known as

Volkswagen special tool VW 1301. The numbers given in the following tests do not indicate ohms.

To test fuel gauge:

1. Disconnect the plug from the sending unit on the fuel tank.

2. Connect VW 1301 to ground on some clean, unpainted metal part of the car and to the striped wire that goes from the plug to the fuel gauge.

3. Turn on the ignition. Allow one full minute for the gauge to stabilize after connecting or selecting the specified dial setting. At the dial settings given, the gauge should read in the ranges indicated in Fig. 11-20.

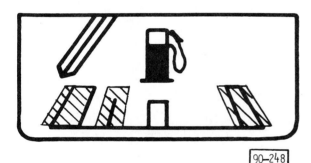

Dial setting	Gauge reading
60	1/1
255	1/4
360	R

Fig. 11-20. Fuel gauge test readings. Shaded areas from left to right indicate ranges of satisfactory R, 1/4, and 1/1 readings.

To test coolant temperature gauge:

1. Disconnect the wire from the temperature gauge sending unit on the engine.

2. Connect VW 1301 to ground on some clean, unpainted metal part of the car and to the disconnected wire.

3. Turn on the ignition. Allow one full minute for the gauge to stabilize after connecting or selecting the specified dial setting. At the dial settings given, the gauge should read in the ranges indicated in Fig. 11-21.

If the gauges are inaccurate, be sure to test the voltage stabilizer as previously described. A faulty voltage stabilizer or a faulty voltage stabilizer ground connection may permit full battery current to reach the gauges, driving their needles above the maximum readings on the dials. This condition may so damage the gauges that they will be inaccurate even after the voltage stabilizer fault has been corrected. Inaccurate gauges should be either replaced or returned to their manufacturer for calibration (VDO Instruments, Ltd., 116 Victor Ave., Detroit, Michigan 48203).

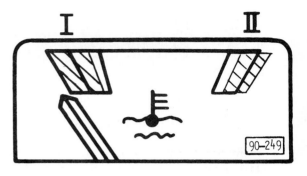

Dial setting	Gauge reading
500	cold range (I)
60 (through 1978)	hot range (II)
58 (from 1979)	hot range (II)

Fig. 11-21. Coolant temperature gauge test readings. Shaded areas at I and II indicate respectively the ranges of satisfactory cold and hot readings.

Disassembling, Checking, and Assembling Instrument Cluster

To disassemble the instrument cluster into the components shown earlier in Fig. 11-17, first remove the screws and the nuts that hold the printed circuit board and the voltage stabilizer to the instruments. Then remove the printed circuit board. Similarly remove the center support and the clock. Carefully pry out the lens holder, then separate the lens holder from the printed circuit board for the LEDs (light emitting diodes) by pulling the holder and the board apart. Take out the screws that hold the gauges and the speedometer so that you can remove these instruments from the cluster.

Assembly is the reverse of disassembly. If there have been electrical problems, check the tightness of the various electrical connections and carefully inspect the printed circuit boards for breaks in the conductive strips.

Either repair broken conductive strips or replace the printed circuit board(s). Fig. 11-22, Fig. 11-23, and Fig. 11-24 can be used to troubleshoot open circuits in the instrument cluster or multiple connector plug. An ohmmeter is the best instrument for making tests.

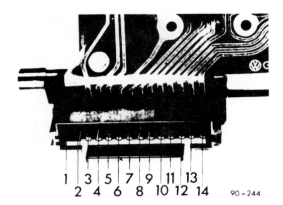

90-244

1. Vacant
2. Vacant
3. Instrument illumination (58b)
4. Ground (31)
5. Coolant temperature sending unit
6. Fuel gauge sending unit
7. Clock positive wire (30)
8. Headlight high beam indicator light
9. Turn signal indicator light (49a)
10. Engine oil pressure warning light (from sending unit)
11. Catalytic converter warning light
12. EGR warning light (Calif. only)
13. Alternator warning light (61)
14. Positive wire (15)

Fig. 11-22. Designations of multiple connector points on printed circuit board. Terminal numbers, where applicable, appear in parentheses in key.

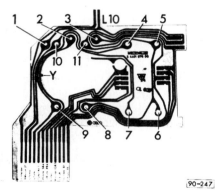

90-247

1. Ground (31)
2. From ignition coil terminal 1
3. Positive connection (15)
4. Coolant temperature gauge connection (to sending unit via printed circuit)
5. Positive connection for coolant temperature gauge (current from voltage stabilizer +A terminal)
6. Positive connection for fuel gauge (current from voltage stabilizer +A terminal)
7. Fuel gauge connection (to sending unit via printed circuit)
8. Vacant
9. Vacant
10. Vacant
11. Vacant
L10. To instrument illumination bulbs
Y. To clock positive connection

Fig. 11-23. Terminal layout of printed circuit board. Terminal numbers, where applicable, appear in parentheses in key.

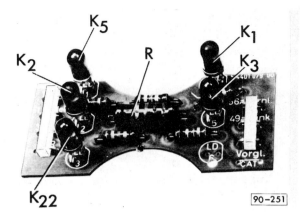

90-251

K1. Headlight high beam indicator light
K2. Alternator warning light
K3. Engine oil pressure warning light
K5. Turn signal indicator light
K22. EGR warning light
R. Resistor for alternator pre-exciter circuit

Fig. 11-24. Terminal designations of printed circuit board for LEDs. Some early cars have a light bulb instead of a resistor for the alternator pre-exciter circuit.

12. WIRING, FUSES, AND RELAYS

The intermittent windshield wiper feature, standard on some 1978 models, can be applied to other 1978 cars by means of a minor change. Simply remove the bridge wire mentioned later in Fig. 12-8, and install relay Part No. 321 955 531 A in its place. Then remove the wedge indicated in Fig. 12-1.

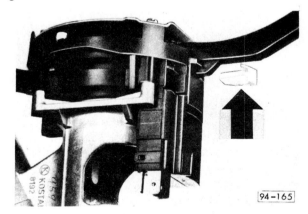

94-165

Fig. 12-1. Wedge (arrow) that prevents wiper switch of cars without intermittent wiper relays from being moved to intermittent position. See **6.2 Removing and Installing Steering Column Switches** for switch housing removal directions.

The fuses and the relays for the electrical system are arranged together in one centralized unit and are protected by a transparent cover. The 1973 and 1974 models have seventeen fuses. Later models have fifteen fuses, though on 1975 models there is room for more fuses in the fuse box. The different fuse/relay boxes are shown in Fig. 12-2, Fig. 12-3, Fig. 12-4, Fig. 12-5, Fig. 12-6, Fig. 12-7, Fig. 12-8, and Fig. 12-9. The main wiring harnesses for the car are connected by plugs and slip-on terminals to the undersides of the fuse/relay boxes. You can determine which circuits are protected by each numbered fuse, either by consulting the Owner's Manual or by studying the current flow diagrams given in **12.2 Wiring Diagrams.**

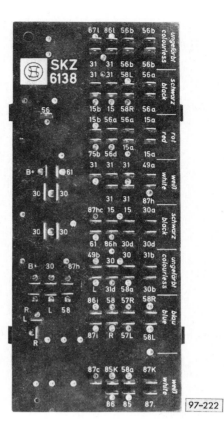

Fig. 12-3. Bottom of 1973-1974 fuse/relay box.

J   — Dimmer relay
J2   — Emergency flasher relay
J9   — Rear window defogger relay
J24 — Windshield wiper and turn signal relay
J25 — Headlight relay
J26 — Radiator cooling fan relay

Fig. 12-2. Top of 1973-1974 fuse/relay box.

J   — Dimmer relay
J2   — Emergency flasher relay
J9   — Rear window defogger relay
J24 — Windshield wiper and turn signal relay
J32 — Air conditioner relay

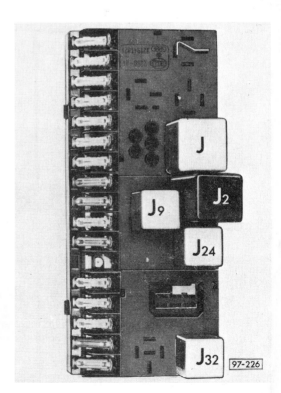

Fig. 12-4. Top of 1975 fuse/relay box.

Fig. 12-5. Bottom of 1975 fuse/relay box.

A - socket for front harness
B - socket for analysis system wiring
C - socket for front harness
D - socket for dashboard wiring
E - socket for dashboard wiring
F - socket for rear harness

G1 - connected to G6 via fuse S15
G2 - connected to terminal E7 and M20
G3 - connected to ignition/starter switch, terminal 15
G4 - connected to fuse S12
G5 - connected to alternator, terminal D+
G6 - connected to G1 via fuse S15
G7 - connected to ignition/starter switch, terminal X
G8 - connected to headlight dimmer switch, terminal 56a
G9 - connected to engine oil pressure switch
G10- connected to light switch, terminal 56

H1
H2
H3
H4 } terminal 30
H5
H6
H7

Fig. 12-6. Bottom of 1976-1977 fuse/relay box. Capital letters A to N and numbers for connections are repeated in test instructions and current flow diagrams.

Fig. 12-7. Top of 1976-1977 fuse/relay box. Capital letters A to N and numbers for connections are repeated in test instructions and current flow diagrams.

Description	Terminal	Terminal on relay	Connected to
Socket J (head light dimmer relay)	1 2 3 4 5 6 7	56 56 56b 56a 56b 30 S	terminal G10, D17, J12 terminal J1 terminal J5, fuse S1 and S2 terminal G8, fuse S3 and S4 terminal J3 terminals H1 to H7 (terminal 30) terminal E8
Socket K (rear window defogger relay)	8 9 10 11	86 30 87 85	terminal D10, L15, M18, N23 (terminal 31) terminal H1 to H7 (terminal 30) fuse S5 terminal D7
Socket L	12 13 14 15 16	86 30 87 31 15	terminal A3 terminals H1 to H7 (terminal 30) terminal A8 terminal D10, K8, M18, N23 (terminal 31) fuse S8, S9
Socket M	17 18 19 20 21	15 31 53s S1 53m	bridged for windshield wiper motor from M9 to M21
Socket N (turn signal/emergency flasher relay)	22 23 24 25	49a 31 +49 C	terminal D1, D3 terminal D10, L15, K8, M18 (terminal 31) terminal D12 terminal D6

Fig. 12-8. Top of 1978 fuse/relay box. This box is essentially the same as the 1976-1977 unit; however, socket K, former location of rear window defogger relay, is now occupied by load reduction relay. Socket M, bridged with a wire on cars without intermittent windshield wipers, is location for intermittent wiper relay, Part. No. 321 955 531 A.

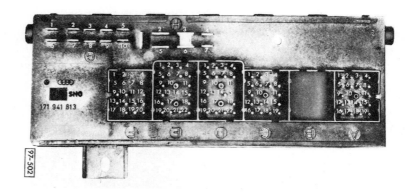

Fig. 12-9. Bottom of 1978 fuse/relay box. Though similar to earlier fuse/relay boxes, all terminals for computer analysis test network (connections **B**) have been eliminated. The 1978 box cannot be installed in earlier cars.

On 1973 through 1975 models, the fuse/relay box is installed in the engine compartment. Beginning with the 1976 models, the fuse box is installed as shown in Fig. 12-10, beneath the left-hand side of the dashboard.

Fig. 12-10. Fuse/relay box installed beneath left side of dashboard on 1976 car.

On 1973 and 1974 cars, you remove the transparent cover by depressing the tab on the left end (Fig. 12-11). To install the cover, first hook it on the right side of the fuse/relay box and then press the cover down so that it engages on the left side with an audible click.

Fig. 12-11. Tab (arrow) that must be depressed to release transparent cover on fuse/relay box.

The 1975 fuse/relay box's transparent cover is held by a clip spring. Carefully disengage the clip spring from the box, then remove the cover. See Fig. 12-12.

Fig. 12-12. Cross section of 1975 fuse/relay box.

4

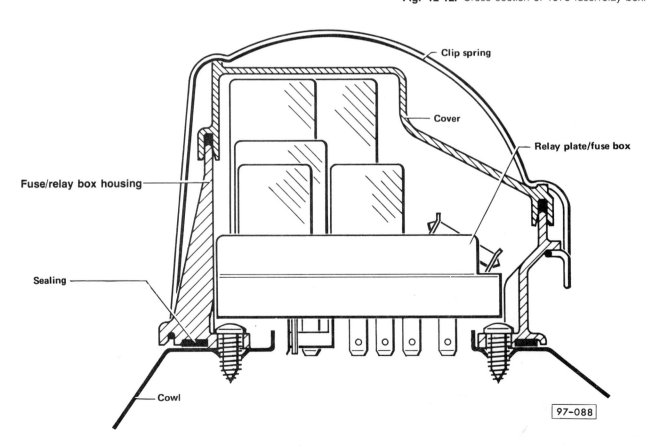

Clip spring

Cover

Relay plate/fuse box

Fuse/relay box housing

Sealing

Cowl

97-088

Replacing Fuses

Always replace white (8-amp) fuses with other white fuses, red (16-amp) with other red fuses, and blue (25-amp) fuses with other blue fuses. If in doubt, consult the Owner's Manual supplied with the car or the current flow diagrams given in **12.2 Wiring Diagrams.**

CAUTION ——

Never patch a burned-out fuse with aluminum foil or replace the fuse with wire or a fuse of greater capacity. Doing this can damage the electrical system.

Replacing Relays

The relays can easily be unplugged or plugged into the fuse box. Because each relay has a different plug pattern, there is no danger of accidentally installing a relay in the wrong location. The relay for the 1974 seat belt interlock and warning system is located under the left-hand side of the dashboard.

12.1 Removing and Installing Wiring Harness

The wiring harnesses attach to the rear of the fuse/relay box. On 1973–1974 models, you must pry outward on the side of the box so that you can lift out the relay plate as shown in Fig. 12-13. The harnesses may then be detached from the bottom of the relay plate. Fig. 12-14

shows the layout of typical wiring harnesses on 1973 through 1975 cars. Fig. 12-15 shows the layout of wiring harnesses on 1976 and later cars.

CAUTION ——

Before you work on any part of the electrical system, disconnect the battery ground strap. Otherwise, the electrical system may be damaged by accidental shorts.

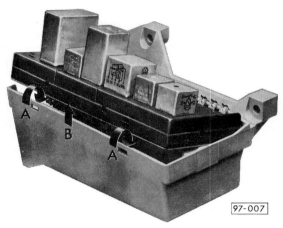

97-007

Fig. 12-13. Relay plate being removed from 1973-1974 fuse/relay box. Pry outward as indicated by arrows **A**, then lift plate as indicated by arrow **B**.

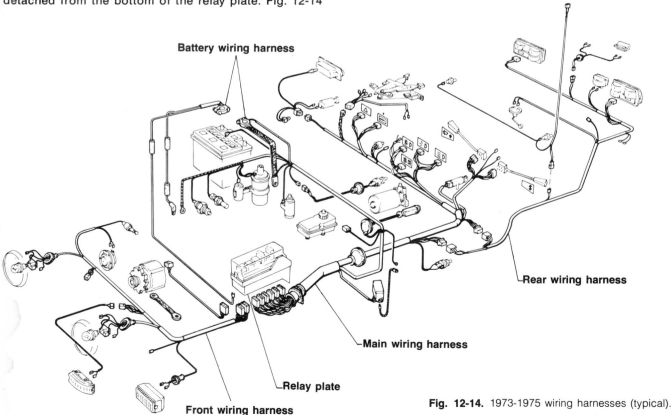

Fig. 12-14. 1973-1975 wiring harnesses (typical).

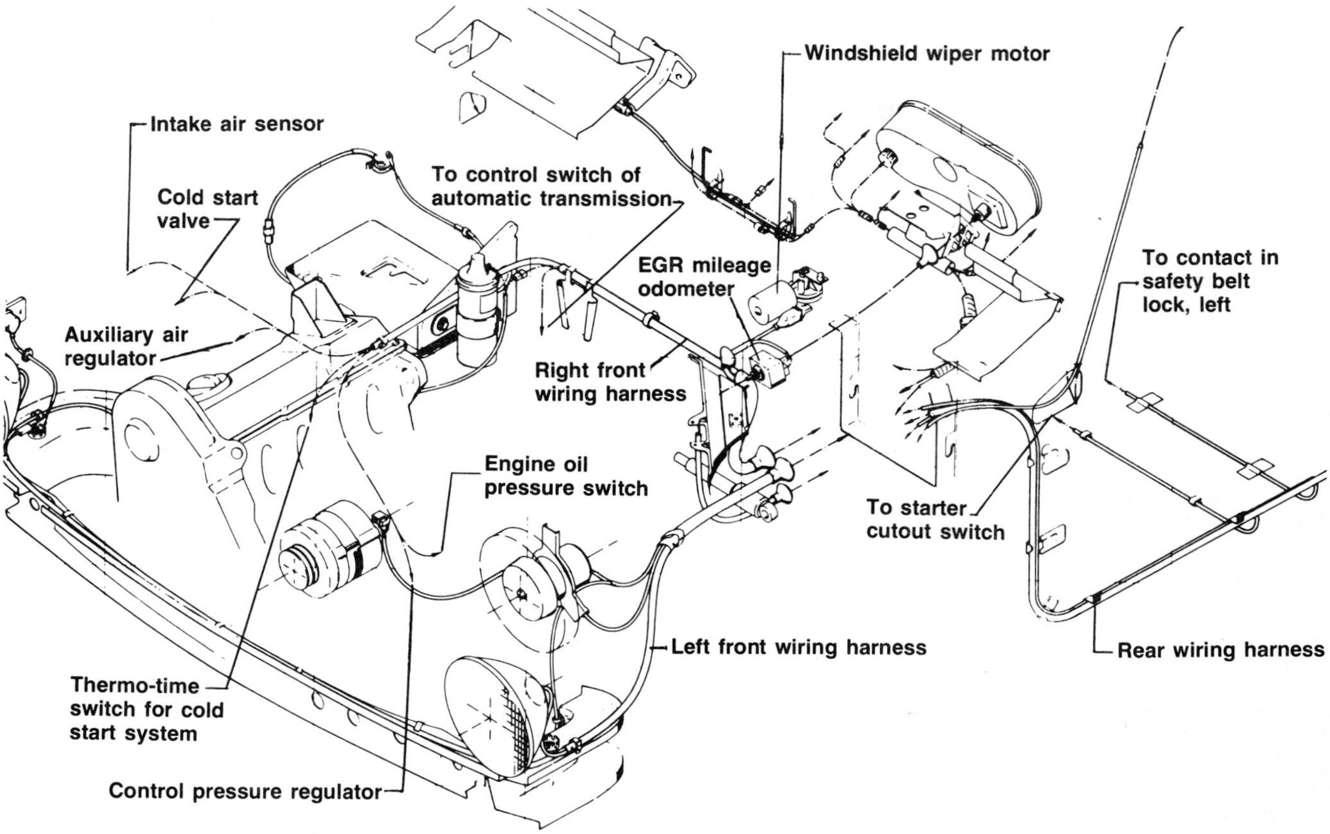

- Intake air sensor
- Cold start valve
- Auxiliary air regulator
- To control switch of automatic transmission
- Windshield wiper motor
- EGR mileage odometer
- Right front wiring harness
- Engine oil pressure switch
- To contact in safety belt lock, left
- To starter cutout switch
- Left front wiring harness
- Rear wiring harness
- Thermo-time switch for cold start system
- Control pressure regulator

Fig. 12-15. 1976 and later wiring harnesses (typical).

4

12.2 Wiring Diagrams

The wiring diagrams given on the following pages are of the current flow type and represent the individual electrical components of the car schematically. The small numbers in the wire lines indicate the wire's gauge in mm². The test connections for the Computer Analysis system are shown throughout these diagrams. Always reconnect the test connection wires when servicing the electrical system.

CAUTION ——

Never connect any device other than the test plug of the Computer Analysis system to the test network socket in the engine compartment. Other test equipment will not guarantee accurate readings and could damage the socket, the test sensors, or the car components containing sensors.

The symbols used in the current flow diagrams are explained in Fig. 12-16. The thin black lines in the current flow diagrams are not actual wires but ground connections via the car's chassis. Along the bottom of each current flow diagram is a yellow or gray band containing numbers that will help you find electrical components easily. Appearing after each component listed in the description are numbers in a column labeled "current track." These numbers indicate the current track in the diagram that contains the part you are looking for.

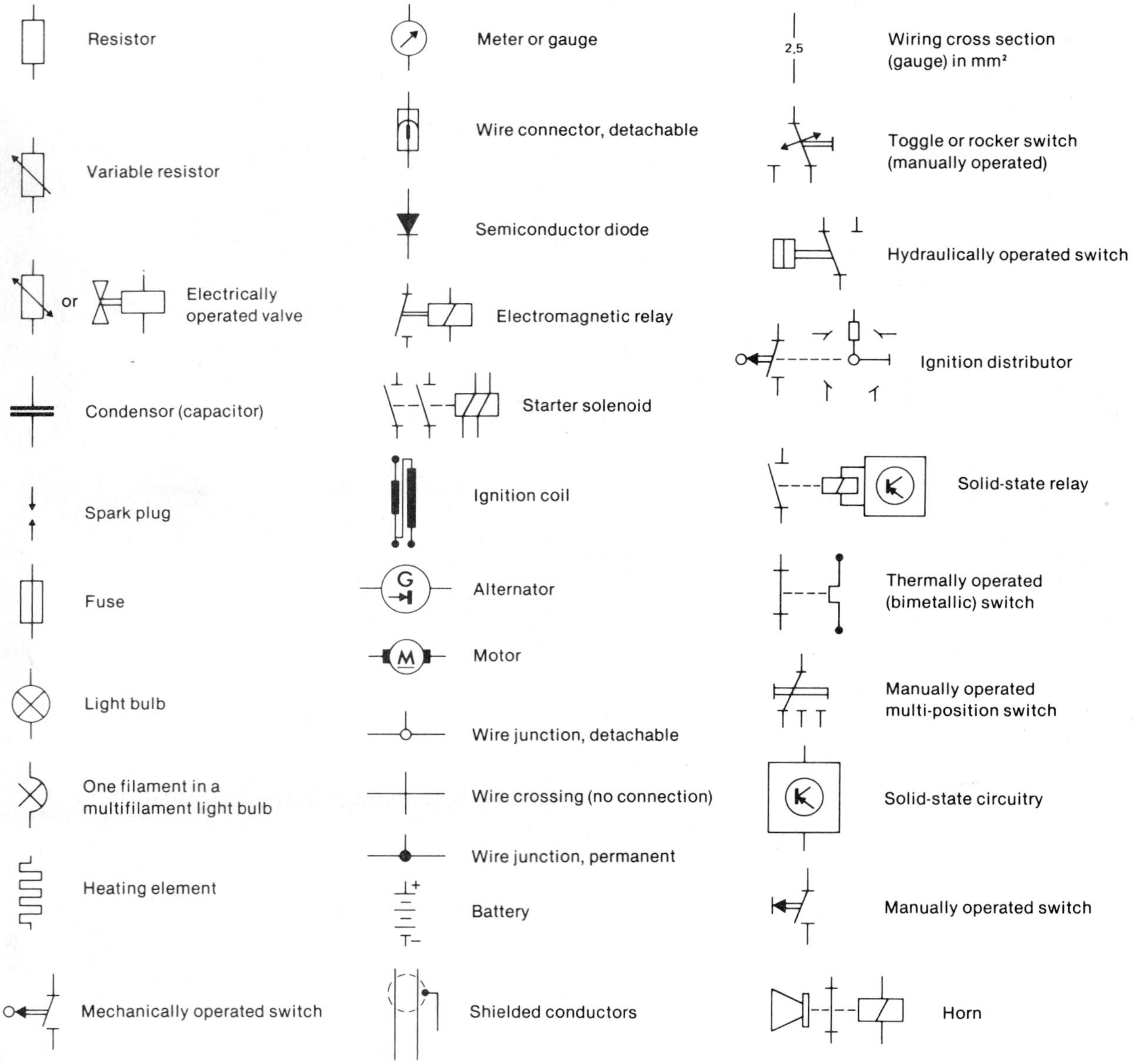

Fig. 12-16. Current flow diagram symbols.

Resistor	Meter or gauge	Wiring cross section (gauge) in mm²
Variable resistor	Wire connector, detachable	Toggle or rocker switch (manually operated)
Electrically operated valve	Semiconductor diode	Hydraulically operated switch
Condensor (capacitor)	Electromagnetic relay	Ignition distributor
Spark plug	Starter solenoid	Solid-state relay
Fuse	Ignition coil	Thermally operated (bimetallic) switch
Light bulb	Alternator	Manually operated multi-position switch
One filament in a multifilament light bulb	Motor	Solid-state circuitry
Heating element	Wire junction, detachable	Manually operated switch
Mechanically operated switch	Wire crossing (no connection)	Horn
	Wire junction, permanent	
	Battery	
	Shielded conductors	

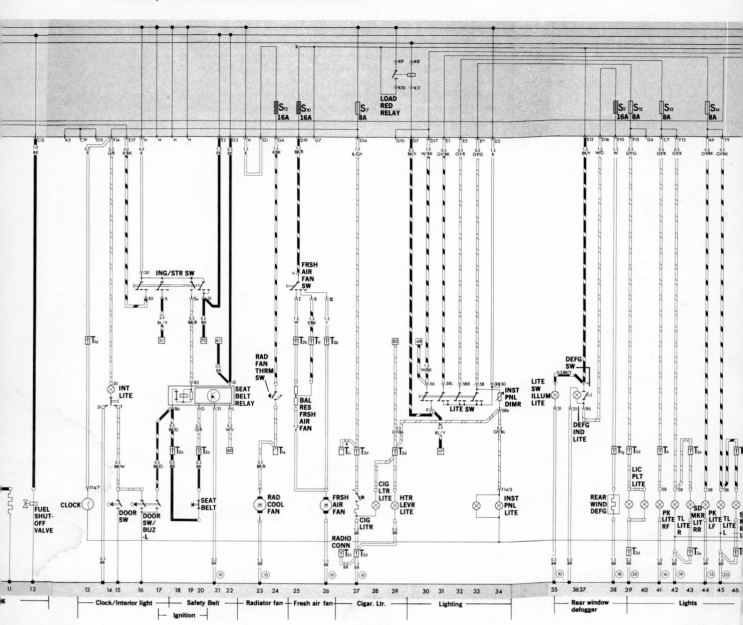

Description	Current track
Alternator	1
Battery	2
Cigarette lighter	27
Cigarette lighter light	28
Clock	13
Coolant fan	23
Coolant fan thermo switch	24
Door switch, right	15
Door switch/buzzer, left	16 – 17
Engine temperature sensor	5
Fresh air/fan ballast resistor	25
Fresh air fan	26
Fresh air fan switch	25
Fuel shutoff valve	12
Fuses S5, S7, S10, S12, S13, S14, S15 on fuse/relay panel	
Fuse S20, in engine compartment	8
Glow plug preheat relay	5 – 8
Heater lever light	29
High beam indicator light	35
Ignition/starter switch	16 – 17, 19 – 20
Instrument panel lights	33 – 34
Instrument panel dimmer	34
Interior light	14
License plate light	39 – 40
Light switch	30 – 34
Light switch illumination light	35
Load reduction relay	29
Radio connector	27
Rear window defogger	38
Rear window defogger switch	37
Rear window defogger warning light	36
Seat belt switch	1
Seat belt warning light	20
Side marker light	18 – 22
Starter	43, 46
Taillight	3 – 4
Voltage regulator	42, 45

T 1a – Wire connector, single; in engine compartment, left front
T 1d – Wire connector, single; rear of dashboard
T 1f – Wire connector, single; rear of dashboard
T 1g – Wire connector, single; rear of dashboard
T 2 – Wire connector, double
T 2a – Wire connector, double; rear of dashboard
T 2b – Wire connector, double; rear of dashboard
T 2c – Wire connector, double; rear of dashboard radio connector
T 2d – Wire connector, double; in luggage compartment, left
T 2e – Wire connector, double; in luggage compartment, right
T 2f – Wire connector, double; in luggage compartment, left
T 3a – Wire connector, 3-point; adjacent to fuse/relay panel
T 3d – Wire connector, 3-point; rear of dashboard
T 4 – Wire connector, 4-point; adjacent to fuse/relay panel
T 14 – Wire connector, 14-point; on instrument cluster
(1) – Ground connector, battery/transmission body
(2) – Ground connector, alternator/engine
(10) – Ground connector, fuse/relay panel
(15) – Ground connector, engine compartment, front left
(16) – Ground connector, engine compartment, front right
(18) – Ground connector, luggage compartment, right
(19) – Ground connector, luggage compartment, rear right
(20) – Ground connector, luggage compartment, rear left

Color code

BK – Black
BR – Brown
CL – Clear
R – Red
Y – Yellow
G – Green
BL – Blue
V – Violet
GY – Gray
W – White

CAUTION ——

*Disconnect the battery ground strap
before starting to work on any part of the
electrical system.*

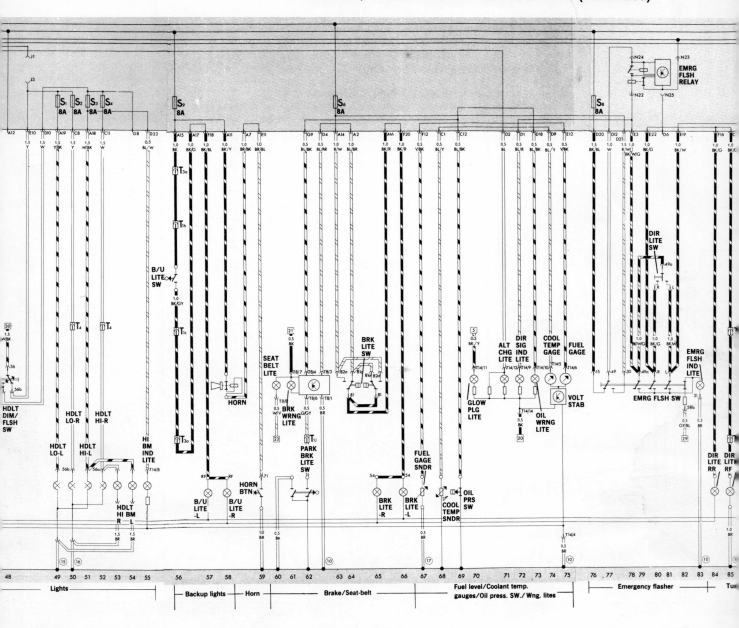

| 48 | 49 | 50 | 51 | 52 | 53 | 54 | 55 | 56 | 57 | 58 | 59 | 60 | 61 | 62 | 63 | 64 | 65 | 66 | 67 | 68 | 69 | 70 | 71 | 72 | 73 | 74 | 75 | 76 | 77 | 78 | 79 | 80 | 81 | 82 | 83 | 84 | 85 |

| Lights | Backup lights | Horn | Brake/Seat-belt | Fuel level/Coolant temp. gauges/Oil press. SW./Wng. lites | Emergency flasher | Tur |

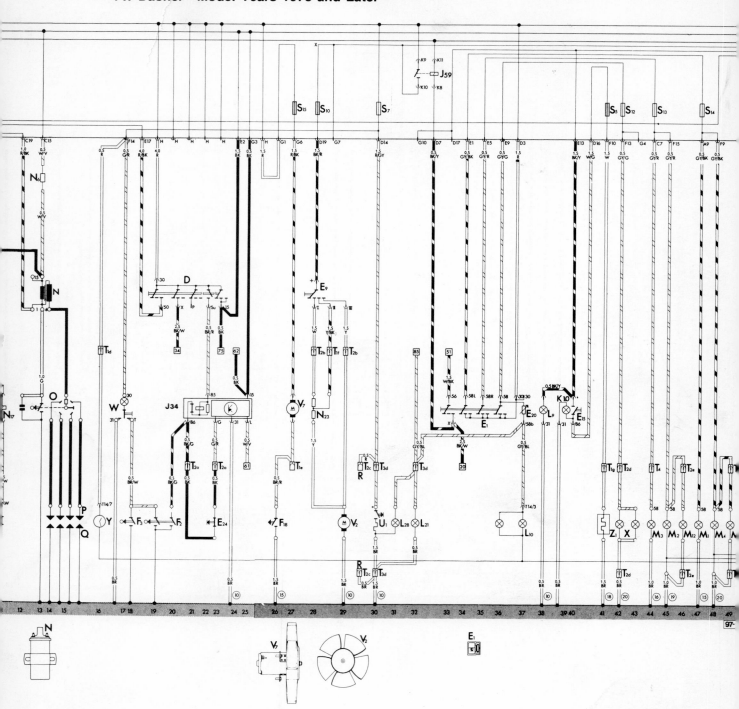

CAUTION ——

Disconnect the battery ground strap before starting to work on any part of the electrical system.

2
1

7

1, 24, 29,
30, 38
26, 47
44

8
41

45

42, 48

Description	Current track
A – Battery	2
B – Starter	3, 4
C – Alternator	1
C 1 – Regulator	1
D – Ignition/starter switch	19–23
E 1 – Light switch	33–36
E 9 – Fresh air fan switch	28, 29
E 15 – Rear window defogger switch	40
E 20 – Instrument panel lighting control switch	37
E 24 – Safety belt switch, left	23
F 2 – Door contact switch for interior light/	
buzzer, left	19, 20
F 3 – Door contact switch for interior light, right	18
F 18 – Radiator cooling fan thermo switch	26
F 26 – Thermo-time switch for cold-start valve	10, 11
G 6 – Electric fuel pump	8
J 17 – Electric fuel pump relay (on fuse/relay panel)	6–9
J 34 – Safety belt warning relay (on fuse/relay panel)	21–25
J 59 – Load reduction relay (on fuse/relay panel)	32
K 10 – Rear window defogger warning light	39
L 9 – Light switch warning light	38
L 10 – Instrument panel lights	36, 37
L 21 – Heater lever warning light	32
L 28 – Cigarette lighter light	31
M 1 – Parking light, left	47
M 2 – Taillight, right	45
M 3 – Parking light, right	44
M 4 – Taillight, left	48
M 12 – Side marker lights, rear	46, 49
N – Ignition coil	13
N 6 – Ballast resistor	13
N 9 – Control pressure regulator	7
N 17 – Cold-start valve	11
N 21 – Auxiliary air regulator	5
N 23 – Speed control resistors for fresh air fan	28
O – Ignition distributor	15
P – Spark plug connectors	15
Q – Spark plugs	15
R – Connectors for radio	30
– Fuses on fuse/relay panel S5, S7, S10,	
S12, S15	
S 31 – Fuse for fuel system components (on front	
of fuel pump relay)	6
T 1 – Wire connector, single; behind dashboard	5–7
T 1a – Wire connector, single; below windshield washer	
fluid container	1
T 1b – Wire connector, single; next to ignition coil	4
T 1c – Wire connector, single; behind dashboard	8
T 1d – Wire connector, single; behind dashboard	16
T 1e – Wire connector, single; in engine	
compartment, left	27
T 1f – Wire connector, single; behind dashboard	28
T 1g – Wire connector, single; in luggage	
compartment, left	41
T 2a – Wire connector, double; under driver's seat	21, 23
T 2b – Wire connector, double; behind dashboard	28, 29
T 2c – Wire connector, double; behind dashboard	30
T 2d – Wire connector, double; in luggage compartment,	
left	30,42
T 2e – Wire connector, double; in luggage compartment,	
right	46
T 2f – Wire connector, double; in luggage compartment,	
left	49
T 3a – Wire connector, 3-point; next to fuse/relay	
panel	4
T 3d – Wire connector, 3-point; behind dashboard	30, 32
T 4 – Wire connector, 4-point; next to fuse/relay	
panel	44
U 1 – Cigarette lighter	30
V 2 – Fresh air fan	29
V 7 – Radiator cooling fan	27
W – Interior light	17, 18
X – License plate light	42
Y – Clock	16
Z 1 – Rear window defogger element	41

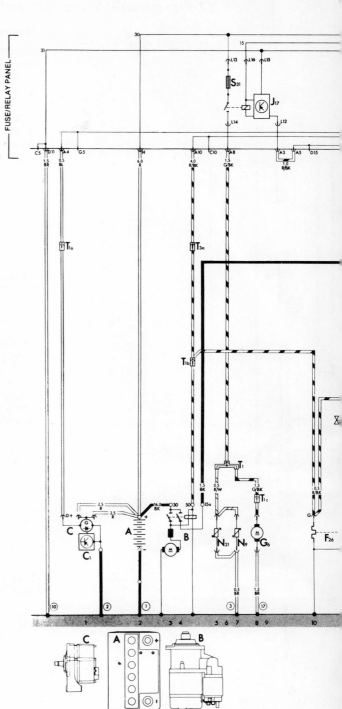

1 – Ground strap battery/body/transmission
2 – Ground strap generator/engine
3 – Ground connector, on cowl reinforcement,
left side
10 – Ground connector, on fuse/relay panel

15 – Ground connector, engine compartment, left
16 – Ground connector, engine compartment, right
17 – Ground connector, in luggage compartment next
to fuel gauge sending unit
18 – Ground connector, luggage compartment, right
19 – Ground connector, luggage compartment, rear
right
20 – Ground connector, luggage compartment, rear
left

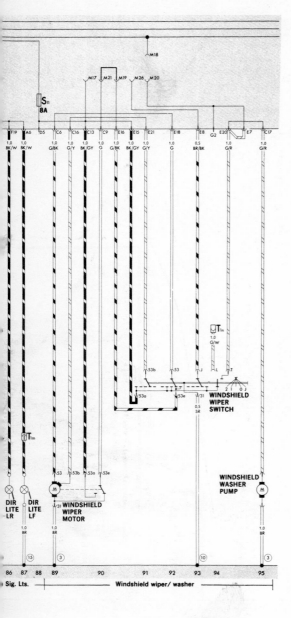

Description	Current track
Alternator charging light	71
Back-up light	57 – 58
Back-up light switch	56
Brake light	65 – 66
Brake light switch	64 – 65
Brake warning light	61
Coolant temperature sender	68
Coolant temperature gauge	74
Directional lights	84 – 87
Directional light switch	80
Directional light indicator light	72
Emergency flasher relay	78 – 81
Emergency flasher switch	77 – 82
Emergency flasher warning light	83
Fuel gauge	75
Fuel gauge sending unit	67
Glow plug preheat light	70
Headlights	49 – 54
Headlight dimmer/flasher switch	47 – 48
Horn	58
Horn button	59
Oil pressure switch	69
Oil pressure warning light	73
Parking brake warning light	61 – 62
Parking brake warning light switch	61 – 62
Seat belt warning relay	60
Voltage stabilizer	75
Windshield washer pump	95
Windshield wiper motor	89 – 90
Windshield wiper switch	91 – 94

T 1c – Wire connector, single; adjacent to glow plug junction

T 1e – Wire connector, single; in engine compartment

T 1h – Wire connector, single; rear of dashboard

T 1j – Wire connector, single; rear of dashboard

T 1m – Wire connector, single; in engine compartment, left

T 1n – Wire connector, single; rear of dashboard

T 3a – Wire connector, 3-point; adjacent to fuse/relay panel

T 4 – Wire connector, 4-point; adjacent to fuse/relay panel

T 8 – Wire connector, 8-point; on dual/park brake warning light circuit

T 14 – Wire connector, 14-point; on instrument cluster

③ – Ground connector, engine compartment left side cowl reinforcement

⑩ – Ground connector, fuse/relay panel

⑮ – Ground connector; engine compartment, front left

⑯ – Ground connector; engine compartment, front right

⑰ – Ground connector; luggage compartment adjacent to fuel gauge sending unit

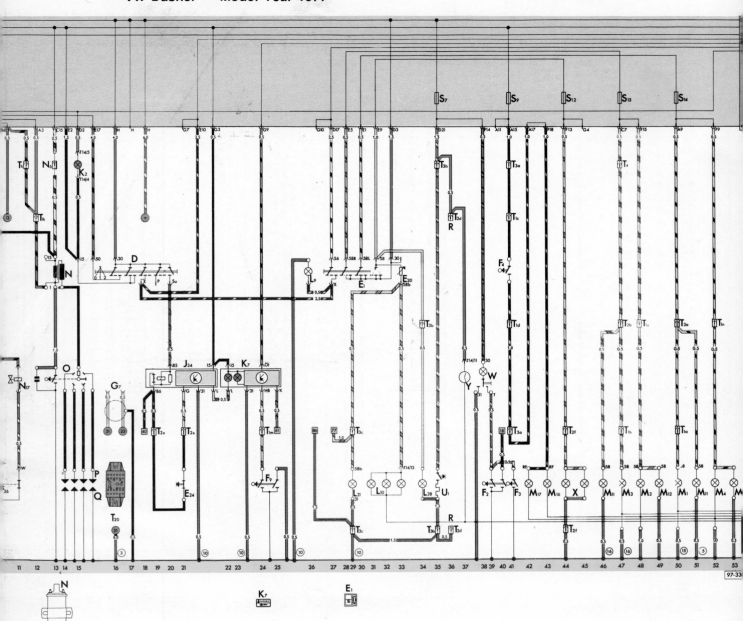

tment,	44
left	4, 41
center	34, 35
center	29, 87
	47, (56, 58, 79)
ster	15 (67 – 70)
	16
	35
	38, 39
	44
	37

eft

ight

NOTE ——

The current track numbers in parentheses indicate wires shown on the other half of the diagram (facing page).

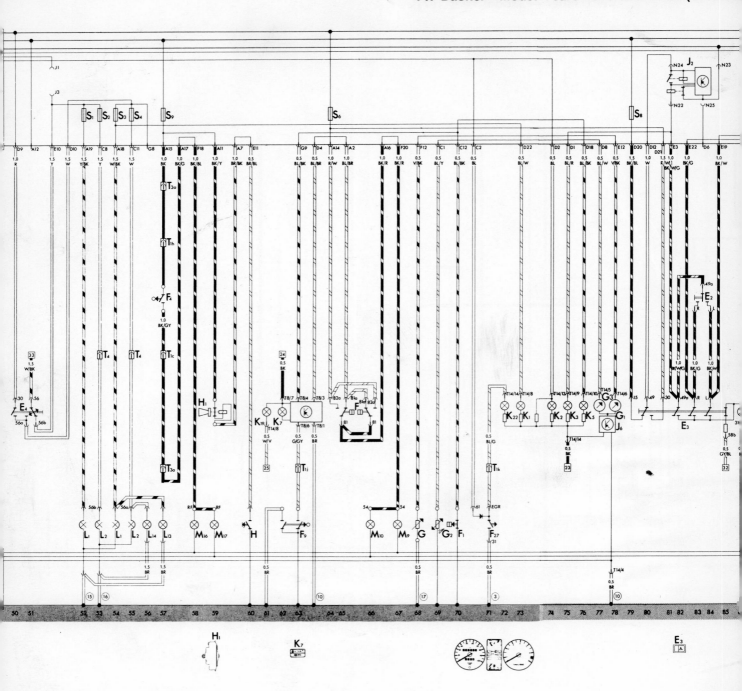

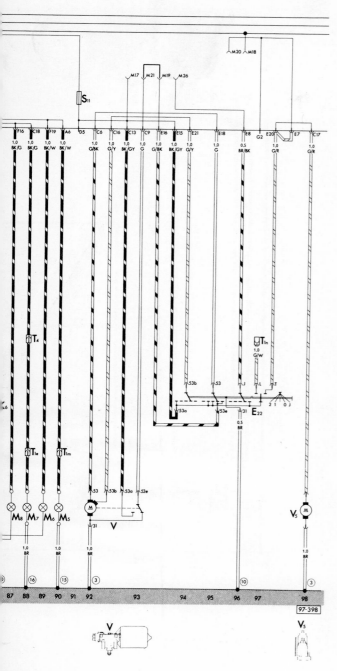

Color code

BK – Black
BR – Brown
R – Red
O – Orange
Y – Yellow
G – Green
BL – Blue
V – Violet
GY – Gray
W – White

Description	Current track
E 2 – Turn signal switch	83, 84
E 3 – Emergency flasher switch	79, 85
E 4 – Headlight dimmer and flasher switch	50, 51
E 22 – Windshield wiper switch	94–97
F – Brake light switch	64–66
F 1 – Engine oil pressure switch	70
F 4 – Back-up light switch	57
F 9 – Parking brake light switch	62, 63
F 27 – Elapsed EGR mileage switch	71
G – Fuel gauge sending unit	68
G 1 – Fuel gauge	78
G 2 – Coolant temperature sending unit	69
G 3 – Coolant temperature gauge	77
H – Horn button	60
H 1 – Horn	59
J 2 – Emergency flasher relay	81–84
J 6 – Voltage stabilizer	78
K 1 – Headlight high beam warning light	73
K 2 – Generator charging warning light	74
K 3 – Engine oil pressure warning light	75
K 5 – Turn signal warning light	76
K 6 – Emergency flasher warning light	86
K 7 – Brake dual circuit/parking brake warning light	62
K 19 – Safety belt warning light	61
K 22 – EGR warning light	72
L 1 – Sealed beam unit, left	52, 54
L 2 – Sealed beam unit, right	53, 55
L 13 – Sealed beam unit, high beam, left	57
L 14 – Sealed beam unit, high beam, right	56
M5 – Turn signal, front left	90
M6 – Turn signal, rear left	89
M7 – Turn signal, front right	88
M8 – Turn signal rear right	87
M9 – Brake light, left	67
M10 – Brake light, right	66
M16 – Back-up light, left	58
M17 – Back-up light, right	59
– Fuses on fuse/relay panel S1, S4, S8, S9, S11	
T 1c – Wire connector, single; next to ignition coil	57
T 1e – Wire connector, single; in engine compartment, right	88
T 1h – Wire connector, single; next to ignition coil	57
T 1j – Wire connector, single; behind dashboard	63
T 1k – Wire connector, single; behind dashboard	71
T 1m – Wire connector, single; in engine compartment, left	90
T 1n – Wire connector, single; behind dashboard	97
T 3a – Wire connector, 3-point, next to fuse/relay panel	57
T 4 – Wire connector, 4-point, next to fuse/relay panel	53, 55, 88
T 8 – Wire connector, 8-point, on brake dual circuit warning light	62–64
T 14 – Wire connector, 14-point, on instrument cluster	61, 72–78
V – Windshield wiper motor	92, 93
V 5 – Windshield washer pump	98
3 – Ground connector, on cowl reinforcement, left side	71, 92, 98
10 – Ground connector, next to fuse/relay panel	63, 78, 86, 96
15 – Ground connector, in engine compartment, front left	52, 90
16 – Ground connector, in engine compartment, front right	53, 88
17 – Ground connector, in luggage compartment next to fuel gauge sending unit	68

NOTE ——

The gray-colored area in the upper part of the current flow diagram indicates the relay plate with fuse box.

Description

		Current track
A	— Battery	2
B	— Starter	3 – 5
C	— Alternator	1
C 1	— Regulator	1
D	— Ignition/starter switch	16 – 21
E 1	— Light switch	27 – 33
E 20	— Instrument panel lighting control switch	33
E 24	— Safety belt switch, left	21
F 2	— Door contact switch, for interior light/buzzer, left	38 – 40
F 3	— Door contact switch, for interior light, right	41
F 4	— Back-up light switch	41
F 9	— Parking brake light switch	24, 25
F 26	— Thermo-time switch for cold-start valve	10, 11
G 6	— Electric fuel pump	8
J 17	— Electric fuel pump relay	6 – 9
J 34	— Safety belt warning system relay	19 – 21
K 2	— Alternator charging warning light	15
K 7	— Dual circuit brake warning light	22 – 25
L 9	— Light switch warning light	26
L 10	— Instrument panel light	31 – 33
L 21	— Heater lever warning light	29
L 28	— Cigarette lighter light	34
M 1	— Parking light, left	50
M 2	— Taillight, right	48
M 3	— Parking light, right	47
M 4	— Taillight, left	52
M 11	— Side marker lights, front	46, 51
M 12	— Side marker lights, rear	49, 53
M 16	— Back-up light, left	43
M 17	— Back-up light, right	42
N	— Ignition coil	13 – 14
N 6	— Ballast resistor	13
N 9	— Control pressure regulator	7
N 17	— Cold-start valve	11
N 21	— Auxiliary air regulator	5
O	— Ignition distributor	14 – 15
P	— Spark plug connectors	14 – 15
Q	— Spark plugs	13 – 15
R	— Connectors for radio, on console	36
	— Fuses S 1 – S 15 in fuse box	
S 31	— Fuse for CIS	7
T 1a	— Wire connector, single; in engine compartment, front left	50
T 1b	— Wire connector, single; in engine compartment, front right	47
T 1c	— Wire connector, single; in engine compartment	47
T 1d	— Wire connector, single; in engine compartment	47
T 1e	— Wire connector, single; in engine compartment	4
T 1i	— Wire connector, single; behind relay plate	11
T 1k	— Wire connector, single; behind dashboard	12
T 1l	— Wire connector, single; in engine compartment	7
T 1m	— Wire connector, single; behind dashboard	24
T 1n	— Wire connector, single; in luggage compartment	52
T 1o	— Wire connector, single; in engine compartment	48
T 2a	— Wire connector, double; in engine compartment, left	50 (81)
T 2b	— Wire connector, double; in engine compartment, right	47 (19)
T 2c	— Wire connector, double; in luggage compartment	8
T 2d	— Wire connector, double; behind dashboard — for radio	36
T 2e	— Wire connector, double; below driver's seat	19, 21

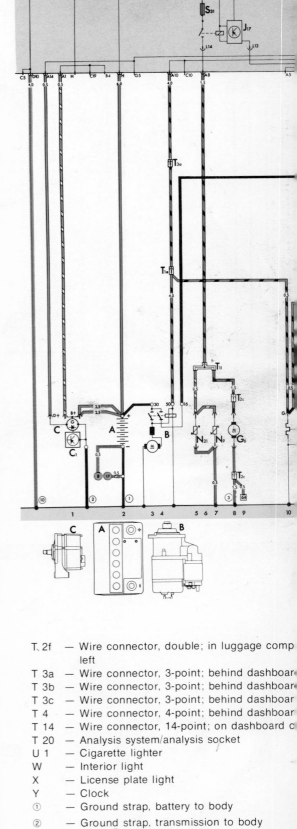

T 2f	— Wire connector, double; in luggage comp. left
T 3a	— Wire connector, 3-point; behind dashboar
T 3b	— Wire connector, 3-point; behind dashboar
T 3c	— Wire connector, 3-point; behind dashboar
T 4	— Wire connector, 4-point; behind dashboar
T 14	— Wire connector, 14-point; on dashboard c
T 20	— Analysis system/analysis socket
U 1	— Cigarette lighter
W	— Interior light
X	— License plate light
Y	— Clock
①	— Ground strap, battery to body
②	— Ground strap, transmission to body
③	— Ground connectors, on firewall
⑩	— Ground connectors, on dashboard
⑮	— Ground connectors, engine compartment,
⑯	— Ground connectors, engine compartment,

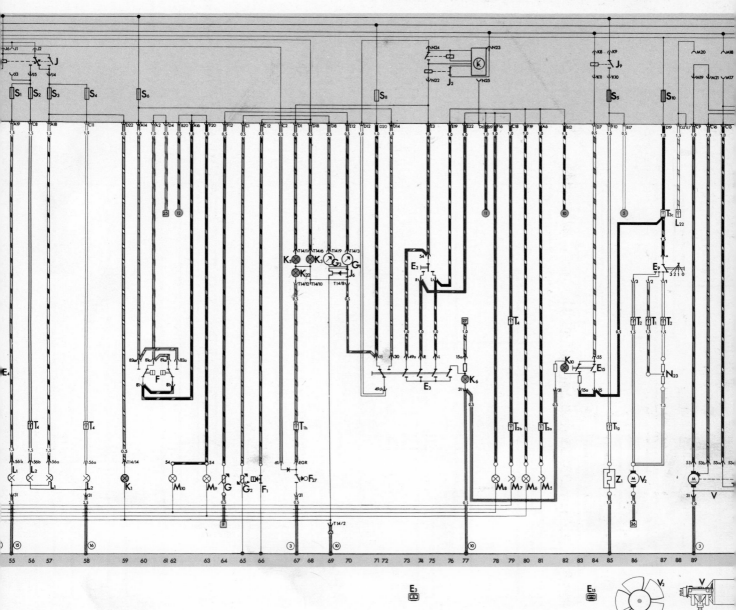

Computer Analysis System ——

The orange-colored spots are connections in the Computer Analysis System that are wired to socket T 20. The numbers in these spots correspond to terminals in the Computer Analysis socket.

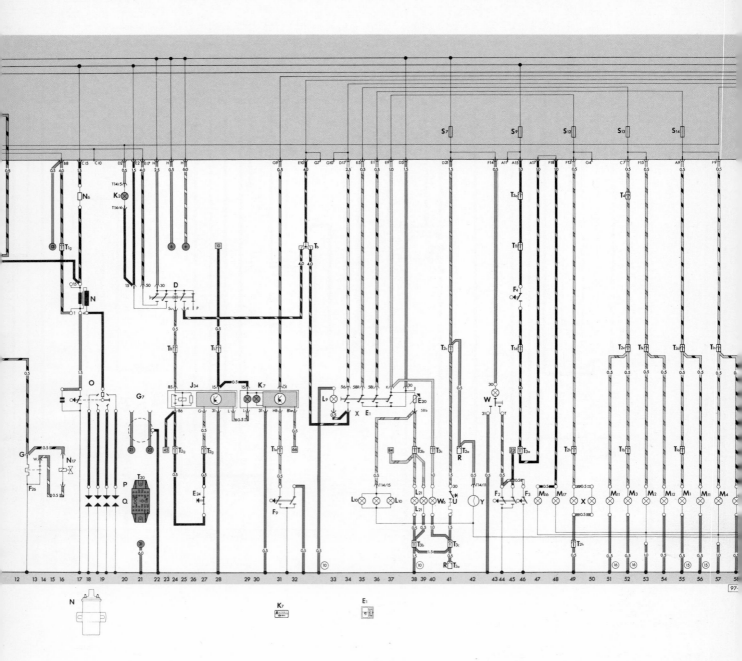

Current track

① — Ground strap, battery/body/engine
② — Ground strap, alternator
⑩ — Ground connector, dashboard
⑮ — Ground connector, engine compartment front left
⑯ — Ground connector, engine compartment front right

Computer Analysis System——
The orange-colored spots are connections in the Computer Analysis System that are wired to socket T 20. The numbers in these spots correspond to terminals in the Computer Analysis socket.

41
8
43
40
49, 50
42

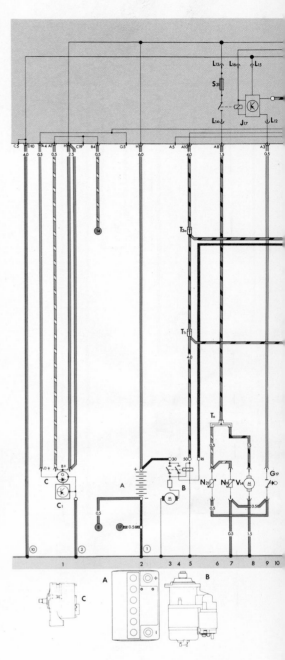

Description

			Current track
A	–	Battery	2
B	–	Starter	3, 4, 5
C	–	Alternator	1
C 1	–	Regulator	1
D	–	Ignition/starter switch	21, 22, 23, 24, 25,26
E 1	–	Light switch	34, 35, 36, 37, 38
E 20	–	Instrument panel lighting control switch	38
E 24	–	Safety belt lock, left	27
F 2	–	Door contact switch, left	44, 45
F 3	–	Door contact switch, right	46
F 4	–	Backup light switch	46
F 9	–	Parking brake control light switch	31, 32
F 26	–	Thermo time switch	13
G 7	–	to TDC indicator sensor	21
G 19	–	Intake air sensor	9
J 17	–	Electric fuel pump relay	6, 7, 8, 9, 10
J 34	–	Safety belt warning system relay	24, 27, 28
K 2	–	Alternator charging warning light	20
K 7	–	Dual circuit brake warning, parking brake and safety belt warning light	29, 30, 31, 32
L 9	–	Light switch warning light	33
L 10	–	Instrument panel light	35, 36, 37
L 21	–	Heater lever warning light	38
M 1	–	Parking light, left	55
M 2	–	Tail light, right	53
M 3	–	Parking light, right	52
M 4	–	Tail light, left	57
M 11	–	Side marker lights, front	51, 56
M 12	–	Side marker lights, rear	54, 58
M 16	–	Backup light, left	47
M 17	–	Backup light, right	48
N	–	Ignition coil	17, 18
N 6	–	Ballast resistor	17
N 9	–	Control pressure regulator	7
N 17	–	Cold start valve	16
N 21	–	Auxiliary air regulator	6
O	–	Ignition distributor	17, 19
P	–	Spark plug connectors	18, 19
Q	–	Spark plugs	18, 19
R	–	Connector for radio	41, 42
	–	Fuses S 7, S 9, S 12, S 13, S 14 in fuse box	
S 31	–	Fuse for CIS	6
Ta	–	Wire connector, multiple, behind dashboard	
Tb	–	Wire connector, multiple, next to light switch	
T 1a	–	Wire connector, single; in engine compartment, front left	
T 1b	–	Wire connector, single; in engine compartment, front right	
T 1c	–	Wire connector, single; in engine compartment, right	
T 1d	–	Wire connector, single; on firewall	
T 1e	–	Wire connector, single; on firewall	
T 1f	–	Wire connector, single; behind dashboard	
T 1g	–	Wire connector, single; behind relay plate	
T 1h	–	Wire connector, single; in engine compartment, front left	
T 1i	–	Wire connector, single; behind relay plate	
T 1k	–	Wire connector, single; in luggage compartment, rear right	
T 1l	–	Wire connector, single; behind dashboard	
T 1m	–	Wire connector, single; in luggage compartment, left	
T 1n	–	Wire connector, single; in luggage compartment, rear left	
T 2a	–	Wire connector, double; behind dashboard (connection for radio)	
T 2b	–	Wire connector, double; behind dashboard	
T 2c	–	Wire connector, double; next to relay plate	
T 2d	–	Wire connector, double; in engine compartment, front left	

Description

T 2e	–	Wire connector, double; in engine compartment, front right
T 2f	–	Wire connector, double; in luggage compartment, rear right
T 2g	–	Wire connector, double; under driver's seat
T 2h	–	Wire connector, double; in luggage compartment
T 3a	–	Wire connector, 3 point; behind dashboard
T 3b	–	Wire connector, 3 point; behind dashboard
T 3c	–	Wire connector, 3 point; behind dashboard
T 4	–	Wire connector, 4 point; next to relay plate
T 20	–	Diagnosis system/diagnosis socket (not on 1976 models)
U	–	Cigarette lighter
V 14	–	Electric fuel pump
W	–	Interior light
W 6	–	Glove compartment light
X	–	License plate light
Y	–	Clock

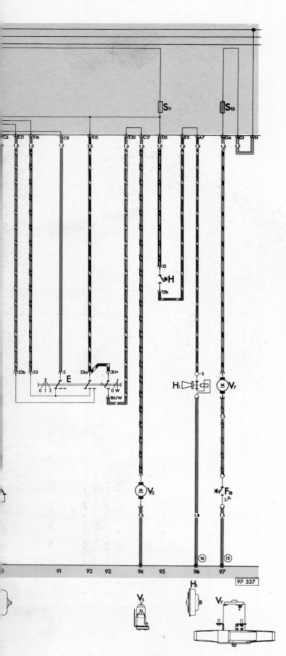

Description		Current track
E	— Windshield wiper switch	90 – 93
E 2	— Turn signal switch	74, 75
E 3	— Emergency flasher switch	71 – 77
E 4	— Headlight dimmer switch	54
E 9	— Fresh air fan switch	86 – 88
E 15	— Rear window defogger switch	82 – 84
F	— Brake light switch	60 – 62
F 1	— Engine oil pressure switch	66
F 18	— Radiator cooling fan thermo switch	97
F 27	— Elapsed EGR mileage switch	67
G	— Fuel gauge sending unit	64
G 1	— Fuel gauge	70
G 2	— Coolant temperature sending unit	65
G 3	— Coolant temperature gauge	69
H	— Horn button	95
H 1	— Horn	95
J	— Headlight dimmer relay	54 – 57
J 2	— Emergency flasher relay	75 – 77
J 6	— Voltage stabilizer	69, 70
J 9	— Rear window defogger relay	84, 85
K 1	— Headlight high beam warning light	59
K 3	— Engine oil pressure warning light	68
K 5	— Turn signal warning light	67
K 6	— Emergency flasher warning light	77
K 10	— Rear window defogger warning light	82
K 22	— EGR warning light	87
L 1	— Sealed beam unit, left	55, 57
L 2	— Sealed beam unit, right	56, 58
L 22	— Connection for fog lights	88
M 5	— Turn signal, front left	81
M 6	— Turn signal, rear left	80
M 7	— Turn signal, front right	79
M 8	— Turn signal, rear right	78
M 9	— Brake light, left	63
M 10	— Brake light, right	62
N 23	— Speed control resistors for fresh air fan	87
	— Fuses S 1 — S 15 in fuse box	
T 1	— Wire connector, single; behind dashboard	86 – 87
T 1g	— Wire connector, single; in luggage compartment, left	85
T 1h	— Wire connector, single; behind dashboard	67
T 2	— Wire connector, double; behind dashboard	86, 87
T 2a	— Wire connector, double; in engine compartment	(50), 81
T 2b	— Wire connector, double; in engine compartment	(47), 79
T 3c	— Wire connector, 3-point; behind dashboard, center	(29), 87
T 4	— Wire connector, 4-point; behind dashboard	(47), 56, 58, 79
T 14	— Wire connector, 14-point, on dashboard cluster	(15), 67 – 70
V	— Windshield wiper motor	89 – 90
V 2	— Fresh air fan	86
V 5	— Windshield washer pump	94
V 7	— Radiator cooling fan	97
Z 1	— Rear window defogger element	85

⑩ — Ground connectors, dashboard

⑮ — Ground connectors, engine compartment, left

⑯ — Ground connectors, engine compartment, right

NOTE ——

The current track numbers in parentheses indicate wires shown on the other half of the diagram (facing page).

NOTE——

The gray-colored area in the upper part of the current flow diagram indicates the relay plate with fuse box.

Description

		Current track
A	– Battery	10
B	– Starter	11, 12
C	– Alternator	2
C1	– Regulator	2
D	– Ignition/starter switch	13, 14, 15, 17, 18
E1	– Light switch	22, 23, 24, 25
E9	– Fresh air fan	32, 33
E20	– Instrument panel lighting control switch	28
E24	– Safety belt lock, left	20
E25	– Safety belt lock, right	18
E31	– Contact strip in driver seat	20
E32	– Contact strip in passenger seat	18
F2	– Door contact and buzzer alarm switch, left	16, 17
F3	– Door contact switch, right	14
F9	– Parking brake control light switch	21, 22
F25	– Throttle valve switch	7
G5	– to tachometer terminal 1	3
G7	– TDC sensor	38
H	– Horn button	31
H1	– Horn	39
J34	– Safety belt warning system relay	13, 14, 17, 18, 19, 20, 21, 22, 23
K2	– Alternator charging warning light	1
K7	– Dual circuit brake warning and safety belt warning system control light	24, 25, 26, 27
L9	– Light switch illumination	27
L10	– Instrument panel light	28, 29
L21	– Heater lever illumination	30
M1	– Parking light, left	46
M2	– Tail light, right	42
M3	– Parking light, right	41
M4	– Tail light, left	44
M11	– Sidemarker lights, front	40, 47
M12	– Sidemarker lights, rear	43, 45
N	– Ignition coil	4
N1	– Automatic choke	8
N3	– Electromagnetic cutoff valve	9
N6	– Series resistance	4
N13	– EGR valve	7
O	– Ignition distributor	4, 6
P	– Spark plug connectors	5, 6
Q	– Spark plugs	5, 6
R	– Radio	33, 34
S	– Fuses S5, S10, S13, S14, S15 in fuse box	
T1a	– Wire connector, single; behind dashboard	
T1b	– Wire connector, single; in engine compartment	
T1c	– Wire connector, single; in engine compartment right	
T1d	– Wire connector, single; in engine compartment right	
T1e	– Wire connector, single; in engine compartment left	
T1f	– Wire connector, single; in engine compartment left	
T1g	– Wire connector, single; in luggage compartment left	
T1h	– Wire connector, single; in luggage compartment right	
T1i	– Wire connector, single; behind dashboard	
T1k	– Wire connector, single; behind dashboard	
T2a	– Wire connector, double; behind dashboard	
T2b	– Wire connector, double; in engine compartment	
T2c	– Wire connector, double; next to radiator	
T2d	– Wire connector, double; in luggage compartment	
T2e	– Wire connector, double; in body bottom	
T2f	– Wire connector, double; below passenger seat	
T2g	– Wire connector, double; below driver seat	
T2h	– Wire connector, double; on body bottom	
T3a	– Wire connector, 3 point; in engine compartment, left front	
T3b	– Wire connector, 3 point; in engine compartment, right front	
T3c	– Wire connector, 3 point; behind dashboard	
T3d	– Wire connector, 3 point; behind dashboard	
T3e	– Wire connector, 3 point; behind dashboard	
T3f	– Wire connector, 3 point; behind dashboard	
T6a	– Wire connector, 6 point; behind dashboard	
T6c	– Wire connector, 6 point; behind dashboard	

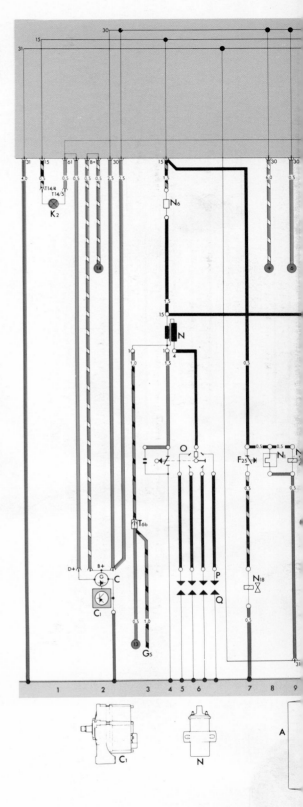

Description

T6d	– Wire connector, 6 point; behind dashboard
T6e	– Wire connector, 6 point; behind dashboard
T14	– Wire connector, 14 point; on dashboard cluster
T20	– Test network/test socket
U	– Cigarette lighter
V2	– Fresh air fan
W6	– Glove compartment light
X	– License plate light
①	– Ground strap —battery/body/engine
⑩	– Ground connector, dashboard cluster

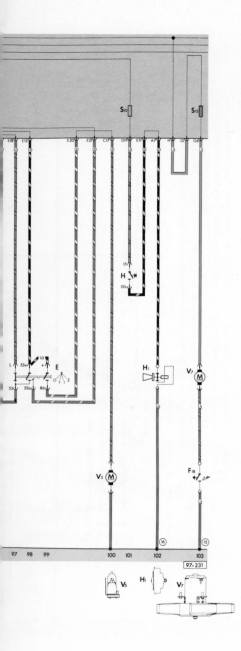

Description		Current track
E	– Windshield wiper switch	97, 98, 99
E 2	– Turn signal switch	80, 81, 82
E 3	– Emergency flasher switch	78, 79, 80, 82, 83
E 4	– Headlight dimmer switch	59
E 9	– Fresh air fan switch	85, 86
E 15	– Rear window defogger switch	87, 88
F	– Brake light switch	65, 67
F 1	– Engine oil pressure switch	71
F 18	– Radiator cooling fan thermo switch	103
F 27	– EGR elapsed mileage odometer	72
G	– Fuel gauge sending unit	69
G 1	– Fuel gauge	77
G 2	– Coolant temperature sending unit	70
G 3	– Coolant temperature gauge	76
H	– Horn button	101
H 1	– Horn	102
J	– Headlight dimmer relay	59, 60, 61, 62, 63
J 2	– Emergency flasher relay	81, 83, 85
J 6	– Voltage stabilizer	77
J 9	– Rear window defogger relay	87, 89
J 31	– Windshield wash/wipe intermittent relay (optional)	95, 96
K 1	– Headlight high beam warning light	64
K 3	– Engine oil pressure warning light	75
K 5	– Emergency flasher warning light	74
K 6	– Emergency flasher warning light	84
K 10	– Rear window defogger warning light	89
K 22	– EGR warning light	72
L 1	– Sealed beam unit, left	60, 62
L 2	– Sealed beam unit, right	61, 63
L 22	– Connection for fog lights	95
M 5	– Turn signal, front left	94
M 6	– Turn signal, rear left	93
M 7	– Turn signal, front right	92
M 8	– Turn signal, rear right	91
M 9	– Brake light, left	68
M 10	– Brake light, right	67
	– Fuses S1, S2, S3, S4, S5, S6, S8, S10, S11, S15 in fuse box	
Ta	– Wire connector, behind dashboard	
Tb	– Wire connector, next to light switch	
T 1a	– Wire connector, single; in engine compartment, front left	
T 1b	– Wire connector, single; in engine compartment, front right	
T 1c	– Wire connector, single; in engine compartment, right	
T 1d	– Wire connector, single; on firewall	
T 1e	– Wire connector, single; on firewall	
T 1f	– Wire connector, single; behind dashboard	
T 1g	– Wire connector, single; behind relay plate	
T 1h	– Wire connector, single; in engine compartment, front left	
T 1i	– Wire connector, single; behind relay plate	
T 1k	– Wire connector, single; in luggage compartment, rear right	
T 1l	– Wire connector, single; behind dashboard	
T 1m	– Wire connector, single; in luggage compartment, left	
T 1n	– Wire connector, single; in luggage compartment, rear left	
T 2a	– Wire connector, double; behind dashboard (connection for radio)	
T 2b	– Wire connector, double; behind dashboard	
T 2c	– Wire connector, double; next to relay plate	
T 2d	– Wire connector, double; in engine compartment, front left	
T 2e	– Wire connector, double; in engine compartment, front right	
T 2f	– Wire connector, double; in luggage compartment, rear right	
T 2g	– Wire connector, double; under driver's seat	
T 2h	– Wire connector, double; in luggage compartment	
T 3a	– Wire connector, 3 point; behind dashboard	
T 3b	– Wire connector, 3 point; behind dashboard	
T 3c	– Wire connector, 3 point; behind dashboard	
T 4	– Wire connector, 4 point; next to relay plate	
V	– Windshield wiper motor	95, 96
V 2	– Fresh air fan	86
V 5	– Windshield washer pump	100
V 7	– Radiator cooling fan	103
Z 1	– Rear window defogger element	90
⑩	– Ground connector, dashboard	
⑮	– Ground connector, engine compartment front left	
⑯	– Ground connector, engine compartment front right	

NOTE——

See also the additional wiring diagram for 1976 and later models at the end of this section.

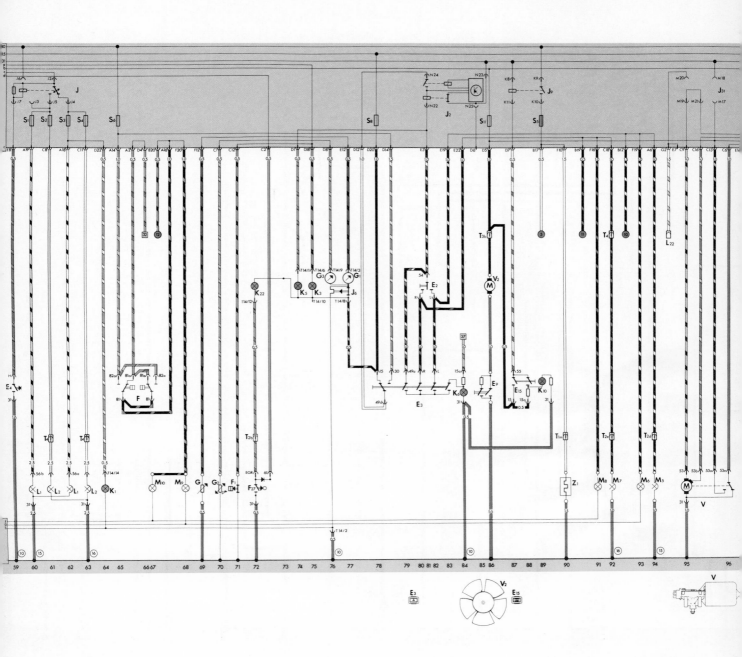

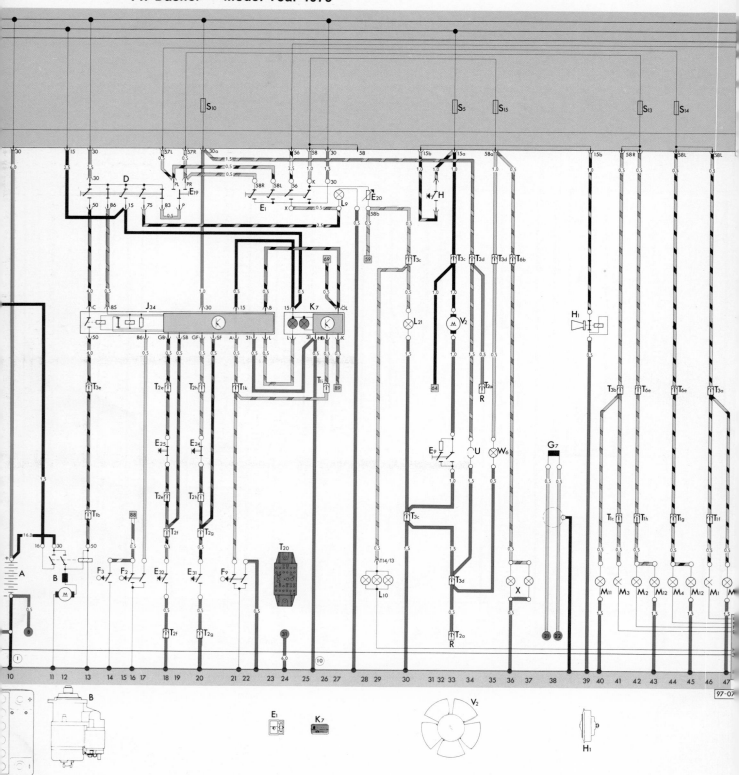

Current track

24	
34	
33	
35	
36	
10	
25	

CAUTION——

Disconnect the battery ground strap before starting to work on any part of the electrical system.

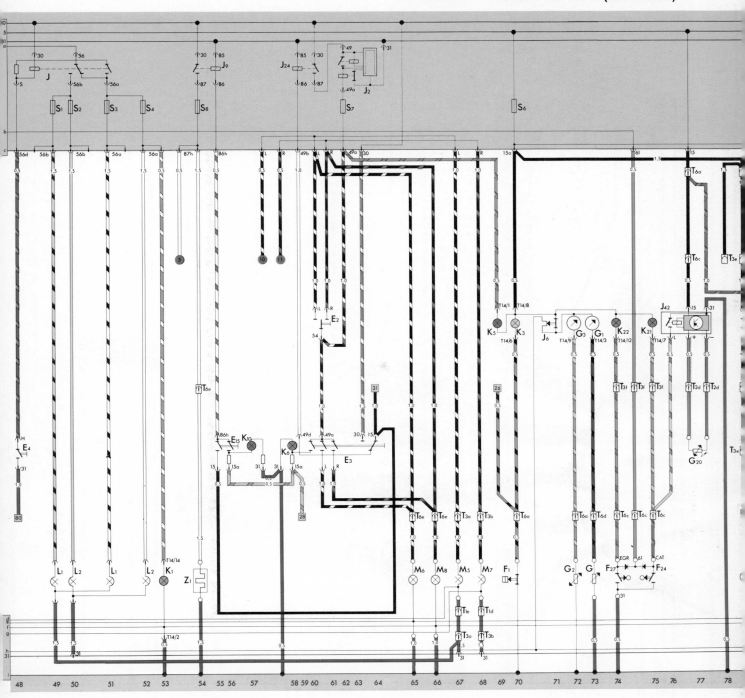

Computer Analysis System——

The orange-colored spots are connections in
the Computer Analysis System that are wired
to socket T 20. The numbers in these spots
correspond to terminals in the Computer
Analysis socket.

Description

E	– Win
E 2	– Turr
E 3	– Eme
E 4	– Hea
E 15	– Rea
F	– Brak
F 1	– Eng
F 4	– Bac
F 18	– Rad
F 24	– Elap
F 27	– Elap

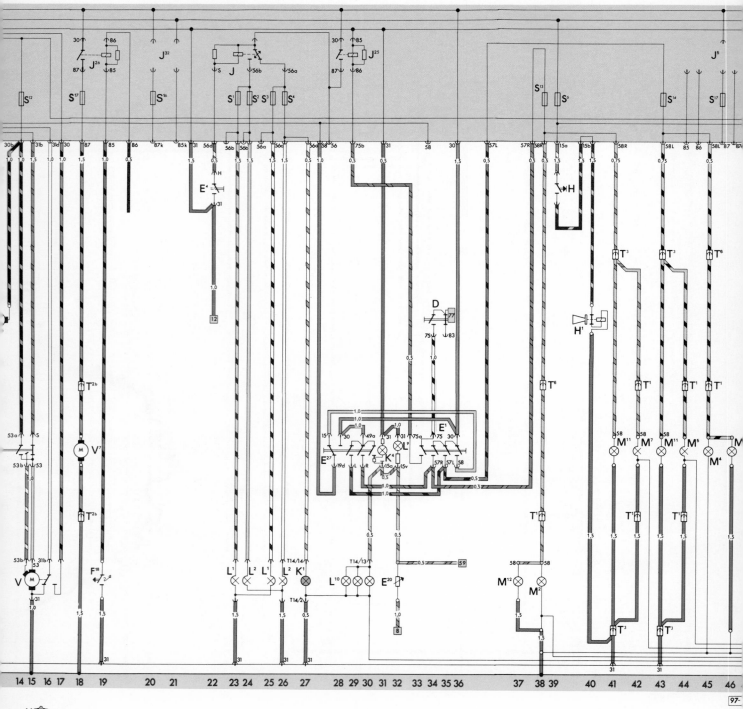

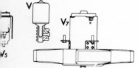

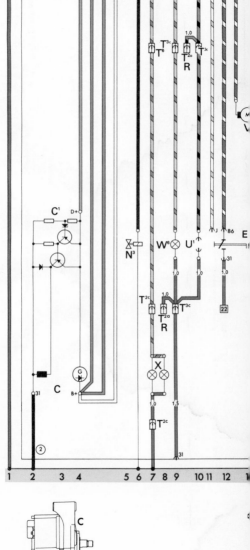

Description

		Current track
C	– Alternator	2, 4
C1	– Regulator	2, 3, 4
D	– Ignition/starter switch	34, 35
E	– Windshield wiper switch	12, 13, 14, 15
E1	– Light switch	33, 34, 35, 36
E4	– Headlight dimmer switch	22
E20	– Instrument panel lighting control	32
E27	– Parking light switch	28, 29, 30, 31
F18	– Radiator fan thermo switch	19
H	– Horn button	39
H1	– Horn	40
J	– Dimmer relay	22, 23, 24, 25, 26
J25	– Headlight relay	28, 29
J32	– Relay for air conditioner	20, 21
K1	– High beam warning light	27
K2	– Alternator charging warning light	3
K4	– Parking light warning light	31
L1	– Sealed beam unit, left headlight	23, 25
L2	– Sealed beam unit, right headlight	24, 26
L9	– Light switch illumination	32
L10	– Instrument panel light	28, 29, 30
M2	– Tail light, right	38
M4	– Tail light, left	45
M5	– Parking light front, left	44
M7	– Parking light front, right	42
M11	– Sidemarker light, front	41, 43
M12	– Sidemarker light, rear	37, 46
N3	– Electromagnetic cutoff valve	6
R	– Radio	8, 10
S	– Fuses	
	S1, S2, S3, S4, S6, S9, S11, S12, S13, S14, S15, S16, S17 in fuse box	
T1a	– Wire connector, single, in luggage compartment	
T1b	– Wire connector, single, in engine compartment, left	
T1c	– Wire connector, single, in engine compartment, right	
T1d	– Wire connector, single, in engine compartment	
T1e	– Wire connector, single, behind instrument panel	
T2a	– Wire connector, double, behind instrument panel	
T2b	– Wire connector, double, in engine compartment	
T2c	– Wire connector, double, in luggage compartment	
T2d	– Wire connector, double, on body bottom	
T3a	– Wire connector, 3 point, in engine compartment, left	
T3b	– Wire connector, 3 point, in engine compartment, right	
T3c	– Wire connector, 3 point, behind instrument panel	
T6	– Wire connector, 6 point, behind instrument panel	
T14	– Wire connector, 14 point, on instrument cluster	
U1	– Cigarette lighter	10
V	– Windshield wiper motor	15, 16, 17
V5	– Windshield washer pump	13
V7	– Radiator fan	18
W6	– Glove compartment light	9
X	– License plate light	7, 8
②	– Ground strap—alternator/engine	2

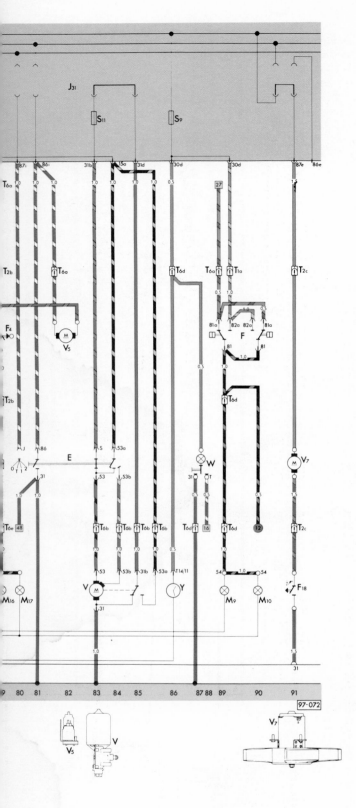

Description	Current track
G – Fuel gauge sending unit	73
G 1 – Fuel gauge	73
G 2 – Coolant temperature sending unit	72
G 3 – Coolant temperature gauge	72
G 20 – Catalytic converter temperature sensor	77
J – Headlight dimmer relay	48, 49, 50, 51, 52
J 2 – Emergency flasher relay	63, 64
J 6 – Voltage stabilizer	71
J 9 – Rear window defogger relay	54, 55
J 24 – Relay activating emergency flasher relay	59, 60
J 31 – Windshield washer/wiper intermittent relay (optional)	80, 81, 83, 85
J 42 – Catalytic converter relay	76, 77
K 1 – Headlight high beam warning light	53
K 3 – Engine oil pressure light	70
K 5 – Turn signal warning light	69
K 6 – Emergency flasher warning light	58
K 10 – Rear window defogger warning light	57
K 21 – Catalytic converter warning light	75
K 22 – EGR warning light	74
L 1 – Sealed beam unit, left	49, 51
L 2 – Sealed beam unit, right	50, 52
M 5 – Turn signal, front left	67
M 6 – Turn signal, rear left	65
M 7 – Turn signal, front right	68
M 8 – Turn signal, rear right	66
M 9 – Brake light, left	89
M 10 – Brake light, right	90
M 16 – Backup light, left	79
M 17 – Backup light, right	80
S – Fuses S1, S2, S3, S4, S6, S7, S8, S9, S11, in fuse box	
T 1a – Wire connector, single; behind dashboard	
T 1b – Wire connector, single; in engine compartment	
T 1c – Wire connector, single; in engine compartment right	
T 1d – Wire connector, single; in engine compartment right	
T 1e – Wire connector, single; in engine compartment left	
T 1f – Wire connector, single; in engine compartment left	
T 1g – Wire connector, single; in luggage compartment left	
T 1h – Wire connector, single; in luggage compartment right	
T 1i – Wire connector, single; behind dashboard	
T 1k – Wire connector, single, behind dashboard	
T 2a – Wire connector, double; behind dashboard	
T 2b – Wire connector, double; in engine compartment	
T 2c – Wire connector, double; next to radiator	
T 2d – Wire connector, double; in luggage compartment	
T 2e – Wire connector, double; on body bottom	
T 2f – Wire connector, double; below passenger seat	
T 2g – Wire connector, double; below driver seat	
T 2h – Wire connector, double, on body bottom	
T 3a – Wire connector, 3 point; in engine compartment, left front	
T 3b – Wire connector, 3 point; in engine compartment, right front	
T 3c – Wire connector, 3 point; behind dashboard	
T 3d – Wire connector, 3 point; behind dashboard	
T 3e – Wire connector, 3 point; behind dashboard	
T 3f – Wire connector, 3 point; behind dashboard	
T 6a – Wire connector, 6 point; behind dashboard	
T 6c – Wire connector, 6 point; behind dashboard	
T 6d – Wire connector, 6 point; behind dashboard	
T 6e – Wire connector, 6 point; behind dashboard	
T 14 – Wire connector, 14 point; on dashboard cluster	
V – Windshield wiper motor	83, 84, 85
V 5 – Windshield washer pump	82
V 7 – Radiator cooling fan	91
W – Interior light	87, 88
Y – Clock	86
Z 1 – Rear window defogger heating element	54

Description	Current track
shield wiper switch	81, 83, 84
signal switch	60, 61
gency flasher switch	59, 60, 61, 62
	63, 64
light dimmer switch	48
window defogger switch	55, 56
e light switch	88, 89, 90
e oil pressure switch	70
up light switch	79
ator cooling fan thermo switch	91
sed CAT mileage odometer	75
sed EGR mileage odometer	74

97-072

NOTE——

The wiring of the electrical fuel pump as shown in the current flow diagram for 1976 and later models (given at the beginning of this section) remains valid for cars built through Chassis No. _ _6 2084 183.

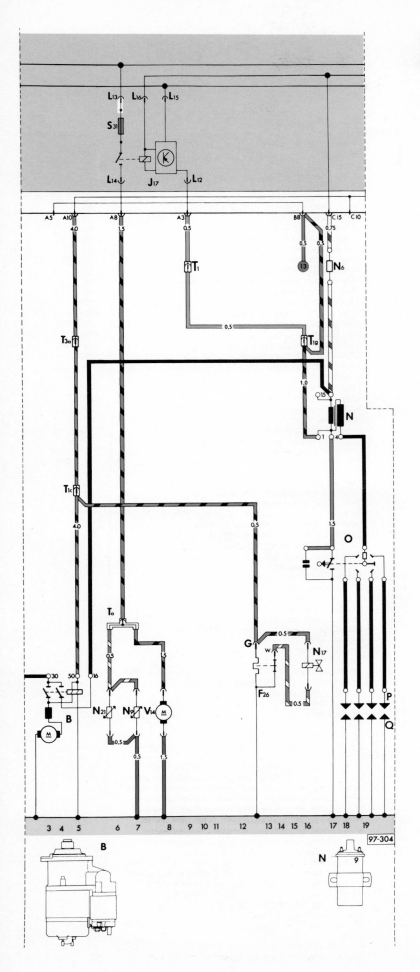

97-304

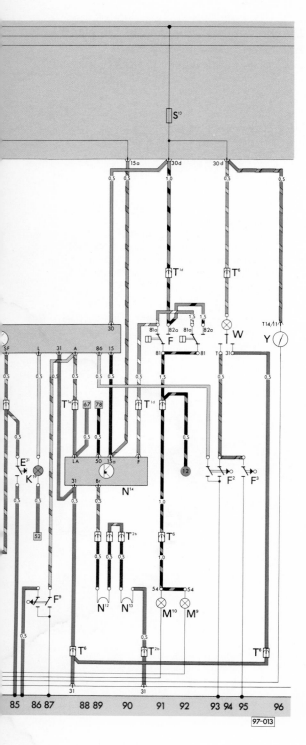

Description

			Current track
A	–	Battery	76
B	–	Starter	76, 77, 79
D	–	Ignition/starter switch	77, 78, 79, 80
E 2	–	Turn signal switch	58, 59
E 3	–	Emergency flasher switch	55, 56, 57, 58, 59
E 15	–	Rear window defogger switch	53
E 24	–	Safety belt lock, left	84
E 25	–	Safety belt lock, right	82
E 31	–	Contact strip in driver seat	85
E 32	–	Contact strip in passenger seat	83
F	–	Brake light switch	91, 92
F 1	–	Oil pressure switch	81
F 2	–	Door contact and buzzer alarm switch, left	93
F 3	–	Door contact switch, right	95
F 4	–	Backup light switch	65
F 9	–	Parking brake control light switch	86, 87
G	–	Fuel gauge sending unit	70
G 1	–	Fuel gauge	70
G 2	–	Coolant temperature gauge sending unit	69
G 3	–	Coolant temperature gauge	69
G 4	–	Ignition timing sensor	74
G 5	–	to tachometer	72
G 7	–	TDC sensor	71
J 2	–	Emergency flasher relay	59, 60
J 6	–	Voltage stabilizer for fuel gauge and coolant temperature gauge	69, 70
J 9	–	Rear window defogger relay	49, 51, 52, 53
J 24	–	Windshild wiper and turn signal relay	54, 55
J 34	–	Safety belt warning system relay (on left side below dashboard)	79, 81, 82, 84
K 3	–	Oil pressure warning light	68
K 5	–	Turn signal warning light	66
K 6	–	Emergency flasher warning light	59
K 7	–	Dual circuit brake warning and parking brake control light	67
K 10	–	Rear window defogger warning light	52
K 19	–	Safety belt warning system light	86
K 21	–	Light for heater lever illumination	51, 52
M 5	–	Turn signal, front, left	63
M 6	–	Turn signal, rear, left	60
M 7	–	Turn signal, front, right	62
M 8	–	Turn signal, rear, right	61
M 9	–	Brake light, left	92
M 10	–	Brake light, right	91
M 16	–	Backup light, left	65
M 17	–	Backup light, right	64
N	–	Ignition coil	73
N 6	–	Series resistance	73
N 12	–	vacant (not connected)	89
N 13	–	vacant (not connected)	90
N 14	–	Electronic switch for dual circuit brake warning system	89
O	–	Ignition distributor	73, 75
P	–	Spark plug connectors	75
Q	–	Spark plugs	75
S	–	Fuses S 5, S 7, S 8, S 10 in fuse box	
T 1a	–	Wire connector, single, in luggage compartment	
T 1b	–	Wire connector, single, in engine compartment, left	
T 1c	–	Wire connector, single, in engine compartment, right	
T 1d	–	Wire connector, single, in engine compartment	
T 1e	–	Wire connector, single, behind instrument panel	
T 2a	–	Wire connector, double, behind instrument panel	
T 2b	–	Wire connector, double, in engine compartment	
T 2c	–	Wire connector, double, in luggage compartment	
T 2d	–	Wire connector, double, on body bottom	
T 3a	–	Wire connector, 3 point, in engine compartment, left	
T 3b	–	Wire connector, 3 point, in engine compartment, right	
T 3c	–	Wire connector, 3 point, behind instrument panel	
T 6	–	Wire connector, 6 point, behind instrument panel	
T 14	–	Wire connector, 14 point, on instrument cluster	
T 20	–	Test network, test socket	82
W	–	Interior light	94
Y	–	Clock	96
Z 1	–	Rear window defogger heating element	49
①	–	Ground strap —battery / body / engine	76

97-013

Computer Analysis System——

The orange-colored spots are connections in the Computer Analysis System that are wired to socket T 20. The numbers in these spots correspond to terminals in the Computer Analysis socket.

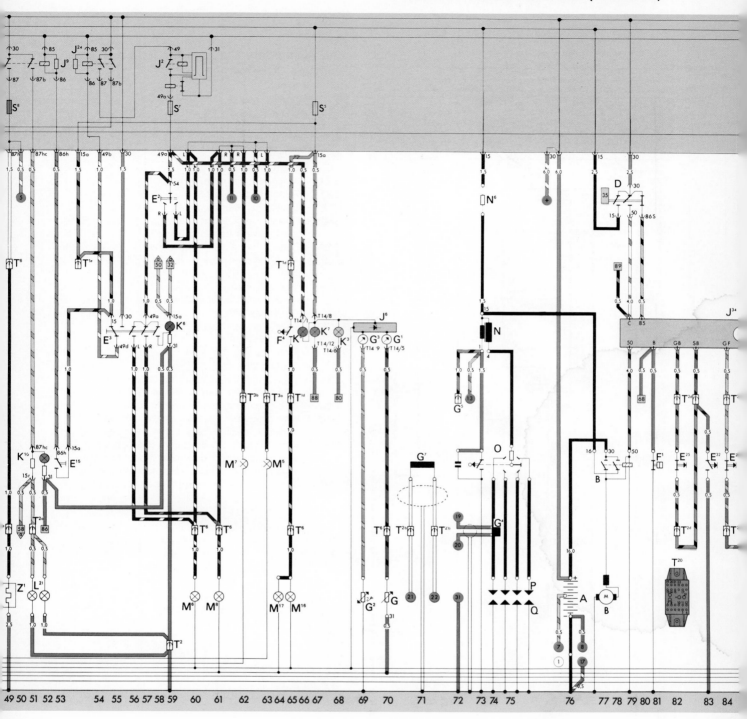

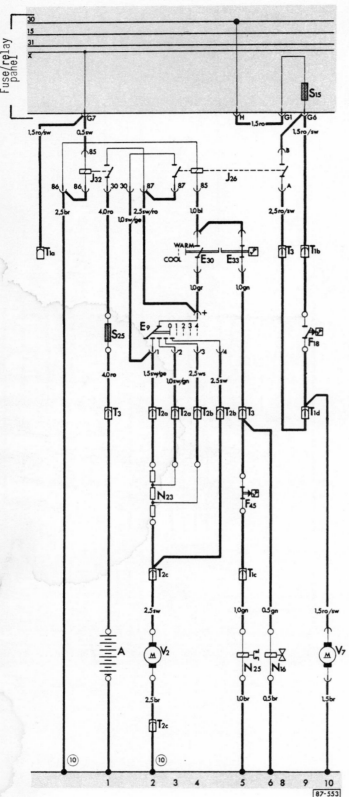

Supplementary Diagram for 1979 and Later Cars with Air Conditioning

Description		Current track
A	– Battery	1
E 9	– Fresh air fan switch	2 –4
E 30	– Air conditioner micro switch	4
E 33	– Temperature switch	5
F 18	– Coolant fan thermo switch	9
F 45	– Coolant circuit air conditioner thermo switch (diesel only)	5
J 26	– Coolant fan relay in relay panel	1 –8
J 32	– Air conditioner relay on fuse/relay panel	1 –2
N 16	– Two-way valve	6
N 23	– Fresh air fan resistor (next to fan)	2
N 25	– Compressor clutch	5
S 15	– Fuse 16 A (on fuse/relay panel)	9
S 25	– Fuse 25 A	1
V 2	– Fresh air fan	2
V 7	– Coolant fan	10
T 1a	– Wire connector, single; on fuse/relay panel	
T 1b	– Wire connector, single; behind dashboard	
T 1c	– Wire connector, single; next to compressor	
T 1d	– Wire connector, single; in engine compartment	
T 2a	– Wire connector, double; behind dashboard	
T 2b	– Wire connector, double; behind dashboard	
T 2c	– Wire connector, double; next to fresh air fan	
T 3	– Wire connector, 3-point; behind dashboard	
⑩	– Ground connector, next to fuse/relay panel	

Color code

bl	– blue
br	– brown
ge	– yellow
gn	– green
gr	– gray
ro	– red
ws	– white
sw	– black

87-553

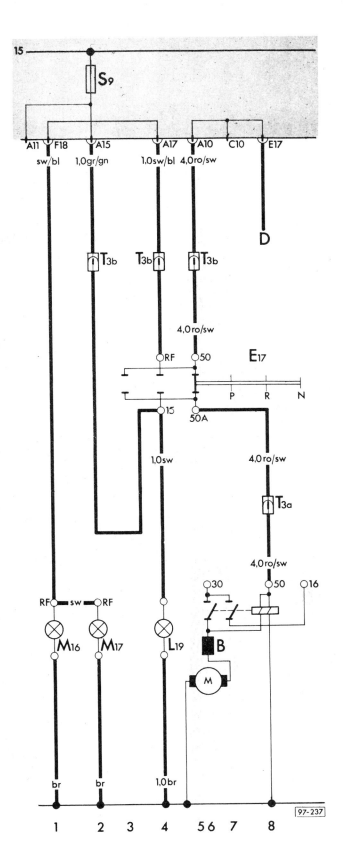

Description		Current track
B	– Starter	5 to 8
D	– To ignition/starter switch, terminal 50	8
E17	– Starter cutout and back-up lights switch	3 to 8
L19	– Shift console light	4
M16	– Back-up light, left	1
M17	– Back-up light, right	2
S9	– Fuse in fuse box	2
T3a	– Wire connector, single; in engine compartment, right	8
T3b	– Wire connector, single; below dashboard	2, 4, 5

4

Color code

bl	– blue
br	– brown
gr	– gray
gn	– green
ro	– red
sw	– black

97-237

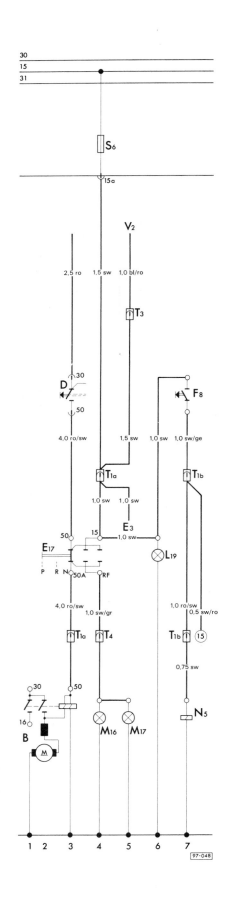

Description		Current track
B	– Starter	1
D	– Ignition/starter switch	3
E3	– To emergency flasher switch	5
E17	– Starter cutout switch and back-up light switch	2
F8	– Kickdown switch	7
L19	– Selector lever console illumination	6
M16	– Back-up light, left	4
M17	– Back-up light, right	5
N5	– Kickdown solenoid	7
S6	– Fuse in fuse box	4
T1a	– Wire connector, single; behind dashboard	3
T1b	– Wire connector, single; in engine compartment	7
T4	– Wire connector, 6-point; behind dashboard	4
V2	– To fresh air fan	5

Color code

bl –	blue
gr –	gray
ro –	red
sw –	black
ge –	yellow

97-048

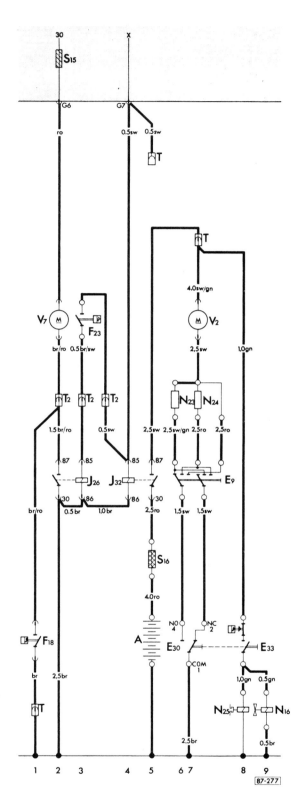

Supplementary Diagram for 1976 and 1977 Cars with Air Conditioning

NOTE ——

Gray-colored area of the diagram indicates the relay plate with the fuse box.

Description		Current track
A	– Battery	5
E9	– Fresh air fan control switch	6, 7
E30	– Micro switch	7
E33	– Temperature switch for compressor clutch	8
F18	– Radiator cooling fan thermo switch	1
F23	– High pressure switch, electric fan (on receiver-drier)	3, 4
J26	– Relay, electric fan	2, 3
J32	– Relay, air conditioner	4, 5
N16	– Two-way valve for increasing engine idle	9
N23	– Resistor, fresh air blower motor	6
N24	– Resistor, fresh air blower motor	7
N25	– Compressor clutch	8
S15	– Fuse 16A	2
S16	– Fuse 25A	5
T	– Wire connector	
T2	– Wire connector	
V2	– Fresh air fan	7
V7	– Radiator cooling fan	2

Color code

br – brown
gn – green
ro – red
sw – black

4

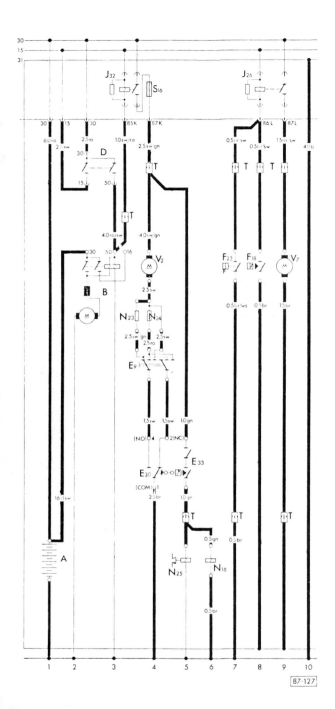

Supplementary Diagram for 1975 Cars with Air Conditioning

Description	Current track
A – Battery	1
B – Starter	2, 3
D – Ignition/starter switch	3
E9 – Fresh air fan control switch	4
E30– Micro switch	4
E33– Temperature switch for compressor clutch	5
F18– Electric fan unit	8
F23– High pressure switch, electric fan (on receiver-drier)	7
J26– Relay, electric fan	7, 8
J32– Relay, air conditioner	3, 4
N16– Two-way valve for increasing engine idle	6
N23– Resistor, fresh air blower motor	4
N24– Resistor, fresh air blower motor	4
N25– Compressor clutch	5
S16– Fuse 25A	4
T – Wire connectors	
V2 – Fresh air fan	4
V7 – Radiator cooling fan	9

Color code

br –	brown
gn –	green
ro –	red
sw –	black

87-127

Supplementary Diagram for 1978 Cars with Air Conditioning

Description	Current track
A – Battery	1
E 9 – Fresh air fan switch	2–3
E 30 – Microswitch	4
E 33 – Temperature switch	5
F 18 – Radiator cooling fan sending unit	9
J 26 – Radiator cooling fan relay	1–8
J 32 – Air conditioner relay	1, 2
N 16 – Idle speed control valve	6
N 23 – Fresh air fan resistor	2
N 25 – Compressor clutch	5
S 15 – Fuse in fuse panel	9
S 25 – Fuse, single	1
T 1a – Wire connector, single; on fuse/relay panel	0
T 1b – Wire connector, single; behind dashboard	5
T 1c – Wire connector, single; next to compressor	5
T 1d – Wire connector, single	9
T 2a – Wire connector, double; behind dashboard	2, 3
T 2b – Wire connector, double; behind dashboard	4
T 2c – Wire connector, double; next to fresh air fan	2
T 3 – Wire connector, 3-point; behind dashboard	1, 5, 8
V 2 – Fresh air fan	2
V 7 – Radiator cooling fan	9
10 – Ground connector next to pedal cluster	0, 2

4

Color code

br – brown
bl – blue
ge – yellow
gn – green
gr – gray
ro – red
sw – black
ws – white

AUTOMATIC TRANSMISSION (THROUGH 1975)

Contents

Automatic Transmission (Through 1975)

5

The automatic transmission covered in this section of the manual has been installed as optional equipment on the 1973, 1974 and 1975 models only. For information on the automatic transmission used on 1976 and later models, see **AUTOMATIC TRANSMISSION (from 1976).** The automatic transmission described here consists of an engine-driven torque converter coupled to a fully automatic three-speed planetary gear system. The automatic transmission's case is held on the separate final drive housing by four studs. Taken as a unit, the combined transmission and final drive is called the transaxle.

The transaxle with automatic transmission operates on entirely different principles from the standard transaxle with manual transmission. However, the constant velocity joints are identical on both the standard and the optional transaxles. See **MANUAL TRANSMISSION** for repairs related to the constant velocity joints and the front wheel driveshafts.

This section should interest almost every car owner, although many of the repair procedures will be of practical value only to the professional mechanic. Some operations require equipment and experience that only a trained mechanic is likely to have. So if you lack skills, tools, or a clean workshop, we suggest that you leave transaxle repairs to an Authorized Dealer or other qualified shop.

The nonprofessional may, however, be able to remove the transaxle, which can help to reduce service time. In this case, we recommend that the transaxle be thoroughly cleaned on the outside and then taken to the shop as is—partial disassembly will not make repairs easier and may indeed complicate them. We especially urge you to consult an Authorized Dealer before attempting repairs on a car still covered by the new-car warranty.

Cleanliness and a careful approach are imperative when repairing the transaxle. Familiarizing yourself with procedures, notes, cautions, and warnings before beginning work is good insurance. Clean and lay out the parts. If necessary, mark them to show their proper assembly order. Also make sure that you have the necessary tools—particularly for procedures given with metric specifications only. Specifications that lack U.S. equivalents require that the related work be carried out only with metric tools and instruments.

1. GENERAL DESCRIPTION

The transaxle with automatic transmission is housed in a case assembled from two main castings. At the rear of the assembly is a cast aluminum transmission case containing the automatic transmission fluid (ATF) pump, the hydraulic controls, and the planetary gear system. Attached at the front of this case by four steel studs is a final drive housing also cast in light alloy. The bellhousing for the torque converter is an integral part of the final drive housing.

The flanged shafts that carry driving torque to the front wheels extend from two openings at either side of the final drive housing. Adjusting rings, threaded into the case, form a support for the differential bearings. A front cover plate, bolted inside the bellhousing, can be removed for access to the differential.

Torque Converter

The torque converter is a large doughnut-shaped assembly located between the engine and the transaxle. The converter not only receives engine output and passes it on to the automatic transmission, but also multiplies engine torque at low vehicle speeds and serves as a fluid coupling between the engine and the transaxle. The converter housing spins with the engine's crankshaft. Curved vanes inside the housing set up a flow of ATF that drives another vaned wheel called the turbine. The turbine drives a hollow shaft that transmits power to the automatic transmission.

ATF Pump

ATF must be circulating under pressure before the automatic transmission can function. The ATF pump that creates this pressure is located at the extreme rear of the transmission case. A long pump driveshaft that passes through the center of the hollow turbine shaft drives the ATF pump.

The pump driveshaft is splined directly to the converter housing. Therefore, the pump circulates ATF whenever the engine is running, regardless of selector lever position. Since the circulating ATF is also the transmission's only lubricant, it is important to remember that the ATF does not circulate when the engine is not running and the car is being towed.

> **CAUTION ——**
>
> *Never tow a car with automatic transmission faster than 30 mph (48 kph) or farther than 30 miles (48 kilometers). Bearings can be damaged by lack of lubrication. If you must tow the car farther, lift the front wheels or remove the driveshafts that connect the front wheels to the transaxle.*

Planetary Gears

A torque converter alone cannot supply the torque multiplication needed for all driving conditions. The output of the torque converter is therefore routed into a planetary gearset. The planetary gearset is located at the front of the transmission case, just behind the final drive housing.

The planetary gear system used in the automatic transmission operates on the same principles as similar gearsets found in other automatic transmissions, though it differs in numerous construction details. The planetary gear system has one large sun gear (51 teeth), one small sun gear (30 teeth), three small planet pinions (16 teeth each), three large planet pinions (35 teeth each), and one large annulus (ring) gear. The planet pinions are all mounted on the planet carrier which is coupled to the final drive pinion (transmission output shaft). The annulus has a one-way roller clutch to provide free wheeling when the driver's foot is removed from the accelerator with the selector lever at **D** and the transmission in 1st gear.

Clutches

Two hydraulically operated multiple disk clutches control the delivery of turbine output to the planetary gear system. The clutch at the rear of the transmission is called the direct and reverse clutch because it transfers power to the small sun gear of the planetary gearset only when the transmission is in direct (3rd gear) or in reverse. The other clutch, located between the direct and reverse clutch and the planetary gearset, is called the forward clutch because it transfers power to the large sun gear in all forward gears.

Brake Bands

Two hydraulically operated brake bands are used to hold various parts of the planetary gear system stationary, thereby obtaining reverse and 2nd gears. One brake band operates on the outer surface of the planetary gearset's annulus (ring) gear. It is called the 1st and reverse brake band because its purpose is to provide reverse operation and to keep the transmission from freewheeling in 1st gear when the selector lever is in **1.** This brake band does not engage when the transmission is in 1st gear and the selector lever is at **D.**

The other brake band locks the drum that houses the direct and reverse clutch and thereby prevents free rotation of the small sun gear in the planetary gearset. It is called the 2nd gear brake band because it is applied in 2nd gear with the selector lever at **D** or at **2,** or during 2nd gear kickdown. Both brake bands are fitted with adjusting screws. However, adjustments can be performed only after the transmission has been removed from the vehicle.

Hydraulic Controls

The hydraulic control system directs and regulates hydraulic pressure from the ATF pump, thereby controlling shifting of the planetary gearset. Shifts are produced by applying ATF pressure to the ring-shaped clutch pistons and the two piston-type brake band servos in the bottom of the transmission case. Hydraulic pressure is directed to the proper clutch or brake band servo by a number of spring-loaded control valves inside cylinders machined into the valve body. See Fig. 1-1.

Three primary control devices regulate the movement of the control valves. One of these devices, the manual valve, is connected to the selector lever by a flexible cable. Moving the lever changes the setting of the valve to produce the necessary application of hydraulic pressure for the drive range selected. A second primary control device, the primary throttle pressure valve, which operates on engine vaccum, makes the transmission responsive to variations in engine speed and load. A third primary control device, the governor, which is gear-driven off the final drive pinion and controls ATF pressure relative to its rotational speed, makes the transmission responsive to variations in vehicle speeds.

NOTE ——

The final drive housing shown in Fig. 1-1 is not the one used on the cars covered by this manual.

1. ATF pump
2. Clutch drum
3. Piston for direct and reverse clutch
4. Direct and reverse clutch
5. Forward clutch drum with ball valve
6. Piston for forward clutch
7. Forward clutch
8. Forward clutch hub
9. Planetary gear carrier
10. Small sun gear
11. Small planet pinion
12. Annulus or ring gear
13. 1st gear one-way clutch
14. Adjusting ring for pinion bearing
15. Turbine shaft
16. Governor drive
17. Final drive housing
18. Bearing web
19. Cooling fins
20. One-way clutch support
21. Impeller
22. Stator
23. Converter housing
24. Turbine
25. One-way clutch
26. Transmission case
27. 2nd gear brake band
28. Control valve
29. Transfer plate
30. ATF strainer
31. Separator plate
32. Valve body
33. Spring for valve
34. Driving shell
35. Large planet pinion
36. Large sun gear
37. 1st and reverse brake band
38. Bearing flange
39. Differential
40. Pinion with shaft
41. Pump shaft
42. Connecting lug

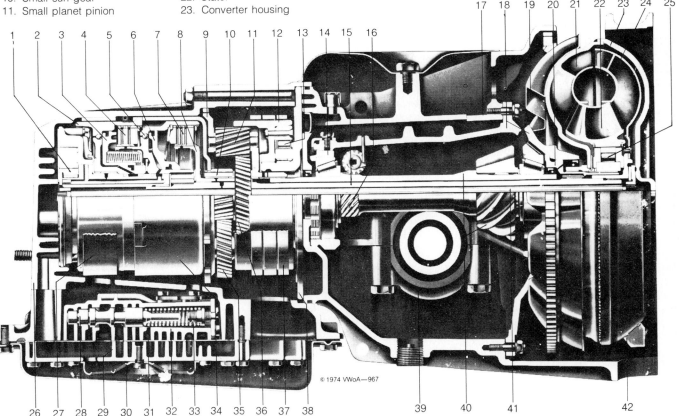

© 1974 VWoA—967

Fig. 1-1. Cutaway view of automatic transmission. Final drive is different on cars covered by this Manual.

Final Drive

The final drive consists of a hypoid drive pinion and ring gear with a differential gearset. The differential gearset, which consists of the two differential gearshafts and the two differential pinions, allows the front wheels to turn at different speeds, as is necessary when making turns (the outside wheel must travel farther than the inside wheel in the same amount of time).

2. MAINTENANCE

Many automatic transmission malfunctions can be traced to dirty ATF, too little or too much ATF, or other improper maintenance and lubrication conditions. Instructions and suggestions for automatic transmission care are found in **LUBRICATION AND MAINTENANCE**. The following operations are covered there:

1. Checking ATF level

2. Checking final drive oil level

3. Checking transmission (ATF) pan bolts

4. Checking kickdown operation

5. Changing ATF; draining and filling transmission, and cleaning the ATF pan and strainer.

3. TROUBLESHOOTING

Before diagnosing automatic transmission troubles, review the history of the unit. Such a review may offer important clues to present difficulties. The following should be checked before making repairs or adjustments:

1. Be sure that the engine is tuned up and running right.

2. Inspect the transaxle for external damage, loose or missing screws, and obvious leaks. Check the final drive hypoid oil for ATF contamination.

3. Check ATF level. Rub some ATF between your fingers and sniff it to detect the burned odor that means burned friction linings. If the ATF is dirty, it may be clogging the automatic controls.

4. Check the adjustment and operation of the kickdown switch and the adjustment of the selector lever cable. See that the vacuum unit on the primary throttle pressure valve is not bent.

3.1 Road Testing

Drive the car in all transmission ranges and under as many road conditions as possible. Note the shift points both up and down. They should take place quickly, without interrupting the power flow. Listen for engine racing between gears, a possible indication of slipping clutches or brake bands. **Table a** may suggest remedies

Table a. Automatic Transmission Troubleshooting

Problem	Probable Cause	Remedy
1. No drive in any selector lever position	a. Automatic transmission fluid level low b. Manual valve not hooked to selector lever c. ATF strainer clogged d. ATF pump clogged or defect in ATF pump or pump drive e. Broken shaft or planetary gearset	a. Check and correct ATF level. Repair any leaks.** b. Replace selector lever cable or attachments. See **13.1**. c. Clean strainer.** *d. Clean, repair, or replace pump. If drive is broken, check pump gears for free movement. See **10.6**. *e. Replace broken parts. See **10**.
2. ATF dark colored and smells burned	This may accompany or signal the start of trouble caused by burned friction linings on the brake bands or clutches	Drain contaminated ATF. Remove as much ATF as possible from converter. Replace with fresh ATF. See **8.5**.**
3. No drive in forward gears	Forward clutch defective	*Repair clutch. See **10.2**, **10.8**.
4. No drive in **R** and no engine braking with lever at **1**	1st and reverse band or servo defective	*Check and repair 1st and reverse band and servo. See **7**, **10.2**, **10.4**.
5. Car will not move off when lever is at **2** or **D**	1st gear one-way clutch in annulus defective	*Replace annulus gear and one-way clutch. See **10.2**, **10.9**.
6. No drive in 2nd gear when lever is at **2** or **D**	2nd gear brake band or servo defective	*Repair brake band or servo. See **7**, **10.2**, **10.4**.
7. Transmission stays in 1st gear with lever at **2** or **D**	a. Governor dirty or defective b. Valve body assembly dirty	a. Clean or repair governor. Fit new lock washer if old one is missing. Remove pan to retrieve old washer. See **6**. b. Remove oil pan. Clean valve body. See **5**.

Table a. Automatic Transmission Troubleshooting (continued)

Problem	Probable Cause	Remedy
8. No drive in 3rd gear or reverse	Direct and reverse clutch defective	*Repair clutch. See **10.2, 10.7**.
9. Erratic power transmission, noisy reverse (accelerator may have to be depressed several times before car moves)	a. ATF level too low or high b. Selector lever out of adjustment c. ATF strainer dirty d. Primary throttle pressure valve sticking	a. Check and correct ATF level. Repair any leaks.** b. Adjust cable. See **13.2**. c. Remove ATF pan, clean strainer.** d. Check valve, replace if necessary. See **3.3, 4**.
10. Engine surges on upshifts. Shift time too long	a. ATF level too low or high b. Primary throttle pressure valve misadjusted c. Direct and reverse clutch defective	a. Check and correct ATF level. Repair any leaks.** b. Adjust primary throttle pressure. See **3.3, 4**. *c. Repair clutch. See **10.2, 10.7**.
11. Shifts take place at too low speeds	a. Primary throttle pressure valve misadjusted b. Governor or governor drive defective c. Valve body assembly dirty	a. Adjust primary throttle pressure. See **3.3, 4**. b. Inspect and repair governor. See **6**. c. Remove ATF pan. Clean valve body. See **5**.
12. Shifts take place at too high speeds	a. Primary throttle pressure valve misadjusted b. Vacuum hose leaky c. Kickdown switch lever bent d. Kickdown solenoid switch defective e. Valve body assembly dirty f. ATF pressure low due to internal transmission leaks	a. Adjust primary throttle pressure. See **3.3, 4**. b. Replace hose. See **4**. c. Repair or replace kickdown switch.** d. Replace solenoid. See **5.2**. e. Remove ATF pan. Clean valve body. See **5**. f. Disassemble transmission and replace all seals and gaskets. See **10, 7, 6, 8.3**.
13. Transmission does not shift into 3rd gear with lever at **D**	a. Governor or governor drive defective b. Valve body assembly dirty c. Direct and reverse clutch defective	a. Inspect and repair governor. See **6**. b. Remove ATF pan. Clean valve body. See **5**. *c. Repair clutch. See **10.2, 10.7**.
14. Heavy jerk when selecting a drive range from neutral	a. Engine idle too fast b. Primary throttle pressure valve misadjusted c. Vacuum hose leaky d. Primary throttle pressure vacuum unit leaking	a. Adjust idle speed. See **FUEL AND EXHAUST SYSTEMS**. b. Adjust primary throttle pressure. See **3.3, 4**. c. Replace hose. See **4**. d. Replace primary throttle pressure vacuum chamber. See **4**.
15. Kickdown will not function	a. Kickdown switch defective or misadjusted b. Kickdown solenoid switch defective	a. Replace kickdown switch.** b. Replace solenoid. See **5.2**.
16. Poor acceleration. Top speed low despite good engine output	a. ATF level too low or high b. Torque converter one-way clutch defective c. Forward clutch defective d. Direct and reverse clutch defective e. 2nd gear brake band or servo defective	a. Check and correct ATF level. Repair any leaks.** b. Replace torque converter. See **8.1**. *c. Repair clutch. See **10.2, 10.8**. *d. Repair clutch. See **10.2, 10.7**. *e. Repair brake band or servo. See **7, 10.2, 10.4**.
17. Screeching noise when moving off or accelerating	a. Torque converter one-way clutch defective b. 1st gear one-way clutch in annulus defective	a. Replace torque converter. See **8.1**. *b. Replace annulus gear and one-way clutch. See **10.2, 10.9**.
18. Scraping, grinding noise from converter. Fluid silver-colored	Thrust washer in converter worn	Replace annulus gear and one-way clutch. See **10.2, 10.9**.
19. High ATF consumption without external leak	a. Leaking vacuum chamber on primary throttle pressure valve (exhaust will be smoky) b. ATF seals for pinion or governor shafts leaking (ATF may be leaking from transmission breather)	a. Replace primary throttle pressure valve vacuum chamber. See **4**. *b. Replace seals. See **7, 11.1, 11.2**.
20. Parking lock will not hold vehicle	a. Selector lever out of adjustment b. Parking lock linkage defective	a. Adjust cable. See **13.2**. b. Repair linkage. See **10.11**.
21. Heavy leakage of ATF. Transmission case and under side of car oily	Leaking converter seal. Welded seam in converter may be leaking	Replace seal, or seal and converter if necessary. See **8, 11.3**.

*Transmission must be out of the car and disassembled for this repair
**See LUBRICATION AND MAINTENANCE

5

for defects you observe. The numbers in bold type in the Remedy column refer to numbered headings in **AUTOMATIC TRANSMISSION.**

When troubleshooting the automatic transmission, try to pin down the main component involved: converter, planetary gear system, or hydraulic controls. If **Table a** has failed to pinpoint the malfunction adequately, the following tests should help to isolate the problem.

3.2 Stall Speed Testing

This test provides a quick check of the torque converter operation, but should be performed only if the car accelerates poorly or fails to reach the specified maximum speed. An electronic tachometer is required.

> *CAUTION —*
>
> *Never extend this test beyond the time it takes to read the gauges—20 seconds maximum. Doing so may overheat the transmission and damage the seals.*

To test:

1. Connect the tachometer according to the instrument manufacturer's instructions.

2. Start the engine.

3. Set the parking brake and depress the foot brake firmly to hold the vehicle stationary.

4. Shift the selector lever to position **D** and floor the accelerator pedal. Instead of revving up, the engine will run at a reduced rpm, known as stall speed.

If the rpm at stall is about 400 rpm below the specified 1900 to 2200 rpm stall speed—and the engine is in a proper state of tune—something is wrong with the torque converter. If the rpm at stall is above 2200 rpm, something is wrong in the forward clutch or the 1st gear one-way clutch located in the annulus gear of the planetary gearset. The test can also be made with the selector lever at **R.** If the reverse stall speed is too high, it indicates slippage in either the direct and reverse clutch or the 1st gear brake band.

3.3 Testing Hydraulic Control Circuit

A stall speed test is valuable mainly for isolating problems in the converter and the planetary gear system. Troubleshooting the hydraulic control system requires pressure testing. Although the pressure tests described here do not include tests for every valve in the hydraulic control system, the tests are adequate for determining whether or not the trouble is in the hydraulic controls. The actual source of the trouble is not significant since

you will have to remove the valve body to correct the trouble, regardless of where it lies. If there are physical defects—even minor ones—the entire valve body and governor must be replaced. In many cases, however, a thorough cleaning will be all that is required.

Pressure Testing

Only two of the four pressure test connections need be used. One is for primary throttle pressure and the other for main pressure. By attaching pressure gauges at these points, it is possible to determine whether there are internal leaks, wear, clogged ATF passages, or sticking valves.

Most automatic transmission malfunctions can be isolated without pressure tests. However, these tests are often valuable for confirming the need for certain repairs or isolating one of two possible causes for the same malfunction. A gauge reading from 0 to 140 psi (0 to 10 kg/cm²) is needed to measure primary throttle pressure and a gauge with a 0 to 350 psi (0 to 25 kg/cm²) range is needed to measure main pressure. Fig. 3-1 shows the test connection points on the transmission case.

> *CAUTION —*
>
> *If you lack the skills, tools, or a suitable workshop for automatic transmission work, we suggest you leave these repairs to an Authorized Dealer or other qualified shop. We especially urge you to consult your Authorized Dealer before attempting repairs on a car still covered by the new-car warranty.*

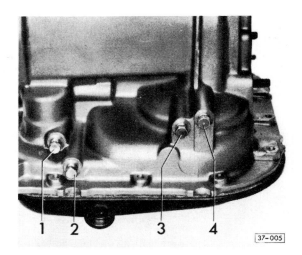

1. Main pressure
2. Primary throttle pressure
3. Main pressure. Release side of 2nd gear brake band servo piston

4. Main pressure. Apply side of 2nd gear brake band servo piston

Fig. 3-1. Pressure test connections. The main pressure **(1)** and primary throttle pressure **(2)** connections are the most important points to know.

To test pressures:

1. Connect the 0 to 350 psi (0 to 25 kg/cm²) gauge to the main pressure test point.

2. Connect the 0 to 140 psi (0 to 10 kg/cm²) gauge to the primary throttle pressure test point.

3. Position the pressure gauges so that you can read them from the driver's seat.

4. Disconnect the vacuum hose from the vacuum unit (Fig. 3-2). Plug the disconnected hose with an 8-mm (⅜-in.) punch.

5. Move the selector lever to **N,** start the engine, and measure both pressures at a fast (1000-rpm) idle. The throttle pressure should be 42.0 psi (3.00 kg/cm²). The main pressure should be 85.0 psi (6.00 kg/cm²).

6. If the throttle pressure is not within specifications, adjust the original vacuum unit—if possible. Alternatively, install a new vacuum unit and adjust it to specifications by turning the socket-head screw inside the vacuum chamber connection (Fig. 3-2).

   NOTE ——

   Always replace vacuum units that will not adjust to specifications. In addition, the vacuum units installed at the factory have their hose connection crimped to lock the socket-head adjusting screw in place. If the screw cannot be turned on these units, install a replacement vacuum unit, then adjust it as shown.

   CAUTION ——

   Be careful not to bend the vacuum unit. It must be perfectly straight to work properly.

7. Reconnect the vacuum hose and again measure the pressures at a fast idle. The throttle pressure

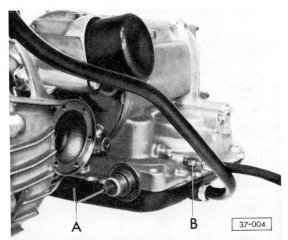

Fig. 3-2. Hex key (**A**) in position to turn the vacuum unit's socket-head adjusting screw. Primary throttle pressure connection is at **B.**

should be 5.0 to 6.0 psi (0.35 to 0.42 kg/cm²), and the main pressure 50.0 to 53.0 psi (3.50 to 3.70 kg/cm²).

8. Move the selector lever to **D.**

9. Check both pressures at full throttle while you hold the car stationary with the foot and parking brakes. The throttle pressure should be 38.0 to 42.0 psi (2.70 to 3.00 kg/cm²), and the main pressure should be 85.0 psi (6.00 kg/cm²).

   CAUTION ——

   Never continue a full-throttle pressure test longer than it takes to read the gauges—20 seconds maximum. Prolonging the test may overheat the transmission and damage the oil seals.

10. Move the selector lever to **R.** Check the main pressure while you hold the car stationary with the foot and parking brakes. The pressure should be 158 to 167 psi (10.70 to 11.70 kg/cm²) at a fast idle and 234 to 305 psi (16.50 to 21.50 kg/cm²) at full throttle.

11. After removing the test hose connections, torque the pressure connection plugs to 1.0 mkg (7 ft. lb.). Then run the engine and check the pressure connection plugs for leaks.

Pressures lower than those specified mean one or more of the following: (1) a worn pump; (2) internal ATF leaks past seals, gaskets, and metal mating surfaces; (3) sticking pressure regulating valves. High pressures always indicate sticking valves or a bent primary throttle pressure valve vacuum unit.

4. REPLACING PRIMARY THROTTLE PRESSURE VACUUM UNIT

The primary throttle pressure vacuum unit screws into the transmission case. A hex below the vacuum chamber provides a grip for the wrench. When installing a new unit, lubricate the threads lightly with a good anti-seize compound. Torque to 2.5 mkg (18 ft. lb.). Make certain that the vacuum hose to the engine is in good condition. Replace it if it is cracked or fits loosely. Do not over-tighten the hose clamps.

NOTE ——

When replacing the primary throttle pressure vacuum unit or installing a new or exchange transmission, check the primary throttle pressure to bring it within the specifications given under step 5 of the pressure testing procedures. A hex key is inserted in the vacuum connection to make any adjustment required as shown in Fig. 3-2.

5

5. SERVICING VALVE BODY AND VALVE BODY ASSEMBLY

Servicing the valve body assembly normally involves only removal and cleaning. However, it may also be necessary to remove the assembly from the transmission in order to replace a faulty kickdown solenoid.

5.1 Removing and Installing Valve Body Assembly

The valve body assembly can be removed with the engine and transmission in the car. The assembly must also be removed for cleaning during more extensive repairs with the transmission out of the car.

To remove:

1. Remove the transmission pan screws. Then take off the transmission pan and the gasket.

2. Disconnect the solenoid electrical wire from its terminal on the transmission case.

3. Fifteen bolts hold the valve body together and fasten it to the transmission. Take out 14 of the bolts, but for the moment leave in place the bolt indicated in Fig. 5-1.

4. Remove the bolt. Take off the valve body assembly, but do not separate it into its three main components as shown in Fig. 5-2 or you may lose the ball valves.

CAUTION ———

If the valve body assembly is removed while the transmission is in the car, the servo piston for the 1st gear band might fall out. Be ready to catch it.

`38-001`

Fig. 5-1. Fasteners for valve body assembly. Arrow points to bolt which is the fifteenth and last fastener to be removed.

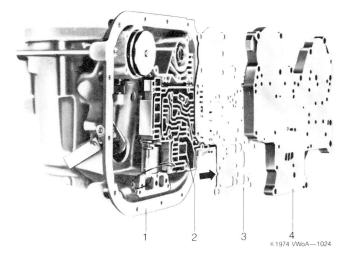

1. Transmission case
2. Valve body
3. Separator plate
4. Transfer plate

© 1974 VWoA—1024

Fig. 5-2. Valve body assembly apart. After removal, disassemble only on a clean workbench.

To disassemble valve body assembly:

1. Place the assembly on a clean workbench with the valve body down. Then remove the 15 Phillips head screws that hold the three components together.

2. Lift off the separator plate and transfer plate as a unit so that the ball valves in the valve body remain in the valve body.

3. Place the transfer plate and separator plate on the workbench with the transfer plate down. Then lift off the separator plate.

Assembly is the reverse of disassembly. The locations for the ball valves are shown in Fig. 5-3 and Fig. 5-4. Torque the Phillips head screws to 0.4 mkg (3 ft. lb.).

© 1974 VWoA—3352

Fig. 5-3. Ball valves in valve body. Ball for direct and reverse clutch valve is at **1**, ball for 1st gear valve is at **2**, ball for 1st and reverse brake band valve is at **3**, and ball and spring for forward pressure relief valve is at **4**.

© 1974 VWoA—3350

Fig. 5-4. Ball valves in transfer plate. Ball and spring for 2nd/3rd gear valve is at **A**; ball and spring for 3rd/2nd gear valve is at **B**.

To install valve body assembly:

1. Attach the valve body assembly to the transmission case with the bolt indicated in Fig. 5-1. The manual valve must be engaged by the operating levers as shown in Fig. 5-5.

2. Install the 14 bolts and washers finger-tight.

3. Working diagonally, torque all bolts to 0.36 mkg (3 ft. lb. or 36 in. lb.).

38-014

Fig. 5-5. Operating lever engaged in manaul valve (arrow).

4. Connect the wire to the kickdown solenoid.

5. Install a new oil pan gasket and then the transmission oil pan. Working diagonally, torque the pan screws to 1 mkg (7 ft. lb.).

6. Wait 5 minutes for the new gasket to compress, then retorque the screws to 1 mkg (7 ft. lb.).

7. Repeat step 6 until the screws remain at 1 mkg (7 ft. lb.).

CAUTION ——

Never tighten the transmission pan screws to more than 1 mkg (7 ft. lb.) in an attempt to cure a leaking gasket. Overtightening will deform the pan and make it impossible to get a good seal. Always install a new gasket to correct leaks.

5.2 Removing and Installing Kickdown Solenoid

The kickdown solenoid is an electromechanical device that moves the kickdown valve in the hydraulic control system. It is operated by an electrical switch under the accelerator. If the transmission will not kick down, use a voltmeter to check the wire leading to the transaxle. If current is reaching the transaxle, the solenoid may be at fault.

Test the solenoid for continuity by removing the wire from the outside of the transaxle. Attach a battery-powered test light to the terminal on the transmission case and to the case itself. If the test light does not come on, the solenoid is faulty or disconnected from the terminal inside the transmission case. Remove the transmission pan in order to inspect the wire's connection.

To replace solenoid:

1. Take off the transmission pan and remove the valve body assembly.

2. Remove the two screws that hold the solenoid to the valve body.

NOTE ——

The solenoid mounting screws are inaccessible while the valve body is in place.

As a rule, the valve body is disassembled only for cleaning. Unless the fluid is very dirty or contaminated by large solid particles, it usually is sufficient to immerse the complete assembly in cleaning fluid and dry it with compressed air. However, be careful not to hold the air jet so close that it moves the valves violently. This could damage the springs.

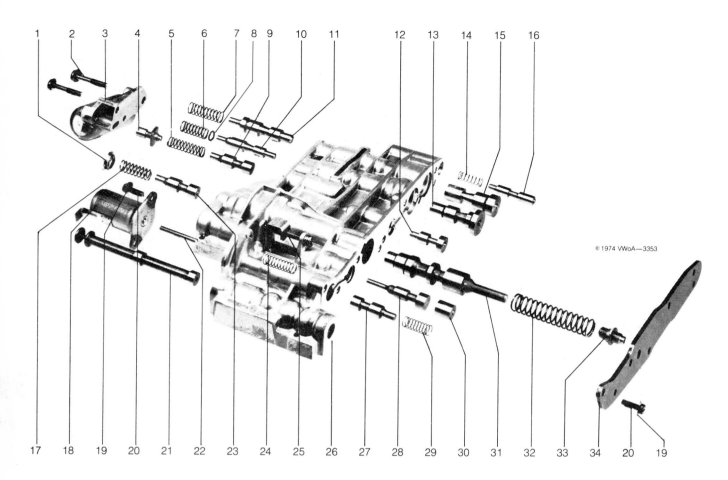

© 1974 VWoA—3353

1. Converter pressure valve spring cup
2. M 5 screw
3. 2nd/3rd gear accumulator
4. Adjusting screw with spring seat
5. Throttle pressure limiting valve spring
6. 1st/2nd gear shift valve spring
7. 2nd/3rd gear shift valve spring
8. Spring seat
9. Throttle pressure limiting valve
10. 1st/2nd gear shift valve
11. 2nd/3rd gear shift valve
12. 2nd/3rd gear control valve
13. 1st/2nd gear governor plug
14. 3rd/2nd gear part throttle valve spring
15. 2nd/3rd gear governor plug
16. 3rd/2nd gear part throttle valve
17. Converter pressure valve spring
18. Kickdown solenoid
19. Spring washer
20. M 5 screw
21. Manual valve
22. Kickdown solenoid plunger
23. Converter pressure valve
24. Secondary throttle pressure valve spring
25. Secondary throttle pressure adjusting screw
26. Valve body
27. Kickdown valve
28. Secondary throttle pressure valve
29. Kickdown valve spring
30. 1st gear plug for secondary throttle pressure valve
31. Main pressure regulating valve
32. Main pressure regulating valve spring
33. Adjusting screw with spring seat
34. Rear endplate

Fig. 5-6. Valve body. The kickdown valve, throttle pressure limiting valve, and converter pressure valve are physically identical. Used valves, however, must not be interchanged.

5.3 Disassembling and Assembling Valve Body

Fig. 5-6 is an exploded view of the valve body. Because many of the parts look alike, it is easy to mix them up. This is especially true of the springs. Unless you keep the springs separated and marked for identification, you will have to measure each spring with a micrometer prior to reassembly in order to find its correct place. See **14. Automatic Transmission Technical Data** for spring dimensions. To avoid the need for such measurements, use a compartmental storage tray. Such a tray will also keep the springs from getting bent or stretched, which would upset their precisely calibrated tensions.

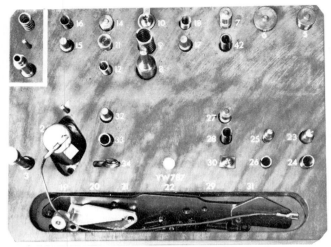

© 1974 VWoA—1027

Fig. 5-7. Storage tray for valve body parts. Number holes to conform with part numbers in Fig. 5-6.

If a storage tray (Fig. 5-7) for the valve body components is not available, you can make one by drilling holes in a thick board and numbering them.

To disassemble:

1. Remove the valve body assembly from the transmission. Then disassemble it into its three main components as described in **5.1 Removing and Installing Valve Body Assembly.**

2. Remove the rear endplate.

> **CAUTION** ———
>
> *Do not, under any circumstances, alter the setting of the main pressure regulating valve adjusting screw that is under the endplate. The screw can be adjusted properly only at the factory. The adjusting screws for the throttle pressure limiting and secondary throttle pressure valves must also be left alone for the same reason.*

3. One at a time, remove each valve and spring and place it in the storage tray. Use a brass rod to carefully press out sticking or tight-fitting valves.

4. Remove the solenoid. Then take out the solenoid plunger and the manual valve. Remove the 2nd/3rd gear accumulator.

5. Remove the remaining valves and springs.

6. Wash all parts in clean kerosene, then dry them with compressed air.

Never use water to clean the valves and valve body, and never dry the parts with fluffy rags or by rubbing them against your clothing. Even a microscopic piece of lint or a small patch of rust can cause a valve to stick in its bore.

Assembly is basically the reverse of disassembly. Clean the workbench before you start to work. Lubricate each valve with ATF as you reinstall it, then make certain that the valve moves freely of its own weight. Used valves that have worn to fit individual bores must be returned to their original locations. When you install the endplate, be careful not to overtighten the screws. Overtightening could easily strip the threads in the valve body.

Join together the three main components of the valve body assembly. Then install the valve body assembly in the transmission. Make certain that moving the selector lever moves the manual valve properly, and that when the valve is fully forward, it contacts the lug on the solenoid.

6. SERVICING GOVERNOR

The governor for the hydraulic control system is located beneath a round, black pressed steel cover just ahead of and slightly above the left driveshaft on the transmission. The cover is held in place by a spring wire clip.

6.1 Removing and Installing Governor

The governor can be removed with the engine and transmission installed in the car. The governor is usually removed for cleaning or for replacing worn parts. However, if a new valve body is being installed, a matching governor is supplied with the new valve body and must be installed whether the old governor is serviceable or not.

To remove:

1. Release the clip and then take off the cover. Allow the governor to turn slightly clockwise as you pull it out of the transaxle.

2. Inspect the needle bearing and (especially if the final drive hypoid oil is contaminated by ATF) the oil seal that are pressed into the final drive housing. If necessary, replace worn parts as described in **11.4 Replacing Governor Bearing, Governor Oil Seal, Speedometer Drive, and Starter Drive Bushing.**

3. Inspect the thrust plate and the drive gear for wear and scoring. Replace worn parts.

> **NOTE** ———
>
> Because replacing the entire governor could possibly change the governor pressure, new governor shafts are available separately to replace those that are worn or damaged.

5

Governor installation is the reverse of removal. Make sure that a new governor is the proper replacement part for the vehicle. Turn the governor counterclockwise as you install it so that the gear on the shaft engages the drive pinion. Always install a new cover O-ring before you install the governor cover.

6.2 Disassembling and Assembling Governor

Disassemble the governor only if it contains debris from burned clutch or brake band linings. Otherwise, just dip it in solvent and dry it with compressed air.

To disassemble the governor, remove the two M 5 × 40 screws and take off the thrust plate and housing. Then take out the transfer plate and the balance weight. The weight has been matched to the governor, so do not exchange the original weight with a weight from another governor. You can remove the weight, valve, spring, and dished washer from the pin by prying off the E-clips. See Fig. 6-1.

Before you assemble the governor, wash all parts in kerosene and dry them with compressed air. Lubricate the parts with ATF as you install them. The drillings in the transfer plate must taper down toward the centrifugal weight. Make sure the angle in the thrust plate is at the center of the housing so that the cover will bear against it.

7. REMOVING AND INSTALLING SERVO PISTONS AND 1ST/2ND GEAR ACCUMULATOR

The servo pistons and accumulator can be removed and installed with the transmission in the car. This job is usually done to replace the piston seals and the O-ring. Fig. 7-1 shows the relative positions of the parts in the transmission case.

To remove:

1. Remove the transmission pan and the valve body assembly.

2. Take out the 1st gear band piston, then remove its seals as shown in Fig. 7-2. Do not use sharp-edged tools that could damage the piston.

3. Remove the sealing cover circlip (Fig. 7-3). Take out the sealing cover for the 2nd gear band piston. Take out the piston. Then, using a procedure similar to that used in removing the seal from the 1st gear band piston, remove the two seals from the 2nd gear band piston.

4. Replace the O-ring on the sealing cover.

5. Take out the accumulator spring and the accumulator piston. Remove the piston seal.

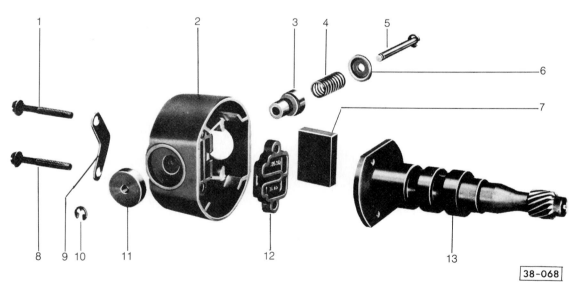

38-068

1. Bolt (2)	8. Spring washer (2)
2. Governor housing	9. Thrust plate
3. Valve	10. E-clip (2)
4. Spring	11. Centrifugal weight
5. Pin	12. Transfer plate
6. Dished washer	13. Governor shaft
7. Balance weight	

Fig. 6-1. Centrifugal governor disassembled.

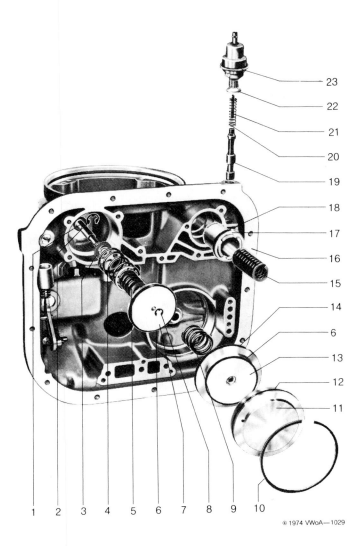

© 1974 VWoA—1029

1. 1st gear band piston rod
2. E-clip
3. Dished washer
4. 1st gear band return spring
5. 1st gear band accumulator spring
6. Piston seal (2)
7. 1st gear band piston
8. E-clip
9. 2nd gear band return spring
10. Sealing cover circlip
11. Sealing cover
12. O-ring
13. Piston with rod
14. 2nd gear band piston seal
15. Accumulator spring
16. Case
17. Accumulator piston
18. Accumulator piston seal
19. Primary throttle pressure valve
20. Primary throttle pressure valve spring
21. Thrust pin
22. Aluminum ring
23. Vacuum unit

Fig. 7-1. Exploded view of servo assemblies.

Fig. 7-2. 1st gear band piston seal being removed. Squeeze seal to one side, forming a loop, and then pull it off.

5

Fig. 7-3. Slot (arrow) for access to circlip. Insert tool and carefully pry out circlip.

To install:

1. Dip the new seals in ATF and install them on their respective pistons. The seal lips must point toward the pressure sides of the pistons, as shown in Fig. 7-4, Fig. 7-5, or Fig. 7-6.

Fig. 7-4. Seal lip position on 1st gear band piston.

Fig. 7-5. Seal lip positions on 2nd gear band position.

Fig. 7-6. Seal lip position on accumulator piston.

2. Lubricate the 2nd gear brake band servo piston with ATF. Then insert it into the sealing cover using a twisting motion. See Fig. 7-7.

3. Insert the cover together with the piston and band

Fig. 7-7. Small drift inserted in hole through piston rod so that piston can be inserted with twisting motion (arrow).

return spring into the transmission case. Then install the circlip.

4. If previously removed, slide the 1st and reverse piston and spring onto the piston rod. Lock them on the rod with the E-clips.

5. Lubricate the accumulator piston and the 1st and reverse brake band servo piston with ATF. Using a twisting motion, install the pistons together with their springs.

6. Install the valve body assembly as described in **5.1 Removing and Installing Valve Body Assembly.**

7. Install a new pan gasket and then the transmission pan.

NOTE ——

Follow a diagonal pattern as you torque the pan bolts to 1 mkg (7 ft. lb.). Wait five minutes for the new gasket to compress, then re-torque the screws to 1 mkg (7 ft. lb.). Do this several times until the screws remain at the specified torque.

CAUTION ——

Never tighten the pan bolts to more than 1 mkg (7 ft. lb.) in an attempt to cure a leaking gasket. Overtightening will deform the pan and make it impossible to get a good seal. Always install a new gasket to correct leaks.

8. TORQUE CONVERTER

Up to this point we have covered service operations that can be carried out with the engine and transaxle in the car—although some may also be carried out with the transaxle removed. Servicing the torque converter demands that the engine or the transaxle be removed from the car.

8.1 Removing and Installing Torque Converter

The torque converter usually requires removal only when you must replace the oil seal, replace the bushing, or clean the converter after a transmission failure has contaminated the ATF. Since the converter is a welded assembly, you must replace it as a unit if it is leaky or noisy, if it has broken welds, or if a stall speed test shows the unit to be faulty.

To remove the torque converter, take the transaxle out of the car as described in **9. Removing and Installing Transaxle.** (This is unnecessary if the engine has already been removed for repair.) Grasp the torque converter with both hands. Remove it by pulling it with a twisting motion off its support tube on the final drive front cover plate.

CAUTION —

Do not rock or tilt the torque converter when removing or installing it. This could damage the oil seal, the stator one-way clutch, or other parts in the hub.

Installation is the reverse of removal. Before installing the torque converter, inspect it thoroughly as described in **8.2 Inspecting Torque Converter.** If the oil seal seat on the hub is rough, worn, or pitted, replace the torque converter. Otherwise the seal will wear out in a very short time. Check that the pump shaft is inserted to the full depth of the pump splines (Fig. 8-1). Slowly turn the

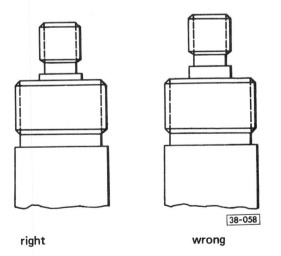

right   wrong

Fig. 8-1. Torque converter installation on pump shaft and turbine shaft. Pump shaft must be fully engaged in pump splines before you install the converter.

converter clockwise and counterclockwise as you install it so that the turbine and pump shafts splines can engage.

8.2 Inspecting Torque Converter

Inspect the converter seal inside the support tube on the final drive front cover plate. Replace the seal if it is hardened, cracked, worn, or otherwise damaged. Check the converter hub for signs of scoring from the oil seal. If the scoring is deep, replace the torque converter. Check for broken welds on the air deflector plate. Insert the turbine shaft (or a suitable substitute) and turn the turbine to see that it spins freely. Check the condition of the torque converter bushing. It should not be scored, nor worn more than 0.03 mm (.001 in.) out of round. Replace worn or damaged bushings.

8.3 Replacing Torque Converter Oil Seal

The torque converter oil seal is located in the final drive front cover plate. If the seal is hardened, worn, cracked, or otherwise damaged, pry it out as shown in Fig. 8-2. Though the final drive front cover plate is shown removed, it is not necessary to remove the cover plate in order to replace the seal.

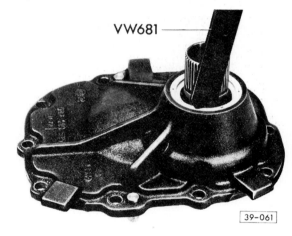

Fig. 8-2. Torque converter oil seal being removed.

Using an appropriate seal-installing tool, carefully drive in a new seal. The seal is soft, easily torn, and weakened by many common solvents. Replace the seal if it has been exposed to cleaning solvents or gasoline or if it has been torn.

8.4 Replacing Torque Converter Bushing

A leaking torque converter oil seal is usually caused by a worn bushing in the torque converter hub, so check the bushing every time you replace a seal. The bushing should not be scored, loose fitting, or more than 0.03 mm (.001 in.) out of round.

To replace the converter bushing, use an extractor and a slide hammer to remove the old bushing, as shown in Fig. 8-3. Drive in the new bushing with a properly fitting bushing driver. Check the bushing for out-of-round following installation.

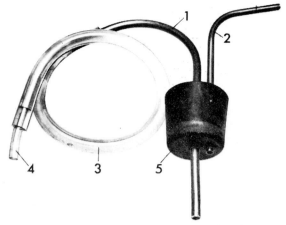

1. Steel or copper tube ³/₁₆ × 8 in. (4 × 200 mm)
2. Steel or copper tube ⅛ × 6 in. (3 × 150 mm)
3. PVC hose ¼ × 14 in. (6 × 350 mm)
4. PVC hose ⅛ × 1¼ in. (3 × 30 mm)
5. Conical rubber plug 1½ in. (35 mm) diam.

Fig. 8-4. Siphon parts available at auto stores. Do not use tubing diameters larger than those specified. Part 4 is needed to restrict flow.

Fig. 8-3. Torque converter bushing being removed. Converter shown is not for a car covered by this manual. Use clean tools to keep dirt out of converter.

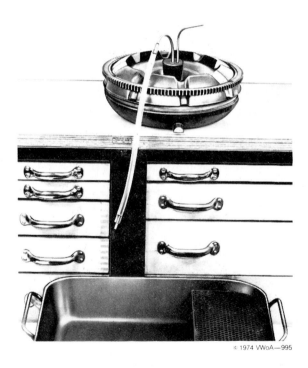

Fig. 8-5. Siphon and oil receptacle in position.

8.5 Cleaning Torque Converter

When charred material from a burned clutch disk or other pollutants have entered the ATF, remove the residual fluid from the converter with the home-made siphon shown in Fig. 8-4.

To drain the converter, install the siphon as shown in Fig. 8-5. Push the siphon line pipe through the rubber plug until it contacts the converter bottom, then place the siphon hose over the oil receptacle. Blow into the short tube to start the siphon. Let the converter drain overnight or for about eight hours.

9. REMOVING AND INSTALLING TRANSAXLE

All the necessary removal points for removing the transaxle are indicated by number in Fig. 9-1. We will refer to this illustration throughout the removal procedure.

5

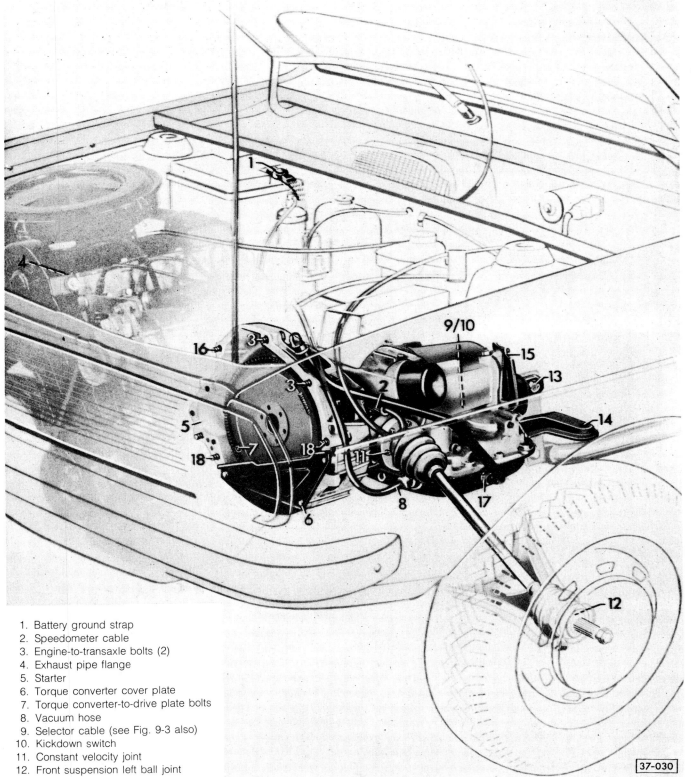

1. Battery ground strap
2. Speedometer cable
3. Engine-to-transaxle bolts (2)
4. Exhaust pipe flange
5. Starter
6. Torque converter cover plate
7. Torque converter-to-drive plate bolts
8. Vacuum hose
9. Selector cable (see Fig. 9-3 also)
10. Kickdown switch
11. Constant velocity joint
12. Front suspension left ball joint
13. Exhaust pipe bracket
14. Transaxle carrier
15. Transaxle rear mount
16. Engine-to-transaxle bolt
17. ATF filler pipe union nut
18. Engine-to-transaxle bolt (2)

Fig. 9-1. Removal points for transaxle with automatic transmission.

37-030

To remove:

1. Disconnect the ground strap (**1** in Fig. 9-1) from the battery's negative (−) post.

2. Disconnect the speedometer cable (**2** in Fig. 9-1).

3. Remove the two upper left engine-to-transaxle bolts (**3** in Fig. 9-1).

4. Remove the nuts, then disengage the exhaust pipe flange from the exhaust manifold (**4** in Fig. 9-1).

5. Disconnect the wires from the starter solenoid. Then remove the three nuts and bolts indicated in Fig. 9-2. Remove the starter from the car.

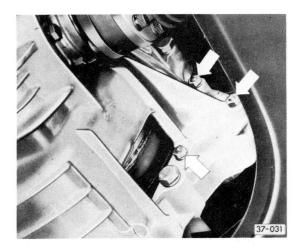

Fig. 9-2. Nuts (arrows) for starter bolts.

6. Take out the bolts and remove the torque converter cover plate (**6** in Fig. 9-1).

7. Working through the opening in the front of the bellhousing, remove the three bolts that hold the torque converter to the engine's drive plate (**7** in Fig. 9-1). Hand-turn the crankshaft to make the bolts accessible by placing a wrench on the bolt that is in the center of the crankshaft pulley at the front of the engine.

8. Pull the vacuum hose off the vacuum unit (**8** in Fig. 9-1).

9. Remove the circlip, then detach the selector cable from the arm on the transmission case (Fig. 9-3).

10. Disconnect the wire from the kickdown switch (**10** in Fig. 9-1).

11. Disconnect the driveshaft constant velocity joints (**11** in Fig. 9-1) from the transaxle as described in **MANUAL TRANSMISSION.** Using home-made wire hooks, suspend the disconnected driveshaft ends from the car body.

Fig. 9-3. Selector cable attachment point.

12. Mark the position of the suspension ball joint on the front suspension's left track control arm. If necessary, consult **SUSPENSION AND STEERING.** Then unbolt the ball joint from the track control arm, swing the road wheel outward, and temporarily reattach the ball joint to the track control arm as shown in Fig. 9-4.

Fig. 9-4. Ball joint temporarily remounted in an outboard position on track control arm.

13. Remove the bolt that holds the exhaust pipe bracket to the transaxle rear mount (**13** in Fig. 9-1).

14. On early models, take out the bolts and nut, then detach the transaxle carrier from the bonded rubber mounting and the body plate. See Fig. 9-5. The transaxle and engine assembly will drop slightly at the rear but no support is necessary.

16. Remove the upper right-hand engine-to-transaxle bolt (**16** in Fig. 9-1).

17. Loosen the union nut on the ATF filler pipe. Then detach and remove the pipe (**17** in Fig. 9-1).

18. Place a floor jack with a transmission adapter under the transaxle. Very slightly raise the engine/transaxle assembly. Then remove the two remaining engine-to-transaxle bolts (**18** in Fig. 9-1).

19. Using the floor jack, pull the transaxle rearward until it is clear of the engine. Make sure that the torque converter separates from the engine's drive plate and is not pulled off its support on the transaxle. When the transaxle is clear of the engine, lower the transaxle to floor level using the jack.

Installation is the reverse of removal. Torque the engine-to-transaxle bolts to 5.5 mkg (40 ft. lb.) and the bolts that hold the converter to the drive plate to 3.0 mkg (22 ft. lb.). Torque the bolt that holds the transaxle carrier to the floor plate to 3.0 mkg (22 ft. lb.) and the bolt that holds the transaxle carrier to the bonded mounting to 4.0 mkg (29 ft. lb.).

The three nuts for the transaxle rear mount should be torqued to 2.5 mkg (18 ft. lb.). The bolt that holds the exhaust pipe to the transaxle rear mount should be torqued to 2.0 mkg (14 ft. lb.) and the bolts that hold the exhaust pipe to the exhaust manifold should be torqued to 2.5 mkg (18 ft. lb.). Torque the converter cover plate bolts to 1.5 mkg (11 ft. lb.), the starter mounting bolt nuts to 2.0 mkg (14 ft. lb.), and the constant velocity joint bolts to 6.5 mkg (47 ft. lb.). Carefully align the suspension ball joint with the mark you made on the track control arm prior to removal. Then install the bolts to a torque of 6.5 mkg (47 ft. lb.).

10. REPAIRING AUTOMATIC TRANSMISSION

Thoroughly clean the outside of the transaxle before disassembly so that dirt will not enter the hydraulic controls or mechanical parts. Study the repair procedures on the following pages. If they require equipment you do not have, the transaxle should be turned over to a specialist before any disassembly.

CAUTION
If you lack the skills, tools, or a suitable workshop for transaxle repairs, we suggest you leave these repairs to an Authorized Dealer or other qualified shop. We especially urge you to consult an Authorized Dealer before attempting repairs on a car still covered by the new-car warranty.

Fig. 9-5. Fasteners (circled) that hold transaxle carrier and exhaust pipe bracket.

NOTE

On later models, which have the transaxle rear mount relocated to the left side of the transmission case, take out the bolts indicated in Fig. 9-6.

Fig. 9-6. Transaxle rear mount used on late models. During installation, tighten the bolts to the torques given in the illustration.

15. On early models, loosen the three nuts. Then remove the transaxle rear mount (**15** in Fig. 9-1).

10.1 Separating Transmission Case from Final Drive Housing

A transmission stand is a great help when it is necessary to make transmission or final drive repairs. Do not disassemble the unit on the shop floor as dirt and debris may get into the working parts.

To disassemble:

1. After cleaning the outside of the transaxle and draining the ATF, remove the torque converter and withdraw the pump shaft and the turbine shaft.

   NOTE ——

   You need not drain the hypoid oil unless you intend to disassemble the final drive.

2. Remove the ATF pan. Remove the four nuts that hold the final drive housing to the transmission case. One nut (Fig. 10-1) is located inside the transmission case.

Fig. 10-1. Nut (arrow) located inside transmission case.

3. Separate the main parts of the transaxle as shown in Fig. 10-2. Cover the converter hub opening and the final drive housing to prevent dirt from entering. Take the transmission itself to the workbench.

Assembly is covered in **10.5 Installing Final Drive on Automatic Transmission.**

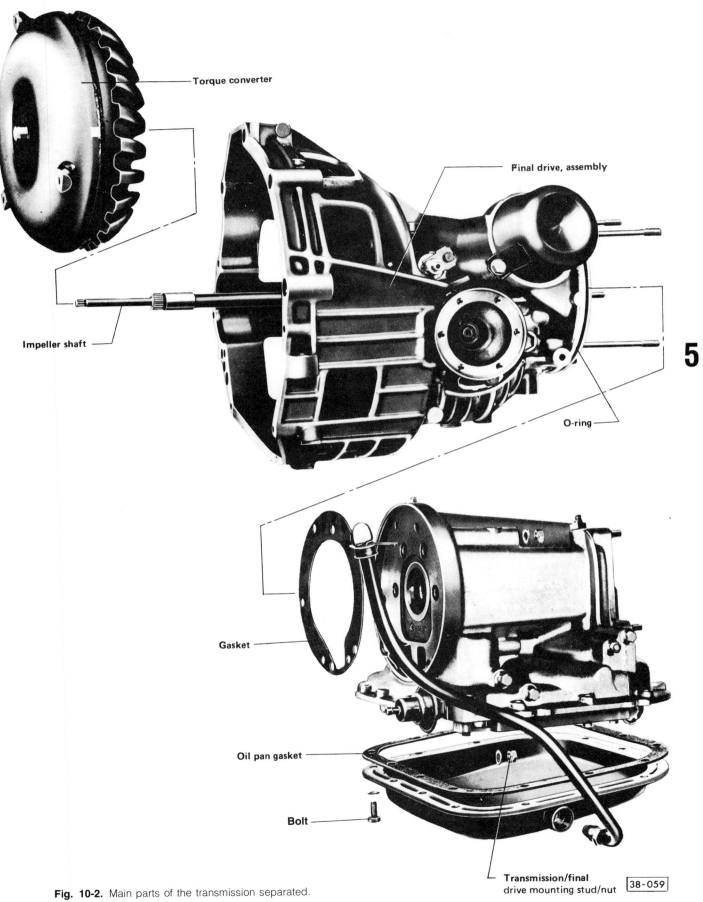

Torque converter

Final drive, assembly

Impeller shaft

O-ring

5

Gasket

Oil pan gasket

Bolt

Transmission/final
drive mounting stud/nut

38-059

Fig. 10-2. Main parts of the transmission separated.

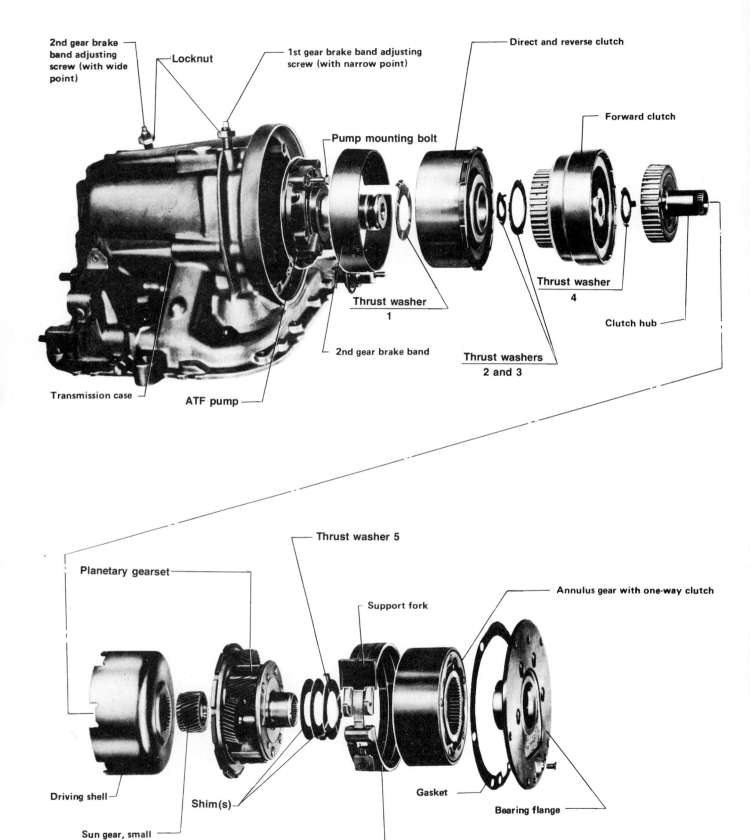

Fig. 10-3. Disassembled planetary gear system. The bearing flange is screwed to the transmission case.

10.2 Disassembling and Assembling Automatic Transmission

Study Fig. 10-3 carefully so that you become familiar with the names of the various parts. These names will be referred to frequently on the following pages. The illustration also shows the positions of the parts inside the transmission case.

To disassemble:

1. Mount the transmission on a stand, as in Fig. 10-4, or secure it to the workbench.

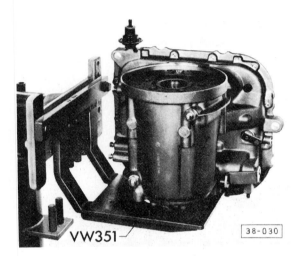

Fig. 10-4. Transmission case mounted on a repair stand.

2. Remove the countersunk bearing flange screw.

3. Using a slide hammer and a puller hook, as shown in Fig. 10-5, pull out the bearing flange.

4. Loosen the 1st gear brake band adjusting screw. Lift out the 1st gear band, the annulus gear with one-way clutch, and the planetary gearset.

NOTE ——
Record the number and thicknesses of the shims you find in the gearset.

Fig. 10-5. Slide hammer being used to pull bearing flange.

5. Remove the driving shell, the small sun gear, the clutch hub, and the forward clutch.

6. Take out the direct and reverse clutch and the 2nd gear brake band. Remove the pump bolts and lift out the ATF pump. (If you are also removing the transmission pan, keep its bolts separate from the bolts you will find in the valve body assembly.)

5

To assemble:

1. Insert the pump in the case so that the single lug and the part number face upward (see Fig. 10-6). Install the five pump bolts together with the spring washers finger-tight. Working diagonally, torque the bolts to 0.4 mkg (3 ft. lb.).

© 1974 VWoA—1001

Fig. 10-6. ATF pump installed. Lower arrow indicates the lug that must face upward. Test the installation by turning the pump as indicated by the curved arrow.

2. Turn the pump with the pump shaft. The pump should turn smoothly and easily.

3. Slide the thrust washer **1** for the direct and reverse clutch over the pump housing and engage the washer on the lug as shown in Fig. 10-7.

4. Install the 2nd gear brake band. Turn the adjusting screw until it enters the recess in the band.

5. Install the direct and reverse clutch, pressing it down in the case until the clutch drum bears on the thrust washer.

Fig. 10-7. Tabs on thrust washer **1** engaged on pump housing lug (arrow).

6. Using grease as an adhesive, stick thrust washers **2** and **3** to the inside of the forward clutch (see Fig. 10-8). Then install the forward clutch in the case.

Fig. 10-8. Thrust washer **3** (arrow **A**) and thrust washer **2** (arrow **B**) in forward clutch.

7. Using a screwdriver, align the internal splines of the forward clutch plates to receive the splines on the clutch hub.

8. Using grease as an adhesive, stick thrust washer **4**

on the forward clutch hub. Then insert the clutch hub into the clutch plate splines.

9. Install the driving shell and the small sun gear. Engage the driving shell's skirt notches with the lugs on the direct and reverse clutch.

10. Install the planetary gearset. All the parts are correctly installed if the planet carrier and parking lock pawl are aligned axially, as in Fig. 10-9.

Fig. 10-9. Transmission parking lock. Arrow indicates the pawl, which snaps into the carrier notches.

11. Measure the axial play as described in **10.3 Adjusting Axial Play.** If necessary, adjust it.

12. If axial play is correct, slip the 1st gear brake band with support fork over the annulus gear. Then turn the adjusting screw until it enters the fork.

13. Install the bearing flange and the gasket with the countersunk flat head screw.

10.3 Adjusting Axial Play

The axial play of the planetary gearset and clutches can be from 0.45 to 1.05 mm (.018 to .041 in.). Measure the play after you have assembled the transmission. If necessary, adjust the play to bring it within the specified range.

To measure and adjust:

1. Assemble the transmission without the shims and the thrust washer. Do not install the 1st gear brake band. Use a new gasket under the bearing flange.

2. With the transmission horizontal, place a dial indicator mounted in a measuring bridge against the face of the bearing flange. The gauge pin should contact the planet carrier of the planetary gearset.

3. Using suitable pliers, push the planet carrier in and out as indicated by the double arrow in Fig. 10-10.

© 1974 VWoA—3337

Fig. 10-10. Axial play being measured. Move the planet carrier as indicated by the double arrow.

4. Compare the measured play with the axial play ranges given in **Table b.** Then assemble the transmission with the proper number and thickness(es) of shim(s) and thrust washer **5.**

5. Recheck the axial play to make sure that it is between 0.45 and 1.05 mm (.018 and .041 in.).

Table b. Axial Play

Measured play range	Number and thickness of shims
1.95–2.25 mm (.077–.089 in.)	Thrust washer only
2.25–2.65 mm (.089–.104 in.)	one 0.4 mm (.0157 in.)
2.65–3.05 mm (.104–.120 in.)	two 0.4 mm (.0157 in.)
3.05–3.45 mm (.120–.136 in.)	one 1.2 mm (.0472 in.)
3.45–3.85 mm (.136–.152 in.)	one 0.4 mm (.0157 in.) and one 1.2 mm (.0472 in.)

10.4 Adjusting Brake Bands

For these adjustments, the transmission must be in a horizontal position. If it is not, any adjustments will be inaccurate.

To adjust:

1. Center the 2nd gear brake band by torquing the adjusting screw to 1.0 mkg (86.8 in. lb.).

2. Loosen the adjusting screw. Then retorque it to 0.5 mkg (43 in. lb.).

3. From this setting, back the screw off exactly 2½ turns. Then, while holding the adjusting screw to prevent it from turning, torque the adjusting screw locknut to 2.0 mkg (14 ft. lb.).

4. After adjusting the 2nd gear brake band, use the same procedure for adjusting the 1st and reverse gear band, but back this screw off from 3¼ to 3½ turns (see Fig. 10-11).

© 1974 VWoA—1007

Fig. 10-11. Torquing 1st and reverse brake band adjusting screw. Arrow indicates 2nd gear brake band screw.

10.5 Installing Final Drive on Automatic Transmission

For this procedure the transmission should be on a repair stand and in a vertical position. When moving or carrying the transmission, do not use the filler tube as a handle. You might bend it or cause it to leak.

To assemble:

1. Inspect the chamfer on the transmission case. Remove burrs, dirt, or rust.

2. Dip the O-ring in ATF.

3. Place a new paper gasket on the transmission case sealing surface and carefully set the final drive housing on it. When you install the housing, be careful not to crush or otherwise damage the O-ring.

4. Working diagonally, torque the four attaching nuts to 3.0 mkg (22 ft. lb.). Install the ATF pan as described in **5.1 Removing and Installing Valve Body Assembly.**

5. Insert the pump and the turbine shafts.

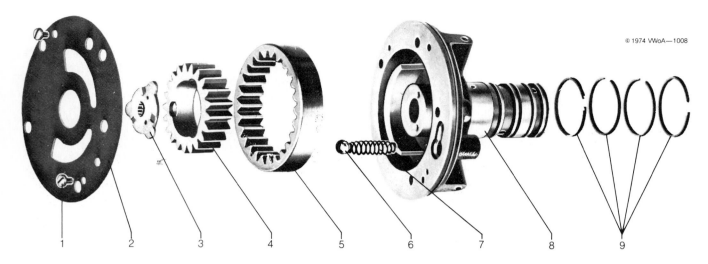

© 1974 VWoA—1008

1. M 4 screw (2)
2. Cover plate
3. Drive plate
4. Inner gear

5. Outer gear
6. 11-mm ball
7. Ball spring
8. Pump housing
9. Piston rings (4)

Fig. 10-12. ATF pump.

6. Set the converter in place over the end of the turbine shaft. Turn the converter clockwise and counterclockwise until it engages the splines of the turbine shaft.

10.6 Disassembling and Assembling ATF Pump

Whenever you remove the ATF pump, carefully inspect the housing, both gears, and the cover plate. Replace the pump if these parts are worn or damaged. The drive plate and the piston rings (Fig. 10-12) can be replaced individually.

To disassemble:

1. Remove the two M4 screws, then remove the cover plate.

2. Remove the 11-mm ball and ball spring, the inner gear, outer gear, and drive plate.

3. Using needle nose pliers, remove the piston rings (Fig. 10-13).

To assemble:

1. Clean all parts thoroughly. Blow out the fluid passages with compressed air.

2. After lubricating all parts thoroughly with ATF, install the gears and the drive plate. Be sure that the drive plate is in the position shown in Fig. 10-12 with the long side of the hub toward the pump body.

© 1974 VWoA—1009

Fig. 10-13 Clutch piston rings being removed from pump.

3. Insert the ball valve spring and the 11-mm ball.

4. Screw on the cover plate.

10.7 Disassembling and Assembling Direct and Reverse Clutch

The direct and reverse clutch and the 2nd gear brake band that operates against the clutch drum are shown in an exploded view in Fig. 10-14. Familiarize yourself with the names of the parts, as they are used frequently in the disassembly and repair procedures.

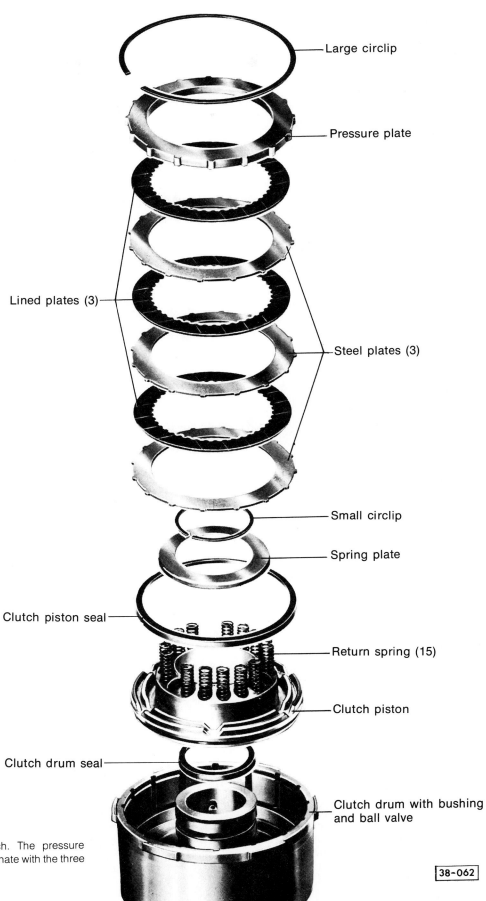

Large circlip

Pressure plate

Lined plates (3)

Steel plates (3)

Small circlip

Spring plate

Clutch piston seal

Return spring (15)

Clutch piston

Clutch drum seal

Clutch drum with bushing and ball valve

5

Fig. 10-14. Direct and reverse clutch. The pressure plate and steel plates alternate with the three lined plates.

38-062

To disassemble:

1. Using a screwdriver, pry out the large circlip.

2. Remove the pressure plate, the three lined plates, and the three steel plates.

3. Put the clutch on a press and force down the spring plate until you can pry out the small circlip. Then raise the press ram and remove the spring plate.

4. With a twisting movement, pull the clutch piston with return springs out of the clutch drum. Remove the piston seal and the clutch drum seal

5. Using an extractor tool and the repair press, withdraw the clutch drum bushing as shown in Fig. 10-15.

Fig. 10-15. Removing clutch drum bushing. Phantom drawing (dashed line) shows extractor.

To check clutch:

1. Check for wear or damage on the friction surfaces of the piston and the clutch drum and in the grooves that the steel clutch plates ride in.

2. Check the ball valve for freedom of movement. Make sure that the drilling is clear.

3. Inspect the steel plates. If any plate is scored or grooved, replace it.

4. Check the lined plates. Replace any plate that is worn, damaged, or burned.

5. Check the 2nd gear brake band. Replace it if it is worn, damaged, or burned.

To assemble:

1. Install new seals on the clutch drum and the piston. The seal lips should point into the drum toward the source of hydraulic pressure.

2. Place a stiff plastic sheet in the clutch drum as

Fig. 10-16. Plastic sheet used to prevent damage to the seals during piston installation.

shown in Fig. 10-16. Lubricate the seals with ATF, then insert the piston into the drum with a twisting motion.

3. Insert the 15 return springs in three groups of 5 each, leaving one hole vacant between groups. Install the spring plate. Press down the spring plate with the repair press until you can snap the small circlip into its groove.

4. Install the clutch lined plates (see Fig. 10-17) and the steel plates. The sequence is important. Check your work by referring to Fig. 10-14. Be sure to soak

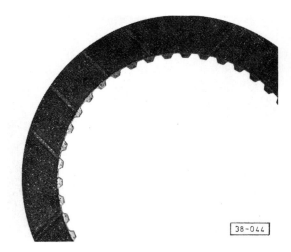

Fig. 10-17. Direct and reverse clutch lined plate. The groove distinguishes these plates from those used on other cars with similar transmissions.

the new lined plates in ATF for at least an hour before you install them.

5. Install the pressure plate and the large circlip. The tolerance range for the thickness of the pressure plate is 6.15 to 6.30 mm (.242 to .248 in.).

6. Check the axial play as shown in Fig. 10-18. There should be 1.70 to 2.20 mm (.067 to .086 in.) of axial play.

Fig. 10-18. A feeler gauge being used to measure the axial play of the clutch plates in the clutch drum.

7. If axial play is outside the prescribed range, install a thicker or thinner large circlip. Circlips are available in thicknesses of 1.50 mm, 1.70 mm, 2.00 mm, 2.30 mm, 2.50 mm, and 2.70 mm (.059 in., .067 in., .079 in., .090 in., .098 in., and .106 in.).

8. When axial play is within the correct range, use the repair press and an appropriate bushing driver to press in a new clutch drum bushing.

10.8 Disassembling and Assembling Forward Clutch

The forward clutch transmits torque from the converter turbine to the direct and reverse clutch and the large sun gear. Fig. 10-19 gives and exploded view.

To disassemble:

1. Using a screwdriver, pry out the outer circlip. Then remove the clutch plates.

2. Pry out the spring circlip. Remove the diaphragm spring.

3. Pull the piston out of the clutch drum. Then remove the small and large piston seals.

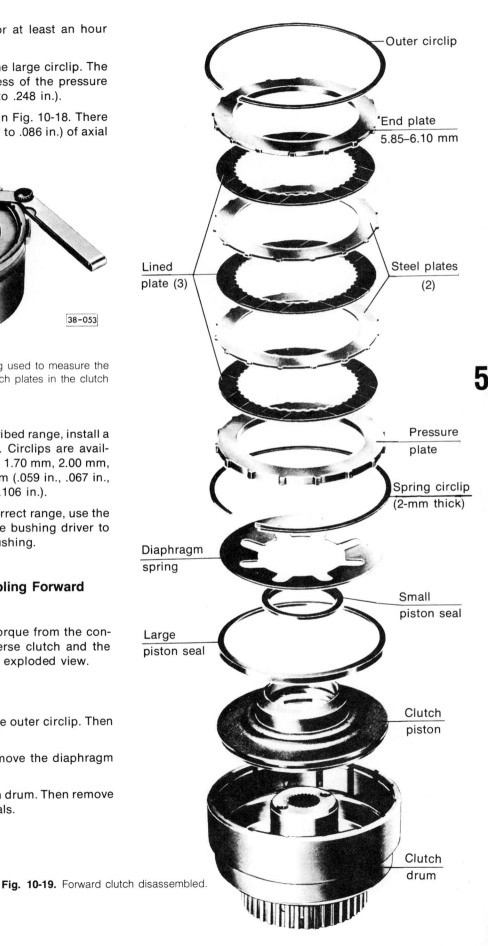

Fig. 10-19. Forward clutch disassembled.

To check clutch:

1. Shake the drum. If the drilling (Fig. 10-20) is clear, you should hear the ball valve rattle.

Fig. 10-20. Ball valve (arrow) in clutch drum.

2. Check the diaphragm spring. When the piston is installed, the spring should reach at least to the lower edge of the circlip groove. Otherwise, replace the spring.

3. Inspect the steel plates. Replace any plate that is scored or grooved.

4. Look for signs of burning and wear on the lined plates. Replace damaged plates.

To assemble:

1. Install new piston seals. The seal lips should point into the drum toward the source of hydraulic pressure.

2. Place a stiff plastic sheet in the clutch drum as illustrated in Fig. 10-16. Lubricate the seals with ATF, then insert the piston into the drum with a twisting motion.

3. Install the diaphragm spring so that the convex side is toward the piston. To retain the diaphragm, use only a spring circlip 2 mm thick with a lug.

   NOTE ——

   The diaphragm spring should be under some tension when the spring circlip is installed and it should not be easy to snap the circlip into its groove. If inserting the circlip does not put the diaphragm spring under tension, replace the diaphragm spring.

4. Install the pressure plate so that the chamfered side is toward the diaphragm spring.

5. Install lines plates alternately with steel plates as

shown earlier in Fig. 10-19. New lined plates (Fig. 10-21) should be soaked for at least an hour before installing. Used plates can simply be lubricated with ATF.

Fig. 10-21. Forward clutch lined plate. The groove pattern distinguishes these plates from the lined plates used on other cars with similar transmissions.

6. Install the end plate and outer circlip. The specified thickness of the end plate is 5.85 to 6.10 mm (.230 to .240 in.).

7. Using a feeler gauge, as shown in Fig. 10-22, check the clearance between the end plate and the outer circlip.

8. If the clearance measured in step 7 is not between 0.80 and 1.20 mm (.031 and .047 in.), select a circlip

Fig. 10-22. Measuring forward clutch end play. Use a feeler guage to measure clearance **a** between the end plate and the large outer circlip.

to give this fit. **Table c** lists the circlips that are available.

Table c. Circlip Thickness

Thickness	Part No.
1.50 mm (.059 in.)	003 323 157 D
1.70 mm (.067 in.)	003 323 157
2.00 mm (.079 in.)	003 323 157 A
2.30 mm (.090 in.)	003 323 157 C
2.50 mm (.098 in.)	003 323 157 B

10.9 Disassembling and Assembling Annulus Gear

The annulus gear assembly includes the annulus gear, the one-way clutch, and the 1st gear brake band. Fig. 10-23 gives an exploded view of the assembly. The annulus engages the small pinions of the planetary gearset.

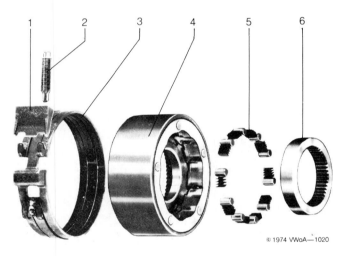

© 1974 VWoA—1020

1. Support fork
2. Adjusting screw
3. 1st gear brake band
4. Annulus gear
5. Spring spacers (10) and rollers (10)
6. One-way clutch inner ring

Fig. 10-23. Annulus gear assembly. The adjusting screw for the 1st gear brake band passes through the transmission case into a recess in the support fork on the end of the band. The spring spacers and rollers are part of the one-way clutch assembly.

37-184

To disassemble the annulus gear, pull out the inner ring. Then lift out the 10 rollers and 10 spring spacers. Inspect the parts. The outer surface of the annulus should not be scored and the annulus gear teeth should not be noticeably worn. The rollers should not be flattened and the spring spacers should be crack-free. The inner and outer rings of the one-way clutch should not show signs of wear from contact with the rollers. Unless the one-way clutch is in perfect condition, it will not hold the annulus gear against the rotation of the turbine shaft.

To assemble:

1. Insert the inner ring of the one-way clutch in the annulus.

2. Insert the 10 rollers into the space between the one-way clutch inner ring and the annulus gear assembly.

3. Place the spring spacers between the lugs and the rollers. As you look down on the gear, the installation sequence should be: lug, spring, roller, lug, spring, roller, . . . and so on.

NOTE ——

Late transmissions, used from early 1975, have a different kind of one-way clutch. The springs are narrower, as shown in Fig. 10-24, and are installed on their sides as indicated in Fig. 10-25. You cannot install the new kind of springs in the older kind of one-way clutch outer ring.

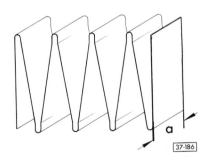

37-186

Fig. 10-24. Spring spacer dimensions. Dimension **a** for older-type springs (Part No. 003 323 643) is 10 mm (⅜ in.). Dimension **a** for newer-type springs (Part No. 010 323 643 D) is 6 mm (¼ in.).

Fig. 10-25. Old-type and new-type spring spacer installation. Notice that the new-type one-way clutch outer ring is different.

4. Install the one-way clutch on the bearing flange so that the splined part of the flange meshes with the inner ring.

5. To check the locking effect and the direction of rotation, try to turn the clutch both clockwise and counterclockwise (Fig. 10-26).

38-039

Fig. 10-26. One-way clutch. When installed on the bearing flange, the clutch turns in direction **A** but holds in direction **B.**

6. Inspect the 1st gear brake band. Check the lining for burning and excessive wear. Remove any embedded bits of metal. Check the operating parts for wear. Replace faulty brake bands.

10.10 Planetary Gears

The planetary gearset shown in Fig. 10-27 should not be disassembled. The planetary pinions run on needle bearings on peened-in shafts that can be properly installed only at the factory. Worn or damaged gearsets must be replaced as a unit since individual parts are not supplied.

To check the planetary gearset, inspect all gear teeth and thrust surfaces, and check for excessive backlash in meshing gears. Check for excessive radial play of the planetary gears. Replace worn gearsets. Check the internal splines and the flange of the parking lock for wear. Remove any burrs that you find on the flange.

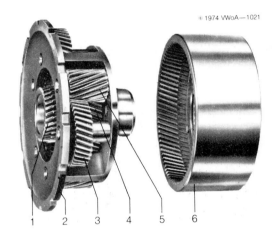

© 1974 VWoA—1021

1. Small sun gear
2. Planet carrier
3. Large planet pinion
4. Large sun gear
5. Small planet pinion
6. Annulus (ring) gear

Fig. 10-27. Planetary gear system with annulus removed. The annulus engages the small pinions only.

10.11 Parking Lock

Disassembly of the parking lock requires removal of the transmission pan and the valve body. The position of the parking lock relative to that of the planetary gearset is shown in Fig. 10-28.

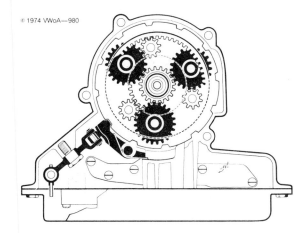

© 1974 VWoA—980

Fig. 10-28. Parking lock in engaged position. The notches around the edge of the planet carrier are shaped to hold the pawl firmly when the vehicle is stationary, but to force the pawl from engagement if the selector lever is accidentally moved to **P** while the car is moving.

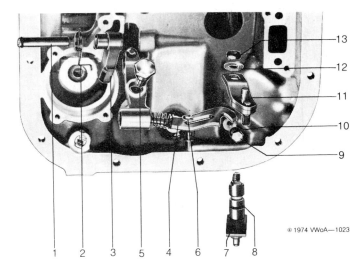

© 1974 VWoA—1023

1. Pawl pin
2. Return spring
3. Pawl
4. Threaded pin
5. Operating lever
6. E-clip (2)
7. Cable lever and shaft
8. O-ring
9. Retaining bolt
10. Spring washer
11. Manual valve lever
12. Washer
13. Self-locking nut

Fig. 10-29. Parking lock assembly (viewed from below). Shapes of some parts are different on cars covered by this Manual.

To disassemble:

1. Remove the transmission pan and the valve body (Fig. 10-29). Unscrew the threaded pin for the operating lever. Remove the E-clip and then the lever.

2. Drive out the pawl pin. Remove the pawl and the return spring.

3. Remove the self-locking nut from the manual valve lever, then remove the lever.

4. Remove the retaining bolt and then the cable lever and shaft.

To assemble:

1. Using a new O-ring, install the cable lever and shaft. Install the manual valve lever with the washer and the self-locking nut. Torque the nut to 1.0 mkg (7 ft. lb.). Install the retaining bolt together with its spring washer and torque to 0.5 mkg (3.5 ft. lb.).

2. Insert the pawl together with the return spring. Holding the pawl away from the planet carrier, drive in the pawl pin.

3. Install the operating lever and then the E-clip. Torque the threaded pin to 2.0 mkg (14 ft. lb.).

4. Check the operation of the parking lock. If it works properly, install the valve body and the transmission pan as described in **5.1 Removing and Installing Valve Body Assembly.**

5

1. Left socket head screw
2. Left flanged shaft
3. Final drive housing
4. Starter drive bushing
5. Pinion oil seal
6. Front tapered-roller bearing outer race
7. Torque converter seal
8. Front cover plate with one-way clutch support
9. Bolt
10. Governor needle bearing
11. O-ring
12. Governor
13. Oil seal
14. Differential
15. Speedometer drive
16. O-ring
17. Lockplate
18. Bolt
19. Right flanged shaft
20. Rear tapered-roller bearing inner race
21. S_3 shim
22. S_4 shim
23. Drive pinion
24. Front tapered-roller bearing inner race
25. Differential bearing outer race
26. O-ring
27. Differential bearing adjusting ring
28. Flanged shaft oil seal
29. Flanged shaft selective shim
30. Right socket head screw
31. O-ring
32. Rear cover plate
33. Pinion oil seal
34. Rear tapered roller bearing outer race

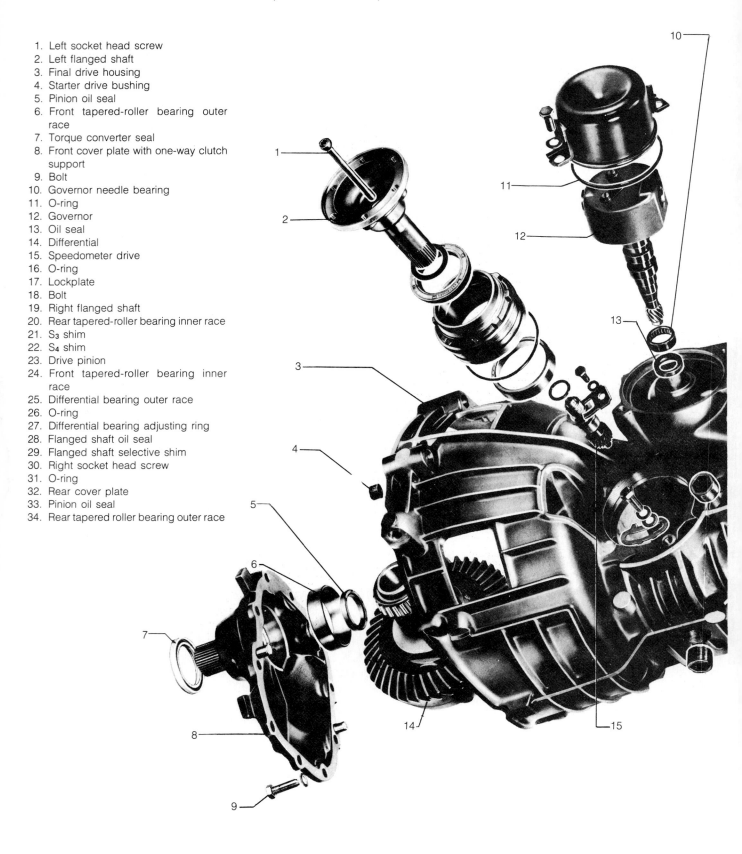

Fig. 11-1. Exploded view of final drive and related parts.

11. FINAL DRIVE

Fig. 11-1 illustrates the disassembly of the final drive. If you replace certain final drive components, it will be necessary to select new shims. The selective shims S_3 and S_4 can be replaced only with the help of special precision measuring equipment. The adjusting rings also require special precision equipment for correct adjustment.

CAUTION

Before you decide to replace any part of the final drive, carefully read **12. Adjusting Final Drive.** *For some replacements you must make precision measurements before you disassemble the final drive. Failure to do this can make proper reassembly difficult.*

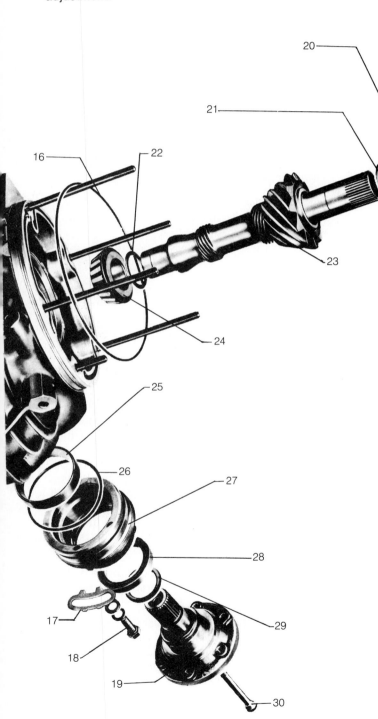

5

11.1 Removing and Installing Drive Pinion

The drive pinion is a matched pair with the ring gear, so the ring and pinion must be replaced as a unit. If you intend to replace the final drive housing, either of the cover plates, one or both of the tapered-roller bearings, or the ring and pinion gearset, please read **12. Adjusting Final Drive** before you undertake any disassembly.

To remove drive pinion:

1. Remove the transaxle from the car. Then separate the transmission from the final drive as described in **10.1 Separating Transmission Case from Final Drive Housing.** Take out the retaining bolt and remove the speedometer drive. Remove the governor.

2. Remove the socket head screws that are in the centers of the left and right flanged shafts. Then, being careful that the flanged shaft splines do not damage the oil seals, pull the flanged shafts out of the final drive.

3. Using a scriber, carefully mark the position of the right differential bearing adjusting ring in the final drive housing. Then remove the bolt and the lockplate.

4. Remove the bolts that hold the front cover plate inside the final drive housing. Use a slide hammer to pull off the cover as shown in Fig. 11-2.

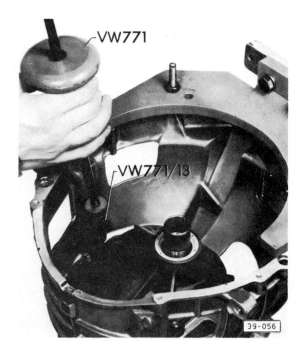

Fig. 11-2. Front cover plate being removed.

5. Remove the five bolts that hold the rear cover plate to the final drive housing. Wrap the splines of the drive pinion with plastic electrical tape so that the splines will not damage the pinion oil seal in the cover plate. Then pull off the rear cover plate with a twisting motion.

6. Turn the final drive housing so that the right differential bearing adjusting ring is down, then remove the ring as shown in Fig. 11-3. Doing this will allow the differential to slip out of mesh with the drive pinion.

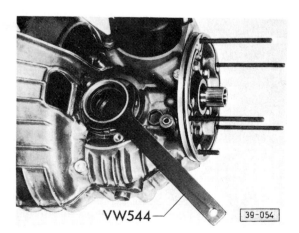

Fig. 11-3. Adjusting ring being removed.

7. Position the differential so that two of the ring gear bolts are aligned with the edge of the final drive housing (Fig. 11-4). Then take the drive pinion out toward the rear of the housing.

Fig. 11-4. Differential positioned so that two ring gear bolts (arrows) are aligned with edge of housing.

To install:

1. If you have replaced the final drive housing, either of the cover plates, either of the tapered-roller bearings, or the ring and pinion gearset, select and install new S_3 and S_4 shims as described in **12. Adjusting Final Drive.**

2. Install the drive pinion and its bearings in the final drive housing so that the teeth of the drive pinion are loosely engaged with the teeth of the ring gear.

3. Lubricate the differential bearings with hypoid oil. Install a new O-ring on the right adjusting ring, then coat the O-ring and the threads with multipurpose grease. With the final drive housing left side up, carefully screw in the right adjusting ring. As you do this, guide the differential upward into the left differential bearing outer race. Be careful that the drive pinion is not caught between the differential and the final drive housing. Do not overtighten the adjusting ring.

4. Install a new O-ring on the rear cover plate. Lubricate the O-ring and the rear tapered-roller bearing with hypoid oil.

5. Install a conical plastic sleeve over the drive pinion splines (Fig. 11-5). Alternatively, you can wrap the splines with plastic electrical tape. Then, while holding the drive pinion stationary, install the rear cover plate with a twisting motion. Install the five bolts to a torque of 2.5 mkg (18 ft. lb.).

6. Lubricate the front tapered roller bearing with hypoid oil. Coat the bolt flange of the front cover

plate with oil resistant sealer. Then install the front cover. Torque the bolts to 2.5 mkg (18 ft. lb.).

Fig. 11-5. Plastic sleeve, W771/14, installed to protect pinion oil seal during rear cover plate installation.

7. Position the right adjusting ring so that the mark you scribed on the adjusting ring is aligned with the mark you scribed on the final drive housing. Then install the lockplate and torque the bolt to 1.0 mkg (7 ft. lb.).

8. Make sure that the correct shim is installed on each flanged shaft. If you have replaced either flanged shaft or any part of the differential, select new shims as described in **12. Adjusting Final Drive.** Then install the flanged shafts. Torque the socket head screws to 2.5 mkg (18 ft. lb.).

9. Install the speedometer drive and torque the retainer bolt to 1.0 mkg (7 ft. lb.). Install the governor. Install the transmission on the final drive as described in **10.5 Installing Final Drive on Automatic Transmission.** Then install the transaxle in the car.

Replacing Pinion Bearings and Oil Seals

If you replace either pinion bearing, you must select new S_3 and S_4 shims as described in **12. Adjusting Final Drive** before you install the tapered-roller bearing inner races on the drive pinion. You can replace the pinion oil seals without replacing the bearings but, if you also replace the bearings, adjust the final drive before you install the new oil seals.

Remove the oil seal from the front cover as shown in Fig. 11-6. Lightly coat the periphery of the new seal with an oil resistant sealer. Then press in the new seal so that its lip is toward the interior of the final drive housing. See Fig. 11-7.

> **NOTE ——**
> If you must adjust the final drive, do not install the new seal until after you have adjusted the drive pinion.

Fig. 11-6. Hooked tool (VW 681) being used to remove pinion oil seal from front cover plate.

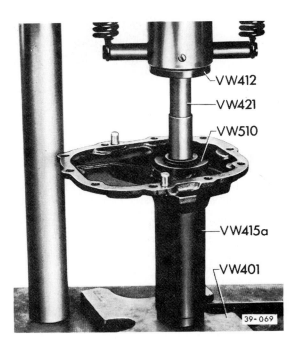

Fig. 11-7. Pinion oil seal being pressed into front cover plate.

A procedure similar to that described for replacing the pinion seal in the front cover plate can be used to replace the torque converter seal in the front cover plate. This work is illustrated in **8.3 Replacing Torque Converter Oil Seal.**

To replace the pinion oil seal that is in the rear cover plate, drive out the old seal with a drift. Lightly coat the periphery of the new seal with an oil resistant sealer.

5

Then drive in the new seal so that its lip is toward the interior of the final drive housing. See Fig. 11-8.

NOTE ——

If you must adjust the final drive, do not install the new seal until after you have adjusted the final drive's drive pinion.

Fig. 11-8. Pinion oil seal being driven into rear cover plate.

An expansion mandril can be used to press the front tapered-roller bearing outer race out of the front cover plate (Fig. 11-9). Press in the new outer race as shown in Fig. 11-10.

CAUTION ——

If you remove both pinion bearing outer races at the same time, be careful not to mix them up. If an outer race is installed in the wrong cover plate, the bearing may make noise or fail.

An expansion mandril can also be used to press the rear tapered–roller bearing outer race out of the rear cover plate (Fig. 11-11). Press in the new outer race as shown in Fig. 11-12.

CAUTION ——

If you remove both pinion bearing outer races at the same time, be careful not to mix them up. If an outer race is installed in the wrong cover plate, the bearing may make noise or fail.

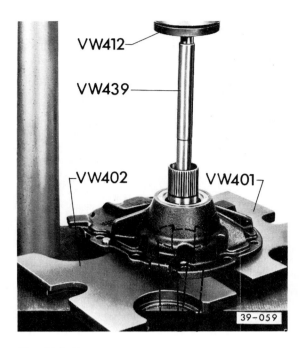

Fig. 11-9. Tapered-roller bearing outer race being pressed out of front cover plate.

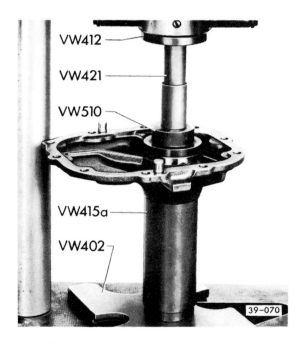

Fig. 11-10. Tapered-roller bearing outer race being pressed into front cover plate.

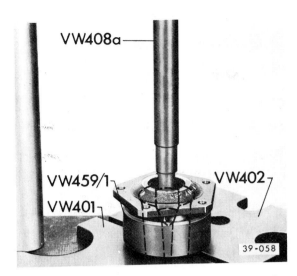

Fig. 11-11. Tapered-roller bearing outer race being pressed out of rear cover plate.

Fig. 11-12. Tapered-roller bearing outer race being pressed into rear cover plate.

You will need a split collet support, such as the one shown in Fig. 11-13, in order to press the drive pinion out of the front or rear tapered-roller bearing inner race. If you do not intend to replace any parts that would make it necessary to adjust the final drive, write down the number and thicknesses of the original S_3 and S_4 shims.

CAUTION ——

If you remove both pinion tapered-roller bearing inner races at the same time, be careful not to mix them up. If their locations are reversed, the bearing may make noise or fail.

If you have replaced any part that makes it necessary to adjust the final drive, select new S_3 and S_4 shims. Otherwise, install original number and thickness of S_3

and S_4 shims on the drive pinion. Heat the pinion tapered-roller bearing inner races to appoximately 100°C (212°F) in a pan of oil placed in a larger pan of boiling water. Then press the bearing races onto the drive pinion as shown in Fig. 11-14.

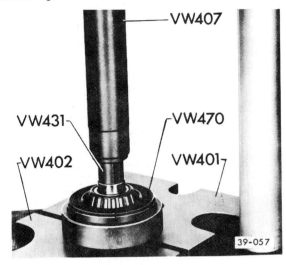

Fig. 11-13. Tapered-roller bearing inner race being removed from drive pinion.

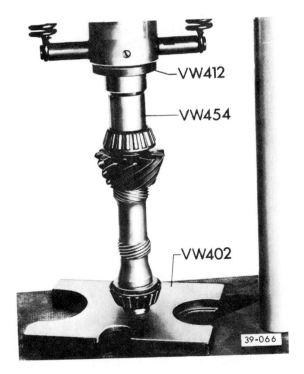

Fig. 11-14. Tapered-roller bearing inner race being pressed onto drive pinion.

11.2 Removing and Installing Differential

The ring gear, which is mounted on the differential, is a matched pair with the drive pinion, so the ring and pinion must be replaced as a unit. If you intend to replace the final drive housing, either of the cover plates, one or both of the differential bearings, one or both of the differential bearing adjusting rings, the differential housing, or the ring and pinion gearset, please read **12. Adjusting Final Drive** before you undertake any disassembly.

To remove differential:

1. Remove the drive pinion as described in **11.1 Removing and Installing Drive Pinion.**

2. Using a depth micrometer, measure the depth to which the left adjusting ring is screwed into the final drive housing. Write down the measurement. Then, using a scriber, carefully mark the position of the left adjusting ring in the final drive housing.

3. Remove the bolt and the lockplate for the left adjusting ring. Then remove the adjusting ring.

4. Lift up the differential, then tilt it and remove it through the front of the final drive housing.

To install:

1. If you have replaced the ring and pinion gearset, the differential housing, the final drive housing, one or both of the differential bearings, or one or both of the adjusting rings, adjust the final drive as described in **12. Adjusting Final Drive.**

2. Position the differential inside the final drive housing. The ring gear should be toward the right side of the housing.

3. Install a new O-ring on the left adjusting ring, then coat the O-ring and the threads with multipurpose grease. If you have made no repair that requires

final drive adjustment, install the right adjusting ring to its original depth and align the mark you scribed on the adjusting ring with the mark you scribed on the final drive housing. Install the lockplate and torque the bolt to 1.0 mkg (7 ft. lb.).

4. Install the drive pinion as described in **11.1 Removing and Installing Drive Pinion.**

11.3 Disassembling and Assembling Differential

An exploded view of the differential is given in Fig. 11-15. If you intend to replace any part of the differential, read **12. Adjusting Final Drive** to determine whether precision adjustments must be carried out following repair. If the final drive is not correctly adjusted following certain repairs, the ring and pinion gearset will be noisy and will wear rapidly.

To disassemble:

1. Loosen the eight bolts, then drive off the ring gear as shown in Fig. 11-16.

> **CAUTION** ——
>
> *When removing the ring gear, be careful not to let it fall against the vise, which could damage the ring gear teeth. A pad of rags placed beneath the ring gear is a worthwhile precaution.*

2. If the differential bearings are to be replaced, pull the inner races off the differential housing and the differential housing cover as shown in Fig. 11-17.

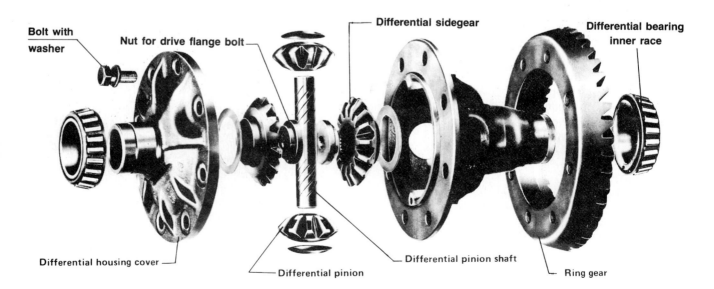

Fig. 11-15. Exploded view of differential.

Fig. 11-16. Rubber mallet being used against bolt heads to drive off ring gear.

Fig. 11-17. Differential bearing inner race being removed.

3. Using a screwdriver, separate the differential housing cover from the differential housing as shown in Fig. 11-18.

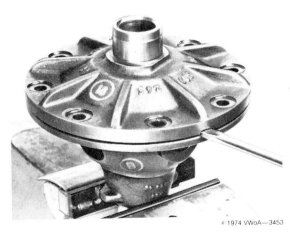

© 1974 VWoA—3453

Fig. 11-18. Cover being pried off differential housing.

4. Using a drift, drive out the differential pinion shaft. Remove the pinions, sidegears, and other internal parts.

To assemble:

1. Examine all thrust surfaces on the differential housing, the cover, the ring gear, the pinion shaft, and the thrust washers. Replace worn parts. Inspect the gear teeth for burrs or excessive wear and replace as necessary.

2. Install the differential sidegears, the large thrust washers, the dished thrust washers, and the differential pinions. Then drive in the differential pinion shaft.

   NOTE ——
   If the pinion shaft does not fit tightly, replace it with a new shaft.

3. Using an oilstone, remove all burrs and pressure marks from the mating surfaces of the housing, the housing cover, and the ring gear. Then install the differential housing cover without the bolts.

4. Heat the ring gear to about 100°C (212°F) in a pan of oil placed in a larger pan of boiling water. Then install the ring gear as shown in Fig. 11-19. If the bolts have spring-type lockwashers, as used on early cars, torque the eight bolts to 6.0 mkg (43 ft. lb.). If the later bolts, with serrated washer surfaces, are used, torque the bolts to 7.0 mkg (50 ft. lb.).

   CAUTION ——
   Do not use spring washers with the later bolts. Doing this will result in poor ring gear mounting.

Fig. 11-19. Ring gear being installed on differential. Use a rag to avoid burning your fingers.

5. If the differential bearing inner races have been

5

removed, heat them in oil also. Then install the bearing races as shown in Fig. 11-20.

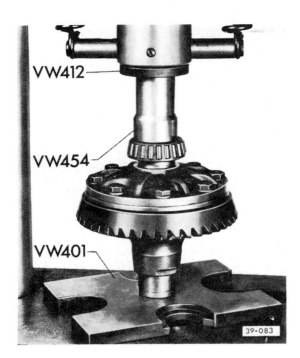

Fig. 11-20. Differential bearing inner race being pressed onto differential. The press tool must not contact the roller cage.

6. A new differential bearing outer race must be installed at the same time as the new inner race. Press out the old outer race, or drive it out of the adjusting ring with a drift. Then press in the new race as shown in Fig. 11-21.

11.4 Replacing Governor Bearing, Governor Oil Seal, Speedometer Drive, and Starter Drive Bushing

A slide hammer, with a suitable toggle washer, can be used to pull the governor needle bearing and the governor oil seal out of the final drive housing. See Fig. 11-22. Drive in the new seal so that its lip is toward the governor, then drive in the new needle bearing. The tool used to drive in the seal and the bearing is shown in Fig. 11-23.

If a special pulling tool such as the one shown in Fig. 11-24 is not available, you can pull out the starter drive bushing by installing a thread cutting tap and pulling the bushing out along with the tap. Drive in the new bushing as shown in Fig. 11-25.

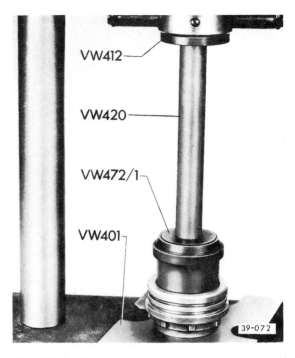

Fig. 11-21. Differential bearing outer race being pressed into adjusting ring.

Fig. 11-22. Governor oil seal and governor needle bearing being removed.

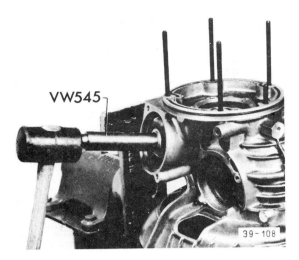

Fig. 11-23. Installing governor bearing or oil seal. One end of special tool is for seal, the other end for bearing.

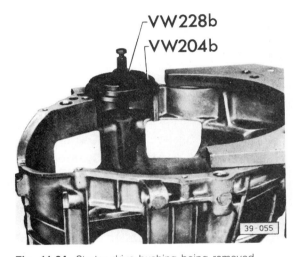

Fig. 11-24. Starter drive bushing being removed.

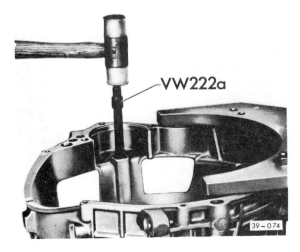

Fig. 11-25. Starter drive bushing being installed.

To remove the speedometer drive, disconnect the speedometer cable by unscrewing the ferrule nut. Remove the retaining bolt and the retaining plate for the speedometer drive, then remove the speedometer drive from the final housing. Installation is the reverse of removal. Torque the retaining bolt to 1.0 mkg (7 ft. lb.). If necessary, you can disassemble the speedometer drive into the components shown in Fig. 11-26 by prying off the spring clip with two screwdrivers.

1. Driven gear
2. Spring clip
3. Drive body

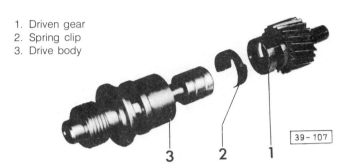

Fig. 11-26. Exploded view of speedometer drive.

11.5 Replacing Flanged Shaft Oil Seal

With the adjusting ring removed during final drive repairs, it is easy to pry out the old flanged shaft oil seal and then install a new one. With the transaxle installed in the car, you must disconnect the inner constant velocity joint from the flanged shaft. This work is covered in detail in **MANUAL TRANSMISSION.** Remove the socket head screw that is in the center of the flanged shaft, then pull the flanged shaft out of the final drive. The old seal can then be removed as shown in Fig. 11-27.

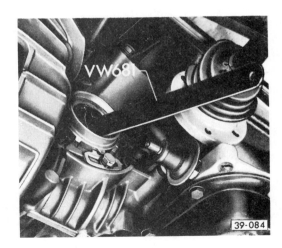

Fig. 11-27. Hooked tool being used to pry out flanged shaft oil seal.

Coat the outer periphery of the new oil seal with oil resistant sealer. Fill the space between the seal lip and seal body with multipurpose grease. Then drive in the new seal so that its lip points into the final drive housing. See Fig. 11-28.

Fig. 11-28. Tool used to drive flanged shaft oil seal into adjusting ring.

12. ADJUSTING FINAL DRIVE

The adjustments described here are necessary to the life of the gearset, the differential bearings, and the drive pinion bearings. They are also necessary to ensure quiet operation. The final drive requires adjustment only when parts directly affecting the adjustment have been replaced or when careless disassembly has resulted in the loss of the original shims or the adjusting ring screw-in depth measurements. **Table d** lists what adjustments must be made when certain parts are replaced.

There are two factors involved in making final drive adjustments: bearing turning torque and the backlash between the ring and pinion gears. The backlash is adjusted by repositioning the ring gear axially. The position of the pinion is determined by the thickness(es) of the S_3 and S_4 shims. The position of the ring gear is determined by the screw-in depth of the differential bearing adjusting rings. The standard symbols used in making final drive adjustments are defined in **Table e**.

The ring gear and pinion are run on special testing machines during transaxle manufacture to check the tooth contact pattern and silent running under both drive and coast conditions. When the optimum relationship of the two gears is found, they are installed in the final drive housing using pinion shims and differential bearing adjusting ring positions that will duplicate the gearset's position in the testing machines. The purpose of all subsequent adjustments is to restore the gearset to this position following repair.

Table d. Required Final Drive Adjustments

Part replaced	Adjust pinion	Adjust ring gear (differential bearings)	Adjust flanged shaft axial play
Final drive housing	X	X	
Differential bearings		X	
Adjusting rings for differential		X	
Differential housing		X	X
Differential housing cover		X	X
Pinion tapered-roller bearings	X		
Front or rear cover plates	X		
Pinion and ring gear. Installation of new gearset requires replacement of tapered-roller bearings	X	X	
Flanged shaft, differential sidegears, or large thrust washer			X

Table e. Standard Symbols

Symbol	Description	Dimension
S_3	Shim between tapered-roller bearing and pinion head (determines bearing preload)	See table for thicknesses
S_4	Shim at front of drive pinion (determines pinion position)	See table for thicknesses
R_0	Length of master gauge used in factory testing machine	41.85 mm (1.6476 in.)
r	Deviation from R_0 marked on gear set	measured in $1/100$ mm
G 933	Gearset: G = Gleason; .933 = 9/33 number of teeth	3.67:1 ratio
e	Measurement obtained with universal bar with total shim thickness behind pinion head	measured in $1/100$ mm

12.1 Adjusting Drive Pinion

If both the drive pinion and the ring gear must be adjusted, adjust the pinion before you adjust the ring gear. The differential must be removed from the final drive housing before you can adjust the pinion. R_o, given in Fig. 12-1, is the length of the master gauge used at the factory (41.85 mm). The actual position of the pinion head differs from the length of the master gauge by the deviation r. Deviation r is stamped on the outer face of the ring gear in $1/100$ mm. For example, the number 42 means that $r = 0.42$ mm.

CAUTION ——

If you lack the skills, special measuring tools, or a clean workshop for adjusting the final drive, we suggest you leave these repairs to an Authorized Dealer or other qualified and properly-equipped shop. We especially urge you to consult your Authorized Dealer before attempting repairs on a vehicle covered by the new-car warranty.

To adjust pinion:

1. Heat the tapered roller bearing inner races to approximately 100°C (212°F) in a pan of oil placed in a larger pan of boiling water. Then press the tapered-roller bearing inner races onto the drive pinion without either the S_3 or the S_4 shims.

2. If not previously removed, remove the differential as described in **11.2 Removing and Installing Differential.**

3. Install the drive pinion and the front and rear cover plates in the final drive housing. You need use only the four bolts indicated in Fig. 12-2 to hold the front cover plate. Torque the bolts to 2.5 mkg (18 ft. lb.).

Fig. 12-2. Four bolts used to hold front cover plate.

Fig. 12-1. Pinion adjustment dimensions and locations of S_3 and S_4 shims.

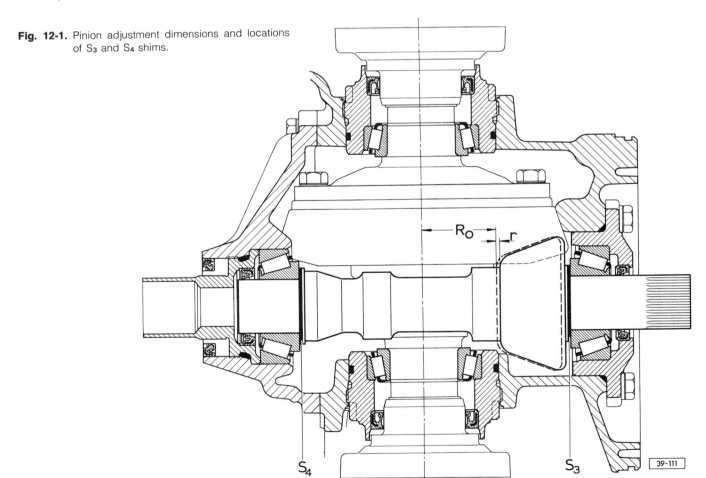

4. Zero a dial indicator against the rear end of the drive pinion as shown in Fig. 12-3. The magnetic plate, VW 385/17, provides a uniform surface for the gauge pin to contact.

5. By reaching inside the final drive housing, raise the pinion fully up. Write down the dial indicator reading.

CAUTION ——

Do not turn the drive pinion as you raise it up. The reading will be inaccurate if the pinion is turned.

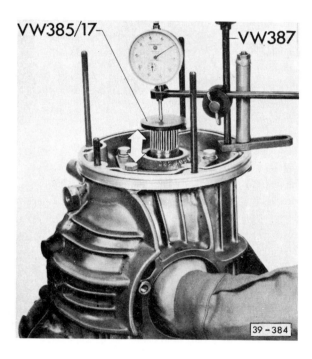

Fig. 12-3. Pinion axial play being measured. Move pinion up and down as indicated by the double arrow.

6. To the dial indicator reading obtained in step 5, add 0.15 mm to provide bearing preload and add 0.10 to compensate for bearing settling. The sum is the total thickness of the combined S_3 and S_4 shims that are required for correct pinion adjustment.

CAUTION ——

Every number or setting in the following example is imaginary. Using them as specifications for a car could cause serious damage.

Example:

Dial indicator reading obtained in step 5	2.38 mm
Amount added for bearing preload	+0.15 mm
Amount added for bearing settling	+0.10 mm
Combined thickness of S_3 and S_4 shims	2.63 mm

7. Remove the front cover plate. Remove the drive pinion.

8. Carefully pull off the tapered-roller bearing that is adjacent to the pinion head. If necessary, consult **11.1 Removing and Installing Drive Pinion.**

9. Select shims that equal the total shim thickness that you computed in step 6. The available range of shims is given later in **Table f.** Install all of the shims on the front of the drive pinion. Then, after heating the tapered-roller bearing inner race to approximately 100°C (212°F) in a pan of oil placed in a larger pan of boiling water, press the tapered-roller bearing onto the drive pinion. See Fig. 12-4.

10. Install the special gauge plate on the drive pinion as shown in Fig. 12-4.

Fig. 12-4. Pinion being prepared for position measurement. Total thickness of combined S_3 and S_4 shims is installed at arrow. Special gauge plate is installed on drive pinion.

11. Install the drive pinion and special gauge plate in the final drive housing. The rear of the housing should be pointing down and the drive pinion supported by the rear cover plate.

12. Adjust the clamp ring on the univeral measuring bar (Tool VW 385/1). Dimension **a** shown in Fig. 12-5 is 58 mm.

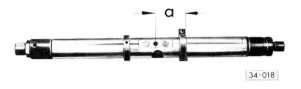

Fig. 12-5. Clamp ring adjustment.

13. Slide the centering discs (VW 385/2) onto the bar until they contact the clamp ring and the setting ring. Then attach measuring pin VW 385/13 with extension VW 385/20 to the gauge pin hole in the center of the bar. Install a dial indicator with a 3-mm range. Using setting block VW 385/5 as shown in Fig. 12-6, zero the dial indicator with no preload.

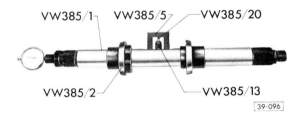

Fig. 12-6. Measuring bar ready for use. Notice how the setting block, VW 385/5, has been placed over the measuring pin extension.

14. Place an O-ring on the left adjusting ring. Lightly lubricate the O-ring and the threads with multipurpose grease, then screw the adjusting ring into the final drive housing until its outer surface is flush with the surface of the final drive housing.

   NOTE ——

   The differential bearing outer races must be installed in the adjusting rings.

15. Insert the measuring bar. Place an O-ring on the right adjusting ring. Lightly lubricate the O-ring and the threads with multipurpose grease, then screw in the adjusting ring.

16. By turning the knurled knob on the end of the measuring bar (Fig. 12-7), move the setting ring and centering disc outward until it is just barely possible to hand-turn the measuring bar.

17. Install the front cover plate. Install all the bolts and torque them to 2.5 mkg (18 ft. lb.).

Fig. 12-7. Setting ring position being adjusted (arrow).

18. Turn the final drive housing over so that its rear end is up. Hand-turn the drive pinion slightly back and forth in order to settle the tapered-roller bearings.

5

   CAUTION ——

   Do not turn the drive pinion too far or the gauge pin will slip off the special gauge plate that is installed on the drive pinion. After settling the bearings, return the drive pinion to its original position. Fig. 12-8 shows the correct arrangement of measuring tools inside the final drive housing.

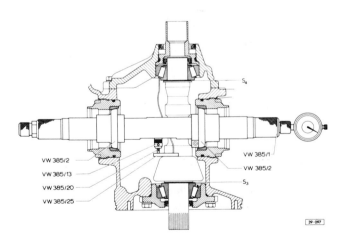

Fig. 12-8. Arrangement of measuring tools inside final drive housing.

19. Rotate the bar back and forth over center (Fig. 12-9). The maximum dial indicator reading should be observed and written down.

Fig. 12-9. Measuring bar being rotated (arrow) back and forth over center.

20. Compute the ideal thicknesses of the S_4 shim. To do this, add the deviation **r** marked on the ring gear to the reading you obtained in step 19. Subtract the computed thickness of the S_4 shim from the total shim thickness you determined previously in step 6 in order to determine the ideal thickness of the S_3 shim.

CAUTION ——

Every number or setting in the following example is imaginary. Using them as specifications for a car could cause serious damage.

Example:

Dial indicator reading obtained in step 19	0.94 mm
Deviation **r** marked on ring gear	+0.42 mm
Ideal thickness of S_4 shim	1.36 mm

Example:

Total shim thickness computed earlier in step 6	2.63 mm
Ideal S_4 shim thickness from first example	−1.36 mm
Ideal thickness of S_3 shim	1.27 mm

21. Select the correct S_3 and S_4 shims from **Table f.**

22. Remove the front cover plate. Remove the universal measuring bar. Remove the drive pinion.

23. Remove both tapered-roller bearings from the drive pinion. Remove the shims from the drive pinion.

Table f. Available S_3 and S_4 Shims

Ideal thickness	Shim to be installed	Part No.
1.05 to 1.100	1.100	082 519 141 AE
1.105 to 1.125	1.125	082 519 141 AF
1.130 to 1.150	1.150	082 519 141 AG
1.155 to 1.175	1.175	082 519 141 AH
1.180 to 1.200	1.200	082 519 141 AJ
1.205 to 1.225	1.225	082 519 141 AK
1.230 to 1.250	1.250	082 519 141 AL
1.255 to 1.275	1.275	082 519 141 AM
1.280 to 1.300	1.300	082 519 141 AN
1.305 to 1.325	1.325	082 519 141 AP
1.330 to 1.350	1.350	082 519 141 AQ
1.355 to 1.375	1.375	082 519 141 AR
1.380 to 1.400	1.400	082 519 141 AS
1.405 to 1.425	1.425	082 519 141 AT
1.430 to 1.450	1.450	082 519 141 BA
1.455 to 1.475	1.475	082 519 141 BB
1.480 to 1.500	1.500	082 519 141 BC
1.505 to 1.525	1.525	082 519 141 BD
1.530 to 1.550	1.550	082 519 141 BE
1.555 to 1.575	1.575	082 519 141 BF
1.580 to 1.600	1.600	082 519 141 BG
1.605 to 1.625	1.625	082 519 141 BH
1.630 to 1.650	1.650	082 519 141 BJ
1.655 to 1.675	1.675	082 519 141 BK
1.680 to 1.700	1.700	082 519 141 BL

CAUTION ——

The tapered-roller bearings must later be reinstalled on their original ends of the drive pinion. Be careful not to mix them up.

24. Heat the tapered-roller bearing inner races to approximately 100°C (212°F) in a pan of oil placed

in a larger pan of boiling water. Install the correct S_3 shim adjacent to the pinion head. Then press on the rear tapered-roller bearing inner race.

25. Install the correct S_4 shim at the front end of the drive pinion. Then press on the front tapered-roller bearing inner race.

26. Reinstall the special gauge plate on the drive pinion. Lightly lubricate the bearings with hypoid oil. Reinstall the drive pinion, the universal measuring bar, and the front cover plate in the final drive housing.

27. By rotating the bar back and forth over center, repeat the measuring procedure you carried out in step 19. The dial indicator reading should correspond with the deviation **r** stamped on the ring gear, within a tolerance of ±0.04 mm. If it does not, you have made an error in selecting the shims or in making previous measurements.

28. If you have installed new pinion tapered-roller bearing, check the pinion turning torque with a torque gauge as shown in Fig. 12-10. If the torque required to turn the pinion is less than 25 cmkg (22 in. lb.) with new bearings, you have not allowed sufficient shim thickness for bearing pre-load and bearing settling. The turning torque with used bearings need not be checked.

Fig. 12-10. Pinion turning torque being measured after the installation of new tapered-roller bearings.

12.2 Adjusting Ring Gear

The ring gear depth-of-mesh backlash must be adjusted after you have adjusted the drive pinion. The backlash is determined by the screw-in depths of the differential bearing adjusting rings. If you have installed new differential bearings, it will also be necessary to check the differential bearing turning torque.

To adjust:

1. After you have adjusted the drive pinion, remove the front and rear cover plates and the drive pinion from the final drive housing.

2. Install the new oil seals in the front and rear cover plates.

3. Install the differential in the final drive housing, but do not install the adjusting rings.

4. With careful attention to the instructions given in **11.1 Removing and Installing Drive Pinion,** install the drive pinion in the final drive housing. Install a new O-ring on the rear cover plate; lubricate the O-ring and the tapered roller bearings with hypoid oil. Coat the bolt flange of the front cover plate with oil resistant sealer. Torque the bolts of the cover plates to 2.5 mkg (18 ft. lb.). This is the final installation of the drive pinion.

5. Install new O-rings on the differential bearing adjusting rings. Lightly coat the O-rings and the threads with multipurpose grease. Lubricate the differential bearings with hypoid oil. Position the final drive housing so that the left side is uppermost, then install each adjusting ring until the surface indicated in Fig. 12-11 is flush with the surface of the final drive housing.

NOTE ——
About halfway through the 1975 model year, a new kind of adjusting ring was introduced. The new ring has the O-ring groove in the threaded (outer) end, whereas the earlier adjusting ring has the O-ring groove at the smooth (inner) end. The new adjusting ring cannot be used in early final drive housings, so replace the O-rings and damaged adjusting rings with new parts of the original kind.

Fig. 12-11. Surface (arrow) between tooth divisions of adjusting ring. This should be adjusted flush with housing, as shown.

6. From its flush position, screw in the right adjusting ring (at the ring gear side of the final drive) until the ring gear meshes fully with the pinion and there is no backlash (play between the teeth of the ring gear and the drive pinion).

7. Screw in the left adjusting ring (at the side opposite the ring gear) as far as possible. Tighten the ring slightly so that all play is removed from the differential bearings.

8. Unscrew the right adjusting ring ½ tooth division; screw in the left adjusting ring 2 tooth divisions (Fig. 12-12). This should correctly set the bearing preload and adjust the gear backlash. However, you should check the backlash and, if necessary, the bearing turning torque as described in the following procedure.

Fig. 12-13. Pinion locked with special clamp plate. Bolt hole in plate should be drilled to 8.5 mm.

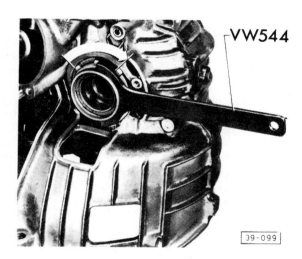

Fig. 12-12. Left adjusting ring being tightened two tooth divisions (arrow).

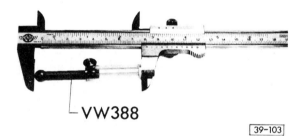

Fig. 12-14. Measuring bar being adjusted with vernier caliper.

To check backlash and turning torque:

1. Hand-turn the drive pinion several rotations in each direction in order to settle the bearings and distribute the lubricant evenly.

2. Using a suitable tool, such as the one shown in Fig. 12-13, lock the drive pinion so that it cannot turn.

3. Adjust the length of the backlash measuring bar to 62 mm as indicated in Fig. 12-14.

4. Install the backlash measuring bar and a dial indicator on the final drive as shown in Fig. 12-15. The gauge pin of the dial indicator must meet the spherical end of the backlash measuring bar at a 90° angle.

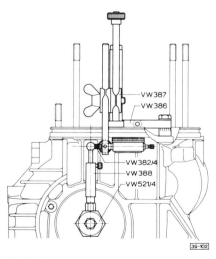

Fig. 12-15. Dial indicator gauge pin positioned at 90° to measuring bar.

5. By grasping the locking sleeve with a wrench, as shown in Fig. 12-16, turn the measuring bar as far as it will go away from the dial indicator before differential rotation is stopped by the locked drive pinion. Then zero the dial indicator. Turn the differential in the opposite direction until it is stopped by the pinion and write down the dial indicator reading. This is the ring gear's backlash.

Fig. 12-16. Ring gear backlash being measured.

6. Loosen the locking bolt on the locking sleeve. Reposition the measuring bar in a location that is 90° from its previous location. Tighten the locking bolt.

7. Loosen the bolt that holds the locking device on the drive pinion. Then turn the differential until the measuring bar is again positioned against the gauge pin of the dial indicator. Lock the pinion.

8. Again measure the backlash and write down the reading. Make two more backlash measurements so that you have four readings taken at four points 90° apart around the circumference of the ring gear.

   NOTE ——

   The difference between the four readings must not exceed 0.05 mm; if it is greater, something is wrong with the gearset or its installation. Left in this condition, the final drive will be noisy and wear rapidly.

9. Add the four measurements, then divide the sum by four. The quotient is the average backlash for the ring and pinion gearset. The average should be between 0.15 mm and 0.25 mm, with no individual measurement greater than 0.25 mm or less than 0.15 mm.

   NOTE ——

   If the backlash is outside the tolerance range given in step 9, you should bring the average backlash within the tolerance range by turning both differential bearing adjusting rings by equal amounts in opposite directions.

10. If you have installed new differential bearings as well as new pinion bearings, recheck the pinion turning torque as described in **12.1 Adjusting Drive Pinion.** With the differential installed, the pinion turning torque should be at least 30 cmkg (26 in. lb.). If it is less, you have not tightened the adjusting rings enough to provide adquate bearing preload.

11. When the backlash and, if applicable, the bearing turning torque is correct, install the lockplates on the adjusting rings. Torque the lockplate bolts to 1.0 mkg (7 ft. lb.).

12.3 Adjusting Flanged Shaft Axial Play

You can adjust the flanged shaft axial play either before or after you have installed the differential in the final drive housing. The adjustment is simpler with the differential removed. The available flanged shaft selective shims for adjusting flanged shaft axial play are listed in **Table g.**

Table g. Available Flanged Shaft Selective Shims

Total Axial play (mm)	Shim thickness (mm)	Part No.
1.05 to 1.13	1.00	003 507 401
1.14 to 1.20	1.07	003 507 402
1.21 to 1.27	1.14	003 507 403
1.28 to 1.34	1.21	003 507 404
1.35 to 1.41	1.28	003 507 405
1.42 to 1.48	1.35	003 507 406
1.49 to 1.55	1.42	003 507 407
1.56 to 1.62	1.49	003 507 408
1.63 to 1.69	1.56	003 507 409
1.70 to 1.76	1.63	003 507 410
1.77 to 1.83	1.70	003 507 411
1.84 to 1.90	1.77	003 507 412
1.91 to 1.97	1.84	003 507 413
1.98 to 2.04	1.91	003 507 414
2.05 to 2.11	1.98	003 507 415
2.12 to 2.14	2.05	003 507 416

To adjust the flanged shaft axial play with the differential removed, install the flanged shaft in the differential with the thinnest available (1.00 mm) shim. Install the socket head screw and torque it to 2.5 mm mkg (18 ft. lb.). Pull the flanged shaft outward. Then, using feeler gauges of various thicknesses as shown in Fig. 12-17, determine the clearance between the flanged shaft and the differential. To the thickness of the feeler gauge, add 1.00 mm—the thickness of the shim you have installed. The sum is the flanged shaft's total axial play.

Fig. 12-17. Axial play being measured with differential removed.

Using the total axial play as a guide, select a shim from **Table g.** Remove the 1.00-mm shim, then reinstall the flanged shaft with the selected shim and repeat the feeler gauge measurement. The clearance between the flanged shaft and the differential should be between 0.05 and 0.15 mm. If it is not within this range, select a slightly thicker or thinner shim in order to bring the axial play within the correct range.

To adjust the flanged shaft axial play with the differential installed, remove the flanged shaft and the original shim. Then install the flanged shaft with the thinnest available (1.00 mm) shim. Install the socket head screw and torque it to 2.5 mkg (18 ft. lb.). Install a dial indicator with a 30-mm gauge pin extension as shown in Fig. 12-18.

Push down the flanged shaft, then zero the dial indicator. Pry the flanged shaft up fully, then write down the dial indicator reading. To this reading, add 1.00-mm—the thickness of the shim you have installed. Use this sum, which is the flanged shaft's total axial play, to select a shim from **Table g.** Install the selected shim in place of the 1.00-mm shim. Then remeasure the axial play, which should be between 0.05 and 0.15 mm. If it is not within this range, select a slightly thicker or thinner shim in order to bring the axial play within the correct range.

Fig. 12-18. Axial play being measured with differential installed.

13. SELECTOR LEVER AND CABLE

The selector lever used with the automatic transmission shares no parts with the gearshift lever used with the manual transmission. A cable couples the selector lever with a lever on the automatic transmission. This cable is not repairable and must be replaced as a unit if either the moving part of the cable or its outer conduit is worn or damaged. Fig. 13-1 is an exploded view of the selector lever and cable used until the end of the 1974 model year. The selector lever introduced on the 1975 models is different in a number of details.

13.1 Removing, Installing and Adjusting Selector Lever

The contact plate for the neutral start switch can be replaced without replacing the entire selector lever assembly. If the selector lever requires adjustment only, you can adjust it after you have removed the center console.

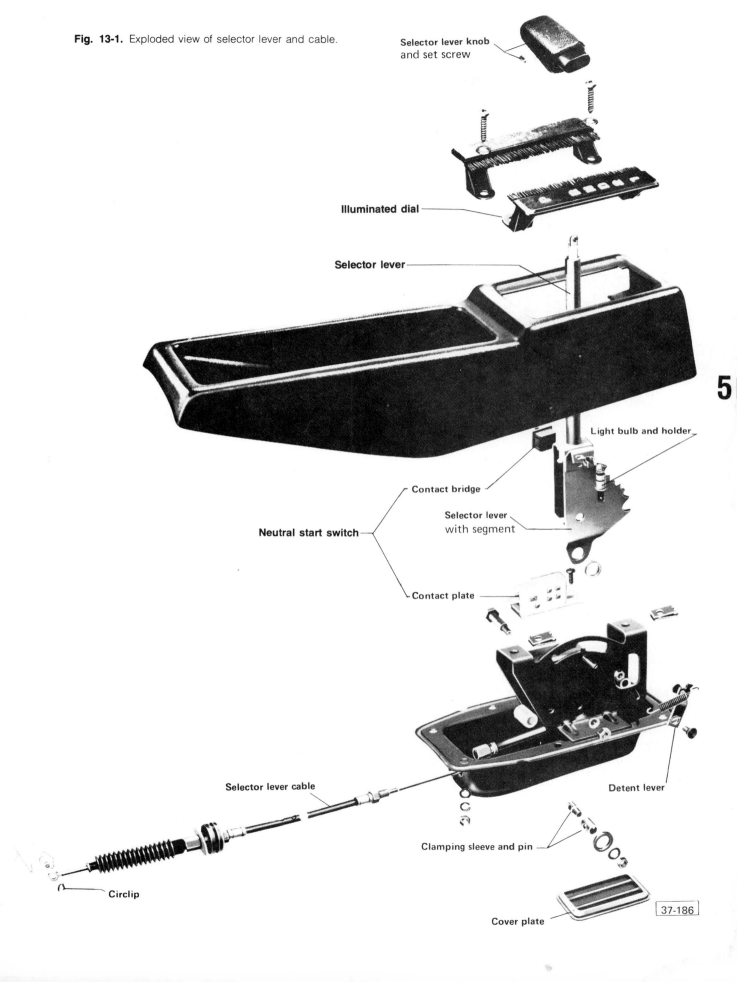

Fig. 13-1. Exploded view of selector lever and cable.

Selector lever knob and set screw

Illuminated dial

Selector lever

Light bulb and holder

Contact bridge

Selector lever with segment

Neutral start switch

Contact plate

Detent lever

Selector lever cable

Clamping sleeve and pin

Circlip

Cover plate

37-186

5

To remove selector lever:

1. Take out the two screws and washers that hold the illuminated dial and its matching trim plate to the selector lever assembly. The screws are located between the dial and the trim plate as indicated in Fig. 13-2.

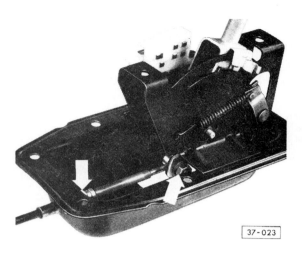

Fig. 13-3. Fasteners that hold cable. Cable conduit ring nut is at left arrow; Clamping sleeve and pin are at right arrow.

Fig. 13-2. Locations (arrows) of screws that hold illuminated dial and trim plate.

2. Remove the fasteners that hold the center console to the floor. Then remove the console. Disconnect the wiring from the illuminating bulb and the contact plate.

3. If you wish to remove the entire selector lever assembly as a unit, remove the bolts that hold the selector lever housing to the floor. Then, being careful not to tear the gasket, lift up the selector lever assembly and detach it from the cable by loosening the clamping sleeve and pin and removing the cable conduit ring nut. See Fig. 13-3.

4. If you wish to remove the selector lever with segment without removing the selector lever housing from the floor, detach the cable from the segment by loosening the clamping sleeve and pin and loosening the cable conduit ring nut. See Fig. 13-3. Then take out the selector lever pivot bolt and remove the selector lever with segment.

5. To remove the handle from the selector lever, take out the setscrew indicated in Fig. 13-4.

6. To replace the contact plate, remove the screws that are visible in Fig. 13-4.

Fig. 13-4. Setscrew (arrow) that holds knob to selector lever.

7. To adjust the selector lever, place the lever in the **P** position as indicated by the white arrow in Fig. 13-5. Then, using a screwdriver as shown in Fig. 13-5, pry the detent lever into position so that the roller contacts both flanks of the groove in the segment.

Assembly and installation are the reverse of removal. If you wish to disassemble the selector lever assembly fully, refer to Fig. 13-1 given earlier. Before you install the center console, attach the wires to the neutral start switch. It should be possible to start the engine only when the selector lever is in the **P** position or the **N** position. Following installation, adjust the selector cable as described under the next heading.

Fig. 13-5. Selector lever being adjusted. To center roller, pry with screwdriver as indicated by double arrow.

13.2 Replacing and Adjusting Selector Cable

If the selector cable needs adjusting, but does not need to be replaced, you can make the adjustment without removing the center console. Always check the cable adjustment after you have adjusted or reinstalled the selector lever and after you have replaced the selector cable. The cable should also be adjusted any time the drive ranges cannot be selected by placing the selector lever adjacent to the correct letter or number on the illuminated dial.

To check and correct cable adjustment:

1. Run the engine at 1000 to 1200 rpm. Firmly set the parking brake and depress the foot brake.

2. Move the selector lever so that it is aligned with the letter **R** on the illuminated dial. There should be a noticeable drop in engine speed and a transmission of reverse power to the front wheels.

> **NOTE** ——
> If the selector lever does not align correctly with the letters and numbers on the illuminated dial, adjust the selector lever as described in **13.1 Removing, Installing, and Adjusting Selector Lever** before you continue with the cable adjustment check.

3. Move the selector lever to **P.** The engine speed should increase, indicating that reverse gear has disengaged.

4. Move the lever to **R.** Again there should be a noticeable drop in engine speed and a transmission of reverse power to the front wheels.

5. Move the selector lever to **N.** The engine speed should increase, indicating that reverse gear has disengaged.

6. Move the selector lever to **D.** There should be a noticeable drop in engine speed and a transmission of forward power to the front wheels.

7. Move the selector lever to **1.** The lever should engage the detent without having to overcome a resistance. If there is excessive resistance, check the selector lever adjustment as described in **13.1 Removing, Installing, and Adjusting Selector Lever.**

8. If the correct result is not obtained in any of the preceeding steps, turn off the engine. Then place the selector lever in **P**—making sure that the lever engages the detent correctly.

9. Raise the car on a hoist or support it on jack stands. Then, working under the car, carefully pry out the rectangular cover plate that is in the bottom of the selector lever housing. See Fig. 13-6.

5

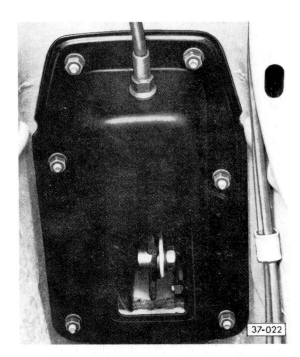

Fig. 13-6. Selector lever housing with cover plate removed.

10. Working through the opening in the bottom of the selector lever housing, loosen the nut on the clamping sleeve. The cable should be able to slide freely in and out in the sleeve.

11. Using a pair of pliers, turn the lever (Fig. 13-7) on the transmission fully rearward against spring tension so that the lever is against its stop. Then, while holding the lever in this position, tighten the nut on the clamping sleeve.

12. Recheck the adjustment as described in the first seven steps of this procedure. If no further adjustment is required, install the cover plate and lower the car to the ground.

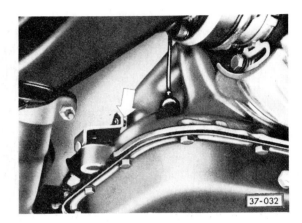

Fig. 13-7. Lever (arrow) on transmission.

To replace cable:

1. Remove the center console as described in **13.1 Removing, Installing, and Adjusting Selector Lever.** Loosen the nut on the clamping sleeve. Remove the ring nut that holds the cable conduit to the selector lever housing.

2. Raise the car on a hoist or support it on jack stands. Working under the car, remove the circlip from the lever on the transmission. Detach the cable conduit from the transmission carrier. See Fig. 13-8.

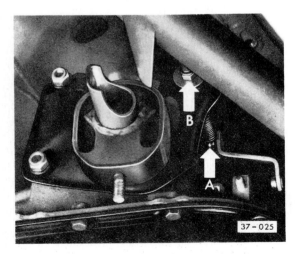

Fig. 13-8. Cable attachment points on transmission. Circlip is at arrow **A**, nut on transmission carrier is at arrow **B**.

3. Pull the cable and conduit out of the selector lever housing and out of the transmission carrier.

Installation is the reverse of removal. Do not tighten the nut on the clamping sleeve until you have adjusted the cable as previously described. Then check the adjustment with the engine running and, if necessary, correct the adjustment.

14. REPLACING TRANSAXLE BONDED MOUNTING

The bonded rubber mounting on early model transaxles can be replaced without replacing the entire transaxle rear mount. To do this, you must first remove the rear mount from the transaxle. Unbolt the exhaust pipe bracket from the rear mount, then remove the transaxle carrier from the body and from the bonded rubber mounting. The transaxle and engine assembly will drop down when you remove the carrier but no support is necessary. Remove the nuts that hold the rear mount to the transmission case. Then take the rear mount, complete with bonded rubber mounting, to the workbench.

To replace bonded mounting:

1. Clamp the transaxle rear mount in a vise. Using a sturdy knife, cut the outer ring off the rubber part of the bonded mounting. Then use a puller, as shown in Fig. 14-1, to remove the rubber part of the bonded mounting from the transaxle rear mount.

   NOTE ——
   Before you pull the old bonded mounting off the transaxle rear mount, mark the distance to which the bonded mounting is pressed onto the rear mount.

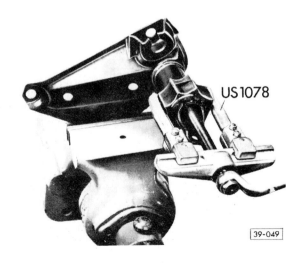

Fig. 14-1. Bonded rubber mounting being removed.

2. Install the new bonded mounting on the transaxle rear mount so that the wide groove in the bonded mounting is aligned with the rib on the rear mount (Fig. 14-2).

Fig. 14-2. Aligning bonded rubber mounting. Wide groove is at arrow **A**, rib is at arrow **B**.

3. Using a press and an appropriate tool, as shown in Fig. 14-3, press on the new bonded rubber mounting until the distance mark you made prior to

removal of the old bonded mounting is aligned with the inner ring of the new bonded mounting.

4. Reinstall the rear mount on the transaxle. Torque the nuts to 2.5 mkg (18 ft. lb.). Install the transaxle carrier, torquing the bolts to 3.0 mkg (22 ft. lb.) and the nut to 4.0 mkg (29 ft. lb.). Torque the bolt for the exhaust pipe bracket to 2.0 mkg (14 ft. lb.).

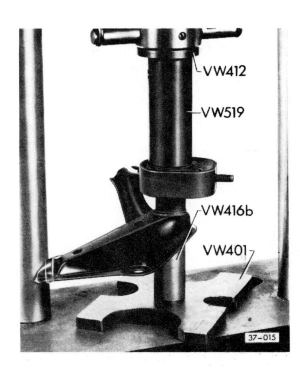

Fig. 14-3. Bonded mounting being pressed onto transaxle rear mount.

15. AUTOMATIC TRANSMISSION TECHNICAL DATA

I. Tolerances and Settings

Designation	Setting or new part tolerance
1. Torque converter bushing .... maximum out-of-round	0.03 mm (.001 in.)
2. Planetary gearset axial play .... setting	0.45–1.05 mm (.018–.041 in.)
3. Brake band adjustment: Torque adjusting screw to 1.0 mkg (86.8 in. lb.). Then loosen and retorque to 0.5 mkg (43 in. lb.). Loosen by specified number of turns. Torque locknut to 2.0 mkg (14 ft. lb.).	
2nd gear brake band .... turns	exactly 2½
1st and reverse gear brake band .... turns	3¼ to 3½
4. Correct axial play of direct and reverse clutch with correct circlip and a pressure plate that is 6.15 to 6.30 mm (.242 to .248 in.) thick. Available circlips: 1.50, 1.70, 2.00, 2.30, 2.50, 2.70 mm (.059, .067, .079, .090, .098, .106 in.)	1.70–2.20 mm (.067–.086 in.)
5. Correct axial play of forward clutch with correct circlip. Available circlips: 1.50, 1.70, 2.00, 2.30, 2.50 mm (.059, .067, .079, .090, .098 in.)	0.80–1.20 mm (.031–.047 in.)
6. Preload of pinion bearings .... turning torque	25 cmkg (22 in. lb.) minimum
7. Total preload of combined pinion and differential bearings	30 cmkg (26 in. lb.) minimum

II. Tightening Torques

Location	Designation	mkg	ft. lb.
Pressure connection plugs in transmission case	threaded plug	1.0	7
Vacuum unit in transmission case	—	2.5	18
Valve body in transmission case	bolt	0.36	36 in. lb.
ATF pan to transmission case	bolt	1.0	7
Late model transaxle rear mount to left side of transmission case	bolt	5.5	40
Late model transaxle rear mount to body	bolt	4.0	29
Early model transaxle carrier to bonded mounting	nut	4.0	29
Early model transaxle carrier to body	bolt	3.0	22
Early model transaxle rear mount to rear of transmission case	nut	2.5	18
Engine to transaxle	bolt	5.5	40
Torque converter to drive plate	bolt	3.0	22
Exhaust pipe bracket to transaxle support	bolt	2.0	14
Exhaust pipe to exhaust manifold	nut	2.5	18
Torque converter cover plate to bellhousing	bolt	1.5	11
Starter to bellhousing	bolt and nut	2.0	14
Constant velocity joint to drive flange	socket-head screw	6.5	47
Suspension ball joint on track control arm	bolt	6.5	47
ATF pump to transmission case	bolt	0.4	3
Locknuts for band adjusting screws	nut	2.0	14
Transmission case to final drive housing	nut	3.0	22
Manual valve lever to shaft	self-locking nut	1.0	7
Retaining bolt for cable lever and shaft in transmission case	bolt	0.5	3.5
Threaded pin for parking pawl relay lever in transmission case	special bolt	2.0	14
Front or rear final drive cover to final drive housing	bolt	2.5	18
Differential bearing adjusting ring lockplate to final drive housing	bolt	1.0	7
Flanged shafts to differential	socket-head bolt	2.5	18
Retaining bolt for speedometer drive in final drive housing	bolt	1.0	7
Ring gear to differential housing	bolt with spring-type lock washer	6.0	43
	bolt with serrated washer surface	7.0	50

III. Valve Body Springs

Description	Part No.	No. of coils	Wire thickness mm (in.)	Free length (approximate) mm (in.)	Coil inner diameter mm ± 0.3 mm (in. ± .012 in.)
Main pressure valve spring	003 325 131 A	16.5	1.50 (.0590)	71.6 ($2^{13}/_{16}$)	11.90 (.469)
Secondary throttle pressure valve spring	003 325 257 B	11.5	0.85 (.0335)	27.7 ($1^3/_{32}$)	7.35 (.289)
Kickdown valve spring	003 325 175	10.5	0.63 (.0248)	23.8 ($^{15}/_{16}$)	7.70 (.303)
2nd/3rd shift valve spring	003 325 207	10.5	0.80 (.0315)	29.2 ($1^5/_{32}$)	8.20 (.323)
1st/2nd shift valve spring	003 325 207	10.5	0.80 (.0315)	29.2 ($1^5/_{32}$)	8.20 (.323)
Throttle pressure limiting valve spring	003 325 227 B	12.5	1.00 (.0393)	31.0 ($1^7/_{32}$)	7.70 (.303)
Converter pressure valve spring	003 325 247	9.5	1.25 (.0492)	27.3 ($1^5/_{64}$)	8.13 (.320)
Part throttle valve spring	003 325 129	6.5	0.40 (.0157)	18.1 ($^{23}/_{32}$)	6.10 (.240)
Pressure relief valve spring (between valve body and separator plate)	003 325 267	15.5	0.80 (.0315)	27.7 ($1^3/_{32}$)	4.70 (.185)
2nd/3rd and 3rd/2nd valve spring	003 325 269	4.5	0.20 (.0078)	5.8 ($^7/_{32}$)	4.30 (.169)
Primary throttle pressure valve spring	003 325 295	10.5	0.63 (.0248)	36.3 ($1^7/_{16}$)	9.00 (.354)
3rd/2nd accumulator spring	003 325 233 B	14.0	2.00 (.0787)	61.7 ($2^7/_{16}$)	11.60 (.457)

IV. Final Drive Ratios

Model	No. of pinion teeth	No. of ring gear teeth	Ratio
From introduction through 1974 cars	11	45	4.09:1
1975	11	43	3.91:1

V. Automatic Transmission Test Data

Stall Speed (1900-2200 rpm) Pressure			
Selector lever position	Pressure	psi (kg/cm²)	Remarks
N	Primary throttle pressure	42.0 (3.0)	Increase idle speed to 1000 rpm with vacuum hose off and plugged
	Main pressure	85.0 (6.0)	
	Primary throttle pressure	5.0–6.0 (0.35–0.42)	Increase idle speed to 1000 rpm with vacuum hose on
	Main pressure	50.0–53.0 (3.5–3.7)	
R	Main pressure	158–167 (10.7–11.7)	
D	Primary throttle pressure	38.0–42.0 (2.7–3.0)	At stall torque speed (1900-2200 rpm at full throttle) with vacuum hose on (do not prolong test beyond 20 seconds)
	Main pressure	85.0 (6.0)	
R	Main pressure	234–305 (16.5–21.5)	
D	Main pressure	85.0 (6.0)	At full throttle with a road speed of over 19 mph (30 kph)

Full-throttle gearshift speeds in mph (kph)	
Gears	Road speeds
1–2	20–22 (32–35)
1–2 kickdown	30–40 (48–64)
2–3	53–60 (85–96)
2–3 kickdown	60–68 (96–109)
3–2	33–42 (53–67)
3–2 kickdown	58–65 (93–104)
2–1	14–16 (22–26)
2–1 kickdown	28–38 (45–61)

5

VI. Driveshaft Lengths (dimension a)

Transmission	Left driveshaft length mm (in.)	Right driveshaft length mm (in.)
Manual	506 (19.92 or 19 59/64)	506 (19.92 or 19 59/64)
Automatic	437 (17.20 or 17 13/64)	531 (20.90 or 20 29/32)

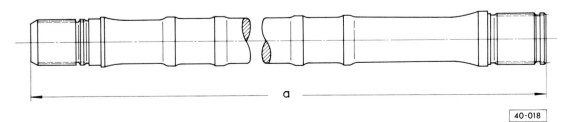

40-018

AUTOMATIC TRANSMISSION
(FROM 1976)

Contents

Automatic Transmission (From 1976)

The automatic transmission covered in this section of the Manual is optional on 1976 and later models as an alternative to the standard manual transmission. This new automatic transmission is completely different from the automatic transmission used on 1975 and earlier cars. With the new transmission, shifting is controlled by the throttle linkage, rather than by engine vacuum. The throttle linkage also operates the kickdown, which was electrically operated on earlier cars.

The detents that were formerly in the selector lever are now built into the transmission itself. Also, the new automatic transmission has separate planetary gearsets for forward and reverse, whereas the earlier automatic transmission had a single, compound planetary gearset. Another significant internal change is the use of a multiple-disk 1st/reverse gear brake instead of a 1st/reverse gear brake band.

6

The automatic transmission is housed in a cast aluminum alloy case that is held by studs to a separate final drive housing. Taken as a unit, the transmission and final drive are called the transaxle. Though the transaxle with automatic transmission operates on entirely different principles from those of the transaxle with manual transmission, the constant velocity joints and front wheel driveshafts of both transaxles are identical, except for driveshaft length. Please consult **MANUAL TRANSMISSION** for repairs related to the driveshafts and constant velocity joints.

Cleanliness and a careful approach are imperative when repairing the transaxle. Familiarize yourself with the instructions before you begin a job and make sure that you have the necessary tools—particularly for procedures given with metric specifications only. Specifications that lack U.S. equivalents require that the related work be carried out with metric tools and instruments only.

Though you may not have the tools or the skills for carrying out actual repairs, you may be able to remove the transaxle, which can help to reduce service time. In this case, we recommend that the transaxle be thoroughly cleaned on the outside and then taken to the shop as is—partial disassembly will not make repairs easier and may indeed complicate them. We especially urge you to consult an Authorized Dealer before attempting repairs on a car still covered by the new-car warranty.

1. GENERAL DESCRIPTION

The transaxle with automatic transmission used on 1976 and later cars is shown in Fig. 1-1. At the front of the transaxle is the final drive housing, which has an integral bellhousing for the torque converter. Inside the final drive housing are the differential and the ring and pinion gearset. The governor for the automatic transmission is located beneath the round cover on the left-hand side of the final drive housing.

The final drive housing, which contains hypoid oil for lubricating the final drive gears, is completely sealed off from the transmission case. There are, however, two ATF (automatic transmission fluid) passages in the final drive housing that are connected to the automatic transmission's hydraulic control system. These passages carry ATF to and from the governor and in no way influence the lubrication or operation of the final drive.

At the rear of the transaxle is the cast aluminum transmission case that contains the ATF pump, the hydraulic controls, and the planetary gear system. The planetary gear system is lubricated solely by the ATF that is circulated through the transmission by the ATF pump. Because the ATF does not circulate unless the engine is running, it is important to remember that the transmission parts are only partially lubricated when the engine is turned off and the car is being towed.

Fig. 1-1. Transaxle used on 1976 and later cars with automatic transmissions.

CAUTION ——

Never tow a car with an automatic transmission faster than 30 mph (48 kph) or farther than 30 mi. (48 km). Bearings can be damaged by lack of lubrication. If you must tow the car farther, lift the front wheels or remove the driveshafts that connect the front wheels to the transaxle.

Torque Converter

The torque converter is a large doughnut-shaped assembly located between the engine and the transaxle. The converter not only receives engine output and passes it on to the transmission, but also multiplies engine torque at low vehicle speeds and serves as a fluid coupling between the engine and the transmission. Curved vanes inside the housing set up a flow of ATF that drives another vaned wheel called the turbine. The turbine drives a hollow shaft that transmits power to the transmission.

ATF Pump

ATF must be circulating under pressure before the automatic transmission can function. The ATF pump that creates this pressure is located at the extreme rear of the transmission case. A long pump driveshaft, which passes through the center of the hollow turbine shaft, drives the ATF pump. Because the pump driveshaft is splined directly to the torque converter housing, the pump circulates ATF whenever the engine is running, regardless of selector lever position.

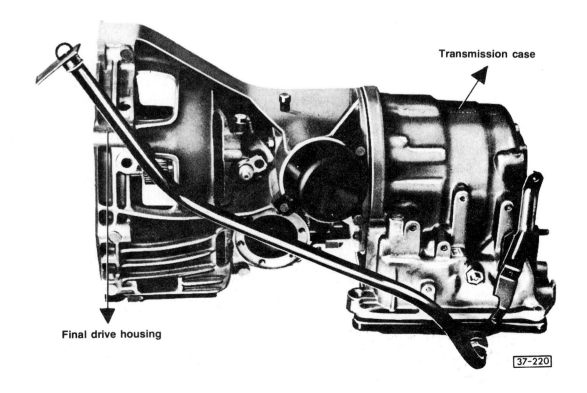

Transmission case

Final drive housing

37-220

Planetary Gear System

A torque converter alone cannot supply the torque multiplication needed for all driving conditions. The output of the torque converter is therefore routed into a planetary gear system. The planetary gear system consists of two clutches, two brakes, and two planetary gearsets—one gearset for forward operation of the vehicle and the other gearset for reverse.

The two hydraulically operated multiple-disk clutches control the delivery of the torque converter's turbine output to the planetary gearsets. The clutch at the front of the transmission is called the forward clutch because it transfers power to the planetary gears in all forward gears. The clutch at the rear of the transmission is called the direct and reverse clutch because it transfers power to the planetary gears only when the transmission is in direct (3rd gear) or in reverse.

One of the two brakes is a band that contracts around the direct and reverse clutch drum in order to provide 2nd gear. For this reason, it is known as the 2nd gear brake band. The second of the two brakes is a multiple-disk brake that is applied hydraulically in order to obtain reverse operation. This brake is also applied when the selector lever is at 1 in order to lock the 1st gear one-way clutch in both directions of rotation and thus provide additional engine braking. Owing to its two functions, the multiple-disk brake is called the 1st/reverse gear brake.

Hydraulic Controls

The hydraulic control system directs and regulates hydraulic pressure from the ATF pump, thereby controlling shifting of the planetary gear system. Shifts are produced by the piston-type servo for the 2nd gear brake band, the ring-shaped piston for the multiple-disk 1st/reverse brake, and the two ring-shaped clutch pistons.

Three primary control devices regulate the movement of the control valves in the automatic transmission's valve body assembly. One of these is the manual valve, which is connected to the selector lever by a flexible cable. Moving the lever changes the setting of the valve and produces the necessary application of hydraulic pressure for the drive range selected. The second primary control device is the throttle pressure valve, which is operated by the accelerator cable and makes the transmission responsive to variations in engine speed and load. A third primary control device, the governor, which is gear-driven off the final drive pinion and controls ATF pressure relative to its rotational speed, makes the transmission responsive to variations in vehicle speeds.

Final Drive

The final drive housing used on 1976 and later cars with automatic transmissions is little different from the final drive housing used on 1975 and earlier cars. The final drive housing flange is modified to accept the new automatic transmission, the drive pinion shaft cover is equipped with an additional oil seal, and the torque converter one-way clutch support has been made integral with the final drive housing front cover. The ring and pinion gearset of 1976 and later cars is not interchangeable with the gearset used in 1973 through 1975 cars.

In this section of the Manual, you will find only the final drive repair and adjustment procedures that are different from those described for the earlier transaxle with automatic transmission. Please consult **AUTOMATIC TRANSMISSION (Through 1975)** for all final drive repairs and adjustments that are not found in this section.

2. MAINTENANCE

The following routine maintenance jobs should be performed at the time or mileage interval prescribed in **LUBRICATION AND MAINTENANCE.** Instructions can be found in **LUBRICATION AND MAINTENANCE.**

1. Checking ATF level and, if necessary, adding ATF
2. Checking kickdown operation
3. Checking final drive hypoid oil
4. Changing ATF

6

3. TROUBLESHOOTING

Before diagnosing automatic transmission troubles, review the history of the unit. Such a review may offer important clues to present difficulties. The following should be checked before making repairs or adjustments:

1. Be sure that the engine is tuned-up and running right.
2. Inspect the transaxle for external damage, loose or missing screws, and obvious leaks. Check the final drive hypoid oil for ATF contamination caused by faulty seals.
3. Check the ATF level. Rub some ATF between your fingers and sniff it to detect the burned odor that means burned friction linings. If the ATF is dirty, it may be clogging the automatic controls.
4. Check the adjustment and operation of the selector lever cable and the throttle cable.

3.1 Road Testing

Drive the car in all drive ranges and under as many road conditions as possible. Note the shift points both up and down. They should take place quickly, without interrupting the power flow. Listen for engine racing between gears, a possible indication of slipping clutches or a slipping 2nd gear brake band. The correct shift points are given in **Table a.**

Table a. Automatic Shift Points

Shift	At full throttle mph (kph)	Kickdown mph (kph)
1st to 2nd gear	19–24 (30–38)	35–39 (56–63)
2nd to 3rd gear	49–53 (79–85)	65–66 (104–106)
3rd to 2nd gear	30–35 (48–56)	62–63 (99–101)
2nd to 1st gear	15–17 (24–27)	32–34 (51–54)

3.2 Troubleshooting Table

Table b may suggest remedies for defects that you observed during road testing. The numbers in bold type in the Remedy column refer to numbered headings in this section of the Manual where the repair or adjustment is described.

When troubleshooting the automatic transmission, try to pin down the main component involved: torque converter, planetary gear system, or hydraulic controls. If **Table b** fails to pinpoint the malfunction adequately, carry out the tests described in **3.3 Stall Speed Testing** and **3.4 Pressure Testing.**

Table b. 1976 and Later Automatic Transmission Troubleshooting

Problem	Selector lever position	Probable cause
1. No drive (car will not move)	R, D, 2, 1	a. ATF level low b. Drive plate broken or not bolted to torque converter c. Manual valve not hooked to selector lever cable d. Sticking main pressure valve e. ATF pump or pump drive faulty—no pressure f. Broken gear or shaft—possibly in final drive
2. No drive in forward gears	D, 2, 1	a. Forward clutch plates burned or worn out b. Forward clutch diaphragm spring borken
3. No drive in 1st gear	D, 2	a. 1st gear one-way clutch slipping b. Forward clutch plates burned or worn out c. Forward clutch diaphragm spring broken
4. No drive in 1st gear (engine braking deceleration gear)	1	a. 1st/reverse brake disks burned or worn out
5. No drive in 2nd gear	D, 2	a. 2nd gear brake band incorrectly adjusted b. 2nd gear brake band burned or worn out
6. No drive in 3rd gear	D	a. Direct/reverse clutch plates burned or worn out
7. No drive in reverse	R	a. 1st/reverse brake disks burned or worn out b. Direct/reverse clutch plates burned or worn out c. Forward clutch seized
8. Irregular drive in all forward gears gears	D, 2	a. ATF level low b. ATF pump pickup strainer partially clogged
9. No upshift into 2nd gear	D, 2	a. Faulty governor drive b. Governor dirty c. Governor incorrectly assembled during repair d. Valve body assembly dirty e. Loose accumulator cover plate f. 1st/2nd gear shift valve sticking
10. No upshift into 3rd gear	D	a. Governor dirty b. Valve body assembly dirty c. Ball valves missing from transfer plate d. 2nd/3rd gear shift valve sticking
11. No downshift into 2nd gear	D	a. Governor dirty b. 2nd/3rd gear shift valve sticking
12. No downshift into 1st gear	1	a. Governor dirty b. 1st/2nd gear shift valve sticking

6

Remedy
a. Check and, if necessary, correct ATF level. **LUBRICATION AND MAINTENANCE** b. Install bolts. If necessary, replace drive plate. **ENGINE AND CLUTCH** c. Connect and adjust selector lever cable. **4.2** d. Remove, disassemble, and clean valve body. **6.1, 6.2** e. Make pressure test **(3.4).** If no pressure, replace faulty fpump or pump driveshaft.   If driveshaft is broken, check pump gears for free movement. **3.4, 11.2, 11.3** f. Remove, disassemble and inspect transaxle. Make necessary repairs. **9, 11.1, 11.2, 12**
a. Repair forward clutch. **11.5** b. Repair forward clutch. **11.5**
a. Repair or replace 1st gear one-way clutch **11.2, 11.6** b. Repair forward clutch. **11.5** c. Repair forward clutch. **11.5**
a. Replace 1st/reverse brake disks. **11.2**
a. Adjust 2nd gear brake band. **5.1** b. Replace and adjust 2nd gear brake band. **11.2, 5.1**
a. Repair direct/reverse clutch. **11.4**
a. Replace 1st/reverse brake disks. **11.2** b. Repair direct/reverse clutch. **11.4** c. Repair forward clutch. **11.5**
a. Check and, if necessary, correct ATF level. **LUBRICATION AND MAINTENANCE** b. Remove ATF pan. Clean strainer. **6.1**
a. Replace governor shaft and, if necessary, ring and pinion gearset. **7, 12** b. Remove and clean governor. **7** c. Assemble governor correctly. **7.3** d. Remove, disassemble, and clean valve body. **6.1, 6.2** e. Remove valve body assembly. Install accumulator cover plate correctly. **6.1** f. Remove, disassemble, and clean valve body. **6.1, 6.2**
a. Remove and clean governor. **7** b. Remove, disassemble, and clean valve body. **6.1, 6.2** c. Separate transfer plate from valve body. Check ball valves. **6.1** d. Remove, disassemble, and clean valve body. **6.1, 6.2**
a. Remove and clean governor. **7** b. Remove, disassemble, and clean valve body. **6.1, 6.2**
a. Remove and clean governor. **7** b. Remove, disassemble, and clean valve body. **6.1, 6.2**

continued on next page

Table b. 1976 and Later Automatic Transmission Troubleshooting (continued)

Problem	Selector level position	Probable cause
13. Downshift to 1st gear delayed (jerky engagement)	D, 2	a. 1st gear one-way clutch slipping
14. Shift(s) take place below normal speed given in **Table a**	D, 2	a. Governor dirty b. Valve body assembly dirty
15. Shift(s) take place above normal speed given in **Table a**	D, 2	a. Governor dirty b. Valve body assembly dirty c. Paper gasket for transmission or intermediate plate damaged
16. Gear engagement jerky when selector lever is moved from N to D or R	D, R	a. Engine idle speed too fast b. ATF level low
17. Gear engagement delayed on upshift from 1st to 2nd gear	D, 2	a. ATF level low b. Valve body assembly dirty c. 2nd gear brake band incorrectly adjusted d. 2nd gear brake band burned or worn out e. Incorrect piston installed in 2nd gear brake band servo during repair
18. Gear engagement delayed on upshift from 2nd to 3rd gear	D, 2	a. ATF level low b. Valve body assembly dirty c. 2nd gear brake band incorrectly adjusted d. 2nd gear brake band burned or worn out e. Incorrect piston installed in 2nd gear brake band servo during repair f. Direct/reverse clutch plates burned or worn out g. Incorrect direct/reverse clutch installed during repair
19. Kickdown fails to operate	D, 2	a. Accelerator cable incorrectly adjusted
20. Vehicle does not accelerate as quickly as it should	D, 2, 1, R	a. Engine needs a tune-up b. Throttle cable incorrectly adjusted c. Accelerator cable incorrectly adjusted
21. Vehicle fails to achieve maximum speed	D	a. Engine needs a tune-up b. Throttle cable incorrectly adjusted c. Accelerator cable incorrectly adjusted
22. Parking lock fails to engage	P	a. Parking lock mechanism damaged b. Selector lever cable misadjusted
23. Front wheels locked (car can not be moved by pushing, rear wheels turn freely)	R	a. Parking lock mechanism jammed
24. ATF needs to be added often, no visible leaks	—	a. Governor shaft seal leaking ATF into final drive housing b. O-ring and gaskets between transmission and final drive leaking ATF into final drive housing c. Drive pinion shaft oil seal leaking ATF into final drive housing
25. ATF needs to be added often, leakage visible externally	—	a. ATF filler tube leaking b. Torque converter seal leaking c. Torque converter bushing worn d. O-ring for governor cover leaking e. Nuts for transmission case/final drive housing studs loose f. O-ring and gaskets between transmission and final drive leaking ATF to outside
26. ATF appears very dirty, smells burnt	—	a. 1st/reverse brake disks burned b. 2nd gear brake band burned c. Direct/reverse clutch linings burned d. Forward clutch linings burned

Remedy
a. Repair or replace 1st gear one-way clutch. **11.2, 11.6**
a. Remove and clean governor. **7** b. Remove, disassemble, and clean valve body. **6.1, 6.2**
a. Remove and clean governor. **7** b. Remove, disassemble, and clean valve body. **6.1, 6.2** c. Separate transmission fromfinal drive. Reassemble with new gaskets   correctly installed. **11.1**
a. Adjust idle. See **FUEL AND EXHAUST SYSTEMS** b. Check and, if necessary, correct ATF level. **LUBRICATION AND MAINTENANCE**
a. Check and, if necessary, correct ATF level. **LUBRICATION AND MAINTENANCE** b. Remove, disassemble, and clean valve body. **6.1, 6.2** c. Adjust 2nd gear brake band. **5.1** d. Replace and adjust 2nd gear brake band. **11.2, 5.1** e. Replace 2nd gear brake band servo piston with correct piston. **8**
a. Check and, if necessary, correct ATF level. **LUBRICATION AND MAINTENANCE** b. Remove, disassemble, and clean valve body. **6.1, 6.2** c. Adjust 2nd gear brake band. **5.1** d. Replace and adjust 2nd gear brake band. **11.2, 5.1** e. Replace 2nd gear brake band servo piston with correct piston. **8** f. Repair direct/reverse clutch. **11.4** g. Replace direct/reverse clutch. **11.4**
a. Adjust accelerator cable. **FUEL AND EXHAUST SYSTEMS**
a. Tune-up engine. **ENGINE AND CLUTCH, FUEL AND EXHAUST SYSTEMS** b. Adjust throttle cable. **FUEL AND EXHAUST SYSTEMS** c. Adjust accelerator cable. **FUEL AND EXHAUST SYSTEMS**
a. Tune-up engine. **ENGINE AND CLUTCH, FUEL AND EXHAUST SYSTEMS** b. Adjust throttle cable. **FUEL AND EXHAUST SYSTEMS** c. Adjust accelerator cable. **FUEL AND EXHAUST SYSTEMS**
a. Repair parking lock mechanism. **11.8** b. Adjust selector lever cable. **4.3**
a. Repair parking lock mechanism. **11.8**
a. Replace governor shaft seal. **7** b. Replace O-ring and gaskets. **11.1** c. Replace drive pinion shaft oil seal. **12.1**
a. Tighten filler tube union or replace filler tube. **6.1** b. Repalce torque converter seal; check bushing. **10, 12.1** c. Replace torque converter bushing and seal. **10, 12.1** d. Replace O-ring. **11.1** e. Torque nuts to 3.0 mkg (22 ft. lb.). **11.1** f. Replace O-ring and gaskets. **11.1**
a. Replace 1st/reverse brake disks. **11.2** b. Replace and adjust 2nd gear brake band. **11.2, 5.1** c. Repair direct/reverse clutch. **11.4** d. Repair forward clutch. **11.5**

6

3.3 Stall Speed Testing

This test provides a quick check of the torque converter and the planetary gear system. You should only test the stall speed if the car accelerates poorly despite a perfectly-tuned engine. A precision electric tachometer must be used for this test, as dashboard instruments are not calibrated with sufficient accuracy.

CAUTION ——

Never extend this test beyond the time it takes to read the tachometer—20 seconds maximum. Prolonging the test may overheat the transmission and damage the seals.

To test:

1. Connect the tachometer according to the instrument manufacturer's instructions. Then start the engine.

2. Set the parking brake and depress the foot brake firmly to hold the car stationary.

3. Place the selector lever in **D** and floor the accelerator pedal. Instead of revving up, the engine should run at a reduced rpm, known as stall speed.

If the rpm at stall is about 400 rpm below the specified 2100 to 2350 rpm stall speed—and the engine is in a proper state of tune—something is wrong with the torque converter. If the rpm at stall is above 2350 rpm, there is slippage in the forward clutch or the 1st gear one-way clutch. The test can also be made with the selector lever at **R**. If the reverse stall speed is too high, it indicates slippage in either the direct and reverse clutch or in the multiple-disk 1st/reverse brake.

NOTE ——

Slippage in the forward clutch—and especially slippage in the 1st/reverse brake—can be caused by inadequate hydraulic pressure as well as by worn clutch or brake components. Indeed, slippage caused by low pressure may lead to clutch or brake wear. This excessive wear will recur if you do not correct the low pressure condition at the same time as you repair the transmission's clutches and brakes. Transmission internal leaks are the usual cause of inadequate hyraulic pressure.

3.4 Pressure Testing

A main pressure test will locate internal leaks and other troubles in the hydraulic controls. Though you can make the full-throttle test while driving the car on a highway, whenever possible this test should be carried out on a dynamometer. The pressure gauge should have a range of 0 to 150 psi or 0 to 10 kg/cm².

NOTE ——

At this printing, the factory had not yet published main pressure specifications for the late valve body (Code Letter L). The specifications given in the following test for transmissions beginning with Transmission No. ET 26 116 are estimates based on field experience. It is impossible to say whether these estimates apply past Transmission No. ET 01 068 because the publisher has had no experience with the latest valve body, code letter AA, which was introduced in Transmission No. ET 02 068. Code letter information appears in **6.1 Removing and Installing Valve Body Assembly.**

To test:

1. Using a long hose so that you can place the gauge inside the car, connect the pressure gauge to the main pressure tap on the transmission (Fig. 3-1). Tie the hose to the car body so that it cannot become entangled with the wheels.

Fig. 3-1. Main pressure tap on transmission case.

2. Start the engine and warm it up to its normal operating temperature. Make sure that the idle speed is adjusted to specifications, as described in **FUEL AND EXHAUST SYSTEMS.**

3. Place the selector lever at **D**. With the car stationary and the engine idling, the main pressure should be between 41 and 42 psi (2.90 and 3.00 kg/cm²)—or between 44.0 and 45.5 psi (3.10 and 3.20 kg/cm²) beginning with Transmission No. ET 26 116.

4. Place the selector lever at **R**. With the car stationary and the engine idling, the main pressure should be between 104 and 105 psi (7.35 and 7.40 kg/cm²)—or between 112 and 118 psi (7.85 and 8.30 kg/cm²) beginning with Transmission No. ET 26 116.

5. With the car's speedometer indicating a speed above 25 mph (40 kph), floor the accelerator. During full-throttle acceleration, the main pressure should be between 83 and 84 psi (5.85 and 5.95 kg(cm²)—or between 91 and 93 psi (6.40 and 6.55

kg(cm²) beginning with Transmission No. ET 26 116.

6. After disconnecting the test gauge hose, install the plug for the pressure tap to 1.0 mkg (7 ft. lb.). Then run the engine and check the plug for leakage.

Main pressures that are higher or lower than those specified usually mean that the valve body is dirt-clogged or that the valves in the valve body are sticking. This trouble can be remedied by removing and cleaning the valve body. But while high pressures always indicate sticking valves, low pressures may also indicate a worn ATF pump or internal ATF leaks past seals, gaskets, and metal mating surfaces.

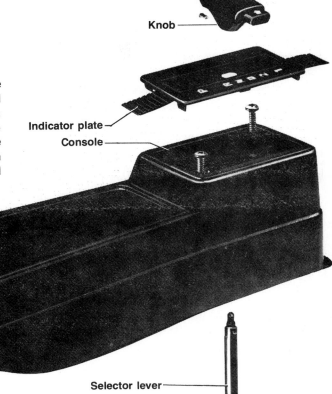

Knob

Indicator plate

Console

6

4. SELECTOR LEVER AND CABLE

The selector lever used on 1976 and later cars is similar except in detail to the selector lever used on 1975 cars. The 1975 selector lever contained the shift detents. The 1976 and later automatic transmission covered in this section of the Manual has internal detents and so the detents were eliminated from the selector lever.

The selector lever shares no parts with the gearshift lever used with the manual transmission. A cable couples the selector lever with the lever on the automatic transmission. This cable is not repairable and must be replaced as a unit if either the cable itself or the conduit is worn or damaged.

4.1 Removing and Installing Selector Lever

The entire selector lever and cable mechanism is shown in Fig. 4-1. There are minor styling differences between the 1975 selector lever console and the console shown in Fig. 4-1.

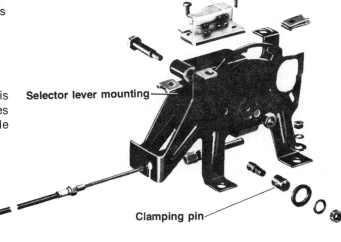

Selector lever

Selector lever mounting

Cable

Clamping pin

37-221

Fig. 4-1. Exploded view of selector lever and cable used on 1976 and later cars. 1975 unit is similar.

To remove selector lever:

1. Disconnect the battery ground strap.

2. Loosen the setscrew that holds the knob to the top of the selector lever. Then remove the knob assembly.

3. Carefully pry loose and remove the indicator plate. Then remove the screws that hold the selector lever console and remove the console.

4. Remove the four nuts and the washers that hold the selector lever assembly to the car's floorboard.

5. Loosen the nut for the cable clamping bolt so that the cable end is free to be withdrawn from the clamping pin in the lower end of the lever. Loosen the cable conduit nut so that the conduit is free from the lever mounting.

6. Disconnect the wires from the indicator light and the neutral safety switch. Then remove the selector lever assembly as a unit. If further disassembly is necessary, use Fig. 4-1 as your guide.

Installation is the reverse of removal. Before you install the console, adjust the cable as described in **4.3 Adjusting Selector Lever Cable.**

4.2 Removing and Installing Selector Lever Cable

The selector lever cable used with the transaxle covered in this section of the Manual is different from the cable installed on 1975 and earlier cars. Individual cable components, other than the rubber boot, are unavailable as replacement parts. If either the cable or its conduit is damaged, replace the cable as a unit.

To remove selector cable:

1. Loosen the setscrew that holds the knob to the top of the selector lever. Then remove the knob assembly.

2. Carefully pry loose and remove the indicator plate. Then remove the screws that hold the selector lever console and remove the console.

3. Loosen the nut for the cable clamping bolt so that the cable end is free to be withdrawn from the clamping pin in the lower end of the lever. Loosen the cable conduit nut so that the conduit is free from the lever bracket.

4. Completely free the cable and conduit from the selector lever assembly so that the cable and conduit can be pulled out from beneath the car. If necessary, loosen the nuts and raise the lever assembly slightly so that you can detach the cable.

5. Working beneath the car, remove the E-clip that holds the cable to the lever on the transaxle.

6. Loosen the locknuts that hold the cable conduit to the bracket beneath the car. Detach the cable from the transaxle; detach the conduit from the bracket. Then pull out the cable and conduit as a unit.

Installation is the reverse of removal. Following installation, adjust the cable as described in **4.3 Adjusting Selector Lever Cable.**

4.3 Adjusting Selector Lever Cable

Adjust the selector lever cable following installation of the cable or the selector lever—or whenever the correct letter or number on the indicator plate is not illuminated with the selector lever in a particular drive range.

To adjust:

1. Select **P.** If the cable is not attached to the lever, as in installing the selector lever following replacement or repair, select **P** by hand-moving the lever on the transaxle (beneath the car). Try to push the car forward and backward in order to make sure that the parking pawl has engaged inside the transmission.

2. Loosen the setscrew that holds the knob to the top of the selector lever. Then remove the knob assembly.

3. Carefully pry loose and remove the indicator plate. Then remove the screws that hold the selector lever console and remove the console.

4. Loosen the nut for the cable clamping bolt so that the cable end is free to slide in the clamping pin in the lower end of the lever.

5. Temporarily reinstall the console and the indicator plate. Move the selector lever so that the letter **P** on the indicator plate is illuminated. Then, being careful not to disturb the position of the selector lever, lift off the indicator plate and the console.

6. Tighten the nut for the cable clamping bolt, thus locking the cable end firmly to the lower end of the lever.

7. Temporarily reinstall the console and the indicator plate. Select all drive ranges in order to make sure that the lever is aligned with the correct letter or number on the indicator plate when the detents inside the transmission engage. If necessary, correct the adjustment.

8. When the adjustment is correct, install the screws that hold the console to the floorboard. Press in the indicator plate, then install the knob and tighten its setscrew.

5. AUTOMATIC TRANSMISSION ADJUSTMENTS

Aside from adjusting the selector lever cable, as described under the preceding heading, the automatic transmission covered in this section of the Manual has only two adjustments. These are adjusting the accelerator cable and adjusting the 2nd gear brake band. Accelerator and throttle cable adjustments are covered in **FUEL AND EXHAUST SYSTEMS.**

5.1 Adjusting 2nd Gear Brake Band

The 2nd gear brake band can be adjusted either with the transaxle in the car or with the transaxle removed. In either case the axis of the planetary gear system must be in a horizontal plane during adjustment, as it would be with the car on level ground. If this precaution is not observed—especially with the transaxle removed—the 2nd gear brake band may jam during adjustment. This would make necessary at least partial disassembly of the transmission in order to realign the band.

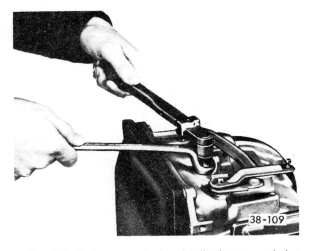

Fig. 5-1. 2nd gear brake band adjusting screw being held stationary while locknut is tightened.

To adjust:

1. Loosen the locknut for the adjusting screw. Then center the 2nd gear brake band by torquing the adjusting screw to about 1.0 mkg (100 cmkg or 87 in. lb.).

2. Loosen the adjusting screw. Then retorque it to 0.5 mkg (50 cmkg or 43 in. lb.).

3. From this setting, back the screw off exactly 2½ turns. Then, while holding the adjusting screw as shown in Fig. 5-1, tighten the locknut. Finally, torque the locknut to 2.0 mkg (14 ft. lb.).

6. SERVICING VALVE BODY AND VALVE BODY ASSEMBLY

Servicing the valve body assembly normally involves removal and cleaning, but sealing balls can be replaced with the valve body installed. (A missing ball will prevent shifting to 3rd gear.) To replace a missing sealing ball (Part No. N 25 652 2), stick a new ball to the tip of an 8-mm ($^{11}/_{32}$-in.) pin with grease. Then drive in the ball as shown in Fig. 6-1.

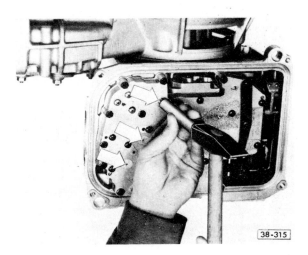

Fig. 6-1. Sealing balls (arrows) in transfer plate (bottom part) of valve body assembly. Remove ATF pan as described under next heading, then drive in new ball(s) as indicated.

6

6.1 Removing and Installing Valve Body Assembly

The valve body assembly can be removed with the transaxle in the car. The valve body assembly must also be removed for cleaning during more extensive repairs with the transaxle out of the car. Beginning with Transmission No. ET 13 038, a screen-type pump-to-valve-body ATF strainer is installed to clean the ATF coming from the pump before the fluid enters the valve body. This second strainer, which requires no routine maintenance, helps to eliminate the need to disassemble the valve body for cleaning in the event that a major transmission failure causes the ATF to be contaminated by foreign matter from broken or damaged transmission components.

To remove:

1. Drain the ATF (automatic transmission fluid). Remove the ATF pan screws. Then take off the ATF pan and the gasket.

2. Remove the screws that hold the pump pickup's ATF strainer to the valve body assembly. Remove the ATF strainer.

3. Eleven bolts hold the valve body assembly to the transmission case. Remove ten of the bolts, keeping installed the bolt indicated in Fig. 6-2—which is near the accumulator piston's spring.

4. While supporting the valve body assembly so that it does not fall, remove the eleventh bolt. Then remove the valve body assembly. Beginning with Transmission No. ET 13 038, remove the pump-to-valve-body ATF strainer.

5. Remove the accumulator cover plate, the accumulator spring, and the accumulator piston. If necessary, use circlip expanding pliers inserted into the spring recess of the piston to withdraw the piston from the transmission case.

NOTE ——

Two kinds of accumulator pistons have been installed. One kind is cast aluminum with a separate sealing ring. If you replace the sealing ring, its lip must point toward the pressure side of the piston (point away from the cover plate). The second kind of piston is stamped from sheet metal with a sealing lip permanently bonded to it. The two kinds of accumulator pistons are readily interchangeable.

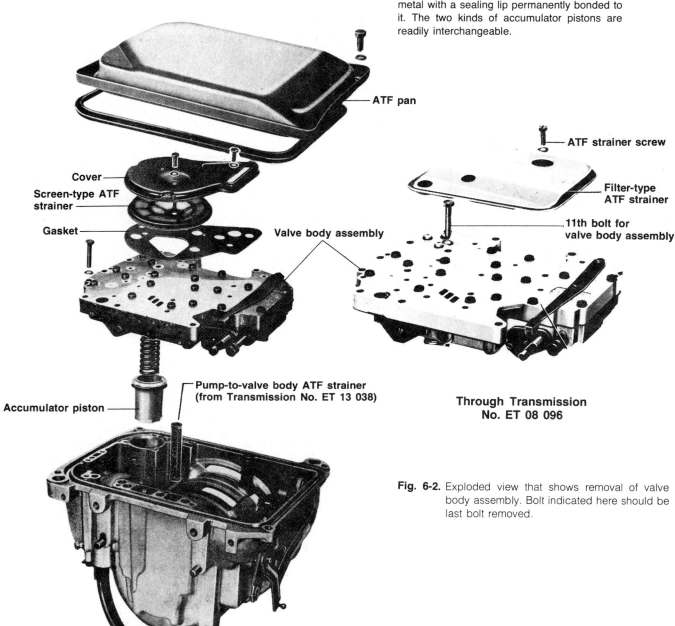

ATF pan

ATF strainer screw

Cover

Screen-type ATF strainer

Filter-type ATF strainer

Gasket

Valve body assembly

11th bolt for valve body assembly

Accumulator piston

Pump-to-valve body ATF strainer (from Transmission No. ET 13 038)

Through Transmission No. ET 08 096

Fig. 6-2. Exploded view that shows removal of valve body assembly. Bolt indicated here should be last bolt removed.

38-352

To disassemble valve body assembly:

1. Place the assembly on a clean workbench with the valve body down. Then remove the 19 Phillips head

screws that hold the valve body, the separator plate, and the transfer plate together. See Fig. 6-3.

2. Lift off the separator plate and transfer plate as a

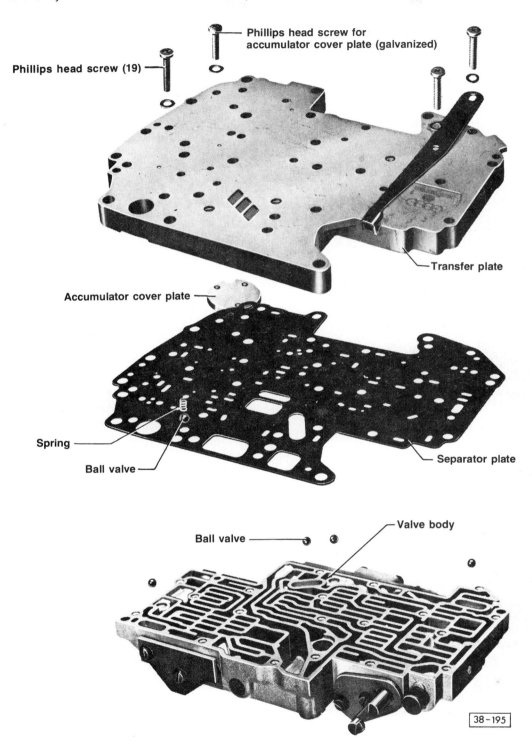

Fig. 6-3. Exploded view of valve body assembly. Ball valve locations are different beginning with Transmission No. ET 02 068.

unit—so that the ball valves in the valve body will remain in the valve body and the ball valve in the transfer plate will be kept in place by the separator plate.

3. Place the transfer plate and separator plate on the workbench with the transfer plate down. Then lift off the separator plate.

If you are replacing either the transfer plate or the separator plate with used parts from a similar transmission, the replacement must have the same markings as the original. See Fig. 6-4, Fig. 6-5, and Fig. 6-6. Do not install components from an automatic transmission that was not originally used in a car covered by this Manual.

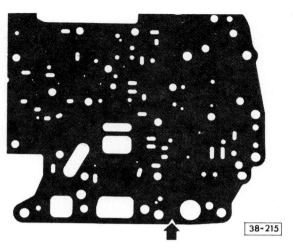

Fig. 6-6. Marking of separator plate used through Transmission No. ET 01 068. There should be only one notch at point indicated by arrow.

Assembly is the reverse of disassembly. The locations of the ball valves are given in Fig. 6-7, Fig. 6-8, and Fig. 6-9. All balls are 6 mm in diameter. Torque the Phillips head screws to 40 cmkg (35 in. lb.).

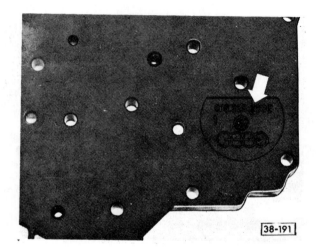

Fig. 6-4. Marking of transfer plate (arrow). For example, 010 325 283 E.

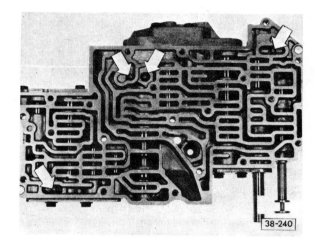

Fig. 6-7. Locations for ball valves in valve body used through Transmission No. ET 01 068, which was installed until partway through 1978 model year.

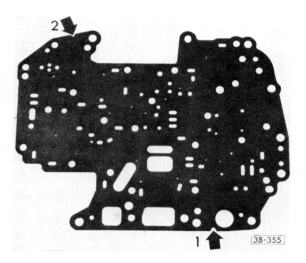

Fig. 6-5. Marking of separator plate used on latest transmissions, beginning with Transmission No. ET 02 068, which was manufactured partway through 1978 model year. There should be one notch only at arrow **1** and one notch only at arrow **2**.

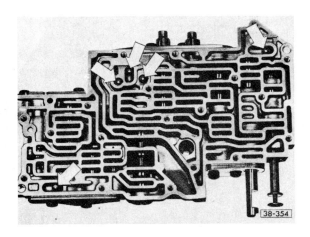

Fig. 6-8. Ball valve locations (arrows) in latest valve body, introduced in Transmission No. ET 02 068 partway through 1978 model year.

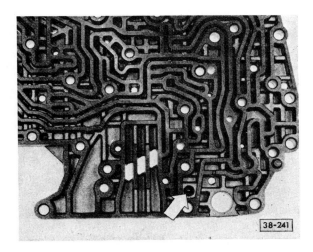

Fig. 6-9. Location for ball valve (arrow) and spring in transfer plate of valve body introduced on 1973 cars and discontinued with Transmission No. ET 01 068 manufactured partway through 1978 model year.

To install valve body assembly:

1. If you have removed the accumulator piston, lubricate its sealing ring with ATF. Then install the piston, the spring, and the cover. Torque the three Phillips head screws to 30 cmkg (26 in. lb.).

   NOTE ——

   The Phillips head screws for the accumulator cover plate are galvanized, whereas the screws that hold the valve body to the separator plate and transfer plate are not. Do not mix up the screws.

2. If you are installing a new valve body assembly, make certain that the correct code letter appears in the location indicated in Fig. 6-10 or Fig. 6-11. This letter is the only reliable indication that the valve body is suitable for a car covered by this Manual. Do not install a valve body that was designed for use in another kind of car.

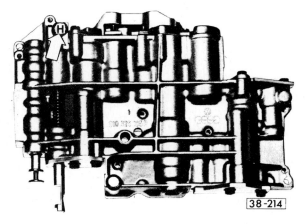

Fig. 6-10. Location of code letter (arrow) that is stamped into boss on valve body used through Transmission No. ET 01 068. Letter must be **H** on replacement valve bodies beginning with Transmission No. ET 26 116, or **L** on earlier transmissions.

Fig. 6-11. Code letter **AA** (arrow) stamped on latest valve body (Part No. 010 325 031 G) introduced partway through 1978 model year and continued on 1979 models.

3. Position the valve body assembly on the transmission case so that the manual valve and the kickdown valve are correctly engaged with their operating levers, as shown in Fig. 6-12.

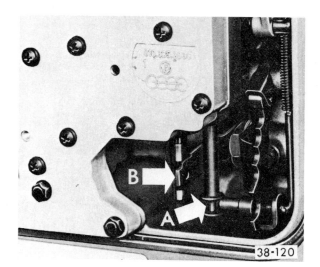

Fig. 6-12. Manual valve (arrow **A**) and kickdown valve (arrow **B**) correctly engaged with operating levers.

4. Attach the valve body assembly to the transmission case with the 11th bolt, indicated previously in Fig. 6-2. Install the 10 remaining bolts. Then, working diagonally, gradually torque all of the bolts to 40 cmkg (35 in. lb.).

5. Install the ATF strainer. Torque the screws to 30 cmkg (26 in. lb.).

> **NOTE ——**
>
> The ATF strainer used prior to Transmission No. ET 09 096 cannot be cleaned, so replace it if the ATF was dirty or contaminated or if the ATF strainer itself is obviously dirty or clogged.

6. Install the ATF pan together with a new gasket. Working diagonally, gradually torque the ATF pan bolts to 2.0 mkg (14 ft. lb.).

> **CAUTION ——**
>
> *Do not use sealer on the gasket, as any surplus may find its way into the ATF and cause the control valves to stick. Never tighten the ATF pan bolts to more than 2.0 mkg (14 ft. lb.) in an attempt to cure a leaking gasket. Overtightening will deform the pan and make it impossible to get a good seal. Always install a new gasket to correct leaks.*

7. Refill the transmission case with ATF as described in **LUBRICATION AND MAINTENANCE.**

6.2 Disassembling and Assembling Valve Body

As a rule, the valve body is disassembled only for cleaning. Unless the ATF is very dirty or contaminated by large solid particles, it usually is sufficient to immerse the complete assembly in cleaning fluid and dry it with compressed air. However, be careful not to hold the air jet so close that it moves the valves violently. This could damage the springs.

The special compartmented storage tray shown in Fig. 6-13 is very useful for disassembling and cleaning the valve body. The tray not only prevents the components from becoming mixed up, but is designed so that its cover can be locked in place and the entire tray, with the valve body components inside, can be immersed in solvent. Such a tray will also keep the springs from getting bent or stretched, which would upset their precisely calibrated tensions.

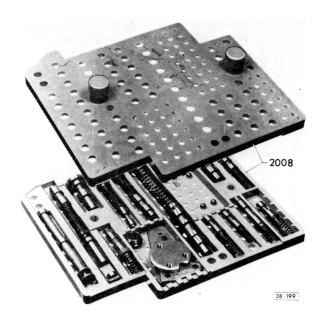

Fig. 6-13. Compartmental storage tray for valve body parts.

Fig. 6-14 and Fig. 6-15 are exploded views of the valve body. Because many of the parts look alike, it is easy to mix them up. This is especially true of the springs and some of the valves that are physically identical. Unless you keep the springs separated and marked for identification, you will have to measure each spring with a micrometer prior to reassembly in order to find its correct place. See **13. Automatic Transmission Technical Data** for spring dimensions. Used valves, which have worn to fit individual bores, must be returned to their original locations. Never install a used valve in place of some other valve that is physically identical.

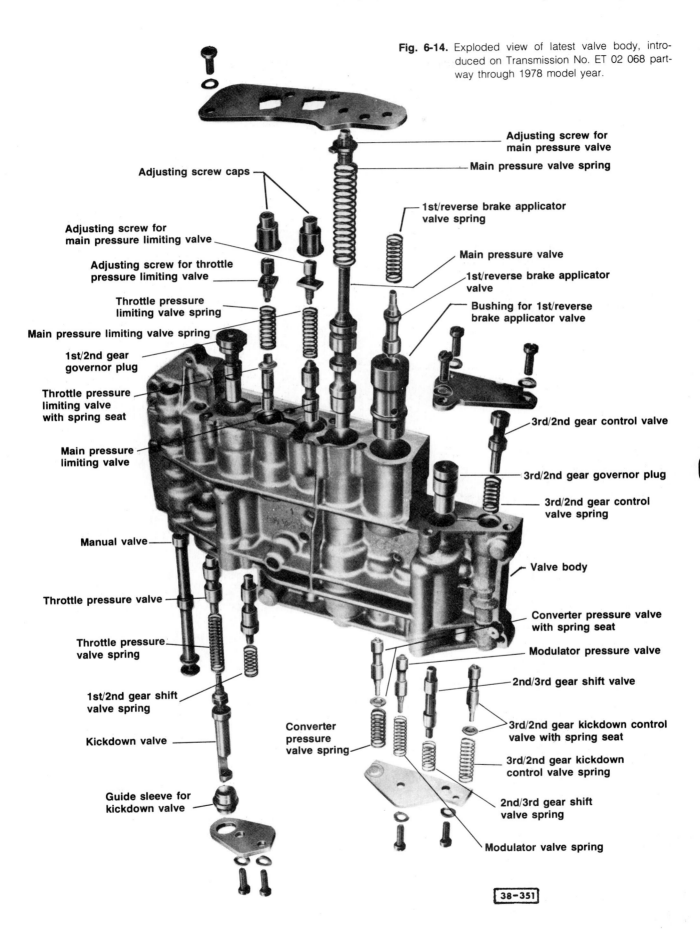

Fig. 6-14. Exploded view of latest valve body, introduced on Transmission No. ET 02 068 partway through 1978 model year.

Adjusting screw for main pressure valve

Main pressure valve spring

Adjusting screw caps

1st/reverse brake applicator valve spring

Adjusting screw for main pressure limiting valve

Main pressure valve

Adjusting screw for throttle pressure limiting valve

1st/reverse brake applicator valve

Throttle pressure limiting valve spring

Bushing for 1st/reverse brake applicator valve

Main pressure limiting valve spring

1st/2nd gear governor plug

Throttle pressure limiting valve with spring seat

3rd/2nd gear control valve

Main pressure limiting valve

3rd/2nd gear governor plug

3rd/2nd gear control valve spring

Manual valve

Valve body

Throttle pressure valve

Converter pressure valve with spring seat

Throttle pressure valve spring

Modulator pressure valve

1st/2nd gear shift valve spring

2nd/3rd gear shift valve

Kickdown valve

Converter pressure valve spring

3rd/2nd gear kickdown control valve with spring seat

3rd/2nd gear kickdown control valve spring

Guide sleeve for kickdown valve

2nd/3rd gear shift valve spring

Modulator valve spring

38-351

Fig. 6-15. Exploded view of valve body used through Transmission No. ET 01 068 (through early 1978 models).

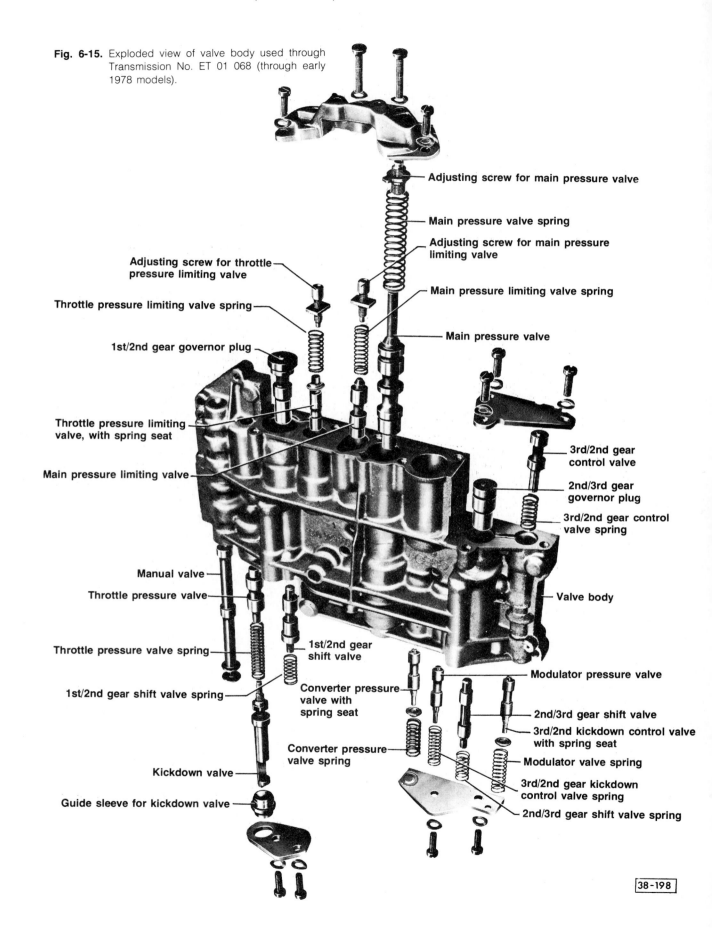

Adjusting screw for main pressure valve

Main pressure valve spring

Adjusting screw for main pressure limiting valve

Main pressure limiting valve spring

Main pressure valve

Adjusting screw for throttle pressure limiting valve

Throttle pressure limiting valve spring

1st/2nd gear governor plug

Throttle pressure limiting valve, with spring seat

Main pressure limiting valve

3rd/2nd gear control valve

2nd/3rd gear governor plug

3rd/2nd gear control valve spring

Manual valve

Throttle pressure valve

Valve body

Throttle pressure valve spring

1st/2nd gear shift valve

1st/2nd gear shift valve spring

Converter pressure valve with spring seat

Modulator pressure valve

2nd/3rd gear shift valve

3rd/2nd kickdown control valve with spring seat

Converter pressure valve spring

Modulator valve spring

Kickdown valve

3rd/2nd gear kickdown control valve spring

Guide sleeve for kickdown valve

2nd/3rd gear shift valve spring

38-198

To disassemble:

1. Remove the valve body assembly from the transmission. Then disassemble it into its three main components as described in **6.1 Removing and Installing Valve Body Assembly.**

2. Remove one of the end plates.

> **CAUTION ——**
>
> *Do not, under any circumstances, alter the settings of any of the adjusting screws located beneath the cast aluminum end plate. These screws can be adjusted properly only at the factory.*

3. One at a time, remove each valve and spring and place it in the storage tray. Use a brass rod to press out sticking or tight-fitting valves carefully.

4. One at a time, remove the other cover plates and repeat the procedure described in the preceding step.

5. Wash all parts in clean kerosene, then dry them with compressed air.

> **CAUTION ——**
>
> *Never use water to clean the valves and valve body—and never dry the parts with fluffy rags or by rubbing them against your clothing. Even a microscopic piece of lint or a small patch of rust can cause a valve to stick in its bore.*

Assembly is basically the reverse of disassembly. Clean the workbench before you start to work. Lubricate each valve with ATF as you reinstall it, then make certain that the valve moves freely of its own weight. Used valves, which will have worn to fit individual bores, must be returned to their original locations. When you install the endplates, be careful not to overtighten the screws. Doing this could easily strip the threads or distort the valve body enough to cause a valve to stick.

7. SERVICING GOVERNOR

The governor for the hydraulic control system is located beneath a round, black pressed steel cover just above and to the rear of the drive flange for the left front wheel driveshaft. The cover is held in place by two bolts.

7.1 Removing and Installing Governor

The governor can be removed with the transaxle in the car. The governor is usually removed for cleaning or for replacing worn parts. However, if a new valve body is being installed, a matching governor may be supplied with the new valve body and should be installed whether the old governor is serviceable or not.

To remove:

1. Thoroughly clean the area around the governor cover so that abrasive road dirt cannot accidentally enter the transaxle as the cover is removed.

2. Remove the two bolts and washers that hold the cover to the final drive housing. Then remove the cover and its O-ring.

3. Withdraw the governor with a clockwise twisting motion that will allow its drive gear to disengage from the helical gear on the drive pinion.

4. Inspect the thrust plate and the drive end of the shaft for wear and scoring.

> **NOTE ——**
>
> Because replacing the entire governor could possibly change the governor pressure, new governor shafts are available separately to replace those that are worn or damaged.

Governor installation is the reverse of removal. Check the oil seal and the needle bearing at the innermost end of the governor shaft bore in the final drive housing—especially if the hypoid oil is contaminated by ATF. If necessary, replace the seal, the bearing, or both, as described under the next heading.

Make sure that a new governor is the correct replacement part for the vehicle. Turn the governor as you install it so that the drive gear will engage. If the O-ring for the cover is broken or deformed, replace the O-ring. Torque the cover bolts to 1.5 mkg (11 ft. lb.).

6

7.2 Replacing Governor Oil Seal and Needle Bearing

Two kinds of governors have been used in the automatic transmissions installed on 1976 and later cars. Each kind of governor has its matching arrangement of the oil seal and the needle bearing, both of which are located in the final drive housing. The condition of the oil seal is very important. If it leaks, it will allow ATF to contaminate the hypoid oil in the final drive.

To replace the oil seal or the needle bearing, both must be taken out. Use a slide hammer and an expansion puller as shown in Fig. 7-1 to remove both the oil seal and the needle bearing race simultaneously. With care, this work can be done while the transaxle is installed in the car. You should, however, be very careful that no dirt or other foreign matter enters the transaxle.

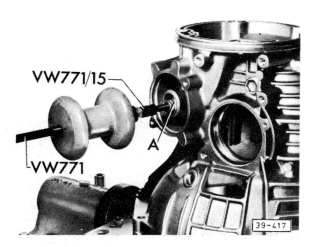

Fig. 7-1. Governor oil seal (**A**) and needle bearing race being removed from final drive housing.

Whether you install the needle bearing or the oil seal first depends on whether the transaxle has the early-type or the late-type governor. The needle bearing races and the oil seals for the two kinds of governors are not identical. Fig. 7-2 is a cross-section of the final drive housing used with the early-type governor. Notice that the oil seal is installed first, and then the needle bearing. Fig. 7-3 is a similar cross-section of the final drive housing used with the late-type governor. On these transaxles, the needle bearing race is installed first.

Whether your transaxle has the early-type or the late-type governor, it is important that you thoroughly clean the recess for the needle bearing race and the oil seal before you install either the bearing or the seal. You should be especially careful not to deform the outer part of the needle bearing race during installation because this will prevent the bearings from moving freely and can lead to early failure of the bearing and possible damage to the governor. The oil seal should not be installed with sealer or any other adhesive. There is a danger that these substances may enter the ATF, thereby causing the valves in the valve body to stick. In addition, you should, if possible, use the special tools shown in the following procedure. Otherwise it is difficult to install the seal and the bearing so that they are not angled in the bore.

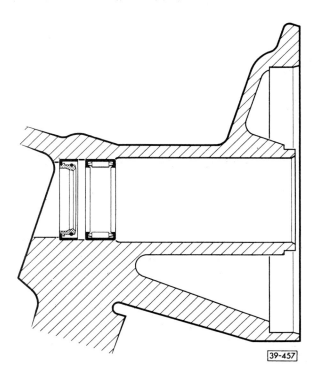

Fig. 7-2. Locations of oil seal and needle bearing by governor in early transmissions. Bearing is lubricated by ATF.

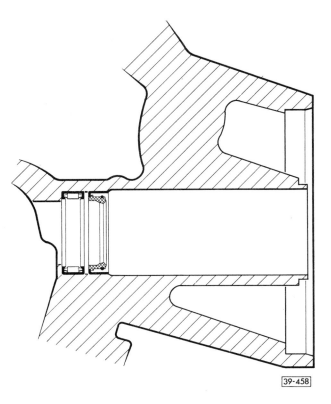

Fig. 7-3. Locations of oil seal and needle bearing for governor in late transmissions. Bearing is lubricated by hypoid oil.

Drive in the new needle bearing race as indicated in Fig. 7-4. The special tool is designed to fit snugly inside the needle bearing race, which keeps the bearing race from entering the bore at an angle. Drive in the oil seal as shown in Fig. 7-5. Make sure that the oil seal's lip points toward the governor.

CAUTION ——

Do not install the oil seal with its lip toward the final drive gears. If you do, the pressure generated by the ATF pump may force ATF past the seal and into the final drive housing of the transaxle.

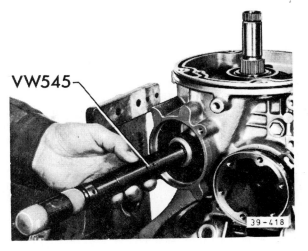

Fig. 7-4. Governor needle bearing race being driven into final drive housing.

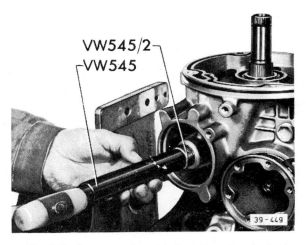

Fig. 7-5. Governor oil seal being driven into final drive housing.

7.3 Disassembling and Assembling Governor

Disassemble the governor only if it contains debris from burned clutch or brake linings. Otherwise, just dip it in solvent and dry it with compressed air.

To disassemble the governor, remove the two M 5 X 40 fillister head screws and take off the thrust plate and the housing. Then take out the transfer plate and the balance weight. The weight has been matched to the governor, so do not exchange the original weight with a weight from another governor. You can remove the centrifugal weight, the valve, the spring, and the dished washer from the pin by prying off one of the E-clips. See Fig. 7-6 or Fig. 7-7.

Before you assemble the governor, wash all parts in kerosene and dry them with compressed air. Lubricate the parts with ATF as you install them. The transfer plate and, on the late-type governor, the strainer must be installed in the positions shown in the illustrations. Make sure that the angle of the thrust plate is at the center of the housing so that the cover will bear against it.

8. SERVICING 2ND GEAR BRAKE BAND SERVO PISTON

The 2nd gear brake band servo piston can be removed with the transaxle in the car. This job is usually done to replace the piston seals and the cover O-rings. The 2nd gear brake band servo piston must also be removed before the 2nd gear brake band can be removed during disassembly of the transmission's planetary gear system.

To remove the cover and the 2nd gear brake band servo piston, first remove the circlip that retains the cover in the transmission case. Then, using a rubber mallet as shown in Fig. 8-1, tap the cover until the servo piston spring forces the piston and the cover out of the case.

Fig. 7-6. Exploded view of early-type governor used through Transmission No. ET 27 015.

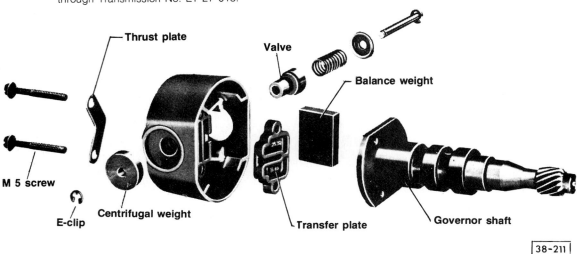

Fig. 7-7. Exploded view of late-type governor used from Transmission No. ET 27 016.

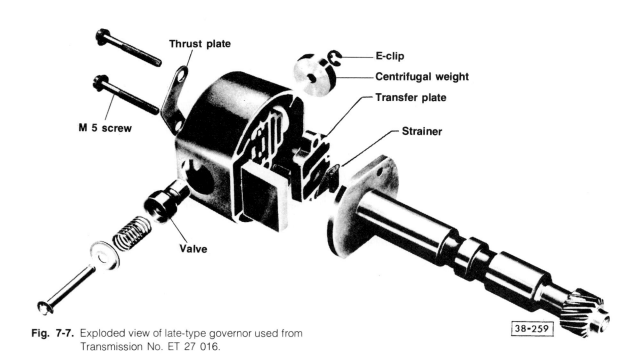

Fig. 8-1. Rubber mallet being used to tap cover for 2nd gear brake band servo piston. After a few taps, cover should pop out under pressure from spring.

sure that the piston seal lips point in the directions indicated in Fig. 8-3.

Fig. 8-3. Correct installed positions of piston seals.

You can separate the 2nd gear brake band servo piston assembly into its individual components as shown in Fig. 8-2. The piston assembly that is supplied as a replacement part is already correctly assembled and adjusted. The shim, used in adjusting the piston, should never be interchanged with a shim from another piston assembly nor replaced by an ordinary washer in the event that the shim is lost.

Dip the piston seals and the cover O-rings in ATF before you install them on the piston or the cover. Make

To install the 2nd gear brake band servo piston, first lubricate the piston with ATF and fully insert it into the cover, which should be thoroughly clean and lightly lubricated with ATF. Insert the piston with a twisting motion, being careful that the piston seals are not damaged or forced out of position.

Lubricate the cover O-rings with ATF. Insert the piston assembly and cover into the case, guiding the piston rod into engagement with the 2nd gear brake band. Then,

Fig. 8-2. Exploded view of 2nd gear brake band servo piston assembly and cover.

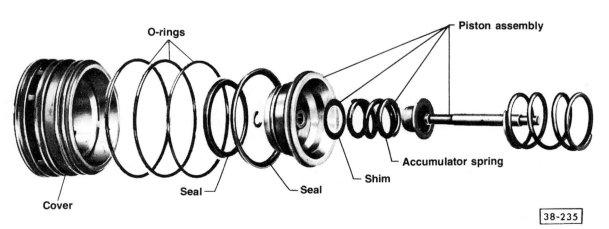

using a suitable lever as shown in Fig. 8-4, press the cover and the piston into the transmission case against spring tension until you can install the circlip. Make certain that the circlip is completely seated in the groove in the transmission case.

Fig. 8-4. Lever being used to press in cover and 2nd gear brake band servo piston assembly.

9. TRANSAXLE REMOVAL AND INSTALLATION

Please follow the instructions given for removing and installing the transaxle that are given in **AUTOMATIC TRANSMISSION (Through 1975)**. The changes in the transaxle used on 1976 and later cars are mainly internal. Only the following differences will be found in the removal and installation procedures:

1. The 1976 and later transaxle with automatic transmission has no vacuum hose or electrical wire to disconnect.

2. You must disconnect the accelerator cable and the throttle cable from the lever on the 1976 and later transaxle.

3. Following installation of the 1976 and later transaxle, you must adjust the throttle cable and the accelerator cable as described in **FUEL AND EXHAUST SYSTEMS.**

10. TORQUE CONVERTER

The torque converter (Part No. 089 323 A, Code Letter M) used on 1976 and later models is for all practical purposes identical to the torque converter used on earlier cars. Please follow the instructions given in

AUTOMATIC TRANSMISSION (Through 1975) for all service and repair operations related to the torque converter. Replacement of the torque converter seal is described in this section under **12.1 Removing and Installing Drive Piston.**

11. REPAIRING AUTOMATIC TRANSMISSION

Thoroughly clean the outside of the transaxle before you disassemble it so that dirt will not enter the hydraulic controls or the mechanical parts. Study the repair procedures on the following pages. If they require equipment that you do not have, the transaxle should be turned over to a specialist before any disassembly.

> *CAUTION* ───
>
> *If you lack the skills, the tools, or a suitable workshop for automatic transmission work, we suggest you leave these repairs to an Authorized Dealer or other qualified shop. We especially urge you to consult an Authorized Dealer before attempting repairs on a car still covered by the new-car warranty.*

11.1 Separating and Rejoining Automatic Transmission and Final Drive

A transmission stand such as the one shown in Fig. 11-1 is a great help when you must take the transaxle apart. Do not disassemble the transaxle on the shop floor as dirt and debris may get into the working parts.

Fig. 11-1. Transaxle installed on transmission repair stand.

To disassemble:

1. After cleaning the outside of the transaxle and draining the ATF, remove the torque converter. Cover the converter's hub opening in order to keep out dirt and foreign matter while the converter is removed.

   NOTE ——
   You need not drain the hypoid oil unless you intend to disassemble the final drive.

2. Withdraw the pump shaft from the center of the turbine shaft. Detach the ATF filler pipe from the transmission's ATF pan.

3. Remove the four M 8 nuts from the steel studs that hold the final drive housing to the transmission case. Separate the main parts of the transaxle as shown in Fig. 11-2.

4. Withdraw the turbine shaft from the final drive. Then cover both ends of the final drive housing in order to keep out dirt and foreign matter while the final drive is removed.

To assemble:

1. If you are installing a new transmission, the correct studs must be installed to the correct length. Fig. 11-3 and Fig. 11-4 give the stud length dimensions.

Fig. 11-3. Correct installed lengths for transmission-to-final drive studs. Dimension **a** should be 31.50 mm (1.240 in.) with stud Part No. N 900 044 01. Dimension **b** should be 138.00 mm (5.433 in.) with stud Part No. N 900 045 01.

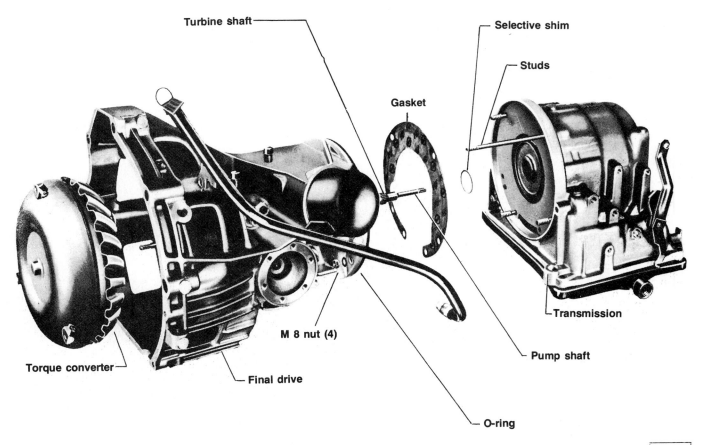

Fig. 11-2. Main parts of transaxle separated.

Fig. 11-4. Correct installed lengths for transmission mounting studs. Dimensions **a** and **b** should both be 18.00 mm (.708 in.) with stud Part No. N 014 523 2.

2. Obtain two new transmission-to-final drive gaskets. The transmission axial play must be adjusted before you assemble the transaxle—whether or not you have replaced any part other than the gaskets. Do not reuse the old gaskets.

3. To adjust the transmission axial play, you must first determine dimensions **a** and **b** as given in Fig. 11-5.

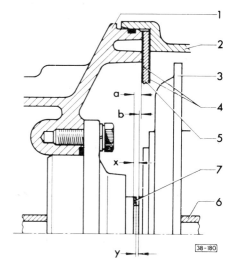

1. Final drive housing
2. Transmission case
3. Annulus (ring) gear flange
4. Gaskets
5. Separating plate
6. Drive pinion shaft
7. Selective shim

Fig. 11-5. Dimensions used in adjusting transmission axial play. Dimension **a** is distance from final drive housing to edge of oil seal race. Dimension **b** is obtained from two measurements made on the transmission. Dimension **x** is computed from dimensions **a** and **b**. Dimension **y** is correct axial play.

From these measurements, you will be able to compute dimension **x** (total axial play with no shim) and the shim thickness required to limit axial play to specifications (dimension **y**). Obtain a straightedge and a vernier depth gauge for making the measurements.

4. To determine dimension **a**, place the straightedge across the final drive housing as shown in Fig. 11-6. Using the vernier depth gauge, measure the distance from the upper surface of the straightedge to the edge of the oil seal race. Write down the measurement.

Fig. 11-6. Method of making first measurement used in determining dimension **a**.

5. Make a second measurement from the top of the straightedge to the edge of the final drive housing, as shown in Fig. 11-7. This measurement will accurately determine the thickness of the straightedge you are using. Write down the measurement.

Fig. 11-7. Method of determining the exact thickness of the straightedge when it is placed on final drive housing.

6. Subtract the straightedge thickness, as determined in step 5, from the measurement you made in step 4. The difference is dimension **a,** which should be written down for use in selecting a new shim.

CAUTION ——

Every number in the following examples is imaginary. Using them for actual adjustments could seriously damage the transmission.

Example:

Distance from top of straightedge to oil seal race	18.70 mm
Distance from top of straightedge to housing	− 8.00 mm
Dimension **a**	=10.70 mm

7. Install first a new gasket and then the separating plate and its screw in the transmission case. Finally, place a second new gasket atop the separating plate.

8. To determine dimension **b,** place the straightedge across the transmission case as shown in Fig. 11-8. Using the vernier depth gauge, measure the distance from the upper surface of the straightedge to the gasket atop the separating plate. Write down the measurement.

Fig. 11-8. Method of making first measurement used in determining dimension **b.**

9. Make a second measurement from the top of the straightedge to the shim surface on the shoulder of the annulus gear flange, as shown in Fig. 11-9. Write down the measurement.

10. Subtract the measurement made in step 9 from the distance from the top of the straightedge to

Fig. 11-9. Method of making second measurement used in determining dimension **b.**

the gasket, which you measured in step 8. The difference is dimension **b,** which should be written down for use in selecting a new shim.

Example:

Distance from top of straightedge to gasket atop separating plate	19.20 mm
Distance from top of straightedge to shim shoulder on annulus gear	−10.00 mm
Dimension **b**	= 9.20 mm

11. To compute dimension **x,** subtract dimension **b** from dimension **a.** Use dimension **x** to select the correct shim combination from **Table c.**

Example:

Dimension **a**	10.70 mm
Dimension **b**	− 9.20 mm
Dimension **x**	= 1.50 mm

Table c. Axial Play Selective Shims

Two shim thicknesses are available:		
Part No. 010 323 345 A	0.40 mm thick	
Part No. 010 323 346 A	1.20 mm thick	

Dimension x (mm)	Number and thicknesses of shims to be installed
0.23–0.84	no shim required
0.85–1.24	1 shim, 0.40 mm thick
1.25–1.64	2 shims, each 0.40 mm thick
1.65–2.04	1 shim 1.20 mm thick
2.05–2.44	1 shim 0.40 mm thick plus 1 shim 1.20 mm thick
2.45–2.84	2 shims 0.40 mm thick plus 1 shim 1.20 mm thick
2.85–3.24	2 shims 1.20 mm thick
3.25–3.64	1 shim 0.40 mm thick plus 2 shims 1.20 mm thick
3.65–3.88	2 shims 0.40 mm thick plus 2 shims 1.20 mm thick

6

12. If previously removed, install the turbine shaft in the final drive. The end of the shaft with the piston rings on it should be toward the transmission. If you have replaced the turbine shaft, make sure that it is the correct part by measuring its length as indicated in Fig. 11-10.

Fig. 11-10. Length of turbine shaft used in cars covered by this Manual. Dimension **a** is 401.7 mm (15 13/16 in.).

13. Install the correct selective shim, then install a new O-ring on the final drive housing and lubricate it with ATF.

14. Check that the piston rings on the turbine shaft are correctly seated (Fig. 11-11). Lubricate the piston rings with ATF. Then install the transmission on the final drive. Torque the four M 8 nuts to 3.0 mkg (22 ft. lb.).

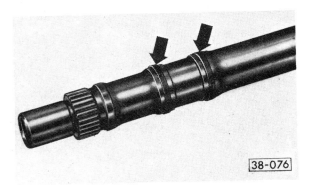

Fig. 11-11. Locations (arrows) of piston rings on turbine shaft.

15. If you are replacing the ATF pump driveshaft, make sure that you have the correct shaft by checking its length, as indicated in Fig. 11-12. Then lubricate the splines with ATF and install the pump shaft through the center of the turbine shaft.

Fig. 11-12. Length of pump shaft used in cars covered by this Manual. Dimension **a** is 453.1 mm (17 27/32 in.).

16. Make sure that the pump shaft is completely seated in the pump inside the transmission by checking the shoulder indicated in Fig. 11-13. Then install the torque converter, turning it slowly clockwise and counterclockwise so that the turbine and pump shaft splines can engage.

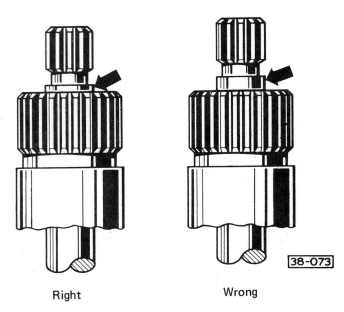

Right   Wrong

Fig. 11-13. Installation of pump shaft being checked prior to installation of torque converter. Shoulder indicated by arrows must not project more than about 2 mm (or 1/16 in.) above end of turbine shaft.

17. Install the ATF filler. Install the transaxle in the car before you refill the transmission with ATF as described in **LUBRICATION AND MAINTENANCE.**

11.2 Disassembling and Assembling Automatic Transmission

Study Fig. 11-14 carefully so that you become familiar with the names of the various parts. These names will be referred to frequently on the following pages. The illustration also shows the positions of the parts inside the transmission case.

To disassemble:

1. Mount the transmission on a stand or secure it to the workbench.

2. Remove the screw that holds the separating plate. Then remove the separating plate and the gasket.

3. Remove the annulus gear and the two thrust washers that are behind the annulus gear.

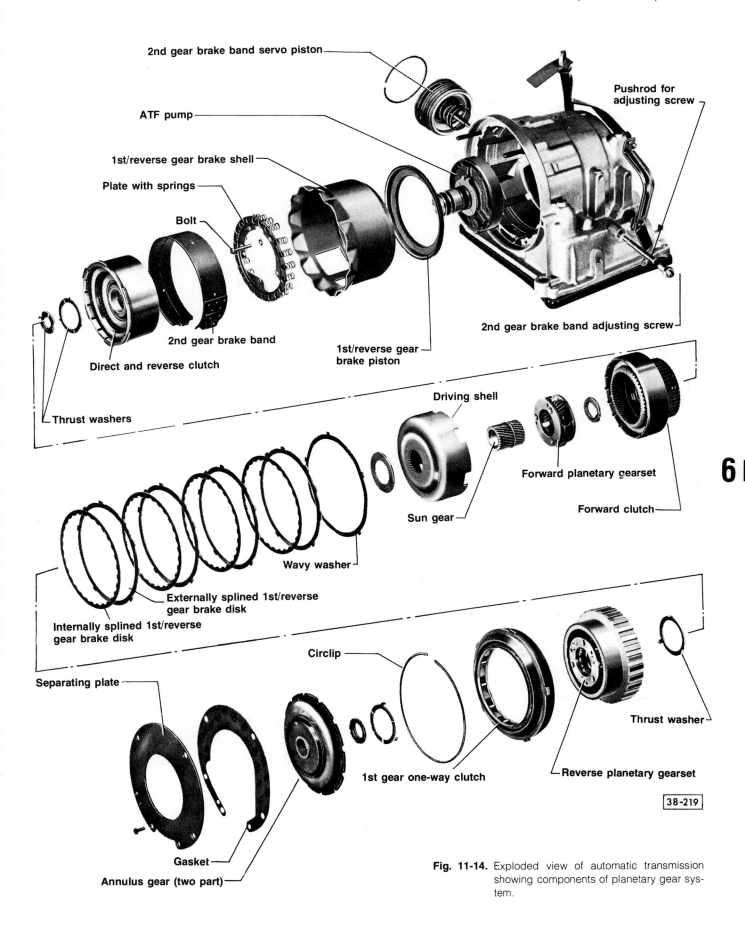

2nd gear brake band servo piston

ATF pump

1st/reverse gear brake shell

Plate with springs

Bolt

2nd gear brake band

Direct and reverse clutch

Thrust washers

Pushrod for adjusting screw

2nd gear brake band adjusting screw

1st/reverse gear brake piston

Driving shell

Sun gear

Forward planetary gearset

Forward clutch

Externally splined 1st/reverse gear brake disk

Internally splined 1st/reverse gear brake disk

Wavy washer

Separating plate

Circlip

Thrust washer

1st gear one-way clutch

Reverse planetary gearset

Gasket

Annulus gear (two part)

38-219

Fig. 11-14. Exploded view of automatic transmission showing components of planetary gear system.

4. Using a screwdriver, carefully pry the circlip out of its groove, beginning near the gap in the circlip as indicated in Fig. 11-15.

Fig. 11-15. Point (arrow) at which you should begin prying circlip out of groove.

5. Remove the 1st gear one-way clutch, the disks for the 1st/reverse gear brake, and the reverse planetary gearset.

6. Lift out the thrust washers. Then remove the sun gear, driving shell, forward planetary gearset, and forward clutch as a unit.

7. Remove the circlip for the 2nd gear brake band servo piston cover. Then, using a rubber mallet, tap the cover as shown in Fig. 11-16 until the cover and the piston pop out under spring pressure. Remove the cover and the piston assembly as a unit.

   NOTE ——
   For detailed instructions on removing, re-pairing, and installing the 2nd gear brake band servo piston, please consult **8. Servicing 2nd Gear Brake Band Servo Piston.**

8. Loosen the locknut for the 2nd gear brake band adjusting screw. Then remove the screw and locknut and withdraw the pushrod for the adjusting screw.

9. Lift out the remaining planetary gear system components that are housed in the 1st/reverse gear brake shell.

10. Take out the five bolts that hold the plate with springs and the ATF pump to the transmission case. Then lift out the plate with springs, the 1st/reverse brake shell, and the ATF pump and 1st/reverse brake piston.

Fig. 11-16. Rubber mallet being used to tap cover for 2nd gear brake band servo piston.

NOTE ——
If you wish to replace the thrust washer that is on the ATF pump, do so as illustrated in **11.3 Disassembling and Assembling ATF Pump.**

To assemble:

1. Lubricate the 1st/reverse gear brake piston with ATF, then install the piston on the ATF pump.

2. Install the ATF pump and brake piston in the transmission case as a unit. Position the pump so that the lug indicated in Fig. 11-17 is toward the top of the transmission case.

Fig. 11-17. Anti-rotation lug for thrust washer on ATF pump (arrow). Install pump so lug is toward top of transmission case.

3. If you replace the 1st/reverse gear brake shell, measure the new shell in order to determine whether it is the correct replacement part for cars covered by this Manual. See Fig. 11-18. Install the 1st/reverse gear brake shell as shown in Fig. 11-19.

Fig. 11-18. Correct 1st/reverse gear brake shell for cars covered by this Manual. Dimension **a** should be 94.9 mm ($3^{47}/_{64}$ in.).

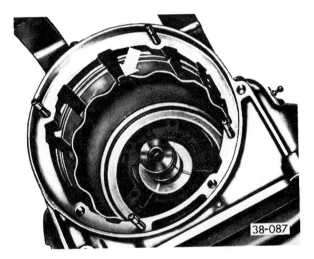

Fig. 11-19. 1st/reverse gear brake shell correctly installed. Lug (arrow) goes in groove at top of transmission case.

4. Assemble the plate with springs as indicated in Fig. 11-20. Then install the plate so that the springs contact the 1st/reverse gear brake shell and the bolt holes in the plate match those in the ATF pump.

5. Loosely install the five bolts that hold the plate with springs and the ATF pump to the transmission case. Working diagonally, gradually tighten the bolts to a final torque of 70 cmkg (61 in. lb.).

CAUTION ——

After you have torqued the bolts, temporarily insert the pump driveshaft so that you can hand-turn the pump gears. If the pump's internal parts are jammed or binding, owing to incorrect installation or overtightened bolts, severe transmission damage could result when the car's engine is started.

Fig. 11-20. Correct installation of springs on plate. If necessary, you can use vaseline as an adhesive to hold loose-fitting springs in place.

6. If you have installed a new transmission case, use an O-ring (Part No. 003 321 419), a cover (011 321 303), a clip (011 321 307), a washer (N 012 038 1), and a bolt (N 010 212 14) to seal the drilling indicated in Fig. 11-21. (The pressed-in caps used in car production from March 1978 are not installed in replacement cases and are not sold as replacement parts.)

Fig. 11-21. Drilling (arrow) correctly sealed.

7. Install new O-rings on the cover for the second gear brake band servo piston. The piston should be correctly installed inside the cover as described in **8. Servicing 2nd Gear Brake Band Servo Piston.** Lubricate the O-rings with ATF. Then press in the

cover and piston against spring tension as shown in Fig. 11-22. Install the circlip.

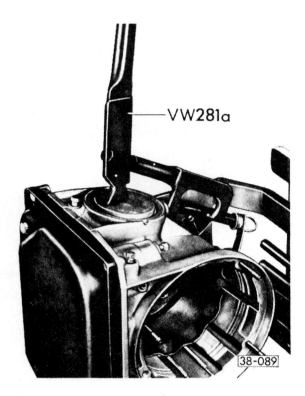

Fig. 11-22. Lever being used to press in cover and 2nd gear brake band servo piston.

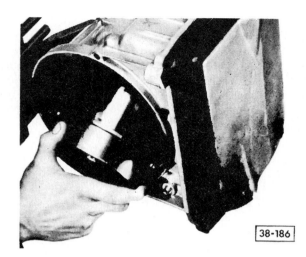

Fig. 11-23. Direct and reverse clutch being installed while transmission case is in its horizontal position.

8. Turn the transmission case to a horizontal position, so that the cover for the 2nd gear brake band servo points down. Then position the 2nd gear brake band inside the case, correctly engaging it with the servo piston. Loosely install the pushrod for the adjusting screw and the adjusting screw and locknut.

9. Keeping the case in its horizontal position, lubricate the direct and reverse clutch with ATF. Then insert the direct and reverse clutch into the transmission case, sliding it onto the neck of the ATF pump and into the 2nd gear brake band. See Fig. 11-23.

10. Torque the 2nd gear brake band adjusting screw to about 100 cmkg (87 in. lb.) in order to prevent the brake band from shifting its position. Then turn the transmission case so that its open end is uppermost.

11. Using petroleum jelly as an adhesive, stick the thrust washers to the forward clutch. Then install the forward clutch atop the direct and reverse clutch. If necessary, consult Fig. 11-14, given earlier.

12. Install the thrust washer, the forward planetary gearset, the sun gear, the drive shell, and the washer with the toothed opening. If necessary, consult Fig. 11-14, given earlier.

13. Using petroleum jelly as an adhesive, stick the thrust washer to the reverse planetary gearset. Then install the gearset.

14. Install the wavy washer. Then install four externally splined 1st/reverse gear brake disks and four internally splined 1st/reverse gear brake disks—alternately, beginning with an externally splined disk. See Fig. 11-24.

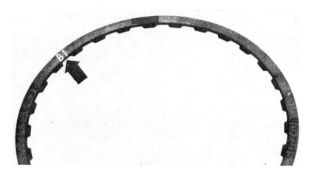

Fig. 11-24. Identification of 1st/reverse gear brake disks introduced in Transmission No. ET 02 068. This kind of disk, with **B1** marked on it (arrow), should be used only with latest-type valve body, which has a 1st/reverse brake applicator valve. Use unmarked disks with earlier valve bodies. Use tip of screwdriver to align externally splined disks with grooves in case and internally splined disks with splines on reverse planetary gearset.

15. Install the 1st gear one-way clutch, turning the planetary gearset's planet carrier as indicated in Fig. 11-25 until the one-way clutch slips into place. On new-type one-way clutches introduced in the summer of 1978, insert the retaining key shown in Fig. 11-25, pressing it in with a brass drift if necessary.

Fig. 11-25. 1st gear one-way clutch being installed. Turn planet carrier clockwise, as indicated by curved arrow. Upper arrow indicates retaining key used in latest transmissions. Earlier 1st gear one-way clutches have five lugs on outer ring.

16. Check the operation of the 1st gear one-way clutch as shown in Fig. 11-26. It should be possible to turn the planet carrier clockwise but, owing to the locking of the one-way clutch, impossible to turn the planet carrier counterclockwise.

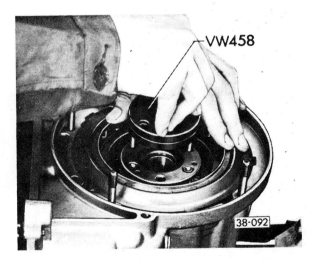

Fig. 11-26. 1st gear one-way clutch being checked. Special tool can be used to turn planet carrier.

17. Install the circlip. If all transmission components have been correctly installed, the circlip groove will be uncovered as indicated in Fig. 11-27. Do not attempt to force in the circlip on an incorrectly assembled transmission.

18. Using a new gasket, install the separating plate. Torque the screws to 70 cmkg (61 in. lb.).

NOTE ——
You should adjust the transmission end play as described in **11.1 Separating and Rejoining Automatic Transmission and Final Drive**—whether or not you have installed new parts in the transmission.

Fig. 11-27. Circlip groove (arrow) uncovered, indicating that transmission is correctly assembled.

19. Place the transmission in a horizontal position as shown in Fig. 11-28. Make sure that the 2nd gear brake band adjusting screw is torqued to 100 cmkg (87 in. lb.), then loosen the adjusting screw. Torque the screw to 50 cmkg (43 in. lb.) and, from this position, back off the screw by exactly 2½ turns. Hold the screw stationary while you torque the locknut to 2.0 mkg (14 ft. lb.). For additional information, consult **5.1 Adjusting 2nd Gear Brake Band.**

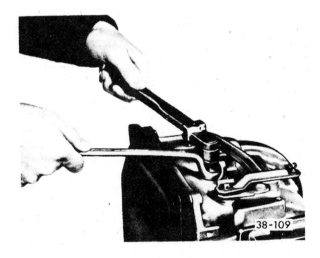

Fig. 11-28. 2nd gear brake band being adjusted. Transmission must be horizontal in order to keep band from slipping or jamming, which could make disassembling the transmission necessary.

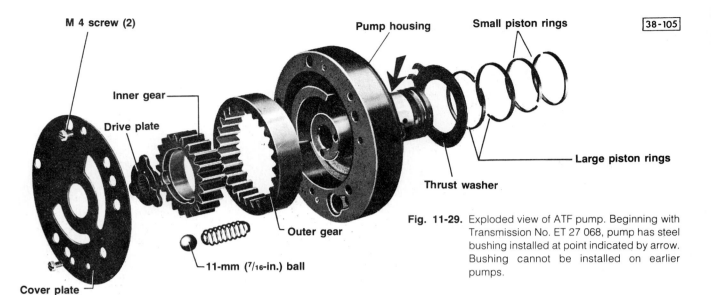

Fig. 11-29. Exploded view of ATF pump. Beginning with Transmission No. ET 27 068, pump has steel bushing installed at point indicated by arrow. Bushing cannot be installed on earlier pumps.

11.3 Disassembilng and Assembling ATF Pump

Whenever you remove the ATF pump, carefully inspect the housing, both gears, and the cover plate. Replace the pump if these parts are worn or damaged. The drive plate and the piston rings (Fig. 11-29) can be replaced individually, as can the thrust washer.

To disassemble:

1. Remove the two M 4 screws, then remove the cover plate.

2. Remove the 11-mm ($^7/_{16}$-in.) ball and the ball spring. Remove the inner gear, the outer gear, and the drive plate.

3. Using needle nose pliers as shown in Fig. 11-30, unhook the ring ends and carefully remove first the small and then the large piston rings.

4. Take off the thrust washer.

To assemble:

1. Thoroughly clean all parts in kerosene. Blow out the ATF passages with compressed air.

2. Install the thrust washer (Fig. 11-31) so that the claws on the washer point away from the piston ring grooves and are engaged on the lug on the pump housing.

3. Carefully install first the large and then the small clutch piston rings, making sure that the ring ends hook correctly.

4. After lubricating all parts thoroughly with ATF, install the gears and the drive plate—making sure that the extended hub of the drive plate is inserted into the shaft opening of the pump housing.

Fig. 11-30. Clutch piston rings being removed from ATF pump.

Fig. 11-31. Thrust washer installed on pump housing. Washer must be installed before clutch piston rings are installed.

5. Insert the ball valve spring and then the 11-mm ($^7/_{16}$-in.) ball.

6. Align the cover plate with the pump housing, then install the two M 4 screws.

7. Check that the pump gears turn freely by hand-turning them with the pump driveshaft. Check this again after the pump has been installed. If the pump's internal parts are jammed or binding, owing to incorrect assembly or installation, severe transmission damage could result when the car's engine is started.

11.4 Disassembling, Checking, and Assembling Direct and Reverse Clutch

The direct and reverse clutch is shown in an exploded view in Fig. 11-32. Familiarize yourself with the names of the parts, as they are used frequently in the disassembly and repair procedure.

To disassemble:

1. Using a screwdriver, pry out the large circlip.

2. Remove the pressure plate, the three internally splined plates, and the three externally splined plates.

3. Put the clutch on a press and force down the spring

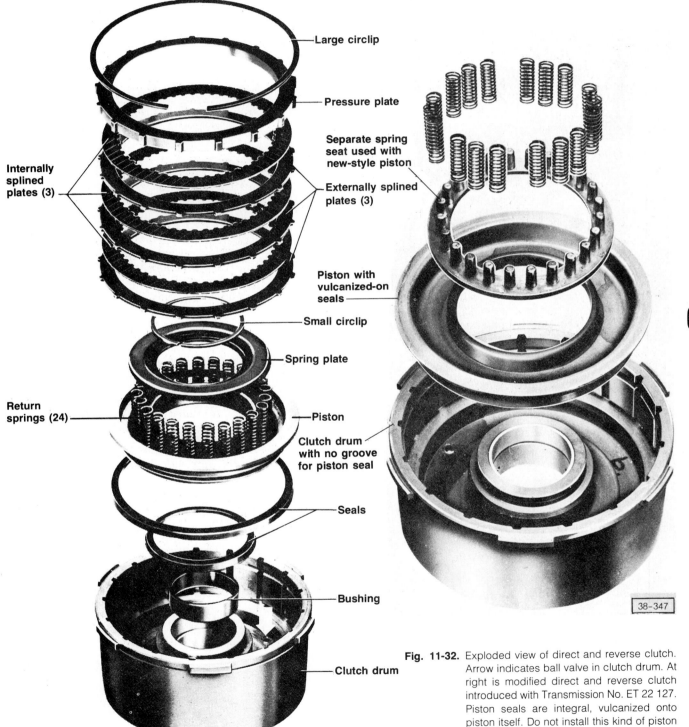

Large circlip

Pressure plate

Separate spring seat used with new-style piston

Internally splined plates (3)

Externally splined plates (3)

Piston with vulcanized-on seals

Small circlip

Spring plate

Return springs (24)

Piston

Clutch drum with no groove for piston seal

Seals

Bushing

Clutch drum

38-347

38-234

Fig. 11-32. Exploded view of direct and reverse clutch. Arrow indicates ball valve in clutch drum. At right is modified direct and reverse clutch introduced with Transmission No. ET 22 127. Piston seals are integral, vulcanized onto piston itself. Do not install this kind of piston in old-style clutch drum that has groove for separate seal.

6

plate until you can pry out the small circlip (Fig. 11-33). Then raise the press ram and remove the spring plate.

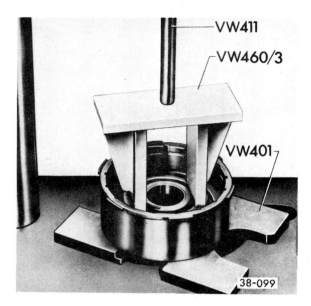

Fig. 11-33. Spring plate being pressed down so that small circlip can be removed or installed.

4. On late direct and reverse clutches with a separate spring seat, lift out the spring seat and the springs. Then remove the piston with a twisting movement. On earlier direct and reverse clutches, pull the clutch piston with return springs out of the clutch drum with a twisting movement, then remove the piston seals and the springs.

5. Using an extractor tool and the repair press, press out the clutch drum bushing as shown in Fig. 11-34.

Fig. 11-34. Clutch drum bushing being removed. Phantom drawing (dashed line) shows extractor.

To check clutch:

1. Check for wear or damage on the friction surfaces of the piston and the clutch drum and in the grooves that the externally splined clutch plates ride in.

> **NOTE ——**
>
> If you replace the clutch drum, make certain that you obtain the correct replacement part by measuring dimension **a** given in Fig. 11-35.

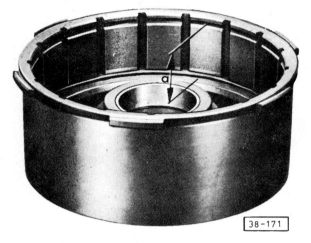

Fig. 11-35. Identification of direct and reverse clutch drum for cars covered by this Manual. Dimension **a** should be 27 mm ($1^1/_{16}$ in.).

2. Check the ball valve for freedom of movement. Make sure that the drilling is clear.

3. Inspect the externally splined plates. If any plate is scored or has radial grooves, replace the plate. Plates that are merely discolored can be reused.

4. Inspect the internally splined plates. Replace any plate that is worn, damaged, or burned.

5. Inspect the springs. Replace springs that are broken or distorted.

To assemble:

1. If you are installing new internally splined plates, soak them in ATF for at least 15 minutes before you install them. Use only plates with lining markings such as those shown in Fig. 11-36.

Fig. 11-36. Pattern on surface of internally splined direct and reverse clutch plates. Do not install plates with a different pattern of markings.

2. Using the setup shown in Fig. 11-37, press in a new clutch drum bushing. On clutch drums with a 13-mm (or ½-in.) bushing recess (used through Transmission No. ET 10 016), press in the bushing until it is flush with the hub of the drum. On clutch drums with a 14-mm (or 9/16-in.) bushing recess (used from Transmission No. ET 10 017), press in the bushing until it is 1.70 mm (.067 in.) below the hub surface, as shown in Fig. 11-38.

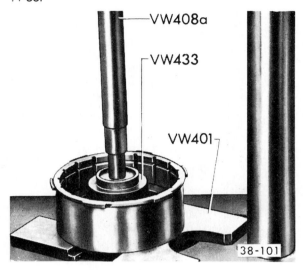

Fig. 11-37. New clutch drum bushing being pressed in.

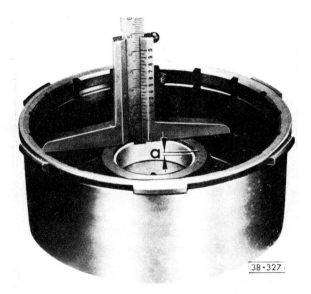

Fig. 11-38. Bushing installed in new-type clutch drum. Dimension **a** is 1.70 mm (.067 in.). You can use old bushing to press in new bushing, after scribing a line 1.70 mm (.067 in.) from edge of old bushing. Press in until line is even with hub surface, then remove old bushing with pliers.

3. Install new piston seals. The seal lips should point into the drum toward the source of hydraulic pressure.

4. Place a stiff plastic sheet in the clutch drum as shown in Fig. 11-39. Lubricate the seals with ATF, then insert the piston into the drum with a twisting motion.

5. If the piston has vulcanized-on seals, install the separate spring seat. Then, on all kinds of pistons, install the return springs and the spring plate. Using the repair press, press down the spring plate until you can snap the small circlip into its groove. See Fig. 11-31 given earlier.

Fig. 11-39. Plastic sheet used to prevent damage to seals during piston installation. Insert piston with twisting motion (arrow). Clutch shown is not for a car covered by this Manual.

6

NOTE ——

If you have installed the modified piston, which has been factory-installed beginning with Transmission No. ET 28 016, you must also install the new-type springs (Part No. 010 323 129 A) that are 24 mm long. (The old-type springs, Part No. 010 323 129, are 26 mm long.) The new-type piston can be identified by checking dimension **a**, given in Fig. 11-40.

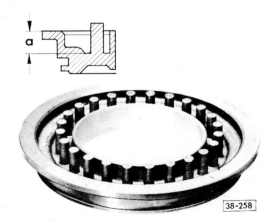

Fig. 11-40. Piston installed beginning with Transmission No. ET 28 016. Dimension **a** is 12 mm. On pistons factory-installed in earlier transmissions, dimension **a** is 14 mm.

6. Install the internally splined and the externally splined plates—alternately, beginning with an externally splined plate.

7. Install the pressure plate and the thinnest available circlip (Part No. 010 323 157 A). Then, using feeler gauges in various combinations, measure the clearance between the pressure plate and the circlip, as shown in Fig. 11-41. If the clearance is greater or smaller than 2.05 to 2.50 mm (.081 to .098 in.), select a different circlip from **Table d** that will bring the clearance within this range.

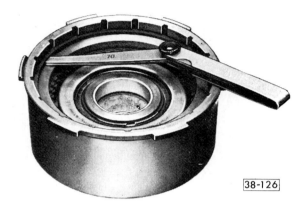

38-126

Fig. 11-41. Clearance between circlip and pressure plate being measured with feeler gauges.

Table d. Available Large Circlips for Direct and Reverse Clutch

Large circlip thickness	Part Number
1.50 mm (.059 in.)	010 323 157 A
1.70 mm (.067 in.)	010 323 157 B
2.00 mm (.079 in.)	010 323 157
2.30 mm (.091 in.)	010 323 157 C
2.50 mm (.098 in.)	010 323 157 D

8. Install the correct circlip. Then recheck the clearance in order to make certain that no mistake has been made.

11.5 Disassembling, Checking, and Assembling Forward Clutch

The forward clutch transmits torque from the torque converter's turbine to the forward planetary gearset and to the sun gear. Fig. 11-42 gives an exploded view of the forward clutch.

Fig. 11-42. Exploded view of forward clutch. Arrow indicates location of ball valve.

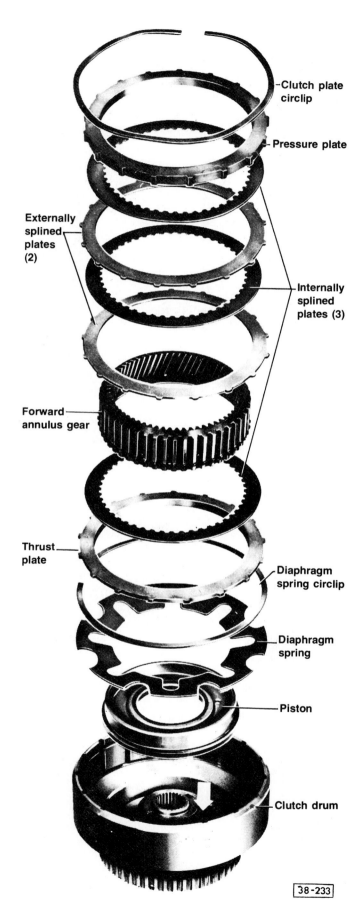

Clutch plate circlip

Pressure plate

Externally splined plates (2)

Internally splined plates (3)

Forward annulus gear

Thrust plate

Diaphragm spring circlip

Diaphragm spring

Piston

Clutch drum

38-233

To disassemble:

1. Using a screwdriver, pry out the clutch plate circlip. Then remove the pressure plate, the forward annulus gear, the internally splined and the externally splined clutch plates, and the thrust plate.

2. Carefully pry out the diaphragm spring circlip. Remove the diaphragm spring.

3. Either pull out the piston or expel it by injecting compressed air.

> **NOTE** ——
> The forward clutch piston sealing lips are vulcanized to the piston. Replace the entire piston if there is leakage past the sealing lips or if the lips are obviously worn or damaged.

To check clutch:

1. Shake the drum. If the drilling is clear, you should hear the ball valve rattle. If not, clean the drilling. Replace faulty drums (the ball valve is not replaceable separately).

2. Check the diaphragm spring. When the piston is installed, the spring should reach at least to the lower edge of the circlip groove.

3. Inspect the externally splined plates. Replace any plate that is scored or has radial grooves. Plates that are merely discolored can be reused.

4. Inspect the internally splined plates. Replace any plate that is worn, damaged, or burned.

To assemble:

1. If you are installing new internally splined plates, soak them in ATF for at least 15 minutes before you install them. Use only plates with lining markings such as those shown in Fig. 11-43.

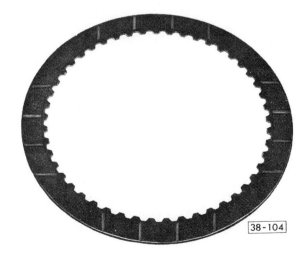

Fig. 11-43. Pattern on surface of internally splined forward clutch plates used on cars covered by this Manual. Do not install plates with a different pattern of markings.

2. If you are installing a new clutch drum, check dimension **a**, given in Fig. 11-44, to make sure that you have obtained the correct replacement part.

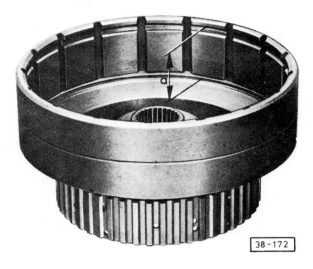

Fig. 11-44. Position of circlip groove on forward clutch drum used on cars covered by this Manual. Dimension **a** should be 26.2 mm (1¹/₃₂ in.).

3. Lubricate the piston's sealing lips with ATF. Install the piston in the clutch drum with a twisting motion—being careful not to damage the sealing lips.

4. Install the diaphragm spring so that the convex side is toward the piston. To retain the diaphragm, use snap ring Part No. 010 323 157 which is 2.03-mm thick.

> **NOTE** ——
> The diaphragm spring should be under some tension when the diaphragm spring circlip is installed—and it should not be easy to snap the circlip into its groove. If inserting the circlip does not put the diaphragm spring under tension, replace the diaphragm spring.

5. Install the thrust plate. If one side is chamfered, install the chamfered side toward the diaphragm spring.

6. Install one internally splined plate. Then install the forward annulus gear so that the short splines beneath its retaining ridge are engaged in the installed internally splined plate.

7. Install (1) an externally splined plate, (2) an internally splined plate, (3) another externally splined plate, and (4) an internally splined plate—in that order.

8. Install the pressure plate and the pressure plate circlip (Part No. 010 323 159 B). Then, using the

6

setup shown in Fig. 11-45, measure the forward clutch end play. Move the annulus gear up and down so that the dial indicator will show the play between the pressure plate and the pressure plate circlip.

Fig. 11-45. Forward clutch end play being measured with dial indicator. Move annulus gear up and down as indicated by double arrow.

9. If the end play measured in step 8 is not between 0.50 and 0.90 mm (.020 and .035 in.), select a new pressure plate from **Table e** that will bring the end play within the prescribed range.

Table e. Available Forward Clutch Pressure Plate Thicknesses

Pressure plate thickness	Part Number
6.00 mm (.236 in.)	010 323 253 F
6.40 mm (.252 in.)	010 323 253 A
6.80 mm (.268 in.)	010 323 253 B
7.20 mm (.283 in.)	010 323 253 C
7.60 mm (.299 in.)	010 323 253 D

11.6 Disassembling and Assembling 1st Gear One-way Clutch

Fig. 11-46 is an exploded view of the 1st gear one-way clutch. Partway through the 1978 model year, a new outer ring was introduced. The new ring has a retaining key (Fig. 11-47) instead of five integral lugs on its periphery. The ring with the key cannot be installed in earlier transmission cases. To disassemble the one-way clutch, first remove the rollers and their springs. Then remove the circlips. Using a plastic hammer, carefully drive the cage out in the direction indicated by the arrow in Fig. 11-46.

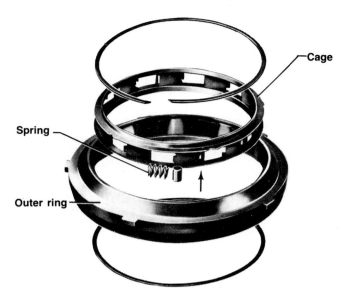

Fig. 11-46. Exploded view of 1st gear one-way clutch.

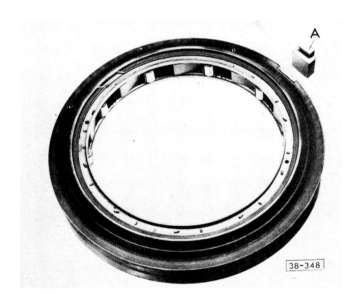

Fig. 11-47. Outer ring with retaining key (**A**), as installed in transmissions built since early summer of 1978.

To assemble:

1. If you replace either the cage or the outer ring, check the markings on the original parts in order to determine the correct replacement part. (Beginning with Transmission No. NF 03 095, the cage seat diameter of the outer ring is decreased) Fig. 11-48 shows the markings on the late-type parts.

2. Install the lower circlip in the groove of the outer ring (Fig. 11-49).

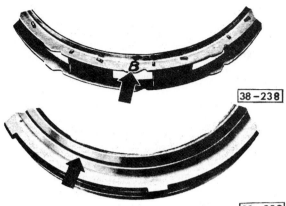

Fig. 11-48. Markings on late-type cage and outer ring. Cage with "B" (top arrow) can be used with both early-type and late-type outer rings. However, clutch will not lock properly if early-type cage (without "B" is installed in late-type outer ring marked with groove (bottom arrow).

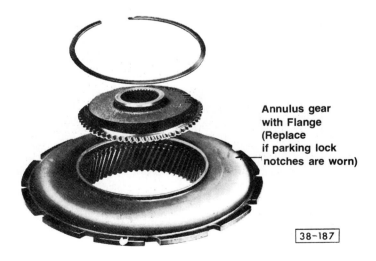

Fig. 11-49. Circlip correctly installed in groove of outer ring. Arrow indicates gap in ring.

3. Heat the outer ring to 150° to 200°C (or 300° to 390°F). Use an oven or a hotplate that has an automatic temperature control.

NOTE ——

It may not be necessary to heat early-type outer rings, owing to their larger inside diameter.

4. Grip the upper shoulder of the cage with two pairs of pliers. Quickly place the cool cage in the heated outer ring, as indicated in Fig. 11-50.

CAUTION ——

The heat from the outer ring will quickly transfer to the cage, causing the cage to stick inside the outer ring. If the cage is not correctly located against the lower circlip and inside the outer ring, do not try to press it into position after the cage has stuck. Instead, carefully knock out the cage, allow it to cool down, then start over again.

5. Install the upper circlip.

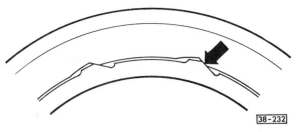

Fig. 11-50. Cage correctly positioned in outer ring. Cage must rest against lower circlip. Short sides of lugs on cage must be firmly against ramps of outer ring, as indicated by arrow.

6. Install the rollers and the springs—making sure that the springs are positioned as shown in Fig. 11-51.

Fig. 11-51. Rollers and springs correctly installed in 1st gear one-way clutch.

11.7 Disassembling and Assembling Annulus Gear (two part)

Fig. 11-52 is an exploded view of the annulus gear that engages the planet gears of the reverse planetary gearset. The two-part gear should be disassembled only if it is necessary to replace one of the components. If you replace the circlip, be sure to obtain the correct replacement part (Part No. 090 323 369).

Annulus gear
with Flange
(Replace
if parking lock
notches are worn)

Fig. 11-52. Exploded view of annulus gear (two part). Disassembly and assembly require only the removal or installation of the circlip.

11.8 Disassembling and Assembling Transmission Internal Linkage

Fig. 11-53 is an exploded view of the transmission's internal linkage. Whenever you disassemble the automatic transmission, check the condition of the parking lock pawl and the detent notches of the selector segment of the manual valve operating lever. Replace worn or damaged parts.

Assembling Parking Lock

In assembling the parking lock mechanism, check the rollers on the parking lock operating lever for ease of movement and freedom from wear. The spring for the parking lock pawl should be installed so that it will retract the parking lock pawl from engagement with the notches in the periphery of the annulus gear flange.

To prevent ATF leaks, the cylindrical end of the pin for the parking lock pawl must be installed flush with the surface of the transmission case. Check the operation of the parking lock mechanism before you install the valve body assembly.

Assembling Operating Lever and Kickdown Lever Linkages

You should install new O-rings during the installation of the levers and shafts. Torque the large nut to 2.0 mkg (14 ft. lb.); torque the small nut to 1.5 mkg (11 ft. lb.). The locking bolt should be torqued to 40 cmkg (35 in. lb.) and the M 8 bolt to 2.0 mkg (14 ft. lb.). Install the operating lever for the kickdown valve so that it is angled toward the center of the transmission, as shown in Fig. 11-54.

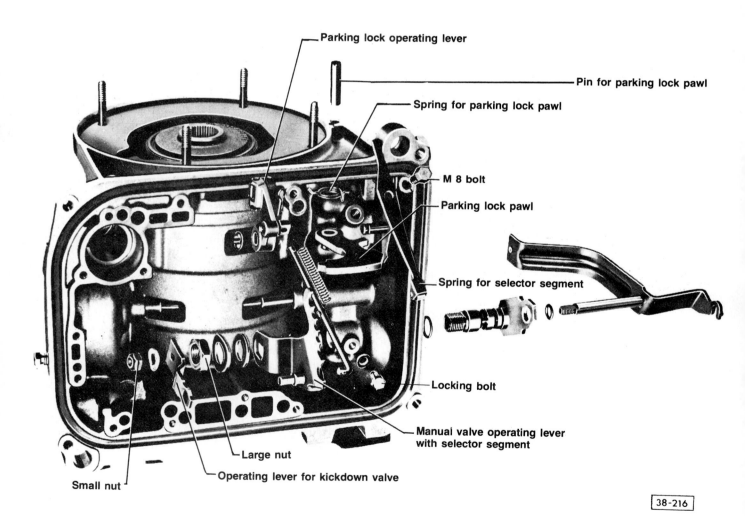

38-216

Fig. 11-53. Exploded view of transmission internal linkage. Valve body assembly must be removed for access to these parts.

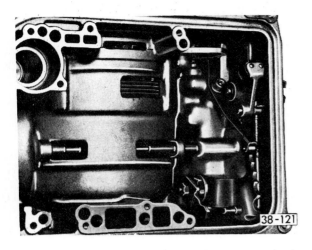

Fig. 11-54. Operating lever for kickdown valve correctly installed.

12. FINAL DRIVE

Fig. 12-1 illustrates the disassembly of the final drive used on 1976 and later cars with automatic transmissions. As mentioned in **1. General Description,** the ring and pinion gearset is not interchangeable with the gearset used on 1973 through 1975 cars. However, the gear ratio is the same as on 1975 cars; namely, 3.91:1, with 11 teeth on the drive pinion and 43 teeth on the ring gear.

The change in ring and pinion gearsets is more fundamental than a change in the gear ratio. The drive pinion head meshes with the front edge of the ring gear on 1976 and later cars whereas, on earlier models, it meshes with the rear edge of the ring gear.

Because of the change in the location of the drive pinion head, the S_3 shim is now located at the front of the drive pinion and the S_4 shim is located at the rear. These

6

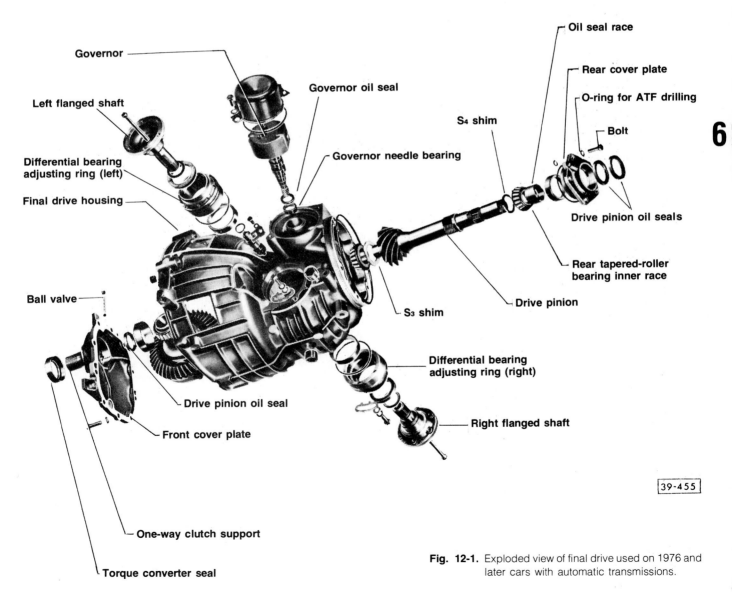

Fig. 12-1. Exploded view of final drive used on 1976 and later cars with automatic transmissions.

selective shims can be replaced only with the help of special precision measuring equipment. The adjusting rings also require special precision equipment for correct adjustments.

Covered in this section of the Manual are only the jobs that require working procedures different from those used on the final drive of 1973 through 1975 cars. To help you locate the necessary supplementary instructions given in **AUTOMATIC TRANSMISSION (Through 1975),** you will find cross references given under some of the following headings.

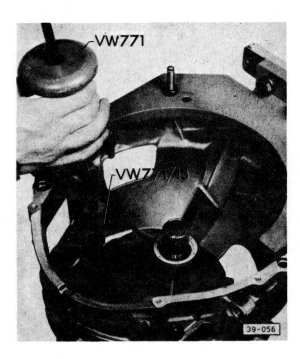

Fig. 12-2. Front cover plate being removed.

12.1 Removing and Installing Drive Pinion

The drive pinion is a matched pair with the ring gear, so the ring and pinion must be replaced as a unit. If you intend to replace the final drive housing, either of the cover plates, one or both of the tapered-roller bearings, or the ring and pinion gearset, please read **13. Adjusting Final Drive** before you undertake any disassembly.

To remove drive pinion:

1. Remove the transaxle from the car. Then separate the transmission from the final drive as described in **11.1 Separating and Rejoining Transmission and Final Drive.** Take out the retaining bolt and remove the speedometer drive. Remove the governor.

2. Remove the bolts that hold the front cover plate inside the final drive housing. Use a slide hammer to pull off the cover as shown in Fig. 12-2.

3. Remove the five bolts that hold the rear cover plate to the final drive housing. Then pull off the rear cover plate.

4. Remove the drive pinion through the front of the final drive housing.

To install:

1. If you have replaced the final drive housing, either of the cover plates, either of the tapered-roller bearings, or the ring and pinion gearset, select and install new S_3 and S_4 shims as described in **13. Adjusting Final Drive.**

2. Install the drive pinion and its bearings in the final drive housing so that the teeth of the drive pinion are loosely engaged with the teeth of the ring gear.

3. Install a new O-ring on the rear cover plate. Lubricate the O-ring and the rear tapered-roller bearing with hypoid oil.

4. Install a new small O-ring for the ATF drilling. If necessary, you can use vaseline as an adhesive to hold the O-ring to the final drive housing until the rear cover plate is installed.

5. Install the conical plastic guide sleeve over the oil seal race of the drive pinion, as shown in Fig. 12-3. Install the rear cover plate. Then install the five bolts to a torque of 2.5 mkg (18 ft. lb.).

6. Lubricate the front tapered-roller bearing with hypoid oil. Coat the bolt flange of the front cover

plate with oil resistant sealer. Then install the front cover. Torque the bolts to 2.5 mkg (18 ft. lb.).

CAUTION ——

Apply the sealer sparingly. There are ATF drillings in the front cover plates used on 1976 and later transaxles. If sealer enters the ATF drillings, it may cause the automatic transmission's control valves to stick.

Fig. 12-3. Rear cover plate being installed. Tool 2058 is plastic guide sleeve. Arrow indicates location of small O-ring for ATF drilling.

7. Install the speedometer drive and torque the retainer bolt to 1.0 mkg (7 ft. lb.). Install the governor. Torque the cover bolts to 1.5 mkg (11 ft. lb.).

8. Install the transmission on the final drive as described in **11.1 Separating and Rejoining Transmission and Final Drive.** Then install the transaxle in the car.

Replacing Pinion Bearings and Oil Seals

If you replace either pinion bearing, you must select new S_3 and S_4 shims as described in **13. Adjusting Final Drive** before you install the tapered-roller bearing inner races on the drive pinion. You can replace the pinion oil seals without replacing the bearings but, if you also replace the bearings, adjust the final drive before you install the new oil seals.

To replace the torque converter seal, use a cold chisel to drive it off the front cover, as indicated in Fig. 12-4. Install the new torque converter seal as shown in Fig. 12-5.

To replace the drive pinion oil seal that is in the front cover plate, carefully pry it out using a screwdriver or

other suitable tool. Then drive in the new oil seal as indicated in Fig. 12-6.

Fig. 12-4. Torque converter seal being removed from front cover plate.

Fig. 12-5. Torque converter seal being installed.

6

Fig. 12-6. Drive pinion oil seal being installed in front cover plate.

There are two drive pinion oil seals in the rear cover plate. Press the seals out one at a time using an expansion tool, as indicated in Fig. 12-7.

Fig. 12.7. One of two oil seals being pressed out of rear cover plate. Tool US 1037 is at **A**.

The first drive pinion oil seal should be driven as shown in Fig. 12-8. The open side of this seal should be toward the final drive gears when the cover is installed. The second drive pinion oil seal should be driven in as shown in Fig. 12-9. The open side should be toward the transmission when the cover is installed.

Fig. 12-8. First drive pinion oil seal being driven in—with seal's open side toward final drive gears.

Fig. 12-9. Second drive pinion oil seal being driven in—with seal's open side toward transmission.

An expansion mandril can be used to press the front tapered-roller bearing outer race out of the front cover plate (Fig. 12-10). Press in the new outer race as shown in Fig. 12-11.

CAUTION ——

If you remove both pinion bearing outer races at the same time, be careful not to mix them up. If either race is installed in the wrong cover plate, the bearing may make noise or fail.

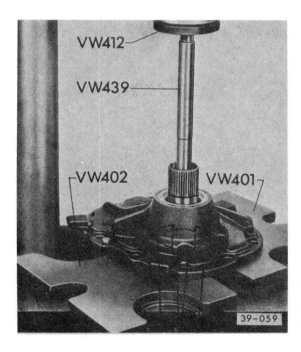

Fig. 12-10. Tapered-roller bearing outer race being pressed out of front cover plate.

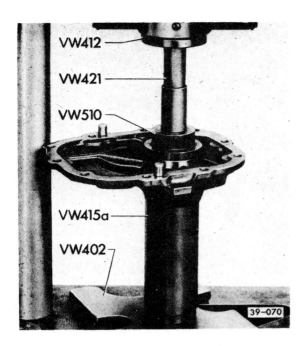

Fig. 12-11. Tapered-roller bearing outer race being pressed into front cover plate.

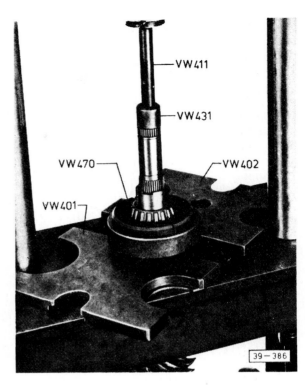

Fig. 12-12. Drive pinion being pressed simultaneously out of tapered-roller bearing inner race and oil seal race.

To remove and install the tapered roller bearing outer race that is in the rear cover plate, use the same tools as shown previously for removing and installing the tapered-roller bearing outer race that is in the front cover plate. As mentioned in the preceding CAUTION, you should be careful not to intermix used outer races that have been installed in the front and the rear cover plates.

You will need a split collet support, such as the one shown in Fig. 12-12, in order to press the drive pinion out of the front or the rear tapered-roller bearing inner race. If you do not intend to replace any parts that make it necessary to adjust the final drive, write down the number and thicknesses of the original S_3 and S_4 shims.

CAUTION ——

If you remove both pinion tapered-roller bearing inner races at the same time, be careful not to mix them up. If their locations are reversed, the bearings may make noise or fail.

If you have replaced any part that makes it necessary to adjust the final drive, select new S_3 and S_4 shims. Otherwise, install the original number and thicknesses of S_3 and S_4 shims on the drive pinion. Heat the pinion tapered-roller bearing inner races and the oil seal race to approximately 100°C (212°F) in a pan of oil placed in a larger pan of boiling water. Then press the bearing races onto the drive pinion as shown in Fig. 12-13.

6

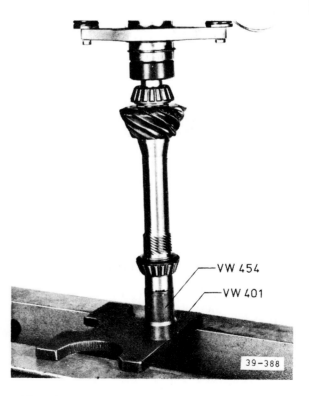

Fig. 12-13. Drive pinion being pressed simultaneously into tapered-roller bearing inner race and oil seal race.

12.2 Removing and Installing Differential

The ring gear, which is mounted on the differential, is a matched pair with the drive pinion, so the ring and pinion must be replaced as a unit. If you intend to replace the final drive housing, either of the cover plates, one or both of the differential bearings, one or both of the differential bearing adjusting rings, the differential housing, or the ring and pinion gearset, please read **13. Adjusting Final Drive** before you undertake any disassembly.

To remove differential:

1. Remove the drive pinion as described in **12.1 Removing and Installing Drive Pinion.**

2. Remove the socket-head screws that are in the centers of the left and right flanged shafts. Then, being careful that the flanged shaft splines do not damage the oil seals, pull the flanged shafts out of the final drive. Remove the flanged shaft shims and store each shim with its own flanged shaft.

3. Using a depth micrometer, measure the depths to which the left and the right adjusting rings are screwed into the final drive housing. Write down each measurement—clearly indicating to which adjusting ring it applies. Then, using a scriber, carefully mark the positions of the left and the right adjusting rings in the final drive housing.

4. Remove the bolts and the lockplates from the adjusting rings. Then remove the adjusting rings.

5. Lift up the differential, then tilt it and remove it through the front of the final drive housing.

To install:

1. If you have replaced the ring and pinion gearset, the differential housing, the final drive housing, one or both of the differential bearings, or one or both of the adjusting rings, adjust the final drive as described in **13. Adjusting Final Drive.**

2. Position the differential inside the final drive housing. The ring gear should be toward the right side of the housing.

3. Install new O-rings on the adjusting rings, then coat the O-rings and the threads with multipurpose grease.

4. If you have made no repair that requires final drive adjustment, lubricate the tapered-roller bearings with hypoid oil. Then install the adjusting rings to their original depths and align the marks you scribed on the adjusting rings with the marks you scribed on the final drive housing.

5. Install the lockplates. Torque the bolts to 1.0 mkg (7 ft. lb.).

6. If you have replaced the differential housing, the differential housing cover, a differential sidegear, a differential sidegear large thrust washer, or a flanged shaft, select new flanged shaft shims. See **13.3 Adjusting Flanged Shaft Axial Play.** Then install the correct shims and the flanged shafts.

7. Install the socket-head bolts in the centers of the flanged shafts. Torque the bolts to 2.5 mkg (18 ft. lb.).

8. Install the drive pinion as described in **12.1 Removing and Installing Drive Pinion.**

12.3 Disassembling and Assembling Differential

To disassemble and assemble the differential, follow the instructions given under heading **11.3** in **AUTOMATIC TRANSMISSION (Through 1975).** Though the ring and pinion gearset is different on 1976 and later cars, the differential components remain unchanged.

12.4 Replacing Speedometer Drive and Starter Drive Bushing

To replace either the speedometer drive or the starter drive bushing, please follow the instructions given under heading **11.4** in **AUTOMATIC TRANSMISSION (Through 1975).** The additional instructions given there for replacing the governor bearings and the governor oil seal should not be used in repairing a 1976 or later transaxle with automatic transmission. For these repairs, use the instructions given in this section of the manual in **7.2 Replacing Governor Oil Seal and Needle Bearing.**

12.5 Replacing Flanged Shaft Oil Seal

To replace the flanged shaft oil seals, please follow the instructions given under heading **11.5** in **AUTOMATIC TRANSMISSION (Through 1975).**

13. Adjusting Final Drive

The adjustments described here are necessary to the life of the gearset, the differential bearings, and the drive pinion bearings. They are also necessary to ensure quiet operation. The final drive requires adjustment only when parts directly affecting the adjustment have been replaced or when careless disassembly has resulted in the loss of the original shims or the adjusting ring screw-in depth measurements. **Table f** lists what adjustments must be made when certain parts are replaced.

Table f. Required Final Drive Adjustments

Part replaced	Adjust pinion	Adjust ring gear (differential bearings)	Adjust flanged shaft axial play
Final drive housing	X	X	
Differential bearings		X	
Adjusting rings for differential		X	
Differential housing		X	X
Differential housing cover		X	X
Pinion tapered-roller bearings	X		
Front or rear cover plates	X		
Pinion and ring gear. Installation of new gearset requires replacement of tapered-roller bearings	X	X	
Flanged shaft, differential sidegears, or large thrust washer			X

There are two factors involved in making final drive adjustments: bearing turning torque and the backlash between the ring and pinion gears. The backlash is adjusted by repositioning the ring gear axially. The position of the pinion is determined by the thicknesses of the S_3 and S_4 shims. The position of the ring gear is determined by the screw-in depth of the differential bearing adjusting rings. The standard symbols used in making final drive adjustments are defined in **Table g.**

NOTE ——

Studying some of the illustrations given in **AUTOMATIC TRANSMISSION (Through 1975)** may help you in understanding the instructions given here for adjusting the 1976 and later final drive.

The ring gear and pinion are run on special testing machines during transaxle manufacture to check the tooth contact pattern and silent running under both drive and coast conditions. When the optimum relationship of the gears is found, they are installed in the final drive housing using pinion shims and differential bearing adjusting ring positions that will duplicate the gearset's position in the testing machines. The purpose of all subsequent adjustments is to restore the gearset to this position following repair.

Table g. Standard Symbols

Symbol	Description	Dimension
S_3	Shim between tapered-roller bearing and pinion head (determines bearing preload)	See table for thicknesses
S_4	Shim at rear of drive pinion (determines pinion position)	See table for thicknesses
R_o	Length of master gauge used in factory testing machine	unavailable
r	Deviation from R_o marked on gear set	measured in $1/100$ mm
G 1143	Gearset: G = Gleason; .1143 = $11/43$ number of teeth	3.91:1 ratio
e	Measurement obtained with universal bar with total shim thickness behind pinion head	measured in $1/100$ mm

13.1 Adjusting Drive Pinion

If both the drive pinion and the ring gear must be adjusted, adjust the pinion before you adjust the ring gear. The differential must be removed from the final drive housing before you can adjust the pinion.

CAUTION ——

If you lack the skills, special measuring tools, or a clean workshop for adjusting the final drive, we suggest you leave these repairs to an Authorized Dealer or other qualified and properly equipped shop. We especially urge you to consult your Authorized Dealer before attempting repairs on a vehicle covered by the new-car warranty.

To adjust drive pinion:

1. Heat the tapered-roller bearing inner races to approximately 100°C (212°F) in a pan of oil placed in a larger pan of boiling water. Then press the tapered-roller bearing inner races onto the drive pinion without either S_3 or S_4 shims—but with a 1.50-mm test shim (Part No. 082 519 141 BC) installed at the point indicated in Fig. 13-1.

   NOTE ——

   Seat the bearings with a pressure of about 3 tons.

Fig. 13-1. Location of 1.50-mm thick test shim between rear tapered-roller bearing inner race and flange on drive pinion (arrow).

2. If not previously removed, remove the differential as described in **12.2 Removing and Installing Differential.**

3. If not previously removed, remove the drive pinion oil seals from the front and rear cover plates. Then install the drive pinion and the cover plates in the final drive housing. You need use only four bolts to hold the front cover plate (Fig. 13-2). Torque the bolts to 2.5 mkg (18 ft. lb.).

4. Zero a dial indicator that has a 10-mm range against the rear end of the drive pinion as shown in Fig. 13-3. The magnetic plate, VW 385/17, provides a uniform surface for the gauge pin to contact.

5. By reaching inside the final drive housing, raise the pinion fully up. Write down the dial indicator reading.

Fig. 13-2. Front cover plate installed with only some of the bolts (arrows).

Fig. 13-3. Drive pinion axial play being measured. Move pinion up and down as indicated by double arrow.

CAUTION ——

Do not turn the drive pinion as you raise it up. The reading will be inaccurate if the pinion is turned.

6. To the dial indicator reading obtained in step 5, add the 1.50-mm thickness of test shim, 0.15 mm to provide bearing preload, and 0.10 mm to

compensate for bearing settling. The sum is the total thickness of the combined S_3 and S_4 shims that are required for correct pinion adjustment.

CAUTION ——

Every number or setting in the following examples is imaginary. Using them as specifications for a car could cause serious damage.

Example:

Dial indicator reading obtained in step 5	1.08 mm
Thickness of the test shim	+1.50 mm
Amount added for bearing preload	+0.15 mm
Amount added for bearing settling	+0.10 mm
Combined thickness of S_3 and S_4 shims	=2.83 mm

7. Remove the front cover plate. Remove the drive pinion.

8. Carefully pull off the tapered-roller bearing that is adjacent to the pinion head. If necessary, consult **12.1 Removing and Installing Drive Pinion.**

9. Subtract the thickness of the 1.50-mm test shim from the total shim thickness that you computed in step 6. Using the difference, select a shim from **Table h** (given later) and install the shim adjacent to the pinion head. After heating the tapered-roller bearing inner race to approximately 100°C (212°F) in a pan of oil placed in a larger pan of boiling water, press the tapered-roller bearing onto the drive pinion atop the shim.

Example:

Combined thickness of S_3 and S_4 shims	2.83 mm
Thickness of the test shim	−1.50 mm
Ideal thickness of shim to be temporarily installed adjacent to pinion head (a 1.350-mm shim would be used)	=1.33 mm

10. Install the drive pinion in the final drive housing. Reinstall the front cover plate.

11. Install the special gauge plate on the drive pinion as shown in Fig. 13-4.

12. Adjust the clamp ring on the universal measuring bar (Tool VW 385/1). Dimension **a** shown in Fig. 13-5 is 58 mm.

13. Slide the centering disks (VW 385/2) onto the bar until they contact the clamp ring and the setting ring. Then attach measuring pin VW 385/13 with extension VW 385/20 to the gauge pin hole in the center of the bar. Install a dial indicator with a 3-mm range. Using setting block VW 383/5 as shown in Fig. 13-6, zero the dial indicator with no preload.

Fig. 13-4. Special gauge plate installed on drive pinion.

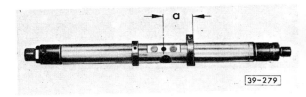

Fig. 13-5. Clamp ring adjustment.

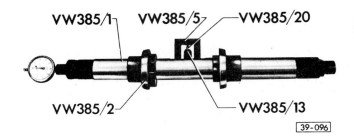

Fig. 13-6. Measuring bar ready for use. Notice how the setting block, VW 385/5, has been placed over the measuring pin extension.

14. Place an O-ring on the left adjusting ring. Lightly lubricate the O-ring and the threads with multipurpose grease, then screw the adjusting ring into the final drive housing until its outer surface is flush with the surface of the final drive housing.

NOTE ——

The differential bearing outer races must be installed in the adjusting rings.

15. Insert the measuring bar. Place an O-ring on the right adjusting ring. Lightly lubricate the O-ring and the threads with multipurpose grease, then screw in the adjusting ring.

16. By turning the knurled knob on the end of the measuring bar (Fig. 13-7), move the setting ring and centering disk outward until it is just barely possible to hand-turn the measuring bar.

Fig. 13-7. Setting ring position being adjusted (arrow).

17. Hand-turn the drive pinion slightly back and forth in order to settle the tapered-roller bearings.

CAUTION ——

Do not turn the drive pinion too far or the gauge pin will slip off the special gauge plate that is installed on the drive pinion. After settling the bearings, return the drive pinion to its original position, with the measuring bar gauge pin resting squarely against the gauge plate.

18. Rotate the bar back and forth over center (Fig. 13-8). The maximum dial indicator reading should be observed and written down.

Fig. 13-8. Measuring bar being rotated (arrow) back and forth over center.

19. Compute the ideal thickness of the S_4 shim. To do this, first subtract the dial indicator reading obtained in step 18 from the 1.50-mm test shim thickness. To the difference, add the deviation **r** marked on the ring gear.

Example:

Thickness of the test shim	1.50 mm
Dial indicator reading obtained in step 18	−0.88 mm
	=0.62 mm
Deviation **r** marked on ring gear	+0.44 mm
Ideal thickness for S_4 shim	=1.06 mm

20. Determine the ideal thickness of the S_3 shim. To do this, subtract the ideal thickness for the S_4 shim from the total combined shim thickness that you determined in step 6.

Example:

Combined thickness of S_3 and S_4 shims	2.83 mm
Ideal thickness for S_4 shim	−1.06 mm
Ideal thickness for S_3 shim	=1.77 mm

21. Select the correct S_3 and S_4 shims from **Table h.**

NOTE ——

Always check shim thicknesses at several points with a micrometer. Also check the shims for burrs and other damage. Use only good shims of the correct thickness.

22. Remove the front cover plate. Remove the universal measuring bar. Remove the rear cover plate and the drive pinion.

23. Remove both tapered-roller bearings from the drive pinion. Remove the shims from the drive pinion.

CAUTION ——

The tapered-roller bearings must later be reinstalled on their original ends of the drive pinion. Be careful not to mix them up.

24. Heat the tapered-roller bearing inner races and the oil seal race to approximately 100°C (212°F) in a pan of oil placed in a larger pan of boiling water. Install the correct S_3 shim adjacent to the pinion head. Then press on the front tapered-roller bearing inner race.

25. Install the correct S_4 shim at the rear end of the drive pinion. Then press on the rear tapered-roller bearing inner race.

26. Reinstall the special gauge plate on the drive pinion. Lightly lubricate the bearings with hypoid

Table h. Available S₃ and S₄ Shims

Ideal thickness	Shim to be installed	Part number
1.050 to 1.100	1.100	082 519 141 AE
1.105 to 1.125	1.125	082 519 141 AF
1.130 to 1.150	1.150	082 519 141 AG
1.155 to 1.175	1.175	082 519 141 AH
1.180 to 1.200	1.200	082 519 141 AJ
1.205 to 1.225	1.225	082 519 141 AK
1.230 to 1.250	1.250	082 519 141 AL
1.255 to 1.275	1.275	082 519 141 AM
1.280 to 1.300	1.300	082 519 141 AN
1.305 to 1.325	1.325	082 519 141 AP
1.330 to 1.350	1.350	082 519 141 AQ
1.355 to 1.375	1.375	082 519 141 AR
1.380 to 1.400	1.400	082 519 141 AS
1.405 to 1.425	1.425	082 519 141 AT
1.430 to 1.450	1.450	082 519 141 BA
1.455 to 1.475	1.475	082 519 141 BB
1.480 to 1.500	1.500	082 519 141 BC
1.505 to 1.525	1.525	082 519 141 BD
1.530 to 1.550	1.550	082 519 141 BE
1.555 to 1.575	1.575	082 519 141 BF
1.580 to 1.600	1.600	082 519 141 BG
1.605 to 1.625	1.625	082 519 141 BH
1.630 to 1.650	1.650	082 519 141 BJ
1.655 to 1.675	1.675	082 519 141 BK
1.680 to 1.700	1.700	082 519 141 BL
1.705 to 1.725	1.725	082 519 141 BM
1.730 to 1.750	1.750	082 519 141 BN
1.755 to 1.775	1.775	082 519 141 BP
1.780 to 1.800	1.800	082 519 141 BQ
1.805 to 1.825	1.825	082 519 141 BR
1.830 to 1.850	1.850	082 519 141 BS
1.855 to 1.875	1.875	082 519 141 BT
1.880 to 1.900	1.900	082 519 141 CA

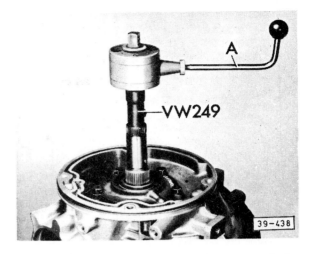

Fig. 13-9. Pinion turning torque being measured after installation of correct shims.

oil. Reinstall the drive pinion, the universal measuring bar, and the cover plates in the final drive housing.

27. By rotating the bar back and forth over center, repeat the measuring procedure you carried out in step 18. The dial indicator reading should correspond with the deviation **r** stamped on the ring gear, within a tolerance of ±0.04 mm. If it does not, you have made an error in selecting the shims or in making this or previous measurements.

28. If you have installed new pinion tapered-roller bearings, check the pinion turning torque with a torque gauge as shown in Fig. 13-9. If the torque required to turn the pinion is less than 14 cmkg (12 in. lb.) with new bearings, you have not allowed sufficient shim thickness for bearing preload and bearing settling.

NOTE ——

You can also check the installation of used bearings in this way—if you measure and write down the turning torque before you disassemble the final drive. When correctly assembled, the turning torque with used bearings should be 2 to 4 cmkg (1.7 to 3.5 in. lb.) greater than it was prior to disassembly.

13.2 Adjusting Ring Gear

The ring gear depth-of-mesh backlash must be adjusted after you have adjusted the drive pinion. To make this adjustment, follow the instructions given under heading **12.2** in **AUTOMATIC TRANSMISSION (Through 1975)**.

13.3 Adjusting Flanged Shaft Axial Play

To adjust the flanged shaft axial play, follow the instructions given under heading **12.3** in **AUTOMATIC TRANSMISSION (Through 1975)**.

14. REPLACING TRANSAXLE BONDED MOUNTING

To replace the transaxle bonded mounting on the transaxle rear mount, follow the instructions given under heading **14** in **AUTOMATIC TRANSMISSION (Through 1975)**.

6

15. AUTOMATIC TRANSMISSION TECHNICAL DATA

I. Tightening Torques

Location	Designation	mkg	ft. lb.	cmkg	in. lb.
Main pressure tap plug in transmission case	threaded plug	1.0	7		
Locknut for 2nd gear brake band adjusting screw	nut	2.0	14		
Accumulator cover to transmission case	Phillips head screw			30	26
Valve body to separator plate and transfer plate	Phillips head screw			40	35
Valve body assembly to transmission case	bolt			40	35
ATF strainer to valve body	Phillips head screw			30	26
ATF pan to case	bolt	2.0	14		
Governor cover to final drive housing	bolt	1.5	11		
Transaxle rear mount to transmission case	nut	5.5	40		
Transaxle rear mount to body	bolt	4.0	29		
Engine to transaxle	bolt	5.5	40		
Torque converter to drive plate	bolt	3.0	22		
Exhaust pipe bracket to transaxle support	bolt	2.0	14		
Exhaust pipe to exhaust manifold	nut	2.5	18		
Torque converter cover plate to bellhousing	bolt	1.5	11		
Starter to bellhousing	bolt and nut	2.0	14		
Constant velocity joint to drive flange	socket-head screw	6.5	47		
Suspension ball joint on track control arm	bolt	6.5	47		
Transmission case to final drive housing	nut	3.0	22		
ATF pump/plate with springs to transmission case	bolt			70	61
Separating plate to transmission case	fillister-head screw			70	61
Spring for selector segment to transmission case	M 8 bolt or fillister-head screw	2.0	14		
Locking bolt for operating lever shaft	bolt			40	35
Operating lever for manual valve to shaft	nut	2.0	14		
Operating lever for kickdown valve to shaft	nut	1.5	11		
Front or rear cover plate to final drive housing	bolt	2.5	18		
Speedometer drive retainer to final drive housing	bolt	1.0	7		
Lockplate for differential bearing adjusting ring to final drive housing	bolt	1.0	7		
Flanged shaft to differential	socket-head bolt	2.5	18		
Ring gear to differential housing	bolt with serrated washer surface	7.0	50		

II. Valve Body Springs

Description	Part No.	No. of coils	Wire thickness mm (in.)	Free length (approx.) mm (in.)	Coil inner diameter mm ± 0.30 mm (in. ± .012 in.)
Throttle pressure limiting valve spring	003 325 119	14.5	1.10 (.043)	35.30 (1.390)	7.70 (.303)
Main pressure limiting valve spring	003 325 119	14.5	1.10 (.043)	35.30 (1.390)	7.70 (.303)
Main pressure valve spring	003 325 131 A	16.5	1.50 (.059)	71.60 (2.819)	11.90 (.469)
Throttle pressure valve spring	010 325 175 B	16.0	1.25 (.049)	43.40 (1.709)	7.75 (.305)
Modulator valve spring	010 325 185	12.0	0.70 (.028)	18.70 (0.736)	5.30 (.209)
1st/2nd gear shift valve spring	010 325 207	6.5	0.90 (.035)	19.90 (0.783)	8.10 (.319)
2nd/3rd gear shift valve spring	010 325 207	6.5	0.90 (.035)	19.90 (0.783)	8.10 (.319)
3rd/2nd control valve spring	003 325 227 A	12.5	1.00 (.039)	32.40 (1.276)	7.70 (.303)
Converter pressure valve spring	003 325 227 A	12.5	1.00 (.039)	32.40 (1.276)	7.70 (.303)
3rd/2nd gear kickdown control valve spring	003 325 207 A	11.5	0.90 (.035)	28.40 (1.118)	8.10 (.319)

NOTE ——

Though the throttle pressure limiting valve spring and the main pressure limiting valve spring are identical, used springs should not be interchanged. Nor should 2nd/3rd gear shift valve springs and converter pressure valve springs be interchanged once they have seen service, though they are identical when new.

III. Driveshaft Lengths (dimension a)

Transmission	Left driveshaft length mm (in.)	Right driveshaft length mm (in.)
Manual	506 (19.92 or 19^{59}/$_{64}$)	506 (19.92 or 19^{59}/$_{64}$)
Automatic	437 (17.20 or 17^{13}/$_{64}$)	531 (20.90 or 20^{29}/$_{32}$)

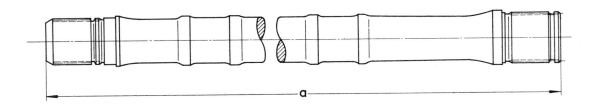

NOTE ——

For all other specifications relative to the automatic transmission used on 1976 and later cars, please see the specifications given in the text under appropriate headings.

6

FUEL AND EXHAUST SYSTEMS

Contents

Fuel and Exhaust Systems

The fuel system handles five main tasks necessary for proper engine operation: (1) it provides storage space for the gasoline; (2) it includes the components necessary for delivering gasoline to the engine; (3) it is responsible for admitting the proper amount of filtered air to the engine; (4) it incorporates a system for mixing fuel and air in precisely controlled proportions and delivering this mixture to the cylinders; and (5) it modifies the density of the incoming air so that the combustion process does not produce an excess of undesirable exhaust emissions. The fourth function mentioned above, that of mixing the fuel with air, is handled on early models by a carburetor and on later models by a fuel injection system.

On the carburetor-engined cars covered by this Manual, the carburetor is a dual-venturi, progressive opening carburetor. That is, the primary venturi's throttle valve is directly controlled by the accelerator pedal and is the only throttle valve in operation during normal driving. During acceleration to high speeds, and when cruising at high speeds, the secondary venturi's throttle valve also opens. By limiting the operation of the second venturi to periods of high-power demand, greater fuel economy is obtained during normal driving—when the power needed is either light or moderate.

The fuel injection system, used on the later cars covered by this Manual, has the same kind of progressive throttle valves as the carburetor already described. The throttle valves, however, are mounted in a separate throttle valve housing and control only the quantity of air that enters the engine's cylinders. The quantity of air going to the throttle valves is accurately measured by a separate unit, known as the air flow sensor.

The air flow sensor is built into a single unit with the fuel distributor. The amount of fuel injected into the engine's intake ports is precisely metered in proportion to the air entering the engine. Unlike a carburetor, fuel injection does not depend on the velocity of the incoming air to draw fuel into the engine. Instead, fuel is injected into the airstream under pressure. The system used on cars covered by this manual is a continuous-flow system—that is, the gasoline is injected in a continuous spray of varying quantity. By contrast, the fuel injection system used on Type 1 and Type 2 VWs injects the fuel in a uniform quantity—but in pulses of varying duration.

The continuous injection system (CIS) is not an electronic system and requires few electrical tests for troubleshooting. A pressure gauge and one or two special tools are, however, required. If you lack the skills, instruments, or other equipment necessary for testing either the carburetion system or the fuel injection system, we suggest you leave these tests or repairs to an Authorized Dealer or other qualified and properly equipped shop. We especially urge you to consult your Authorized Dealer before attempting repairs on a car still covered by the new-car warranty.

7

1. GENERAL DESCRIPTION

As noted earlier, the fuel system may conveniently be divided into five subsystems, each with a separate function. For brevity, these will be called fuel storage, pump and lines, air cleaner, carburetor or fuel injection, and emission controls.

Fuel Storage

The fuel tank is at the rear of the car, beneath the floor of the trunk. It has a capacity of 12.1 U.S. gallons (10.1 Imperial gallons or 46 liters), which includes a reserve of 1.3 U.S. gallons (1.1 Imperial gallons or 5.0 liters).

The tank is equipped with a sending unit for the electrical fuel gauge, a pickup tube for the transfer of fuel to the engine, and a vent tube routed into the evaporative emission control system. The unvented filler cap is concealed beneath a flap in the right rear fender.

Pump and Lines

Engines with carburetors have a mechanical fuel pump located on the left-hand side of the engine block. This pump is operated by an eccentric on the engine's intermediate shaft.

Engines with fuel injection have an electrical fuel pump located beneath the rear of the car—just ahead of the right-hand end of the fuel tank. The electric fuel pump draws fuel from the tank and pumps the fuel into the pressure line to the fuel distributor.

The fuel lines that pass beneath the floor of the car are steel tubes housed in the floor pan tunnel. Hoses connect the steel lines to the fuel pump and to the carburetor or the fuel injection system. On fuel injection cars, the hoses are connected to banjo unions so that the unions can easily be disconnected without removing and installing the hoses on their connections.

Air Cleaner

All cars covered by this Manual have dry-type pleated paper filter elements. A ring-shaped filter element is used on cars with carburetors whereas a flat rectangular filter element is used on cars with fuel injection.

1.1 Carburetor

The 1973 and 1974 models are equipped with Solex 32/35 DIDTA carburetors. The 1975 models with carburetors have a Zenith 2B3 carburetor. The Solex and Zenith units are both dual-venturi designs. A small 32-mm throttle valve is used for idle and midrange operation. This gives a good economy and throttle response with a minimum of exhaust emissions. At full

load, a second 35-mm throttle valve opens in addition to the 32-mm throttle valve. The operating stages can be seen in Fig. 1-1. Once the primary throttle valve has opened beyond a predetermined point, the secondary throttle valve is able to open to a degree that is proportional to engine vacuum—thus avoiding the hesitation that might occur if both throttle valves were fully opened at low speed on an engine tuned for maximum fuel economy.

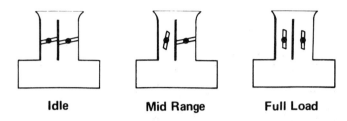

Idle   **Mid Range**   **Full Load**

Fig. 1-1. Stages of dual-venturi carburetor operation. Secondary throttle valve is opened by a vacuum chamber attached to the carburetor.

On all models, the carburetor has a built-in automatic choke operated by a thermostatic spring. The thermostatic spring closes the choke valve when the engine is cold. As the engine warms up, heated coolant is conducted to the carburetor by hoses, warming the thermostatic spring and causing the choke to open at a predetermined rate. Whenever the throttle valve is closed—as at idle or during deceleration—a vacuum diaphragm overrides the thermostatic spring and causes the choke to open slightly.

1.2 Fuel Injection

Fig. 1-2 is a schematic view of the CIS (continuous injection system) that is used on the latest cars covered by this Manual. To help you understand this diagram, a brief explanation is given here of the function of each of the system's components. A detailed description of each component can be found under the heading for the particular component; for example **7.8 Testing and Replacing Cold-start Valve.**

For the sake of description, it is convenient to divide the fuel injection system into two subsystems. These subsystems are the fuel circuit and the air system.

Fuel Circuit

The electric fuel pump draws fuel from the tank and pumps it through the fuel accumulator and the fuel filter to the fuel distributor. The function of the fuel accumulator is to absorb the initial pressure surge when the pump starts, thereby preventing the control plunger of the fuel distributor's metering unit from being forced up before an adequate stable pressure has been reached.

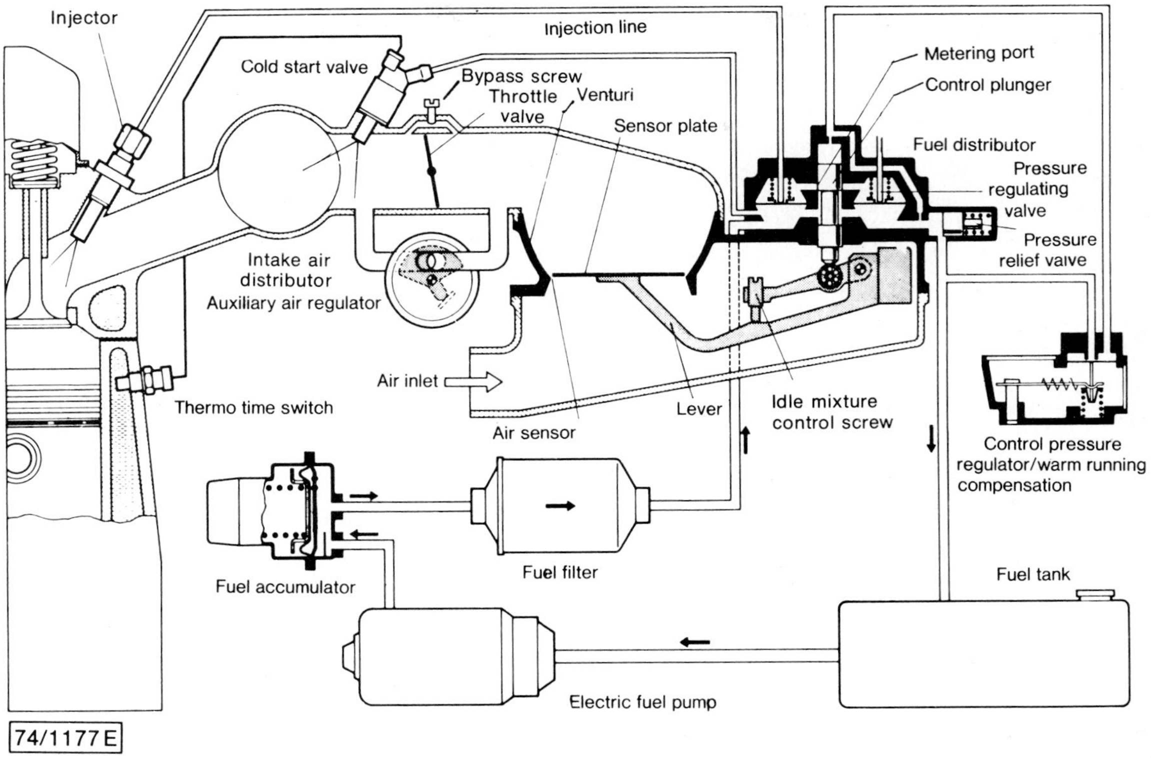

Fig. 1-2. Schematic view of CIS fuel injection.

The fuel accumulator also serves as a reservoir to keep the system under pressure (1.5 to 2.5 bar) for a short time after the engine has been turned off. This residual fuel pressure is necessary to prevent vapor lock.

A pressure relief valve, built into the fuel distributor, keeps the pressure in the system at a predetermined level by allowing surplus fuel from the pump to flow back to the tank. The pressure is modulated according to engine temperature by the control pressure regulator. It too regulates pressure in the system by allowing a varying amount of fuel to flow back to the tank. In addition to being warmed by contact with the engine and engine oil, the control pressure regulator is warmed by an electrically heated thermostatic spring. The electric heating element ensures that the pressure will not be excessive when the outside air temperature is very cold.

In addition to the richer mixture produced for cold running by the control pressure regulator, there is a cold-start valve that injects additional fuel during starter operation when the engine is cold. The function of the cold-start valve is analogous to the function of a choke on a carburetor. The cold-start valve, sometimes called the fifth injector, is operated electrically by current from the starter solenoid. However, the thermo-time switch interrupts the current if the engine is hot or after the starter has been in constant operation for more than a few seconds. The purpose of the thermo-time switch is to prevent flooding.

The main function of the four injectors is to atomize the continuous flow of fuel that is injected under pressure into the intake ports of the engine. Valves in the nozzles stop the flow of fuel when the fuel pressure drops below a certain point. The quantity of fuel injected is regulated by the fuel distributor's metering unit and, secondarily, by the control pressure regulator. The metering function of the fuel distributor is controlled by the quantity of air entering the engine, which is measured by the sensor plate.

Air System

The sensor plate of the mixture control unit is the heart of the fuel injection system. (The mixture control unit consists of the air volume sensor and the fuel distributor.) The greater the amount of air admitted to the engine past the throttle valve or the auxiliary air regulator, the higher the sensor plate is raised above the narrowest part of the venturi. A lever connected to the sensor plate raises or lowers the control plunger in the fuel distributor's metering unit—increasing the quantity of fuel to the injection nozzle when air flow increases or reducing the quantity of fuel when air flow diminishes.

In addition to the throttle valve, which is connected to the accelerator pedal, the quantity of air entering the engine can be changed by two other devices. The first of these is the auxiliary air regulator. When the engine is cold, the auxiliary air regulator admits additional air to the intake air distributor at closed throttle in order to provide a faster idle until the engine has warmed up. The auxiliary air regulator consists of a rotary valve operated by an electrically heated thermostatic spring. The spring begins to heat up as soon as the engine is started, gradually closing the valve and returning the engine to its normal idle rpm at a predetermined warm-up rate.

A second throttle valve bypass is adjustable by means of the bypass screw. This bypass screw, which is located in the throttle valve housing, is used to adjust the engine's idle speed.

As installed on the car, the intake air distributor is a large, cylindrical cast aluminum chamber with four integral manifold tubes that conduct air to the intake ports of the engine. The intake air distributor provides mounting points for the throttle valve housing, the cold-start valve, and for various air and vacuum hoses.

1.3 Emission Controls

The EEC (evaporative emission control) consists of the fuel tank ventilation hoses, an activated charcoal filter canister, and the hoses from the canister to the engine. Its purpose is to keep fuel tank fumes from polluting the air. All of the engines covered by this Manual have a closed PCV (positive crankcase ventilation) system. The system contains no PCV valve that requires periodic cleaning or replacement but does include an oil separator.

An EGR (exhaust gas recirculation) system is installed on most of the cars covered by this Manual. Some cars are equipped with an AI (air injection) system and others have a CAT (catalytic converter). Which of these systems is on a given vehicle can be determined by inspecting the emission decal located on the engine. Cars that are equipped with catalytic converters are also identifiable by a fuel filler that will accept only the small pump nozzles used for lead-free gasoline.

2. MAINTENANCE

There are only a few maintenance operations that must be carried out at a specified mileage or after a certain period of service. These are listed below and covered in **LUBRICATION AND MAINTENANCE** or under the listed headings in this section of the Manual.

1. Servicing the air cleaner
2. Replacing the fuel filter (for fuel injection cars only; see **7.4**)
3. Checking emission controls (see **5.** and **9.**)
4. Replacing catalytic converter (see **9.**)
5. Replacing activated charcoal filter canister
6. Checking PCV system.

3. FUEL TANK

If the fuel tank must be removed for cleaning or repairs, it is important that the connections leading to the tank be reinstalled correctly and in their original locations. Errors can lead to fuel starvation, or to the improper venting of fumes.

3.1 Removing and Installing Fuel Tank

To avoid the hazard of spilled fuel, the tank should be as near empty as possible during removal. Surplus fuel should be drained off. Removal and testing of the fuel gauge sending unit is described in conjunction with the instruments in **ELECTRICAL SYSTEM.**

> **WARNING ——**
> *Disconnect the battery ground strap. Do not smoke or work near heaters or other fire hazards. Have a fire extinguisher handy.*

To remove:

1. Raise up the trunk mat or rear luggage compartment mat. Remove the sending unit access plate from the floor of the trunk or rear luggage area.
2. Disconnect the wires from the fuel gauge sending unit. Also pry off the clamp(s) and disconnect the ventilation hose(s) from the sending unit.
3. Remove the fuel filler cap by taking off the snap ring (Fig. 3-1) and remove the rubber boot that seals the space between the fuel tank filler neck and the car body.
4. Working under the car, use a pinch clamp or clamps to squeeze the fuel hose(s) shut at a point near the tank connection(s). Then detach the hose(s) from the tank and quickly insert small corks or other suitable plugs in the tank outlet(s) if the tank is not fully empty.
5. Remove the bolts that hold the tank straps to the car body. Then remove the tank from the car.

Installation is the reverse of removal. Use new clips on the fuel and the ventilation hoses. The hoses must not be installed in a twisted position or bent so sharply that they collapse. See Fig. 3-1.

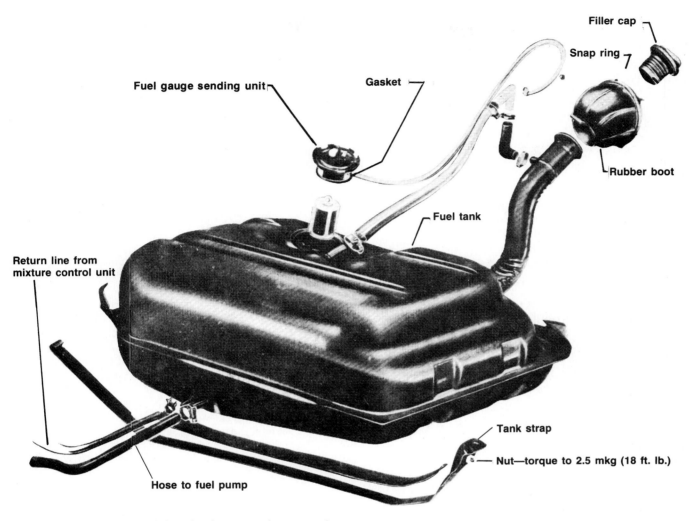

Fig. 3-1. Exploded view showing connections to spark-ignition fuel tank of cars with fuel injection.

Filler cap

Snap ring

Rubber boot

Gasket

Fuel gauge sending unit

Fuel tank

Return line from mixture control unit

Tank strap

Nut—torque to 2.5 mkg (18 ft. lb.)

Hose to fuel pump

7

4. MECHANICAL FUEL PUMP
(CARBURETOR ENGINES ONLY)

On cars with carburetors, the fuel pump is mounted on the engine. It is a mechanical pump, operated by an eccentric on the engine's intermediate shaft. The stroke of the pump is non-adjustable.

4.1 Removing and Installing Mechanical Fuel Pump

(carburetor engines only)

1. Where applicable, pry off or loosen the clamps, then disconnect the fuel hoses from the fuel pump.

> **WARNING ——**
>
> *Fuel will be expelled as you disconnect the hoses. Disconnect the battery ground strap. Do not smoke or work near heaters or other fire hazards. Have a fire extinguisher handy.*

2. Remove the bolts that hold the pump to the engine. Then take off the pump. See Fig. 4-1.

3. Remove the seal, the spacer, and the gasket—as applicable to the car you are working on.

Fig. 4-1. Nuts (arrows) that hold pump to engine. Fuel outlet is indicated by arrow superimposed on fuel hose. Hose clamp is circled.

Installation is the reverse of removal. Use a new seal and a new gasket as applicable to the car you are working on. Torque the bolts to 2.0 mkg (14 ft. lb.). If the hose clamps are the clip kind, without screws, replace them.

> **NOTE ——**
>
> If the original hoses are to be reinstalled, carefully inspect their ends to see that they have not been weakened or deformed by the previous installation of hose clamps. A new clamp may not seal hoses that have lost resiliency. In this case, a new hose should always be installed.

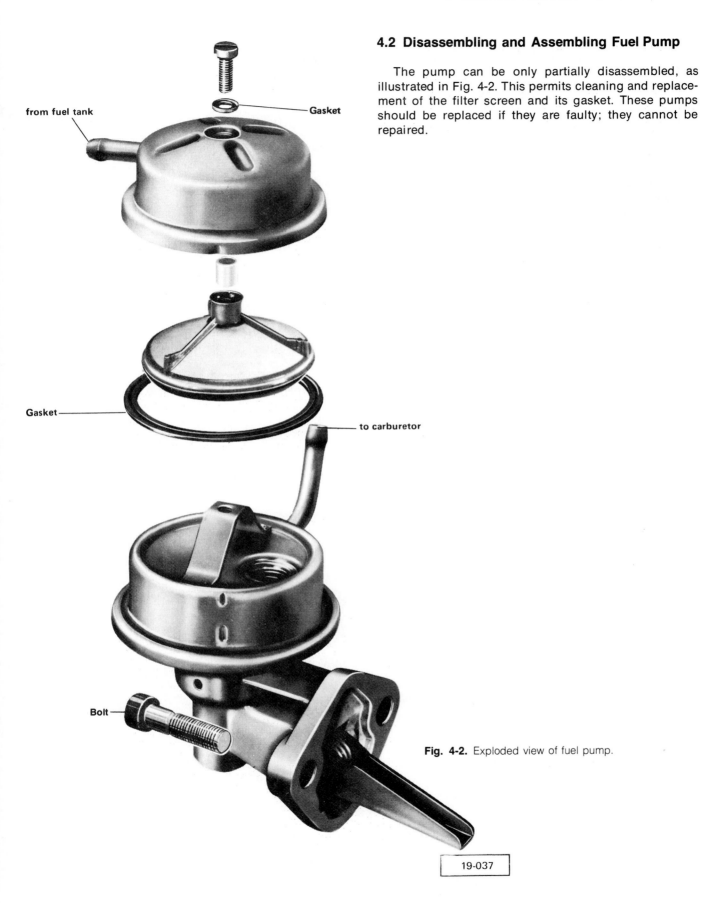

4.2 Disassembling and Assembling Fuel Pump

The pump can be only partially disassembled, as illustrated in Fig. 4-2. This permits cleaning and replacement of the filter screen and its gasket. These pumps should be replaced if they are faulty; they cannot be repaired.

from fuel tank

Gasket

Gasket

to carburetor

Bolt

Fig. 4-2. Exploded view of fuel pump.

19-037

7

Clean the filter screen with compressed air. Always use a new gasket between the cover and the pump body and between the screw head and the cover. In installing the cover, the notch (Fig. 4-3) must engage the projection on the pump body.

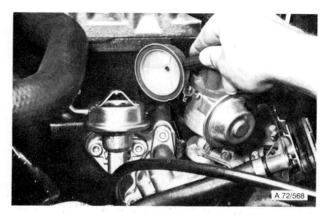

Fig. 4-3. Notch (arrow) on pump cover.

5. ADJUSTING IDLE

Because haphazard idle adjustments will adversely affect exhaust emissions, please follow the instructions carefully and use the specified equipment. Professional mechanics should find out whether state authorization is required before a repair shop can make adjustments that influence exhaust emissions.

During routine maintenance, you should adjust the idle speed only. This is done by turning the bypass screw in the carburetor or on the throttle valve housing of the fuel injection system. Do not adjust the idle speed by turning the throttle valve adjustment, which is the procedure used on some other makes of cars. You need not adjust the idle mixture (CO content) unless (1) you have installed a different carburetor or, on fuel injection cars, a new mixture control unit, (2) you have removed, repaired, or rebuilt the carburetor or the mixture control unit, (3) the engine has been extensively rebuilt, or (4) there are excessive exhaust emissions.

In troubleshooting the engine, eliminate all other possible trouble sources before you touch the carburetor or fuel injection system adjustments. Also, adjusting the idle rpm should be the last step in a tune-up. Otherwise, valve and ignition adjustments will upset the previously made idle adjustment. A preliminary idle speed adjustment should be made earlier only if the engine is idling too fast to check the ignition timing.

CAUTION ——

If you lack the skills, tools, or test equipment for adjusting the carburetor or the fuel injection, we suggest you leave this work to an Authorized Dealer or other qualified shop. We especially urge you to consult your Authorized Dealer before attempting repairs on a car still covered by the new-car warranty.

5.1 Adjusting Idle on Cars with Solex Carburetors

The idle adjustments of the Solex carburetor are shown in Fig. 5-1. The bypass screw is used for adjusting the idle speed. Turning this screw will not alter exhaust emissions so long as the idle rpm is adjusted to the prescribed range. The idle mixture control screw will alter emissions if it is turned and should not be adjusted without the aid of an exhaust gas analyzer.

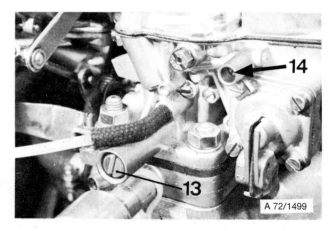

Fig. 5-1. Solex carburetor idle adjustment. Bypass screw for adjusting idle speed is at **13**; idle mixture control screw is at **14**.

Adjusting Idle Speed

If you suspect that someone has altered the factory throttle valve adjustments or has otherwise used incorrect procedures in adjusting the carburetor, you should check the various adjustments as described in **6.1 Removing, Rebuilding, and Installing Solex Carburetor** before you attempt to adjust the idle speed. Always use the procedure given here to adjust the idle speed. Do not adjust the idle speed by turning the throttle valve adjustment.

To adjust idle speed:

1. Drive the car until the engine has reached an operating temperature of 60° to 80°C (140° to 176°F).

2. Stop the car and set the parking brake firmly. Raise the hood and connect a dwell meter/tachometer according to the instructions furnished by the instrument's manufacturer. Set the instrument to measure rpm for a four-cylinder engine.

3. With the engine running, read the idle rpm. If the idle speed is not between 850 and 1000 rpm, adjust it to specifications by turning the bypass screw. Turning the bypass screw counterclockwise will increase the idle speed, turning it clockwise will decrease the idle speed.

   NOTE ——

   If turning the bypass screw makes little difference in the idle speed, it is likely that someone has tampered with the throttle valve adjustment. If the engine refuses to idle at all, test the electromagnetic cutoff valve as described in **6.1 Removing, Rebuilding, and Installing Solex Carburetor.**

Adjusting Idle Mixture
(CO content)

Do not attempt to adjust the idle mixture without a good quality infrared exhaust gas analyzer such as the Sun® EPA 75 Performance Analyzer. The instrument that you use for making idle mixture adjustments should measure parts per million of hydrocarbons and CO percentages.

To adjust idle mixture:

1. Adjust the idle speed as described under the preceding heading.

2. Disconnect the evaporative emission purge hose that goes between the activated charcoal filter canister and the air cleaner. On cars with air injection, disconnect the hose between the air pump and the diverter valve (Fig. 5-2) and plug the hose.

3. Connect the exhaust gas analyzer to its power source and turn it on. Insert the probe into the car's tailpipe.

Fig. 5-2. Point where hose should be disconnected from air pump (circled). Pump is used only on California cars.

7

4. With the engine idling, compare the exhaust analyzer readings with the prescribed ranges for CO emissions and, where applicable, for hydrocarbon emissions. The applicable specifications are listed on the engine's emissions decal or are prescribed by the state government. If the decal is missing, check that the CO volume percentage at idle is within the specifications given in **Table a.**

NOTE ——

The cooling fan should not be running.

Table a. CO Percentage Specifications for Solex Carburetor

Vehicle	Specification
VW cars sold in California (air injection & EGR)	1.0% to 2.0%
VW cars sold outside California (EGR only)	0.4% to 1.0%
Audi cars sold in California (air injection & EGR)	1.5%
Audi cars sold outside California (EGR only through engine No. XW 001 013)	0.7% to 1.3%
Audi cars sold outside California (EGR only from engine No. XW 001 014)	0.6% to 1.0%

5. If the CO level is outside the prescribed range, use a screwdriver to turn the idle mixture control screw (Fig. 5-3).

NOTE ——

Turning the idle mixture control screw clockwise (screwing it in) makes the mixture leaner.

Fig. 5-3. Location of idle mixture control screw (arrow).

6. If necessary, connect a dwell meter/tachometer and readjust the idle speed to 850 to 1000 rpm by turning the bypass screw.

7. On California cars, which have the air injection system, reconnect the hose to the air pump. The CO percentage should drop below 1.0%. If not, test the air injection system as described in **9. Emission Controls.**

8. If both the idle speed and the idle mixture (CO content) are correct, stop the engine. Disconnect the dwell meter/tachometer and the exhaust gas analyzer. Then reconnect the EEC hose.

5.2 Adjusting Idle on Cars with Zenith Carburetors

The idle speed is adjusted by turning a bypass screw. Turning this screw will not alter exhaust emissions so long as the idle rpm is adjusted to the prescribed range. The idle mixture screw will alter emissions if it is turned and should not be adjusted without the aid of an exhaust gas analyzer.

Adjusting Idle Speed

If you suspect that someone has altered the factory throttle valve adjustment or has otherwise used incorrect procedures in adjusting the carburetor, you should check the various adjustments as described in **6.2 Removing, Rebuilding, and Installing Zenith Carburetor** before you attempt to adjust the idle speed. Always use the procedure given here to adjust the idle speed. Do not adjust the idle speed by turning the throttle valve adjustment.

To adjust idle speed:

1. Drive the car until the engine has reached an oil temperature of approximately 60°C (140°F).

2. Stop the car and set the parking brake firmly. Raise the hood and connect a dwell meter/tachometer according to the instructions furnished by the instrument's manufacturer. Set the instrument to measure rpm for a four-cylinder engine.

3. With the engine running, read the idle rpm. If the idle speed is not between 850 and 1000 rpm, adjust it to specifications by turning the bypass screw (Fig. 5-4). Turning the bypass screw counterclockwise will increase the idle speed, turning it clockwise will decrease the idle speed.

> **NOTE** ——
> If turning the bypass screw makes little difference in the idle speed, it is likely that someone has tampered with the throttle valve adjustment.

Fig. 5-4. Location of bypass screw used to adjust idle speed.

Adjusting Idle Mixture
(CO content)

Do not attempt to adjust the idle mixture without a good quality infrared exhaust gas analyzer such as the Sun® EPA 75 Performance Analyzer. The instrument that you use for making idle mixture adjustments should measure parts per million of hydrocarbons and CO percentages.

To adjust idle mixture:

1. Adjust the idle speed as described under the preceding heading.

2. Disconnect the evaporative emission purge hose that goes between the activated charcoal filter canister and the air cleaner. Disconnect the hose between the air injection pump and the diverter valve and plug the connection as indicated in Fig. 5-5.

Fig. 5-5. Rubber plug (arrow) installed on connection of diverter valve.

7

3. Connect the exhaust gas analyzer to its power source and turn it on. Insert the probe into the port provided in the EGR filter (Fig. 5-6). Do not insert the probe in the tailpipe; because of the catalytic converters used on some cars, a tailpipe reading would not be accurate.

Fig. 5-6. Exhaust analyzer probe connected to EGR filter (arrow).

4. With the engine idling, compare the exhaust analyzer readings with the prescribed ranges for CO emissions and, where applicable, for hydrocarbon emissions. The applicable specifications are listed on the engine's emissions decal or are prescribed by the state government. If the decal is missing, check that the CO volume percentage at idle is at 2.0% ± 0.5%.

   NOTE——
   The cooling fan should not be running. The engine oil temperature must be between 50° and 70°C (122° and 158°F).

5. If the CO level is outside the prescribed range, use a screwdriver to turn the idle mixture control screw (Fig. 5-7).

   NOTE——
   Turning the idle mixture control screw clockwise (screwing it in) makes the mixture leaner.

6. If necessary, connect a dwell meter/tachometer and readjust the idle speed to 850 to 1000 rpm by turning the bypass screw.

7. Reconnect the hose to the diverter valve. The CO percentage should drop noticeably. Measured at the tailpipe, the CO reading should be less than 0.4%. If not, test the air injection system as described in **9. Emission Controls.**

Fig. 5-7. Location of idle mixture control screw (arrow).

8. If both the idle speed and the idle mixture (CO content) are correct on cars with catalytic converters, check the CO percentage with the exhaust gas analyzer probe inserted into the car's tailpipe. The CO reading should be less than 0.4%. If not, the catalytic converter is probably faulty and should be replaced.

9. If the tailpipe reading is satisfactory, disconnect the dwell meter/tachometer and the exhaust gas analyzer. Then reconnect the EEC hose.

5.3 Adjusting Idle on Cars with Fuel Injection

The idle speed is adjusted by turning a bypass screw in the throttle valve housing. Turning this screw will not alter exhaust emissions so long as the idle rpm is adjusted to the prescribed range. The idle mixture screw, located in the fuel distributor, will alter emissions if it is turned. It should not be adjusted without the aid of an exhaust gas analyzer.

CAUTION——
Do not try to cure engine operating problems by making idle adjustments. Incorrect adjustments are seldom the cause of such things as hard starting, rough running, or lack of power. If the engine does not seem to be running right, refer to **7.1 Troubleshooting Fuel Injection.** *Carry out the checks and tests suggested there before you attempt to adjust the idle.*

Adjusting Idle Speed

Always use the procedure given here to adjust the idle speed. Do not adjust the idle speed by altering the throttle valve position.

To adjust idle speed:

1. Drive the car until the engine has reached an oil temperature between 50° and 70°C (122° and 158°F).

2. Stop the car and set the parking brake firmly. Raise the hood and make sure that the auxiliary air regulator has fully closed. To check this, temporarily disconnect the hose from the end of the auxiliary air regulator that is opposite the electrical connection. You should feel no vacuum when you place your thumb against the connection on the valve. If you do, check the valve as described in **7.9 Testing and Replacing Auxiliary Air Regulator.**

3. If the auxiliary air regulator is closed, reconnect the hose. Then connect a dwell meter/tachometer according to the instructions furnished by the instrument's manufacturer. Set the instrument to measure rpm for a four-cylinder engine.

4. Turn the headlights on to high beam. With the engine running, read the idle rpm. If the idle speed is not between 850 and 1000 rpm, adjust it to specifications by turning the bypass screw (Fig. 5-8). Turning the bypass screw counterclockwise will increase the idle speed, turning it clockwise will decrease the idle speed.

NOTE

If the car is so equipped, turn on the air conditioner during idle adjustments.

NOTE

If turning the bypass screw makes little difference in the idle speed, either someone has tampered with the throttle valve adjustment, there is a leak in the air system somewhere on the intake air distributor (which will also cause a rough idle), or the auxiliary air regulator is not fully closed.

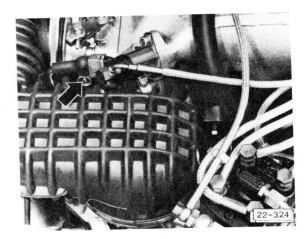

Fig. 5-8. Location of bypass screw (arrow) on throttle valve housing. This screw is used to adjust the idle speed.

Adjusting Idle Mixture

(CO content)

Do not attempt to adjust the idle mixture without a good quality infrared exhaust gas analyzer such as the Sun® EPA 75 Performance Analyzer. The instrument that you use for making idle mixture adjustments should measure parts per million of hydrocarbons and CO percentages.

To adjust idle mixture:

1. Adjust the idle speed as described under the preceding heading. The headlight high beams and, when installed, the air conditioner should be turned on during idle speed adjustment and left on while you adjust the mixture.

2. Disconnect the evaporative emission purge hose that goes between the activated charcoal filter canister and the air cleaner.

3. Connect the exhaust gas analyzer to its power source and turn it on. Insert the probe into the tailpipe—including the tailpipes of most cars with catalytic converters.

NOTE

Only on 1975 Audi models sold in California should you attach the probe at the port provided ahead of the catalytic converter.

4. With the engine idling, compare the exhaust analyzer readings with the prescribed ranges for CO emissions and, where applicable, for hydrocarbon emissions. The applicable specifications are listed on the engine's emissions decal (Fig. 5-9) or are prescribed by the state government. If the decal

7

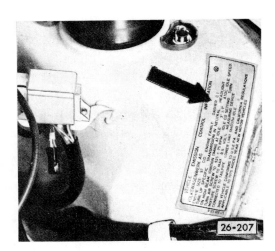

Fig. 5-9. Location of emissions decal (arrow).

is missing, check that the CO volume percentage at idle conforms to the specifications given in **Table b.**

NOTE ——

The cooling fan should not be running. The engine oil temperature must be between 50° and 70°C (122° and 158°F).

Table b. CO Percentages for Cars with Fuel Injection

Car model	CO volume percentage
1975 cars	1.0% ±0.5%
1976 and later USA and Canada cars with manual transmissions	1.5% maximum
1976 and later USA and Canada cars with automatic transmissions	1.0% maximum
1976 and later California cars with manual transmissions	0.5% maximum
1976 and later California cars with automatic transmissions	0.5% maximum

5. If the CO level is outside the prescribed range, remove the rubber plug from the top of the mixture control unit's housing. There is a looped wire handle attached to this plug so that the plug can easily be pulled out of its hole.

6. Use the adjusting tool as shown in Fig. 5-10 to turn the idle mixture control screw. Remove the tool after each adjustment, install the plug, and accelerate the engine briefly before you read the CO% with the engine idle.

CAUTION ——

Do not push the adjusting tool down or accelerate the engine while the tool is in place. Doing these things can damage the air flow sensor.

NOTE ——

You can readily see what mechanical change your adjustment will accomplish by studying the schematic diagram given in **1.2 Fuel Injection**. Turning the screw clockwise makes the mixture richer; turning it counterclockwise makes the mixture leaner.

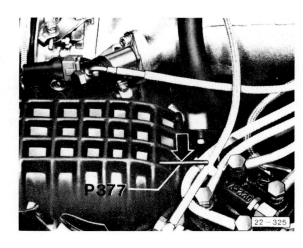

Fig. 5-10. Idle mixture (CO content) being adjusted.

7. If necessary, connect a dwell meter/tachometer and readjust the idle speed to 850 to 1000 rpm by turning the bypass screw on the throttle valve housing.

8. If both the idle speed and the idle mixture (CO content) are correct, reinstall the rubber plug in the fuel distributor.

9. Disconnect the dwell meter/tachometer and the exhaust gas analyzer. Then reconnect the EEC hose.

6. REPAIRING CARBURETORS

Carburetor repairs consist of cleaning the carburetor, replacing the soft parts (gaskets, O-rings, and seals), replacing the jets and similar hard components, and making various pre-installation adjustments. If you install a new carburetor or a factory rebuilt carburetor, you should still check the various adjustments before you install the new carburetor on the car.

6.1 Removing, Rebuilding, and Installing Solex Carburetor

If a carburetor must be replaced, it is important that the new carburetor have the same part number as the original, or that the new carburetor be the correct replacement for the car model being serviced. Always obtain replacement carburetors and carburetor parts with reference to the carburetor part number and the engine number.

To remove Solex carburetor:

1. Release the clips that hold the cover to the body of the air cleaner. Remove the cover. Disconnect the EEC hose from the air cleaner body.

2. Remove the nut indicated in Fig. 6-1. Then, being careful not to damage the intake air preheating duct as you disengage it from its connection on the exhaust manifold, lift up the air cleaner and disconnect the PCV hose. Remove the air cleaner from the car.

Fig. 6-1. Air cleaner body mounting nut (arrow).

3. Obtain two corks of appropriate diameter. Disconnect the coolant hoses from the automatic choke and quickly plug them with the corks to prevent the loss of coolant.

4. Pry off the spring clip (Fig. 6-2). Then disconnect the accelerator cable from the throttle arm.

Fig. 6-2. Spring clip (arrow) that holds accelerator cable to throttle arm.

5. Disconnect the electrical wire(s) from the electromagnetic cutoff valve and, where applicable, from the automatic choke.

WARNING ——

Fuel will be spilled during removal of the carburetor. Do not smoke. Disconnect the battery ground strap to prevent accidental electrical sparks. Do not work near heaters or other fire hazards. Have a fire extinguisher handy.

6. Disconnect the fuel hose and the vacuum hose(s) from the carburetor. Plug the disconnected fuel hose with a screw, a pencil, or a golf tee.

7. Remove the four nuts that hold the carburetor to the intake manifold. Then remove the carburetor and its gasket from the manifold.

7

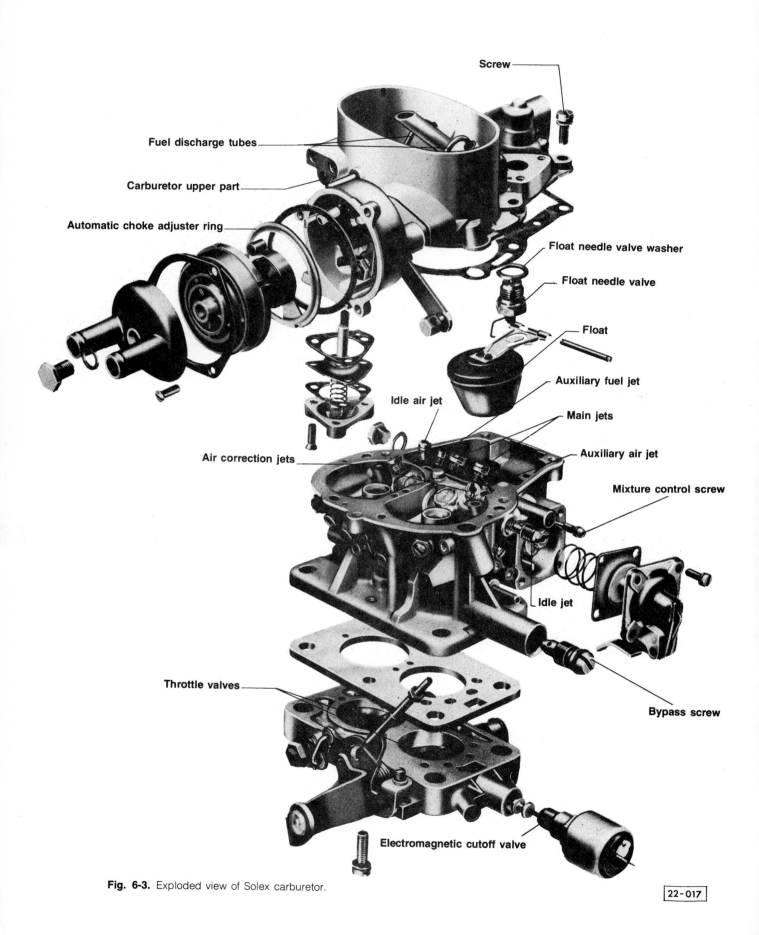

Fig. 6-3. Exploded view of Solex carburetor.

22-017

Disassembling and Assembling Carburetor

Disassembly of the Solex carburetor is illustrated in Fig. 6-3. The jet sizes and other specifications for this carburetor can be determined from the table that appears in **12. Fuel and Exhaust Systems Technical Data.** The following basic disassembly sequence should be followed:

1. Remove the carburetor upper part from the carburetor body.

2. Remove the various jets and adjustment screws from the carburetor body. Remove the float valve and the choke components from the carburetor upper part.

3. Disassemble the accelerator pump and linkage.

4. Take out the screws and remove the throttle body and the spacer from the bottom of the carburetor body.

5. Remove the electromagnetic cutoff valve from the throttle body.

CAUTION ——

It is not recommended that you try to disassemble the throttle valves and shafts. The screws that hold the throttle valves to the shafts are peened and are likely to strip or break if you try to remove them.

Obtain a rebuilding kit. With the exception of the choke heating element (on carburetors that have a supplemental electrical heating element), the pump diaphragm, the float, the vacuum diaphragm and similar non-metallic parts, was all old parts that are to be reused in lacquer thinner, acetone, or a commercial carburetor cleaner.

WARNING ——

Do not smoke or work near heaters or other fire hazards. The cleaning agents are highly combustible.

Blow out all jets, valves, and drillings with compressed air. Do not clean them with pins or pieces of wire, which could upset the precise calibration of these parts. Assembly of the carburetor is the reverse of disassembly. As you assemble the carburetor, install the new components from the rebuilding kit and carry out the adjustments described under the following unnumbered headings.

Adjusting Automatic Choke

The automatic choke is correctly adjusted when the three index marks indicated in Fig. 6-4 are in line with one another. The looped end of the thermostatic spring must be slipped over the cranked end of the choke valve shaft.

1. Notch on choke cover
2. Notch on adjuster ring
3. Notch on choke housing

Fig. 6-4. Choke index marks correctly aligned.

In order to make adjusting the choke easier, there is a notch in the adjuster ring that you can push against with the tip of a screwdriver, thus rotating the adjuster ring. See Fig. 6-5.

Fig. 6-5. Adjusting notch for insertion of screwdriver **(1)**. The adjusting notch is approximately opposite the index notch **(2)**.

Adjusting Throttle Valve Gaps

The throttle valve gaps need only be adjusted if the factory settings have been unintentionally altered. Never move the throttle valve adjustments from their factory settings unless this is necessary during repair of the carburetor. After you have adjusted either throttle valve, it is necessary to readjust the idle mixture (CO content) as described in **5.1 Adjusting Idle on Cars with Solex Carburetors.**

7

To adjust primary throttle valve gap:

1. Hold the choke valve fully open. If necessary, secure it in this position with a rubber band.

2. Loosen lock nut **a,** as given in Fig. 6-6. Then turn screw **b** counterclockwise until its tip no longer contacts the boss on the throttle body when the primary throttle valve is fully closed.

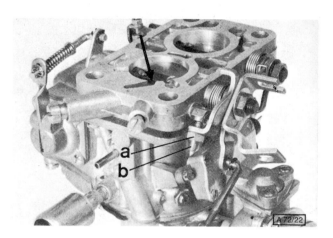

Fig. 6-6. Primary throttle valve adjustment. Lock nut is at **a,** adjusting screw is at **b.** Arrow indicates the primary throttle valve.

3. Hold the primary throttle valve closed—exerting no more than light pressure. Then, using a depth micrometer or the depth tang of a vernier caliper, measure dimension **y,** as given in Fig. 6-7.

4. From dimension **y,** measured in step 3, subtract 0.90 mm (.035 in.) if the carburetor is for a car with air injection. Subtract 0.40 mm (.016 in.) if the carburetor is for a car without air injection. The remainder is dimension **x.**

> **CAUTION ——**
> *The dimension* **y** *used in the following example is a fictitious number that is used only for instruction. Do not use this number in adjusting a carburetor.*

Example:

Dimension **y**	6.29 mm (.248 in.)
	−0.40 mm (.016 in.)
Dimension **x**	=5.89 mm (.232 in.)

5. Set the depth micrometer or vernier caliper to dimension **x,** which you computed in the preceding step. Then turn in the throttle valve adjusting screw (**b** in Fig. 6-6) until the edge of the throttle valve is set at dimension **x,** as given in Fig. 6-7. Tighten the lock nut and seal it with paint.

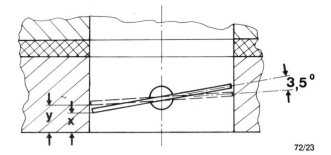

72/23

Fig. 6-7. Primary throttle valve adjustment. Dimension **y** is measured with throttle valve closed. Dimension **x** must be computed as described in the procedure steps. The 3.5° angle shown is applicable to carburetors used on cars that have air injection.

To adjust secondary throttle valve gap:

1. Loosen the locknut on the adjusting screw indicated in Fig. 6-8.

2. Loosen the adjusting screw until the secondary throttle valve is fully closed and the screw no longer makes contact.

3. Turn in the screw until it just makes contact, then turn it in one-half turn more. Lock the screw in this position by tightening the lock nut.

Fig. 6-8. Secondary throttle valve adjusting screw (circled).

Adjusting Fast Idle

The fast idle setting must be adjusted any time the carburetor has been disassembled. Do not alter the fast idle setting on a carburetor that is installed on a car. The carburetor must be removed for this adjustment.

To adjust fast idle:

1. Loosen the bolt indicated in Fig. 6-9. On carburetors that have two nuts threaded onto the connecting rod, loosen both nuts.

Fig. 6-9. Connecting rod adjustment bolt (arrow). Connecting rod with nuts and threaded end is illustrated earlier in Fig. 6-3.

Fig. 6-10. Vacuum pull-down unit being positioned. Press pull-down rod downward as indicated by lower arrow and rotate choke valve as indicated by the upper arrow. Drive lever **a** should contact upper stop on pull-down rod.

2. Obtain a drill bit for use as a gauge rod. Use an 0.80-mm (.032-in.) drill if the car is any VW model (except California VWs with manual transmissions) or an Audi model with an automatic transmission. Use an 0.65-mm (.026-in.) drill if the car is a California VW with a manual transmission or an Audi model with manual transmission.

3. Hold the choke valve fully closed. Then adjust the connecting rod—using either the adjusting bolt indicated in Fig. 6-9 or the two nuts shown earlier in Fig. 6-3—until the correct drill bit can just be inserted between the primary throttle valve and the carburetor bore as shown in Fig. 6-9. Tighten the adjusting bolt or the nuts.

4. Recheck the throttle valve clearance with the choke valve held fully closed. The drill bit should enter the gap exactly or within a tolerance range of ±0.05 mm (±.002 in.).

Adjusting Choke Vacuum Pull-down

Use a screwdriver to press the pull-down rod as far as possible into the vacuum chamber, as indicated by the downward-pointing arrow in Fig. 6-10. While holding the pull-down rod in this position, move the choke valve toward its closed position, as indicated by the curved arrow in Fig. 6-10. Move the choke valve until drive lever **a** is resting against the upper stop in the cutout of the pull-down rod. A 3.50-mm (.138-in.) drill should then fit between the edge of the choke valve and the carburetor air horn with a tolerance of ±0.15 mm (±.006 in.). See Fig. 6-11. If necessary, correct the choke gap by slightly bending drive lever **a.**

Fig. 6-11. Drill bit (arrow) being used as a gauge rod to determine choke valve vacuum pull-down opening.

7

Adjusting Accelerator Pump

The accelerator pump's injection quantity is adjustable. The adjustment is made by means of a bellcrank and cam located on the end of the primary throttle valve shaft.

To measure the injection quantity, first be sure that the float bowl is filled with fuel. Then attach a length of hose or tubing to the end of the accelerator pump discharge tube so that the expelled gasoline can be caught and measured in a glass graduate (Fig. 6-12). Hold the glass graduate under the end of the tubing and operate the throttle valve slowly and steadily exactly ten times. Divide the amount caught by ten to get the average quantity of a single injection pulse. The average quantity should be 0.9 cc ± 0.15 cc. With rapid movement of the throttle valve, the average quantity should be at least 0.4 cc ± 0.1 cc.

Fig. 6-12. Accelerator pump injection quantity being measured.

If the injection quantity is not correct, loosen the lock screw shown in Fig. 6-13. Move the bellcrank on the cam either to increase or to decrease the injection quantity as required. Then tighten the lock screw.

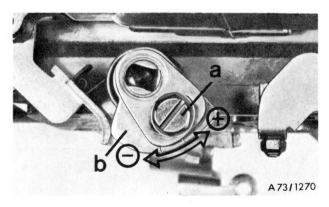

Fig. 6-13. Accelerator pump adjustment. Lock screw is at **a**, cam is at **b**. Turn bellcrank in directions indicated by double arrow to increase (+) or decrease (−) the injection quantity.

Recheck the injection quantity again after making the adjustment to see that it is within specifications. Best economy is obtained with the adjustment at the specified quantity. Exhaust emissions will be adversely affected if the quantity is increased above this point.

Checking Electromagnetic Cutoff Valve

The electromagnetic cutoff valve can be checked while it is installed. Turn on the ignition without starting the engine, then remove the wire from the terminal on the electromagnetic cutoff valve. Touch the wire to the terminal several times. The valve should make a clicking sound each time contact is made.

The same test can be carried out with the electromagnetic cutoff valve removed from the car. Connect negative battery current to the valve's outer casing and apply positive battery current to the terminal. You may have to apply slight finger pressure to the electromagnetic cutoff valve before the plunger will retract into the solenoid.

Checking Fuel Level in Float Bowl

The carburetor upper part must be removed before you can check the float level. Invert the carburetor upper part on a tapered block that will support the carburetor upper part at a 45° angle. See Fig. 6-14. Install the special gauge. The pointers of the gauge should align with the uppermost edge of the float collar. If you lack the special gauge, the upper edge of the collar on the float should be 16.5 mm ±1.0 mm (.649 in. ±.039 in.) above the surface of the carburetor upper part. If necessary, correct the level by bending the tongue of the float hinge that contacts the needle valve.

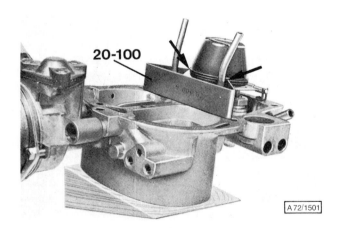

Fig. 6-14. Float position being measured with float needle valve closed. Pointers (arrows) on gauge should align with top of bead on float.

Adjusting or Replacing Throttle Dashpot

(except California models)

Make sure that the choke valve is fully open and that the primary throttle valve is closed. Push the plunger fully into the dashpot. Clearance **a**, given in Fig. 6-15, should be 1.00 mm (.039 in.). If not, loosen the dashpot mounting nuts and reposition the dashpot in its mounting until the clearance is correct. Then tighten the nuts.

Fig. 6-15. Dashpot adjustment. Measure clearance at **a**. It should be 1.00 mm (.039 in.) with the throttle closed and the dashpot plunger pressed in.

Beginning with Chassis No. __4 2155 256, the following additional steps also apply: First, open the throttle valve fully. Then fill gap **b**, given in Fig. 6-16, with the spacers supplied with the new dashpot. Use only as many of the spacers as are necessary to fill the gap.

NOTE——

The bushing supplied with the kit should be pressed into the plunger guide bracket from the side that is toward the dashpot.

Fig. 6-16. Spacers installed in gap between bushing and locking ring on plunger.

Replacing and Adjusting Secondary Throttle Valve Vacuum Unit

Replacement vacuum units for the secondary throttle valve must be adjusted during installation. Do this before you connect the vacuum unit operating rod to the throttle valve arm. Hold the choke valve fully open and both throttle valves fully closed. Then, by loosening the locknut and turning the operating rod, adjust the length of the vacuum unit operating rod until the hole in the rod end extends 1 to 2 mm (or $1/32$ to $1/16$ in.) beyond the pin on the throttle valve arm. Then tighten the locknut and connect the operating rod to the pin.

Installing Carburetor

Lightly lubricate the choke valve shaft and the throttle valve shafts with engine oil and the external linkage with molybdenum grease. Using a new gasket, install the carburetor on the intake manifold, then torque the nuts to 2.0 mkg (14 ft. lb.). Secure the fuel hose with a new hose clamp. Make sure that all wires and vacuum hoses have been installed in their original locations. After you have reconnected the accelerator cable, make certain that full throttle can be obtained before you install the air cleaner. See **8. Accelerator Cable.** Torque the air cleaner body mounting nut to 1.0 mkg (7 ft. lb.). Replace the intake air preheating duct hose if it is torn or otherwise damaged.

6.2 Removing, Rebuilding, and Installing Zenith Carburetor

If a carburetor must be replaced, it is important that the new carburetor have the same part number as the original, or that the new carburetor be the correct replacement for the car model being serviced. Always obtain replacement carburetors and carburetor parts with reference to the carburetor part number and the engine number.

7

To remove Zenith carburetor:

1. Release the clips that hold the cover to the body of the air cleaner. Remove the cover. Disconnect the EEC hose from the air cleaner body.

2. Remove the nut that holds the air cleaner body to its support. Then, being careful not to damage the intake air preheating duct as you disengage it from its connection on the exhaust manifold, lift up the air cleaner and disconnect the PCV hose. Remove the air cleaner from the car.

3. Obtain two corks of appropriate diameter. Disconnect the coolant hoses from the automatic choke and quickly plug them with the corks to prevent the loss of coolant.

4. Disconnect the accelerator cable from the pin on the throttle arm. Then remove the three screws that hold the accelerator cable conduit bracket to the carburetor and remove the bracket, leaving it attached to the cable conduit. By removing the bracket, you will avoid the job of having to adjust the accelerator cable.

5. Disconnect all electrical wires from the carburetor, marking them for correct reinstallation, if necessary.

WARNING —

Fuel will be spilled during removal of the carburetor. Disconnect the battery ground strap to prevent accidental electrical sparks. Do not work near heaters or other fire hazards. Have a fire extinguisher handy.

6. Disconnect the fuel hose and the vacuum hose(s) from the carburetor. Plug the disconnected fuel hose with a screw, a pencil, or a golf tee.

7. Remove the bolts that hold the carburetor to the intake manifold. Then remove the carburetor and its gasket from the manifold.

Disassembling and Assembling Carburetor

Fig. 6-17 and Fig. 6-18 show the locations of the various jets. In disassembling and assembling the Zenith carburetor, follow the exploded view given in Fig. 6-19. The jet sizes and other specifications for this carburetor can be determined from the table that appears in **11. Fuel and Exhaust Systems Technical Data.**

1. Secondary full load enrichment
2. Primary air correction jet
3. Secondary air correction jet
4. Primary idle air and idle fuel jets
5. Secondary idle air and idle fuel jets
6. Primary auxiliary air jet and auxiliary fuel jet (fuel jet is below air jet)

Fig. 6-17. Locations of jets that are accessible after the air cleaner is removed.

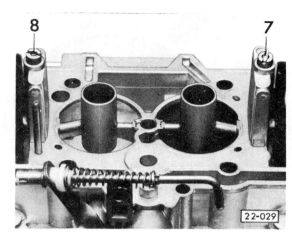

7. Primary jet
8. Secondary main jet

Fig. 6-18. Locations of jets that are accessible after removing carburetor upper part.

The following basic sequence should be followed in disassembling the carburetor:

1. Remove the carburetor upper part from the carburetor body.

2. Remove the various jets and adjustment screws. Remove the float valve and the choke components from the carburetor upper part.

3. Disassemble the accelerator pump and linkage.

4. Take out the screws and remove the throttle body and the spacer from the bottom of the carburetor body.

5. Remove the electromagnetic cutoff valve from the throttle body.

CAUTION —

It is not recommended that you try to disassemble the throttle valves and shafts. The screws that hold the throttle valves to the shafts are peened and are likely to strip or break if you try to remove them.

With the exception of the choke heating element (on carburetors that have a supplemental electrical heating element), the pump diaphragm, the floats, the vacuum diaphragm, and similar non-metallic parts, wash all old parts that are to be reused in lacquer thinner, acetone, or a commercial carburetor cleaner.

WARNING —

Do not smoke or work near heaters or other fire hazards. The cleaning agents are highly combustible.

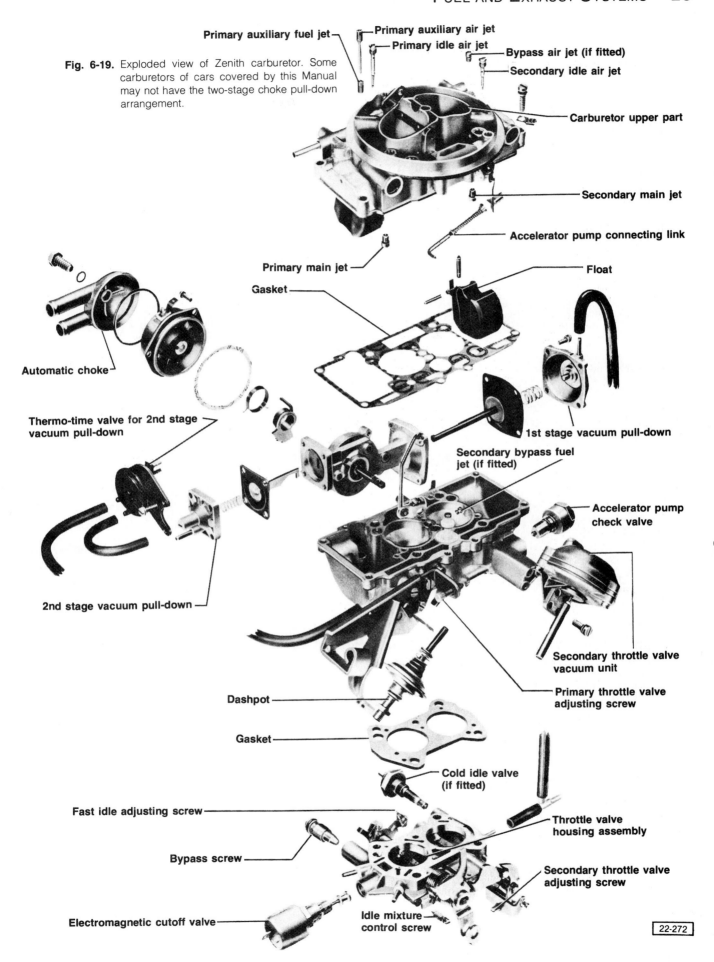

Primary auxiliary fuel jet

Primary auxiliary air jet

Primary idle air jet

Bypass air jet (if fitted)

Secondary idle air jet

Fig. 6-19. Exploded view of Zenith carburetor. Some carburetors of cars covered by this Manual may not have the two-stage choke pull-down arrangement.

Carburetor upper part

Secondary main jet

Accelerator pump connecting link

Primary main jet

Float

Gasket

Automatic choke

Thermo-time valve for 2nd stage vacuum pull-down

1st stage vacuum pull-down

Secondary bypass fuel jet (if fitted)

Accelerator pump check valve

2nd stage vacuum pull-down

Secondary throttle valve vacuum unit

Primary throttle valve adjusting screw

Dashpot

Gasket

Cold idle valve (if fitted)

Fast idle adjusting screw

Throttle valve housing assembly

Bypass screw

Secondary throttle valve adjusting screw

Electromagnetic cutoff valve

Idle mixture control screw

7

22-272

Blow out all jets, valves, and drillings with compressed air. Do not clean them with pins or pieces of wire, which could upset the precise calibration of these parts. Assembly of the carburetor is the reverse of disassembly. As you assemble the carburetor, install the new components from the rebuilding kit and carry out the adjustments described under the following numbered headings.

Installing and Adjusting Automatic Choke

In installing the automatic choke, the end of the choke valve operating lever must be inserted between the two tabs on the spring end (Fig. 6-20). Install the choke cover so that its index mark is aligned with the index mark on the choke housing of the carburetor.

Fig. 6-20. Choke installation. End of operating lever must go between tabs on spring end, as indicated by arrow.

Adjusting Throttle Valve Gaps

The throttle valve gaps need be adjusted only if the factory settings have been unintentionally altered. Never move the throttle valve adjustments from their factory settings unless this is necessary during carburetor repairs. After you have adjusted either throttle valve, it is necessary to readjust the idle mixture (CO content) as described in **5.2 Adjusting Idle on Cars with Zenith Carburetors.**

To adjust primary throttle valve gap:

1. Remove the plastic cap from the slotted end of the throttle valve adjusting screw (Fig. 6-21).

2. Turn the adjusting screw out until there is a gap between the throttle valve lever and the screw.

3. Turn in the adjusting screw until it just contacts the throttle valve lever with the choke valve fully open. Then turn the adjusting screw in one-quarter turn further so that there will be a slight amount of clearance between the throttle valve and the carburetor bore, thus preventing bore wear.

4. Reinstall the plastic cap on the slotted end of the adjusting screw.

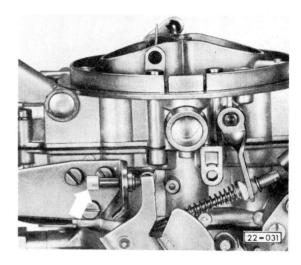

Fig. 6-21. Plastic cap (arrow) on end of throttle valve adjusting screw.

To adjust secondary throttle valve gap:

1. Hold the choke valve fully open; hold both throttle valves fully closed.

2. Turn in the secondary throttle valve adjusting screw until there is no clearance noticeable between the activating cam and the roller.

3. From this no-clearance position, turn the adjusting screw out one-half turn.

Adjusting Fast Idle

The fast idle setting must be adjusted any time the carburetor has been disassembled. Do not alter the fast idle setting on a carburetor that is installed on a car.

To adjust fast idle:

1. Hold the choke valve fully closed.

2. You should be able to insert a 0.45-mm (.018-in.) drill between the primary throttle valve and its bore (Fig. 6-22) but you should not be able to insert a 0.50-mm (.020-in.) drill.

3. If the gap is not between 0.45 and 0.50 mm (.018 and .020 in.), as measured in step 2, adjust the gap by turning the screw indicated in Fig. 6-22.

Fig. 6-22. Drill being used to measure fast idle opening. Arrow indicates fast idle adjusting screw.

Adjusting Choke Vacuum Pull-down

Using the tip of a screwdriver, push the pull-down rod fully into the choke vacuum chamber. With the pull-down rod in this position, hold the choke valve as nearly closed as possible. Then use a drill bit or gauge rod as shown in Fig. 6-23 to measure the gap between the choke valve and the air horn. The gap should be between 3.80 and 4.20 mm (.150 and .165 in.). If the gap is not correct, adjust the vacuum pull-down by turning the screw indicated in Fig. 6-23.

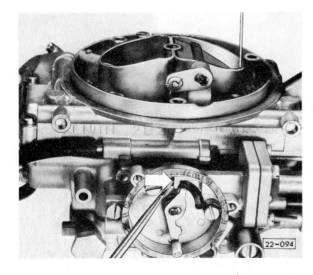

Fig. 6-23. Vacuum pull-down being measured. Push pull-down rod in direction of arrow. Insert drill or gauge rod as shown.

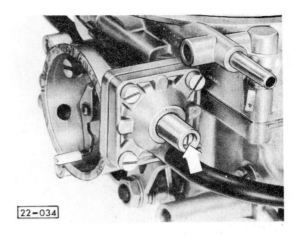

Fig. 6-24. Choke vacuum pull-down adjusting screw (arrow).

Adjusting Accelerator Pump

The accelerator pump's injection quantity is adjustable. The adjustment is made by turning a threaded adjusting sleeve that is on the end of the accelerator pump connecting link.

To measure the injection quantity, first be sure that the float bowl is filled with fuel. Then place a funnel in the top of a glass graduate and hold the carburetor over the funnel so that fuel expelled by the accelerator pump will run out of the carburetor's primary throttle bore and into the funnel. Slowly and steadily open the throttle valve exactly ten times—while holding the choke valve open. Divide the amount of fuel caught by ten to get the average quantity of a single injection pulse. The average quantity should be 0.75 to 1.05 cc.

If the injection quantity is not correct, turn the adjusting sleeve indicated in Fig. 6-25 either to increase or to decrease the injection quantity as required.

7

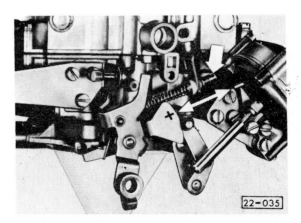

Fig. 6-25. Accelerator pump adjustment. Threaded adjusting sleeve is indicated by the broad arrow. Screw the sleeve further onto the connecting link to increase the quantity (+) or further off the link to decrease the quantity (−).

Recheck the injection quantity again after making the adjustment to see that it is within specifications. Best economy is obtained with the adjustment at the specified quantity. Exhaust emissions will be adversely affected if the quantity is increased above this point.

Checking Electromagnetic Cutoff Valve

The electromagnetic cutoff valve can be checked while it is installed. Turn on the ignition without starting the engine, then remove the wire from the terminal on the electromagnetic cutoff valve. Touch the wire to the terminal several times. The valve should make a clicking sound each time contact is made.

The same test can be carried out with the electromagnetic cutoff valve removed from the car. Connect negative battery current to the valve's outer casing and apply positive battery current to the terminal. You may have to apply slight finger pressure to the electromagmetic cutoff valve before the plunger will retract into the solenoid.

Checking Fuel Level in Float Bowl

The carburetor upper part must be removed before you can check the float level. Invert the carburetor upper part. Then measure from the uppermost part of the float to the surface of the carburetor upper part to determine dimension **a,** as given in Fig. 6-26. Dimension **a** for the float on the carburetor's primary side should be 28 mm ±0.50 mm (1.102 in. ±.020 in.). Dimension **a** for the float on the carburetor's secondary side should be 30 mm ±0.50 mm (1.181 in. ±.020 in.). If necessary, correct the level by bending the tongue of the float hinge that contacts the needle valve.

Fig. 6-26. Float position being measured (dimension **a**) with float needle valve closed.

Adjusting Throttle Dashpot

(except California models)

Make sure that the choke valve is fully open and that the primary throttle valve is closed. Push the plunger fully into the dashpot. Clearance **a,** given in Fig. 6-27, should be 3 mm (or 1/8 in.). If not, loosen the dashpot mounting nuts and reposition the dashpot in its mounting until the clearance is correct. Then tighten the nuts.

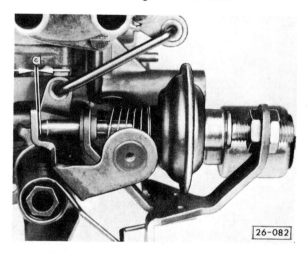

Fig. 6-27. Dashpot adjustment. Measure clearance at **a.** It should be 3 mm (or 1/8 in.) with the throttle closed and the dashpot plunger pressed in.

Replacing and Adjusting Secondary Throttle Valve Vacuum Unit

Replacement vacuum units for the secondary throttle valve must be adjusted during installation. Do this before you connect the vacuum unit operating rod to the throttle valve arm. Hold the choke valve fully open and both throttle valves fully closed. Then, by loosening the locknut and turning the operating rod, adjust the length of the vacuum unit operating rod until the ball socket in the rod extends 1 to 2 mm (or 1/32 to 1/16 in.) beyond the ball on the throttle valve arm. Then tighten the locknut and connect the operating rod to the ball.

Installing Carburetor

Lightly lubricate the choke valve shaft and the throttle valve shafts with engine oil and the external linkage with molybdenum grease. Using a new gasket, install the carburetor on the intake manifold, then torque the nuts to 2.0 mkg (14 ft. lb.). Secure the fuel hose with a new hose clamp. Make sure that all wires and vacuum hoses have been installed in their original locations. After you have reconnected the accelerator cable, make certain that full throttle can be obtained before you install the air cleaner. See **8. Accelerator Cable.** Torque the air cleaner body mounting nut to 1.0 mkg (7 ft. lb.). Replace the intake air preheating duct hose if it is torn or otherwise damaged.

7. FUEL INJECTION TROUBLESHOOTING AND REPAIR

Before you begin troubleshooting or repairing the CIS (continuous injection system), you should be thoroughly familiar with the diagram and the general description of the system that appears in **1.2 Fuel Injection.** The system has very few electrical components and a minimum knowledge of electrical circuits should suffice for troubleshooting purposes.

7.1 Troubleshooting Fuel Injection

Before you begin troubleshooting the fuel injection system, make sure that the engine trouble is not caused by something other than a fuel system problem. As with carburetors, no fuel injection test or adjustment should be made until you are confident that the engine has adequate compression and that the ignition system is not faulty.

Misfiring is not a typical symptom of a faulty fuel injection system. If you encounter misfiring—or if the car starts hard, fails to start, or has inadequate power—check for carbon tracking at the distributor rotor and distributor cap (Fig. 7-1), and the coil (Fig. 7-2). Replace faulty components. Also check the resistance of the spark plug connectors and the distributor rotor as described in **ENGINE AND CLUTCH.** Neither rotor nor connector resistance should exceed 10,000 ohms.

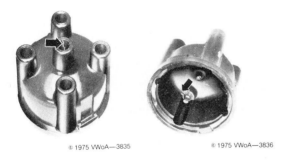

© 1975 VWoA—3835   © 1975 VWoA—3836

Fig. 7-1. Typical carbon tracks in distributor cap.

© 1975 VWoA—3837

Fig. 7-2. Typical carbon track on coil tower.

Finally, do not overlook incorrect valve clearances, faulty spark plugs, a dirty air cleaner, or a restricted exhaust system as possible causes of engine trouble. Because the fuel metering is highly dependent on the measurement of intake air volume, any air entering the engine that does not pass through the mixture control unit will cause the engine to operate incorrectly. Typically, it will start hard, idle slowly or stall at idle, and give symptoms of lean operation at driving speeds. Look for a loose-fitting oil filler cap, leaking or disconnected ventilation hoses, or a leaking cylinder head cover gasket.

Troubleshooting Procedures

The Bosch CIS (continuous injection system) has been designed so that you can make all the necessary electrical tests using only a test lamp and an ohmmeter. In addition to these two electrical instruments, you will need a fuel pressure gauge to test the fuel pump and the control pressure regulator.

Do not try to correct engine trouble by adjusting the idle speed or the idle mixture (CO content). Changing these adjustments will hinder you in locating trouble in other parts of the fuel injection system. Before you adjust the idle on an engine that is not running right owing to a fuel system problem, make a thorough inspection of the system in the following sequence:

1. Inspect the system visually for loose hoses, disconnected wires, and damaged components. See **7.2 Visual Inspection.**

2. Make electrical tests in order to determine whether current is reaching the right places at the right times. See **7.3 Electrical Tests.**

3. Make pressure tests and a pump delivery rate test so that you will know whether or not adequate fuel pressure is available under all conditions. See **7.4 Testing and Replacing Fuel Pump, Filter, and Fuel Pressure Accumulator.**

4. Inspect and test the individual injection system components—testing those that seem most likely to be trouble sources in light of the engine running conditions, the fuel pressure tests, and the electrical tests previously made. See headings for **7.5** through **7.12.** Correct the trouble.

5. Adjust the idle. See **5.3 Adjusting Idle on Cars with Fuel Injection.**

Troubleshooting Table

As previously stated, you should always check the engine for ignition and mechanical problems before doing any fuel injection system troubleshooting. Make sure that there is fuel in the tank and that the battery is not run down.

Table c lists engine operating problems, their possible causes, and where the applicable fuel injection system troubleshooting or repair procedures can be found. The numbers listed after each possible cause indicate the heading in this section of the Manual where appropriate testing and repair instructions are described. Troubleshoot the possible causes in the order in which they appear. To troubleshoot fuel injection problems not covered by this table, use the sequence given under the preceding heading.

Table c. Fuel Injection System Troubleshooting

I. Engine hard to start or fails to start when cold (battery not discharged, starter current draw not excessive)
1. Cold-start valve not opening. See **7.8.**
2. Thermo-time switch defective. See **7.7.**
3. Wiring or pump relay faulty. See **7.3.**

II. Engine is hard to start or fails to start when hot (battery not discharged, engine not overheated, oil supply and viscosity adequate)
1. Cold-start valve leaking or operating continuously. See **7.8.**
2. Control pressure regulator faulty. See **7.6.**
3. Wiring or pump relay faulty. See **7.3.**
4. Fuel leaks in the system. See **7.4.**

III. Engine fails to start under any condition (battery not discharged, fuel in tank)
1. Large air leaks. See **7.2.**
2. Insufficient fuel. See **7.4.**
3. Cold-start valve faulty. See **7.8.**
4. Thermo-time switch faulty. See **7.7.**
5. Decel valve faulty. See **7.9.**
6. Mixture control unit faulty. See **7.5.**
7. Auxiliary air regulator faulty. See **7.10.**
8. Control pressure regulator faulty. See **7.6.**

IV. Idle speed varies
1. Check the idle speed and mixture (CO content). See **5.3.**
2. Small air leaks. See **7.2.**
3. Control pressure regulator faulty. See **7.6.**
4. Injection nozzles or nozzle seals faulty. See **7.11.**
5. EGR valve faulty or not being switched off at idle. See **9.**
6. Leaking fuel lines. See **7.12.**
7. Cold-start valve leaking. See **7.8.**
8. Mixture control unit faulty. See **7.5.**

V. Engine starts but stall at idle
1. Control pressure regulator faulty. See **7.6.**
2. Cold-start leaking or operating continuously. See **7.8.**
3. Thermo-time switch faulty. See **7.7.**
4. Auxiliary air regulator faulty. See **7.10.**
5. "Engine warm" control pressure incorrect. See **7.4.**
6. Idle incorrectly adjusted. See **5.3.**

VI. Engine rpm fails to drop to idle speed when accelerator is relesed
1. Binding accelerator linkage or cable; lubricate linkage. See **8.**
2. Auxiliary air regulator not closing. See **7.10.**
3. Decel valve leaking. See **7.9.**

VII. Engine hesitates on acceleration (if engine backfires into intake air distributor, check engine for valve and other mechanical faults)
1. Air leaks. See **7.2.**
2. Injection nozzles not delivering uniform quantities. See **7.11.**
3. Fuel distributor faulty. See **7.5.**
4. Cold-start valve leaking. See **7.8.**
5. "Engine warm" control pressure incorrect. See **7.4.**
6. Idle mixture incorrectly adjusted. See **5.3.**

VIII. High fuel consumption
1. Leaking fuel lines. See **7.12.**
2. Control pressures incorrect. See **7.4.**
3. Control pressure regulator faulty. See **7.6.**
4. Cold-start valve leaking. See **7.8.**
5. Idle mixture incorrectly adjusted. See **5.3.**

continued on next page

Table c. Fuel Injection System Troubleshooting (continued)

IX. Engine continues to run after ignition is turned off
  1. Sensor plate stuck above "off" position. See **7.5.**
  2. Injection nozzles leaking. See **7.11.**
  3. Fuel pressures excessive. See **7.4.**

7.2 Visual Inspection

You should visually inspect the entire system for fuel and air leaks before undertaking any adjustments or tests on the CIS (continuous injection system). Before you make any electrical tests, please read **7.3 Electrical Tests.** Unless the precautions described there are observed, you could accidentally damage solid state components in the car. However, loose wires that you may find during your visual examination can be reconnected so long as the ignition is turned off and you are sure that you are reconnecting the wires to their correct terminals. Fig. 7-3 and Fig. 7-4 show the locations of the various fuel injection components on the engine.

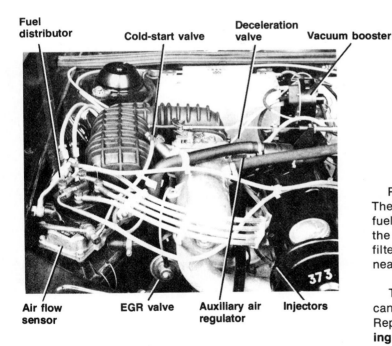

Fig. 7-3. Fuel injection components on the right-hand side of the engine. EGR valve, deceleration valve, and vacuum booster are covered in **9.3 1975 and Later Fuel Injection Engine Emission Controls.**

Fig. 7-4. Fuel injection components on the left-hand side of engine.

Checking Fuel Line Connections

Place the car on a hoist or support it on jack stands. Then check the fuel line connections at the fuel tank, the fuel pump, and the fuel pressure accumulator. Moving to the front of the car, check the connections at the fuel filter, which is located on the front floor plate, underneath the left side of the firewall.

The fuel line connections in the engine compartment can be examined while the car is sitting on its wheels. Replace damaged fuel lines as described in **7.11 Replacing Plastic Fuel Lines.** If there are leaks around the banjo unions, torque them to no more than 1.0 mkg (7 ft. lb.) in an attempt to stop the leak. If torquing is not adequate to seal the leaking gasket, replace the gasket. Do not overtighten the union.

Checking Air System

Leaks in the air system that will affect engine operation are leaks that allow air to enter at some point between the mixture control unit's sensor plate and engine's intake valves. Only a large air leak will prevent the engine from starting. Look for a torn or loose connecting duct between the mixture control unit and the throttle valve housing. The engine will start if there are only small leaks, such as disconnected vacuum hoses, a loose-fitting oil filler cap, or a loose duct clamp. Typically, small air leaks will cause the engine to run or idle irregularly.

Any air leak in the critical area between the sensor plate and the intake valves will cause uncontrolled lean mixtures and result in poor engine output. Check especially the connecting duct, the hoses connected to the auxiliary air regulator, the intake air distributor flange gaskets, air hose connections on the intake air distributor, the cold-start valve flange gasket, the injection nozzle seals, the vacuum lines at the vacuum powered brake booster, the vacuum lines at the throttle valve housing, and the vacuum connection at the EGR valve. Make sure that the wires are connected to the auxiliary air regulator. Otherwise the auxiliary air regulator may not be closing completely.

7.3 Electrical Tests

The electrical testing of individual components is described under the heading for that component: for example, **7.8 Testing and Replacing Cold-start Valve.** In making electrical tests, refer to the current flow diagram given in the Wiring Diagrams topic of **ELECTRICAL SYSTEM.**

Except for the cold-start valve, which receives current from terminal 50, all other electrical components of the fuel injection system receive positive current via the pump relay. This relay is located in the car's fuse/relay box. In making electrical tests, keep in mind that terminals numbered 30 are permanently connected to positive battery current. Terminals numbered 50 provide positive battery current only while the starter is being operated; they are connected to the control circuit of the starter solenoid. Terminals numbered 15 provide positive battery current whenever the ignition is turned on.

> *CAUTION* ———
>
> *Before you make any electrical tests on an engine that is not running but has the ignition turned on, disconnect the plug from the air sensor switch (on cars that have it) and disconnect the positive wire from the alternator. Otherwise, testing may damage the diode on the alternator. Disconnect the high tension cable from terminal 4 of the ignition coil so that the engine will not start when you run the starter.*

7.4 Testing and Replacing Fuel Pump, Filter, and Fuel Pressure Accumulator

Absolute cleanliness is essential when you work with fuel circuit components of the CIS. Even a minute particle of dirt may cause trouble if it reaches an injector. Before you disconnect any of the fuel line connections, thoroughly clean the unions. Use clean tools.

Pressure Tests

Special care is required when you check the control pressure because the control pressure influences all engine operating characteristics—such as idle, partial throttle and full throttle response, starting and warm-up, engine power, and emission levels.

To test "Engine cold" control pressure:

1. Disconnect the control pressure line from the center of the top of the fuel distributor. Connect the outlet hose of the pressure gauge's 3-way valve to the fuel distributor in place of the control pressure line. See Fig. 7-5 and Fig. 7-6.

> **NOTE** ———
>
> The engine must be completely cold for an "Engine cold" control pressure test. For this test, the vehicle should not be operated for several hours—preferably left unused overnight.

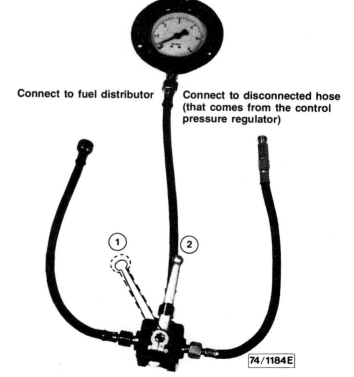

Connect to fuel distributor   Connect to disconnected hose (that comes from the control pressure regulator)

74/1184E

Fig. 7-5. Pressure gauge used for testing control pressures and system pressure, and for detecting leakage.

Fig. 7-6. Pressure gauge correctly installed. Operating lever of 3-way valve is at **A**.

2. Connect the hose you disconnected from the fuel distributor to the inlet hose of the pressure gauge's 3-way valve.

3. Disconnect the electrical plug from the control pressure regulator; disconnect the positive wire from the alternator.

4. Allow the pressure gauge to hang down so that the 3-way valve is uppermost. This is necessary in order to bleed air from the pressure gauge.

5. Remove the fuel pump relay from the relay plate of the fuse box. Then bridge terminals L13 and L14 as indicated in Fig. 7-7. While the pump is running, move the operating lever on the 3-way valve at 10-second intervals about five times between position 1 (lever toward hose connected to fuel distributor, i.e., flow blocked) and position 2 (lever toward hose attached to pressure gauge, i.e., flow to the control pressure regulator).

NOTE ──

It is not necessary to switch on the ignition.

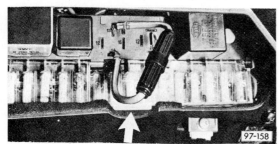

Fig. 7-7. Terminals L13 and L14 bridged with jumper wire.

6. With the gauge bled, hang the gauge from the hood so that it can be easily read. Keep the ignition on and the fuel pump running. Move the 3-way valve to position 2 (toward the hose attached to the pressure gauge). See Fig. 7-8. The pressure gauge reading should be in the nominal range for the corresponding ambient temperature, as shown in Fig. 7-9. If not, replace the control pressure regulator.

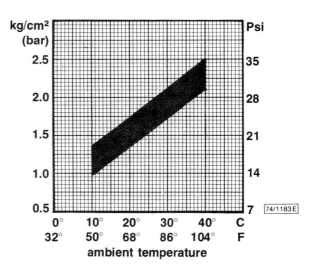

Fig. 7-8. 3-way valve lever in position **2**. Car shown is not one of those covered by this Manual.

7

Fig. 7-9. Graph of acceptable "Engine cold" control pressures. For example, at 30°C the "Engine cold" control pressure should be between 1.70 and 2.10 bar.

To test "Engine warm" control pressure:

1. Conduct the "Engine cold" test just described. If no fault is found, keep the jumper wire on terminals L13 and L14.

2. Observe the pressure gauge. As the warm running compensation heating element in the control pressure regulator warms up, the control pressure should rise and stabilize between 3.40 and 3.80 bar (48 to 54 psi).

3. If an "Engine warm" control pressure between 3.40 and 3.80 bar (48 to 54 psi) cannot be obtained, replace the control pressure regulator.

To check system pressure:

1. Move the 3-way lever on the pressure gauge to position 1 (lever pointed toward the gauge hose attached to the fuel distributor). This will block the flow of fuel to the fuel distributor, thus eliminating the escape of fuel past the fuel distributor's pressure relief valve.

2. Bridge terminals L13 and L14 as before. The pressure should build up to 4.50 to 5.20 bar (64 to 74 psi).

3. If the system pressure is not within the prescribed range, the fuel pump is probably faulty. However, you should check for leaks between the pump and the control pressure regulator before replacing the pump.

4. If the system pressure is within the prescribed range, but the engine is operating with an excessively lean mixture, the pump's check valve may be faulty. To test the check valve, again bridge terminals L13 and L14 until the pressure is between 4.50 and 5.20 bar (64 to 74 psi). Then disconnect the jumper wire. If, within 10 minutes, the pressure drops below 1.8 bar (25 psi), replace the check valve as described in the next two steps.

5. To replace the fuel pump check valve, remove the right rear wheel. Then remove the fuel tank filler cap in order to release any pressure. Thoroughly clean the fuel line union. Disconnect the fuel line at the point indicated in Fig. 7-10 or Fig. 7-11.

   NOTE ——
   Beginning with the 1978 models, the same kind of fuel pump is used as on later 1977 cars, but on some cars the pump is now located nearer the right rear wheel, as shown in Fig. 7-12.

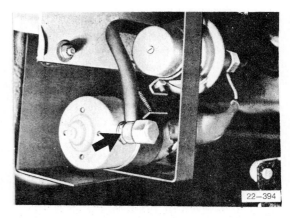

Fig. 7-10. Fuel line that must be removed from 1975 through early 1977 pump before you can replace pump's check valve.

Fig. 7-11. New-type electric fuel pump introduced early in 1977 model year. Arrow indicates fuel line connection that must be removed before you can replace pump's check valve.

Fig. 7-12. Location of fuel pump on some 1978 and later cars.

6. Remove the screw connector, which contains the check valve (Fig. 7-13 or Fig. 7-14). Using a new seal washer, install a new check valve—Part No. 810 906 112 for the pump shown in Fig. 7-10 or Part No. 810 906 093 for the pump shown in Fig. 7-11 and Fig. 7-12. Torque the screw connector to no more than 15 to 20 cmkg (13 to 17 in. lb.) for the early pump or 2.0 mkg (14 ft. lb.) for the later pump.

7. If the system maintains pressure, but the engine still operates with an excessively lean mixture, the fuel pressure may be adequate but the fuel delivery rate may be too low. First replace the fuel filter as described under the next heading. Then test the delivery rate as described in the following procedure.

Fig. 7-13. Screw connector (arrow) that contains check valve on early-type pump.

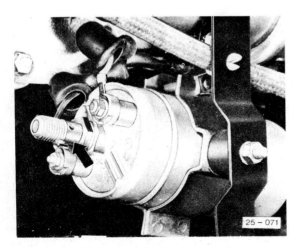

Fig. 7-14. Screw connector (arrow) that contains check valve on late-type pump.

To test fuel pump delivery rate:

1. Disconnect the high tension cable from terminal 4 of the ignition coil.

2. Disconnect the fuel return line from the fuel distributor.

> *CAUTION* ——
> *Fuel will be expelled as you disconnect the union. Do not disconnect any wires that could cause electrical sparks. Do not smoke or work near heaters or other fire hazards. Have a fire extinguisher handy.*

3. If previously removed, install the fuel pump relay. Then place the end of the return line hose in an 800-cc or 1000-cc glass graduate. See Fig. 7-15.

4. Run the starter for exactly 30 seconds so that the fuel pump operates for precisely that period of time. On pumps that have the wires attached with nuts, you should have collected at least 900 cc (about 30 oz.) of fuel. On pumps that have the wires attached with flat spade terminals, you should have collected at least 750 cc (about 25 oz.) of fuel.

5. If the delivery rate is low, check that the fuel filter is not clogged; replace the filter if necessary, then repeat the delivery rate test. If the delivery rate is still low, replace the pump. If the pump did not run, make the tests described later under **Fuel Pump Electrical Tests.**

Fig. 7-15. Glass graduate being used to measure fuel delivery rate.

7

Replacing Fuel Filter

On 1975 through 1977 cars with fuel injection, the fuel filter is located on the left-hand side of the front floor plate, underneath the firewall (Fig. 7-16). Beginning with the 1978 models, the fuel filter is in the engine compartment, attached to the firewall between the ignition coil and the vacuum powered brake servo (Fig. 7-17).

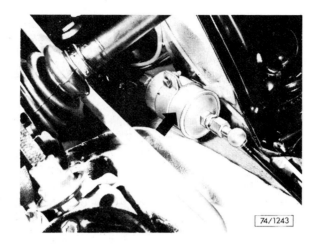

Fig. 7-16. Location of 1975-1977 fuel filter (arrow).

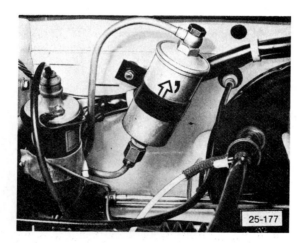

Fig. 7-17. Location of 1978 and later fuel filter. This filter will not fit earlier cars. Arrow on filter indicates direction of flow (toward engine).

Thoroughly clean both connections before you attempt to remove the filter. Then disconnect the fuel line unions from the filter, loosen the clamp bolt that holds the filter in the bracket, and remove the old filter from the car.

WARNING —

Fuel will be discharged as you disconnect the unions. To minimize fuel loss, insert rubber plugs into the disconnected lines. Do not smoke or work near heaters or other fire hazards. Have a fire extinguisher handy.

In installing the new filter, notice the direction of flow indicated on the filter housing (Fig. 7-18). The arrow on the housing should point toward the hose that conducts fuel to the engine. After you have connected the line unions to the new filter, run the starter so that the pump operates. Check for leaks at the filter connections.

Fig. 7-18. Arrows on fuel filter that indicate direction of fuel flow (toward engine).

Fuel Backpressure Valve(s)

Near the beginning of the 1977 model year, fuel backpressure valves were introduced to help eliminate pressure variations in the system. These valves are installed in the supply line and the return line at the points indicated in Fig. 7-19. Beginning with the 1978 models, the valves shown in Fig. 7-19 were eliminated and replaced by a single fuel backpressure valve located in the fuel filter fitting for the fuel supply line. See Fig. 7-20.

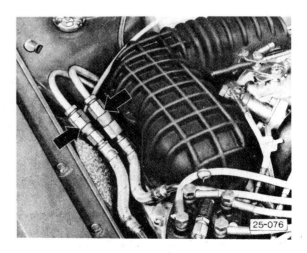

Fig. 7-19. Locations of fuel backpressure valves of 1977 car.

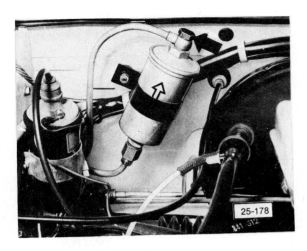

Fig. 7-20. Location of fuel backpressure valve introduced on 1978 cars (arrow).

Fuel Pump Electrical Tests

Cars through VW Chassis No. __6 2084 184 and Audi Chassis No. __6 2042 541 have a fuel pump relay with six terminals. Later cars have a fuel pump relay with five terminals. Early 1975 Audi models have the fuel pump fused through fuse No. 10, but after sedan Chassis No. __5 2064 873 and wagon Chassis No. __5 2002 285, the pump is connected to relay plate terminal 30d through an in-line 16-amp fuse (Fig. 7-21). Many earlier 1975 Audi models have had the in-line fuse service installed after manufacture. Some cars have the fuse located atop the pump relay itself.

The following electrical tests should be made if the pump does not run or if the pump fails to deliver adequate volume or fuel pressure owing to erratic pump operation. Before you make any other test, check the fuel pump relay. Checking the relay will determine whether the fault is in the relay or in the pump and wiring.

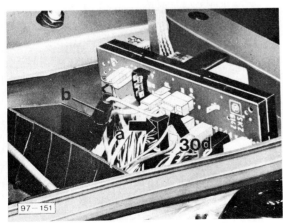

Fig. 7-21. In-line fuse holder (**b**) installed in 1975 Audi. Pump wire is at arrow **a**; terminal 30d is indicated by the right-hand arrow.

To check pump relay:

1. Check the fuse for the electric fuel pump. This fuse is sometimes located atop the pump relay (Fig. 7-22).

Fig. 7-22. Fuel pump fuse atop relay.

2. Remove the cover from the fuse/relay box. Remove the fuel pump relay. If necessary, consult **ELECTRICAL SYSTEM** in order to determine the relay's location.

3. Make a test jumper such as the one shown in Fig. 7-23. Use 1.5 mm² (14-gauge) wire and an 8-amp fuse in the in-line fuse holder.

4. Turn on the ignition.

> **CAUTION ──**
>
> *Before you make any electrical tests on a car that is not running but has the ignition turned on, disconnect the plug from the air sensor switch (on cars that have it) and disconnect the positive wire from the alternator. Otherwise, testing may damage a diode at the alternator.*

5. Using the test jumper, bridge terminals L13 and L14. If the pump did not run previously (or ran erratically) with the relay installed, but runs smoothly when the terminals are bridged, the relay is faulty and should be replaced. If the fuse blows or the fuel pump fails to run correctly, there is trouble in the pump or the wiring to the pump.

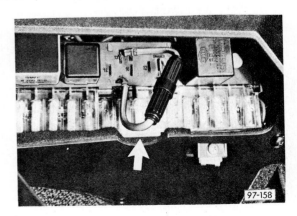

Fig. 7-23. Fuel pump relay being checked.

7

To determine whether current from the pump relay is reaching the fuel pump, install a pump relay that you know is in good condition. Alternatively, keep the test jumper installed between terminal L13 and terminal L14. Working under the rear of the car, disconnect both wires from the fuel pump. Then, with the ignition turned on, measure the voltage at the disconnected wires with a voltmeter. See Fig. 7-24. If there is no voltage, there is a faulty wire or connection between the pump relay and the fuel pump. If the voltage is less than full battery voltage, there is a corroded connector or other high-resistance connection somewhere between the relay and the pump.

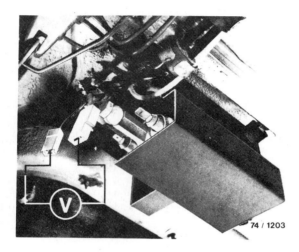

Fig. 7-24. Voltmeter connections used to test current delivered to the fuel pump. Pump is located beneath the car, just ahead of the front right-hand corner of the fuel tank.

To test the fuel pump's current draw, disconnect the positive wire from the pump as shown in Fig. 7-25. Connect an ammeter in series between the disconnected positive wire and the pump terminal. Turn on the ignition so that the pump operates. The current draw indicated by

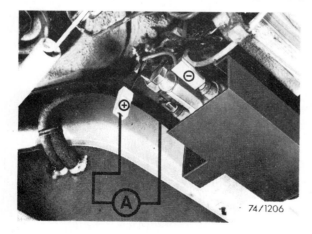

Fig. 7-25. Ammeter connections used to test current draw of fuel pump. Notice that negative wire is connected to the pump.

the ammeter must not exceed 8.5 amperes. If the current draw is higher, replace the pump. Though the current draw is not excessive, you should still replace the pump if it fails to attain the minimum delivery rate prescribed earlier under **Pressure Tests.**

Replacing Fuel Pump and Fuel Pressure Accumulator

The fuel pressure accumulator on 1975 through 1977 cars is mounted directly above the fuel pump. The pump and the pressure accumulator on these models are located beneath the car, just ahead of the front right-hand corner of the fuel tank (Fig. 7-26). The accumulator used on most 1977 and all later models is shaped differently and is slightly larger. On some of the 1978 models, the fuel pressure accumulator is mounted separately, as shown in Fig. 7-27. See Fig. 7-12, given earlier, for the pump location on 1978 and later cars.

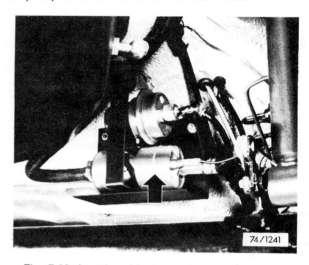

Fig. 7-26. Location of fuel pump (arrow) and fuel pressure accumulator through 1977.

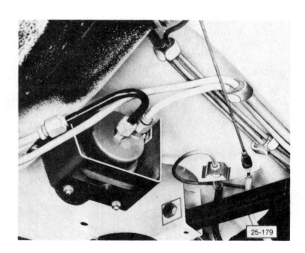

Fig. 7-27. Location of fuel pressure accumulator on some 1978 and later cars.

To replace pump:

1. Make certain that the ignition is turned off. Disconnect the electrical connections from the fuel pump.

2. Thoroughly clean the fuel line unions before you disconnect them. Then disconnect both fuel lines from the fuel pump. Quickly insert a rubber plug into the hose that comes from the tank.

WARNING —

Fuel will be discharged as you disconnect the unions. Do not smoke or work near heaters or other fire hazards. Have a fire extinguisher handy.

3. Loosen the screw that holds the pump to the mounting bracket. Then remove the pump from the car.

Installation is the reverse of removal. See Fig. 7-28. If either electrical connector is broken, corroded, or otherwise damaged, replace it. Following installation, turn on the ignition so that the fuel pump operates. Check for leaks around the unions on the fuel pump.

The fuel pressure accumulator should be replaced if it is leaking or if it fails to maintain residual pressure in the

system for a few minutes after the engine has been turned off. The failure to maintain residual pressure can cause vapor lock. The fault is usually a ruptured diaphragm in the fuel pressure accumulator. See Fig. 7-29.

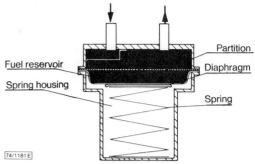

Fig. 7-29. Schematic cross-section of fuel pressure accumulator. The unit cannot be disassembled for repair.

To replace pressure accumulator:

1. Thoroughly clean the fuel line unions before you disconnect them from the fuel pressure accumulator.

2. Disconnect both fuel lines from the fuel pressure accumulator. To minimize the loss of fuel, quickly insert rubber plugs into the disconnected lines.

WARNING —

Fuel will be discharged as you disconnect the unions. Do not smoke or work near heaters or other fire hazards. Have a fire extinguisher handy.

3. Loosen the screw that holds the fuel pressure accumulator to the mounting bracket. Then remove the pressure accumulator from the car.

Installation is the reverse of removal. Following installation, turn on the ignition so that the fuel pump operates. Check for leaks around the unions on the fuel pressure accumulator.

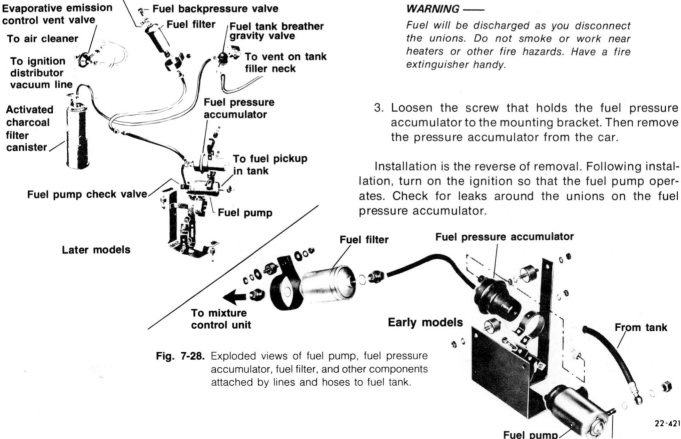

Fig. 7-28. Exploded views of fuel pump, fuel pressure accumulator, fuel filter, and other components attached by lines and hoses to fuel tank.

7.5 Testing and Repairing Mixture Control Unit

The mixture control unit governs the fuel/air ratio. It consists of an air flow sensor and the fuel distributor. The sensor plate of the air flow sensor is connected to the control plunger of the fuel distributor's metering unit. A simplified diagram of the mixture control unit is given in Fig. 7-30.

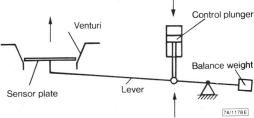

Fig. 7-30. Simplified diagram of mixture control unit.

As air enters from the air cleaner, it must pass between the sensor plate and its venturi before it can enter the connecting duct and flow toward the throttle valves. The balance weight partially offsets the weight of the lever and the sensor plate. The intake air lifts the air sensor plate until an equilibrium is reached between the air flow rate and the hydraulic counterpressure that acts on the lever through the control plunger.

The control plunger, in moving up or down in its cylinder, uncovers or covers the square-shaped metering ports of the fuel distributor's metering unit. Each injection outlet of the fuel distributor has its own metering port. Thus, the flow of fuel to the injectors is always in direct proportion to the quantity of air entering the engine.

A detailed layout of the fuel distributor's metering unit appears in Fig. 7-31. There are four of the steel-diaphragm pressure regulating valves—one for each injector hose outlet. These valves maintain a constant pressure drop in the metering ports regardless of fuel flow, fuel pump pressure, or injector opening pressure.

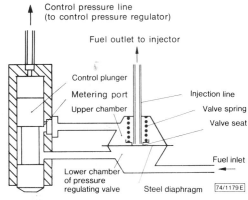

Fig. 7-31. Schematic layout of fuel distributor's metering unit.

To test mixture control unit:

1. Disconnect the connecting duct from the outlet of the mixture control unit's air flow sensor. This is the large rubber duct that connects the mixture control unit with the throttle valve housing.

2. Remove the fuel pump relay from the relay plate of the fuse box. Then bridge terminals L13 and L14 for about 5 seconds so that the fuel pump will operate and pressurize the system. This pressure will press the fuel distributor metering unit's control plunger against the sensor plate lever. See Fig. 7-32.

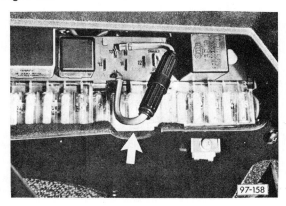

Fig. 7-32. Terminals L13 and L14 bridged with jumper wire.

3. Using a magnetic tool, lift the sensor plate by hand, as indicated in Fig. 7-33. There should be uniform resistance throughout the plate's entire range of travel. (With rapid downward movement, the lever will encounter more resistance owing to the residual hydraulic pressure being exerted on the control plunger.)

4. If the sensor plate is hard to move, or moves with uneven resistance, remove the top of the air flow sensor in order to determine why the sensor plate is hard to move. If the pivot is dirty or lacks lubrication, you should clean and relubricate it so that it moves smoothly.

5. If the resistance encountered in moving the sensor plate is caused by a binding control plunger, replace the fuel distributor as described in the next two steps. Faulty control plungers cannot be replaced separately because each plunger is a precision fit with its own fuel distributor.

6. To replace the fuel distributor, first disconnect the fuel line banjo unions from the old fuel distributor.

WARNING ——
Fuel will be expelled as you remove the unions. Do not smoke or work near heaters or other fire hazards. Have a fire extinguisher handy.

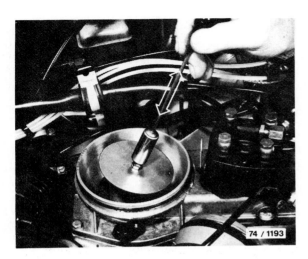

Fig. 7-33. Magnetic tool being used to raise and lower sensor plate (double arrow).

7. Remove the screws that hold the fuel distributor to the cover of the air flow sensor housing (Fig. 7-34).

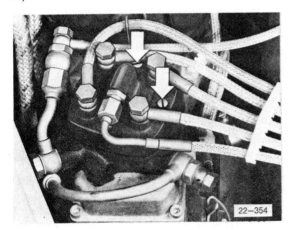

Fig. 7-34. Screws (arrows) that hold fuel distributor to air flow sensor.

8. Remove the old fuel distributor. Then, using a new gasket (Fig. 7-35), install the new fuel distributor. Adjust the idle as described in **5.3 Adjusting Idle on Cars with Fuel Injection.**

CAUTION ——

The control plunger can easily fall out of the fuel distributor (Fig. 7-36). So it is best to hold the cover of the air flow sensor housing in an inverted position during removal or installation of the fuel distributor. If the plunger of the new fuel distributor is allowed to fall, it may be damaged —thereby rendering the entire fuel distributor unserviceable. Always wash the plunger with gasoline before you install the plunger in the fuel distributor.

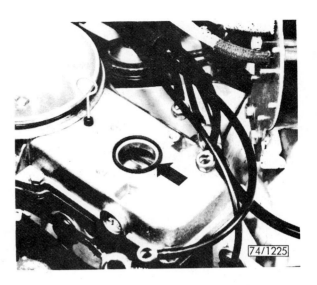

Fig. 7-35. Gasket for fuel distributor. In installing the fuel distributor on the air flow sensor housing, torque the screws to 35 to 40 cmkg (30 to 35 in. lb.).

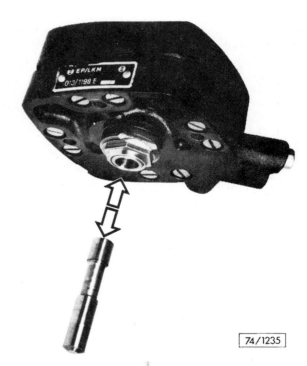

Fig. 7-36. Control plunger and fuel distributor. The plunger can easily be removed or inserted, as indicated by the arrows. Notice that the longest land on the plunger should be toward the sensor plate lever.

9. If the sensor plate moved with uniform resistance in step 3, check the rest position of the sensor plate. To do this, install a pressure gauge, VW 1318 or P 379, in the line that connects the fuel

7

distributor with the control pressure regulator (Fig. 7-37). Set the gauge lever to the open position.

NOTE ——

The control pressure regulator is located on the left-hand side of the engine block. The control pressure line is the fuel line that connects the control pressure regulator with the center of the top of the fuel distributor.

WARNING ——

Fuel will be expelled as you loosen the union. Do not smoke or work near heaters or other fire hazards. Have a fire extinguisher handy.

Fig. 7-37. Mixture control unit being prepared for testing. Lever (**a**) is in open position. Connecting duct at **B** should be removed.

10. Install a jumper wire on relay socket terminals L13 and L14, as previously shown in Fig. 7-32. (It is not necessary to switch on the ignition.) Wait until the pressure gauge reads 3.40 to 3.80 bar (48 to 54 psi). (This is the "Engine warm" control pressure test described earlier.)

11. Disconnect the jumper wire. With the wire off, the pressure should drop, then stabilize between 2.00 and 2.60 bar (28 to 37 psi).

12. If the pressure is incorrect in step 10, the control pressure regulator is faulty and should be replaced; if the pressure falls rapidly below the minimum pressure given in step 11, the fuel pump's check valve is faulty and should be replaced. If the pressure is correct in both steps, check the rest position of the sensor plate while the pressure is between 2.00 and 2.60 bar (28 and 37 psi). See Fig. 7-38.

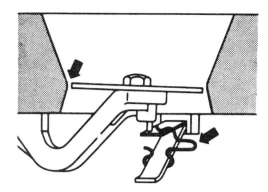

Fig. 7-38. Correct sensor plate position. Edge of plate (left arrow) should be neither above nor more than 0.50 mm (.020 in.) below narrowest point of venturi. Height can be adjusted by bending wire spring stop at right arrow.

13. If the sensor plate position is incorrect, take out the screws, then remove the cover from the air flow sensor.

14. Bend the U-shaped part of the spring stop (Fig. 7-39) so that the sensor plate is correctly aligned with the narrowest point of the venturi when the sensor plate is in its rest position.

NOTE ——

When you check the adjustment by temporarily placing the cover back on the air flow sensor, make sure that the fuel pressure is still between 2.00 and 2.60 bar (28 and 37 psi). If necessary, temporarily reinstall the jumper wire to run the fuel pump and restore the pressure to its correct range.

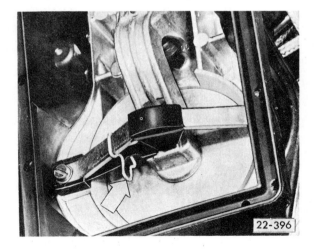

Fig. 7-39. Spring stop (arrow).

15. When the adjustment is correct, reinstall the cover using a new gasket. Then remove the pressure gauge and reconnect the fuel line. Install the rubber elbow.

16. Reinstall the fuel pump relay. Start the engine, then adjust the idle rpm and the idle mixture as described in **5. Adjusting Idle.**

Removing and Installing Mixture Control Unit

Fig. 7-40 is an exploded view of the entire fuel injection system. Before the mixture control unit can be disassembled as shown, you must remove it from the car using the procedure given here. If you must remove the fuel distributor, use the procedure given earlier.

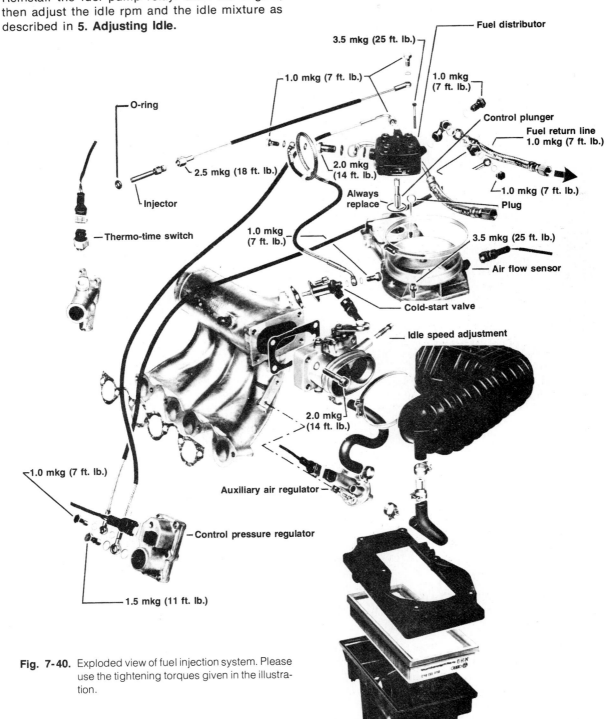

Fig. 7-40. Exploded view of fuel injection system. Please use the tightening torques given in the illustration.

7

To remove mixture control unit:

1. Thoroughly clean the fuel unions on the fuel distributor. Then disconnect all fuel lines from the fuel distributor. Attach tags to the removed banjo unions so that later you will be able to install them in their original positions. Fig. 7-41 and Fig. 7-42 show the new fuel distributors introduced during the 1977 model year.

> **WARNING ——**
>
> *Fuel will be discharged as you remove the unions. Disconnect the battery ground strap. Do not smoke or work near heaters or other fire hazards. Have a fire extinguisher handy.*

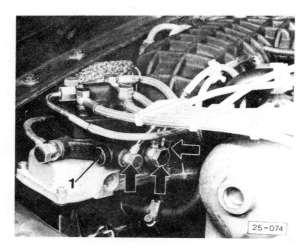

Fig. 7-41. New-type fuel distributor introduced early in 1977 model year. Arrows indicate new connections for fuel return lines. New check valve (**1**) prevents loss of system pressure if the control pressure regulator fails, thus making it possible to drive the car.

Fig. 7-42. Fuel distributor with aluminum casting (previously iron) and revised diaphragm (arrow). This unit is used on some 1977 cars, beginning with Engine Nos. YK 30 130, YH 55 237, and YG 28 395. It is used on all 1978 California models.

2. Loosen the hose clamp. Then disconnect the connecting duct from the air flow sensor outlet.

3. Using the tip of a screwdriver, snap loose the retainers that hold the bottom part of the air cleaner to the bracket on the car body. Steady the mixture control unit as you loosen the retainers so that the unit does not fall.

4. Being careful not to damage the intake air preheating duct as you disengage it from its connection on the exhaust manifold, remove the mixture control unit and the air cleaner from the car.

Installation is the reverse of removal. After you have reinstalled the mixture control unit, connect the battery ground strap. Then turn on the ignition so that the fuel pump operates. Check for leaks at the fuel line unions on the fuel distributor. Following installation of a new or a repaired mixture control unit, you must adjust the idle as described in **5.3 Adjusting Idle on Cars with Fuel Injection.**

7.6 Testing and Replacing Control Pressure Regulator

To test the control pressure regulator, use the "Engine cold" and "Engine warm" control pressure tests described in **7.4 Testing and Replacing Fuel Pump, Filter, and Fuel Pressure Accumulator.** Replace the control pressure regulator if it fails to maintain fuel pressures that are within the prescribed ranges.

Fig. 7-43 is a schematic diagram that shows the relationship of the control pressure regulator to the fuel distributor's metering unit. If the pressure on the top of the control pressure regulator's diaphragm increases owing to the wider metering port openings in the fuel distributor, the control pressure regulator's diaphragm is pressed down—thus allowing more fuel to flow to the injectors. As the diaphragm's movement increases the flow to the injectors, the increased pressure from the fuel distributor is relieved and the pressure in the system is balanced to maintain its regulated level. The control pressure regulator serves, therefore, to permit increases or reductions in the quantity of fuel delivered to the injectors without any change in the pressure at the nozzles.

A coil spring exerts pressure on the diaphragm of the control pressure regulator. The coil spring pressure works counter to the fuel pressure. When the engine is cold, a flat thermostatic spring works in conjunction with the fuel pressure to compress the coil spring. This increases the quantity of fuel flowing to the injectors—thereby preventing the excessively lean mixture that would otherwise result owing to the cold air that is entering the engine.

As the engine and engine oil warm up, the thermostatic spring is deflected, placing less compressing force on the coil spring. The coil spring then exerts greater pressure on the diaphragm, reducing the quantity of fuel reaching the injectors.

In addition to responding to heat from the engine and engine oil, the control pressure regulator's thermostatic spring responds to an electrical heating element. See Fig. 7-44. This heating element prevents the fuel pressure from remaining high for an excessively long period of time in cold weather. The following electrical tests should be made to detect trouble in the warm running compensation heating element.

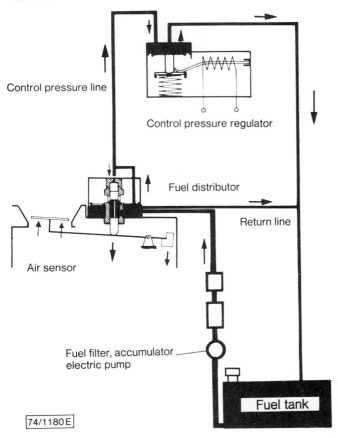

Fig. 7-43. Schematic diagram of control pressure regulator and related components. Notice the electrical heating element wound around the control pressure regulator's thermostatic spring.

Fig. 7-44. Electrical plug (arrow) for heating element of control pressure regulator's warm running compensation device. The control pressure regulator is located on the left side of the engine, just ahead of the ignition distributor.

To test heating element:

1. Disconnect the electrical plug from the air flow sensor of the mixture control unit (on cars that

have this plug); disconnect the positive wire from the alternator. Turn on the ignition without starting the engine.

2. Disconnect the electrical plug from the control pressure regulator. Then measure the voltage available at the plug as indicated in Fig. 7-45.

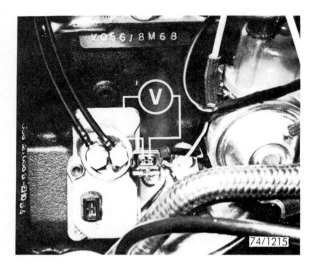

Fig. 7-45. Voltmeter hookup used to check voltage at connecting plug.

3. If there was no voltage at the electrical plug when you made the test described in step 2, test the power relay and the pump relay as described in **7.3 Electrical Tests.** If voltage is available at the pump relay, then there is trouble in the wire that connects the control pressure regulator plug with the relay.

4. If voltage is reaching the electrical plug correctly, test the heating element with an ohmmeter as shown in Fig. 7-46. If the heating element is open (infinite ohms), or if the resistance is not between 16 and 22 ohms, replace the control pressure regulator.

Fig. 7-46. Ohmmeter being used to test resistance and continuity of heating element.

To replace control pressure regulator:

1. Disconnect the fuel unions from the control pressure regulator.

> **WARNING ——**
>
> *Fuel will be expelled as you disconnect the unions. Disconnect the battery ground strap. Do not smoke or work near heaters or other fire hazards. Have a fire extinguisher handy.*

2. Disconnect the electrical plug (arrow) on the control pressure regulator (Fig. 7-47).

Fig. 7-47. Electrical plug (arrow) on control pressure regulator.

3. Remove the bolts that hold the control pressure regulator to the engine block. Remove the regulator and its gasket.

Installation is the reverse of removal. Use a new gasket. Torque the mounting bolts to 1.5 mkg (11 ft. lb.).

7.7 Testing and Replacing Thermo-time Switch

The thermo-time switch (Fig. 7-48) controls the operation of the cold-start valve. When the engine temperature is above the cutoff temperature stamped on the hexagon of the thermo-time switch, the cold-start valve does not inject fuel during starter operation. If the starter is operated for longer than normal, the thermo-time switch cuts off the cold-start valve in order to prevent engine flooding. The time limit is also stamped on the hexagon of the thermo-time switch. It is not possible to check the timing and cutoff temperature exactly with normal workshop equipment.

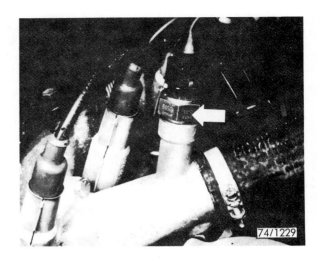

Fig. 7-49. Location of thermo-time switch (arrow).

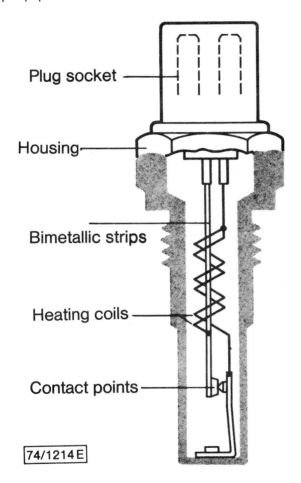

Plug socket

Housing

Bimetallic strips

Heating coils

Contact points

74/1214E

Fig. 7-48. Cross-section of thermo-time switch. The contact points are opened either by engine heat or, if the starter is operated for a longer-than-normal period of time, by the heating coils.

2. Carefully disconnect the electrical plug from the cold-start valve. Disconnect the ignition high tension cable from terminal 4 of the ignition coil in order to prevent the engine from starting.

3. Attach the leads of a test lamp or a voltmeter to the terminals of the disconnected plug (Fig. 7-50). Operate the starter without interruption for 15 to 20 seconds. The test lamp should first light brightly and then become noticeably dimmer—or go out—before the starter has operated for the time prescribed above. Alternatively, the voltmeter should at first indicate battery voltage and then fall off toward zero.

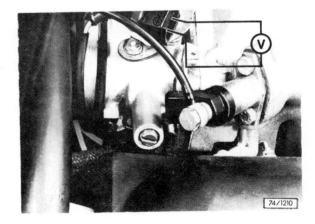

Fig. 7-50. Voltmeter hook-up used to test thermo-time switch.

To test thermo-time switch:

1. Make sure that the temperature of the thermo-time switch is below the cutoff temperature marked on its hexagon (below 35°C or 95°F). If necessary, allow the engine to sit overnight or cool the thermo-time switch with ice. The location of the thermo-time switch is shown in Fig. 7-49.

4. If the test lamp does not light at all, attach one of the test lamp leads to ground on some clean, unpainted metal part of the engine. The other lead should remain connected to one of the plug terminals.

5. Operate the starter. If the test lamp does not light, repeat the test with the test lamp connected to the other terminal of the disconnected plug. If the lamp lights in neither test, the wiring to the starter solenoid is faulty.

> **NOTE**
>
> If the test lamp lights whether the starter is operating or not, someone has misconnected the wires at the starter solenoid, installing the wire that belongs on terminal 50 on terminal 30 instead.

6. If battery current is reaching the plug, but the test lamp did not light when the starter was operated in step 3, the thermo-time switch is faulty and should be replaced.

To replace thermo-time switch:

1. Drain the cooling system as described in conjunction with replacing hoses in **ENGINE AND CLUTCH.**

> **CAUTION**
>
> Do not drain the coolant while the engine is hot. Doing this could warp the cylinder head or the engine block.

2. Disconnect the electrical plug from the thermo-time switch.

3. Using a socket wrench, unscrew the thermo-time switch from the engine block.

4. Using a new gasket, install a new thermo-time switch in the engine block. Reconnect the electrical plug to the thermo-time switch. Then refill the cooling system as described in **ENGINE AND CLUTCH.**

7.8 Testing and Replacing Cold-start Valve

The cold-start valve (Fig. 7-51), sometimes called the fifth injector, sprays fuel into the intake air distributor only during the first few seconds of starter operation and only when the engine and the surrounding air are cold. The valve's operation is controlled by the thermo-time switch and by current from terminal 50 of the starter solenoid. The cold-start valve is located at the right-hand side of the intake air distributor, just ahead of the bypass screw on the throttle valve housing.

If the cold-start valve fails to inject fuel during the cranking of a cold engine, it will be difficult or impossible to start the engine. If the cold-start valve is leaky, the engine may flood during starting—especially if the engine is hot.

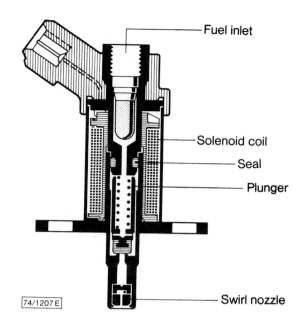

Fig. 7-51. Cross-section of cold-start valve.

Labels: Fuel inlet, Solenoid coil, Seal, Plunger, Swirl nozzle

74/1207 E

To test cold-start valve:

1. Carefully disconnect the electrical plug from the cold-start valve. Put tape over the plug terminals to prevent accidental electrical sparks. Disconnect the electrical plug from the mixture control unit's air flow sensor (on cars that have this terminal) and disconnect the positive wire from the alternator.

2. Remove the two screws that hold the cold-start valve to the intake air distributor. Remove the valve from the intake air distributor but leave the fuel hose connected to the valve.

3. Disconnect the ignition high tension cable from terminal 4 of the ignition coil so that the engine will not start.

4. Wipe dry the nozzle of the cold-start valve. Turn on the ignition so that the fuel pump operates. No drops of fuel should form on the nozzle within one minute from the time that the pump began to operate.

> **WARNING**
>
> Do not smoke or work near heaters or other fire hazards. Have a fire extinguisher handy.

5. If the cold-start valve leaks fuel with the ignition on, owing to normal pressure from the fuel pump, replace the cold-start valve.

6. If the valve did not leak, reconnect the electrical plug to the cold-start valve. Then disconnect the

electrical plug from the thermo-time switch and, using a jumper wire, connect the terminal for the green/white wire to ground on some clean, unpainted metal part of the engine.

7. To test the cold-start valve's operation, place the in Fig. 7-52. This will permit you to examine the spray pattern without spilling the fuel that is expelled.

Fig. 7-52. Cold-start operation being checked.

WARNING ——
Fuel will be expelled. Do not smoke or work near heaters or other fire hazards. Have a fire extinguisher handy.

8. Have someone operate the starter while you observe the spray from the cold-start valve. The valve should spray fuel in an even conical pattern. An irregular pattern indicates a dirty or damaged valve, which should be replaced.

9. If the cold-start valve is working correctly, it can be reinstalled on the intake air distributor. Test the thermo-time switch if you suspect that the cold-start valve is failing to operate when the engine is cold.

10. If no fuel is expelled from the cold-start valve during starter operation, disconnect the electrical plug from the cold-start valve. Then connect one lead of a test lamp or a voltmeter to the positive plug terminal (Fig. 7-53). Connect the other test lead to ground on some clean, unpainted metal part of the engine.

11. Operate the starter. If the test lamp does not light, or the voltmeter indicates no battery voltage, the wiring to the starter solenoid terminal 50 is faulty.

NOTE ——
If the test lamp lights whether the starter is operating or not, someone has misconnected the wires at the starter solenoid, installing the wire that belongs on terminal 50 on terminal 30 instead.

Fig. 7-53. Plug for cold-start valve. Negative terminal is grounded by thermo-time switch. The test described here is made independently of the thermo-time switch.

12. If battery current is reaching the cold-start valve, but the valve does not operate, the valve is faulty and must be replaced. You can also use an ohmmeter to test for continuity between the two terminals on the cold-start valve. If there is no continuity, the valve is definitely faulty.

7

To replace cold-start valve:

1. Disconnect the electrical plug from the cold-start valve. Disconnect the fuel union.

WARNING ——
Fuel will be expelled as you remove the union. Disconnect the battery ground strap. Do not smoke or work near heaters or other fire hazards. Have a fire extinguisher handy.

2. Remove the two screws that hold the cold-start valve to the intake air distributor. Then remove the cold-start valve and its gaskets.

3. Install the new cold-start valve and a new gasket. Then reconnect the fuel union, the electrical plug, and the battery ground strap. Reconnect any other wires that you removed earlier during testing.

7.9 Testing and Replacing Auxiliary Air Regulator

Fig. 7-54 is a schematic view of the auxiliary air regulator. When open, a rotary valve in the auxiliary air regulator provides additional air—and consequently additional fuel—during engine warm-up. The auxiliary air regulator's function in the air system can be seen in Fig. 1-2 in **1.2 Fuel Injection.**

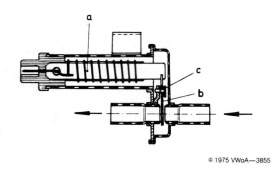

© 1975 VWoA—3855

a. Bimetallic strip   b. Rotary valve   c. Pivot

Fig. 7-54. Schematic view of auxiliary air regulator. Arrows indicate air flow through open valve.

On the car, the auxiliary air regulator is located on the No. 4 cylinder manifold tube of the intake air distributor. When the engine is started, current from the pump relay begins to warm the heating element that is wound around the auxiliary air regulator's bimetallic strip. Heat—whether from the heating element or from hot air surrounding the engine—causes the bimetallic strip to deflect gradually, closing the rotary valve and cutting off the additional air.

To test the auxiliary air regulator, disconnect both hoses from it. Also disconnect the electrical plugs at the control pressure regulator and at the mixture control unit's air flow sensor, and disconnect the positive wire from the alternator. Turn on the ignition. After about five minutes the rotary valve of the auxiliary air regulator should be closed completely—in a workshop that is heated to room temperature. You can check this by looking through the auxiliary air regulator as indicated in Fig. 7-55.

If the auxiliary air regulator does not close after five minutes (outside, in cold weather, considerably more time may be required), stop the engine. Disconnect the electrical plug from the auxiliary air regulator. Using an ohmmeter, measure the resistance between the terminals on the auxiliary air regulator. The reading should be 30 ohms. If the ohmmeter reads infinity, or if the resistance is considerably less than 30 ohms, replace the auxiliary air regulator.

22-398

Fig. 7-55. Inspection point for auxiliary air regulator (arrow). You should be able to see the rotary valve close by looking into the hose connections.

If the auxiliary air regulator resistance is in the correct range, use a test light as shown in Fig. 7-56 to determine whether battery voltage is reaching the heating element while the engine is running. If not, you should make further tests at the power relay and the pump relay. Especially check that someone has not accidentally exchanged the positions of the wires that go to terminals 30 and 50 on the starter solenoid.

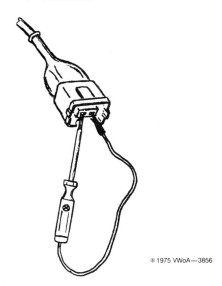

© 1975 VWoA—3856

Fig. 7-56. Test light being used to check for current at the auxiliary air regulator plug while engine is running.

To replace auxiliary air regulator:

1. Disconnect both air hoses from the auxiliary air regulator.

2. Disconnect the electrical plug from the auxiliary air regulator. Then remove the two screws that hold the auxiliary air regulator to the No. 4 cylinder manifold tube of the intake air distributor.

3. Remove the old auxiliary air regulator. Then install the new auxiliary air regulator using a reverse of the removal procedure.

7.10 Checking and Replacing Injectors

The injectors are held in the manifold tubes of the intake air distributor by their rubber seals. You can remove individual injectors by pulling them out as indicated in Fig. 7-57. By removing an injector, you can check its operation with the ignition turned on.

Fig. 7-57. Injection nozzle (injector) being removed. Pull out as indicated by arrow.

To check injector:

1. Remove one injector from the manifold tube, leaving the fuel hose attached to the injector. Pull the injector straight out, as indicated previously in Fig. 7-57.

2. Disconnect the ignition high tension cable from terminal 4 of the ignition coil in order to prevent the engine from starting.

3. Point the injector into a glass jar. Have someone operate the starter for about 15 seconds while you observe the injector's spray pattern—which should be an even, cone-shaped spray.

WARNING ——

Fuel will be discharged during this check. Do not smoke or work near heaters or other fire hazards. Have a fire extinguisher handy.

4. Turn off the ignition. Hold the injector in a horizontal position. It must not drip fuel.

5. If any injector has an irregular spray pattern, or if it dribbles fuel after the ignition is turned off, replace the injector.

6. In installing an injector in the manifold tube, first moisten the rubber seal with gasoline. Soak new seals in gasoline for several minutes before installing them. Then press the injector fully into its seat.

If the idle speed varies, there may be air leaks around the injectors where they are pressed into the engine. Replace the rubber seals. If you suspect that the four injectors are not delivering equal amounts of fuel, owing to foreign matter in the injectors or defective injector valves, replace all four injectors and hoses with new injectors and hoses. This is the only sure test for faulty injectors. Run the engine in order to determine whether the new injectors have cured the operating problem.

To replace injector:

1. Pull the injector out of its seat in the manifold tube. See Fig. 7-57 given earlier.

2. Detach the union that holds the fuel line to the injector and remove the injector from the fuel line.

WARNING ——

Fuel will be discharged as you disconnect the fuel line union. Do not smoke or work near heaters or other fire hazards. Have a fire extinguisher handy.

3. If you intend to install a new injector—or if the old rubber seal is hard, cracked, deformed, or otherwise damaged—remove the rubber seal from the injector.

NOTE ——

A new-type injector was introduced on the 1978 models. This injector (Fig. 7-58) has the same Part No. as the old-type injector and can be used in 1975 through 1977 cars.

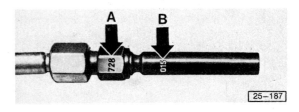

Fig. 7-58. Identification mark 728 (arrow **A**) designates injector introduced on 1978 cars. Earlier injector is marked 725. Bosch No. 015 is at arrow **B**.

7

4. Thoroughly clean the holes in the engine, removing all loose dirt and hardened foreign matter.

Installation is the reverse of removal. Before you install the rubber seal, soak it in gasoline for a few minutes. Always lubricate the seals with fuel before you press the injectors into the engine. Torque the fuel line union to 2.5 mkg (18 ft. lb.).

7.11 Replacing Plastic Fuel Lines

The special tool shown in Fig. 7-59 is used for installing new plastic fuel lines on the banjo unions or at other points. Damaged fuel injection lines should always be replaced. Do not attempt to repair them.

Fig. 7-59. Special tool used for installing new plastic fuel lines. This tool will install lines of two different diameters.

To remove a plastic fuel line, heat it with a soldering iron as shown in Fig. 7-60. If the line has a braided sheath, push back the sheath before you apply the soldering iron.

WARNING ——

Do not heat the fuel line with a torch or other open flame. This could cause a fire or explosion. Never cut the old lines open, because this would damage the cone-shaped connections on the unions or adaptors, causing incurable leakage.

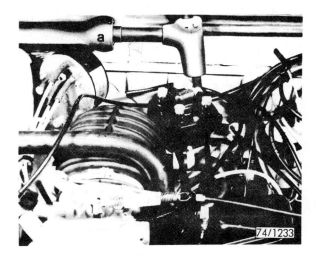

Fig. 7-60. Plastic fuel line being heated with soldering iron (**a**).

Use the special tool to install the new plastic fuel line, as shown in Fig. 7-61. The new fuel line should protrude from the tool for a distance that is equal to the length of the cone-shaped connection on the union or adaptor. Grip the plastic line in the tool by tightening the wing nut.

CAUTION ——

Never heat the new plastic fuel line preparatory to installation. Doing this may prevent a tight fit. The fuel line should be shoved onto the connection cold. Once removed, it should not be reinstalled. Replace removed plastic lines.

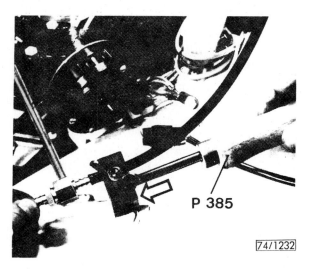

Fig. 7-61. New plastic fuel line being shoved onto connection with special tool.

7.12 Removing and Installing Throttle Valve Housing and Intake Air Distributor

The intake air distributor of cars with fuel injection is the part that corresponds to the intake manifold of cars with carburetors. Normally, you will need to remove the intake air distributor only when you are preparing to remove the cylinder head. If you must remove the intake air distributor with the engine installed, follow the procedure given here.

To remove:

1. Disconnect the battery ground strap.

2. Remove the mixture control unit and air cleaner as described in **7.5 Testing and Repairing Mixture Control Unit.**

3. Loosen the hose clamp and disconnect the connecting duct from the throttle valve housing.

4. Disconnect the hoses from the intake air distributor and the throttle valve housing. Mark each hose as you remove it so that you will be able to install it in its original location.

5. Loosen the setscrew, then disconnect the accelerator cable from the throttle valve lever. If necessary, consult **8. Accelerator Cable.**

6. Disconnect the EGR pipe and the vacuum hose from the EGR valve.

7. Remove all four injectors as described in **7.10 Inspecting and Replacing Injectors.**

8. Remove the cold-start valve as described in **7.8 Testing and Replacing Cold-start Valve.**

9. Remove the six bolts that hold the intake air distributor to the cylinder head. Then remove the intake air distributor and its gasket from the engine.

Installation is the reverse of removal. Thoroughly clean all old gasket material from the port face of the cylinder head and from the manifold tube flange of the intake air distributor. Use a new gasket when you install the intake air distributor on the engine. Torque the bolts to 2.5 mkg (18 ft. lb.). Use a new gasket on the cold-start valve and use new rubber seals, soaked in gasoline, on the injectors.

Adjust the accelerator cable as you install it, using the procedure described in **8. Accelerator Cable.** When installation of all components is complete, adjust the idle as described in **5.3 Adjusting Idle on Cars with Fuel Injection.**

7

8. ACCELERATOR CABLE

The accelerator cables used on cars with fuel injection are different from the accelerator cables used on cars with carburetors. Once the supply of the old type cables is used up, only the cable(s) for fuel injection cars will be available as replacement parts. The new type cable can be used in earlier cars with the modifications listed in **Table d.** To replace a cable, disconnect it at the points shown in Fig. 8-2, Fig. 8-3, and Fig. 8-4. Then adjust the cable(s) as described in **8.1 Adjusting Accelerator Cable.**

CAUTION ——

Be very careful not to kink the cable during installation. A kinked cable will cause erratic throttle operation. New cables bend easily in one direction only and should be installed in that position. The installed cable must be perfectly straight from the bracket on the engine to the throttle valve lever. If necessary, bend the bracket to align the cable. The cable must also be perfectly straight between the grommet in the floorboard and the accelerator pedal. If necessary, bend the cable end of the pedal to align the cable.

8.1 Adjusting Accelerator Cable

Beginning with the 1976 models, cars that have automatic transmissions have two accelerator cables. One cable extends from the accelerator pedal to a lever on the automatic transmission. A second cable extends from the lever on the automatic transmission to the throttle valve lever of the fuel injection system. On engines with carburetors, there is a single accelerator cable that extends from the accelerator pedal to the carburetor's throttle valve lever.

To adjust cable on carburetor engines:

1. Detach the throttle return spring from the carburetor's throttle valve shaft lever.

2. Loosen the nut for the clamp bolt (Fig. 8-1) until you can just move the lever on the pedal shaft.

3. Push the accelerator pedal down to its full throttle position. Then, while holding the pedal down, pull the cable lever up to full throttle, as indicated in Fig. 8-1, and tighten the nut for the clamp bolt.

Table d. Accelerator Cable Applications

Transmission	Model year	Use cable part No.	Necessary modifications
Automatic	1976 and later	321 723 555 C	None
Manual	1976 and later	849 721 555 B	None
Manual/automatic	1975	849 721 555 A	Englarge hole in firewall to about 15 mm (9/16 in.) and use accelerator pedal 823 721 539
Manual/automatic	1973–1974	824 723 555 B	

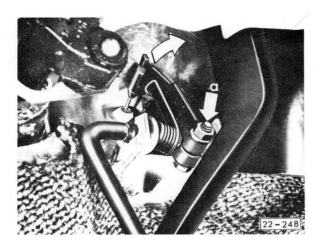

Fig. 8-1. Cable adjustment (carburetor engines). Lock nut for clamp bolt is at **a**. With pedal depressed, pull cable lever fully up, as indicated by curved arrow.

Fig. 8-2. Accelerator cable connections in engine compartment. Cable is at **1**, cable conduit is attached to bracket at **2**, and clamp bolt on throttle valve lever is at **3**.

4. Operate the accelerator several times and check that there is no more than about 1 mm (.040 in.) of play at the carburetor's throttle valve lever with the accelerator fully depressed.

   NOTE ——

   On cars with automatic transmissions, the distance between the accelerator pedal and the kickdown switch must be between 5 and 8 mm ($^3/_{16}$ and $^5/_{16}$ in.) when the throttle is in its fully open position.

**To adjust cable on fuel injection engines:
(manual transmission only)**

1. Push the accelerator pedal to its stop. Keep it in that position with a weight.

2. Working in the engine compartment, loosen the clamp bolt on the throttle valve lever. See Fig. 8-2.

3. Adjust the position of the throttle valve arm on the cable so that both throttle valves just reach their fully open positions. Then tighten the clamp bolt.

Operate the accelerator several times and check that there is no more than about 1 mm (.040 in.) of play at the throttle valve lever when the accelerator is fully depressed.

**To adjust cable on fuel injection engine:
(automatic transmission through 1978 only)**

1. Loosen the clamp bolt on the throttle valve lever. See Fig. 8-2.

2. Press the operating lever on the transmission to its end position as indicated in Fig. 8-3.

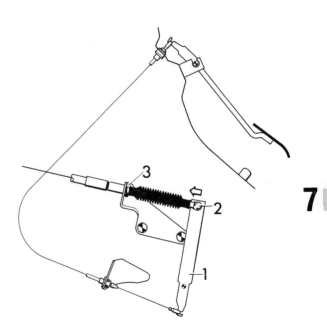

Fig. 8-3. Cable layout on fuel injection cars with automatic transmissions. Operating lever is at **1**. Cable ball socket is at **2**, and accelerator cable conduit is attached to bracket at **3**. To press the operating lever to its end position, move it as indicated by the arrow.

3. With the operating lever held in its end position, adjust the cable at the throttle valve lever so that no play remains in the cable. Then tighten the clamp bolt on the throttle valve lever.

4. To adjust the pedal cable, first loosen the locknut

7

indicated in Fig. 8-4. Then place a 10-mm (⅜-in.) spacer between the accelerator pedal and the pedal stop, and weight the pedal in order to hold it down against the spacer.

5. Press the lower end of the operating lever forward until the lever is in the kickdown position and hold it there. With the accelerator pedal still against the spacer you installed in step 4, tighten the locknut against the bracket in order to remove all play from the conduit.

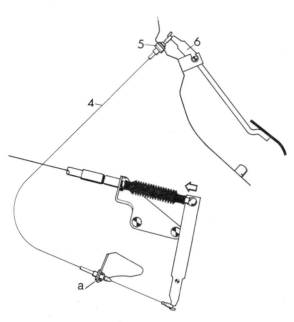

Fig. 8-4. Pedal cable adjustments. Locknut is at **a**, pedal at **6**. Pedal cable is at **4** and cable conduit mounting is at **5**.

6. Remove the spacer from beneath the accelerator pedal. Press the accelerator pedal to its kickdown position, then check that there is no play at the operating lever on the transmission.

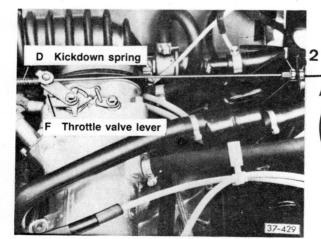

**To adjust cable on fuel injection engine:
(automatic transmission 1979 and later cars)**

1. Fully loosen the adjusting knob (item **3** in Fig. 8-5), which is beneath the car on the side of the transaxle.

2. Press the operating lever (item **C** in Fig. 8-5) in the direction indicated by the white arrow in the illustration. If possible, have someone hold the lever in this position (against the closed-throttle stop inside the transmission), or use a large rubber band.

3. Working in the engine compartment, loosen the locknut (item **1** in Fig. 8-5). Turn the adjusting nut (item **2**) until the cable is slack, then turn the adjusting nut in the opposite direction until all slack is removed from the cable—but not so much that the kickdown spring (item **D**) is compressed. Tighten the locknut to keep the cable conduit in this position.

4. Remove the pedal stop bolt, which is beneath the accelerator pedal. Remove the floor mat.

5. To make the adjustment bolt indicated in Fig. 8-5, obtain two M 8 nuts and an M 8 bolt that is 135 mm (5⁵⁄₁₆ in.) long. Install the nuts on the bolt so that dimension **a**, given in Fig. 8-6, is 124 mm (4⅞ in.). Tighten the nuts against one another to hold them in place.

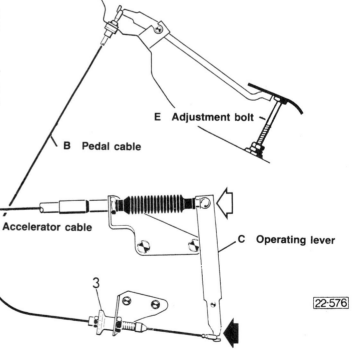

Fig. 8-5. Cable layouts on 1979 and later fuel injection cars with automatic transmissions. Locknut is at **1**, adjusting nut at **2**, and adjusting knob at **3**. Item **E** is for temporary installation only.

6. Temporarily install the adjustment bolt beneath the accelerator pedal, screwing it onto the hole for the pedal stop bolt as far as the nuts will permit.

7. Keeping the operating lever in its closed-throttle position as previously described, turn the adjusting knob until the pedal cable pulls the pedal down into contact with the temporarily installed adjusting bolt.

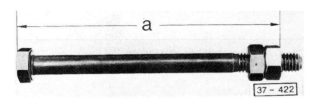

Fig. 8-6. Adjusting bolt, which is for temporary installation beneath the accelerator pedal. Dimension **a** is 124 mm (4⅞ in.) long.

8. Move the operating lever on the transaxle in the direction indicated by the black arrow given previously in Fig. 8-5. Then, working inside the car, remove the adjusting bolt and reinstall the floor mat and the throttle stop bolt.

9. Press the accelerator pedal into its full-throttle position (but not into its kickdown position). The operating lever on the transaxle should be against the full-throttle stop inside the transmission.

10. Press the accelerator pedal into its kickdown position. The kickdown spring at the throttle valve lever should be compressed by 10 to 11 mm (⅜ to 7/16 in.) and the operating lever on the transaxle should be fully against its kickdown stop inside the transmission.

NOTE ——

If the system does not function correctly in step 9 or step 10, you have not carried out the adjustment procedure correctly.

9. EMISSION CONTROLS

Several kinds of emission controls have been used on the cars covered by this Manual. The procedures given here are designed to keep these controls in good working order.

9.1 1973 and 1974 Emission Controls

Not all of the emission controls covered here are used on every 1973 and 1974 model. An inspection of the vehicle, and of the emission decal on the engine, will help you in identifying the emission controls that are installed on your particular car.

1973 Intake Air Preheating

Fig. 9-1 shows the temperature control valve for the intake air preheating system. This valve is installed in the intake manifold, beside the carburetor. You can test the temperature control valve using the procedure given later for checking 1974 California models. If you replace the temperature control valve, connect the hose from the carburetor to the angled connection on the valve. Con-

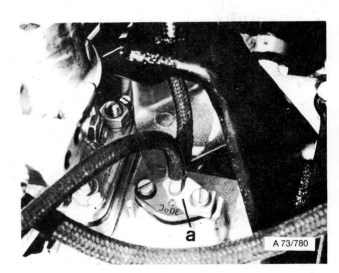

Fig. 9-1. 1973 Temperature control valve **(a)**.

7

nect the hose from the air cleaner's vacuum motor to the straight connection on the valve. The vacuum motor and related components are shown in Fig. 9-2.

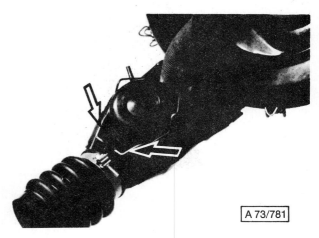

A 73/781

Fig. 9-3. Vacuum motor being removed. Press down spring holder as indicated by arrows in order to disengage it from the air cleaner duct.

A 73/779

b. Warm air duct   c. Vacuum motor   d. Cool air duct

Fig. 9-2. Intake air preheating system components on air cleaner.

To replace the vacuum motor on the air cleaner, press off the spring retainer as indicated in Fig. 9-3. Then remove the vacuum motor together with the flap. If necessary, you can detach the flap as indicated in Fig. 9-4. Installation is the reverse of removal.

A 73/782

Fig. 9-4. Flap being removed from vacuum motor. Press down diaphragm plunger as indicated by arrow. Then disengage flap at both holders.

1974 Intake Air Preheating

Fig. 9-5 shows the temperature control valve for the intake air preheating system that is used on cars sold in California. This system is almost identical to the system used on 1973 models. To check the operation of the temperature control valve, the engine must be cold. Start the cold engine and allow it to idle. Then pull the vacuum hose off the vacuum motor. The flap in the air intake should close, cutting off preheated air to the engine, and you should be able to feel a vacuum at the disconnected hose.

If the flap was already closed and there is no vacuum, the temperature control valve is faulty and should be replaced. In replacing the temperature control valve, connect the hose from the carburetor to the angled connection on the valve. Connect the hose from the air cleaner's vacuum motor to the straight connection on the valve. Fig. 9-6 shows the temperature control valve removed from the engine.

Fig. 9-5. 1974 California intake air preheating system. Temperature control valve is at **a**, vacuum motor on air cleaner is at **b**.

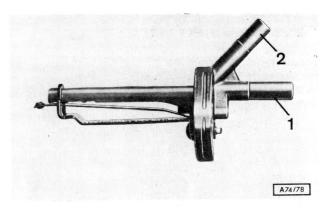

Fig. 9-6. Temperature control valve. Connection for vacuum motor is at **1**; connection for carburetor is at **2**.

If, in checking the temperature control valve, you find that vacuum is present at the disconnected hose but the flap does not move, replace the vacuum motor. Use the procedure given earlier for 1973 cars.

7

Fig. 9-7 shows the intake air preheating system used on 1974 cars sold outside California. The engine must be cold when you check the operation of the temperature control valve. Start the cold engine and allow it to idle. Then pull the vacuum hose off the vacuum motor. The flap in the air intake should close, cutting off preheated air to the engine, and you should be able to feel vacuum at the disconnected hose.

If the flap was already closed and there is no vacuum, the temperature control valve is faulty and should be replaced. In replacing the temperature control valve, connect the hose from the carburetor to the brass pipe on the valve. Connect the hose from the air cleaner's vacuum motor to the plastic pipe on the valve. Fig. 9-8 shows the temperature control valve removed from the air cleaner.

Fig. 9-7. Intake air preheating system for 1974 cars sold outside California. Temperature control valve is at **a**; vacuum motor is at **b**.

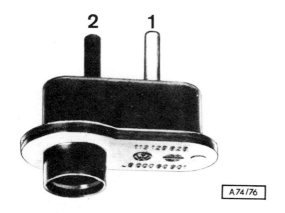

Fig. 9-8. Temperature control valve. Brass pipe for carburetor hose is at **1**; plastic pipe for hose from vacuum motor is at **2**.

If, in checking the temperature control valve, you find that vacuum is present at the disconnected hose but the flap does not move, replace the vacuum motor. Use the procedure given earlier for 1973 cars.

Exhaust Gas Recirculation

Fig. 9-9 shows the EGR (exhaust gas recirculation) system. Exhaust gas is diverted from the exhaust manifold at the No. 4 cylinder. The gas passes through the EGR filter before it is admitted to the intake manifold by the EGR valve.

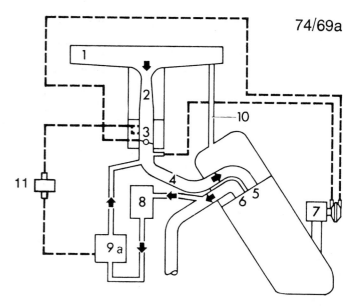

1. Air cleaner
2. Carburetor venturi
3. Carburetor throttle valve
4. Intake manifold
5. Intake port in cylinder head
6. Exhaust port in cylinder head
7. Ignition distributor
8. EGR filter
9. EGR valve
10. PCV hose
11. Throttle delay valve (Audi only)

Fig. 9-9. 1974 EGR system. Vacuum hoses are shown by the dashed lines.

1974 cars sold in California have an air injection system in addition to the EGR system. On these cars, there are two vacuum lines to the EGR valve, as shown in Fig. 9-10.

73/1413 b

1. Air cleaner
2. Carburetor venturi
3. Carburetor throttle valve
4. Intake manifold
5. Intake port in cylinder head
6. Exhaust port in cylinder head
7. Ignition distributor
8. EGR filter
9. EGR valve (double stage)
10. PCV hose
11. Air injection pump belt
12. Air injection pump
13. Air injection filter
14. Diverter valve
15. Check valve
16. Anti-backfire valve

Fig. 9-10. EGR and air injection systems on a car sold in California. The EGR system has a two-stage valve with two vacuum connections.

To check EGR valve:

1. Start the engine and allow it to idle.

2. On cars with a single vacuum line to the EGR valve, disconnect the retard hose from the inner connection of the ignition distributor's vacuum unit and connect it to the vacuum connection on the EGR valve. The idle speed should drop, indicating that exhaust gases are being recirculated.

3. On cars with air injection that have two vacuum lines to the EGR valve, disconnect the retard hose from the inner connection of the ignition distributor's vacuum unit and connect it alternately to the two connections on the EGR valve. The idle speed should drop during both tests, indicating that exhaust gases are being recirculated.

4. If the idle speed does not drop during the tests described in step 2 or step 3, check for the following conditions: (1) EGR filter clogged, (2) EGR valve faulty or clogged, (3) EGR line or fitting in exhaust manifold clogged.

NOTE ——
The EGR filter and lines are shown in Fig. 9-11. Clean the EGR valve as indicated in Fig. 9-12.

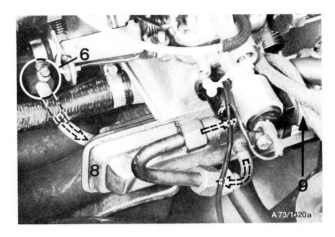

Fig. 9-11. EGR filter and connections. Filter is at **8**, EGR valve is at **9**. The connection at the exhaust manifold is at **6**. Orifice in manifold connection is 4 mm ($^5/_{32}$ in.) on cars with manual transmissions and 7 mm ($^9/_{32}$ in.) on cars with automatic transmissions.

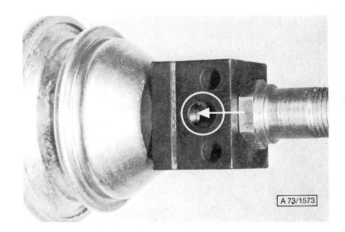

Fig. 9-12. EGR valve being cleaned. Make sure that passage (arrow) is clear and that plunger moves when vacuum is applied to the EGR valve connection(s).

Air Injection

To test the components of the air injection system shown earlier in Fig. 9-10 (California cars only), refer to the air injection tests described in **9.2 1975 Carburetor Engine Emission Controls.**

7

9.2 1975 Carburetor Engine Emission Controls

Fig. 9-13 shows the vacuum hose connections on the emission control components used on 1975 cars with carburetors. The anti-backfire valve and the diverter valve are parts of the air injection system. The two-way valve and the EGR valve are parts of the EGR (exhaust gas recirculation) system. Emission control system components cannot be repaired and must be replaced if testing shows them to be faulty.

CAUTION ——

Be careful not to interchange the vacuum hose connections when removing or installing emission control system components. Doing this will cause poor running and possible engine damage. The connections for each vacuum circuit should be the same color; for example, both connections for the hose from the carburetor to the anti-backfire valve are dark blue.

Fig. 9-13. Emission control components of 1975 cars with carburetors, showing vacuum line connections.

EGR (Exhaust Gas Recirculation)

Fig. 9-14 illustrates the operation of the EGR system. At idle and at low speeds, the EGR valve operates at its first stage only—as controlled by the temperature valve. (The temperature valve does not permit exhaust gas recirculation at low speeds and at idle until the engine has warmed up.) The second stage is controlled by a microswitch on the carburetor. Vacuum is always applied to the two-way valve but the two-way valve does not apply vacuum to the EGR valve's second stage port until the carburetor's throttle valve has opened far enough to trigger the microswitch.

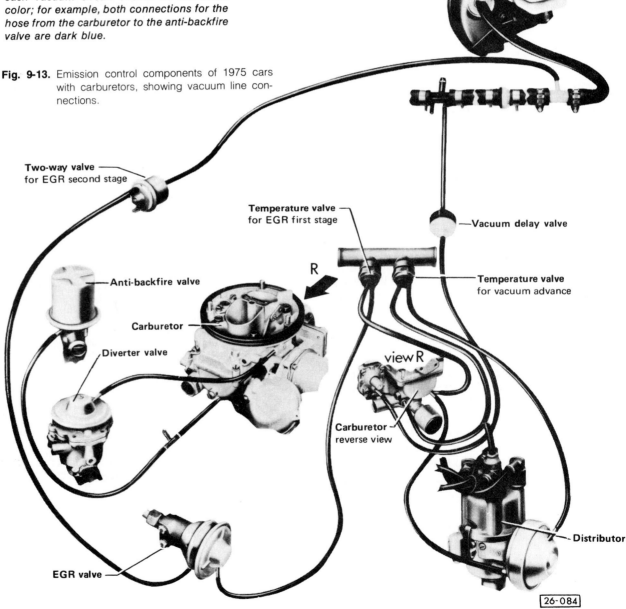

Two-way valve for EGR second stage

Temperature valve for EGR first stage

Vacuum delay valve

Temperature valve for vacuum advance

Anti-backfire valve

Carburetor

R

Diverter valve

view R

Carburetor reverse view

Distributor

EGR valve

26-084

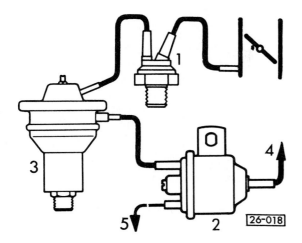

Fig. 9-14. Schematic layout of EGR system. Temperature valve is at **1**, two-way valve at **2**, and EGR valve at **3**. **4** is the vacuum connection from the engine. **5** is the electrical connection from the microswitch.

To test EGR valve first stage:

1. Start the engine and allow it to idle.

2. Disconnect the EGR valve vacuum hose that is indicated by the arrow in Fig. 9-15.

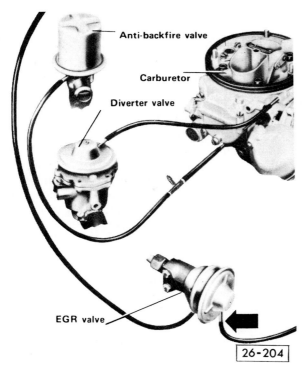

Fig. 9-15. First stage vacuum hose (arrow) that must be disconnected from EGR valve.

3. Pull the vacuum hose off the anti-backfire valve and attach it to the first stage port on the EGR valve. The idle speed should drop, indicating that exhaust gases are being recirculated.

4. If the idle speed does not drop during the test, check for the following conditions: (1) EGR filter clogged, (2) EGR valve faulty or clogged, (3) EGR line or fitting in exhaust manifold clogged.

NOTE ——

You can clean the EGR valve and lines as shown previously for 1974 cars in Fig. 9-11 and Fig. 9-12. Faulty or clogged filters should be replaced.

To test EGR first stage temperature valve:

1. Remove the temperature valve and place its threaded end in a pan of water that contains a thermometer.

2. Heat the water. Attach a piece of hose to the angled connection of the temperature valve (Fig. 9-16). By placing the hose in your mouth, you should not be able to suck air through the valve until the water temperature reaches $46° \pm 3°C$ ($115° \pm 5°F$).

3. If the valve fails to open at the prescribed temperature, or if the valve is open at low temperatures, replace the temperature valve.

Fig. 9-16. Temperature valve test. Attach hose at connection indicated by arrow.

To check EGR valve second stage:

1. Start the engine and allow it to idle.

7

2. Operate the microswitch (Fig. 9-17) on the carburetor by hand—without moving the carburetor's throttle valve. The idle speed should drop, or the engine stall, indicating that exhaust gases are being recirculated.

Fig. 9-17. Microswitch on carburetor. Lift up on the roller indicated by arrow in order to hand-operate microswitch.

3. If the idle speed does not drop or the engine stall during the test, check for the following conditions: (1) microswitch or electrical wiring and connections faulty, (2) two-way valve faulty, (3) EGR filter clogged, (4) EGR valve faulty or clogged, (5) EGR line or fitting in exhaust manifold clogged.

> **NOTE** ──
>
> You can clean the EGR valve and lines as shown previously for 1974 cars in Fig. 9-11 and Fig. 9-12. Faulty or clogged filters should be replaced. When battery current is applied to the terminal and to the case of the two-way valve, you should be able to hear it click. Test the microswitch and the wiring with a voltmeter or a test light in order to make sure that battery voltage is reaching the terminals. If necessary, refer to the wiring diagrams given in **ELECTRICAL SYSTEM.** If you replace the microswitch, you must adjust it as described in the next procedure.

To adjust microswitch:

1. Remove the automatic choke's water housing as a unit, leaving the coolant hoses attached.

2. Remove the nut from the throttle valve shaft and then install a protractor as shown in Fig. 9-18.

3. Check that the throttle valve is closed. (It may be necessary to open the choke by hand in order to release the fast-idle mechanism.) Then zero the protractor.

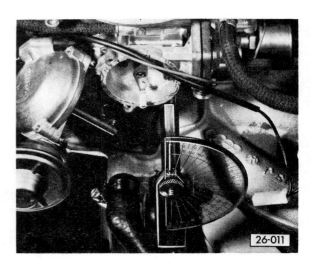

Fig. 9-18. Protractor installed on carburetor's primary throttle valve shaft.

4. Slowly open the throttle valve. The microswitch should click at the following switching points: (1) at 30° and 67° for cars with manual transmissions; (2) at 23° and 63° for cars with automatic transmissions.

5. If the adjustment is incorrect, correct it by moving the microswitch on its mounting bracket.

Air Injection System

During routine maintenance, you should check the air injection system as follows: first, pull the hose off the air distributor tube on the cylinder head and plug the distributor tube. Then start the engine and allow it to idle while you check whether air is flowing out of the disconnected hose. If not, test the components as described under the next procedures. If the system seems to be working well, but emissions do not drop when the air injection hose is connected following idle mixture adjustment, the distributor tube may be clogged. Take out the union bolts indicated in Fig. 9-19 and remove the distributor tube. Then clean out the bores in the bolts and in the engine. You can clean the banjo unions and the tube with solvent and compressed air.

If air is not being injected owing to a stuck check valve, you can clean the check valve by blowing it out with compressed air. The valve should be removed from the engine and air blown through the valve in the direction of normal air flow.

Occasionally, there will be too much air injected owing to a faulty pressure valve on the air pump. To check, disconnect the hose from the pressure valve (Fig. 9-20), then cover the air outlet with your finger. At idle, there should be only insignificant pressure. If the valve is blowing off excessively, replace the complete pump and valve assembly.

Fig. 9-19. Union bolt(s) that hold air injection distributor tube to engine.

Fig. 9-20. Pressure valve test. Pressure valve of pump is at **14**. Cover the outlet with your finger in order to determine the amount of air blowing past valve (arrow).

To check anti-backfire valve:

1. Disconnect the air hose from the anti-backfire valve as indicated in Fig. 9-21.

2. Start the engine and allow it to idle until full oil pressure has been established.

3. Place your hand over the connection on the anti-backfire valve. Run the engine at high rpm for a

moment, then allow the throttle to snap closed suddenly. You should feel a vacuum at the anti-backfire valve for a period of from 1 to 3 seconds.

4. If no vacuum can be felt—and the hoses connected to the anti-backfire valve are neither clogged nor kinked—the anti-backfire valve is faulty and should be replaced.

Fig. 9-21. Hose removed from anti-backfire valve. Place your hand over the hose's connection on the valve (arrow).

To check diverter valve:

1. Pull the vacuum hose off the diverter valve. See Fig. 9-22.

2. Disconnect the vacuum hose from the anti-backfire valve, then connect this hose to the diverter valve.

3. Start the engine and allow it to idle. You should be able to feel air flow from the diverter valve muffler (at the arrow in Fig. 9-22).

7

Fig. 9-22. Diverter valve test. Diverter valve vacuum hose is at **1**, anti-backfire valve vacuum hose is at **2**. The arrow indicates the diverter valve muffler.

4. If the air pump, the air pump filter, and the hoses have already been checked and found to be in good condition, the diverter valve is faulty and should be replaced.

NOTE ———

Air pump tests are described earlier under this heading. If the pump is found to be faulty, it must be replaced, as no repairs are possible.

Temperature Controlled Vacuum Advance

Fig. 9-23 is a schematic view of the temperature controlled vacuum advance system. Vacuum from the carburetor is shut off by the temperature valve whenever engine coolant temperatures are below 58° ± 3°C (136° ± 5°F). Higher temperatures open the valve, allowing vacuum to reach the vacuum unit of the ignition distributor.

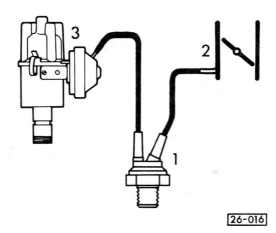

26-016

Fig. 9-23. Schematic view of temperature controlled vacuum advance. Temperature valve is at **1**, carburetor at **2**, and ignition distributor at **3**.

To test temperature valve:

1. Remove the temperature valve and place its threaded end in a pan of water that contains a thermometer.

2. Heat the water. Attach a piece of hose to the angled connection of the temperature valve. (See Fig. 9-23 given earlier.) By placing the hose in your mouth, you should not be able to suck air through the valve until the water temperature reaches 58° ± 3°C (136° ± 5°F).

3. If the valve fails to open at the prescribed temperature, or if the valve is open at low temperatures, replace the temperature valve.

Catalytic Converter

The catalytic converter is shown in Fig. 9-24. Catalytic converter overheating and incipient damage, which are indicated by a flickering of the CAT light in the speedometer, can be caused by the following:

1. Misfiring owing to bad spark plugs, spark plug cables, and other ignition system components

2. Incorrect ignition timing that causes the engine to get too hot

3. CO value too high ahead of the converter (mixture too rich)

4. A faulty diverter valve in the air injection system that does not shut off at high rpm

5. A faulty temperature sensor on the catalytic converter.

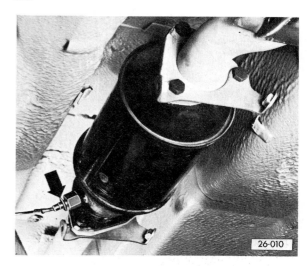

26-010

Fig. 9-24. Catalytic converter. Arrow indicates the temperature sensor that controls the CAT light in the speedometer.

The CAT light may flicker when the engine is under extreme load owing to trailer towing, prolonged high speed driving in hot weather and other similar conditions. Normally, the CAT light will go out if the driver reduces speed. The converter should be checked as described below if there has been prolonged driving with a flickering CAT light or if there is (1) poor engine output, (2) stalling at idle, (3) a rattle in the exhaust system, (4) CO value (at tailpipe) of more than 0.4 volume % at idle.

To check catalytic converter:

1. Hold the catalytic converter up to strong light and look through both ends. You should not see any evidence of damage to the ceramic insert.

CAUTION ——

Do not drop or hit the catalytic converter. Any sharp blow will destroy the ceramic insert and ruin the catalytic converter.

2. Check the ceramic insert for blockage. Air should pass through easily.

3. If the catalytic converter is blocked, or if the ceramic insert is damaged, replace the converter. Then reset the elapsed mileage odometer.

Elapsed Mileage Odometer

The elapsed mileage odometer indicates catalytic converter maintenance intervals of 30,000 miles (48,000 km) by causing the CAT light in the speedometer to come on. It indicates EGR maintenance intervals of 15,000 miles (24,000 km) by causing the EGR light in the speedometer to come on. You should reset the elapsed mileage odometer only after the indicated maintenance has been carried out. See Fig. 9-25 and Fig. 9-26.

Fig. 9-25. CAT indicator light reset button. Press to reset the elapsed mileage odometer.

Fig. 9-26. EGR indicator light reset button. Press to reset the elapsed mileage odometer.

7

9.3 1975 and Later Fuel Injection Engine Emission Controls

Fig. 9-27 shows the vacuum hose connection on the emission control components of a fuel injection engine. Owing to the reduced emissions made possible by the use of fuel injection, there are fewer emission control components on fuel injection engines than on carburetor

1. Throttle valve assembly
2. From auxiliary air regulator
3. To intake air duct
4. Deceleration valve (manual transmission only)
5. Vacuum accumulator (all California cars and all USA cars from early 1977)
6. EGR valve
7. Vacuum booster
8. EGR temperature control valve
9. Two-way valve (for air conditioner)
10. Distributor advance
11. Distributor retard
12. To air conditioning vacuum motors
13. Vacuum accumulator (cars with air conditioner only)
14. Brake booster

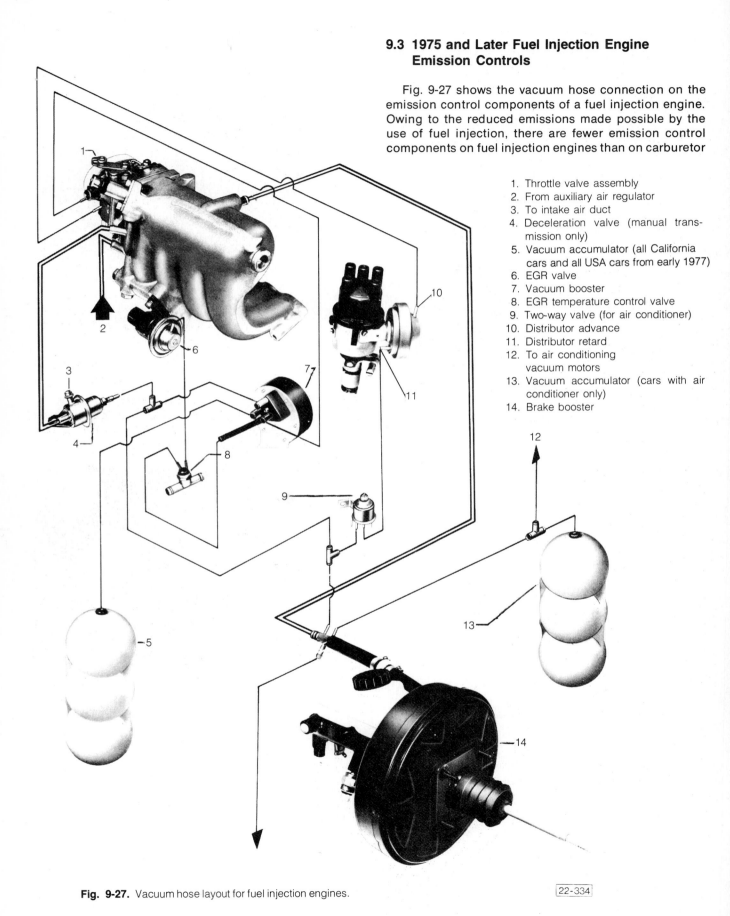

Fig. 9-27. Vacuum hose layout for fuel injection engines.

22-334

engines. The procedures given under this heading will allow you to check the operation of the individual components. Emission control system components cannot be repaired and must be replaced if testing shows them to be faulty.

EGR (Exhaust Gas Recirculation)

Owing to the vacuum characteristics of fuel injection engines, a vacuum accumulator (reservoir) has been used in some applications (Fig. 9-28) and a vacuum booster (vacuum amplifier) has been used in the EGR system. Always check the condition of the vacuum hoses—making sure that they are installed on the right connections—before you begin checking or troubleshooting the EGR system.

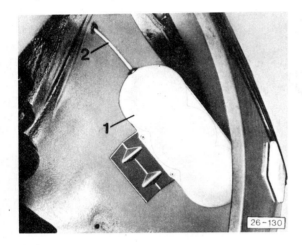

Fig. 9-28. Vacuum accumulator (**1**) located under right front fender.

To check EGR valve:

1. Start the engine and allow it to idle.

2. Check that the exhaust gas line from the engine's front exhaust pipe to the EGR valve is not leaking. If necessary, replace the pipe.

3. Disconnect the vacuum hose from the EGR valve.

4. Disconnect the vacuum retard hose from the innermost connection of the ignition distributor's vacuum unit. Then connect the retard hose to the EGR valve. The idle speed should drop or the engine stall.

5. If the idle speed does not slow or the engine does not stall, the EGR valve is faulty or clogged—or the exhaust gas line is clogged or damaged.

NOTE ———
To clean the EGR valve, follow the procedure given earlier for 1974 cars in Fig. 9-12.

To test EGR temperature control valve:

1. With the engine idling, attach a vacuum gauge to the vacuum line for the EGR valve (Fig. 9-29).

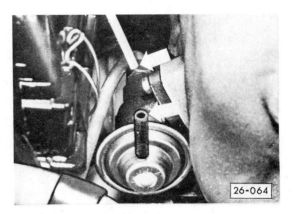

Fig. 9-29. Vacuum hose disconnected from EGR valve. Lower arrow indicates connection on valve. Attach vacuum gauge to hose at upper arrow.

2. With the engine idling, the vacuum gauge should indicate 50 to 90 mm/Hg (2 to 4 in./Hg).

3. If the correct vacuum is not indicated, allow the engine to cool, and then partially drain the coolant as described in **ENGINE AND CLUTCH**. Replace the EGR temperature control valve (Fig. 9-30).

Fig. 9-30. EGR temperature valve (arrow). After installing a new valve, make sure that you connect the vacuum hoses as indicated previously in Fig. 9-27.

7

To check vacuum booster (vacuum amplifier):

1. Start the engine and allow it to idle.

2. Using a T-fitting, connect a vacuum gauge between the vacuum line from the part-throttle port and its connection on the vacuum booster (Fig. 9-31).

   NOTE ——

   Beginning early in 1977, there is a vacuum delay valve installed on the vacuum booster (vacuum amplifier), as indicated in Fig. 9-32. Install the T-fitting between this delay valve and the connection on the vacuum booster. The vacuum delay valve has also been dealer-installed on some earlier cars.

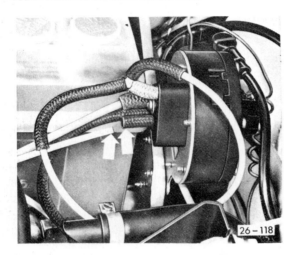

Fig. 9-31. Part-throttle line (left arrow) and its connection (right arrow) on the vacuum booster. By connecting the vacuum gauge with a T-fitting, you will check both the part-throttle port and the booster.

Fig. 9-32. Vacuum delay valve (**1**) for EGR introduced on USA cars early in 1977. In replacing delay valve, always install with white cover away from vacuum booster as shown.

3. With the engine idling, the vacuum gauge should indicate 5 to 8 mm/Hg (0.2 to 0.3 in./Hg). If not, check the throttle valve for correct position and check the part-throttle vacuum port for a possible obstruction.

   NOTE ——

   If the vacuum reading is correct when the vacuum gauge is connected only to the part-throttle line—but the reading falls when you use the T-fitting—there is an internal leak in the vacuum booster and the booster should be replaced.

4. Using a T-fitting, connect the vacuum gauge between the vacuum booster and the temperature valve (Fig. 9-33). With the engine idling, the gauge should indicate 50 to 90 mm/Hg (2 to 4 in./Hg). If not, the vacuum booster is faulty and should be replaced.

Fig. 9-33. Ends of disconnected booster-to-temperature valve vacuum hose (arrows). Install vacuum gauge with T-fitting.

To check deceleration valve (manual transmission only):

1. Disconnect the air hose from the large side connection of the decel (deceleration) valve (Fig. 9-34).

2. Run the engine at about 3000 rpm, while covering the decel valve connection with your finger.

3. Allow the throttle to snap closed suddenly. You should feel suction at the decel valve for a second or more.

4. Disconnect the decel valve's vacuum hose from the T-fitting indicated in Fig. 9-35. With the engine running at about 3000 rpm, you should feel no suction at the decel valve's side air connection.

5. If the decel valve operates incorrectly in either the test described in step 3 or the test described in step 4, replace the decel valve.

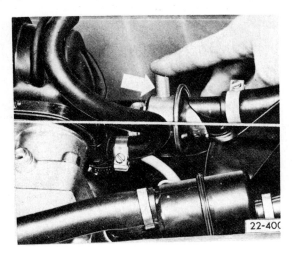

Fig. 9-34. Air connection on side of decel valve (arrow) being covered with finger.

Fig. 9-35. Decel valve vacuum hose disconnected (right arrow). Left arrow indicates finger over decel valve's side air connection.

Evaporative Emission Control

On 1975 through 1977 cars with fuel injection, the evaporative emission control requires no service checks other than to insure that the canister is neither clogged nor leaking. Beginning with the 1978 models, there is a vent valve near the canister. The vent valve should be checked using the procedure given here.

To check vent valve:

1. Remove the vent valve (Fig. 9-36) by detaching the three hoses that are connected to it.

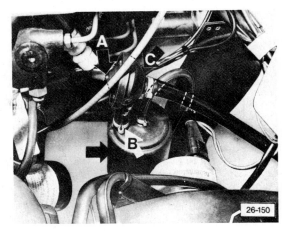

Fig. 9-36. Vent valve located above activated charcoal filter canister for evaporative emission control. Connection **A** is to vacuum hose, connections **B** and **C** are for ventilation hoses.

2. Blow into the vent valve at connection **B**. No air should flow from connection **C**. If it does, the vent valve is faulty and should be replaced.

3. Disconnect the vacuum hose from the engine's ignition distributor and connect this vacuum hose to the vent valve. Start the engine and allow it to idle. When you blow into valve connection **B**, air should flow out at connection **C**. If it does not, the vent valve is faulty and should be replaced.

Beginning with the 1978 models, there is a fuel tank breather gravity valve in the evaporative emission control system (Fig. 9-37). The valve is located on the car body, to the right and above the fuel tank.

7

Fig. 9-37. Fuel tank breather gravity valve. Connection **A** goes to charcoal filter canister, connection **B** is blocked, and connection **C** goes to fuel tank.

To check gravity valve operation:

1. Remove the gravity valve. Attach short pieces of clean hose to connections **A** and **C**, as given in Fig. 9-37.

2. Immerse the hose for connection **A** in a container filled with water. With the valve held vertically, blow into the hose for connection **C**. If air bubbles do not appear in the water, the valve is faulty and should be replaced.

3. While continuing to blow into connection **C**, gradually tilt the valve. If the bubbles do not stop when the valve reaches a 45° angle, the valve is faulty and should be replaced.

10. EXHAUST SYSTEM

The servicing of the catalytic converter used on some late models is covered in **9.2 1975 Carburetor Engine Emission Controls.** In installing exhaust system components, please observe the procedures shown in Fig. 10-1, Fig. 10-2, and Fig. 10-3.

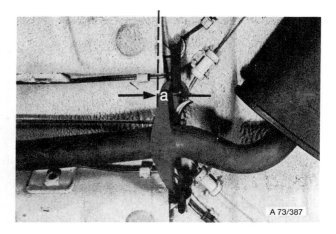

Fig. 10-1. Resonator being aligned. Distance between crossmember and rear surface of mounting hook (dimension **a**) should be 20 to 23 mm (¹³/₁₆ to ¹⁵/₁₆ in.).

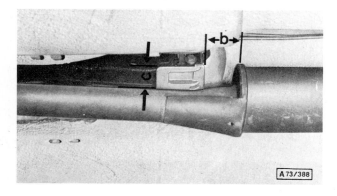

Fig. 10-2. Muffler being aligned. Dimension **b**, between edge of shift gate and primary muffler, should be 42 to 47 mm (1⅝ to 1⅞ in.). Dimension **c**, vertical clearance between shift gate and exhaust pipe, should be 19 to 24 mm (¾ to ⅞ in.).

Fig. 10-3. Rear clamp being aligned. The side of the clamp with the bolt (arrow) should face outward, toward the car's wheel.

11. FUEL AND EXHAUST SYSTEMS TECHNICAL DATA

I. CIS Fuel Injection Specifications

Item	Specification
Fuel pump delivery rate	750 cm³ (24 oz.)/30 sec. minimum
Control pressure (engine cold) **NOTE——** Control pressure varies with ambient temperature. See graph.	*(graph: bar/psi vs. ambient temperature; 22-259)*
Control pressure (engine warm—oil temp. 50–70°C or 122–158°F)	3.40–3.80 bar (48–54 psi)
System pressure	4.50–5.20 bar (64–74 psi)
Pressure test for leaks: after 10 min., minimum pressure after 20 min., minimum pressure	1.8 bar (25 psi) 1.6 bar (23 psi)
Fuel injectors: opening pressure pressure difference between injectors	2.5–3.5 bar (35–50 psi) 0.6 bar (8.5 psi) max.

II. 1973 Carburetor Jets and Settings

Designation	Manual transmission	Automatic transmission
Model	32/35 TDID two-stage, idle air/fuel control carburetor	same
Main jet	x120/x140	x115/x114
Air correction jet	140/140	same
Idle jet (with cutoff valve)	g45 (reserve 50)	same
Idle air jet	200/100	same
Venturi diameters	24/27 mm	same
Float needle valve diameter	1.75 mm	same
Float valve gasket thickness	2.0 mm	same
Float weight	7.3 g	same
Throttle valve gap (choke closed)	0.65 ±0.05 mm	0.8 ±0.15 mm
Injection rate per stroke (slow)	0.9 ±0.15 cm³	same
Injection rate per stroke (fast)	0.4 ±0.1 cm³	same
Injection tube	45	same

III. 1974 Carburetor Jets and Settings

Transmission		USA and Canada (except California)		California only	
		Manual	Automatic	Manual	Automatic
Engine Code letter		XW	XV	XZ	XY
Engine No.		XW 000 090	XV 000 123	SZ 000 057	XY 000 052
Carburetor Type		32/35 DIDTA	32/35 DIDTA	32/35 DIDTA	32/35 DIDTA
Spare Part No.		055 129 015 B	055 129 015 G	056 129 015 G	056 129 015 L
Venturi diameters		24/27 mm	24/27 mm	24/27 mm	24/27mm
Main jet		x135/x140	x130/x140	x122.5/x142.5	x120/x145
Air correction jet		150/140	140/140	130/140	140/140
Idle jet		52.5/50	52.5/50	45/50	45/50
Idle air jet		180/100	180/100	180/100	180/100
Auxiliary fuel jet		42.5	42.5	60	60
Auxiliary air jet		110	110	130	130
Power fuel system (without ball)		57.5/80	57.5/80	57.5/80	57.5/80
Injection quantity		0.9 ±0.15 cm³/stroke	0.9 ±0.15 cm³/stroke	0.9 ±0.15 cm³/stroke	0.9 ±0.15 cm³/stroke
Float needle valve diameter		1.75 mm	1.75 mm	1.75 mm	1.75 mm
Throttle valve gap (choke closed)		0.8 ±0.05 mm	0.8 ±0.05 mm	0.65 ±0.05 mm	0.8 ±0.05 mm

IV. 1975 and Later Carburetor Jets and Settings

Transmission		USA including California	
		Manual	Automatic
Engine Code letter		XS	XR
Engine No.		XS 000 001	XR 000 001
Carburetor Type		2B3	2B3
Spare part No.		055 129 017 F	055 129 017 G
	Venturi diameters	24/27 mm	24/27 mm
	Main jet	117.5/137.5	117.5/137.5
	Air correction jet	140/92.5	140/92.5
	Idle jet	52.5/65	52.5/65
	Idle air jet	130/110	130/110
	Auxiliary fuel jet	—/42.5	—/42.5
	Auxiliary air jet	—/127.5	—/127.5
	Power fuel system (with ball)	—/1.1	—/1.1
	Injection quantity	0.75–1.05 cm³/stroke	0.75–1.05 cm³/stroke
	Float needle valve diameter	2 mm	2 mm
	Float adjustment		
	1st stage	28 ±0.5 mm	28 ±0.5 mm
	2nd stage	30 ±0.5 mm	30 ±0.5 mm
	Choke valve gap	3.8–4.2 mm	3.8–4.2 mm
	Throttle valve gap (choke closed)	0.45–0.5 mm	0.45–0.5 mm

7

SUSPENSION AND STEERING

Contents

8

Suspension and Steering

Strut-type independent front-wheel suspension is used on all cars covered by this Manual. The struts, with their built-in shock absorbing capability, are similar in many respects to the landing wheel struts used on commercial airliners. In addition to providing excellent steering and handling for modern driving conditions, the system has the combined advantages of compact size and comparatively light weight.

The front struts have been designed to provide a negative roll radius. That is, each wheel's steering axis intersects the road at a point outboard of the wheel's vertical centerline. The resulting suspension geometry tends to steer the car automatically in the direction of incipient skids caused by unequal front wheel traction. Conventional front suspension geometry, which places the steering axis inboard of the tire centerline, tends to steer the car away from the direction of such a skid—thereby increasing its severity.

The design of the rack and pinion steering gearbox is unique. The steering tie rods are anchored at the center of the rack—rather than at the ends of the rack as with most such systems. Thus, the tie rods can be longer, permitting greater front suspension travel and larger steering angles for increased riding comfort and improved maneuverability.

The rear suspension has been designed for low unsprung weight, easy replacement of springs and shock absorbers, and good handling. The U-section axle beam houses a tubular torsion bar. Both the beam and the torsion bar are free to twist and, together with the trailing arms, act as an anti-roll bar whenever one rear wheel is deflected upward more than the other. A diagonal rod locates the rear axle laterally to prevent sway in cornering.

Though the front suspension struts and track control arms can be disassembled for repair, this work requires special tools, experience, and clean shop conditions. If you lack the skills, tools, or a suitable workshop for suspension and steering work, we suggest you leave such repairs to an Authorized Dealer or other qualified shop. We especially urge you to consult your Authorized Dealer before attempting any repairs on a car still covered by the new-car warranty.

8

1. GENERAL DESCRIPTION

A general view of the suspension and steering is given in Fig. 1-1. The subframe, on which the track front suspension track arms and the stabilizer bar are mounted, is a separate welded assembly that is bolted to the car's unit-construction body. The engine and transaxle are also mounted on the subframe. If necessary, the engine, transaxle, subframe, and front suspension can be removed from the car as a unit.

Front Suspension Struts

Each front suspension strut consists of a hydraulic shock absorber inside a tubular strut housing and a concentrically-mounted coil spring. The front wheel bearing housing and the steering arm are both welded permanently onto the strut housing. To prevent the transfer of road vibrations to the body, the top of each strut is mounted on the body with a rubber bushing. The front suspension's upward travel is limited by a hollow rubber buffer, its lower limit of travel by a rubber stop inside the shock absorber.

Front Track Control Arms and Stabilizer Bar

The two A-shaped track control arms locate the suspension struts both longitudinally and laterally. For easy replacement, the suspension ball joints are bolted on the track control arms and to the suspension struts.

Front wheel camber is adjustable by repositioning the ball joints on the track control arms. The stabilizer bar's only function is that of anti-roll stabilization. The bar does not serve as a longitudinal locating member as on some other cars with strut front suspensions.

Rear Suspension

The U-section pressed-steel rear axle beam is located longitudinally by two trailing arms, which are welded to the axle beam, and laterally by a diagonal strut. For easy replacement, the rear wheel spindles are bolted to the axle beam's steel end plates. Not visible in Fig. 1-1 is the torsion bar which is housed within the rear axle beam and attached to the axle beam end plates.

Steering

The rack and pinion steering gearbox is located behind the engine, above the transaxle. This location not only protects the gearbox from the weather, but also shields the steering from damage in all but the most severe collisions. A hydraulic steering damper is linked to the steering rack to minimize the road shock transmitted to the steering wheel. Neither the steering gearbox nor the tie rod ends require lubrication or adjustment throughout their service lives. Because the left tie rod's ends are threaded, you can adjust front wheel toe simply by loosening the locknuts and turning the left tie rod.

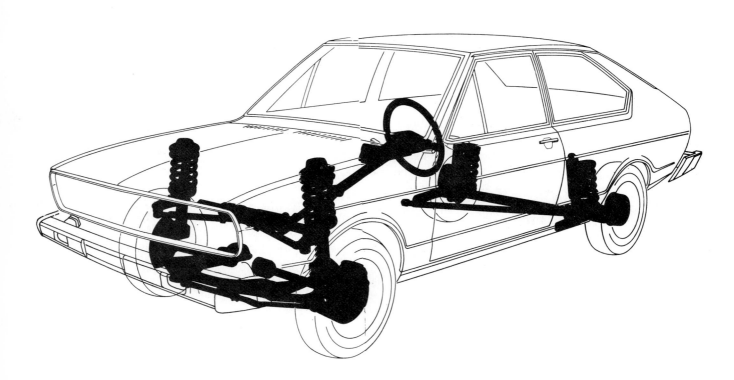

Fig. 1-1. General view of the steering system and the front and rear suspension systems.

2. MAINTENANCE

The suspension and steering are virtually maintenance-free. The following items only are covered in **LUBRICATION AND MAINTENANCE** or under the listed heading in this section of the Manual.

1. Checking ball joint dust seals and tie rod end dust seals

2. Checking steering play

3. Checking steering gearbox boots for leaks, tearing, or other damage

4. Checking front wheel camber and toe. See **3. Wheel Alignment.**

3. WHEEL ALIGNMENT

Only camber and toe are adjustable. Caster angle and king pin inclination are determined by the manufactured dimensions of the suspension parts, so damaged parts must be replaced to correct these alignment factors.

The following preparatory steps are essential to accurate alignment measurements.

1. Have the car on a level surface.

2. Inflate the tires to specifications and unload the car except for the spare wheel and a full fuel tank. Then jounce the car several times and let it settle into its normal position.

3. Check for excessive steering gearbox play. If play is excessive, adjust or replace the gearbox.

4. Make sure there is no play in the tie rod ends or other parts of the steering linkage.

Measuring wheel camber and toe requires suitable gauges. Although professional-grade instruments may cost several hundred dollars, modestly priced gauges that are adequate to home use are available from mail order houses. Instructions are supplied by the manufacturer.

3.1 Checking and Adjusting Front Wheel Camber

Camber is the angle at which wheels depart from the true vertical when viewed from directly in front of the car. If the tops of the wheels lean slightly outward, they are said to have positive camber. If they lean inward, they are said to have negative camber.

To check:

1. After placing the car on a level surface with the steering centered, apply a bubble protractor as shown in Fig. 3-1.

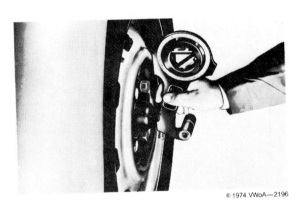

© 1974 VWoA—2196

Fig. 3-1. Bubble protractor against front wheel.

2. Using chalk, mark the wheel at the points where it contacts the protractor.

3. Turn the spirit level carrier on the protractor until the bubble is centered, then read the camber angle on the scale.

   NOTE ——
   If you are using a different type of gauge, follow the manufacturer's instructions.

4. Roll the car forward a half-turn on the wheels and repeat the measurement at the chalk-marked points.

5. Take the new reading and average it with the one you obtained earlier. The result is the camber angle for the wheel.

6. Repeat the entire procedure on the other front wheel.

The front wheels should have 25′ ± 30′ of positive camber. Also, the difference in camber between the wheels should not vary more than 1°. If the camber of each wheel is not within specifications, it should be adjusted to as near 25′ positive camber as possible.

8

To adjust camber:

1. Loosen the nuts and bolts visible in Fig. 3-2.

NOTE ——

The car must be standing on its wheels while adjustments are being made.

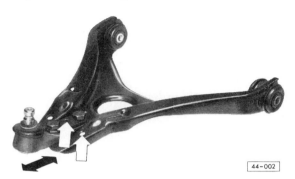

Fig. 3-2. Suspension ball joint mounting on track control arm (arm removed for clarity). With nuts and bolts loosened, ball joint can be moved as indicated by the black double arrow. White arrows indicate holes that accommodate lever tool 40-200.

2. Set the spirit level carrier on the protractor to the specified angle of 25' positive camber.

3. Insert the adjusting lever (tool 40–200) in the holes indicated by white arrows in Fig. 3-2. In adjusting the right-hand front wheel, insert the lever from the front of the car; in adjusting the left-hand front wheel, insert the lever from the rear of the car.

4. Using the lever, pry the ball joint one way or the other (Fig. 3-3) until the bubble in the protractor is centered when the protractor is applied to the chalk-marked points on the wheel.

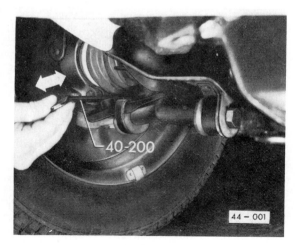

Fig. 3-3. Lever being moved (double arrow) to pry ball joint sideways on track control arm.

5. Torque the nuts and bolts to 6.5 mkg (47 ft. lb.). Again check the camber and repeat the adjustments, if necessary, to bring the camber within specifications.

6. Check the toe and adjust it if necessary.

3.2 Checking and Adjusting Front Wheel Toe

The cars covered by this manual are designed to operate with a small amount of toe-in. This means that the front edges of the tires are slightly closer together than the rear edges. Shops with optical aligning devices should follow the equipment manufacturer's instruction to obtain a toe angle of + 10' ± 15', or + 25' ± 15' after adding 8 to 12 kg (18 to 26 lb.) of extra weight above the wheel. The maximum toe change produced by the added weight should not exceed 15'.

Most small shops and individual car owners check toe with a track gauge. This device is used to measure the distance between two points at the front edges of the rims, then the distance between the same two points after the car has been rolled ahead so that these points are at the rear. The measurement made at the rear should be 1.00 mm (.040 in., or approximately 3/64 in.) greater than the measurement made at the front ± 1.50 mm (.060 in., or approximately 1/16 in.). This should increase to 1.50 mm (.060 in., or approximately 1/16 in.) ± 2.5 mm (.100 in., or approximately 3/32 in.) with weight added above the wheels.

NOTE ——

These specifications apply only with the wheels in their straight-ahead position.

To check and adjust toe:

1. Turn the steering to its centered position (steering wheel spokes horizontal).

2. Measure the toe. If a track gauge is used, mark the measuring points with chalk. Doing this will allow you to make measurements between the same two points after you have rolled the car forward a half-turn of the wheels.

3. If the toe is not within specifications, loosen the locknut and the clamp on the left-hand tie rod (Fig. 3-4). Then rotate the top of the left tie rod toward the front of the car to increase toe-in or rotate the top of the left tie rod toward the rear of the car to decrease toe-in.

4. When the toe-in is correct, position the left tie rod so that the outer tie rod end ball joint is not angled. Torque the locknut at the outer end of the tie rod to 4.0 mkg (29 ft. lb.); torque the clamp bolt at the inner end of the tie rod to 3.0 mkg (22 ft. lb.).

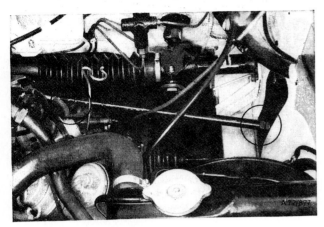

Fig. 3-4. Clamp and locknut (circled) on left-hand tie rod. The left circle contains the pinch clamp used at the inner end of the tie rod; the right circle contains the locknut used at the outer end of the tie rod.

If, after adjusting the toe to specifications, the steering wheel is not centered while you are driving straight ahead on a level surface, either there are damaged steering parts or the steering wheel has been incorrectly installed. However, you should never assume that the steering wheel has been installed incorrectly unless a careful and thorough inspection reveals no damage to the steering or the front suspension.

> **CAUTION** ——
>
> *If there are damaged steering or suspension parts, never center the steering wheel either by altering its position on the column, or by moving the column on the steering gearbox. Doing this leaves the real fault uncorrected.*

3.3 Checking Rear Wheel Alignment

The rear wheel alignment cannot be adjusted. Incorrect alignment can be corrected only by replacing damaged parts. If you wish to check the rear wheel alignment, please refer to **5.3 Checking Axle Beam for Distortion.**

4. FRONT SUSPENSION

Though the cars covered by this manual have front wheel drive, the front suspension is no more complex than that of a rear-drive automobile. All the front suspension parts that are subject to wear are quickly and easily replaceable. Some repairs, however, require equipment other than common hand tools. To avoid undertaking a task that you may not be able to complete, please read the entire procedure for the job before you begin work.

> **CAUTION** ——
>
> *If you lack the skills, tools, or a suitable workshop for repairing the front suspension we suggest you leave this work to an Authorized Dealer or other qualified shop. We especially urge you to consult your Authorized Dealer before attempting repairs on a car still covered by the new-car warranty.*

4.1 Checking Suspension Ball Joints

A special lever and a vernier caliper should be used to check ball joint play.

To check:

1. Lift the car so that the front wheels and suspension are unsupported.

2. Install the special lever as shown in Fig. 4-1. Move the lever as indicated by the curved arrow to compress the spring inside the ball joint. With the ball joint compressed, place a vernier caliper on the suspension in the position shown.

Fig. 4-1. Lever and vernier caliper in position. Lever hook goes under stabilizer bar, lever bar goes above the wheel bearing housing on strut.

3. Note the reading on the vernier caliper. Then, while slowly releasing the lever, note the caliper's travel. The increase in the reading is the ball joint play. Replace the ball joint if play is 2.50 mm (.100 in.) or more. The play in new ball joints is 1.00 mm (.040 in.).

8

4.2 Removing and Installing Suspension Ball Joint

Before you remove a suspension ball joint, scribe or otherwise mark its position on the track control arm. In doing this you will simplify—or eliminate—the job of adjusting the front wheel camber since the ball joint or its replacement can easily be installed in the original location.

To remove a ball joint, first loosen the clamp bolt that holds the ball joint stud in the bottom of the wheel bearing housing on the suspension strut. Then unbolt the ball joint from the track control arm. Pull the ball joint downward out of the suspension strut.

Installation is the reverse of removal. Install a new clamp bolt and nut, then torque the clamp bolt for the ball joint stud to 3.5 mkg (25 ft. lb.) on 1973 through 1977 cars with 8-mm bolts, or to 5.0 mkg (36 ft. lb.) on 1978 and later cars with 10-mm bolts. With the ball joint positioned in the location you marked for it prior to removal, torque the nuts and bolts that hold the ball joint on the track control arm to 6.5 mkg (47 ft. lb.). Check the front wheel camber and toe and, if necessary, adjust them as described in **3. Wheel Alignment.**

4.3 Removing and Installing Suspension Strut

Suspension strut removal is illustrated in the exploded view given in Fig. 4-2. If you wish to remove the drive shafts before you remove the suspension strut, use the procedure given in **MANUAL TRANSMISSION.**

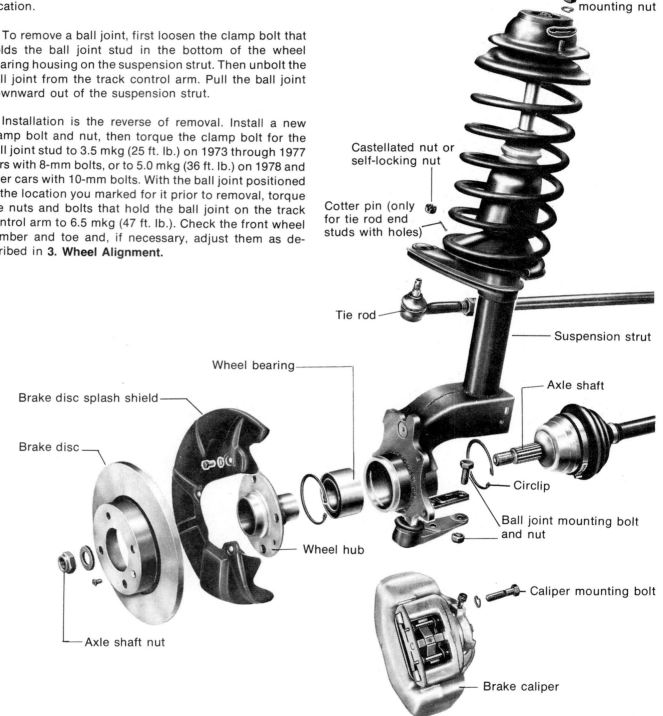

Fig. 4-2. Exploded view of front suspension strut and related parts.

To remove:

1. Pry off the dust cap that is pressed into the center of the wheel hub. Then loosen, but do not remove, the axle shaft nut.

> **WARNING ——**
>
> *Loosen axle shaft nuts with the car on the ground. The leverage needed for this job is enough to topple a car off the lift.*

2. Raise the vehicle on a lift. Remove the road wheel. Remove the brake caliper, the brake hose clips, the brake disc, and the brake disc splash shield as described in **BRAKES AND WHEELS.**

3. Remove the cotter pin from cars that have it. Then remove the nut from the tie rod end stud. Press the tie rod end out of the steering arm with a tool such as the one shown in Fig. 4-3.

> **CAUTION ——**
>
> *Do not hammer out the tie rod end. Doing this will ruin the threads and make reinstallation impossible.*

Fig. 4-3. Puller in position for tie rod end removal.

4. Loosen the clamp bolt that holds the suspension ball joint stud in the bottom of the suspension strut. Unbolt both ends of the stabilizer bar from the track control arms. Then pull down on the track control arm so that the ball joint stud is withdrawn from the suspension strut. Alternatively, you can unbolt the suspension ball joint from the track control arm. However, you will avoid the necessity of correcting the camber adjustment if you leave the ball joint mounted on the track control arm.

5. Remove the axle shaft nut and washer. Support the driveshaft with a wire hook connected to the car body so that the driveshaft will not fall suddenly. Then pull the suspension strut outward and off the axle shaft.

6. Remove the two upper mounting nuts and washers (Fig. 4-4). Support the suspension strut as you remove the second nut. When both nuts and washers have been removed, lower the suspension strut and remove the strut from the car.

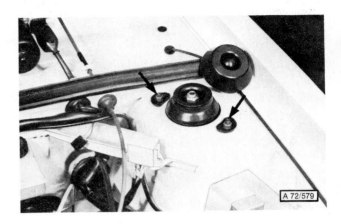

Fig. 4-4. Nuts that hold the suspension strut's upper mounting onto the body.

Installation is the reverse of removal. Torque the strut upper mounting nuts to 2.5 mkg (18 ft. lb.). Use a new clamp bolt and nut to hold the suspension ball joint stud in the strut. The bolt head must be toward the front of the car. Torque the clamp bolt to 3.5 mkg (25 ft. lb.) on 1973 through 1977 cars with 8-mm bolts, or to 5.0 mkg (36 ft. lb.) on 1978 and later cars with 10-mm bolts.

Torque the nut for the tie rod end stud to 3.0 mkg (22 ft. lb.). Castellated nuts should be advanced, if necessary, to uncover the cotter pin hole and a new cotter pin installed. If you removed the ball joint from the track control arm, torque the mounting bolts to 6.5 mkg (47 ft. lb.). Torque the bolts for the stabilizer bar clamps to 1.0 mkg (7 ft. lb.).

Torque the brake disc splash shield to 1.0 mkg (7 ft. lb.), the brake disc mounting bolts to 0.7 mkg (5 ft. lb.), and the brake caliper mounting bolts to 6.0 mkg (43 ft. lb.). Install the axle shaft nut but do not tighten it. Lower the vehicle to the ground. Torque axle shaft nuts with M 18 × 1.5 threads to 20 mkg (145 ft. lb.); torque axle shaft nuts with M 20 × 1.5 threads to 24 mkg (175 ft. lb.). Install the dust cap, then check the front wheel camber and toe.

> **WARNING ——**
>
> *Tighten the axle shaft nuts with the car on the ground. The leverage needed for this job is enough to topple a car off the lift.*

8

4.4 Replacing Front Wheel Bearing

The double-row front wheel ball bearings need not be replaced unless they are noisy or have excessive play. No periodic lubrication is required. You must remove the front suspension strut before you can replace a front wheel bearing.

To replace:

1. Press the wheel hub out of the bearing as shown in Fig. 4-5.

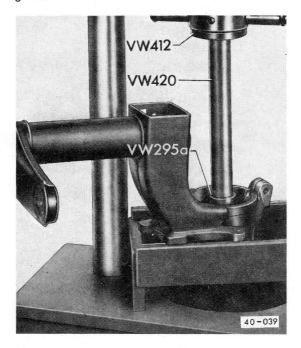

Fig. 4-5. Front wheel hub being pressed out of wheel bearing race in suspension strut.

NOTE ——

If the outboard inner bearing race comes out along with the hub, remove the race from the hub as shown in Fig. 4-6.

CAUTION ——

The wheel bearing is destroyed in pressing out the hub. Once either the wheel hub or the bearing has been removed from the suspension strut, a new bearing must be installed.

2. Remove the two circlips that are inside the bearing housing—one circlip at each end of the bearing (Fig. 4-7).

3. Using a press tool that will apply pressure to only the bearing's outer race, press out the bearing toward the outboard end of the bearing housing.

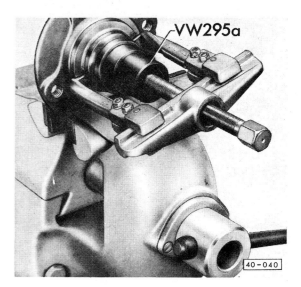

Fig. 4-6. Puller being used to remove bearing inner race from front wheel hub.

Fig. 4-7. Circlip being removed.

4. Install the circlip at the outboard end of the bearing housing. Then, using a press tool that will apply pressure to only the bearing's outer race, press in a new wheel bearing as shown in Fig. 4-8.

5. Install the inboard circlip.

NOTE ——

Though new bearings are lubricated during manufacture, you should add just enough molybdenum grease to compensate for any that is lost during handling and installation.

6. With the wheel hub supported as shown in Fig. 4-9, use a press tool—one that will apply pressure to the inner bearing race only—to press down the bearing and suspension strut onto the hub. Advance the press carefully until the bearing inner race just contacts the wheel hub flange.

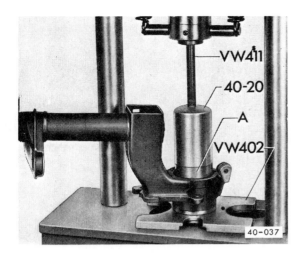

Fig. 4-8. New wheel bearing **(A)** being pressed into bearing housing. Advance the press tool carefully until the bearing outer race just contacts the circlip.

Fig. 4-9. Wheel hub being installed in bearing.

4.5 Disassembling and Assembling Front Suspension Strut

Fig. 4-10 illustrates the disassembly of a front suspension strut. You can replace the end collar without removing the strut. Always install a new suspension strut nut in place of a nut that has been removed. To disassemble a strut fully, you must have a proper spring compressing appliance.

WARNING ——

Do not attempt to tension the spring with makeshift tools. If a compressed spring slips free, it can inflict severe injury.

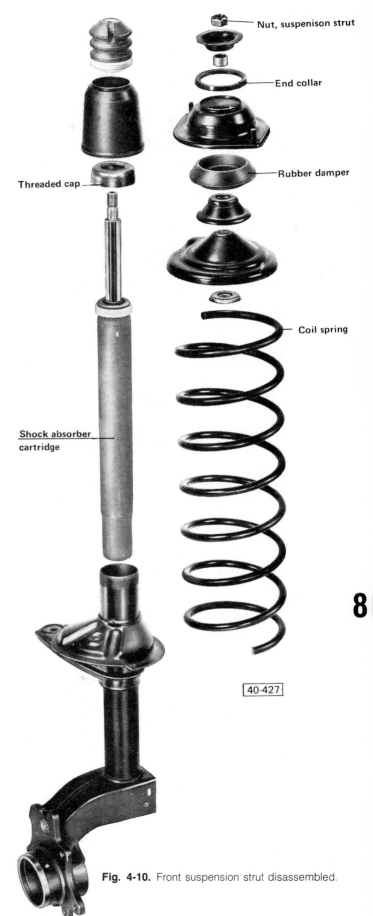

Fig. 4-10. Front suspension strut disassembled.

To disassemble strut:

1. Remove the strut from the car. Install the spring compressing appliance in a bench vise, then install the strut in the spring compressing appliance.

2. To compress the spring, tighten the long bolts a few turns at a time, working alternately (Fig. 4-11).

Fig. 4-11. Strut mounted in spring compressing appliance.

3. Using an offset box wrench and an Allen wrench as shown in Fig. 4-12, remove the nut from the shock absorber piston rod.

4. Working alternately, gradually loosen the two long bolts on the compressing appliance until spring tension is relieved. Then take off the upper mounting components and the spring.

> **NOTE ——**
>
> Consult **Table a** if a spring must be replaced. It is unnecessary to replace both springs if one spring is faulty, even though the original springs have a different number of paint marks than the standard replacement springs.

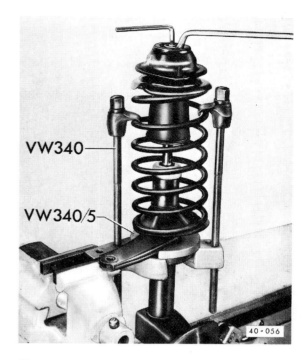

Fig. 4-12. Removing nut from piston rod.

Table a. Replacement Front Springs

Model	Paint marks on original spring	Paint marks on replacement spring
1973 and 1974 through Chassis No __4 2119 990	1 white 2 white 3 white	1 white 2 white 3 white
1974 from Chassis No. __2119 991 through 1977	2 red 2 red 3 red	1 red 2 red 2 red
1978	1 orange 2 orange 1 gray 2 gray 3 gray	2 orange 2 orange 2 gray 2 gray 2 gray

5. If the shock absorber must be replaced, install a special tool that will engage the hexagonal recess in the top of the threaded cap. Then remove the threaded cap as shown in Fig. 4-13.

> **NOTE ——**
>
> You can check the shock absorber without removing it from the strut housing.

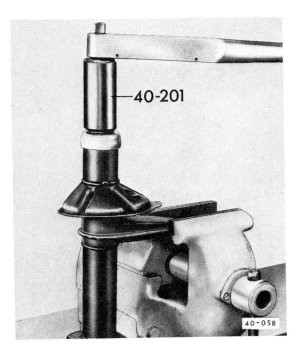

Fig. 4-13. Threaded cap being removed from strut.

6. Withdraw the shock absorber from the strut housing. If the shock absorber is stuck inside the
housing, install the old suspension strut nut on the
shock absorber's piston rod. Place an undersize
open end wrench beneath the nut. Then drive the
shock absorber out of the housing as shown in Fig.
4-14.

Fig. 4-14. Shock absorber being driven out of strut
housing.

Assembly is the reverse of disassembly. If it was
removed during disassembly, torque the threaded cap to
15.0 mkg (108 ft. lb.). Install a new end collar and a new
suspension strut nut. Torque the suspension strut nut to
6.0 mkg (43 ft. lb.) as shown in Fig. 4-15.

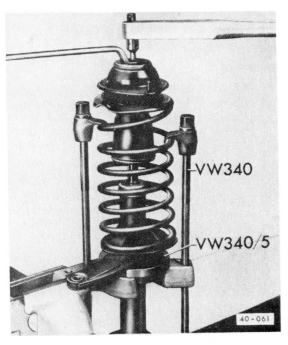

Fig. 4-15. Suspension strut nut being torqued. Use a
box wrench to hold the nut stationary. Then,
using a hexagonal driver on the torque
wrench, turn the shock absorber piston rod
counterclockwise until the correct torque is
attained.

Checking Shock Absrober

Defective shock absorbers often make knocking
noises when the car is driven. You can hand-check a
shock absorber by extending and compressing it while
holding it in its installed position. It must operate
smoothly and with uniform resistance throughout its
entire stroke. If possible, compare the used unit with a
new shock absorber. New shock absorbers that have
been in storage may have to be pumped several times
before they reach full efficiency.

Shock absorbers do not require maintenance. An
adequate supply of fluid is placed in them during manufacture to compensate for small leaks. Minor traces of
fluid are acceptable if the shock absorber still functions
efficiently. Defective shock absorbers cannot be serviced
and must be replaced.

8

4.6 Removing and Installing Stabilizer Bar and Track Control Arm

Fig. 4-16 shows the stabilizer bar and a track control arm in relation to the front suspension subframe. The rubber bushings can be replaced after the stabilizer bar and the track control arm(s) have been removed.

To remove:

1. With the car on a lift that does not support the front wheels or the front suspension, remove the bolts that hold the stabilizer bar clamps on both track control arms and on the subframe. Then remove the clamps, the rubber bushings, and the stabilizer bar.

2. Loosen the clamp bolt that holds the suspension ball joint stud in the bottom of the wheel bearing housing. Then pull down on the track control arm so that the ball joint stud is withdrawn from the suspension strut. Alternatively, you can unbolt the suspension ball joint from the track control arm.

3. Bend up the tabs on the locking plates (1973 cars only). Then remove the bolts for the track control arm and remove the track control arm from the subframe.

To install:

1. Inspect the rubber bushings in the track control arm. If either is worn, cracked, or damaged, replace both bushings as described in **4.7 Replacing Bushings in Track Control Arm.**

2. If the car has been in an accident or if the front wheels cannot be aligned to specifications, you can check the track control arm for distortion using the checking appliance illustrated in Fig. 4-17.

3. Using new locking plates, bolt the track control arm to the subframe. Torque the bolts for the track control arm to 7.0 mkg (50 ft. lb.), then bend over the tabs on the locking plate so that the tabs engage the flats on the bolt heads.

4. Attach the track control arm to the suspension strut. If you removed the ball joint stud from the strut, torque the clamp bolt to 3.5 mkg (25 ft. lb.). If

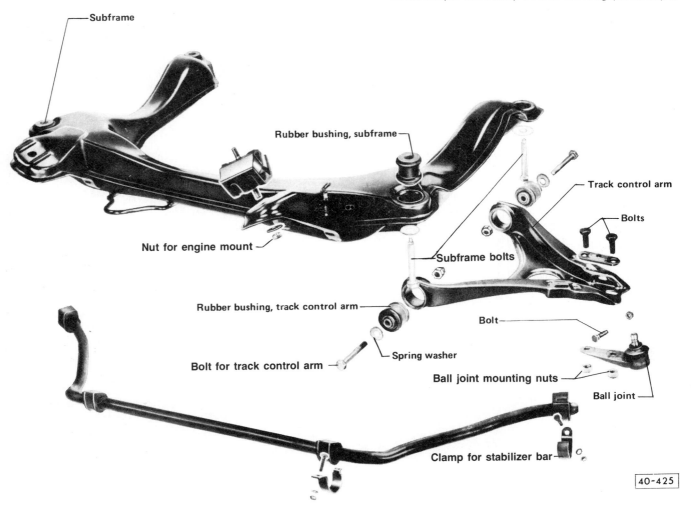

Fig. 4-16. Exploded view of front suspension.

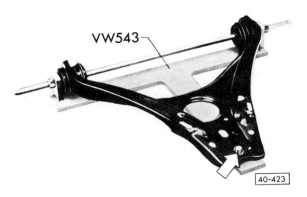

Fig. 4-17. Track control arm being checked for distortion. Pin on appliance must readily enter the hole in the track control arm (arrow).

you removed the ball joint from the track control arm, install the ball joint mounting nuts loosely. Then torque the nuts to 6.5 mkg (47 ft. lb.) after you have adjusted the front wheel camber as described in **3.1 Checking and Adjusting Front Wheel Camber.**

5. Install the stabilizer bar on the track control arms. Use water pump pliers to compress the clamps around the rubber bushings while you start the bolts in their holes. Torque the bolts to 1.0 mkg (7 ft. lb.).

6. Install the stabilizer bar on the subframe. Torque the mounting bolts to 1.0 mkg (7 ft. lb.).

7. Check and adjust the front wheel camber and toe as described in **3. Wheel Alignment.**

4.7 Replacing Bushings in Track Control Arm

If inspection reveals wear, cracks, or other damage to the rubber bushings in the track control arm, press out the damaged bushings as shown in Fig. 4-18. Be sure to support the track control arm as illustrated. The arm may be distorted if you attempt to press out a bushing with the opposite bushing eye supported on the press bed.

To ensure that the new rubber bushing will enter the track control arm correctly, bolt the new bushing to a guide piece as shown in Fig. 4-19. The diameter of the guide piece should be such that it forms a smooth fit with the inside of the support piece that is beneath the bushing eye in the track control arm. The 1978 and later bushings have less shore hardness than do earlier bushings.

Lightly lubricate the new bushing with brake cylinder paste (see **BRAKES AND WHEELS**) or with silicone spray. Then press in the bushing as shown in Fig. 4-20. Notice how the guide piece enters the support piece, thereby preventing the bushing from entering the bushing eye at an angle.

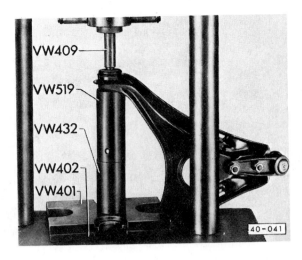

Fig. 4-18. Rubber bushings being pressed out of track control arm. Notice how the bushing eye in the track control arm is being supported.

Fig. 4-19. New bushing bolted to guide piece.

8

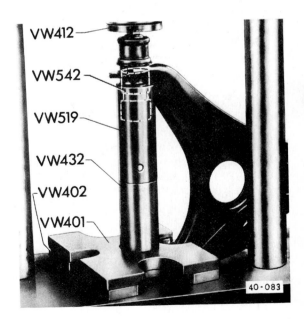

Fig. 4-20. Rubber bushing being pressed into track control arm. The position of the guide piece inside the support piece is shown by dashed lines.

4.8 Removing and Installing Subframe

To support the engine while the subframe is off, install a support on the lug at the rear of the cylinder head as shown in Fig. 4-21.

Fig. 4-21. A support bar installed across the engine compartment. A threaded rod attaches the support bar to the lug on the cylinder head.

To remove:

1. Remove the stabilizer bar and both track control arms as described in **4.6 Removing and Installing Stabilizer Bar and Track Control Arm.**

2. Remove the two nuts that hold the side engine mounts on the sub frame.

3. Remove the four bolts that hold the subframe on the body. Support the subframe as you remove the last bolt so that the subframe does not fall suddenly.

Installation is the reverse of removal. Thoroughly clean all dirt—and especially undercoating material—from the subframe bolts, then lightly lubricate the bolt threads with engine oil. Torque the subframe bolts to 7.0 mkg (50 ft. lb.). Torque the nuts for the engine mounts to 4.0 mkg (29 ft. lb.). After you have installed the stabilizer bar and the track control arms, check and adjust the front wheel camber and toe as described in **3. Wheel Alignment.**

Replacing Bushings in Subframe

If the rubber bushings in the subframe are worn, cracked, or otherwise damaged, press out the damaged bushings as shown in Fig. 4-22.

Fig. 4-22. Rubber bushing being pressed out of subframe.

Lubricate the new bushings with brake cylinder paste (see **BRAKES AND WHEELS**) or with silicone spray. Then, using a press tool that has a projection that will fit inside the new bushing, drive in the new bushing as shown in Fig. 4-23. This kind of tool will prevent the bushing from entering the subframe at an angle.

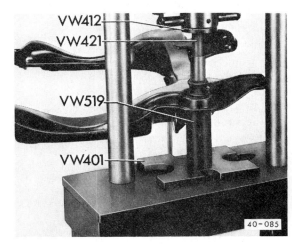

Fig. 4-23. Rubber bushing being pressed into subframe.

4.9 Removing and Installing Subframe Complete with Engine, Transaxle, and Front Suspension

When both the engine and the transaxle require repairs, or when the transaxle, engine, and front suspension must be removed preparatory to body repairs, it is convenient and efficient to remove the subframe complete with engine, transaxle, and front suspension. In doing this, you will avoid many smaller jobs which would be required if the engine, transaxle, and front suspension were removed separately.

To remove:

1. Drain the cooling system as described in **ENGINE AND CLUTCH.**

2. Disconnect the battery ground strap. Remove the front road wheels.

3. Working beneath the car, drain the coolant (arrows **1** and **2** in Fig. 4-24). Disconnect the radiator lower hose (arrow **3**), disconnect the starter cable and wires (arrow **4**), and unbolt the exhaust pipe from the exhaust manifold flange (arrow **5**).

4. Working at the left side of the engine compartment, disconnect the radiator upper hose (arrow **8** in Fig. 4-25). Disconnect the heater hose (arrow **9**).

5. Loosen the clutch cable adjusting nuts (arrow **10** in Fig. 4-25) so that you can disengage the clutch cable housing from the bracket that is on the side engine mount. With the housing disengaged from the bracket, unhook the cable end from the clutch operating lever which is on the side of the transaxle bellhousing.

6. Disconnect the speedometer cable (arrow **11** in Fig. 4-25) from the transaxle. Disconnect the high tension cable (arrow **12**) from the center of the

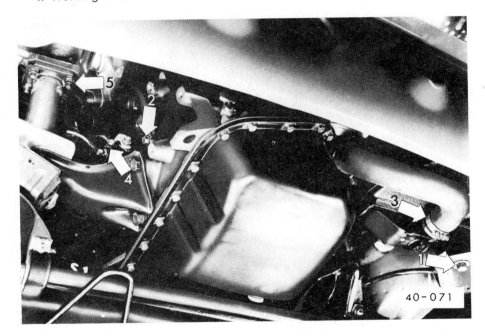

Fig. 4-24. Jobs to be performed while working beneath the car.

Fig. 4-25. Jobs to be performed while working at the left-hand side of the engine.

8

Fig. 4-26. Jobs to be performed while working at the left-hand side of the engine.

distributor cap. Disconnect the primary wire from terminal 1 on the ignition coil (arrow **13**), then unbolt the engine ground strap (arrow **14**).

7. Disconnect the fuel hose (arrow **15** in Fig. 4-25) from the fuel pump. Using a punch, pencil, or golf tee, quickly plug the hose.

WARNING ——

Do not smoke or work near heaters or other fire hazards. Have a fire extinguisher handy.

8. Remove the air cleaner as described in **LUBRICATION AND MAINTENANCE.** Remove the nuts that hold the suspension struts on the body (see **4.3 Removing and Installing Suspension Strut**).

9. Working at the right-hand side of the engine, disconnect the wire from the electromagnetic cutoff valve (arrow **18** in Fig. 4-26). Then remove the electromagnetic cutoff valve (arrow **19**) from the carburetor.

10. Pry off the accelerator cable retaining clip and then disconnect the accelerator cable from the throttle valve lever (arrow **20** in Fig. 4-26). Remove the accelerator cable housing mounting nut (arrow **21**). Then withdraw the accelerator cable and its housing from the bracket on the engine.

11. Unbolt the front engine mount from the engine and from the body (arrow **22** and **23** in Fig. 4-26).

12. Working under the car, unbolt the exhaust system from the transaxle and from the body (arrows **24, 25,** and **26** in Fig. 4-27). Unhook the exhaust system rubber support rings. Then pull the exhaust system to the rear so that it will not interfere with the lowering of the engine, transaxle, suspension, and subframe. See **FUEL AND EXHAUST SYSTEMS** for detailed procedures.

13. On cars with manual transmissions, remove the

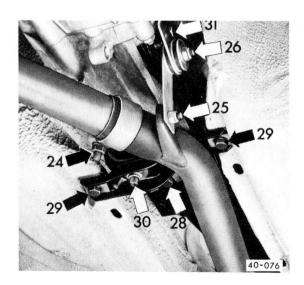

Fig. 4-27. Exhaust system and transaxle mounting fasteners located near the rear of the transaxle.

clutch operating rod (arrow **28** in Fig. 4-27). Remove the bolts for the transaxle carrier (arrows **29**). Then remove the bonded rubber mounting nut (arrow **30**).

14. Cut the locking wire, then remove the shift rod coupling setscrew that is on the rear of the manual transmission transaxle (arrow **31** in Fig. 4-27).

15. On cars with automatic transmission transaxles, remove the transaxle rear support and disconnect the selector cable as described in **AUTOMATIC TRANSMISSION.** Disconnect the kickdown wire from the terminal on the transaxle.

16. Remove the cotter pin from cars that have it. Then remove the nut from the tie rod end stud. Using a puller, as described in **4.3 Removing and Installing Suspension Strut,** press the tie rod end out of the steering arm (arrow **32** in Fig. 4-28).

> *CAUTION* ——
>
> *Do not hammer out the tie rod end. Doing this will ruin the threads and make reinstallation impossible.*

17. Disconnect the brake hose at the point indicated by arrow **33** in Fig. 4-28. Use clean bleeder valve dust seal to plug the brake line and prevent the loss of brake fluid.

18. Slightly loosen the four bolts that hold the subframe on the body (arrows **36** in Fig. 4-28). If you intend to separate the engine from the subframe following removal, remove the nuts for the side engine mounts (arrow **35** in Fig. 4-28).

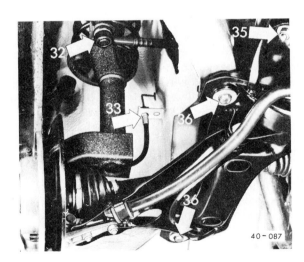

Fig. 4-28. Fasteners that join the suspension struts and the subframe to the body.

19. Position a floor jack with an engine/transaxle adapter beneath the engine, transaxle, and subframe. With the engine, transaxle, subframe, and suspension thus supported, remove the four bolts that hold the subframe on the body.

20. Slightly lower the engine, transaxle, suspension, and subframe assembly. Then disconnect the wire from the back-up light switch which is at the rear of the transaxle.

21. Lower the engine/transaxle/suspension/subframe assembly from the car as shown in Fig. 4-29.

Fig. 4-29. Engine/transaxle/suspension/subframe assembly being lowered from car body.

To install:

1. Raise the engine/transaxle/suspension/subframe assembly until you can connect the back-up light wire to the switch on the rear of the transaxle (Fig. 4-30).

8

Fig. 4-30. Wire connected to back-up light switch (arrow).

2. Thoroughly clean all dirt—and especially under-coating material—from the subframe bolts and then lightly lubricate the bolt threads with engine oil. Raise the engine/transaxle/suspension/subframe assembly into position on the body. Align the hole for the left rear subframe mounting bolt with the hole in the body, then install the bolt. Align the subframe with the remaining three mounting bolts that hold the subframe on the body to 7.0 mkg (50 ft. lb.). If necessary, torque the nuts for the side engine mounts to 4.0 mkg (29 ft. lb.).

3. Push up the rear of the transaxle. Then loosely bolt the transaxle carrier to the body.

4. On cars with manual transmissions, connect the shift rod coupling to the transaxle, then install the setscrew and lock it with wire. On cars with automatic transmissions, connect and, if necessary, adjust the selector cable and other transmission controls. See **AUTOMATIC TRANSMISSION.**

5. Install the tie rod ends in the steering arms. Torque the nuts to 3.0 mkg (22 ft. lb.). Advance the castellated nuts, if necessary, to uncover the cotter pin holes, then install new cotter pins.

6. Install the brake hoses. Then bleed the brakes as described in **BRAKES AND WHEELS.**

7. Install the exhaust system. Connect the wires to the starter.

8. Loosely install the front engine mount. Install the front suspension struts on the body. Torque the nuts to 2.5 mkg (18 ft. lb.).

9. Reconnect the fuel line to the fuel pump. Install the electromagnetic cutoff valve.

   WARNING ——

   Do not smoke or work near heaters or other fire hazards. Have a fire extinguisher handy.

10. Connect all remaining hoses and wires to the engine—including the engine ground strap. Connect the speedometer cable to the transaxle. Then connect the battery ground strap.

11. On cars with manual transmissions, install the clutch cable and adjust the clutch pedal freeplay to 15 mm (⅝ in.) as described in **ENGINE AND CLUTCH.**

12. Install the road wheels. Fill the cooling system as described in **LUBRICATION AND MAINTENANCE.**

13. With the car resting on its wheels, align the engine/transaxle assembly so that the bonded rubber mountings are not under tension. First shift the transaxle carrier on the body so that the side engine mounts are not twisted. Then torque the bolts that hold the carrier to 2.5 mkg (18 ft. lb.). Torque the nut for the bonded rubber bushing to 4.0 mkg (29 ft. lb.).

   NOTE ——

   The torque specifications given here apply only to cars with manual transmissions. Torque specifications for the automatic transmission can be found in **7. Suspension and Steering Technical Data.** Additional information about aligning the automatic transmission transaxle mountings can be found in **AUTOMATIC TRANSMISSION.**

14. With the engine/transaxle assembly aligned as described in step 12, torque the front engine mount bolts to 2.5 mkg (18 ft. lb.).

15. If the engine or the transaxle were drained during removal or repair, refill the engine or the transaxle as described in **LUBRICATION AND MAINTENANCE** before you start the engine.

16. Install the accelerator cable. See **FUEL AND EXHAUST SYSTEMS.**

17. Install the air cleaner as described in **LUBRICATION AND MAINTENANCE.** Then adjust the carburetor as described in **FUEL AND EXHAUST SYSTEMS.**

5. REAR SUSPENSION

Early 1973 Audi models have a rear axle that is different from that of later Audi and VW models. This early axle has the shock absorbers and the springs installed concentrically, assembled into a strut arrangement. The later axle has the shock absorbers and springs installed as separate units. The new version permits greater vertical suspension travel and simplifies shock absorber replacement.

Though the rear wheel bearings do not routinely require lubrication and adjustment, this work is a necessary part of brake service. Therefore, many of the jobs described here will be carried out in conjunction with those described in **BRAKES AND WHEELS.**

5.1 Checking and Replacing Shock Absorbers

The shock absorbers do not require maintenance. An adequate supply of fluid is placed in them during manufacture to compensate for small leaks. Minor traces of fluid are acceptable if the shock absorber still functions efficiently. Damaged or worn-out shock absorbers cannot be serviced and must be replaced.

Worn-out shock absorbers often make knocking noises when the car is driven or produce a rough, bouncy ride except when the rear seat and trunk are heavily loaded. The best way to check the shock absorbers is to remove them.

To remove early 1973 Audi shock absorber:

1. With the car resting on its wheels, remove the rear seat cushion and backrest as described in **BODY AND INTERIOR.**

2. Remove the rubber cover from the upper shock absorber mounting. Then remove the mounting nut indicated in Fig. 5-1, the cupped washer, and the rubber upper bearing ring disk.

Fig. 5-1. Location of upper mounting nut (arrow).

3. Raise the body until the spring is no longer under load. Then remove the bolt indicated in Fig. 5-2 and pull the coil spring/shock absorber assembly out downward.

Fig. 5-2. Lower shock absorber mounting bolt (arrow).

4. With the coil spring/shock absorber assembly clamped in a vise, use the special tool indicated in

Fig. 5-3 to remove the slotted nut. A second wrench can be used on the double flats of the shock absorber rod to prevent the rod from turning.

NOTE ——
Removing the slotted nut will gradually relieve tension from the coil spring.

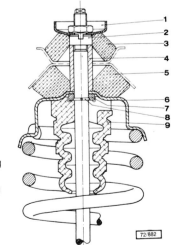

Fig. 5-3. Slotted nut being removed.

Installation is the reverse of removal. In assembling the upper coil spring/shock absorber mounting, install the components as indicated in Fig. 5-4. Torque the lower mounting bolt to 5.5 to 6.5 mkg (40 to 47 ft. lb.). Torque the upper mounting nut to 3.5 to 4.0 mkg (25 to 29 ft. lb.).

8

1. Cupped washer
2. Slotted nut
3. Upper rubber bearing ring
4. Distance piece
5. Lower rubber bearing ring
6. Upper spring retainer
7. Spacer ring
8. Snap ring
9. Rubber jounce stop

Fig. 5-4. Installed positions of upper mounting components.

To remove late-type shock absorber:

1. Support the car on its wheels or on jack stands placed beneath the outer ends of the axle beam.

2. Remove the nut and the bolt that hold the shock absorber to the axle beam's spring support.

3. Remove the bolt that holds the top of the shock absorber to the body and remove the shock absorber from the car.

4. Check the upper mounting. If distance **a,** as given in Fig. 5-5, is 27 mm (1 1/16 in.), install the old-type shock absorber with the small upper eye and rubber bushing; if distance **a** is 37 mm (1 15/23 in.), install the new-type shock absorber with the large upper eye and rubber bushing, as introduced on cars built after Chassis No. 8 2181 769.

Fig. 5-5. Upper shock absorber mounting. Dimension **a** is measured from lower edge of bolt hole to upper edge of mounting.

Installation is the reverse of removal. Torque the upper and the lower mounting bolts to 6.0 mkg (43 ft. lb.).

Once removed from the car, you can hand-check a shock absorber by extending and compressing it while holding it in its installed position. It must operate smoothly and with uniform resistance throughout its entire stroke. If possible, compare the used unit with a new shock absorber. (New shock absorbers that have been in storage may have to be pumped several times before they reach full efficiency.)

5.2 Rear Wheel Bearings

The rear wheel bearings, the brake assembly, and the stub axle are shown in relation to the axle beam in Fig. 5-6. Repairs related to the brake assembly are described in **BRAKES AND WHEELS.**

Removing and Installing Rear Wheel Bearings

You can remove the wheel bearing inner races with common hand tools. The outer races, however, are pressed into the brake drum and should be installed with a hydraulic press and appropriate mandrels.

To remove bearing races:

1. Fully back off the brake adjuster (see **BRAKES AND WHEELS**). Remove the road wheel. Pry off the dust cover.

2. Remove the cotter pin and the nut lock. Remove the nut from the stub axle.

3. Pull off the brake drum, being careful not to let the thrust washer and the outer tapered-roller bearing inner race fall out and onto the floor.

4. Place the brake drum on the workbench, then carefully remove the thrust washer and the outer bearing's inner race. Store them in a clean, dust-free place.

5. Pry the grease seal out of its recess in the rear of the drum. Then lift out the inner tapered-roller bearing's inner race. Store it with the outer bearing's inner race.

To install inner races:

1. Carefully clean the bearing inner races with solvent, then dry them with compressed air.

   CAUTION ——

   Do not use solvents such as gasoline because they remove all lubrication. Also, do not let blasts of compressed air spin the races. Unlubricated bearings can be damaged by rapid movement.

2. Inspect the inner bearing races. Replace them if they are worn, burred, rough or heat-blued.

3. Clean the brake drum hub and inspect the outer bearing races. Replace them if they are worn, burred, rough, or heat-blued.

4. To replace the outer races, first use a brass drift to drive out the inner tapered-roller bearing's outer race. (The brake drum hub has three recesses for this purpose, as shown in Fig. 5-7.)

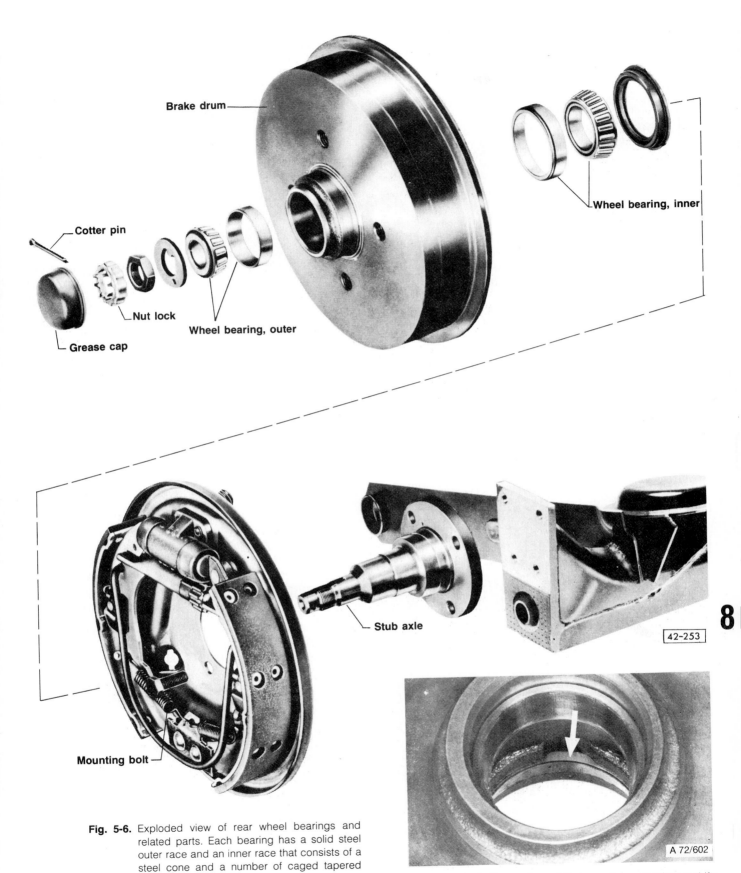

Brake drum

Wheel bearing, inner

Cotter pin

Nut lock

Grease cap

Wheel bearing, outer

Stub axle

42-253

8

Mounting bolt

Fig. 5-6. Exploded view of rear wheel bearings and related parts. Each bearing has a solid steel outer race and an inner race that consists of a steel cone and a number of caged tapered rollers.

A 72/602

Fig. 5-7. Recess (arrow) that permits you to place a drift against the inner bearing's outer race.

5. To remove the outer bearing's outer race, remove the circlip from 1973 cars only (Fig. 5-8). Then press (or drive) out the outer bearing's outer race toward the outboard side of the brake drum.

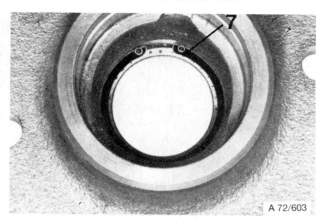

Fig. 5-8. Circlip (**7**) that is behind the outer bearing's outer race on 1973 models.

6. To install the outer races, first install the circlip. Then use a repair press and appropriate mandrels to press in the outer bearing's outer race as shown in Fig. 5-9; press in the inner bearing's outer race as shown in Fig. 5-10.

Fig. 5-9. Outer bearing outer race being pressed into brake drum. Press in until race just contacts circlip or machined shoulder.

Fig. 5-10. Inner bearing outer race being pressed into brake drum hub.

7. Pack the inner bearing's inner race with multipurpose grease. If a pressure bearing lubricator is not available, get a palmful of multipurpose grease and thrust the edges of the roller bearing race into it, continuing around the bearing until it is completely filled. Coat the races inside the hub with the same lubricant. Do not pack large quantities of grease inside the hub; just coat the interior lightly to prevent corrosion.

CAUTION ——

Use only multipurpose (lithium) grease to lubricate the rear wheel bearings. Other greases will not maintain adequate lubrication and may lead to bearing failure.

8. Carefully place the inner bearing's inner race in the brake drum hub. Then, using clean tools, press in a new grease seal.

9. Inspect the stub axle for burrs or blued areas. If satisfactory, lightly coat the stub axle with multipurpose grease.

10. Carefully slide the brake drum onto the stub axle so that the grease seal or bearing races are not accidentally damaged by the sharp threads.

11. Using the same procedure you used in packing the inner bearing's inner race, pack the outer bearing's inner race with multipurpose grease. Then carefully slide it onto the stub axle and into the hub.

12. Install the thrust washer and the nut. Tighten the nut until the bearings just contact their outer races.

13. Before you install the nut lock and a new cotter pin, adjust the rear wheel bearings as described under the following heading.

14. Fill the dust cap with approximately 10 g ($^5/_{16}$ oz.) of multipurpose grease. Then install the dust cap and the road wheel.

15. Adjust the brakes as described in **BRAKES AND WHEELS**.

Adjusting Rear Wheel Bearings

The rear wheel bearings must turn smoothly and not have excessive axial play. If the bearings feel gritty, have tight spots, or make noises as the brake drum turns, they probably need to be replaced. Excess axial play, though, can be corrected by adjusting.

To adjust bearings:

1. Raise the wheel, then pry off the dust cap.

2. If the bearings have just been installed, torque the nut on the stub axle to about 1.0 mkg (7 ft. lb.) while you hand-turn the brake drum.

> **CAUTION** ——
>
> *Never torque the nut to more than 1.3 mkg (9.5 ft. lb.). Doing this may damage the bearing races.*

3. To measure the bearing axial play, install a dial indicator on one of the wheel lugs (or use a dial indicator with a magnetic base).

4. Position the dial indicator pin against the end of the stub axle as shown in Fig. 5-11.

5. Move the brake drum in and out by hand. Turn the nut one way or the other until the axial play is between 0.03 and 0.07 mm (.001 and .0027 in.).

> **NOTE** ——
>
> Turn the brake drum and repeat the measurement at several different points. The readings should not vary greatly and their average should fall within the prescribed range. Replace bearings that will not adjust properly. In the event that you do not have a dial indicator, a less precise adjustment can be made using the procedure given in the following step.

Fig. 5-11. Dial indicator being used to measure wheel bearing axial play. Move wheel as indicated by double arrow.

6. Alternatively, you can determine rear wheel bearing axial play indirectly by testing the friction that is exerted on the thrust washer. To do this, turn the nut one way or the other until you can just move the thrust washer sideways with the tip of a screwdriver as shown in Fig. 5-12.

Fig. 5-12. Friction on thrust washer being checked by moving thrust washer with screwdriver.

7. When the bearings have been adjusted using the procedures given in step 5 or step 6, install the nut lock so that its projections do not cover the cotter pin hole. Then install a new cotter pin.

8. Install the dust cover and lower the wheel to the ground.

8

Removing, Checking, and Installing Stub Axle

To remove the stub axle, first remove the brake drum and the wheel bearings. Then unbolt the rear brake assembly. The same mounting bolts that hold the brake assembly on the stub axle hold the stub axle on the axle beam. By pulling the brake assembly outward and toward the front of the car, you can remove the stub axle without disconnecting the brake line or the parking brake cable.

You can check the stub axle for distortion using a vernier caliper and a machinist's square as shown in Fig. 5-13. Make your measurements at a minimum of three points around the stub axle. The difference between any two measurements must not exceed 0.25 mm (.010 in.). Replace distorted stub axles.

Fig. 5-13. Vernier caliper and machinist's square being used to check stub axle for distortion.

In installing the stub axle and the brake assembly on the axle beam, use new spring washers and torque the mounting bolts to 6.5 mkg (47 ft. lb.). Make certain that there is no dirt between the stub axle flange and the axle beam (which could upset wheel alignment) or between the brake backing plate and the stub axle (which could produce uneven braking or uneven brake lining wear).

5.3 Checking Axle Beam for Distortion

To check the rear axle beam for distortion, first raise the car and then remove the road wheels. Using a bubble protractor as shown in Fig. 5-14, determine how much, if any, the axle beam departs from the horizontal. Write down the reading because you will need to add it to, or subtract it from, later protractor readings.

Using the bubble protractor, measure the camber of each brake drum as shown in Fig. 5-15. If the axle beam is exactly horizontal, the camber angle on each side should be $-30'$ $\pm30'$ on 1973 through 1977 models, or $-40'$ $\pm40'$ on 1978 and later models—with a maximum differ-

ence on all models of 30' between sides. If the axle beam is not horizontal, add the reading you obtained with the protractor on the axle beam to the camber angle of the brake drum on the higher end of the axle; subtract the reading you obtained with the protractor on the axle beam from the camber angle of the brake drum on the lower end of the axle. The results of these calculations should give $-30'$ $\pm30'$ (1973 through 1977) or 40' $\pm40'$ (1978 and later) for each brake drum. If one or both of the camber measurements are outside the specified range, replace the rear axle beam.

Fig. 5-14. Bubble protractor being used to determine how far the axle beam departs from the horizontal.

Fig. 5-15. Bubble protractor being used to determine the camber angle of a rear wheel brake drum.

Rear wheel toe can be checked using procedures similar to those given for measuring and adjusting front wheel toe. See **3.2 Checking and Adjusting Front Wheel Toe.** Rear wheel toe in or toe out on 1973 through 1977 cars should not exceed $\pm0°$ 25', with a maximum difference of 15' between wheels. Rear wheel toe in or toe out on 1978 and later cars should not exceed $\pm0°$ 50', with a maximum difference of 20' between wheels. If there is greater toe, replace the rear axle beam.

5.4 Removing, Repairing, and Installing Rear Suspension

Fig. 5-16 shows the early-type rear axle that was installed only on early 1973 Audi models. Removal and disassembly of the coil spring/shock absorber assembly is described in **5.1 Checking and Replacing Shock Absorbers.** In removing this rear axle, you need not dismount the upper ends of the shock absorber from the body unless the shock absorber or spring requires service or replacement.

Replacement springs for the early-type rear axle are identified by red paint marks. There is one paint mark on springs for two-door cars and two paint marks on springs for four-door cars.

Fig. 5-16. Early-type Audi rear axle.

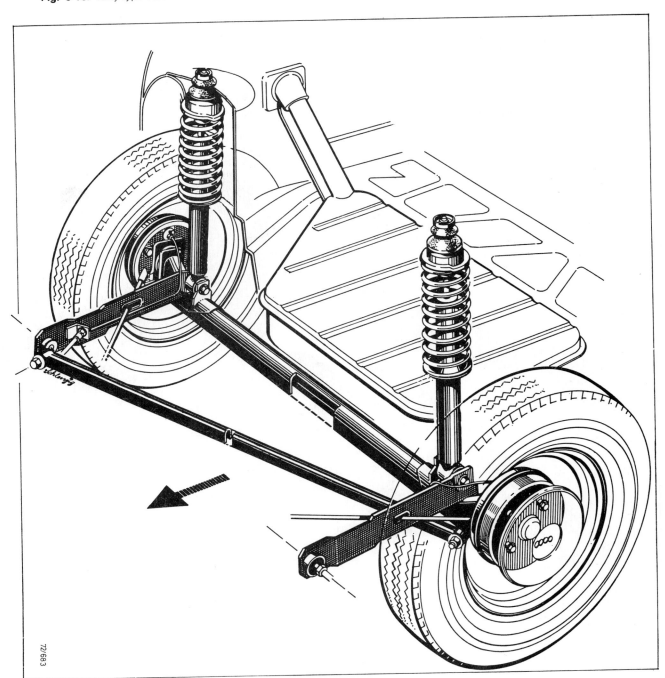

72/68-3

8

Fig. 5-17 shows the components of the later-type rear suspension. The rear suspension trailing arms are welded to the axle beam. Though the rear springs installed at the factory may be marked with 1, 2, or 3 paint marks, replacement springs always have 2 paint marks. It is unnecessary to replace both springs if one spring is faulty, even though the original springs have a different number of paint marks than the standard replacement springs. Axle beams for 1978 and later cars are redesigned, with a different angle for the stub axle mount-

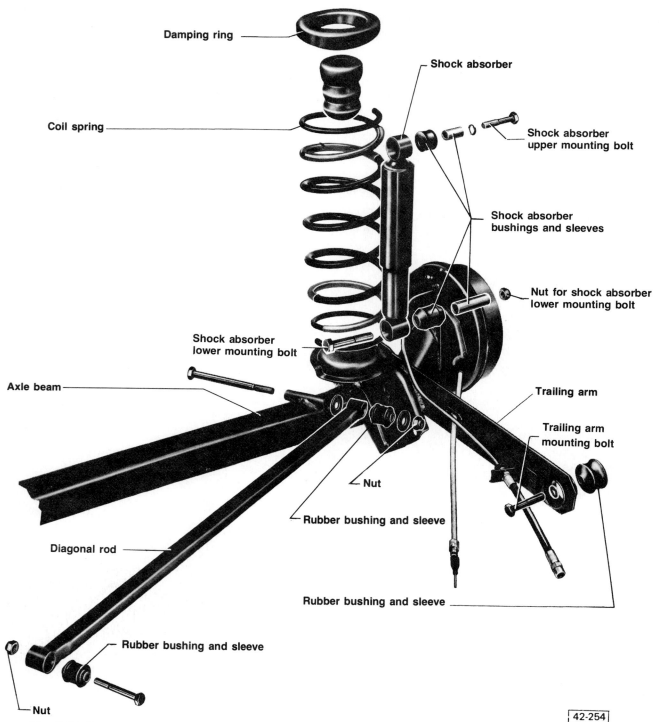

Damping ring

Shock absorber

Coil spring

Shock absorber
upper mounting bolt

Shock absorber
bushings and sleeves

Nut for shock absorber
lower mounting bolt

Shock absorber
lower mounting bolt

Axle beam

Trailing arm

Trailing arm
mounting bolt

Nut

Rubber bushing and sleeve

Diagonal rod

Rubber bushing and sleeve

Rubber bushing and sleeve

Nut

42-254

Fig. 5-17. Components of later-type rear suspension disassembled. Diagonal rod mountings and hardware were changed early in 1977 model year. To obtain correct replacement parts, take along old parts for comparison.

ings, 5-mm thick trailing arms (were 4-mm), and a 3.0-mm thick torsion tube (was 2.2-mm).

To remove rear suspension:

1. Except on early 1973 Audi models with the early-type rear axle, use two tools, similar to the ones shown in Fig. 5-18, in order to compress the rear springs.

   NOTE ——

   Alternatively, you can unbolt the rear shock absorbers and the diagonal rod while the car is resting on its wheels. Then raise the car body off the rear springs before you unbolt the trailing arms from the body.

Fig. 5-18. Special tool and home-made hook (**A**) being used to compress rear spring.

2. Working under the car, remove the nut and the locknut on the parking brake equalizer bar (arrow **1** in Fig. 5-19). Pry the plastic bushings (arrow **2**) out of the clips on the body. Then unhook the exhaust system rubber support rings as shown.

Fig. 5-19. Jobs to be performed under car. Notice the hook that is being used to remove the exhaust system rubber support rings.

3. Working near the rear axle, disconnect the parking brake cable (arrow **4** in Fig. 5-20) and detach its housing from the body. Disconnect the brake hose (arrow **5**), then plug the brake line with a clean brake bleeder dust cap to prevent the loss of brake fluid.

4. Remove the trailing arm mounting bolts (arrow **6** in Fig. 5-20).

Fig. 5-20. Jobs to be performed near rear axle. One side of the axle is illustrated, but there are similar parts to be disconnected at the other side.

8

5. Unhook the exhaust system rubber support rings at the rear of the muffler (arrow **7** in Fig. 5-21). Unbolt the diagonal rod (arrow **8**) and the shock absorbers (arrow **9**) from the axle.

NOTE ——

By swinging the shock absorbers aside, they can be left installed on the body while the rear axle is removed. Push the exhaust system to one side for clearance.

Fig. 5-21. Jobs to be performed at rear axle.

6. Remove the nut and the bolt that hold the diagonal rod on the body. Remove the diagonal rod.

7. With the rear axle supported by two helpers or a jack, remove the spring compressing tools and lower the rear suspension from the car. If the rear wheels are resting on the floor, raise the body off the rear suspension.

To install:

1. Inspect the rubber bushings and metal sleeves in the diagonal rod. If the bushings or sleeves are worn, cracked, or otherwise damaged, replace them as shown in Fig. 5-22.

Fig. 5-22. New rubber bushing and metal sleeve being pressed into diagonal rod. Press out the old bushing and sleeve. Then, before you press in the new bushing and sleeve, lubricate the rubber bushing with silicone spray or brake cylinder paste (see **BRAKES AND WHEELS**).

2. Inspect the rubber bushings and metal sleeves in the trailing arms. If either is worn, cracked or otherwise damaged, remove it as shown in Fig. 5-23.

Fig. 5-23. Puller being used to remove the rubber bushing and metal sleeve from a trailing arm.

3. To install a new rubber bushing and metal sleeve in the trailing arm of an Audi car or a VW car built before Chassis No. __4 2098 434, first bolt a guide piece onto the bushing sleeve. Lubricate the rubber bushing with silicone spray or brake cylinder paste (see **BRAKES AND WHEELS**). Then pull in the bushing and sleeve as shown in Fig. 5-24.

Fig. 5-24. Rubber bushing and metal sleeve being pulled into a trailing arm (except VW from Chassis No. __4 2098 434). Notice the steel guide piece that is bolted onto the bushing and sleeve.

4. To install a new rubber bushing and metal sleeve in the trailing arm of a VW car beginning with Chassis No. __4 2098 434, position the slots of the new bushing as indicated in Fig. 5-25. Then press in the rubber bushing and metal sleeve as shown in Fig. 5-26.

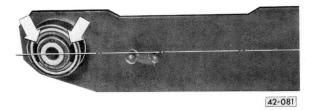

Fig. 5-25. Slots (arrows) of rubber bushing with rubber bushing and metal sleeve correctly installed.

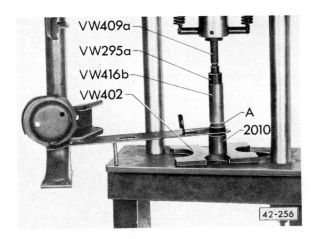

Fig. 5-26. Rubber bushing and metal sleeve being pressed into trailing arm (from VW Chassis No. __4 2098 434).

NOTE ——

Knocking or cracking noises in the rear suspension are sometimes caused by the torsion tube contacting the axle beam or by spring coils knocking together. If the rear alignment is within specifications, you can correct the torsion tube noise as described in step 5. If the rear springs have not sagged excessively, correct the spring noise as described in step 6.

5. To correct torsion tube/axle beam contact, slit a piece of spring damping hose (Part No. 461 511 123 A) down one side, then install it over the torsion tube at the point where the torsion tube is knocking against the axle beam. See Fig. 5-27.

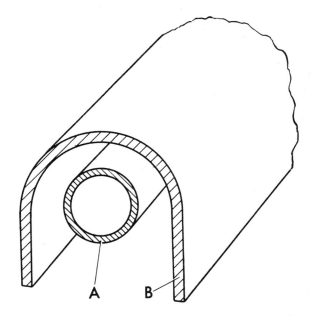

Fig. 5-27. Cross section of rear axle. Torsion tube is at **A**, axle beam is at **B**.

8

6. To correct spring coil noises, install damping hoses (Part No. 321 511 123 A) first over the top and then over the bottom of the spring. Lubricate the inside of each hose with vaseline, then expand the hose as shown in Fig. 5-28 as you slide it onto the spring.

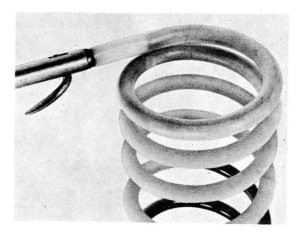

Fig. 5-28. Damping hose being installed with help of compressed air. When correctly installed, the hose must not project more than 5 mm ($^3/_{16}$ in.) beyond the end of the spring coil.

7. Using new bolts and new lock washers (Part No. 321 501 119 A) instead of spring washers, loosely bolt the trailing arms onto the body. Install the rear springs, the rubber buffers, and the damping rings.

> **NOTE**
>
> The damping rings for the left and right sides of the car are different. Be careful not to interchange them. A replacement damping ring should be the correct one for the side of the car it will be installed on. If, in an emergency, you must reuse the old bolts, thoroughly clean them of all dirt—and especially undercoating material. Then lightly lubricate the threads with engine oil.

8. Using special tools such as those illustrated earlier in Fig. 5-18, compress the rear springs. Alternatively, have the road wheels on the floor, then carefully lower the body onto the springs. Compress the springs until the center of the stub axle is approximately 70 mm (2¾ in.) higher than the center of the bushing in the trailing arm. See Fig. 5-29.

9. With the springs correctly compressed, torque the trailing arm bushing bolts to 6.0 mkg (43 ft. lb.).

10. On early 1973 Audi models that have the rear shock absorbers mounted inside the coil springs, torque the upper nut to 3.5 to 4.0 mkg (25 to 29 ft. lb.) and the lower bolt to 5.5 to 6.5 mkg (40 to 47 ft.

a. 70 mm (2¾ in.)
b. 270 mm (10⅝ in.)

Fig. 5-29. Rear springs compressed, preparatory to torquing of the trailing arm bolts. Do not tighten the trailing arm bushing bolts prior to compressing the springs.

lb.). On all other cars, which have the rear shock absorber separate from the rear spring, install the shock absorbers and torque the upper and lower bolts to 6.0 mkg (43 ft. lb.).

11. Install the diagonal rod and torque the bolts to 8.5 mkg (61 ft. lb.).

12. The remainder of installation is the reverse of removal. Following installation, adjust and bleed the brakes as described in **BRAKES AND WHEELS.**

> **NOTE**
>
> Because of the diagonal dual-circuit braking system, it is advisable to bleed the front wheel brakes as well as the rear wheel brakes if very much fluid was lost when you disconnected the rear brake hoses.

6. STEERING

Until the early months of 1974, the rack and pinion steering gearbox was non-adjustable. Cars built after that time have an adjustable steering gearbox. If an early, non-adjustable steering gearbox has become worn, it can be converted to an adjustable gearbox by installing repair kit Part. No. 321 498 061A.

Fig. 6-1 shows the rack and pinion steering gearbox and the components of the steering system that are connected to it. The unit normally requires no lubrication during its service lifetime. New rubber boots are available to replace steering rack boots that have become cracked or otherwise damaged.

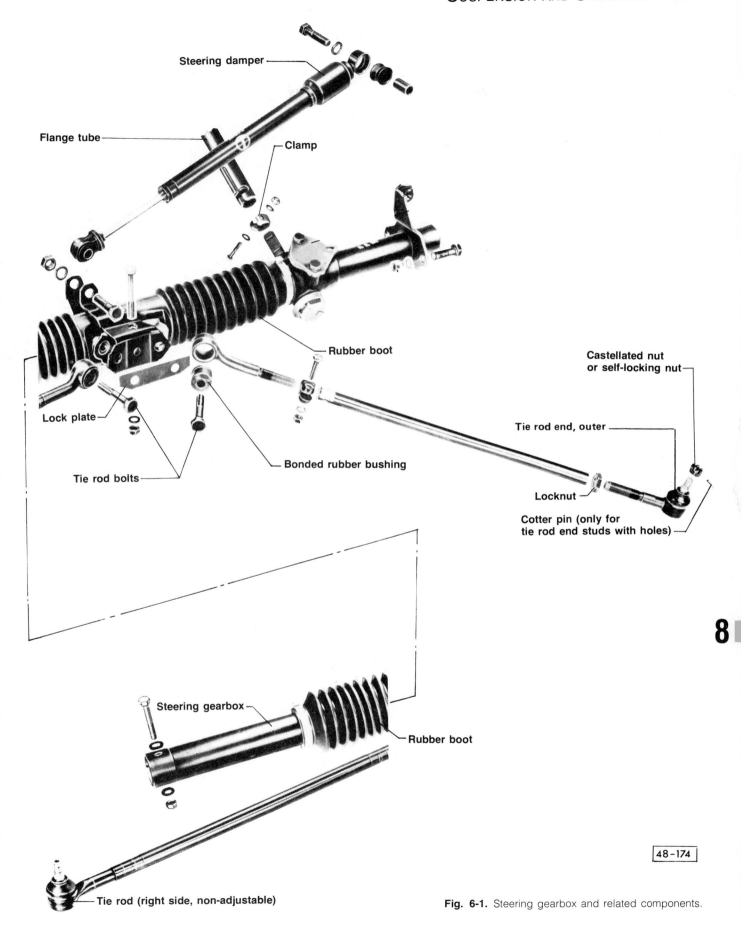

Steering damper

Flange tube

Clamp

Rubber boot

Castellated nut or self-locking nut

Tie rod end, outer

Lock plate

Locknut

Tie rod bolts

Bonded rubber bushing

Cotter pin (only for tie rod end studs with holes)

Steering gearbox

Rubber boot

48-174

Tie rod (right side, non-adjustable)

Fig. 6-1. Steering gearbox and related components.

8

6.1 Removing and Installing Tie Rods, Tie Rod Ends, and Rubber Bushings

You can replace the tie rod ends on the left tie rod only. To replace the right tie rod's ends, you must replace the entire tie rod. During the 1977 model year a new, 4-mm ($5/32$-in.) shorter right tie rod was introduced on cars designed to be fitted with optional wheels. This new tie rod is not available as a spare part for cars with manual transmissions, so you must use the adjustable left tie rod, Part No. 823 419 801 D, as a replacement. This is done by adjusting its length to the dimension shown in Fig. 6-2. Beginning with the 1978 models, new left tie rods were introduced. However, the earlier-type left tie rod (Part No. 823 419 801 D) must still be used as a replacement right tie rod on 1978 cars with manual transmissions.

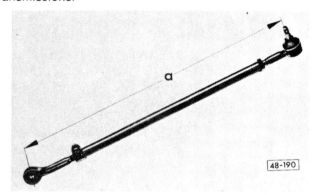

Fig. 6-2. Adjustment length for installing left tie rod on right side of late cars with optional wheels. Dimension **a** (from center of tie rod end stud to center of bonded rubber bushing) should be 542 mm ± 1 mm (21 $11/32$ in. ± $1/32$ in.).

To remove tie rod:

1. Remove the nut that holds the tie rod end stud in the steering arm on the suspension strut; if it is a castellated nut, you must first remove the cotter pin.

2. Using a puller as shown in Fig. 6-3, press the tie rod end stud out of the steering arm.

   CAUTION ——

   Do not hammer out the tie rod ends. Doing this will ruin the threads and make reinstallation impossible.

3. Bend up the tab on the locking plate. Then unbolt the tie rod's inner end from the steering gearbox.

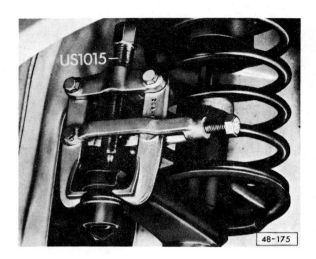

Fig. 6-3. Puller being used to press tie rod end stud out of steering arm on suspension strut.

To install:

1. Inspect the outer tie rod end. If the ball joint has visible play, if the rubber boot is torn, or if the tie rod end is otherwise damaged, replace the tie rod end.

   NOTE ——

   To replace the right-side tie rod end, replace the entire tie rod. To replace the left-side tie rod end, loosen the locknut and then unscrew the tie rod end from the tie rod. After you have installed a new tie rod end on the left-side tie rod, do not tighten the locknut until you have adjusted the front wheel toe. You can use the latest-type tie rod end with the 17.5-mm ($11/16$-in.) long stud and no cotter pin hole in place of the old-type tie rod end with the 14-mm ($9/16$-in.) long stud and a hole for the cotter pin. With the new-type tie rod end you must use self-locking nut Part No. N 011 189 3. The self-locking nut must not be used on the old-type tie rod end with the cotter pin hole.

2. Insepct the rubber bushing in the inner tie rod end. If the bushing is worn, cracked, or otherwise damaged replace the bushing as shown in Fig. 6-4.

3. Install a new locking plate and both tie rod bolts (Fig. 6-5). Remove one bolt and install the tie rod. With one tie rod installed, remove the other bolt and then install the other tie rod. Torque the bolts to 5.5 mkg (40 ft. lb.). Secure the bolts by bending over the tabs on the locking plate so that the tabs engage the flats on the bolt heads.

4. Install the outer tie rod end stud in the steering arm on the suspension strut. Torque the nut to 3.0 mkg (22 ft. lb.). Advance the castellated nuts, if necessary, to uncover the cotter pin hole, then install a new cotter pin.

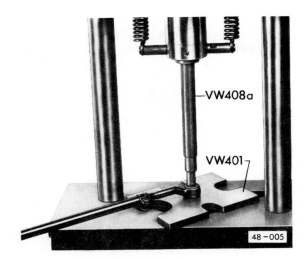

Fig. 6-4. A new rubber bushing being pressed into an inner tie rod end. Press out the old bushing. Then lubricate the new bushing with silicone spray or brake cylinder paste (see **BRAKES AND WHEELS**) before you press in the new bushing.

Fig. 6-5. Bolts that hold tie rod inner ends on the steering gearbox.

5. Adjust the front wheel toe as described in **3.2 Checking and Adjusting Front Wheel Toe.** Then torque the locknut for the outer left tie rod end to 4.0 mkg (29 ft. lb.). Torque the clamp bolt at the tie rod inner end to 3.0 mkg (22 ft. lb.).

6.2 Removing and Installing Steering Damper

The steering damper is a kind of miniature hydraulic shock absorber installed between the steering rack and steering gearbox housing. It is designed to prevent road shocks from being transmitted to the steering wheel.

To remove:

1. By taking out the bolt, detach the steering damper piston rod from the bracket on the steering gearbox's steering rack.

2. Unbolt the steering cylinder from the bracket on the steering gearbox housing.

3. Remove the steering damper from the car.

Hand-check the steering damper by extending and compressing it while holding it in its installed position. It must operate smoothly and with uniform resistance throughout its entire stroke. If necessary, compare the used unit with a new steering damper. Minor fluid leakage does not make replacement necessary as long as efficiency is not impaired.

Installation is the reverse of removal. Torque the bolt that holds the steering damper to the body to 6.0 mkg (43 ft. lb.). Torque the bolt that holds the steering damper's piston rod to the steering rack to 4.0 mkg (29 ft. lb.). Check to see that the steering operates freely before taking the car out on the road.

6.3 Adjusting Steering

Fig. 6-6 is a cross section of the adjustable steering gearbox that was introduced during the early months of 1974. The adjustment makes it possible to correct excessive steering wheel play and eliminate rattles from the steering rack.

If, when you drive the car, the steering seems stiff or fails to self-center, the steering adjustment is probably too tight. If the steering rattles while you drive or if there

8

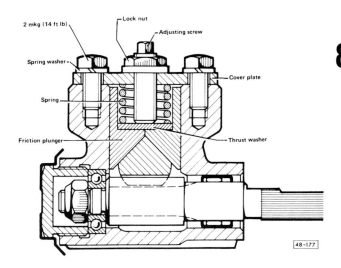

Fig. 6-6. Cross section of adjustable steering gearbox.

is any visible play in the steering wheel with the road wheels pointed straight ahead, the adjustment is probably too loose. If the steering gearbox is the early, non-adjustable kind, you can adjust it after installing repair kit Part No. 321 498 061 A, which consists of the components shown in Fig. 6-7.

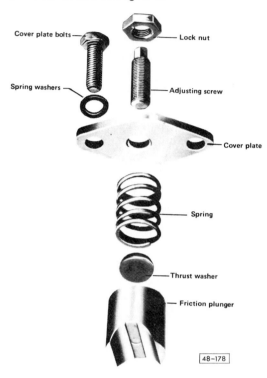

Fig. 6-7. Components of repair kit Part No. 321 498 061A.

To adjust the steering gearbox, loosen the locknut indicated in Fig. 6-8. Hand-turn the adjusting screw until it just contacts the thrust washer. While holding the adjusting screw in this position, tighten the locknut. Then re-check the steering in order to determine whether or not your adjustment has corrected the steering fault that you observed earlier.

NOTE ——

If, after correctly adjusting the steering, there is still excessive play or rattling, check for loose tie rod ends, loose steering gearbox mounting bolts, or loose parts in the front suspension.

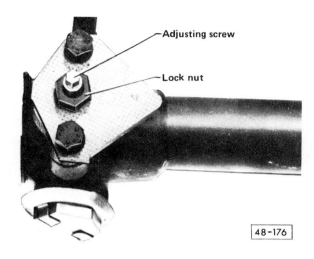

Fig. 6-8. Adjusting screw and locknut.

6.4 Removing and Installing Rack and Pinion Steering Gearbox

Except for replacement of the rubber boots and the adjusting mechanism, the rack and pinion steering gearbox cannot be repaired and must be replaced if it is faulty.

To remove:

1. Remove the nut and the bolt from the clamp that holds the steering column flange tube on the steering gearbox pinion shaft. Then, using a drift, drive the flange tube upward until it is off the pinion shaft.

2. Bend up the tabs on the locking plate. Then remove the bolts that hold the tie rods on the center of the steering rack. The tie rods need not be disconnected from the steering arms on the suspension struts.

3. Remove the nuts and the bolts that hold the left-hand end of the steering gearbox on the car body. If necessary, have someone reach under the left front fender to hold the bolts while you remove the nuts.

4. Unbolt the right-hand end of the steering gearbox from the car body. Then remove the gearbox from the car together with the steering damper.

To install:

1. Inspect the rubber boots on the steering gearbox. If they are worn, cracked, torn, or otherwise damaged, replace them. To do so, remove the hose clamps that hold the boots on the rack and the housing. Then cut off the old boots. Slide on both new boots from the side of the gearbox that is opposite the steering pinion. Then install new hose clamps.

   NOTE ——
   In order to install the left-side boot, you must unbolt the steering damper and the tie rod mounting bracket from the center of the rack. During reinstallation of these parts, torque the bolt for the tie rod mounting bracket to 2.0 mkg (14 ft. lb.). Torque the bolt for the steering damper piston rod to 4.0 mkg (29 ft. lb.).

2. Before you install the gearbox, install a new lockplate and the two bolts indicated in Fig. 6-9.

Fig. 6-9. Bolts that hold tie rod inner ends on the steering gearbox.

3. Using all three mounting bolts and their nuts and washers, loosely install the steering gearbox on the car body.

4. Center the steering gearbox. Center the steering wheel (spokes horizontal). Make sure that the column tube bushings are in place on the pins at the lower end of the steering column.

5. Being careful that the holes in the flange tube slide down over the pins on the steering column, use a drift to drive the flange tube down and onto the pinion shaft on the steering gearbox. Drive down the flange tube until the tube contacts the stop on the pinion, align the bolt recesses that are in the flange tube and the pinion shaft, then install the clamp and torque the clamp bolt to 3.0 mkg (22 ft. lb.).

6. Torque the three nuts and bolts that hold the steering gearbox on the car body to 2.0 mkg (14 ft. lb.).

7. Turn the steering wheel to the right. Remove the bolt for the right-hand tie rod, install the tie rod, then torque the bolt to 5.5 mkg (40 ft. lb.). Bend over a tab on the locking plate so that it engages a flat on the bolt head.

8. Turn the steering wheel to the left. Remove the bolt for the left-hand tie rod, then install the left-hand tie rod using the same procedure you used to install the right-hand tie rod.

9. Check the front wheel toe and, if necessary, adjust it as described in **3.2 Checking and Adjusting Front Wheel Toe.**

8

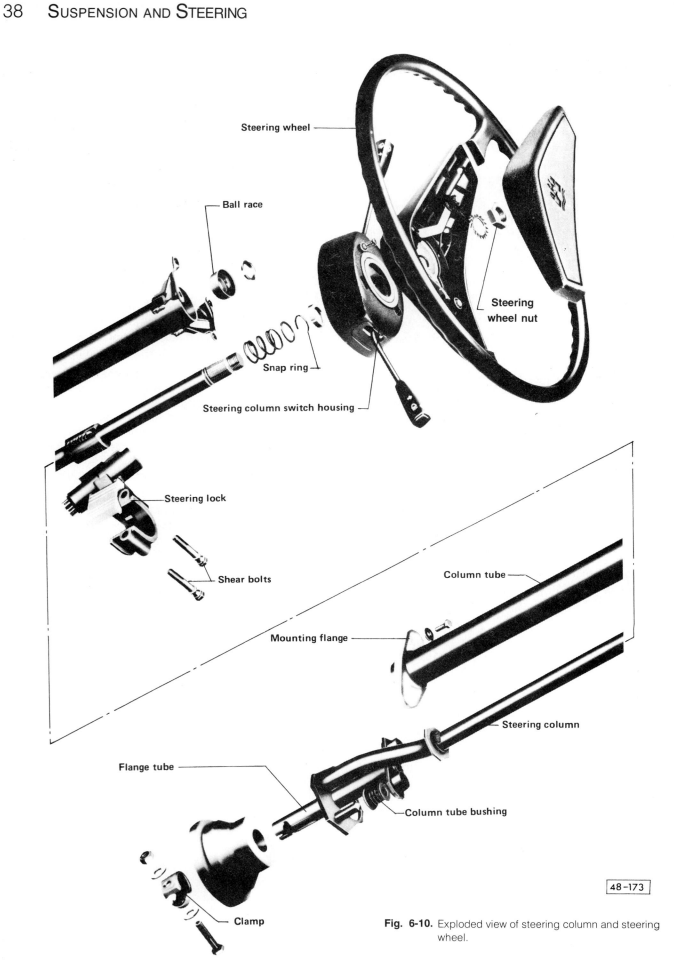

Steering wheel

Ball race

Steering wheel nut

Snap ring

Steering column switch housing

Steering lock

Shear bolts

Column tube

Mounting flange

Steering column

Flange tube

Column tube bushing

Clamp

48-173

Fig. 6-10. Exploded view of steering column and steering wheel.

6.5 Removing, Repairing, and Installing Steering Column and Steering Wheel

Before you can remove the steering column from the car, you must remove the steering wheel so that the steering column switches can be disconnected from the wiring harness. The steering lock can be replaced without fully removing the steering column. Fig. 6-10 is an exploded view of the steering column, steering wheel, and related parts.

To remove and disassemble:

1. Disconnect the battery ground strap. Hand-pull the horn control and padding off the steering wheel (Fig. 6-11). Then disconnect the ground wire at the horn control.

2. Remove the steering wheel nut. Pull the steering wheel off the steering column.

Fig. 6-11. Horn control and padding removed from steering wheel.

3. Remove the steering column switches as described in **ELECTRICAL SYSTEM.** Remove the steering column trim.

4. Working under the hood, remove the nut and the bolt from the clamp that holds the steering column flange tube on the steering gearbox pinion shaft. Then, using a drift, drive the flange tube upward until it is off the pinion shaft.

5. Unbolt the steering column tube's mounting flange from the bracket that is above the brake pedal.

6. Disconnect the wires from the ignition/starter switch. Insert the key and turn the ignition/starter switch to its ON position.

7. Centerpunch the shear bolts that hold the steering lock on the steering column mounting. Then, using an 8.5-mm (5/16-in.) twist drill, drill out the shear bolts as shown in Fig. 6-12.

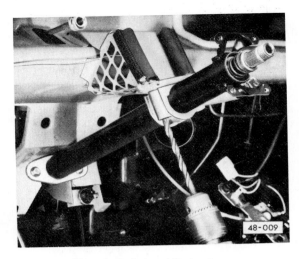

Fig. 6-12. Shear bolts being drilled out.

8. Remove the steering lock. Then remove the steering column and steering column tube as a unit.

9. To remove the steering column from the column tube, remove the steering wheel spacer ring and the snap ring indicated in Fig. 6-13. Then remove the washer and the spring.

Fig. 6-13. Snap ring that holds steering column in column tube. Use circlip pliers at points indicated by arrows to remove the snap ring from the steering column.

10. Pull the steering column out through the bottom of the column tube. If necessary, press the ball race out of the column tube.

To assemble and install:

1. Inspect the ball race. Replace it if it is worn or otherwise damaged.

2. Using Fig. 6-10, given earlier, as a guide, install the steering column in the column tube with a new snap ring. Then position the steering column in the car.

8

3. Install the steering lock. Position the lock so that the lock lug will engage the recess in the steering column (Fig. 6-14). Loosely install two new shear bolts.

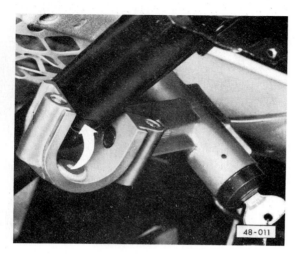

Fig. 6-14. Recess (arrow) that steering lock lug must engage as the lock is rotated into position beneath the steering column.

WARNING ——

If the deformation element (Fig. 6-15) in the steering column mounting has been deformed or torn by collision damage, replace it. If you straighten a damaged deformation element, it may not collapse properly and could cause injury to the driver in an accident.

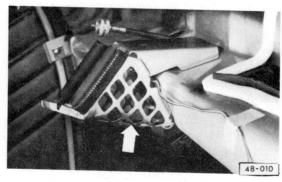

Fig. 6-15. Deformation element in steering column mounting. New elements must be welded in place.

4. Bolt the mounting flange onto its bracket so that the long side of the flange is toward the right-hand side of the car. Torque the bolts to 2.0 mkg (14 ft. lb.).

5. Tighten the shear bolts—but not enough to shear off their heads.

6. Connect the wires to the ignition/starter switch.

Install the steering column trim. Then install the steering column switches as described in **ELECTRICAL SYSTEM.**

7. Place the front wheels in their straight-ahead position.

8. Make sure that the column tube bushings are in place on the pins at the lower end of the steering column. Then, being careful that the holes in the flange slide down over the pins on the steering column, use a drift to drive the flange tube down and onto the pinion shaft on the steering gearbox. Drive down the flange until the tube contacts the stop on the pinion.

9. Align the bolt recesses that are in the flange tube and the pinion shaft. Then install the clamp and torque the clamp bolt to 3.0 mkg (22 ft. lb.).

10. If necessary, reposition the steering column slightly until the steering lock works smoothly. Then tighten the shear bolts until the heads shear off.

11. Install the steering wheel so that its spokes are horizontal with the front wheels in their straight-ahead position. Torque the steering wheel nut to 5.0 mkg (36 ft. lb.).

12. Connect the horn ground wire. Then hand-press the horn control and padding onto the steering wheel.

Removing and Installing Ignition/Steering Lock Cylinder

(1973 through 1977 models)

The procedure described here applies only to 1973 through 1977 models. The ignition/steering lock on 1978 and later cars is integral with the other steering column switches, so removal and installation of its lock cylinder is covered in **ELECTRICAL SYSTEM** in conjunction with the removal and installation of steering column switches.

To remove early lock cylinder:

1. Disconnect the battery ground strap.

2. Turn on the ignition so that the steering column is no longer locked. Remove the steering wheel and the steering column switches as described in **ELECTRICAL SYSTEM.**

3. Remove the dashboard as described in **BODY AND INTERIOR.**

4. Using a 3-mm (or ⅛-in.) drill, make a hole in the mounting for the lock as indicated in Fig. 6-16.

5. Using a pin inserted into the hole you have drilled, press down the spring that holds the lock cylinder. Then pry out the cylinder with a small screwdriver as indicated in Fig. 6-17.

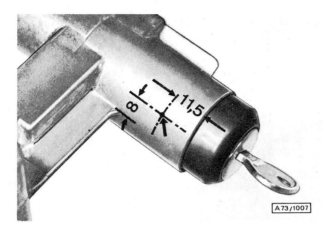

Fig. 6-16. Location for hole in lock mounting (bottom arrow). Dimensions, given as 8.0 mm and 11.5 mm, equal ⁵/₁₆ in. and ²⁹/₆₄ in. respectively.

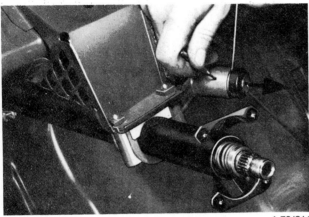

A 72/811

Fig. 6-17. Lock cylinder being pried out (arrow). Notice pin inserted through hole in mounting.

To install the lock cylinder, insert the key. Then push the cylinder into its mounting until the spring engages. See Fig. 6-18. The remainder of installation is the reverse of removal. Removal and installation of the ignition/starter switch is covered in **ELECTRICAL SYSTEM.**

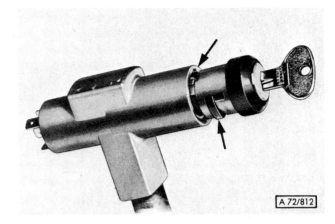

Fig. 6-18. Lock cylinder being installed. Align with groove (top arrow) then push in until spring (bottom arrow) engages.

7. SUSPENSION AND STEERING TECHNICAL DATA

I. Steering Specifications

Designation	Specification
1. Steering ....type	rack and pinion
2. Steering ....ratio	20.2:1
3. Vehicle turning circle ....minimum	10.08 m (33.1 ft.)
4. Steering wheel................turns, lock to lock	3.94
5. Steering gearbox....number of pinion teeth	7
6. Steering gearbox......number of rack teeth	30

II. Front Wheel Alignment

Designation	Value
Front wheel alignment	
1. Total toe angle of front wheels, not pressed	+10′ ± 15′
2. Total toe angle of front wheels, pressed	+25′ ± 15′
3. Pressure applied to wheels	12 ± 2 kg (22 ± 4 lb.)
4. Maximum permissible difference between total toe angle with wheels pressed and not pressed	15′
5. Front wheel camber with wheel straight ahead (adjust as close as possible to +25′)	+25′ ± 30′
6. Maximum permissible difference between sides	1°
7. Toe-out angle at 20° lock to left and right (not pressed)	−1°15′ ± 30′
8. Stub axle offset in direction of motion	max. 5 mm (³/₁₆ in.)
9. Caster angle of a wheel..	+10′ ± 30′
10. Corresponds to the camber difference of a wheel on a lock from 20° left to 20° right..	+5′ ± 20′
11. Maximum permissible difference between left and right	max. 1°
Rear wheel alignment	
1. Rear wheel camber..	−30′ ± 30′
2. Maximum permissible difference between sides of the car	30′
3. Rear wheel toe angle..	0° ± 25′
4. Total toe..	0° ± 50′
5. Maximum permissible difference in toe between sides of car	15′

8

III. Tightening Torques

Location	Designation	mkg	ft. lb.
Front suspension ball joint to track control arm	nut and bolt	6.5	47
Locknut for left outer tie rod end	nut	4.0	29
Clamp for left inner tie rod end	nut and bolt	3.0	22
Clamp bolt for front suspension ball joint stud	M 8 nut and bolt	3.5	25
	M 10 nut and bolt	5.0	36
Front suspension struts to car body	nut	2.5	18
Tie rod end to steering arm	castellated nut or self-locking nut	3.0	22
Stabilizer bar mounting clamp to subframe/track control arm	bolt	1.0	7
Brake caliper to front suspension strut	bolt	6.0	43
Brake disc splash shield to front suspension strut	bolt	1.0	7
Brake disc to front wheel hub	bolt	0.7	5
Front wheel hub to axle shaft	M 18 × 1.5 nut	20.0	145
	M 20 × 1.5 nut	24.0	175
Shock absorber in front suspension strut	threaded cap	15.0	108
Front shock absorber piston rod to front suspension strut upper mounting	nut	6.0	43
Front track control arm to subframe	bolt	7.0	50
Subframe to car body	bolt	7.0	50
Side engine mount to subframe	nut		
Transaxle carrier to car body (manual trans.)	bolt	2.5	18
Bonded rubber mounting to transaxle carrier (manual trans.)	nut	4.0	29
Late model transaxle rear mount to left side of automatic transmission case	bolt	5.5	40
Late model transaxle rear mount to body (automatic trans.)	bolt	4.0	29
Early model transaxle carrier to bonded mounting (automatic trans.)	nut	4.0	29
Early model transaxle carrier to body (automatic trans.)	bolt	3.0	22
Early model transaxle rear mount to rear of transaxle	nut	2.5	18
Front engine mount to engine/car body	bolt	2.5	18
Rear shock absorber to car body (1973 Audi with shock absorber inside coil spring)	nut	3.5–4.0	25–29
Rear shock absorber to axle (1973 Audi with shock absorber inside coil spring)	bolt	5.5–6.5	40–47
Rear shock absorber to axle or to car body (all cars with shock absorber mounted separately from rear spring)	bolt	6.0	43
Nut on rear stub axle prior to rear wheel bearing adjustment	nut	1.0–1.3 (while turning wheel)	7–max. 9.5 (while turning wheel)
Stub axle and brake backing plate to rear axle beam	bolt	6.5	47
Rear suspension trailing arm to car body	bolt	6.0	43
Diagonal arm to rear axle beam/car body	bolt	8.5	61
Tie rod inner ends to steering rack	bolt	5.5	40
Tie rod mounting bracket to steering rack	nut and bolt	2.0	14
Steering damper piston rod to steering rack	nut and bolt	4.0	29
Steering damper cylinder to steering gearbox housing	bolt	6.0	43
Clamp for steering column flange tube on steering gearbox pinion shaft	nut and bolt	3.0	22
Steering gearbox to car body	nut and bolt	2.0	14
Steering column tube lower mounting flange to car body	bolt	2.0	14
Steering wheel to steering column	nut	5.0	36

IV. Tolerances, Wear Limits, and Settings

Designation	New Installation mm (in.)	Wear Limit mm (in.)
1. Front suspension ball joints............................play	1.00 (.040)	2.50 (.100) using VW 281a
2. Rear stub axle....................................distortion	0.25 (.010)	—
3. Rear wheel bearing.............................axial play	0.05–0.07 (.002–.0027)	—
4. Clutch pedal ....freeplay	15 (⅝)	—
5. Front track ....width	1340 (52.76)	—
6. Rear track...width	1335 (52.56)	—
7. Wheelbase ....length	2470 (97.24)	—

BRAKES
AND WHEELS

Contents

9

Brakes and Wheels

The diagonal dual-circuit hydraulic foot brakes operate on all four wheels. Brake pedal pressure is reduced by a vacuum powered servo installed between the pedal and the master cylinder. Floating caliper disc brakes are used on the front wheels and drum brakes on the rear wheels. On certain models, there is a pressure regulator, or two pressure regulators, in the hydraulic lines to the rear brakes. The regulators prevent the rear brakes from locking when the brakes are being used to their maximum.

A dual-chamber master cylinder provides operating pressure to both brake circuits. The system is designed so that leaks in one circuit cannot affect the other. One circuit operates on the right front wheel and the left rear wheel. The other circuit operates on the left front wheel and the right rear wheel. An electrical warning system in the master cylinder causes a red warning indicator in the instrument panel to light up if hydraulic pressure is too low in either brake circuit. If you see this light while you are driving, it is imperative that the brake system be given a thorough check, even though braking action may still seem satisfactory. Complete loss of pressure in one of the brake circuits will cause the pedal to fall closer to the floor during braking and will result in abnormally long stopping distances.

Because safe vehicle operation depends very heavily on the brakes, all brake system service and repair work must be carried out with extreme cleanliness, careful attention to specifications, and proper working procedures. All necessary information is given here, although some of the operations that are described may be of practical value only to professional mechanics.

If you lack the skills, the special tools, or a clean workshop for servicing the brake system, we suggest you leave these repairs to an Authorized Dealer or other qualified shop. We especially urge you to consult your Authorized Dealer before attempting repairs on a car still covered by the new-car warranty.

The pages devoted to wheels and tires should have practical interest to all drivers, whether they service their own cars or not. A great many cases of abnormal tire wear or poor vehicle handling are the direct result of improperly fitted tires, tires incorrectly inflated, or driving practices that damage the tires. It is our belief that following the advice offered here will not only save you money but also make your driving safer.

9

1. GENERAL DESCRIPTION

Fig. 1-1 is a simplified schematic diagram of the diagonal dual-circuit brake system. Each chamber of the dual-chamber master cylinder is connected to one of the circuits. The front chamber of the master cylinder operates the brakes on the right front wheel and the left rear wheel. The rear chamber of the master cylinder operates the brakes on the left front wheel and the right rear wheel. Each circuit is capable of operating independently of the other.

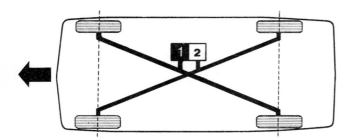

Fig. 1-1. Simplified schematic diagram of the diagonal dual-circuit brake system. Arrow indicates front of car.

Master Cylinder and Hydraulic Lines

The master cylinder generates the hydraulic pressure needed to operate the brakes and is connected to the wheel cylinders by the brake lines and hoses. When the driver depresses the brake pedal, the movement is transmitted by a rod to a valve inside the vacuum powered brake servo. Depending on the movement of the valve, engine vacuum acts upon the servo piston. The piston is connected to a pushrod that moves the master cylinder pistons. The system fails safe so, if the servo ceases to function, the foot brakes can still be applied. However, the pedal pressure required will be somewhat greater than normal.

Calipers and Wheel Cylinders

The rear wheel cylinders are of the rigidly-mounted, dual opposed piston type. When hydraulic pressure is applied to the cylinder, the pistons move outward, applying mechanical pressure to the brake shoes.

Three different kinds of front disc brake calipers have been used on the cars covered by this Manual. All are of the floating caliper type. The Teves (ATE) caliper used on 1973 through 1977 cars and the Girling caliper introduced on the 1978 models both have single pistons. The third unit, a Girling caliper used on 1973 through 1977 cars, has two opposed pistons that move outward through opposite ends of the same cylinder.

Pressure Regulator(s)

Except for VW Sedans with manual transmissions, the cars covered by this manual have pressure regulated rear brakes. On Audi models through Chassis No. __3 2198 442, there are two pressure regulators mounted on the vacuum powered brake servo. The same system is used on VW Sedans with automatic transmissions through Chassis No. __ 4 2143 624 and on all VW station wagons through Chassis No. __ 4 2045 520. Thereafter, again with the exception of VW Sedans with manual transmissions, a single pressure regulator located near the rear axle is used.

Parking Brakes

The cable-operated parking brake works on the rear wheels only. The hand lever is held or released by a ratchet and is centrally located between the front seats.

2. MAINTENANCE

The following routine maintenance operations are covered briefly in **LUBRICATION AND MAINTENANCE.** Additional information can be found in this section under the headings listed after each maintenance check.

1. Checking and changing brake fluid. **9.1**

2. Checking brake linings. **7.1, 8.2**

3. Checking brakes for correct adjustment (through 1978 models only). **8.1**

4. Checking parking brake adjustment and lubricating compensator. **10.1**

5. Checking brake lines and hoses for leaks and damage. **6**

6. Checking brake lights. **4.1**

7. Checking tires for wear, damage, and correct inflation pressures. **11.**

3. BRAKE TROUBLESHOOTING

Table a lists brake problems, probable causes, and suggested remedies. The numbers in bold type in the Remedy column refer to the numbered headings in this section of the Manual under which the suggested repairs are described.

Table a. Brake Troubleshooting

Problem	Probable Cause	Remedy
1. Pedal goes all the way to floor in braking	a. Linings worn b. No fluid, low fluid	a. Adjust brake shoes (never adjust at pedal). See **8.1**. b. Find and repair leaks. Fill and bleed system. See **9**.
2. Low pedal even after adjustment and bleeding	Master cylinder defective	Replace or rebuild master cylinder. See **4.2**, **4.3**.
3. Pedal spongy or brakes work only after pedal is pumped	a. Insufficient fluid in reservoir b. Air in system c. Spring weak in master cylinder	a. Top up fluid and bleed system. See **9**. b. Check for leaks and bleed system. See **9**. c. Replace or rebuild master cylinder. See **4.2**, **4.3**.
4. Braking action decreases after shoes have been adjusted	a. Brake lines leaking b. Defective master or wheel cylinders	a. Tighten connections or fit new lines and hoses. See **6**. b. Replace or rebuild faulty cylinder. See **4.2**, **4.3**, **7.2**, **7.3**, **8.5**, **8.6**.
5. Brakes overheat	a. Compensating port blocked b. Pushrod misadjusted c. Brake shoe return spring weak d. Rubber parts swollen	a. Clean master cylinder. See **4.2**, **4.3**. b. Adjust pushrod length. See **5.2**. c. Fit new return springs. See **8.2**, **8.3**, **8.4**. d. Flush system, replace fluid and all rubber parts. See **9**.
6. Brakes inefficient despite high pedal	a. Linings oiled up b. Unsuitable brake linings c. Loose or leaking vacuum hose to power brake servo d. Servo diaphragm leaking e. Poor seal between servo and master cylinder f. Check valve in vacuum line not working properly	a. Clean drums. Replace linings and seals. See **8.2**, **8.3**, **8.4**. b. Fit new linings. See **7.1**, **8.3**, **8.4**. c. Replace leaking vacuum hoses or tighten hose clamps. See **5.3**. d. Replace the servo. See **5.3**. e. Replace large sealing ring. Check piston rod for damage and, if necessary, replace it. See **4.2**. f. Replace faulty valve. See **5.1**.
7. Brakes bind while car is in motion	a. Compensating port blocked b. Brake fluid unsuitable c. Pushrod misadjusted	a. Disassemble master cylinder and clear port. See **4.2**, **4.3**. b. Flush system and refill. See **9**. c. Adjust pushrod length. See **5.2**.
8. Brakes chatter and tend to grab	a. Linings worn b. Drums out-of-round	a. Fit new linings. See **7.1**, **8.3**, **8.4**. b. Recondition or replace drums. See **8.2**, **8.8**.
9. Drum brakes squeak	a. Unsuitable or badly fitted linings b. Brake linings dirty c. Backing plates distorted d. Brake shoe return springs weak e. Poor lining contact pattern due to shoe distortion	a. Fit new linings properly. See **8.3**, **8.4**. b. Clean brakes. See **8.2**. c. Check backing plates for distortion and fit new parts if necessary. See **8.2**, **8.7**. d. Fit new return springs. See **8.3**, **8.4**. e. Align shoes with backing plate with 0.20 mm (.008 inch) clearance at lining ends and contact across full width. See **8.3**, **8.4**.
10. Disc brakes squeak	a. Unsuitable pads b. Spreader spring faulty or missing c. Pad guide surfaces dirty or rusted d. Pads dirty or glazed e. Lining loose on pad	a. Fit new pads. See **7.1**. b. Install new spreader spring. See **7.1**. c. Clean pads and calipers. See **7.1**. d. Clean and replace pads. See **7.1**. e. Replace pads. See **7.1**.
11. Brakes give uneven braking	a. Oil or grease on linings b. Brake pressure regulator defective c. Poor contact between lining and drum due to brake shoe distortion d. Brake shoes too tight in the adjusting screw slots or in wheel cylinder pistons e. Different types of linings on same axle f. Incorrect tire pressures or unevenly worn tires g. Drums or discs out-of-round or scored h. Disc brake pads sticking in caliper i. Disc brake pads reinstalled in wrong location	a. Clean drums. Fit new linings and seals or wheel cylinders if necessary. See **8.2**, **8.3**, **8.4**, **8.5**. b. Adjust or replace brake pressure regulator. See **4.4**. c. Shape shoes to leave 0.20 mm (.008 inch) clearance at lining ends. See **8.3**, **8.4**. d. Free up shoes. See **8.3**, **8.4**. e. Fit new shoes or pads. See **7.1**, **8.3**, **8.4**. f. Correct pressures or replace worn tires. See **11.2**, **11.6**. g. Recondition or replace discs or drums. See **7.4**, **8.2**. h. Clean caliper and pads. See **7.1**. i. Install new pads. See **7.1**.

9

continued on next page

Table a. Brake Troubleshooting (continued)

Problem	Probable Cause	Remedy
	j. Brake shoes not in contact with backing plate k. Pistons tight in wheel cylinders l. Dirt in brake lines or hoses	j. Reposition shoes or align or replace backing plate. See **8.3**, **8.7**. k. Free up pistons. See **8.6**. l. Clean system and replace defective parts. See **6**, **9**.
12. Brakes pulsate	a. Drums out-of-round (drum brakes only) b. Excessive disc runout or thickness variations (disc brakes only) c. Mating surface between discs and hubs dirty d. Brake pads worn out	a. Recondition or replace drums. See **8.2**, **8.8**. b. Recondition or replace discs. See **7.4**. c. Clean surface. Reinstall disc. See **7.4**. d. Fit new pads. See **7.1**.
13. Foot pressure on brake pedal must be increased when the pedal reaches a certain position	Groove worn in piston rod that allows air from ventilation drilling to enter servo as groove goes past sealing cup	Replace or rebuild master cylinder. See **4.2**, **4.3**.

4. MASTER CYLINDER AND PRESSURE REGULATOR(S)

The master cylinder is mounted on the vacuum powered brake servo, inside the engine compartment. A
translucent plastic brake fluid reservoir is mounted atop
the brake master cylinder.

4.1 Testing and Replacing Brake Light/Warning Light Switches

The brake light/warning light electrical connections
are shown in Fig. 4-1. The dashboard-mounted brake
warning light should light up when the engine is being
started (key position 3). This is a functional check to
show whether or not the bulb is burned out. The light
goes off when the key has been released to position 2. If
the light comes on during braking, it indicates either a
leak or a pressure loss in one of the brake circuits.

To test brake light switch contacts:

1. Check the brake light bulbs. Replace if necessary.

2. Disconnect the outside wires from the front brake
   light/warning light switch (**81** and **81a**, black-red
   and blue-brown wires; see Fig. 4-1).

3. Switch the ignition on and depress the brake pedal.
   The brake lights should go on. If they do, reconnect
   the wires to the front switch and remove the wires
   (**81** and **82a**) from the rear switch. Repeat the test.
   The brake lights should go on.

4. If the brake lights do not work in one of the tests,
   replace the defective switch (the one that remained
   connected during the test).

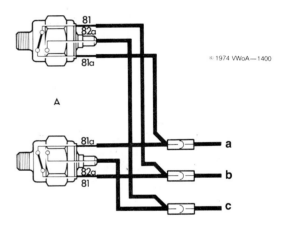

© 1974 VWoA—1400

A. Brake light/warning light switches
a. Blue-brown wire to terminal K on dual-circuit brake warning and safety belt warning system control light
b. Black-red wire to brake lights
c. Yellow-red wire to terminal 30d on fuse box

Fig. 4-1. Electrical wiring and terminals of brake light/
warning light switches.

To replace switch:

1. Disconnect all wires from the defective switch.

2. Unscrew the switch from the master cylinder. Keep
   the sealing washer.

3. Install the sealing washer and the new switch.
   Torque to 2.0 mkg (14 ft. lb.). Then connect the
   wires as indicated in Fig. 4-1.

NOTE ——

For additional information about the electrical circuits, consult the wiring diagrams in
ELECTRICAL SYSTEM.

To test brake warning light contact:

1. Check the socket and the light bulb. If necessary, replace them.

2. Operate the starter. The warning light should come on.

3. Open the bleeder valve at the left rear wheel. (See **9. Bleeding Brakes.**)

4. Start the engine and depress the brake pedal. The brake warning light should come on.

5. Close the bleeder valve of the left rear brake and open the bleeder valve at the right rear wheel. Repeat the test described in step 4.

6. Close the bleeder valve. Check the fluid level in the brake fluid reservoir. If necessary, add fluid.

> *CAUTION* ——
>
> *Use only new, unused brake fluid that meets SAE recommendation J 1703 and conforms to Motor Vehicle Safety Standard 116 DOT 3*

4.2 Removing and Installing Master Cylinder

The master cylinder is mounted on two studs on the vacuum powered brake servo. In removing or installing the master cylinder, be careful not to bend any of the brake lines or damage the union nuts that hold the lines to the master cylinder.

To remove:

1. Using a clean syringe, remove the brake fluid from the reservoir. Discard the fluid.

> *WARNING* ——
>
> *Do not start a siphon with your mouth or spill fluid onto the car. Brake fluid is both poisonous and damaging to paint.*

2. Disconnect the battery ground strap. Then disconnect the wires from the brake light/warning light switches. If necessary, attach tags to the wires so that later you can reinstall the wires in their original positions.

3. Disconnect the brake lines from the master cylinder.

4. Remove the two nuts that hold the master cylinder to the vacuum powered brake servo. Then remove the master cylinder from the car. Discard the old vacuum seal O-ring that is between the master cylinder and the servo.

To install:

1. Install a new vacuum seal O-ring in the annular groove of the master cylinder.

> **NOTE** ——
>
> The master cylinder pushrod inside the vacuum powered brake servo is factory-machined to precise tolerances and does not require adjustment prior to installation of the master cylinder—even if a new servo has been installed.

2. Position the master cylinder on the servo and, while you hold the cylinder in position, screw the brake line union nuts into the master cylinder by a few turns.

3. Install the nuts that hold the master cylinder to the brake servo. Torque the nuts to a maximum of 1.3 mkg (9.4 ft. lb.). Over-tightening the nuts may damage the servo.

4. Torque the brake line unions to 1.5 to 2.0 mkg (11 to 14 ft. lb.).

5. Reconnect the wires to the brake light/warning light switches. If necessary, refer to the wiring diagram given in **4.1 Testing and Replacing Brake Light/Warning Light Switches.**

6. Fill the brake fluid reservoir with new, unused brake fluid that meets SAE recommendation J 1703 and conforms to Motor Vehicle Safety Standard 116 DOT 3. Then bleed the entire brake system as described in **9. Bleeding Brakes.**

7. Reconnect the battery ground strap. Then check the brake operation with a road test. Make sure that pedal travel is not excessive and that the pedal does not feel spongy—which could indicate that the bleeding operation needs to be repeated. The brake warning light should not come on during braking.

4.3 Rebuilding Master Cylinder

In rebuilding the brake master cylinder, always use all of the parts that are included in the repair kit. To prevent wear and leakage, use the lubricants specified in the following procedure.

9

> *WARNING* ——
>
> *Rebuilding the master cylinder requires skill, special tools, and perfectly clean working conditions. Because the master cylinder has a vital influence on safe vehicle operation, you should not attempt to repair a master cylinder that has a worn cylinder bore or other physical damage.*

To disassemble:

1. Remove the master cylinder as described in **4.2 Removing and Installing Master Cylinder.** Remove the residual pressure valves and the brake light/ warning light switches.

2. Carefully remove the fluid reservoir from the master cylinder by pulling its outlet pipes out of the rubber plugs. Then remove the rubber plugs from the master cylinder.

3. Remove the stop screw and its seal from the top center part of the master cylinder. Push the pistons slightly in, then use snap ring pliers to remove the circlip. See Fig. 4-2.

Fig. 4-2. Circlip being removed from master cylinder.

4. Withdraw the stop washer/primary piston assembly from the rear chamber of the master cylinder. Then, by tapping the cylinder on a piece of soft wood, or by injecting compressed air, remove the secondary piston assembly from the front chamber of the master cylinder.

5. Carefully inspect the bore of the master cylinder. If the bore surface is scored, corroded, or in any way damaged, replace the entire master cylinder.

Minor scratches and hardened deposits can be removed from the cylinder with a brake cylinder hone. When using a brake cylinder hone, lubricate the stones with brake fluid only, never with mineral oil or kerosene. While the hone is spinning, move it in and out of the bore rapidly in order to achieve an even polish over the entire cylinder wall.

After honing, check the fit between the new pistons and the cylinder bore. If the clearance exceeds 0.10 mm (.004 in.), the entire master cylinder should be replaced. The clearance can be measured by inserting a feeler gauge between the piston and the cylinder wall. However, a brake cylinder bore measuring tool or a snap (telescope) gauge and micrometer are preferable tools.

WARNING ——
After honing the master cylinder, clean any burrs from the compensating ports. Otherwise, the burrs may damage the rubber cups.

To assemble:

1. Thoroughly clean the master cylinder with new, unused brake fluid that meets SAE recommendation J 1703 and conforms to Motor Vehicle Safety Standard 116 DOT 3.

WARNING ——
Never wash brake parts in gasoline or other petroleum-based solvents since they are damaging to rubber parts in the system.

2. Check the repair kit to make sure that it contains all the necessary new seals, cups, and pistons. Fig. 4-3 is an exploded view that shows all the master cylinder components.

3. Check that there is no foreign matter on the new parts. If necessary, wash the parts in new, unused brake fluid that meets SAE recommendation J 1703 and conforms to Motor Vehicle Safety Standard 116 DOT 3.

4. Install the new small-diameter cups, washers, and spring seats on the new pistons. In installing the small-diameter cups, it is helpful to have a conical cup sleeve such as the one shown in Fig. 4-4. If this tool is unavailable, liberally lubricate the new cups with new, unused brake fluid and be careful not to cut or tear the cups when you pass them over the piston lands.

NOTE ——
The lips of the cups must point in the directions shown in Fig. 4-3.

5. Lightly coat the pistons and the installed cups with VW brake cylinder paste. Alternatively, you can fully lubricate the cylinder bore, the pistons, and the cups with new, unused brake fluid that meets SAE recommendation J 1703 and conforms to Motor Vehicle Safety Standard 116 DOT 3.

NOTE ——
Brake cylinder paste is available from your Authorized Dealer and should be the preferred form of lubrication when brake cylinders are repaired. Brake fluid should be considered a satisfactory substitute only if you are unable to reach an Authorized Dealer. Brake cylinders will give longer service when lubricated with VW brake cylinder paste than when lubricated by brake fluid alone.

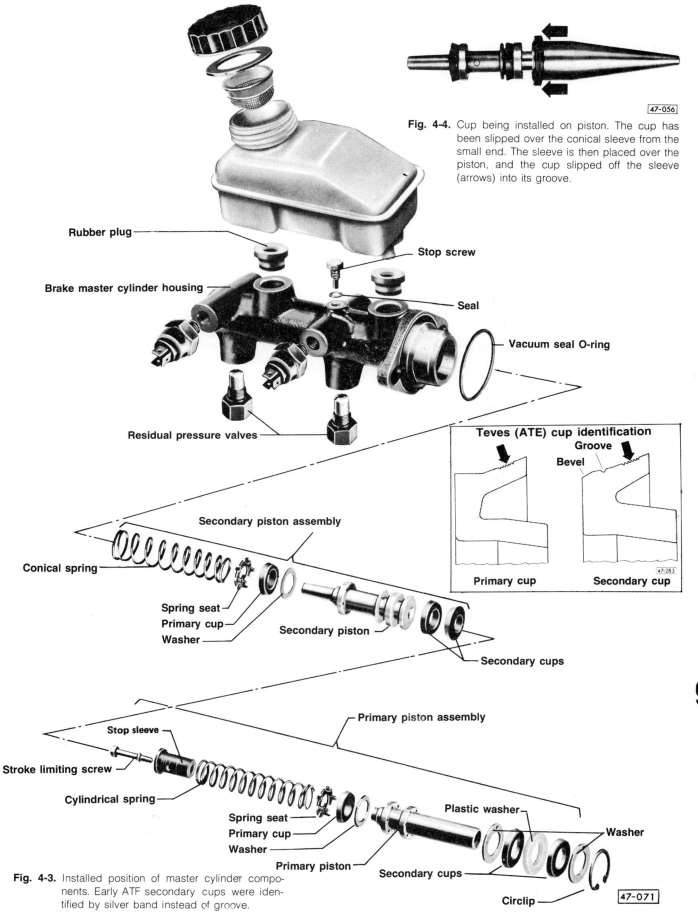

Fig. 4-4. Cup being installed on piston. The cup has been slipped over the conical sleeve from the small end. The sleeve is then placed over the piston, and the cup slipped off the sleeve (arrows) into its groove.

Rubber plug

Stop screw

Brake master cylinder housing

Seal

Vacuum seal O-ring

Residual pressure valves

Teves (ATE) cup identification

Groove

Bevel

Primary cup   Secondary cup

Secondary piston assembly

Conical spring

Spring seat
Primary cup
Washer

Secondary piston

Secondary cups

Primary piston assembly

Stop sleeve

Stroke limiting screw

Cylindrical spring

Spring seat
Primary cup
Washer

Primary piston

Plastic washer

Secondary cups

Washer

Circlip

Fig. 4-3. Installed position of master cylinder components. Early ATF secondary cups were identified by silver band instead of groove.

9

6. Hold the master cylinder with its closed end down. Install the conical spring—large end first. Then install the secondary piston assembly, pushing it as far as possible into the cylinder.

7. Lubricate the shaft of the primary piston with a light coat of silicone grease (provided in the repair kit). Also fill the annular grooves in the large-diameter secondary cups with silicone grease.

8. Install the metal washers, the large-diameter secondary cups, and the plastic washer on the shaft of the primary piston. The lips of both the large-diameter secondary cups should point into the cylinder, and the radial hole in the plastic washer should point upward when the master cylinder is installed on the car.

9. Start the secondary piston into the cylinder. While holding the cylinder with its open end down, fully install the secondary piston assembly as indicated in Fig. 4-5. Then install the circlip.

Fig. 4-5. Secondary piston assembly being installed (arrow).

10. Install the stop screw and a new seal. Torque to 0.5 to 1.0 mkg (3.5 to 7.0 ft. lb.).

CAUTION ——

Be sure the stop screw hole is clear. If it is blocked by the piston, damage will result as the screw is installed.

11. Screw the brake light/warning light switches and

the residual pressure valves into the master cylinder. Torque to 2.0 mkg (14 ft. lb.).

12. Coat the rubber plugs with new, unused brake fluid. Then press them into the cylinder. Lubricate the fluid reservoir outlet pipes with new, unused brake fluid and install the reservoir on the master cylinder.

13. Install the master cylinder as described in **4.2 Removing and Installing Master Cylinder.**

4.4 Testing and Replacing Rear Brake Pressure Regulator(s)

Audi cars through Chassis No. _ _3 2198 442, VW station wagons through Chassis No. _ _4 2045 521, and VW sedans with automatic transmissions through Chassis No. _ _4 2143 625 are equipped with two brake pressure regulators mounted on the vacuum powered brake servo (Fig. 4-6). The pressure regulator on the right side of the car controls the hydraulic pressure delivered to the right rear wheel. The pressure regulator on the left side controls the pressure to the left rear wheel.

You can quickly check the dual pressure regulators by having someone firmly depress the brake pedal once. As the pedal is released, you should hear a slight knock from each regulator. This knock indicates that the regulator pistons are returning and are not stuck.

Fig. 4-6. Dual pressure regulators installed on brake servo.

Audi cars from Chassis No. _ _4 2000 051. VW station wagons from Chassis No. _ _4 2045 522, and VW sedans with automatic transmissions from Chassis No. _ _4 2143 626 are equipped with a single brake pressure regulator located on the body, just ahead of the rear axle. This kind of regulator is operated mechanically by a coil spring attached to the rear axle beam.

Neither the early-type dual regulators nor the late-type single regulator can be repaired. Faulty regulators must be replaced as a unit. However, the late-type single regulator can be adjusted if the front and rear brake pressures are not correctly proportioned.

To pressure-test either kind of brake regulator, you must install two pressure gauges as shown in Fig. 4-7 and Fig. 4-8. The pressure gauges should have a capacity of 160 kg/cm² (2300 psi) and have hoses equipped with threaded ends that can be installed in place of the brake bleeder valves.

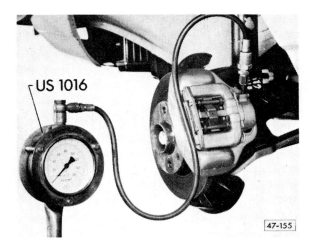

Fig. 4-7. Pressure gauge attached to bleeder valve hole of front brake caliper.

Fig. 4-8. Pressure gauge attached to bleeder valve hole of rear wheel cylinder.

To pressure-test early (dual) regulators:

1. Remove the brake bleeder valve from the left rear wheel cylinder. Then connect a pressure gauge. Remove the brake bleeder valve from the right front brake caliper and connect a second pressure gauge.

2. Using the bleeder valves on the gauges, bleed both hoses and gauges. See **9. Bleeding Brakes.**

3. Firmly depress the brake pedal several times. Then depress the brake pedal until the gauge on the right front brake caliper reads 35 kg/cm² (497 psi). The gauge on the left rear wheel cylinder should then read 27 ±2 kg/cm² (384 ± 28 psi).

4. Depress pedal further until the gauge on the right front brake caliper reads 100 kg/cm² (1422 psi). The gauge on the left rear wheel cylinder should then read 57 ±3 kg/cm² (810 ±42 psi).

5. If the correct rear brake pressures are not indicated, replace the left brake pressure regulator.

6. Disconnect the gauge from the right front brake caliper and reconnect it to the left front brake caliper. Disconnect the gauge from the left rear wheel cylinder and reconnect it to the right rear wheel cylinder. Bleed the gauges and hoses.

7. Repeat the pressure tests described in steps 2 and 3. If the correct rear brake pressures are not indicated, replace the right brake pressure regulator.

To test late (single) regulators:

1. Remove all luggage and other cargo from the car. Fill the fuel tank.

2. Have one person, approximately 75 kg (165 lb.), sit in the driver's seat. Jounce the car several times at the rear and allow it to settle into its natural attitude.

3. Without having the person leave the driver's seat,

9

install spring tensioners as shown in Fig. 4-9 and Fig. 4-10. Tighten the wing nuts until the tensioner hooks just make contact. The object of installing the tensioners is to keep the rear springs in the exact positions they assumed after you carried out step 2.

Fig. 4-9. Tensioner correctly installed on left rear spring support.

Fig. 4-10. Tensioner correctly installed on right rear spring support.

WARNING ——

Be sure that the tensioners are firmly attached to the lower spring supports. Otherwise, when the person gets out of the driver's seat, a tensioner may fly off and cause injury.

4. Remove the brake bleeder valve from the right rear wheel cylinder. Then connect a pressure gauge. Remove the brake bleeder valve from the left front brake caliper and connect a second pressure gauge.

5. Using the bleeder valves on the gauges, bleed both hoses and gauges. See **9. Bleeding Brakes.**

6. Firmly depress the brake pedal several times. Then depress the brake pedal until the gauge on the left front brake caliper reads 50 kg/cm^2 (710 psi). The gauge on the right rear wheel cylinder should then read 31 to 35 kg/cm^2 (440 to 497 psi).

7. Depress the pedal further until the gauge on the left front brake caliper reads 100 kg/cm^2 (1422 psi). The gauge on the right rear wheel cylinder should then read 53 to 57 kg/cm^2 (753 to 810 psi).

8. If the rear wheel pressures measured in the two preceeding steps are too low, reduce the spring tension at the regulator. If the pressures are too high, increase the spring tension at the regulator. See Fig. 4-11.

CAUTION ——

Do not adjust the spring tension with the brake pedal depressed. Doing this could damage the pressure regulator.

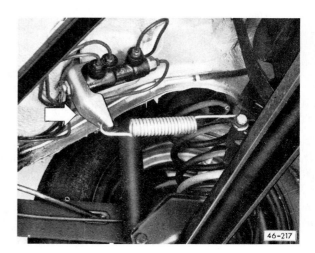

Fig. 4-11. Location of late-type brake pressure regulator. Notice the spring that connects the operating lever to the rear axle beam. Arrow indicates operating lever.

NOTE ——

Increasing the spring tension increases the pressure at the rear wheels. The spring tension is adjusted by loosening the locknut on the screw for the operating lever on the pressure regulator. Then turn the screw clockwise to increase spring tension, or counterclockwise to reduce spring tension. When the correct tension is obtained, tighten the locknut.

9. Repeat the pressure comparisons and adjustments until the correct rear brake pressures are indicated. If the correct rear brake pressures cannot be obtained by adjusting the spring tension, replace the pressure regulator.

10. When the correct pressures have been obtained, remove the gauges and bleed the brake system as described in **9. Bleeding Brakes.** Remove the spring tensioners.

NOTE ——

It is unnecessary to repeat the pressure tests at the opposite wheel on each axle.

Replacing Brake Pressure Regulators

The single late-type pressure regulator is held to the car body by two bolts. After disconnecting the spring from the operating lever and disconnecting the brake lines from the regulator, you can remove the regulator from the car by taking out the bolts. Installation is the reverse of removal. Torque the mounting bolt to 1.5 mkg (11 ft. lb.). Torque the brake line unions to 1.5 to 2.0 mkg (11 to 14 ft. lb.). Following installation, bleed the entire brake system as described in **9. Bleeding Brakes.** Then adjust the pressure regulator as previously described.

The early-type dual regulators are individually mounted on a bracket on the vacuum brake servo. Disconnect the brake lines from the regulator, then remove the bolt that holds the regulator to the bracket. Installation is the reverse of removal. Following installation, bleed the brake circuit that is controlled by the regulator you have replaced. See **9. Bleeding Brakes.** (The regulator on the left side of the car controls the left rear wheel and the right front wheel. The regulator on the right side of the car controls the right rear wheel and the left front wheel.)

5. BRAKE PEDAL AND BRAKE SERVO

Two kinds of vacuum powered brake servos (Fig. 5-1 and Fig. 5-2) have been used in the cars covered by this Manual. Both kinds have the same specifications and can be interchanged with no modification.

Fig. 5-1. Brake servo and master cylinder manufactured by Bendix.

9

Fig. 5-2. Brake servo and master cylinder manufactured by Teves (ATE).

5.1 Servicing Vacuum Powered Brake Servo

There is a filter in the rear of the vacuum powered brake servo. This filter does not need to be replaced unless the adaptor housing has been removed. Nevertheless, it is wise to replace the filter any time that the servo is removed from the car. Instructions for replacing the filter are given in **5.3 Removing and Installing Vacuum Powered Brake Servo.**

If the vacuum powered brake servo is faulty, it must be replaced; no repairs are possible. The troubleshooting table given in **3. Brake Troubleshooting** will help you to determine troubles that can be caused by a faulty servo.

If the vacuum powered brake servo is faulty, it must be replaced; no repairs are possible. The troubleshooting table given in **3. Brake Troubleshooting** will help you to determine troubles that can be caused by a faulty servo. When installing current replacement servos in older cars, it may be necessary to enlarge the retaining pin hole in the brake pedal to 10 mm (⅜ in.) and to use the late-type retaining pin and yoke—the latter part being 16 mm (⅝ in.) longer to compensate for the shorter pedal pushrod of the latest servo.

Before you assume that there is trouble in the master cylinder or the vacuum powered brake servo, check the vacuum hoses carefully. If they are disconnected from either the engine or the servo, or if they are cracked and leaking, the servo will not operate. Also test the vacuum check valve as described under the next heading.

Testing Vacuum Check Valve

There is a check valve installed in the vacuum line from the engine to the brake servo. The purpose of this valve is to prevent an engine backfire from producing pressure rather than vacuum in the brake servo vacuum chamber.

To test the vacuum check valve, remove it from the vacuum line. Blow into the valve in the direction indicated by the arrow. The valve should lift from its seat and permit pressure to escape from the top. The valve must seal if you blow into its opposite end. Install the valve with the arrow toward the brake servo.

5.2 Removing and Installing Brake Pedal and Clutch Pedal

On cars with manual transmissions, the clutch pedal is mounted on the same shaft (Fig. 5-3) with the brake pedal. If you wish to remove the clutch pedal as well as the brake pedal, disconnect the clutch cable from the clutch pedal. It may be necessary to slacken the clutch cable adjustment beforehand. If so, see **ENGINE AND CLUTCH.**

To remove:

1. Remove the left-hand under-dash panel as described in **BODY AND INTERIOR.**

2. Using pliers, remove the retaining pin from the pedal pushrod yoke. To do this, pull the spring-clip end of the pin downward off the yoke, then withdraw the pin from the yoke and the pedal.

3. Disconnect the return spring from the pedal.

4. Carefully pry off the spring clip that is on the right-hand end of the pedal cross shaft.

5. Slide the cross shaft out to the left until it is possible to remove the brake pedal and, if necessary, the clutch pedal.

Installation is the reverse of removal. Before you install the pedal pushrod yoke retaining pin, check the pedal pushrod adjustment as described under the next heading.

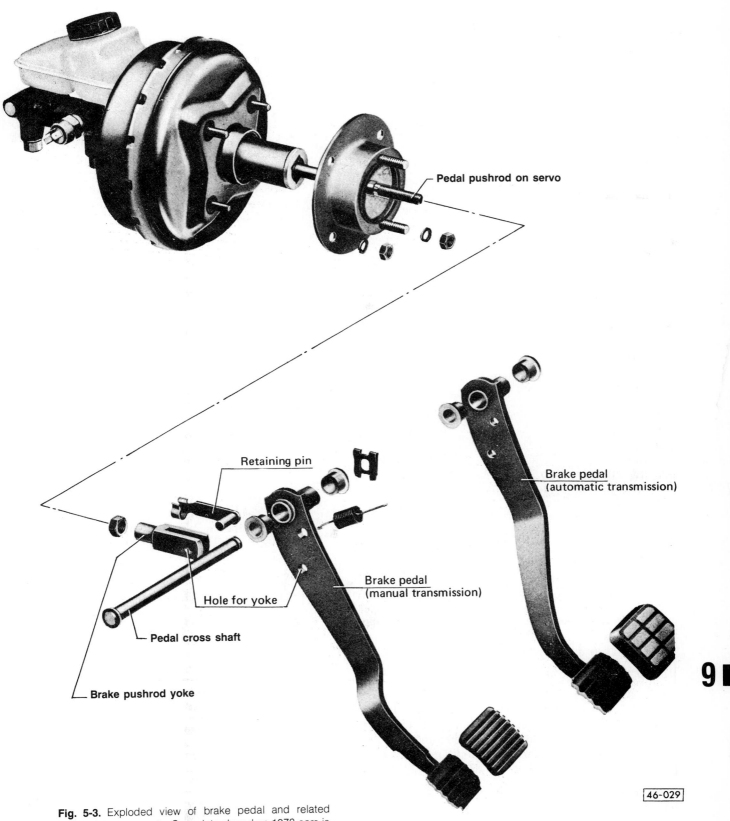

Pedal pushrod on servo

Retaining pin

Brake pedal
(automatic transmission)

Hole for yoke

Brake pedal
(manual transmission)

Pedal cross shaft

Brake pushrod yoke

9

46-029

Fig. 5-3. Exploded view of brake pedal and related
components. Servo introduced on 1978 cars is
larger—230 mm (9 in.) in diameter. Yoke is also
longer, pushrod shorter, on cars built after
August 1976.

Adjusting Pedal Pushrod

Unlike some other cars, there should be no clearance between the pedal pushrod and the internal parts of the servo. In installing the brake pedal, installing a new servo, or correcting the pedal pushrod adjustment, first disconnect the pedal pushrod yoke from the brake pedal. To do this, use pliers to pull the spring-clip end of the retaining pin downward off the yoke. Then withdraw the pin from the yoke and the pedal.

Make sure that the pedal is fully up, against its stop. Loosen the locknut for the pedal pushrod yoke. Then turn the yoke on the threaded end of the pushrod until the retaining pin hole in the yoke is aligned with the retaining pin hole in the pedal. When the holes are aligned, the pedal must be against its stop and there must be no clearance between the pedal pushrod and the servo. When the correct adjustment is obtained, install the retaining pin and then tighten the locknut. On 1978 and later cars, you can check the adjustments as shown in Fig. 5-4.

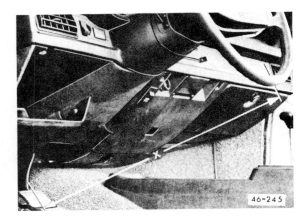

Fig. 5-4. 1978 and later pushrod adjustment being checked. Dimension **x**, from pedal face to steering wheel, should be 605 mm (23^{13}/$_{16}$ in.).

5.3 Removing and Installing Vacuum Powered Brake Servo

You should not attempt to remove the vacuum powered brake servo without removing the master cylinder. Even when the master cylinder is unbolted from the servo, the attached brake lines will not permit the master cylinder to be moved far enough aside for removal of the servo. Attempting to force it aside will damage the brake lines.

To remove servo:

1. Using a clean syringe, remove the brake fluid from the master cylinder reservoir. Discard the fluid.

2. Disconnect the battery ground strap. Then disconnect the wires from the brake light/warning light switches. If necessary, attach tags to the wires so that later you can reinstall the wires in their original positions.

3. Disconnect the brake lines from the master cylinder and, on cars with dual brake pressure regulators, from the regulators. Disconnect the vacuum hose from the servo.

4. Working inside the passenger compartment, remove the left-hand under-dash panel as described in **BODY AND INTERIOR.**

5. Using pliers, remove the retaining pin from the pedal pushrod yoke. To do this, pull the spring-clip end of the pin downward off the yoke, then withdraw the pin from the yoke and the pedal. If necessary, refer to Fig. 5-3 given earlier.

6. Remove the two nuts that hold the vacuum powered brake servo to the car body. Then, working under the hood, remove the servo and master cylinder as a unit.

7. If necessary, remove the master cylinder from the servo and discard the vacuum seal O-ring that is between the master cylinder and the servo.

8. To service the filter, remove the four nuts that hold the adaptor housing. Remove the housing and the seals. Take the cap off the end of the servo, then withdraw the damping ring and the filter. See Fig. 5-5.

To install:

1. Install a new filter, damping ring, gasket, and sealing washer. The slot in the filter should be offset 180° from the slot in the damping ring. Install the adaptor housing and torque the nuts to 1.5 mkg (11 ft. lb.).

NOTE ——
The filter and the damping ring for the Teves (ATE) servo are not the same as corresponding parts for the Bendix servo.

2. Install a new vacuum seal O-ring in the annular groove of the master cylinder. Then install the master cylinder on the servo. Torque the nuts to a maximum of 1.3 mkg (9.4 ft. lb.). Over-tightening the nuts may damage the servo.

3. Position the servo and master cylinder in the car. Working beneath the dashboard, loosely install the nuts that hold the servo to the car body.

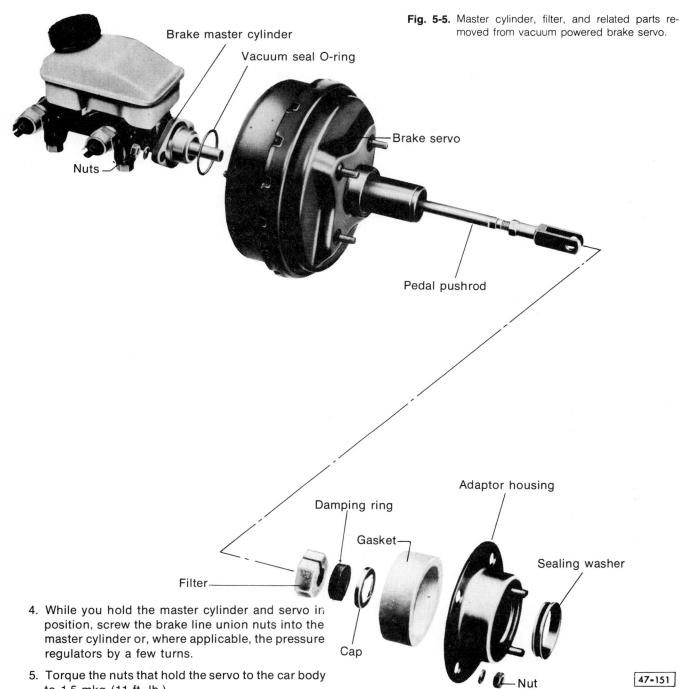

Fig. 5-5. Master cylinder, filter, and related parts removed from vacuum powered brake servo.

Brake master cylinder

Vacuum seal O-ring

Nuts

Brake servo

Pedal pushrod

Damping ring

Gasket

Adaptor housing

Sealing washer

Filter

Cap

Nut

47-151

9

4. While you hold the master cylinder and servo in position, screw the brake line union nuts into the master cylinder or, where applicable, the pressure regulators by a few turns.

5. Torque the nuts that hold the servo to the car body to 1.5 mkg (11 ft. lb.).

6. Adjust the pedal pushrod and install the retaining pin as described in **5.2 Removing and Installing Brake Pedal and Clutch Pedal.** Install the under-dash panel.

7. Torque the brake line unions to 1.5 to 2.0 mkg (11 to 14 ft. lb.). Reconnect the vacuum hose to the servo.

8. Reconnect the wires to the brake light/warning light switches. If necessary, refer to the wiring diagram given in **4.1 Testing and Replacing Brake Light/Warning Light Switches.**

9. Fill the brake fluid reservoir with new, unused brake fluid that meets SAE recommendation J 1703 and conforms to Motor Vehicle Safety Standard 116 DOT 3. Then bleed the entire brake system as described in **9. Bleeding Brakes.**

10. Reconnect the battery ground strap. Then check the brake operation with a road test. Make sure that pedal travel is not excessive and that the pedal does not feel spongy—which could indicate that the bleeding operation needs to be repeated. The brake warning light should not come on during braking.

5.4 Repairing Brake Servo Vacuum Pump

(VW diesel models only)

Because of the low intake manifold vacuum of the VW diesel engine, it is necessary for VW diesel models with vacuum powered brakes to have a vacuum pump installed on the engine. This pump is gear driven by the intermediate shaft and installed in the location occupied by the ignition distributor on spark ignition engines. An exploded view of the vacuum pump is given in Fig. 5-6. Repairs consist mainly of replacing the diaphragm and cleaning the pump interior.

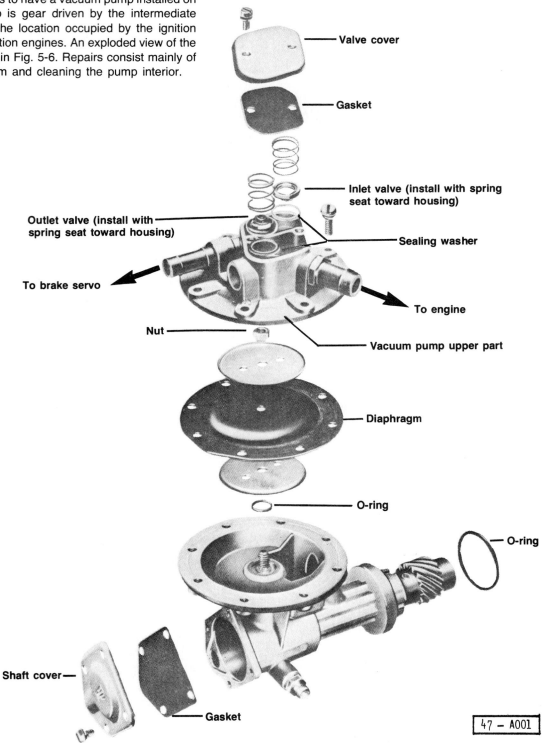

Valve cover

Gasket

Inlet valve (install with spring seat toward housing)

Outlet valve (install with spring seat toward housing)

Sealing washer

To brake servo

To engine

Nut

Vacuum pump upper part

Diaphragm

O-ring

O-ring

Shaft cover

Gasket

47 – A001

Fig. 5-6. Exploded view of vacuum pump for diesel cars.

To remove, repair, and install vacuum pump:

1. Loosen the hose clamps, then pull the vacuum hoses off the vacuum pump upper part. Disconnect the oil line from the union on the vacuum pump body.

2. Remove the hold-down bolt and the hold-down clamp that retain the vacuum pump to the engine block. Withdraw the pump from the engine.

3. Mark the vacuum pump upper part and the vacuum pump body so that these components can be reassembled in their original locations relative to one another.

4. Remove the eight screws that hold the vacuum pump upper part to the vacuum pump body. Then separate the two halves of the pump.

5. Clean the pushrod stud threads and the nut to remove all traces of oil, grease or sealing compound. Remove the nut, the diaphragm and its center plates, and the O-ring for the pushrod.

6. By taking out the four screws, remove the shaft cover and its gasket. If the pump is oily inside, owing to a ruptured diaphragm, also remove the valve cover, its gasket, the springs, and the valves. Wash all components in solvent.

7. Install the new pushrod O-ring. Install the new diaphragm and its center plates—positioning the diaphragm so that its molded (raised) center is away from the pump body.

8. Coat the threads of the new nut with sealing compound, then install the nut and torque it to 0.7 mkg (5 ft. lb.).

   NOTE ——
   During installation of the diaphragm, make sure that the screw holes in its periphery are aligned with those in the pump body.

9. With reference to the alignment marks made prior to disassembly, loosely install the vacuum pump upper part on the vacuum pump body. (With the pump installed on the engine, the connection for the hose to the brake servo should point straight up.)

10. Remove the circlip and the washer from the drive shaft (Fig. 5-7). Then push the drive shaft out gear-end first until the pushrod is free of the driveshaft—thus removing tension from the diaphragm.

11. Working diagonally, tighten the eight screws that hold the vacuum pump upper part to the vacuum pump body.

12. Using the tip of a screwdriver, press the pushrod toward the diaphragm as indicated in Fig. 5-8. Hold it in this position while you push the driveshaft back into place. Install the washer and the circlip on the driveshaft.

Fig. 5-7. Circlip on end of pump driveshaft.

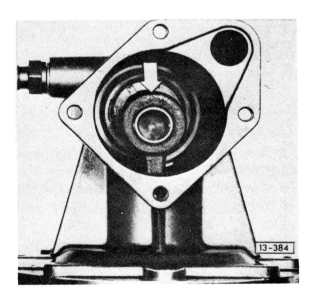

Fig. 5-8. Arrow indicating direction pushrod must be pressed in order to return driveshaft to its installed position.

13. If you have removed the valves and the springs, install them with careful reference to Fig. 5-8 given earlier. Then, using new gaskets, install the valve cover and the shaft cover.

14. Reinstall the vacuum pump on the engine using a reverse of the removal procedures. Torque the hold-down bolt to 1.5 mkg (11 ft. lb.).

9 ■

6. BRAKE LINES AND HOSES

The brake lines are steel tubes mounted on the car's body. They carry brake fluid from the master cylinder to the flexible brake hoses that serve the wheel cylinders.

The brake lines are so routed that they are not exposed to moisture and to the hazard of flying stones. The steel clips that secure the lines to the body at short intervals prevent vibration and chafing that might weaken the tubing.

6.1 Removing and Installing Brake Lines

The brake lines should be inspected regularly, certainly whenever there is brake trouble or the brakes are being serviced. Look for signs of corrosion, leaks around the unions, leaks in the lines themselves, and dents or cracks that may soon cause trouble.

Replacement lines can be obtained from your Authorized Dealer. The unions are factory-installed on the replacement lines, and the lines themselves are pre-formed to the correct shape for immediate installation.

To remove brake line:

1. Unscrew the unions on the line ends (Fig. 6-1).

2. Remove the spring steel clips that hold the line to the body.

3. Remove the brake line from the vehicle.

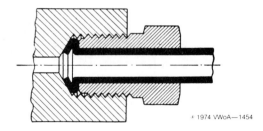

ε 1974 VWoA—1454

Fig. 6-1. Cross section of brake line union. Notice the double flare that holds the union on the tubing.

To install brake lines:

1. Route the new line so that it follows the routing of the old line.

2. Lubricate the flared ends of the brake lines with brake fluid, then insert the unions and torque them to 1.5 to 2.0 mkg (11 to 14 ft. lb.).

> **NOTE ——**
> Use a properly fitting wrench to avoid round-ing off the union.

3. Carefully install the clips to hold a new line.

4. Bleed the brakes as described in **9. Bleeding Brakes.**

> **WARNING ——**
> *When installing brake lines, be very careful not to dent, flatten, or bend the tubing enough to collapse it. The resulting restriction can upset brake balance and will create stress points in the tubing that may later cause it to crack. Never attempt to straighten a bent or dented brake line.*

6.2 Removing and Installing Brake Hoses

Being flexible, brake hoses are much more subject to wear than brake lines. The hoses should, therefore, be inspected very carefully every time routine maintenance is being carried out.

To remove brake hose:

1. Remove the road wheel.

2. Unscrew the union that holds the hose to the brake line.

3. Remove the spring steel hose clip from the bracket on the frame or axle.

4. Pull the hose off the line and plug the line with a new brake bleeder dust cap.

5. Unscrew the hose from the brake caliper or wheel cylinder.

> **NOTE ——**
> Girling brake caliper hose connections have left-hand threads.

To install brake hose:

1. Obtain a new hose of the correct length. See Fig. 6-2.

> **WARNING ——**
> *If the hose is too long, it may rub the wheel or moving suspension parts. If too short, it could break when drawn tight by wheel travel or steering movements. In either case, partial brake failure could result. Hoses must never be painted, and they can be damaged by grease, oil, gasoline, or kerosene. Brake hoses that bulge or appear oil-soaked or cracked must be replaced immediately.*

2. Install the hose, following the removal steps in reverse. The hose must hang down and be free of twists.

Fig. 6-2. Hose for Girling caliper (top) and hose for Teves (ATE) caliper (bottom), as used on 1973 through 1977 cars. Shorter Girling hose, identified by groove (arrow), has left-hand thread at caliper end. 1978 and later Girling calipers use different hose, Part No. 849 611 707 A.

3. Torque the hose ends to 1.5 mkg (11 ft. lb.) in disc brake calipers and to 1.5 to 2.0 mkg (11 to 14 ft. lb.) in other locations.

4. Check the hose position and the routing in all steering and suspension travel positions.

7. FRONT BRAKES

The brake calipers are mounted at the trailing edges of the discs. On 1973 through 1977 cars, the calipers may be of either Girling or Teves (ATE) manufacture (Fig. 7-1 and Fig. 7-2). All 1978 and later cars have Girling calipers—different from the Girling calipers of earlier models. Each kind of caliper has its own kind of brake hose, and faulty calipers must always be replaced with calipers of the same design and manufacture.

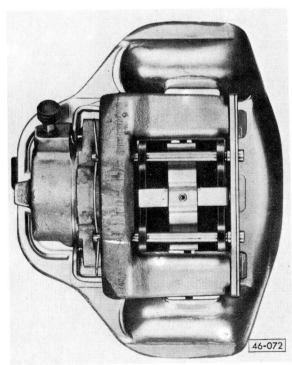

Fig. 7-1. Teves (ATE) caliper.

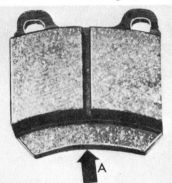

Fig. 7-2. Girling caliper.

7.1 Removing and Installing Brake Pads

Some 1973 through 1977 cars have a built-in brake pad wear indicator system (Fig. 7-3). When the lug on the disc contacts the extension on the pad, the driver feels a pulsation in the brakes. If a 1973 through 1977 car is not

Fig. 7-3. Brake pad wear indicator system used on some 1973 through 1977 cars. Extension of pad's lining material is at **A**; lug on brake disc friction surface is at **B**.

equipped with the brake pad wear indicator system, you should replace the pads when the friction material has worn to a remaining thickness of 2.00 mm (.080 in.).

On 1978 and later cars, you can check the pads through the wheel openings, as shown in Fig. 7-4. On these cars, the pads should be replaced if the total thickness of any pad (including the steel backing plate) is less than 7 mm (or $^9/_{32}$ in.). The total thickness of new pads is 14 mm (or $^9/_{16}$ in.). Each 1 mm (.040 in.) of friction material gives a minimum of approximately 600 mi. (or 1000 km) of service.

Fig. 7-4. Brake pad total thickness being checked through wheel opening of 1978 or later car. Dimension **a** should not be less than 7 mm (or $^9/_{32}$ in.).

Removing and Installing 1973 through 1977 Brake Pads

Though the pads for Girling calipers are the same as the pads for Teves (ATE) calipers on 1973 through 1977 cars, the procedure for replacing the pads is different for each kind of caliper. Each caliper will be covered separately.

To remove Girling caliper pads:

1. Remove the front wheel. Then carefully pry off the spreader spring (Fig. 7-5).

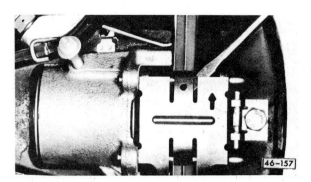

Fig. 7-5. Girling caliper spreader spring being pried off. Notice screwdriver blade position.

2. Remove the bolt that holds the clip for the U-shaped pad retainer to the caliper frame. Then pull out the retainer as indicated in Fig. 7-6.

3. Pull the brake pads out of the caliper as shown in Fig. 7-7.

   NOTE ——
   If the discs are deeply scored, it may be necessary to press the pistons slightly into the caliper in order to free the pad.

WARNING ——

If the pads are to be reused, mark each pad and its original position in the caliper. Changing the location of used pads will result in uneven braking.

Fig. 7-6. Pad retainer being removed. Use pliers to pull retainer out in direction indicated by arrow.

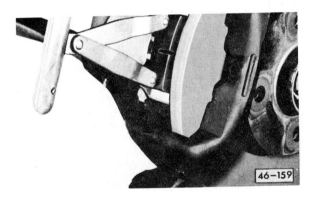

Fig. 7-7. Brake pad being removed with T-handled puller. Tool is convenient, but not necessary.

To install:

1. Inspect the spreader spring and the retainer. If either part is worn, cracked, deformed, or badly corroded, replace both parts, which are included in repair kit Part No. 171 689 445.

2. Scrape clean the pad seating and sliding surfaces in the caliper, then blow out the dirt with compressed air. Make sure that the floating part of the caliper moves smoothly in the frame.

3. Check the rubber dust seals for the pistons. They must not be cracked, hard, or swolen. If necessary, remove the caliper from the car as described in **7.2 Removing and Installing Brake Caliper.** Then replace the seals as described in **7.3 Brake Caliper Repair.**

4. Check the brake disc for wear as described in **7.4 Brake Disc.** If necessary, replace or recondition the disc.

5. Push both pistons into the cylinder with a piston retracting device as shown in Fig. 7-8.

NOTE ——

As you push in the pistons, brake fluid will be forced back into the reservoir. So first remove some fluid to prevent the reservoir from overflowing.

WARNING ——

Do not start a siphon with your mouth or spill fluid on the car. Brake fluid is both poisonous and damaging to paint.

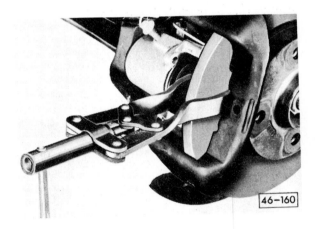

Fig. 7-8. Pistons being pushed into cylinder bore.

6. Install the pads in the caliper.

WARNING ——

Install used pads in the positions you marked for them during removal. If the pads are in the wrong locations, or bind in the caliper, uneven braking will result.

9

7. Install the U-shaped pad retainer, the clip, and the bolt. Torque the bolt (Fig. 7-9) to 2.0 mkg (14 ft. lb.).

WARNING ——

Do not grease the retainer. Heat produced by braking can melt the lubricant and cause it to flow onto the pads or the disc.

Fig. 7-9. Bolt (arrow) that holds clip for U-shaped retainer.

8. Install the spreader spring as shown in Fig. 7-10. The arrow must point in the direction of forward wheel rotation (point up).

Fig. 7-10. Spreader spring being installed.

9. Check the level of the brake fluid in the reservoir. If necessary, add fresh fluid.

CAUTION ——

Use only new, unused brake fluid that meets SAE recommendation J 1703 and conforms to Motor Vehicle Safety Standard 116 DOT 3.

To remove Teves (ATE) caliper pads:

1. Remove the retaining pin spring clip. Using a punch and a hammer, drive out the pad retaining pins. Take out the cross-shaped spreader spring. Then pull out the inner pad as shown in Fig. 7-11. The pins on the removing tool engage the retaining pin holes in the pad.

NOTE ——

If the discs are deeply scored, it may be necessary to press the piston slightly into the caliper in order to free the pad.

2. The outer brake pad is positioned in a notch (Fig. 7-12). To disengage the pad from the notch, press in the floating frame and brake cylinder. Then pull the pad out of the caliper.

WARNING ——

If the pads are to be reused, mark each pad and its original position in the caliper. Changing the locations of used pads will result in uneven braking.

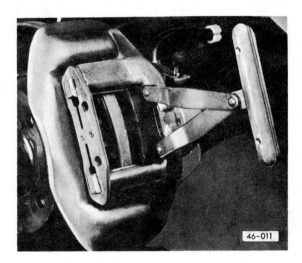

Fig. 7-11. Inner brake pad being removed with T-handled puller. Tool is convenient, but not necessary.

Fig. 7-12. Outer brake pad being removed. Floating frame must be pressed inward to disengage pad from notch (arrow).

To install:

1. Inspect the spreader spring, the retaining pins, and the retaining pin spring clip. If any part is worn, cracked, deformed, or badly corroded, replace it.

2. Scrape clean the pad seating and sliding surfaces in the caliper, then blow out the dirt with compressed air. Make sure that the floating part of the caliper moves smoothly in the frame.

3. Check the rubber dust seal for the piston. It must not be cracked, hard, or swollen. If necessary, remove the caliper from the car as described in **7.2 Removing and Installing Brake Caliper.** Then replace the seals as described in **7.3 Brake Caliper Repair.**

4. Check the brake disc for wear as described in **7.4 Brake Disc.** If necessary, replace or recondition the disc.

5. Push the piston into the cylinder with a piston retracting device as shown in Fig. 7-13.

   NOTE ——
   As you push in the piston, brake fluid will be forced back into the reservoir. So first remove some fluid to prevent the reservoir from overflowing.

   WARNING ——
   Do not start a siphon with your mouth or spill fluid on the car. Brake fluid is both poisonous and damaging to paint.

6. Check the 20° angle of the piston face recess as shown in Fig. 7-13. If necessary, rotate the piston to obtain the correct angle as shown in Fig. 7-14.

Fig. 7-13. Piston being pushed into cylinder bore.

Fig. 7-14. Gauge with 20° angle being used to check piston position. Arrow indicates direction of forward wheel rotation.

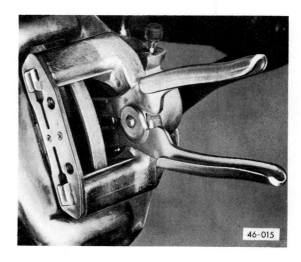

Fig. 7-15. Piston rotating pliers being used to correct piston position.

9

7. Install the pads in the caliper.

WARNING ——

Install used pads in the positions you marked for them during removal. If the pads are in the wrong locations, or bind in the caliper, uneven braking will result.

8. Install the cross-shaped spreader spring and the retaining pins as shown in Fig. 7-16. Then install the retaining pin spring clip.

WARNING ——

Do not grease the retaining pins. Heat produced by braking can melt the lubricant and cause it to flow onto the pads or the disc.

Fig. 7-16. Retaining pin being installed (arrow).

Removing and Installing 1978 and Later Brake Pads

A new kind of Girling brake caliper is used on the 1978 and later models. This caliper shares no parts with the Girling brake caliper used on earlier cars. The total thickness of the brake pads should be checked whenever the car is serviced—regardless of mileage. A quick method of checking the brake pads is shown earlier in Fig. 7-4.

To remove 1978 and later Girling caliper pads:

1. Remove the front wheel. Then hand-press the caliper in the direction indicated in Fig. 7-17, so that the piston is pushed into the cylinder.

NOTE ——

As you push in the piston, brake fluid will be forced back into the reservoir. So first remove some fluid to prevent the reservoir from overflowing.

WARNING ——

Do not start a siphon with your mouth or spill fluid on the car. Brake fluid is both poisonous and damaging to paint.

Fig. 7-17. Piston being pushed into cylinder by pressing caliper outward (arrow).

2. Using an open end wrench, hold the guide pin's head stationary while you fully remove the cylinder housing's lower mounting bolt. See Fig. 7-18.

Fig. 7-18. Guide pin head being held stationary with open end wrench while cylinder housing's lower mounting bolt is removed with box wrench.

3. Swing the caliper's cylinder housing upward as shown in Fig. 7-19, then lift out the pads.

WARNING ——

If the pads are to be reused, mark each pad and its original position in the caliper. Changing the locations of used pads will result in uneven braking.

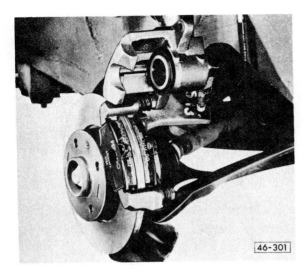

46-301

Fig. 7-19. Caliper cylinder housing swung upward so that pads can be lifted out of caliper's brake pad carrier.

To install:

1. Scrape clean the pad seating and sliding surfaces in the caliper's brake pad carrier, then blow out the dirt with compressed air. Make sure that the rubber boots for the guide pins are not torn or cracked, and that the guide pins slide smoothly in the housing.

   NOTE ——
   New rubber boots, and new guide pins to replace those that are worn, scored, or corroded, are available only together with a new brake pad carrier.

2. Check the dust seal for the piston. It must not be cracked, hard, or swollen. If necessary, remove the caliper from the car as described in **7.2 Removing and Installing Brake Caliper.** Then replace the seals as described in **7.3 Brake Caliper Repair.**

3. Check the brake disc for wear as described in **7.4 Brake Disc.** If necessary, replace or recondition the disc.

4. Install the brake pads. In installing new brake pads, be sure to use the new bolt and any other parts included in the brake pad replacement kit.

5. Swing down the brake caliper's cylinder housing.

CAUTION ——
It may be necessary to hand-press the piston further into the cylinder. Be sure that you have removed enough brake fluid from the reservoir so that the reservoir does not overflow. Do not force a protruding piston against the brake pad in an attempt to force down the cylinder housing. Doing this could damage the piston and the cylinder.

6. Install the cylinder housing's lower mounting bolt. Then, while holding the guide pin stationary with an open end wrench, torque the bolt to 3.5 mkg (25 ft. lb.).

7. Depress the brake pedal firmly several times while the car is stationary in order to seat the brake pads fully against the brake disc.

8. Check the level of the brake fluid in the reservoir. If necessary, add fresh fluid.

CAUTION ——
Use only new, unused brake fluid that meets SAE recommendation J 1703 and conforms to Motor Vehicle Safety Standard 116 DOT 3.

9 ■

7.2 Removing and Installing Brake Caliper

You must remove the brake pads as described in **7.1 Removing and Installing Brake Pads** before you can remove the caliper from the car. Caliper removal is illustrated in Fig. 7-20. Never attempt to remove a brake caliper until it has cooled.

If the brake caliper is to be completely removed from the car, unscrew the brake hose from the caliper and seal it with a clean bleeder valve dust cap. Support the caliper as it is being unbolted. If the caliper is being only partially removed, for example to obtain clearance for removal of the brake disc, the brake line need not be disconnected. Simply hang the caliper by a stiff wire hook from one of the steering tie rods. Doing this will eliminate the need for bleeding the brakes, which is necessary if the hose is disconnected. Never allow the caliper to hang by its hose.

> **CAUTION** ——
>
> *You must use a 15-mm wrench to remove or install the caliper mounting bolts. There is no suitable U.S. standard wrench size. A ⅝-in. wrench will fit too loosely and round-off the corners of the bolt head.*

When you install the caliper, make sure that the bleeder valves are uppermost. Though there may originally be spring washers on the mounting bolts, install the bolts without washers. Torque the bolts to 6.0 mkg (43 ft. lb.). Consult **6. Brake Lines and Hoses** before you replace a brake hose. The hoses for Girling calipers are shorter than those for Teves (ATE) calipers and have a left-hand thread at the caliper end.

> **NOTE** ——
>
> New replacement Girling calipers for 1973 through 1977 cars must be converted before you can install them. See Fig. 7-21 and Fig. 7-22. To convert the calipers, it is necessary to disassemble them as described in **7.3 Brake Caliper Repair.** Left calipers of either make are different from right calipers of the same make. Cars that were originally equipped with calipers of one design or make should not be re-equipped with calipers of another design or make.

Fig. 7-20. 1978 brake caliper and related parts removed from suspension strut. Installation is similar on other models.

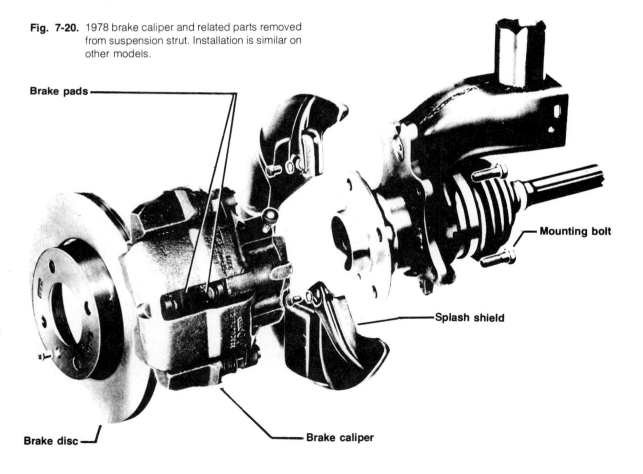

Brake pads

Mounting bolt

Splash shield

Brake disc

Brake caliper

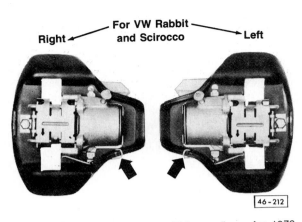

Fig. 7-21. New replacement Girling calipers for 1973 through 1977 cars, which are factory-assembled for installation on the VW Rabbit and Scirocco. Locating springs (arrows) are opposite bleeder valves. Spreader spring arrows point in opposite direction from bleeder valves.

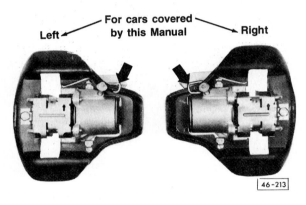

Fig. 7-22. Girling calipers converted for use on 1973 through 1977 cars covered by Manual. Locating springs (arrows) are on same side as bleeder valves. Spreader springs (arrows) point in direction of bleeder valves.

After you have installed the brake pads and related parts, as described in **7.1 Removing and Installing Brake Pads,** depress the brake pedal several times while the car is stationary to ensure that the pads are seated against the disc. If the hose has been disconnected, bleed the brakes as described in **9. Bleeding Brakes.**

7.3 Brake Caliper Repair

Though the pads for the Girling calipers are the same as the pads for the Teves (ATE) calipers on 1973 through 1977 cars, no other parts are interchangeable. Similarly, no parts for the Girling calipers introduced on the 1978 models are interchangeable with parts for earlier cars. The repair of each kind of caliper is covered separately under the headings that follow.

> *CAUTION* ———
>
> *If you lack the skills, tools, or a clean workshop for servicing the brake calipers, we suggest you leave these repairs to an Authorized Dealer or other qualified shop. We especially urge you to consult your Authorized Dealer before attempting repairs on a car still covered by the new-car warranty.*

Repairing 1973 through 1977 Brake Calipers

Be sure to determine whether your car has Girling or Teves (ATE) calipers before you attempt to buy replacement parts. If possible, take the used parts with you so that they can be compared to the new parts you obtain.

To disassemble Girling caliper:

1. Remove the caliper from the car as described in **7.2 Removing and Installing Brake Caliper.** Thoroughly clean the exterior of the caliper using a wire brush and compressed air.

2. Hand-press the cylinder assembly out of the frame as indicated in Fig. 7-23.

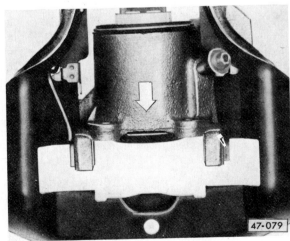

Fig. 7-23. Cylinder assembly being removed (arrow) from caliper frame.

9

3. Remove the retaining rings from the dust seals. Then remove the dust seals. Using compressed air, as shown in Fig. 7-24, blow the pistons out of the cylinder.

Fig. 7-24. Pistons being removed from cylinder. Soft jaws on vise prevent pistons from being blown completely out of cylinder.

4. If necessary, remove the bleeder valve from the cylinder or remove the retaining springs and locating spring from the caliper frame.

5. Remove the piston seals from the inside of the cylinder.

To assemble:

1. Clean all parts with brake fluid only. Check the parts for wear. If the cylinder is damaged, replace the entire brake caliper. Do not hone the cylinder.

2. Lightly coat the pistons and the new piston seals with VW brake cylinder paste. Alternatively, you can fully lubricate the cylinder bore, the pistons, and the seals with new, unused brake fluid that meets SAE recommendation J 1703 and conforms to Motor Vehicle Safety Standard 116 DOT 3.

NOTE ——

Brake cylinder paste is available from your Authorized Dealer and should be the preferred form of lubrication when brake cylinders are repaired. Brake fluid should be considered a satisfactory substitute only if you are unable to reach an Authorized Dealer. Brake cylinders will give longer service when lubricated with VW brake cylinder paste than when lubricated by brake fluid alone.

3. With soft jaws installed on the vise, install the pistons and seals in the cylinder as shown in Fig. 7-25.

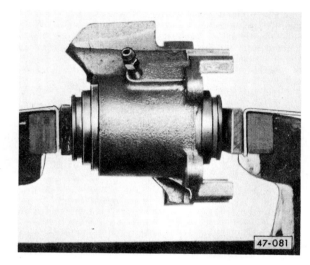

Fig. 7-25. Pistons and piston seals being pressed into cylinder.

4. Lightly rub VW brake cylinder paste into the inside of the rubber dust seal. Install the the dust seal and lock it in place with the retaining ring. See Fig. 7-26.

5. Install the support in the hollow of the piston that presses against the caliper frame. Slide the cylinder assembly into the caliper frame as shown in Fig. 7-27. The retaining springs must be between the sliding surfaces of the frame and the cylinder. The locating spring must exert pressure against the upper edge of the cylinder assembly.

6. If necessary, install the bleeder valve. Then install the caliper on the car.

Fig. 7-27. Cylinder assembly being slid into frame. Retaining springs are indicated by the arrows.

Fig. 7-26. Exploded view of Girling brake caliper. Relative positions of piston seals, pistons, dust seals, and retaining rings are shown.

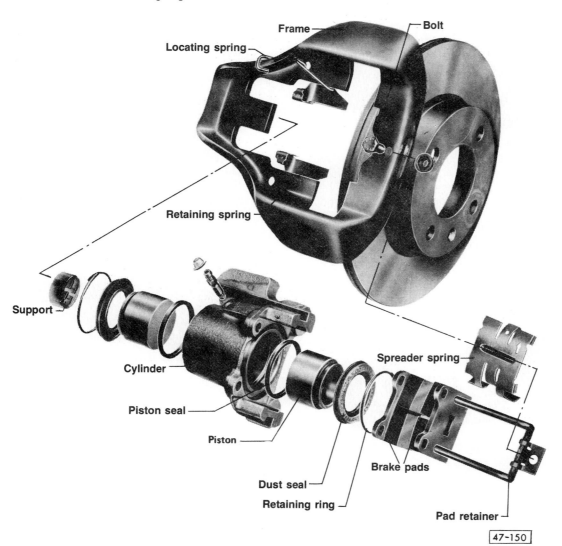

To disassemble Teves (ATE) caliper:

1. Remove the caliper from the car as described in **7.2 Removing and Installing Brake Caliper.** Thoroughly clean the exterior of the caliper using a wire brush and compressed air.

2. Hand-press the cylinder sideways so that its closed end is against the floating frame. Push the mounting frame away from the cylinder as shown in Fig. 7-28. Then lift the mounting frame out of the floating frame.

Fig. 7-28. Mounting frame being pushed away from cylinder.

3. To avoid damaging the piston, place a hardwood block in the floating frame as shown in Fig. 7-29. Then press the cylinder assembly out of the floating frame. Remove the guide spring.

Fig. 7-29. Hardwood block installed in floating frame. Push cylinder assembly out of frame as indicated by the arrow.

4. Remove the retaining ring from the dust seal. Then remove the dust seal. Using compressed air, as shown in Fig. 7-30, blow the piston out of the cylinder.

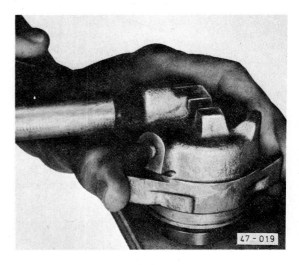

Fig. 7-30. Piston being removed from cylinder. Place piston against wooden block so that it is not blown completely out of cylinder.

5. Remove the piston seal from the cylinder with a plastic rod as shown in Fig. 7-31.

Fig. 7-31. Piston seal being removed from groove in the cylinder bore.

6. If necessary, remove the bleeder valve from the cylinder.

To assemble:

1. Clean all parts with brake fluid only. Check the parts for wear. If the cylinder is damaged, replace the entire brake caliper. Do not hone the cylinder.

2. Lightly coat the piston and the new piston seal with VW brake cylinder paste. Then install the seal. Alternatively, you can fully lubricate the cylinder bore, the piston, and the seal with new, unused brake fluid that meets SAE recommendation J 1703 and conforms to Motor Vehicle Safety Standard 116 DOT 3.

NOTE ——

Brake cylinder paste is available from your Authorized Dealer and should be the preferred form of lubrication when brake cylinders are repaired. Brake fluid should be considered a satisfactory substitute only if you are unable to reach an Authorized Dealer. Brake cylinders will give longer service when lubricated with VW brake cylinder paste than when lubricated by brake fluid alone.

3. With soft jaws installed on the vise, install the piston in the cylinder as shown in Fig. 7-32.

Fig. 7-32. Piston being pressed into cylinder.

4. Lightly rub VW brake cylinder paste into the inside of the rubber dust seal. Install the dust seal and lock it in place with the retaining ring. See Fig. 7-33.

Fig. 7-33. Exploded view of Teves (ATE) brake caliper. Relative positions of piston seal, piston, dust seal, and retaining ring are shown.

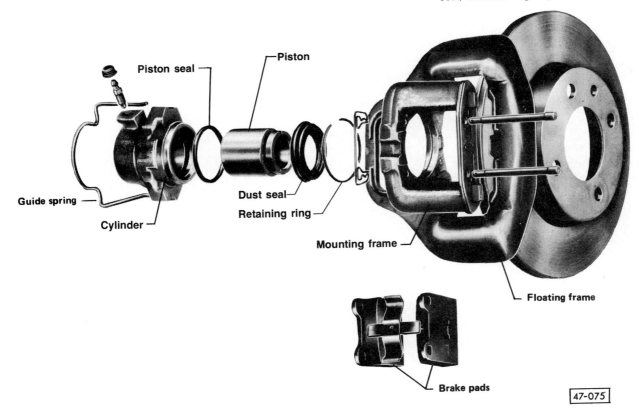

9

5. Install the guide spring on the cylinder. Working on alternate sides of the cylinder assembly (Fig. 7-34), use a brass drift and a hammer to drive the cylinder fully onto the floating frame.

Fig. 7-34. Cylinder assembly being driven onto floating frame. Apply drift alternately to the two surfaces indicated by arrows.

6. Place the mounting frame in the guide spring and push the mounting frame onto the floating frame. There are two grooves (Fig. 7-35) in the mounting frame that must be pushed over the ribs on the floating frame.

Fig. 7-35. Mounting frame being installed in floating frame. Grooves in mounting frame are indicated by the arrows.

7. Check the 20° angle of the piston face recess as shown in Fig. 7-36. If necessary, rotate the piston to obtain the correct angle.

8. If necessary, install the bleeder valve. Then install the caliper on the car.

Fig. 7-36. Gauge with 20° angle being used to check piston position. Arrow indicates direction of forward wheel rotation.

Repairing 1978 and Later Brake Calipers

Complete new brake calipers for 1978 and later cars are not available at this time. However, replacement components are readily available so that worn or damaged calipers can be repaired. Cylinder housings and brake pad carriers for left calipers are not interchangeable with the corresponding parts of right calipers.

To disassemble 1978 and later Girling caliper:

1. Remove the caliper from the car as described in **7.2 Removing and Installing Brake Caliper.** Thoroughly clean the exterior of the caliper using a wire brush and compressed air.

2. Using an open end wrench to keep the guide pins from turning, remove both of the cylinder housing mounting bolts. Then separate the cylinder housing from the brake pad carrier.

3. To avoid damaging the piston, place a hardwood block in the cylinder housing. Then, using compressed air as shown in Fig. 7-37, blow the piston out of the cylinder.

CAUTION ——

Use the minimum air pressure that will gradually push out the piston. The piston may be damaged if it is expelled with excessive force or velocity.

4. Remove the dust seal from the piston or the housing. Then, using a plastic rod as shown in Fig. 7-38, remove the piston seal from the cylinder.

5. If necessary, remove the bleeder valve from the cylinder.

Fig. 7-37. Compressed air being used to remove piston from cylinder. Notice position of hardwood block.

Fig. 7-38. Piston seal being removed from groove in cylinder bore. Though screwdriver is shown, a plastic rod or knitting needle should be used in order to avoid damage to cylinder.

To assemble:

1. Clean all parts with brake fluid only. Check the parts for wear. If the cylinder is damaged, replace the cylinder housing and the piston as a matched set. Do not hone the cylinder.

NOTE ——
New rubber boots, and new guide pins to replace those that are worn, scored, or corroded, are available only together with a new brake pad carrier.

2. Lightly coat the piston, the cylinder bore, and the new piston seal with VW brake cylinder paste. Then install the piston seal in the cylinder. Install the dust seal on the piston as shown in Fig. 7-39.

NOTE ——
Brake cylinder paste is included in the seal replacement kit sold by Authorized Dealers. It is the preferred form of lubrication when brake cylinders are repaired. Brake fluid should be considered a satisfactory substitute only if you are unable to reach an Authorized Dealer. Brake cylinders will give longer service when lubricated with VW brake cylinder paste than when lubricated by brake fluid alone.

Fig. 7-39. Dust seal correctly installed on piston preparatory to installing piston in cylinder.

3. Carefully insert the piston into the cylinder, clipping the inner lip of the dust seal into the cylinder housing's recess as shown in Fig. 7-40.

Fig. 7-40. Dust seal being clipped into cylinder housing recess with piston partially installed.

4. Press the piston fully into the cylinder, as shown in Fig. 7-41. Then engage the outer lip of the dust seal in the groove of the piston.

Fig. 7-41. Piston being pressed into cylinder. Tool shown is not absolutely necessary.

5. Assemble the remaining parts of the caliper using Fig. 7-42 as your guide. Hold the guide pin stationary with an open end wrench while you torque the cylinder housing's upper mounting bolt to 3.5 mkg (25 ft. lb.). Do not install the cylinder housing's lower mounting bolt until you have mounted the caliper on the car and installed the brake pads.

NOTE ──

Assembling the caliper will be easier if you first mount the pad carrier on the suspension strut, torquing the bolts to 6.0 mkg (43 ft. lb.). Then install the cylinder housing on the pad carrier.

Fig. 7-42. Exploded view of Girling caliper introduced on 1978 models. Relative positions of components are shown.

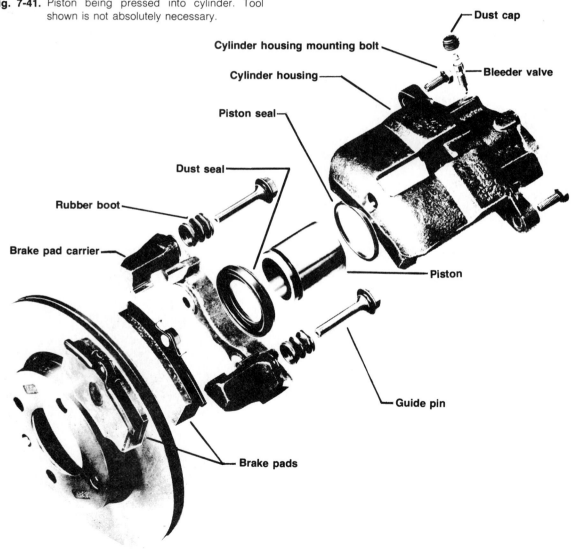

7.4 Brake Disc

Cars with Girling brake calipers have the same discs as cars with Teves (ATE) brake calipers. The brake discs are separate from the front wheel hub and are easily removable once the caliper is off the suspension strut.

Checking Brake Disc

The brake discs should be checked for wear each time repair work is done on the front brakes. Replace the discs if they are worn, scored with sharp ridges, or cracked. Also replace brake discs that have worn down, or have been machined, to a thickness of 10.50 mm (.413 in.) or less.

Check the discs for excessive runout. If a low-speed front end shimmy goes away when you release the brakes, excessive brake disc runout is probably the cause of the shimmy.

To measure runout:

1. Remove the front wheel. Put the transmission in neutral.

2. Install the measuring appliance on the pad retaining pins or pad retainer as shown in Fig. 7-43. Tighten the wing nut to hold it solidly in position.

© 1974 VWoA—1461

Fig. 7-43. Brake disc runout being measured. A dial indicator on a magnetic base can also be used. Brake assembly shown here is not for a car covered by this Manual.

3. Install the dial indicator on the appliance with its gauge pin against the disc surface. Then zero the gauge.

4. Slowly hand-turn the brake disc to check the runout. On 1973 through 1977 cars, the maximum allowable runout is 0.10 mm (.004 in.); on 1978 and later cars the maximum allowable runout is 0.06 in. (.002 in.).

5. If the brake disc runout exceeds specifications, replace or recondition the brake disc.

9

Removing and Installing Brake Disc

The brake caliper must be removed from the suspension strut before the brake disc can be taken off. Hang the caliper from the steering tie rod with a stiff wire hook. Leaving the brake hose attached will save you the job of bleeding the brakes.

CAUTION ——

Always remove the brake caliper. Never try to remove the disc by using force. Force may cause the caliper mounting frame to crack or break.

To remove the brake disc from the front wheel hub, remove the countersunk flathead screw that is located midway between two of the wheel bolt holes. Then pull the disc off the wheel hub. Installation is the reverse of removal.

CAUTION ——

Normally, the disc can be easily pulled off the hub. However, you should not use a steel hammer to drive off the disc if it is rusted tight. Doing this could ruin the disc. Instead, use a rubber hammer or a large three-arm wheel puller.

Reconditioning Brake Discs

Discs that have not worn to a thickness of 11.00 mm (.433 in.) or less can be reconditioned by an Authorized Dealer or a qualified automotive machine shop—if the following restrictions are observed:

1. The minimum allowable thickness after rework is 10.50 mm (.413 in.). New brake discs are 12.00 mm (.472 in.) thick.

CAUTION ——

Never rework brake discs to a lesser thickness. Doing this will allow the pistons to travel farther out in their cylinders. This may severely damage the calipers and the pistons.

2. After reworking a brake disc, its thickness should not vary by more than 0.02 mm (.0008 in.) measured at several locations on the disc.

3. The brake disc must be reworked equally on both sides to prevent squeaking, chattering, or brake pedal pulsation.

4. The maximum allowable runout of a reworked brake disc is 0.10 mm (.004 in.).

7.5 Removing and Installing Brake Disc Splash Shield

The brake disc splash shield must be removed whenever the wheel hub or suspension strut is serviced extensively or if the splash shield itself is damaged. Over the years, minor changes have been made to the shape of the splash shield to accommodate different brake calipers. Replace damaged splash shields with splash shields that are suitable to the brake calipers on the car. Left and right splash shields are different.

To remove the splash shield, remove the brake caliper as described in **7.2 Removing and Installing Brake Caliper.** Then remove the brake disc as described in **7.4 Brake Disc.** Take out the three bolts that hold the splash shield to the suspension strut. See Fig. 7-20, given earlier. Then remove the splash shield.

Installation is the reverse of removal. Torque the three bolts that hold the splash shield to 1.0 mkg (7 ft. lb.).

8. REAR BRAKES

All cars covered by this Manual have drum-type rear brakes. Servicing, replacing, and adjusting the wheel bearings are covered in **SUSPENSION AND STEERING.** The parking brake lever, which is connected by cables to the drum-type rear brakes, is covered in **10. Parking Brake.**

8.1 Adjusting Rear Brakes
(through 1978 models only)

The clearance between the brake linings and the drums gradually increases owing to normal wear. This change is indicated by increasing pedal travel in applying the brakes. When pedal travel becomes excessive, the brake shoes must be adjusted to position the linings nearer the drums. These adjustments are made at the individual wheels. The disc brakes used on the front of the car require no adjustment. Beginning with the 1979 models, the rear brakes are self-adjusting.

To adjust:

1. Raise the car and fully release the parking brake.

2. Depress the brake pedal as far as it will go several times. This centers the brake shoes in the drums.

   NOTE ——
   If the brakes are far out of adjustment, it may be necessary to recenter the shoes once or twice during the course of adjustments.

3. Remove the rubber plugs from the holes in the backing plate.

4. By looking through the hole near the edge of the backing plate, check the remaining thickness of the brake lining. If the lining thickness is less than 2.50 mm (.100 in.), replace the brake linings as described in **8.3 Removing and Installing Brake Shoes (through 1978 models only).**

5. Using a screwdriver or an adjusting lever as shown in Fig. 8-1, turn the star wheel of the adjuster—working through the hole that is right below the brake hose connection. Turn the adjuster until a slight drag is noted when the wheel is turned by hand. Then back off the adjuster three or four clicks so that the wheel turns freely.

   NOTE ——
   Residual pressure in the brake pressure regulator may make turning the right rear wheel difficult. If so, press the lever of the pressure regulator in the direction indicated in Fig. 8-2. Do not back off the brake adjuster unnecessarily.

© 1974 VWoA—1652

Fig. 8-1. Kind of lever used to adjust drum brakes. The brake assembly shown here is not for one of the cars covered by this Manual.

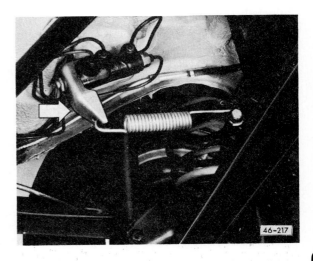

Fig. 8-2. Residual pressure being relieved from pressure regulator. Press lever in direction indicated by arrow.

6. Repeat the entire procedure on the other rear wheel. Then install the rubber plugs. Replace plugs that are cracked or that no longer fit tight.

7. Road-test the car to check the pedal travel.

9

8.2 Removing and Installing Brake Drum

The brake drum can be removed without contaminating the lubricant in the hub. However, dirt usually gets onto the stub axle, which must be cleaned and lubricated before you reinstall the brake drum. If you wish to clean and repack the wheel bearings, please use the procedure given in **SUSPENSION AND STEERING** instead of the procedure given here.

To remove:

1. Fully back off the brake adjustor as described in **8.1 Adjusting Rear Brakes (through 1978 models only)** or in **8.4 Removing and Installing Brake Shoes (1979 and later cars).** Pry off the dust cover.

2. Remove the cotter pin and the nut lock. Remove the nut from the stub axle.

3. Pull off the brake drum, being careful not to let the thrust washer and the outer tapered-roller bearing inner race fall out and onto the floor.

4. Store the brake drum in a clean place. Cover the hub with a clean cloth so that dirt cannot enter.

To install:

1. Wipe clean the stub axle. Then coat it lightly with multipurpose grease.

   NOTE ——

   If you are unsure of the kind of grease that is in the wheel bearings, or if you cannot obtain the same kind of grease, either repack the bearings with the new kind of grease or lightly coat the stub axle with some of the original grease obtained from inside the dust cover. Mixing two different kinds of grease will sometimes cause a chemical reaction that reduces the effectiveness of the lubricant.

2. Carefully slide the brake drum onto the stub axle so that the grease seal or bearing races are not accidentally damaged by the sharp threads.

3. Install the thrust washer and the nut. Tighten the nut until the bearings just contact their outer races.

4. Adjust the position of the nut until you can just move the thrust washer sideways with the tip of a screwdriver as shown in Fig. 8-3.

5. Install the nut lock so that its projections do not cover the cotter pin hole. Then install a new cotter pin.

6. Install the dust cover and the road wheel.

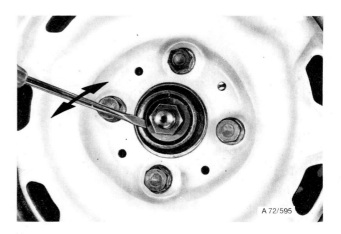

A 72/595

Fig. 8-3. Friction on thrust washer being checked by moving thurst washer with screwdriver.

8.3 Removing and Installing Brake Shoes

(through 1978 models only)

Installing brake shoes on cars covered by this Manual is basically similar to installing brake shoes on other kinds of cars. The components mentioned in this procedure can be identified by referring to Fig. 8-1, which was given earlier.

To remove:

1. Remove the brake drum as described in **8.2 Removing and Installing Brake Drum.**

2. Pull forward the parking brake lever that is on the rear brake shoe, then disconnect the cable from the lever.

3. Check the wheel cylinder for sticking pistons by having someone slowly depress the brake pedal while you watch to see whether the brake shoes move out the same distance at a uniform rate.

   NOTE ——

   Insert two screwdrivers behind the backing plate flange. Press them against the shoes to limit their travel. Also lift the wheel cylinder boot to check for fluid leakage. If the cylinder is sticking, leaking, or if the bleeder valve is rusted tight, rebuild or replace the cylinder.

4. Remove the spring clips and the shoe retaining pins.

5. Using brake spring pliers, remove the lower return springs.

6. Lift one brake shoe outward at the bottom. Then remove the adjuster.

7. Lift each brake shoe outward at the bottom. Then detach the shoe and its upper return spring from the brake cylinder and the backing plate.

To install:

1. Inspect the brake drum and compare it to the specifications given in **8.8 Reconditioning Brake Drums.** Make sure that the same type linings are used at both rear wheels.

    WARNING ——

    Using linings of different size or composition on opposite sides of the car can cause dangerously uneven braking.

2. Disassemble the adjuster and clean the threads. Lubricate the threads with molybdenum grease or zinc oxide grease and reassemble the adjuster.

3. Install the upper return spring on each brake shoe. Then attach the shoe and the spring to the backing plate.

4. After both shoes have been loosely installed, move one shoe outward at the bottom so that you can install the adjuster. The adjuster should be in its fully backed-off position.

5. Install the shoe retaining pins and the spring clips. Using brake spring pliers, install the lower return springs.

6. Install the brake drum as described in **8.2 Removing and Installing Brake Drum.**

7. Adjust the brakes as described in **8.1 Adjusting Rear Brakes (through 1978 models only).**

8.4 Removing and Installing Brake Shoes
(1979 and later cars)

Beginning with the 1979 models, the rear brakes are self-adjusting. This design change has made necessary different brake shoes and related parts. The brake drum reconditioning specifications are not affected by this modification, nor are the specifications and working procedures used in repairing or replacing the wheel cylinder. There are, however, important differences in the procedure for removing and installing the brake shoes.

The self-adjusting action of the redesigned rear brakes is accomplished by means of a variable-length push-bar and an adjusting wedge. The adjusting wedge is held down by spring tension between the push-bar and the leading brake shoe.

The correct clearance between the brake shoes and the brake drum is set by depressing and releasing the brake pedal. When the brake linings wear, the movement of the shoes in braking becomes greater than the correct, predetermined clearance. Under these conditions the adjusting wedge is moved further down by spring tension, thus filling the increased space between the pushbar and the primary brake shoe and automatically restoring the brake shoes to their correct clearance with the brake drum.

9

You can identify the components mentioned in the preceding description by referring to Fig. 8-4. The part names given in the illustration are also used in the procedures that follow.

The rear brake linings should be replaced when the remaining thickness of the riveted linings is 2.50 mm (.100 in.) or less. There is a plug in the brake backing plate that

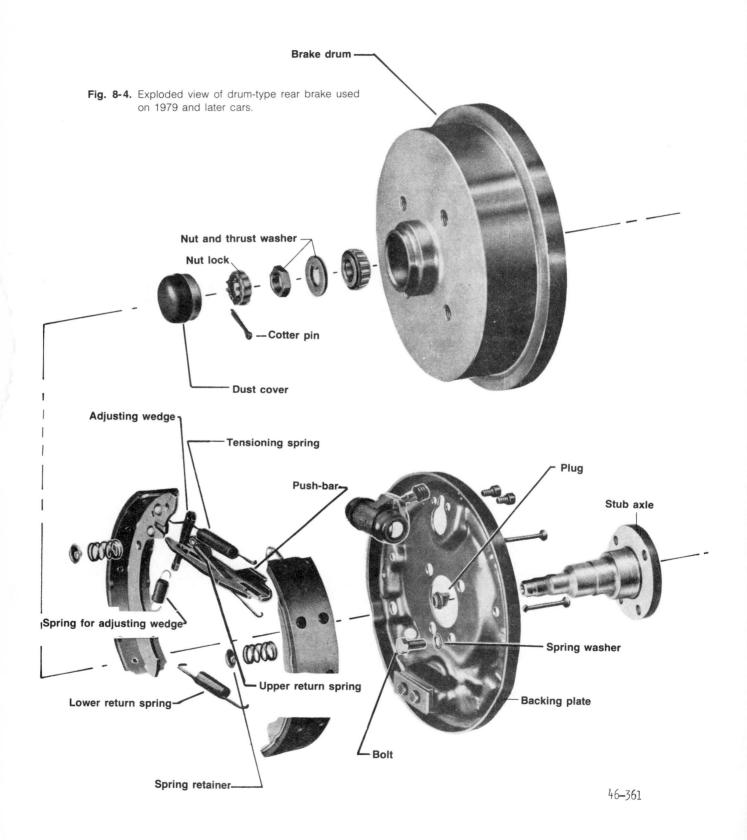

Fig. 8-4. Exploded view of drum-type rear brake used on 1979 and later cars.

Brake drum

Nut and thrust washer

Nut lock

Cotter pin

Dust cover

Adjusting wedge

Tensioning spring

Push-bar

Plug

Stub axle

Spring for adjusting wedge

Spring washer

Backing plate

Lower return spring

Upper return spring

Bolt

Spring retainer

46-361

allows you to inspect the lining thickness without removing the brake drum. This plug is located at the point indicated in Fig. 8-5. Be sure to reinstall the plug after you have checked the brake linings.

Fig. 8-5. Plug (arrow) for hole through which brake lining thickness can be checked.

To remove brake shoes:

1. Loosen one wheel bolt on each wheel that you plan to work on. Then release the parking brake and raise the car on a hoist. Alternatively, you can chock the front wheels to keep the car from rolling and jack the wheel that you are working on off the ground.

2. Fully remove the loosened wheel bolt. Insert a screwdriver as indicated in Fig. 8-6 and push the adjusting wedge upward until it contacts its stop.

Fig. 8-6. Screwdriver being used to push up adjusting wedge. Rotate wheel as necessary.

3. Remove the brake drum as described in **8.2 Removing and Installing Brake Drum.** If you wish, you can leave the road wheel attached to the brake drum when you remove it.

> **NOTE ——**
> Do not apply and release the brake pedal or the parking brake. If you do, the adjusting wedge will pull down again, advancing the adjustment and making it difficult or impossible to remove the brake drum.

4. Check the wheel cylinder for sticking pistons by having someone slowly depress the brake pedal while you watch to see whether the brake shoes move out the same distance at a uniform rate.

> **NOTE ——**
> Insert two screwdrivers behind the backing plate flange. Press them against the shoes to limit their travel. Also lift the wheel cylinder boot to check for fluid leakage. If the cylinder is sticking or leaking, or if the bleeder valve is rusted tight, rebuild or replace the cylinder.

5. Make sure that the adjusting wedge is pushed fully up. Reach behind the backing plate and hold in the head of each shoe retaining pin while you push each spring retainer in against spring tension, and then rotate the retainer 90° in order to remove the retainer and the spring from the pin.

6. Disengage the shoes from the support (Fig. 8-7), then remove the lower return spring.

Fig. 8-7. Support for brake shoes (arrow).

7. Pull forward the parking brake lever that is on the rear brake shoe, then disconnect the cable from the lever.

8. Using pliers, unhook the spring for the adjusting wedge from the adjusting wedge.

9

9. Using pliers, unhook the upper return spring and remove the brake shoes from the car. Then clamp the push-bar in a vise (Fig. 8-8) and use pliers to unhook and remove the tensioning spring.

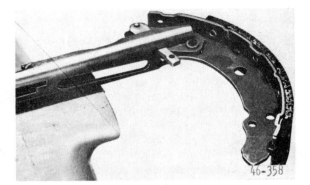

Fig. 8-8. Push-bar clamped in vise so that tensioning spring can be removed.

To install:

1. Inspect the brake drum and compare it to the specifications given in **8.8 Reconditioning Brake Drums.** Make sure that the same type linings are used at both rear wheels.

> **WARNING** ——
>
> *Using linings of different size or composition on opposite sides of the car can cause dangerously uneven braking.*

2. With the push-bar clamped in a vise, attach the brake shoe as indicated in Fig. 8-9—hooking the tensioning spring to the shoe and the bar as indicated and then shoving the shoe into position on the push-bar.

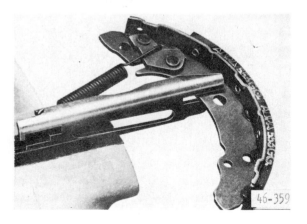

Fig. 8-9. Shoe being attached to tensioning spring and push-bar.

3. Insert the adjusting wedge so that its lug is toward the backing plate. Lubricate the contact surfaces of the push-bar with a grease approved for use on brake parts. Then attach the brake shoe with the parking brake lever as indicated in Fig. 8-10.

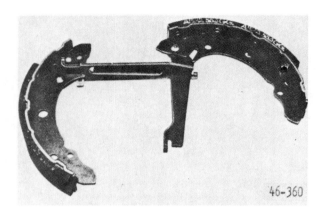

Fig. 8-10. Brake shoe with parking brake lever being attached to push-bar.

4. Install the upper return spring. Then, holding the shoes near the car, reattach the parking brake cable.

5. Place the brake shoes in contact with the brake cylinder pistons, install the lower return spring, then engage the shoes in the support.

6. Reattach the spring for the adjusting wedge to the wedge and to the brake shoe.

7. Reinstall the spring retainers and their springs. Install the brake drum as described in **8.2 Removing and Installing Brake Drum.** Then firmly apply the brake pedal once to set the self-adjusting mechanism.

8.5 Removing and Installing Wheel Cylinder

To remove a wheel cylinder, first carry out the procedure for removing the brake shoes as given in **8.3 Removing and Installing Brake Shoes (through 1978 models only)** or in **8.4 Removing and Installing Brake Shoes (1979 and later cars)**. Disconnect the brake hose from the rear of the brake assembly and seal it with a clean bleeder valve dust cap. Working behind the backing plate, remove the two bolts that hold the wheel cylinder to the backing plate. Then take the wheel cylinder off the front of the backing plate.

Installation is the reverse of removal. Torque the mounting screws to 1.0 mkg (7 ft. lb.). Torque the brake hose to 1.5 mkg (11 ft. lb.). Install the brake shoes as described in **8.3 Removing and Installing Brake Shoes (through 1978 models only)** or in **8.4 Removing and Installing Brake Shoes (1979 and later cars)**. Then bleed the brakes as described in **9. Bleeding Brakes.**

8.6 Wheel Cylinder Repair

Because replacement wheel cylinders are inexpensive, it is usually more economical to replace them as a unit. However, repair kits are available. Other than a very light honing to remove tarnish or gummy deposits, no machine work should be done.

At least two different kinds of wheel cylinders have been used on the cars covered by this Manual. So, when you buy replacement parts, take the old cylinder with you for comparison. Fig. 8-11 shows the components of a rear wheel cylinder.

The internal parts can be hand-pressed out of the housing once the boots are removed. Prior to assembly, clean all parts with brake fluid only.

Check the cylinder for wear. Do not machine or hone metal from the cylinder bore. A new, lubricated piston must be an airtight fit. If it is not, replace the cylinder.

NOTE ——
Vacuum should keep a new piston (lubricated with brake fluid) from falling out of the cylinder when the bleeder valve and brake hose holes are sealed and when you cover the opposite end of the cylinder with your thumb.

Lubricate the cups with brake fluid during installation. Coat the pistons with VW brake cylinder paste and insert them in the cylinder. Install the remaining parts.

NOTE ——
Brake cylinder paste is available from your Authorized Dealer and should be the preferred form of lubrication when brake cylinders are repaired. Brake fluid should be considered a satisfactory substitute only if you are unable to reach an Authorized Dealer. Brake cylinders will give longer service when lubricated with VW brake cylinder paste than when lubricated by brake fluid alone.

Fig. 8-11. Exploded view of rear wheel cylinder.

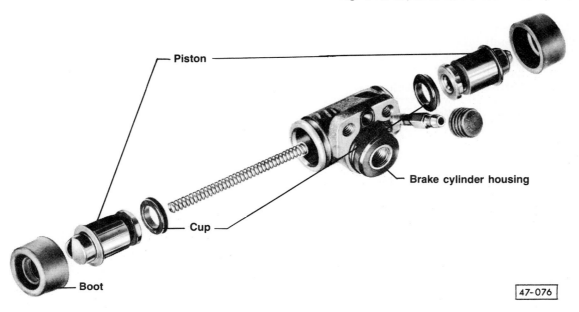

47-076

9

8.7 Removing and Installing Backing Plate

If the backing plate is bent, or if the raised areas that the brake shoes ride against are badly worn, replace the plate. Otherwise, the brake linings will not line up properly with the drum and will wear to a taper.

Remove the brake shoes as described in **8.3 Removing and Installing Brake Shoes (through 1978 models only)** or in **8.4 Removing and Installing Brake Shoes (1979 and later cars).** Remove the wheel cylinder as described in **8.5 Removing and Installing Wheel Cylinder.** Detach the parking brake cable conduit from the backing plate. Then take out the four bolts that hold the backing plate and the stub axle to the axle beam. Remove both the backing plate and the stub axle.

Installation is the reverse of removal. Prior to installation, make sure that the mating surfaces on the backing plate and the stub axle are completely clean. Use new spring washers for the bolts. Torque the four mounting bolts to 6.5 mkg (47 ft. lb.). Then install the wheel cylinder, the brake shoes, and the brake drum as described under preceding headings.

8.8 Reconditioning Brake Drums

Check the brake drums whenever new linings are installed. Taper, scoring, or other wear must, if possible, be corrected on a special machine by an Authorized Dealer or a qualified automotive machine shop. Both rear drums must be machined to the same dimensions. The linings must be ground to the new radius with a special machine by an Authorized Dealer or other qualified shop. Unless the linings are radiused to fit the reconditioned drums, uneven or ineffective braking may result.

The accuracy of the machine work will be improved if the road wheel can be mounted on the brake drum during machining and the wheel bolts tightened to 9.0 mkg (65 ft. lb.). The specified brake drum dimensions and wear limits are given in **Table b.**

Table b. Brake Drum Specifications

Maximum permissible radial runout or out-of-round for used or reconditioned drums	0.05 mm (.002 in.)
Maximum permissible inside diameter for drums that are to be reconditioned	200.50 mm (7.894 in.)
Inside diameter wear limit	201.00 mm (7.913 in.)
Maximum permissible lateral runout at road wheel contact surface	0.50 mm (.020 in.)
Maximum permissible lateral runout at friction surface	0.20 mm (.008 in.)

9. BLEEDING BRAKES

Bleeding the brakes removes air from the hydraulic system. This task must be performed whenever the brake lines have been disconnected or after a brake cylinder has been replaced or repaired. If the brake pedal feels spongy when you apply the brakes, it is an indication that air has entered the system. If bleeding fails to correct the problem, there are probably leaks to be fixed.

Brake Fluids

Additional fluid must be added to the system when it is bled. The quality of the new brake fluid is important. All Audi and VW brake fluids have similar chemical and performance characteristics and may be mixed regardless of differences in color. Using a brake fluid that does not conform with SAE recommendation J 1703 and Motor Vehicle Safety Standard 116 DOT 3 can cause brake failure, premature wear, or erratic operation.

9.1 Changing Brake Fluid

Change the brake fluid in your car every two years. Brake fluid tends to absorb moisture from the air, and water can initiate corrosion. Water can also cause the fluid to boil when the brakes are used very hard.

It is particularly important that the brake systems of vehicles with disc brakes have a fluid with a high boiling point. Since the brake calipers surround the friction linings, they pick up a great deal of heat from them.

> **NOTE ——**
> Whenever you change brake fluid, you should at the same time test the brake light/warning light switches as described in **4.1 Testing and Replacing Brake Light/ Warning Light Switches.**

To change fluid:

1. Attach suitable hoses to the bleeder valves for draining the fluid into containers.

2. Open the left rear and the right front bleeder valves and pump the brake pedal until fluid ceases to flow out of them.

3. Open the right rear and the left front bleeder valves and pump the brake pedal until fluid ceases to flow out of them.

4. Close all bleeder valves.

5. Fill the fluid reservoir with new, unused brake fluid that meets SAE recommendation J 1703 and conforms to Motor Vehicle Safety Standard 116 DOT 3. Then bleed the system by either of the methods described.

9.2 Bleeding with Pressure Bleeder

Whenever possible, brake bleeding should be done with a pneumatic pressure bleeder similar to that shown in Fig. 9-1. Connect this device to the brake fluid reservoir. The bleeder fills the system with fluid under pressure and will complete the job in a very short time. Simply open the bleeder valve, quickly depress and slowly release the pedal several times, and then close the bleeder valve. A fluid receptable supplied with the bleeding device must be fitted to the wheel being bled.

Fig. 9-1. Pressure bleeder for bleeding brake system.

9.3 Bleeding by Pumping

For car owners, the pumping method of bleeding the brakes is usually more practical, even though it requires two persons. Have your helper sit in the car to pump the brake pedal. You will then be free to move from wheel to wheel to perform the actual bleeding.

To bleed:

1. Fully fill the fluid reservoir with brake fluid that meets SAE recommendation J 1703 and conforms to Motor Vehicle Safety Standard 116 DOT 3.

2. Take the dust cap off the bleeder valve at the right-hand rear wheel. Slip a 4-mm (5/32-in.) I.D. hose over the bleeder valve and submerge the other end in a clear glass jar partially filled with clean brake fluid. The jar must be clear so that you can see air bubbles coming out of the hose.

3. Open the bleeder valve a half turn. Have your helper slowly depress the brake pedal until it reaches the floor and keep it there while you close the bleeder valve.

4. Have your helper slowly release the pedal until it is completely up. Repeat the preceding step until no more air bubbles emerge from the hose.

5. Repeat the entire bleeding procedure on the other three wheels in the sequence given in Fig. 9-2.

> **NOTE ——**
> Refill the reservoir after bleeding each wheel cylinder. If the system contains a great deal of air or if the brake fluid is being changed, it will be necessary to add more fluid once or twice while bleeding each wheel cylinder. Never let the reservoir be emptied completely, or you will have to start bleeding the brakes all over again.

> **CAUTION ——**
> Do not allow brake fluid to come in contact with painted surfaces. Brake fluid contains a solvent damaging to most finishes.

> **WARNING ——**
> Do not use soft drink bottles or other food containers to store brake fluid or to bleed the brakes. Brake fluid is poisonous.

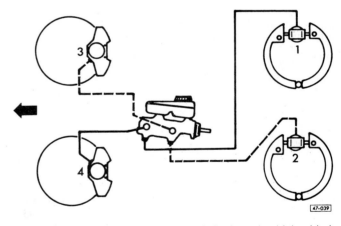

Fig. 9-2. Sequence in which brakes should be bled. Arrow indicates front of car.

9.4 Flushing Brake System

Never use anything but brake fluid to flush the brake system. Alcohol must not be used since it will destroy residual lubrication and will encourage the accumulation of water in the system.

> **NOTE ——**
> Do not rely on flushing alone to clean a brake system contaminated by dirt or rust. To remove all foreign matter, you must disassemble the system and clean the parts individually.

9

10. PARKING BRAKE

The components of the parking brake lever are shown in Fig. 10-1.

The parking brake operates only on the rear wheels. It is completely mechanical and independent of the hydraulic brake system. Once the parking brake handle has been pulled up, it is held in position by a ratchet. The lever will remain in the same position until the ratchet is released by pressing in the button on the end of the handle and allowing the parking brake lever to move down.

A U-shaped cable extends from the parking brake lever, the closed end of the U being looped around the cable compensator and the ends of the U attached to the individual rear wheels. Pulling the parking brake handle upward tightens the cable and moves the rear brake shoe into contact with the rear brake drums. The cable operates on a lever attached to the rear brake shoe of

each rear brake. The movement of the lever is transmitted to the front shoe of each rear brake by the brake adjuster assembly.

10.1 Adjusting Parking Brake

The parking brake should be adjusted whenever the rear brake linings have worn enough so that it is possible to raise the brake handle three clicks without noticeable braking action.

To adjust:

1. Raise the car on a hoist or support the rear axle on jack stands placed at the outermost ends of the rear axle.

2. Adjust the rear brakes as described in **8.1 Adjusting Rear Brakes (through 1978 models only).**

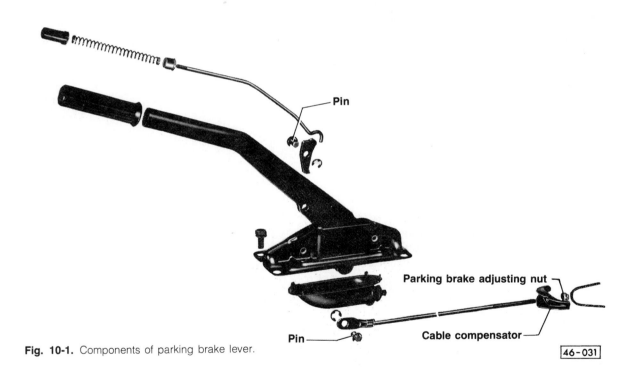

Fig. 10-1. Components of parking brake lever.

46-031

3. Clean the cable compensator that is attached to the rod on the lower end of the parking brake lever. Lubricate the threads and the cable groove with multipurpose grease.

4. Pull the parking brake lever up two clicks.

5. Tighten the nut indicated in Fig. 10-2 until it is just barely possible to hand-turn the rear wheels.

6. Release the parking brake. Then check that both rear wheels rotate freely.

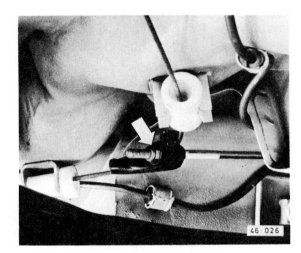

Fig. 10-2. Parking brake adjusting nut (arrow).

10.2 Removing and Installing Parking Brake Lever

It will be helpful if you study Fig. 10-1 (given earlier) before you attempt to remove the parking brake lever. To prevent dirt and corrosion from affecting the operation of the parking brake lever, you should always replace the under-car rubber boot if it is torn, cracked, or loose-fitting.

To remove:

1. Working under the car, detach the rubber boot from the bottom of the parking brake lever assembly. Then pull down on the boot so that you can remove the E-clip and the pin that hold the pull rod to the bottom of the lever.

2. Remove the boot, the pull rod, and the cable compensator as a unit.

3. Working inside the car, carefully detach the parking brake trim panel boot from the hooks at its four corners.

4. Raise the trim panel boot. Remove the four bolts that hold the parking brake lever assembly to the floor.

5. Remove the parking brake lever assembly as a unit. If necessary, you can disassemble the parking brake lever by pulling off the grip and the trim panel boot so that you can remove the E-clip and the ratchet pawl pivot pin.

Installation is the reverse of removal. Following installation, adjust the parking brake as described in **10.1 Adjusting Parking Brake.** If you have disassembled the parking brake lever—or if the lever does not work smoothly—lubricate all pins and sliding surfaces with multipurpose grease.

10.3 Removing and Installing Brake Cable

To remove the parking brake cable, take off both rear brake drums as described in **8.2 Removing and Installing Brake Drum.** Detach the cable ends from the levers on the rear brake shoes. Detach the cable conduits from the brake backing plates. Then carefully pull the conduits, cables, and grommets out of the backing plates and the rear suspension trailing arms. Then you can disconnect the cable and its nylon guides from the car body and the cable compensator. Installation is the reverse of removal.

> **NOTE ——**
> After you have installed the cable, adjust the parking brake as described in **10.1 Adjusting Parking Brake.** If you have installed a new cable, check the adjustment again after about 300 mi. (500 km).

11. WHEELS AND TIRES

Tires are subject to many stresses. If they are to perform as intended, they must be inflated to specifications and correctly balanced. Properly maintained, the factory-installed tires will provide long service with comfort and safety. But they must never be kept in service when worn out or damaged by accidents or careless driving.

11.1 Wheels

The cars dovered by this Manual are equipped with 4½J × 13 rims. An optional 5J × 13 rim is also available. Both kinds of wheels have an offset of 45 mm (1 $^{49}/_{64}$ in.).

Offset is the difference between the center of rim width and the mounting face that bolts to the brake drum or brake disc. The use of wheels other than those standard for a given year and model is discouraged. Many of the wider wheels sold by accessory companies do not have the correct offset dimension. This may

9

impose excessive stress on the wheel bearings or alter steering behavior.

The wheels on all models covered by this Manual are suitable for use with tube or tubeless tires of the correct size, including radials. Tires of nonstandard size may be used only if the tire manufacturer specifies them for your particular make and model car.

11.2 Tire Types and Pressures

Radial ply tires are factory-installed on all cars covered by this Manual. It is recommended that replacement tires also be of radial ply construction. Use 155 SR 13 or 165 SR 13 tires with 4½J × 13 wheels; use 175/70 SR 13 tires with 5J × 13 wheels.

Conventional Tires

Conventional bias ply tires offer very good riding characteristics and are well suited to highways and rough roads alike. Bias-constructed tires can be made extremely strong through the use of an almost infinite number of plies. The basic simplicity of bias ply design also results in lower construction costs.

Radial Tires

There is less friction between the fabric layers in radial ply tires, so they generate less heat. This makes them especially suitable for long-distance, high-speed driving. They also do not heat up so much when carrying heavy loads. Their rigid tread improves wet-weather traction, but tends to produce a harsher ride and increased road noise on some kinds of surfaces.

Winter Tires

Although inferior to regular tires for dry-road wear and handling, winter (mud and snow) tires can greatly improve operation on snowy or slushy roads. Studded winter tires improve traction on icy surfaces, but can be damaged by fast driving on dry roads and may damage some road surfaces. They should be used only if icy conditions predominate throughout the winter months. Also check your local vehicle laws. The use of studded tires may be restricted in your area.

CAUTION —

If you install winter tires on only two of the four wheels, the winter tires should be installed on the front wheels. Also, to prevent dangerous handling, your winter tires must be of radial ply construction if the normal radial tires are kept on the rear wheels. If you install winter tires on all four wheels, the tires should all have the same kind of construction.

Tire Pressures

The inflation pressures given in **Table c** apply to the standard radial tire sizes that are installed at the factory. If you install tires of another kind, follow the inflation recommendation made by the tire manufacturer for your particular car and tire combination.

Table c. Standard Radial Tire Pressures

Car model	Standard and optional wheel sizes	Standard and optional tire sizes	Loads	Front pressure	Rear pressure
1973–1976 2-door or 4-door Sedans	4½J × 13 4½J × 13 5J × 13	155 SR 13 165/70 SR 13 175/70 SR 13	all loads all loads all loads	28 psi 28 psi 28 psi	28 psi 28 psi 28 psi
1977 and later Sedans	4½J × 13 4½J × 13 5J × 13 5J × 13	155 SR 13 155 SR 13 175/70 SR 13 175/70 SR 13	half load max. load half load max. load	27 psi 27 psi 27 psi 27 psi	27 psi 31 psi 27 psi 31 psi
1973–1976 Station Wagon	4½J × 13 4½J × 13 4½J × 13 4½J × 13 5J × 13 5J × 13	155 SR 13 155 SR 13 165/70 SR 13 165/70 SR 13 175/70 SR 13 175/70 SR 13	half load max. load half load max. load half load max. load	28 psi 28 psi 28 psi 28 psi 28 psi 28 psi	28 psi 34 psi 28 psi 34 psi 28 psi 34 psi
1977 and later Station Wagon	4½J × 13 4½J × 13 5J × 13 5J × 13	155 SR 13 155 SR 13 175/70 SR 13 175/70 SR 13	half load max. load half load max. load	27 psi 27 psi 27 psi 27 psi	27 psi 31 psi 27 psi 34 psi

Because steel and textile cord radial tires have different traction characteristics, it is important that all four tires on the car have the same cord material. Tire effectiveness under various road conditions is shown in the following chart:

Operating conditions	Dry	Wet	Snow	Ice
Snow w/studs radial ply	0	—	X	X
Snow w/studs bias ply	0	—	X	X
Snow radial ply	X	X	X	0
Snow bias ply	X	X	X	0
Standard radial ply	X	X	0	0
Standard bias ply	X	X	0	—

X = Effective   0 = Restricted effectiveness   — = Noneffective

11.3 Normal Tire Wear

The original equipment tires on your car have built-in tread wear indicators. These indicators are molded into the bottom of the tire tread grooves. The indicators eventually appear as the result of normal wear. They are about 13 mm (½ in.) wide in visible bands when the tire tread depth gets down to 1.5 mm (1/16 in.).

When these indicators appear in two or more adjacent grooves of a tire tread, as shown in Fig. 11-1, the tire must be replaced well before the indicators are as visible as shown. Worn tires cannot grip even a dry road surface properly and are almost completely ineffective on a wet road surface.

WARNING ——

Do not assume that a tire is sound merely because the tread wear indicators have not yet appeared. Always check for cuts, cracks, rubber separation, and internal damage. Normal wear is only one factor in determining tire serviceability.

© 1974 VWoA—3539

Fig. 11-1. Indicator showing on worn-out tire.

For best all-round handling, always replace all four tires at the same time. If this is not possible, replace both tires on one axle. Do not combine tires of different ply construction, size, or tread pattern.

WARNING ——

Break in new tires by driving at moderate speeds for the first 60 to 100 mi. (100 to 160 km). New tires do not have full traction when first installed.

Normal tire wear is accelerated by higher speeds. Wear at a constant 35 mph (56 kph) is only about a third of that produced at a constant 70 mph (112 kph)—not half, as might seem logical.

Weather also affects normal tire wear. Hot weather is the most damaging and when heat is combined with high speeds and underinflation, tire structure is seriously endangered. Cold weather prolongs tire life; so does wet weather, which reduces the friction between tire and road.

11.4 Removing and Installing Wheels

The Owner's Manual supplied with the car lists the proper procedures for this job. The following points, however, deserve mention to mechanics not familiar with the Owner's Manual or with the cars.

First, use the hubcap remover on cars with hubcaps. This is a wire hook that can be slipped into holes in the edges of the hubcaps. It prevents scratches on the painted wheel and makes the job quicker and easier.

Next, use only the jack supplied with the vehicle. Never attempt to lift the car with an ordinary bumper jack. The cross section of the bumpers is not contoured for the lifting hood on such jacks, and the vehicle cannot be lifted safely by them. If a hydraulic-type floor jack is used, be certain to position it carefully. Place blocks ahead and behind the wheels that remain on the ground to prevent the vehicle from rolling.

CAUTION ——

Under no circumstances must the car be lifted by placing a jack under the engine, transmission, the middle of the rear axle or floor pan. Serious damage can result from these practices.

All wheel bolts are removed by turning them counterclockwise. When tightening the wheel bolts, torque them to 9.0 mkg (65 ft. lb.). Use a torque wrench. Pneumatic tools are seldom capable of attaining the prescribed torque with accuracy.

9

11.5 Wheel Rotation

Although the tires will develop a normal wear pattern under most conditions, abnormal road surfaces or variations in driving technique may produce unequal wear of the four tires on a car. If, after a period of service, the tires on your vehicle show uneven wear, all four wheels can be rotated as shown in Fig. 11-2.

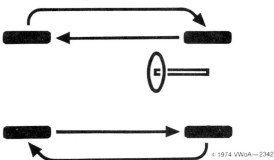

Fig. 11-2. Pattern of recommended wheel rotation. Wheel rotation is not required but may be desirable if tires are wearing unevenly.

11.6 Changing Tires

Dismounting or mounting tires on the rims requires a tire appliance with power enough to force the tire bead over the inner hump on the rim. When carrying out these operations, be sure that the rubber lining on the inner wall of the tire and tire beads is not damaged.

To dismount tire:

1. Take off the valve cap, carefully unscrew the valve core, and let the air out of the tire. Then press the tire bead off the rim as shown in Fig. 11-3.

Fig. 11-3. Pressing tire bead off rim.

2. Pry the tire sidewalls, one after the other, over the rim edges as shown in Fig. 11-4.

Fig. 11-4. Prying tire sidewalls over rim edges.

3. Check the airtight lining inside the tire for damage and bruises between the lining and casing. Carefully inspect the outside of the tire for embedded stones, cuts, grease, and signs of uneven wear.

4. Check the rubber part of the valve for cracks and damage. If the valve is faulty, remove it from the rim. Lubricate a new valve with soapy water. Then install the new valve as shown in Fig. 11-5.

Fig. 11-5. A valve tool being used to install a new valve in the rim.

To mount tire:

1. Check the rim for damage. Radial runout must not exceed 1.25 mm (.050 in.); lateral runout must not exceed 1.50 mm (.060 in.).

> **WARNING** ——
> *Never attempt to straighten bent, dented, or otherwise distorted rims. Doing so could weaken them. Make certain that all wheels are as originally fitted with J-type rims before installing tubeless radial tires. Other rim types are unsuitable for use with radial tires unless tubes are installed.*

2. Using a wire brush, remove any dirt from the rim shoulders and flanges. Smooth any sharp edges before mounting the tire on the wheel.

3. Insert the valve with the valve installing tool.

> **NOTE** ——
> Use inner tubes with radial tires if the vehicle will be used on rough roads or off road.

4. Mount the tire on the rim as shown in Fig. 11-6. If there is a red dot on the sidewall, position it toward the valve.

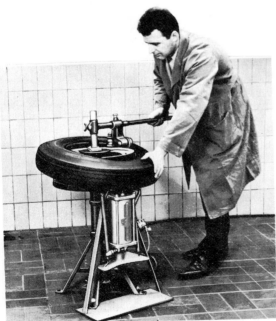

© 1974 VWoA—491

Fig. 11-6. Tire being mounted on rim. Use soft soap or a special rubber lubricant on the rim for safe, easy mounting.

5. Remove the valve core, if not already removed.

6. Inflate the tire to at least the maximum inflation pressure listed on the sidewall.

> **NOTE** ——
> Use a bead expander strap, if necessary, to obtain an airtight seal. When inflating the tire you should hear the bead snap over the inner hump on the rim.

7. Install the valve core and inflate the tire to the correct running pressure, as listed earlier in **11.2 Tire Types and Pressures.**

8. Immerse the wheel in water. Check for leaks.

9. Balance the wheel and install it on the car.

11.7 Abnormal Wear

Following are the six most common causes of abnormal tire wear (extra wear):

1. Underinflation or overinflation

2. Hard driving (high speed driving, violent braking, sudden cornering)

3. Rough or abrasive road surfaces, high crown roads, and very uneven road surfaces

4. Poorly aligned wheels (front or rear)

5. Poorly balanced wheels (front or rear)

6. Vehicle overloading or carrying too much weight for tire capacity.

Improper Inflation

Tire life depends greatly on correct inflation. Unfortunately, there are many ways for a tire to lose air. Every tire normally loses some air pressure due to the diffusion of air molecules through the rubber. Although tubeless tires hold air pressure longer than tires with inner tubes, it is recommended that you check the pressure even of tubeless tires once a week.

Tire pressures should be checked before driving, when the tires are still cold. If tire pressures are checked after driving, the pressures will have increased from the heat of road friction and internal flexing. If air is bled from a warm tire to obtain the pressure recommended for a cold tire, the tire will actually be underinflated. A tire that is driven while underinflated will overheat because of increased tire flexing and will rapidly lose its road-holding ability as tire strength begins to diminish.

There is always a reason when a tire loses a significant amount of air in a short period of time. Aside from a hole in the tire, the possible causes are a leaky rim or valve, loose-fitting tire beads, foreign matter in the rim, or an uneven surface between the rim shoulder and the tire.

9

Fig. 11-7 shows three tire inflation conditions. The shape of the tire is changed by the degree of inflation. This can cause abnormal wear. An underinflated tire wears at its edges; an overinflated tire wears at its center. The profile of an underinflated tire is similar to that of an overloaded tire. The same kind of wear will result from overloading, with the added possibility of severe heat damage and possible structural failure.

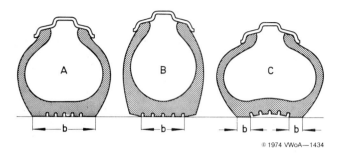

© 1974 VWoA—1434

Fig. 11-7. Tire inflation. Condition **A**, normal inflation; condition **B**, overinflation; condition **C**, underinflation. Dimension **b** is the width of the tire tread in contact with the road.

Fig. 11-8 shows typical tire wear due to overinflation. Because a narrower portion of the tread is in contact with the road, wear occurs faster than normal. This tire is worn out despite the good tread remaining at the edges.

© 1974 VWoA—1438

Fig. 11-8. Overinflation wear. Tire worn out by running it with excessive air pressure.

Fig. 11-9 shows the tread wear pattern of an underinflated tire. This worn-out tire still has deep tread in its center, although the edges are completely bald. Such tires should be removed from service immediately. As with tires worn unevenly by overinflation, they provide very limited adhesion in wet weather and almost no traction in deep snow. In addition, side grip for cornering is seriously impaired.

© 1974 VWoA—1435

Fig. 11-9. Underinflation wear. Tire worn out by running it with too low an air pressure.

Hard Driving

Tires may wear abnormally because of excessive speed, heavy braking (see Fig. 11-10), high speed cornering, and similar violent or abrupt maneuvers. Conservative driving preserves tire life.

© 1974 VWoA—1439

Fig. 11-10. Abnormal tire wear due to locking the brakes. Uneven braking forces can also cause heavy tire wear.

Road Surfaces

Some road surfaces tend to increase tire wear. Rough, anti-skid surfacing materials abrade the tread and accelerate normal wear. Roadways with high crowns necessitate constant steering correction to keep the car headed parallel to the highway. This will eventually produce the kind of abnormal wear usually associated with improper front wheel alignment. Obstructions and road hazards can cause severe tire damage and can even break the casing internally, as shown in Fig. 11-11.

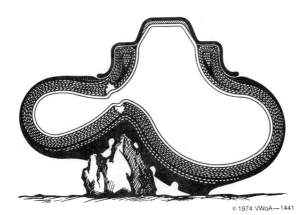

© 1974 VWoA—1441

Fig. 11-11. Internal damage. Striking an obstacle in the road may tear the ply layers. Such damage renders the tire unfit for use. You may have to take the tire off its rim to see such defects.

Faulty Wheel Alignment

Excessive tire wear will result from misalignment of any of the four wheels on the car. If irregular tire wear appears, check the front wheel track, the front wheel angles at full steering lock, the ride height and rear wheel track, the position of the axles relative to each other, the wheelbase on both sides of the car, the front and rear wheel camber, the condition of the rear springs, and the condition of the shock absorbers. The abnormal wear caused by misalignment usually takes the form of greater wear at one edge of the tread than on the other. Alignment specifications are given in **SUSPENSION AND STEERING.**

Wheels Out of Balance

Wheels that are out of balance cause abnormal tire wear and constitute a driving hazard. Unbalanced wheels bounce, tramp, and wobble. The faster you drive, the more dangerous these wheel vibrations are.

Wheel imbalance is always more evident on the front wheels, and usually more dangerous. Fig. 11-12 shows the condition that static balancing of the wheel and tire can detect. The effect of such imbalance is shown in the right-hand part of the illustration.

Fig. 11-13 shows the type of imbalance that only dynamic balancing can detect. Although in perfect static balance, the concentrations of mass are not in line with one another or with the tire centerline. The wheel wobbles sideways when it spins, as shown on the right-hand side of the illustration. This causes deep wear in the form of cupped areas on the tread. Check that wheel runout does not exceed 1.25 mm (.050 in.) either radially or laterally before dynamic balancing the wheel. Replace the wheel if it does.

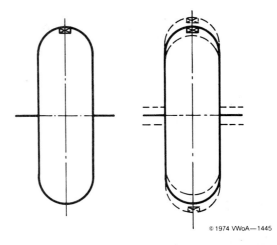

© 1974 VWoA—1445

Fig. 11-12. Imbalance that can be cured by static balancing. Vibration of the spinning wheel is shown at the right.

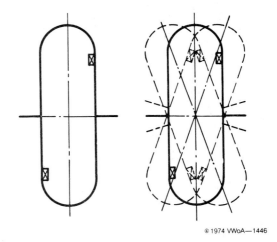

© 1974 VWoA—1446

Fig. 11-13. Imbalance that can be cured only by dynamic balancing. Vibration of the spinning wheel is shown at the right.

Overloading

Overloading the tires causes damage similar to that produced by underinflation. The excessive heat generated by an overloaded tire weakens the tire and causes difficult vehicle handling. The maximum load capacity (given in the Owner's Manual), added to the weight of the vehicle, must never exceed the total load capacity of the four tires (marked on their sidewalls).

12. BRAKES AND WHEELS TECHNICAL DATA

The following tables give all specifications related to the brake system, tires, and wheels. Wheel alignment specifications are given in **SUSPENSION AND STEERING.**

9

I. Tightening Torques

Location	Designation	mkg	ft. lb.
Stop screw in master cylinder housing	special screw	1.5 to 2.0	11 to 14
Residual pressure valve in master cylinder	—	2.0	14
Brake light/warning light switch in master cylinder	—	2.0	14
Brake line to master cylinder	union nut	1.5 to 2.0	11 to 14
Master cylinder to vacuum powered brake servo	nut	1.3 maximum	9.4 maximum
Vacuum powered brake servo to car body	nut	1.5	11
Brake caliper to front suspension strut	bolt	6.0	43
1978 and later Girling caliper cylinder housing to pad carrier	bolt	3.5	25
Brake hose in brake caliper	—	1.5	11
1973–1977 Girling caliper pad retainer clip to caliper frame	bolt	2.0	14
Brake hose in brake caliper	—	1.5	11
Girling caliper pad retainer clip to caliper frame	bolt	2.0	14
Brake disc splash shield to front suspension strut	bolt	1.0	7
Rear wheel brake cylinder to backing plate	screw	1.0	7
Brake hose in rear wheel brake cylinder	—	1.5	11
Rear brake backing plate and stub axle to axle beam	bolt	6.5	47
Pressure regulator to car underbody	bolt	1.5	11
Brake line unions	union nut	1.5 to 2.0	11 to 14
Brake hoses—except in caliper or wheel cylinder	—	1.5 to 2.0	11 to 14
Road wheel to brake disc or brake drum	lug bolt	9.0	65

II. Tolerances, Wear Limits, and Settings

Designation	New Part	Wear Limit
A. Front Brakes		
1. Front wheel brake discs .... thickness	12.00 mm (.472 in.)	
minimum thickness before machining	—	11.00 mm (.433 in.)
minimum permissible thickness	—	10.50 mm (.413 in.)
minimum thickness after machining	—	10.50 mm (.413 in.)
maximum permissible runout (1973–1977)	—	0.10 mm (.004 in.)
maximum permissible runout (1978 and later)	—	0.06 mm (.002 in.)
maximum permissible thickness variation	—	0.02 mm (.0008 in.)
2. Front wheel brake pad linings (1973–1977) .... remaining thickness	—	2.00 mm (.080 in.)
Front wheel brake pad linings (1978 and later) .... total thickness	14 mm ($^9/_{16}$ in.)	7.00 mm ($^9/_{32}$ in.)
B. Rear Brakes		
1. Rear wheel brake drums .. maximum inside diameter before machining	—	200.50 mm (7.894 in.)
maximum permissible inside diameter	—	201.00 mm (7.913 in.)
maximum inside diameter after machining	—	201.00 mm (7.913 in.)
maximum radial runout or out-of-round	—	0.05 mm (.002 in.)
maximum permissible lateral runout at road wheel contact surface	—	0.50 mm (.020 in.)
maximum permissible lateral runout at friction surface	—	0.20 mm (.008 in.)
2. Rear wheel brake shoe linings .... remaining thickness	—	2.50 mm (.100 in.)

LUBRICATION AND MAINTENANCE

Contents

10

Lubrication and Maintenance

The service life of your car depends on the kind of maintenance it receives. The Owner's Manual originally supplied with the car contains valuable information concerning correct car maintenance, which should be used in conjunction with this Manual. Because several model years are covered in this Manual, some of the procedures described may not apply to your car. If you are in doubt, always take the Owner's Manual and the Maintenance Record booklet as your guides.

Some maintenance procedures, such as oil change service, require no special tools and can be carried out by almost all car owners, regardless of their mechanical experience. However, certain other diagnosis and maintenance operations require tools and equipment specifically designed for those operations. Wheel alignment checks, ignition timing, and emission control checks are a few examples. If you lack the skills, tools, or a suitable workshop for performing any of the service steps described, we suggest you leave this work to an Authorized Dealer or other qualified shop. We especially urge you to consult your Authorized Dealer before attempting any repairs on a car still covered by the new-car warranty.

Some of the early cars covered by this Manual are equipped with a system of sensors and test wiring that terminates in a central socket located in the engine compartment. This socket is designed to receive a plug from the cable of the Computer Analysis system. Never connect any device other than the test plug of the Computer Analysis system to the test network central socket. Incorrect equipment may damage the plug connections, the test sensors, or the vehicle components that contain sensors. Any test or diagnosis equipment that you use in maintaining your car should be connected to the vehicle in the manner that is recommended by the instrument manufacturer.

10 ■

1. LUBRICANTS

Because of the recent improvements in the quality of commercially available lubricating oils, completely new oil recommendations became effective in 1975. These new oil recommendations, given below, should be applied to all the cars covered by this Manual.

The superseded oil recommendations, given in the Owner's Manuals supplied with 1973 and 1974 cars can still be used in servicing 1973 and 1974 models. You will find, however, that there are many advantages to be gained in adopting the new recommendations. Only the new oil recommendations, given in this Manual, should be applied to 1975 and later cars.

The lubricants used in your car have a vital influence on its operation. Use only name brand oils labeled "for Service SD" (or "For Service SE" or both) in the spark-ignition engine; oils used in 1975 and later cars must be labeled "For Service API/SE." Use only name brand oils labeled "For Service API/CC" or "MIL-L 46152" in diesel engines; the term CC should appear on the oil container singly or in combination with other designations.

Automatic transmission fluid (ATF) must be labeled Dex-ron®. The hypoid oil used in the manual transmission must meet specification MIL-L 2105 API/GL4. Use a hypoid oil that meets specification MIL-L 2105 B API/GL5 for the final drive of the automatic transmission. No additives should be used in the engine oil, hypoid oil, or ATF. Experience has shown that name brand lubricants of the correct specification and viscosity meet all operating needs of the engine and transmission.

Oil viscosity must be suitable to climatic conditions. Viscosity is a term used to describe how readily a liquid flows. High viscosity oils seem thicker and pour more slowly at room temperature than do low viscosity (thinner) oils. When heated, however, oil loses some of its viscosity. A high viscosity oil heated to 93°C (200°F) may pour as readily as a low viscosity oil at room temperature. If an oil has too low a viscosity, it will not maintain an adequate lubricating film between moving parts. A thin, low viscosity oil may maintain this film at low temperatures but become so much thinner after it has warmed up that it leaves the engine parts unprotected.

It might seem that a high viscosity oil is all that is necessary to lubricate an engine properly. Unfortunately, this is not true. If a high viscosity oil is used during cold weather, it will become so thick and resistant to flow that it cannot properly circulate and reach the parts of the engine requiring lubrication. A thick, high viscosity oil will also become so gummy in cold weather that the starter cannot turn the engine fast enough to start it. The proper viscosity oil will remain fluid enough after the engine has cooled to permit easy starting, yet, after the engine has reached operating temperature, will retain sufficient viscosity to maintain an adequate lubricating film.

Single-grade engine oils, such as SAE 30, were formerly recommended for high-temperature use because of the unreliable quality of the then available multi-grade engine oils. The new high standard for engine oils that conform to the API (American Petroleum Institute) ratings has made multi-grade oils suitable for use at nearly all temperatures. Car owners will find that high-quality multi-grade oils with the correct API ratings for their cars offer many advantages in convenience, performance, and economy—even on older models.

For example, a single-grade oil may have to be discarded after a short period of service owing to the early arrival of winter temperatures. A multi-grade oil, suitable for both summer and winter temperatures, can be left in the engine until the normal oil change mileage has been reached. This feature of multi-grade oils can save the expense of oil changes necessitated by climatic conditions.

Also to be considered is that some oil grades and ratings, as originally recommended for 1973 and 1974 models, may eventually become unavailable. As old stocks of motor oil become depleted, new containers bearing the identifying marks of the new rating system will replace those bearing the identifying marks of older systems. By becoming familiar with the new oil recommendations, you can be sure that the oil you buy is the correct kind for your car. Inferior lubricants, no matter how attractively priced, are not a good investment; using the wrong oil will greatly shorten the service life of your car.

Oil Viscosities

The viscosity grade of oil is designated by an SAE (Society of Automotive Engineers) standard number. An oil designated SAE 40 has a higher viscosity (greater resistance to flow) than an oil designated SAE 30. Multi-grade oils have an extended viscosity range and can be used in place of a number of single-grade oils. For example, an SAE 10W-30 oil is suitable for use within a range of temperatures that would require three different single-grade oils in order to cover it (SAE 10W, SAE 20W/20, and SAE 30). **Table a** or **Table b** lists the proper oil viscosity for VW engines under specific climatic conditions. Particularly with the diesel engine, the viscosity SAE number of the oil should be selected for the lowest anticipated temperature at which engine starting will be required, and not for the temperature at the time of the oil change. Because the temperature ranges of the different oil grades overlap, brief variations in outside temperatures are no cause for alarm.

Table a. Spark-ignition Engine Oil Viscosity Specifications

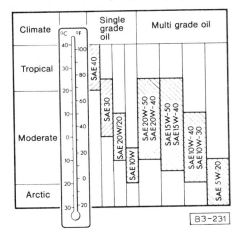

Table b. VW Diesel Engine Oil Viscosity Specifications

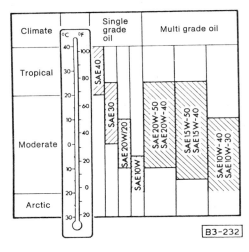

CAUTION

Avoid high-speed, long distance driving when using SAE 5W or SAE 10W oil—especially if the outside temperature rises above the limits given for these lubricants. If you anticipate continuous operation that will impose maximum loads on the engine, or if you expect to drive at sustained speeds above 60 mph (100 kph), use the next higher viscosity oil. Under these conditions, SAE 5W or SAE 10W oil may be inadequate to maintain a proper lubricating film between the moving parts of the engine.

The viscosity of transmission oil is also designated by SAE numbers. Use SAE 80W or SAE 80W/90 for general year-round service in the manual transmission. Always use SAE 90 hypoid oil in the final drive of the automatic transmission. ATF is not graded for viscosity and requires no seasonal change.

Greases

Two types of grease are used for lubrication of chassis and driveline parts. Multipurpose grease (lithium grease) has a wider temperature tolerance range than ordinary grease and should be used for most lubrication purposes. The additives in multipurpose grease give it increased pressure resistance and anticorrosion capabilities. It is suitable for use both in plain bearings and in roller bearings. Molybdenum grease is lithium grease with a friction-reducing molybdenum disulfide additive. It is used in the constant velocity joints of the front axle. Use dry stick lubricant in the hood locks and on the sliding surfaces of the door striker plates. The battery terminals should be coated with either silicone spray or petroleum jelly.

2. MAINTENANCE SCHEDULES

The maintenance schedules given in **Table c** should be followed carefully even if your car is not being serviced by an Authorized Dealer. The right-hand column on page 6 tells where each maintenance job is covered in this Manual. For example, the first operation listed in the table, changing the engine oil, is covered in Section 10 (Lubrication and Maintenance) under heading 3.1 (Changing Engine Oil). The sixth operation listed in the table, checking the valve clearances, is covered in Section 3 (Engine and Clutch) under heading 5.2 or, for VW diesel engines, in section 11 (Diesel Engine) under heading 4.2.

10

NOTE

Though no replacement interval is prescribed by VW, the publisher recommends that you replace the VW diesel engine's camshaft drive belt each 50,000 mi. (80,000 km).

Table b. Scheduled Maintenance Services

Maintenance operations			Where operation is covered in Manual
Changing engine oil and checking the oil level			SECTION 10 HEADING 3.1
Replacing oil filter			SECTION 10 HEADING 3.1
Servicing and replacing spark plugs			SECTION 3 HEADING 3.5
Replacing ignition points and, if necessary, distributor cap, distributor rotor, and secondary cables			SECTION 3 HEADING 3.2
Checking ignition point gap or dwell, checking ignition timing			SECTION 3 HEADING 3.2
Checking valve clearance and replacing cylinder head cover gasket	VW Diesel: SECTION 11 HEADING 4.2	Other: SECTION 3 HEADING 5.2	
Checking cylinder compression			SECTION 10 HEADING 4.3
Cleaning and inspecting air cleaner filter element			SECTION 10 HEADING 4.2
Replacing air cleaner filter element			SECTION 10 HEADING 4.2
Checking exhaust system			SECTION 10 HEADING 5.1
Checking clutch pedal freeplay			SECTION 3 HEADING 9.3
Checking V-belt adjustment and belt condition	VW Diesel: SECTION 11 HEADING 4.6	Other: SECTION 3 HEADING 5.4	
Checking and adjusting idle	VW Diesel: SECTION 11 HEADING 10.1	Other: SECTION 7 HEADING 5	
Checking cooling system	VW Diesel: SECTION 11 HEADING 3	Other: SECTION 3 HEADING 4	
Replacing fuel filter (drain diesel filter between changes)	VW Diesel: SECTION 11 HEADING 10.6	Other: SECTION 7 HEADING 7.4	
Checking injectors and, if necessary, cleaning or rebuilding them			SECTION 11 HEADING 10.7
Checking operation and condition of emission controls			SECTION 7 HEADING 5 & 9
Replacing EGR filter			SECTION 7 HEADING 9
Checking and, if necessary, cleaning air injection pump filter			SECTION 10 HEADING 4.5
Replacing air injection pump filter			SECTION 10 HEADING 4.5
Replacing catalytic converter			SECTION 7 HEADING 9
Replacing activated charcoal filter canister			SECTION 10 HEADING 4.4
Checking PCV system			SECTION 10 HEADING 4.1
Visually checking fuel tank, EEC hoses, and charcoal filter canister			SECTION 7 HEADING 3
Checking operation of lights and switches			SECTION 10 HEADING 6.4
Checking headlight aim			SECTION 4 HEADING 8.1
Checking windshield wipers and washers			SECTION 4 HEADING 7
Checking battery			SECTION 4 HEADING 3.1
Testing charging and starting systems			SECTION 4 HEADING 5.1 & 4.1
Checking constant velocity joint screws and boots			SECTION 10 HEADING 5.4
Checking and correcting transmission hypoid oil level (manual and automatic transmission)			SECTION 10 HEADING 5.3
Changing manual transmission hypoid oil and cleaning magnetic drain plug			SECTION 10 HEADING 5.3
Checking automatic transmission ATF level			SECTION 10 HEADING 5.2
Checking automatic transmission ATF pan bolts			SECTION 10 HEADING 5.2
Changing ATF: draining and filling automatic transmission, cleaning ATF pan and strainer			SECTION 10 HEADING 5.2
Checking automatic transmission kickdown operation			SECTION 10 HEADING 6.4
Checking brake fluid level			SECTION 9 HEADING 9.1
Changing brake fluid and checking brake warning light operation			SECTION 9 HEADING 9.1
Checking brake pressure regulator pressures			SECTION 9 HEADING 4.4
Visually checking brake pressure regulator			SECTION 9 HEADING 4.4
Checking remaining thickness of brake pads and linings			SECTION 9 HEADING 8.2
Checking for brake adjustment (pedal height)			SECTION 10 HEADING 6.4
Checking parking brake adjustment and lubricating compensator			SECTION 9 HEADING 10.1
Checking brake lines and hoses for leaks and damage			SECTION 9 HEADING 6
Checking brake lights			SECTION 9 HEADING 4.1
Checking tires for wear, damage, and correct inflation pressures			SECTION 9 HEADING 11
Checking ball joint dust seals and tie rod end dust seals			SECTION 10 HEADING 5.6
Checking steering play			SECTION 10 HEADING 6.4
Checking steering gearbox boots for leaks, tears, or other damage			SECTION 10 HEADING 5.5
Checking front wheel camber and toe			SECTION 8 HEADING 3
Lubricating door hinges and door checks			SECTION 10 HEADING 6.1
Lubricating hood and trunk lid hinges and locks			SECTION 10 HEADING 6.1
Lubricating oil can points (throttle linkage, clutch linkage, etc.)			SECTION 10 HEADING 6.2

Service intervals (given in thousands of miles/thousands of kilometers)		
1973-1974 models	**1975 models**	**1976 and later models**
5/8	5/8	7.5/12
10/16	15/24	15/24
10/16	15/24	15/24*
10/16	15/24	15/24*
10/16	15/24	15/24*
20/32	15/24	15/24
10/16	15/24	15/24
10/16 or every 2 years min.	15/24	15/24
20/32	30/48	30/48
10/16	15/24	15/24
10/16	15/24	15/24
10/16	15/24	15/24 (replace VW diesel belt 30/48)
10/16	15/24	15/24
10/16	5/8	7.5/12
N/A	N/A	15/24
N/A	N/A	60/96 (VW diesel only)
10/16	15/24	15/24*
20/32	15/24	replace when EGR light comes on*
10/16	15/24	N/A
20/32 or every 2 years min.	30/48	N/A
N/A	30/48	replace when CAT light comes on*
50/80	when inspection shows need	when inspection shows need
10/16	15/24	15/24
10/16	15/24	15/24
10/16	15/24	15/24
10/16	15/24	15/24
10/16	15/24	15/24
10/16	15/24	15/24
10/16	15/24	15/24
10/16	15/24	15/24
30/48	unnecessary except after repair	unnecessary except after repair
10/16	15/24	15/24
10/16	30/48	30/48
30/48	30/48	30/48
10/16	15/24	15/24
10/16	15/24	15/24
every 2 years	every 2 years	every 2 years
every 2 years	every 2 years	every 2 years
N/A	15/24	15/24
10/16	15/24	15/24
10/16	15/24	15/24
10/16	when inspection shows need	when inspection shows need
10/16	15/24	15/24
10/16	15/24	15/24
10/16	15/24	15/24
10/16	15/24	15/24
10/16	15/24	15/24
10/16	15/24	15/24
20/32	15/24	15/24
10/16	15/24	15/24

*Except VW diesel

10

3. OIL CHANGE SERVICE

In addition to the operations described under **3.1 Changing Engine Oil,** you should check the coolant level in the radiator at each oil change. Do not remove the radiator cap until the engine has had an opportunity to cool. Otherwise, the radiator may overflow and some coolant will be lost. The coolant level should reach the full mark, as indicated in Fig. 3-1, or by the Min. and Max. marks on cars with expansion tanks (see Fig. 3-2). If it is necessary to add coolant, follow the instructions given in **ENGINE AND CLUTCH** or **DIESEL ENGINE.**

Fig. 3-1. Radiator full mark (arrow).

While you are changing the oil, it is wise to check the battery electrolyte as described in **ELECTRICAL SYSTEM.** First test the specific gravity of the electrolyte with a hydrometer. Then, if necessary, add distilled water in order to bring the electrolyte level above the cell separators or to the bottom of the filler tubes on batteries that are so equipped.

3.1 Changing Engine Oil

The oil should be drained from the engine while it is hot. Drive the car to a level place and stop the engine. Drain the oil by placing a pan of at least 6 liters (or 6 quarts) capacity beneath the engine. Then remove the oil drain plug from the engine's oil pan and allow the oil to drain into the collecting pan. If you are going to change the oil filter, as described under the next heading, you can do this job while the oil is draining.

When the flow has diminished to one drop per minute, reinstall the drain plug. Torque the plug to 3.0 mkg (22 ft. lb.). Then, if you have changed the oil filter, refill the crankcase with 3.7 U.S. quarts (3.2 Imperial quarts, 3.5 liters) of oil labeled "For Service SE" on spark-ignition engines or "For Service CC" on VW diesel engines. If you have not changed the oil filter, you will need only 3.2 U.S. quarts (2.7 Imperial quarts, 3.0 liters) of this oil.

NOTE ——

Always make a final check of the oil level after the engine has been run long enough to fill the filter and has been stopped long enough for oil to drain down off internal engine parts. Make sure that the level is correct on the dipstick before you drive the car. See Fig. 3-2.

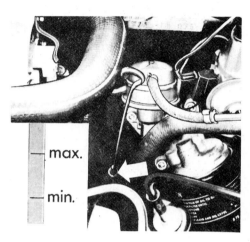

Fig. 3-2. Engine oil dipstick (arrow). The oil should be between the min. and the max. marks on the dipstick. The difference between the marks is about 1 U.S. quart (.85 Imperial quart or 1 liter).

Replacing Oil Filter

The oil filter is located on a flange, on the left-hand side of the engine. To change the filter, place a drip pan beneath the filter location. Then, using an oil filter wrench, turn the filter counterclockwise until it is off the flange. Wipe clean the gasket surface of the flange. Coat the gasket of the new filter with engine oil, then screw on the filter as tightly as you can using your bare hand only.

After you have refilled the engine with oil, run the engine until the new filter is filled and under pressure. Check visually for leaks around the filter. Stop the engine and, after waiting for the oil to drain down off the engine's internal parts, recheck the oil level.

4. ENGINE COMPARTMENT MAINTENANCE OPERATIONS

Because the automatic transmission fluid dipstick is located in the engine compartment, you should check the ATF level before you raise the car on a hoist. Instructions for checking the ATF level are given in **5.2 Checking and Correcting ATF Level.**

4.1 Checking PCV (Positive Crankcase Ventilation) System

The engine has no PCV valve that requires periodic cleaning or replacing. The PCV system consists of a hose that connects the cylinder head cover with the air cleaner. You can quick-check the system by disconnecting the hose from the cylinder head cover and blowing through it.

At the prescribed service interval, remove the PCV hose. Soak the hose in a low volatility petroleum-base solvent. Scrub out the inside of the hose with a suitable brush. Then blow the hose dry with compressed air.

4.2 Servicing Air Cleaner

The air cleaner used on fuel injection engines is different from the air cleaners used on engines with carburetors. All the dust that is present in the air drawn into the engine is trapped and retained by the pleated paper filter element in the air cleaner.

To service carburetor air cleaner:

1. Release the clips (**A** in Fig. 4-1), then lift the cover off the air cleaner.

2. Cover the carburetor's air intake (**C** in Fig. 4-1) in order to prevent the accidental entry of dirt.

3. Lift out the pleated paper filter element (**B** in Fig. 4-1).

4. If you have removed the filter element for inspection purposes only, first tap the element lightly on a hard surface in order to knock off all loose dust. Never wash the filter element in solvent or blow it off with a powerful blast of compressed air. This can ruin the filter. After knocking off the dust, hold the filter up to a bright light and check for cracks in the pleats. If any crack or hole is found, replace the filter element.

Fig. 4-1. Carburetor engine air cleaner. Components indicated by letters are identified in text.

5. Before installing either a new or a used filter element, wipe clean the air cleaner housing (**D** in Fig. 4-1) using a lightly oiled, lint-free cloth.

6. Install the filter element and the cover.

To service fuel injection air cleaner:

For access to the rectangular pleated paper filter element, release the clips indicated in Fig. 4-2. Lift up on the mixture control unit, then withdraw the filter element. If you have removed the filter element for inspection purposes only, first tap the element lightly on a hard surface in order to knock off all loose dust. Never wash the filter element in solvent or blow it off with a powerful blast of compressed air. This can ruin the filter. After knocking off the dust, hold the filter up to a bright light and check for cracks in the pleats. If any crack or hole is found, replace the filter element. Installation is the reverse of removal.

CAUTION ——

In installing either a new or used filter, the word UP, which is printed in large letters on one side of the filter element, must be toward the mixture control unit. This is especially important when you install a used filter because, with the filter inverted, previous accumulations of dirt will be drawn into the engine.

Fig. 4-2. Air cleaner of fuel injection engines. Clips **A** hold air cleaner to bracket on body. Clips **B** hold the mixture control unit to the air cleaner.

10

To service VW diesel engine air cleaner:

1. Release the clips that hold the air cleaner's plastic housing to the engine's air intake manifold (Fig. 4-3). Then pull the plastic housing off the manifold.

2. Lift out the pleated paper filter element.

Fig. 4-3. VW diesel engine air cleaner. Plastic housing is at **a**, one of clips is at **b**.

3. If you have removed the filter element for inspection only, first tap the element lightly on a hard surface in order to knock off all loose dust. Never wash the filter element in solvent or blow it off with a powerful blast of compressed air. This can ruin the filter. After knocking off the dust, hold the filter up to a bright light and check for cracks in the pleats. If any crack or hole is found, replace the filter element.

4. Before installing either a new or a used filter element, wipe clean the air cleaner housing using a lightly oiled, lint-free cloth.

5. Install the filter element and the front part of the air cleaner.

CAUTION ——

In installing either a new or a used filter, the word UP, which is printed in large letters on one side of the filter element, must be toward the air cleaner's plastic cover. This is especially important when you install a used filter because, with the filter reversed, previous accumulations of dirt will be drawn into the engine.

4.3 Testing Engine Compression

To check the cylinder compression on a spark-ignition engine, remove the spark plugs. Then install a compression testing gauge in one of the spark plug holes. Crank the engine with the starter for a few moments while the accelerator is pressed to the floor or while the throttle valves are

held wide open. Normal compression pressure is 142 to 184 psi (10 to 13 atu). If the pressure for any cylinder is below 107 psi (7.5 atu)—or if the pressure differential between any two cylinders exceeds 42 psi (3.0 atu)—the valves may need to be ground, piston rings replaced, or the cylinders bored to accept new oversize pistons.

To check the cylinder compression on a VW diesel engine, remove the electrical wire from the stop control on the injection pump; insulate the wire end with tape. Remove the injector pipes and the injectors, as described in **DIESEL ENGINE**. Install adaptor VW 1323/2 and a compression gauge as indicated in Fig. 4-4—using the old injector heat shield between the adaptor and the injector seat in the cylinder head. Crank the engine with the starter for a few moments, then read the compression gauge. Normal compression pressure is 398 to 483 psi (28 to 34 kg/cm²). If the pressure for any cylinder is below the 398 psi (28 kg/cm²) wear limit—or if the pressure differential between any two cylinders exceeds 71 psi (5 kg/cm²)—the valves may need to be ground, the piston rings replaced, or the cylinders bored to accept new oversize pistons.

CAUTION ——

Remove the heat shields from the injector holes of the three cylinders not being tested. Otherwise, the shields may be sucked into the engine. To prevent leakage, always use new heat shields when you install the injectors.

Fig. 4-4. Compression gauge installed in VW diesel engine. All injectors must be removed during a compression test.

To determine whether it is the piston rings or the valves that are causing low compression, squirt a small quantity of SAE 40 oil into the low-reading cylinder(s) through the spark plug hole(s). Then repeat the compression test. If the readings are significantly higher, the piston rings, pistons, or cylinders are at fault. If the compression pressure reading(s) are still low, suspect faulty valves.

Before assuming the problem is in the valves, however, check the valve adjustment to make sure that there is at least a small amount of clearance between the camshaft lobes and the adjusting discs. If there is no measurable gap, adjust the valves as described in **ENGINE AND CLUTCH** or **DIESEL ENGINE,** then repeat the compression test. If the pressure is still low, the valves need grinding.

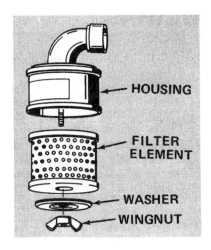

Fig. 4-5. Components of air pump air cleaner.

4.4 Replacing Activated Charcoal Filter Canister

The activated charcoal filter canister is located in the engine compartment. It is connected by a hose to the air cleaner.

To replace the canister, remove the hoses that are connected to it, then take out the Phillips head screw in the canister mounting bracket. Note the positions of the hose installations, so the hoses will be installed on the new canister in their correct positions. Installation is the reverse of removal.

4.5 Cleaning and Replacing Air Injection Pump Air Filter

The air cleaner for the air pump has a pleated paper filter element. Remove the hose clamp that holds the air cleaner to the pump. Then remove the air cleaner and disassemble it as shown in Fig. 4-5. To clean the filter element, tap it against a hard surface in order to knock off all loose dirt. Replace torn or damaged filters. Assemble and install the air cleaner using either a cleaned or a new filter, as specified in **2. Maintenance Schedules.**

> **WARNING** ——
> *Never wash the filter element in solvent. This will not only ruin the filter but could cause a fire or explosion.*

4.6 Adjusting or Replacing VW Diesel Engine Water Pump V-belt

The V-belt tension and condition should be checked each 15,000 mi. (24,000 km), and the belts should be replaced each 30,000 mi. (48,000 km). Adjustment and replacement of the alternator V-belt are covered in **ELECTRICAL SYSTEM,** in conjunction with the procedure given for removing and installing the alternator. The procedure given here applies only to the water pump V-belt. During inspection, replace any V-belt that is cracked, oil-soaked, deteriorating, or worn at any point so that it contacts the bottom of the pulley grooves.

To remove the water pump V-belt, or to adjust its tension, remove the three bolts that hold the water pump pulley to the water pump. Then remove the pulley components and the V-belt. To increase the belt tension, remove one or more shims from between the pulley halves; to decrease the belt tension, add one or more shims between the pulley halves. When the tension is correct you should just be able to depress the belt 10 to 15 mm (⅜ to ⁹/₁₆ in.) at a point midway between the crankshaft pulley and the water pump pulley.

Place ahead of the pulley front half any shim removed from between the pulley halves when you reassemble the pulley and bolt it to the water pump. By doing this you will keep all of the shims supplied with the car available for future use. (Shims must usually be moved from the storage point to a position between the pulley halves when a new V-belt is installed.) An illustration showing the arrangement of shims and other pulley components can be found in the cooling system topic of **DIESEL ENGINE.**

10 ■

5. UNDER-CAR MAINTENANCE OPERATIONS

Except for checking the level of the automatic transmission fluid (ATF), which should be done with the car on the ground, the maintenance operations described under the next six numbered headings should be done with the car raised on a hoist. Alternatively, you can support the car on jack stands.

> **WARNING** ——
>
> *Never work beneath a car that is supported solely by a jack. There is a very real danger that the jack may fail or accidently release, allowing the car to fall.*

5.1 Checking Exhaust System

Momentarily cover the tailpipe opening with a pad of rags while the engine is running. Hissing sounds coming from under the car signal leakage. Darker or lighter areas around joints in the system may indicate escaping gases. Check that the exhaust pipe and muffler mountings are secure and that the rubber parts of the mountings are in good condition.

5.2 Checking and Correcting ATF Level

(automatic transmission only)

The dipstick for the ATF in the automatic transmission is inserted into the ATF filler tube on the left-hand side of the engine (Fig. 5-1). The dipstick is attached to the cap for the ATF filler tube. The level should be checked with the ATF warm and the engine idling. The transmission selector lever must be in neutral and the parking brake set. Correct ATF level is very important for the proper functioning of the automatic transmission.

Pull out the dipstick and wipe it clean. The ring-shaped handle should be in a vertical position when you reinsert the dipstick to measure the fluid level.

Fig. 5-1. ATF dipstick handle (arrow), located near oil filter.

The ATF level is correct only if it falls between the two marks on the dipstick. Add ATF, if necessary, but only as much as is needed. Keep in mind that the difference between the lower and the upper marks is only 13.5 U.S. oz. (11.25 Imperial oz., 398 cm³). To add ATF, use a clean funnel with a 50-cm (20-in.) hose attached. The ATF added must be labeled Dexron®.

Changing ATF and Cleaning Sump and Strainer

The task of changing the ATF, cleaning the ATF pan and cleaning or replacing the strainer should always be done at the specified mileage. Do this work twice as frequently as specified if the car is used under severe conditions, such as trailer towing, stop-and-go driving, or extended mountain driving.

On cars with ATF drain plugs, remove the drain plug from the transmission ATF pan and allow as much ATF as possible to drain. See Fig. 5-2. On cars without ATF drain plugs, detach the filler tube and allow as much ATF as possible to drain. On all transmissions, remove the bolts that hold the ATF pan. Pry the pan loose, if necessary, then carefully lower it. Pour out the remaining ATF.

> **CAUTION** ——
>
> *Do not tow the car or run the engine while there is no ATF in the transmission. This could ruin the transmission bearings.*

Wash the ATF pan in solvent and dry it with compressed air. Never use fluffy rags when cleaning the automatic transmission. Lint from them could cause the control valves in the transmission to jam.

    b. ATF drain plug
    c. Hypoid oil drain plug
    d. Hypoid oil filler plug
    x. Pan bolts

Fig. 5-2. Automatic transmission drain and filler plugs.

Inspect the filter-type ATF strainer used only on 1976 cars and on 1977 cars through Transmission No. ET 20 096. If it is obviously dirty or clogged with debris from burned clutch or brake linings, replace it; this kind of strainer cannot be cleaned. The screen-type strainers used on 1973 through 1975 cars (Fig. 5-3) and on 1977 and later cars from Transmission No. ET 21 096 should be cleaned if they are dirty or clogged. During installation of either type of strainer, torque the screws or the bolt to 30 cmkg (26 in. lb.).

© 1974 VWoA—986

1. Manual valve
2. Kickdown solenoid
3. ATF strainer
4. Transfer plate
5. Valve body
6. Vacuum unit for primary throttle pressure valve

Fig. 5-3. Pre-1976 automatic transmission, pan removed. ATF strainer should be removed, cleaned with solvent, and dried carefully with compressed air.

Install the pan, using a new gasket. Working diagonally, tighten the pan screws to 1.0 mkg (7 ft. lb.) on pans with 13 bolts or to 2.0 mkg (14 ft. lb.) on pans with four bolts. Wait five minutes for the new gasket to compress, then retorque the screws. Repeat this sequence several times until the screws remain at torque.

> **CAUTION ——**
> *Never exceed the torque specifications in an attempt to cure a leaking gasket. Overtightening will deform the pan and make it impossible to get a good seal. Always install a new gasket to correct leaks.*

Refill the transmission with 6.3 U.S. pints (5.3 Imperial pints; 3.0 liters) of ATF. Do not fill above the top mark on the dipstick, as checked with the ATF warm, the engine idling in neutral, and the parking brake set. The ATF used must be labeled Dexron®.

5.3 Checking and Changing Hypoid Oil

The hypoid oil level in both the manual transmission and the final drive of the automatic transmission should be kept at the lower edge of the filler hole in the side of the transmission case or the final drive housing. The level is correct if hypoid oil just barely drips from the hole with the plug removed. The level may be considered satisfactory if you can feel it with your fingertip just below the edge of the filler hole. Hypoid oil is added, if necessary, through the oil filler hole (Fig. 5-4).

Fig. 5-4. Drain hole **(A)** and filler hole **(B)** of manual transmission. Locations are similar on automatic transmissions. See Fig. 5-2 given earlier.

The drain plug in the bottom of the manual transmission contains a magnet that traps metallic particles as they settle in the oil. The accumulation can be cleaned from the magnet periodically by removing the plug. Have a cork of appropriate size ready to plunge into the transmission drain hole as soon as the magnetic plug is removed. Very little hypoid oil will be lost if the filler plug is left installed so that air cannot enter readily. After cleaning the magnetic plug and reinstalling it, correct the hypoid oil level to make up for any that was lost.

Changing Hypoid Oil

It is unnecessary to change the hypoid oil of the transaxle with automatic transmission—unless the oil has become contaminated or a temperature change makes it necessary to use an oil of a different viscosity. However, the hypoid oil in either the automatic transmission transaxle or the manual transmission transaxle should always be changed 600 mi. (1000 km) after rebuilding the manual transmission or the final drive of the automatic transmission transaxle.

The hypoid oil in the manual transmission transaxle should be changed according to the mileage specified in **2. Maintenance Schedules.** The oil will drain faster if it is warm. Remove both the filler plug and the drain plug. Install the drain plug after drips have slowed to one every 20 seconds.

10

Refill with hypoid oil of the correct specification and viscosity. See **1. Lubricants.** On manual transmission trans-axles, pause occasionally while refilling to give the oil time to flow into the final drive portion of the case. If you attempt to put the oil in too rapidly, it may overflow and give the impression that the case is already full although only 2 or 3 pints have been put in. See **Table d.**

Table d. Hypoid Oil Refill Quantities

Final drive of automatic transmission transaxle	3.0 pints (2.5 Imperial pints, 1.4 liters)
Manual transmission transaxle	Initial filling: 4.2 pints (3.5 Imperial pints, 2.0 liters) At change: 3.4 pints (2.8 Imperial pints, 1.6 liters)

5.4 Checking Constant Velocity Joint Screws and Boots

The rubber boots over the constant velocity joints should not be cracked or torn. Instructions for removing the driveshafts and replacing the boots can be found in **MANUAL TRANSMISSION.**

The socket-head screws that hold the constant velocity joints to the flanges should be torqued to 3.5 mkg (25 ft. lb.).

5.5 Checking Steering Gearbox Boots

The rubber boots of the steering gearbox should not be cracked or torn. If dirt has entered the steering through a tear in a boot, the steering gearbox should be removed, disassembled, and cleaned before you install a new boot. See **SUSPENSION AND STEERING.**

5.6 Checking Ball Joint and Tie Rod Seals

The rubber seals on the suspension ball joints and the tie rod ends should be checked to make certain that none is torn or cracked. To replace seals, use the procedures given in **SUSPENSION AND STEERING.**

6. BODY AND INSIDE-VEHICLE MAINTENANCE OPERATIONS

There are only a few routine maintenance steps for the body and interior of your car, but they are important steps. Especially make sure that the driving controls are in good working order before you take the car on a road test following servicing.

6.1 Body Lubrication

Lubricate the door locks and the lock cylinders with lock lubricant. The body hinges, hood latch, auxiliary hood catch, and the door check straps should be lubricated with SAE 30 or SAE 40 engine oil or with polyethylene grease. To lubricate the door hinges, pry off the caps out of the tops of the hinges (Fig. 6-1). Then fill the cavities with SAE 40 engine oil. Use polyethylene or multipurpose grease on the seat runners, seat back pivots, and the trunk latch.

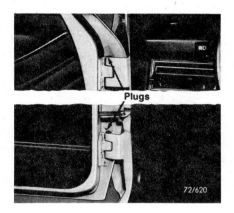

Fig. 6-1. Plugs in door hinges (arrows).

6.2 Oil Can Points

In addition to such things as the hood latches, already mentioned, you should check for other parts that require lubrication with an oil can. The clutch linkage (Fig. 6-2) and the carburetor linkage (Fig. 6-3) are two examples. Oil the adjustment points of the parking brake linkage in order to prevent corrosion. However, under no circumstances should you ever apply oil to rubber parts. Squeaking suspension bushings and similar rubber components should be lubricated with brake fluid or glycerine.

Fig. 6-2. Clutch linkage.

Fig. 6-3. Carburetor linkage.

6.3 Seat Belt Inspection

The seat belts should be kept clean. If cleaning is necessary, wash the belts with mild soap solution without removing them from the car. Do not bleach or dye the seat belts or use any other cleaning agents. They may weaken the webbing.

Carefully check the condition of the webbing while you are cleaning the belts or the interior of the car. Frayed or damaged belts should be replaced. Also check that the belts operate properly and are correctly installed.

6.4 Checking Controls

During inside-vehicle maintenance, be sure to check the headlight switch positions to see whether all tail lights, headlights, parking lights, instrument panel lights, and interior lights are in proper working order. Check the headlight high beams and low beams, the turn signals and, where applicable, the back-up lights.

Depress the foot brake pedal, making sure that there is good pedal height. If not, adjust the brakes as described in **BRAKES AND WHEELS.** Also check the operation of the parking brake. Turn the steering wheel from side to side with the car stationary. There should be no play. If there is excessive play, check the steering linkage for worn tie rod ends, worn suspension parts, or a worn or misadjusted steering gearbox. See **SUSPENSION AND STEERING.**

On cars with automatic transmissions, check the automatic transmission kickdown operation during a road test. If the kickdown fails to operate, or if the kickdown produces a forced downshift before the accelerator pedal reaches its full-throttle position, adjust the accelerator pedal and cable as described in **FUEL AND EXHAUST SYSTEMS.**

6.5 Body Preventive Maintenance

Clean debris from the body drain holes, including any holes in the bottoms of the doors. Make sure that the seat back latches hold the seat backs securely. If necessary, lubricate the latches with polyethylene or multipurpose grease.

Door weatherstrips should be lubricated with silicone spray or with talcum powder. If any weatherstrip is loose, clean away the old cement. Then reglue the weatherstrip with trim cement (available from automotive supply stores).

7. BASIC CAR CARE

The following brief guide will help you keep your car looking as good as it runs.

7.1 Care of Car Finish

The longer dirt is left on the paint, the greater the risk of damaging the glossy finish, either by scratching or simply by the chemical effect dirt particles have on the painted surface.

Washing

Never wash the car in direct sunlight. Beads of water not only leave spots when dried rapidly by the sun's heat, but act as tiny magnifying glasses that burn spots into the finish. Use plenty of water, a car-wash soap, and a soft sponge.

Begin by spraying water over the dry car to remove all loose dirt. Then apply lukewarm soapy water. Rinse the car after sponging off the soapy water, using plenty of clear water under as little pressure as possible. Wipe the car dry with a chamois or soft terrycloth towel to prevent water-spotting.

Waxing

For a long-lasting, protective, and glossy wax finish, apply a hard wax, such as Classic Car Wax, after the car has been washed and dried. Waxing is not needed after every washing, and a more effortless shine can be obtained by using a car-wash liquid containing wax. You can tell when waxing is required by looking at the finish while it is wet. If the water coats the paint in smooth sheets instead of forming beads that roll off, waxing is in order.

10 ■

Polishing

Use paint polish only if the finish assumes a dull look after long service. You can use polish on the car's brightwork to remove tar spots and tarnish, but afterwards apply a coat of wax to protect the clean plating.

Washing Chassis

The best time to wash the underside of the car is just after it has been driven in the rain. Spray the chassis with a powerful jet of water to remove dirt and deicing salt that may have accumulated there.

Special Cleaning

Tar spots can be removed with tar remover. Never use gasoline, kerosene, nail polish remover, or other unsuitable solvents. Insect spots also respond to tar remover. A bit of baking soda dissolved in the wash water will facilitate their removal. This method can also be used to remove spotting from tree sap.

The windshield wiper blades can be removed periodically and scrubbed with a hard bristle brush and alcohol or a strong detergent solution to remove debris. The windows themselves can be cleaned with a sponge and warm water, then dried with a chamois or soft towel. If you use commercial window washing preparations, make certain they are not damaging to automotive finishes.

7.2 Care of Interior

Clean the carpet with a vacuum cleaner or whisk broom. Dirt spots can usually be removed with lukewarm soapy water. Use spot remover for grease and oil spots. Do not pour the liquid directly on the carpet, but dampen a clean cloth and rub carefully, starting at the edge of the spot and working inward. Do not use gasoline, naptha, or other flammable substances to clean the carpeting.

Leatherette Upholstery and Trim

Use a dry foam cleaner. Grease or paint spots can be removed by wiping with a cloth soaked with this cleaner. Use the same cleaner, applied with a soft cloth or brush, on the headliner and side trim panels.

7.3 Tires and Accessories

Never use tar remover, gasoline, or any other petroleum-based substance for cleaning tires. These liquids damage rubber. Whitewall tires can be cleaned with tire sidewall cleaner. Rubber paints, commonly sold as tire dressing, are largely cosmetic.

Accessories

Most chrome-plated accessories can be polished and waxed along with the rest of the car's bright trim. The radio antenna should be lubricated only if hardened grease and collected dirt are interfering with raising or lowering the antenna. Do not use abrasive polish or cleaners on aluminum trim or accessories. They will destroy the mirror-like shine of anodized surfaces.

DIESEL ENGINE

Contents

Diesel Engine

The amazing flexibility and high-revving 5000-rpm performance of the lightweight Volkswagen diesel sets it well apart from the heavy, slow-turning diesels of yesteryear. Rated at 48 horsepower (SAE Net) at 5000 rpm (compared to 78 horsepower at 5500 rpm for the 1979 spark-ignition engine), the diesel is able to propel the Dasher to a top speed of 142 kph (88 mph). Nevertheless, it is in city traffic where the diesel shows to best advantage. According to VW engineers, the diesel uses about 50 percent less fuel in heavy traffic than does the available spark-ignition engine. One reason for this extra economy is that the diesel's good low-speed torque makes it possible to drive at low speeds in a higher gear. Also, the piston displacement of the diesel is a modest 1471 cm³ (89.7 in.³).

Driving the diesel is similar to driving the gasoline-powered Dasher, but on a chilly day starting the diesel takes slightly more time. Each of the cylinders has an electric glow plug to preheat the combustion pre-chamber for cold starts. Depending on how cold it is, the driver must wait from 15 to 60 seconds before starting. A light on the dashboard indicates when preheating is completed. Once the engine is warmed up, there is no need to preheat for subsequent restarting, and warm weather starts are immediate, as with a spark-ignition engine.

A major advantage of a diesel engine is that it eliminates the complication of spark ignition with its spark plugs, breaker points, condenser, ignition cables, distributor rotor and other components that may have to be replaced many times during the life of the car. However, for most owners it is the fuel economy that is the diesel's most attractive feature, and operating costs are further reduced by having no carburetor or emission controls to service periodically.

Quite a large number of special tools are needed to service some parts of the diesel engine. So if you lack the skills, tools, or a suitable workshop for repairing the diesel engine, we suggest you leave these repairs to an Authorized Dealer or other qualified shop. We especially urge you to consult your Authorized Dealer before attempting any repairs on a car still covered by the new-car warranty.

11

1. GENERAL DESCRIPTION

In most respects, the diesel engine is similar to the spark-ignition engine described in the **ENGINE AND CLUTCH** section of this Manual. Each kind of engine is water-cooled, with an overhead camshaft driven by a toothed belt. On the diesel engine, however, the belt also drives the fuel injection pump.

Engine Mounting

The engine and the transaxle are supported as a single unit by bonded rubber mountings. Bolts join the engine to the bellhousing of the transaxle. The engine can be removed without removing the transaxle, though the transaxle and the diesel engine can also be removed as a unit with the front subframe, as described in **SUSPENSION AND STEERING.**

Engine Block, Crankshaft, and Bearings

The cast-iron engine block is identical to that used on spark-ignition Volkswagen Dasher engines. There are, however, minor differences in how the casting is machined; the most notable difference is the cylinder bore diameters. Short block assemblies are of course quite different and crankshafts, bearings, and related parts should always be selected individually using the part numbers that are applicable to the diesel engine.

Cylinder Head and Valve Train

While the camshaft, the cam followers, and the valves are similar in design to those used in spark-ignition engines, individual components are likely to be different in many respects when designed for diesel service. By comparison to the cylinder head of the spark-ignition engine, the diesel head is a totally new design. However, the diesel head is aluminum so that it offers the same excellent heat dissipation qualities that are typical of other VW engines.

Connecting Rods and Pistons

Though the forged steel connecting rods are not unlike those used in the spark-ignition engines, the pistons are of far more robust dimensions and totally different in design. In the diesel, the pistons must be capable of attaining very high compression pressures and withstanding the shock of compression ignition. As on other VW engines, full-floating piston pins secured by circlips are used.

Construction and Accessories

The flywheel and clutch are similar to those used with spark-ignition engines. There are, however, detail differences in the lubrication system, the most noticeable of which are a larger, heavy-duty oil filter and a revised oil pump drive—the latter made necessary by the absence of an ignition distributor.

The cooling system is also somewhat different from that of the spark-ignition engine. Owing to the location of the diesel's fuel injection pump, the radiator top hose connection has been relocated to the opposite end of the cylinder head. The bottom hose connection is also changed slightly.

Diesel Engine Operation

Instead of using an electrical spark to ignite the fuel/air mixture in the combustion chamber, the diesel engine ignites its fuel by spontaneous combustion, working on the principle that air becomes hot when it is compressed. To obtain maximum compression pressure at all times, there is no throttle valve in the system—the intake ports are always "wide open." During the air intake stroke (Fig. 1-1), rotation of the crankshaft drives a toothed belt that turns the overhead camshaft so that the intake valve is open. As the piston moves downward, fresh air is drawn into the cylinder.

Fig. 1-1. Air intake stroke. Arrows indicate entry of air through intake valve and downward movement of piston.

The diesel engine's compression ratio is 23.5:1, almost three times as high as the compression ratio of the spark-ignition engine. On the compression stroke (Fig. 1-2), the piston moves upward with both valves closed. There is no fuel in the cylinder, only air, and this air is compressed into a space 23.5 times smaller than its original volume. At maximum pressure, the air temperature is forced up to 900°C (1650°F)—far above the flashpoint for diesel fuel.

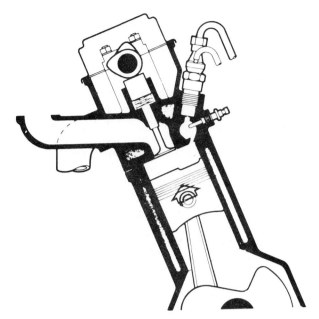

Fig. 1-2. Air compression stroke. Arrow indicates upward movement of piston.

Combustion takes place when the diesel fuel is injected (Fig. 1-3). As the piston reaches the top of its stroke, and the temperature of the compressed air is at its maximum, a mist of diesel fuel is injected at high pressure into the spherical pre-chamber. The hot air ignites the fuel and its burning causes the mixture to expand while the flame front spreads quickly from the pre-chamber to the cylinder. As the piston is now past TDC, it is driven downward by the force of the expanding gases produced by combustion, driving the crankshaft and the car.

Fig. 1-3. Fuel injection and combustion. Expanding gases (shading) drive piston downward on its power stroke (arrow).

As the energy of the fuel/air combustion is spent, the piston begins to move upward on its exhaust stroke (Fig. 1-4). The exhaust valve opens, releasing the burned gases from the cylinder so that the upward stroke of the piston pushes out the last of the combustion residuals. On the next downstroke of the piston, the entire cycle begins again with another air intake stroke. Thus, the VW is a four-stroke cycle diesel, having an intake stroke, a compression stroke, a power stroke, and an exhaust stroke as in the spark-ignition version of the powerplant.

Fig. 1-4. Exhaust stroke. Arrows indicate exit of exhaust gases and upward movement of piston.

2. MAINTENANCE

The following routine maintenance steps are covered briefly in **LUBRICATION AND MAINTENANCE** or in this section under the headings listed after some of the items.

1. Changing engine oil and checking oil level

2. Servicing fuel filter. **10.6**

3. Checking compression

4. Servicing the air cleaner

5. Checking the exhaust system

6. Checking clutch pedal freeplay. See **ENGINE AND CLUTCH**

7. Checking and adjusting idle and maximum rpm. **10.1**

8. Checking the cooling system. **3**

9. Checking V-belt adjustment. **3.3**

10. Checking valve clearance. **4.2**

11. Checking PCV hose

12. Checking fuel tank, lines, and connections for leaks

13. Checking injectors. **10.7.**

3. COOLING SYSTEM

To maintain the anti-corrosion properties of the coolant, you should use a permanent-type anti-freeze year-round. If coolant must be added, use the same proportion of water to anti-freeze that is already in the cooling system. Typical proportions are given in **Table a.**

> *CAUTION ——*
> *Never add cold water or coolant while the engine is hot or overheated. Doing this could crack the engine block or the cylinder head.*

The cooling system is unusual in that the thermostat is mounted in the external-type water pump and the cooling fan is powered by an electric motor. The cooling fan does not operate constantly, but only after the coolant has reached a temperature of about 90°C (194°F) or above. The advantages of this system are fast warm-up, stable operating temperature, low noise level while driving, fast heater reaction, and more available power from the engine. The thermo switch turns off the fan when the coolant temperature falls to between 85° and 90°C (185° and 194°F) or below.

3.1 Replacing Hoses

Hoses can be replaced using the procedures described for spark-ignition engines. Please refer to **ENGINE AND CLUTCH.**

3.2 Cooling System Troubleshooting

The cooling system troubleshooting topic of **ENGINE AND CLUTCH** also applies to cars that have diesel engines. However, in the cooling system troubleshooting table given in that section, all suggested repairs that are listed as being described under headings 4.3 and 4.4 of **ENGINE AND CLUTCH** should be performed as described under headings 3.3 and 3.4 of the **DIESEL ENGINE** section instead.

3.3 Removing and Installing Water Pump

The front part of the water pump, which contains the shaft, the seals, the bearing, and the impeller, can be replaced separately. However, you can avoid removing the camshaft drive belt and sprockets by removing the water pump as a unit before you disassemble it.

To remove:

1. Loosen the mounting bolts and nuts for the alternator and its adjusting bracket. Push the alternator toward the engine, then remove the V-belt.

2. Remove the expansion tank cap from the cooling system. Place a receptacle beneath the water pump for catching the draining coolant.

3. Detach the thermostat housing from the water pump (Fig. 3-1), remove the thermostat, and allow the coolant to drain. Also remove the drain plug from the right side of the engine block, if there is a plug (many late engines have none).

> *CAUTION ——*
> *Never drain the coolant while the engine is hot. Doing this could warp the engine block or the cylinder head.*

4. Using a screwdriver, loosen the hose clamps, two of which are indicated in Fig. 3-1. Slide the clamps toward the centers of the hoses, then pull the hoses off their connections on the water pump.

5. Unbolt the V-belt pulley from the water pump. Remove the pulley and the belt.

6. Take out the bolts that hold the water pump to the engine block. Remove the pump as you take out the last bolt.

Table a. Anti-freeze-to-Water Proportions

For outside temperatures down to	Anti-freeze			Water		
	Quarts	Imp. Quarts	Liters	Quarts	Imp. Quarts	Liters
−25°C (−13°F)	2.3	2.0	2.2	3.6	3.0	3.4
−30°C (−22°F)	2.7	2.3	2.6	3.2	2.7	3.0
−35°C (−31°F)	2.95	2.5	2.8	2.95	2.5	2.8
−40°C (−40°F)	3.2	2.7	3.0	2.7	2.3	2.6

Fig. 3-1. Hose clamps (**1**) and thermostat housing (**2**).

To install:

1. Install a new O-ring in the recess that surrounds the water outlet in the pump's mounting flange. Clean the surface of the engine block where it will be contacted by the pump and the O-ring.

   NOTE ──

   Do not use sealer between the water pump mounting flange and the engine block.

2. Using all four mounting bolts, loosely install the water pump on the engine. Then, tightening each bolt a little at a time, torque the mounting bolts to 2.0 mkg (14 ft. lb.).

3. Reinstall the water pump V-belt and the water pump's V-belt pulley. Adjust the belt tension using the pulley shims, as described in **LUBRICATION AND MAINTE-NANCE.** Torque the bolts for the pulley to 2.0 mkg (14 ft. lb.).

4. Reconnect the hoses and the thermostat housing to the water pump, using water resistant sealer on the hose connections and a new gasket between the thermostat housing and the water pump. Torque the bolts for the thermostat housing to 1.0 mkg (7 ft. lb.).

5. Push the alternator toward the engine and install the alternator's V-belt. By pulling the alternator away from the engine, adjust the V-belt tension so that you can depress the V-belt 10 to 15 mm (⅜ to ⁹/₁₆ in.) at a point midway between the alternator pulley and the crankshaft pulley.

6. When the V-belt tension is correct, torque the mounting bolts and nuts to 2.5 mkg (18 ft. lb.).

   CAUTION ──

   Do not tension either V-belt too tightly. Doing this may cause the alternator bearings or the water pump bearings to fail after only a short period of service.

7. To refill the cooling system, fully open the heater control valve. Then pour in coolant until the level is up to the full mark on the expansion tank. Install the cap and run the engine in order to bleed air out of the coolant circuit. After stopping the engine, add coolant if it is necessary to bring the level back up to the mark.

3.4 Disassembling and Assembling Water Pump

By working under the car, you can easily remove the thermostat housing and the thermostat with the water pump installed on the engine. Once you have removed the thermostat, you can test it as described in **ENGINE AND CLUTCH.** The mechanical (front) part of the water pump can also be removed from the water pump housing with the pump installed, but it is usually more convenient to remove the water pump first.

To disassemble:

1. If not removed previously, remove the three bolts and washers that hold the pulley on the water pump shaft.

   NOTE ──

   Though it is not absolutely necessary to remove the pulley, removing it will improve access to the bolts that hold the water pump together.

2. Remove the seven bolts and washers that hold the front part of the pump to the housing. Then remove the front part of the pump and the gasket.

11

3. Remove the two bolts and washers that hold the thermostat housing to the water pump housing. Then remove the thermostat housing, the O-ring, and the thermostat as shown in Fig. 3-2.

Assembly is the reverse of disassembly. Use a new O-ring between the thermostat housing and the water pump housing and a new gasket between the water pump housing and the front part of the pump. Tighten each of the seven bolts a little at a time until all are torqued to 1.0 mkg (7 ft. lb.). Torque the bolts that hold the pulley to the water pump hub to 2.0 mkg (14 ft. lb.) and torque the bolts for the thermostat housing to 1.0 mkg (7 ft. lb.).

3.5 Removing and Installing Radiator, Cooling Fan, and Air Ducts

The cooling fan, the radiator, and related parts are the same as on cars with spark-ignition engines. Please use the removal and installation procedures given in **ENGINE AND CLUTCH.**

4. VALVES, CAMSHAFT, AND CYLINDER HEAD

The camshaft drive belt, the camshaft, and the cylinder head can be removed from the engine without first removing the engine from the car. You do not need to replace the camshaft drive belt unless inspection shows it to be faulty.

Fig. 3-2. Exploded view of diesel engine cooling system, showing disassembly of water pump.

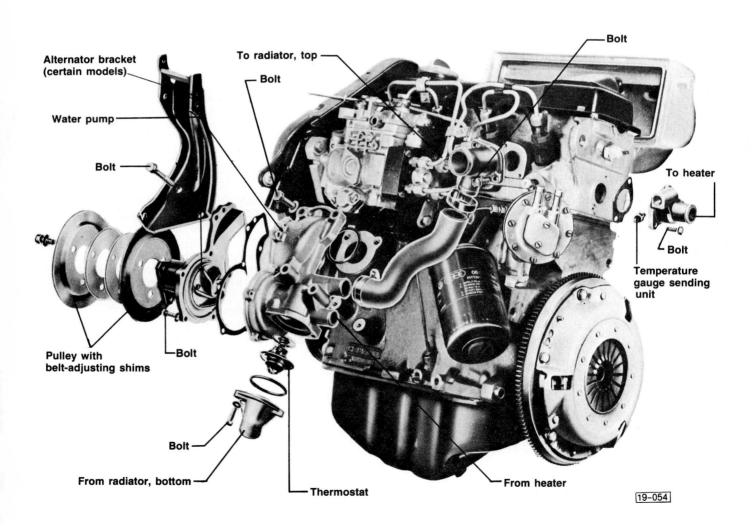

19-054

4.1 Removing, Installing, and Adjusting Camshaft Drive Belt

The removal of the camshaft drive belt and related parts is illustrated in Fig. 4-1. In replacing the drive belt, you need not remove the drive belt sprockets. Removal and installation of the injection pump is covered in **10.4 Removing and Installing Injection Pump.**

To remove camshaft drive belt:

1. Loosen the alternator mounting and adjusting bracket bolts. Push the alternator toward the engine, then remove the alternator V-belt.

2. Take out the four socket-head bolts that hold the crankshaft pulley to the crankshaft sprocket, then remove the pulley and the water pump V-belt.

3. Remove the nuts and bolts that hold the drive belt cover and remove the cover from the engine.

4. Remove the air cleaner, its duct, and the air filter.

5. Remove the eight bolts and cylinder head cover retaining plates. Then carefully lift off the cylinder head cover and its gasket. If the gasket is stuck to the cylinder head, use a dull knife to separate the gasket from the head.

Fig. 4-1. Camshaft drive belt removal.

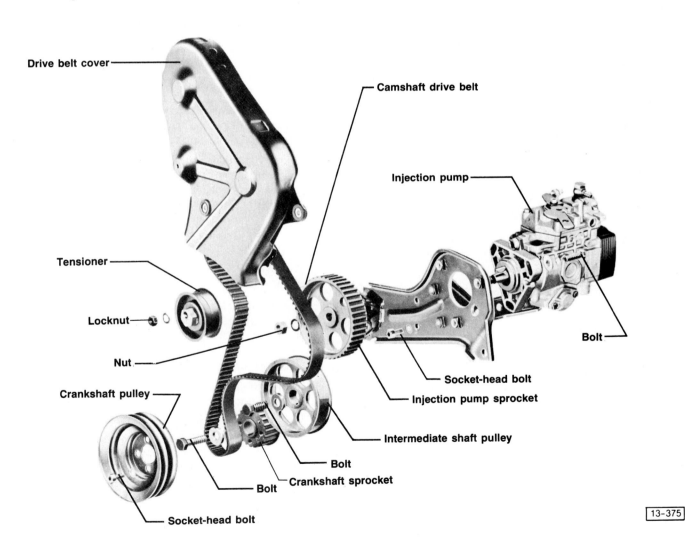

13-375

11

6. Using a wrench on the bolt that is in the center of the crankshaft sprocket, hand turn the crankshaft until the TDC mark on the flywheel is aligned with the pointer (Fig. 4-2) and both valves for the No. 1 cylinder are closed (cam lobes pointed upward).

7. If the drive belt has neither broken nor jumped time, lock the camshaft in position as shown in Fig. 4-2. Otherwise, do this when you are preparing to install the new drive belt.

Fig. 4-2. TDC marks aligned (arrow). Special tool 2065 is used to lock camshaft in position.

8. If the drive belt has neither broken nor jumped time, lock the injection pump sprocket in position as indicated in Fig. 4-3. Otherwise, do not attempt to install the pin until you are ready to install the new drive belt.

9. Loosen the camshaft drive belt tension adjuster locknut. Using a wrench on the tension adjuster, turn the adjuster counterclockwise so that tension is removed from the drive belt. Then remove the drive belt. (Work it off the sprockets toward the front of the car.)

Fig. 4-3. Injection pump sprocket locked in position with special pin 2064.

To install and adjust drive belt:

1. If you have not already done so, lock the camshaft and the injection pump in the No. 1 cylinder TDC positions as previously shown in Fig. 4-2 and Fig. 4-3.

2. Check that the TDC mark on the flywheel is still correctly aligned with the pointer.

3. Loosen the camshaft sprocket bolt ½ turn. Then loosen the sprocket from the camshaft tapered end by tapping the sprocket with a rubber hammer.

4. Check that the injection pump sprocket is still locked in place. Install the drive belt so that there is no slack between the camshaft sprocket and the injection pump sprocket or between the injection pump sprocket (via the intermediate shaft pulley) and the crankshaft sprocket. Then tighten the tension adjuster just enough to keep the belt firmly in place.

5. Remove the special locking pin from the injector pump sprocket.

6. Install the belt tension tester VW 210, as shown in Fig. 4-4. Then, by turning the tension adjuster one way or the other, tension the belt so that the tension tester reads 12 to 13. When the tension is correct, torque the tensioner locknut to 4.5 mkg (32 ft. lb.).

7. Torque the camshaft sprocket bolt to 4.5 mkg (32 ft. lb.). Then remove the locking tool from the camshaft.

8. Turn the crankshaft two full turns in the direction of normal crankshaft rotation (clockwise at the drive belt end). Strike the belt once with a rubber hammer between the camshaft sprocket and the injection pump sprocket. Then recheck the tension and, if necessary, correct it.

9. Check and, if necessary, correct the injection pump timing as described in **10.5 Adjusting Injection Timing.**

Fig. 4-4. Drive belt tension tester, VW 210, installed on engine.

The remainder of installation is the reverse of removal. Torque the bolts for the crankshaft pulley to 2.0 mkg (14 ft. lb.). By pulling the alternator away from the engine, adjust the V-belt tension so that you can depress the V-belt 10 to 15 mm (⅜ to ⁹⁄₁₆ in.) at a point midway between the alternator pulley and the crankshaft pulley. When the adjustment is correct, torque the alternator mounting nuts and bolts to 2.5 mkg (18 ft. lb.). If necessary, adjust the water pump's V-belt as described in **LUBRICATION AND MAINTENANCE.**

4.2 Adjusting Valves

The clearance between the heel of the cam lobe and the bucket-type cam follower is adjustable by means of replaceable adjusting disks (shims), as on the spark-ignition engine. (If you are unfamiliar with this system of adjustment, it will be helpful to refer to Fig. 5-6 given in **ENGINE AND CLUTCH.**)

The adjusting disks are available in twenty-six different thicknesses from 3.00 to 4.25 mm (.1181 to .1673 in.). The disks most frequently required in making adjustments fall in the thickness range of 3.55 to 3.80 mm (.1397 to .1496 in.). **Table b** lists the available disks by thickness and part number. The thickness of each disk is etched on its underside.

You can adjust the valves with the engine hot—coolant temperature approximately 35°C (95°F)—or with the engine cold. However, the clearance will be different depending on whether the engine is hot or cold.

Table b. Adjusting Disk Thicknesses and Part Numbers

Thickness mm	Part No.	Thickness mm	Part No.
3.00	056 109 555	3.65	056 109 568
3.05	056 109 556	3.70	056 109 569
3.10	056 109 557	3.75	056 109 570
3.15	056 109 558	3.80	056 109 571
3.20	056 109 559	3.85	056 109 572
3.25	056 109 560	3.90	056 109 573
3.30	056 109 561	3.95	056 109 574
3.35	056 109 562	4.00	056 109 575
3.40	056 109 563	4.05	056 109 576
3.45	056 109 564	4.10	056 109 577
3.50	056 109 565	4.15	056 109 578
3.55	056 109 566	4.20	056 109 579
3.60	056 109 567	4.25	056 109 580

To adjust valve clearance:

1. Remove the air cleaner, the duct, and the air filter. Remove the eight bolts and cylinder head cover retaining plates. Then carefully lift off the cylinder head cover and its gasket. If the gasket is stuck to the cylinder head, use a dull knife to separate the gasket from the head.

2. Using a wrench on the bolt that is in the center of the crankshaft pulley, hand-turn the crankshaft clockwise until both cam lobes for the No. 1 (front) cylinder are pointing upward. Then, to determine the valve clearance, insert feeler gauges of various thicknesses between the cam lobes and the adjusting disks (Fig. 4-5).

Fig. 4-5. Valve clearance being measured. Notice that both cam lobes for No. 1 cylinder are pointing up, away from the cam followers. The feeler gauge is inserted between the cam lobe and the adjusting disk that is on top of the cam follower.

11

The cylinders are numbered consecutively from the front to the rear of the engine. For example, the No. 4 cylinder is at the end of the engine that is bolted to the flywheel bellhousing of the transaxle.

With the engine hot, the intake valve clearance should be between 0.20 and 0.30 mm (.008 and .012 in.); exhaust valve clearance should be between 0.40 and 0.50 mm (.016 and .020 in.). With the engine cold, the intake valve clearance should be between 0.15 and 0.25 mm (.006 and .010 in.); exhaust valve clearance should be between 0.35 and 0.45 mm (.014 and .018 in.).

3. If either the intake or the exhaust valve clearance is incorrect, write down the actual clearance that you have measured. Then depress the cam followers with special tool VW 546 and lift out the adjusting disk(s) with special pliers (Fig. 4-6).

CAUTION ——

When you depress the cam followers of the diesel engine the piston must not be at TDC. Turn the crankshaft about ¼ turn past TDC so that the valves will not contact the piston when the cam followers are pressed down.

Fig. 4-6. Adjusting disk being removed. Special tool depresses both cam followers simultaneously. Special pliers (Tool 10-208) are used to remove disk from cam follower.

4. Read the thickness that is etched on the underside of the removed disk. (If the number has worn off, check the disk thickness with a micrometer.) Then determine the thickness of the required replacement disk as described in one of the next two steps.

5. If the measured clearance was less than the specified clearance range for the valve, subtract the measured clearance from the specified maximum clearance. Then subtract the difference from the thickness of the original disk in order to determine the thickness of the required replacement disk. If the computed thickness comes out equal to a standard disk thickness, or if the computed thickness is less than a standard disk thickness, use the next thicker disk.

6. If the measured clearance was greater than the specified clearance range for the valve, subtract the specified maximum clearance from the measured clearance. Then add the difference to the thickness of the original disk in order to determine the thickness of the required replacement disk. If the computed thickness comes out equal to a standard disk thickness, or if the computed thickness is less than a standard disk thickness, use the next thicker disk.

7. Install the required replacement disk(s) with the etched numbers toward the cam follower. Remove the special cam follower depressing tool. Then recheck the clearance to make sure that it is within the specified range.

8. Using a wrench on the bolt that is in the center of the crankshaft pulley, hand-turn the crankshaft 180° clockwise and repeat steps 1 through 7 on the No. 3 cylinder. Hand-turn the crankshaft another 180° and adjust the valves of the No. 4 cylinder, and, finally, 180° farther to adjust the valves of the No. 2 cylinder.

9. Install the cylinder head cover. Torque the bolts to 1.0 mkg (7 ft. lb.).

4.3 Removing and Installing Cylinder Head and Manifolds

The cylinder head can be removed (Fig. 4-7) without removing the engine from the car and without removing the camshaft or other valve gear prior to cylinder head removal.

To remove cylinder head and manifolds:

1. Remove the air cleaner, the duct, and the air filter. Then remove the camshaft drive belt as described in **4.1 Removing, Installing, and Adjusting Camshaft Drive Belt.**

2. Remove the expansion tank cap. Place a receptacle beneath the water pump for catching the draining coolant. Then unbolt the thermostat housing from the water pump, remove the thermostat, and allow the coolant to drain.

CAUTION ——

Never drain the coolant while the engine is hot. Doing this could warp the engine block or the cylinder head.

Fig. 4-7. Main components involved in cylinder head removal.

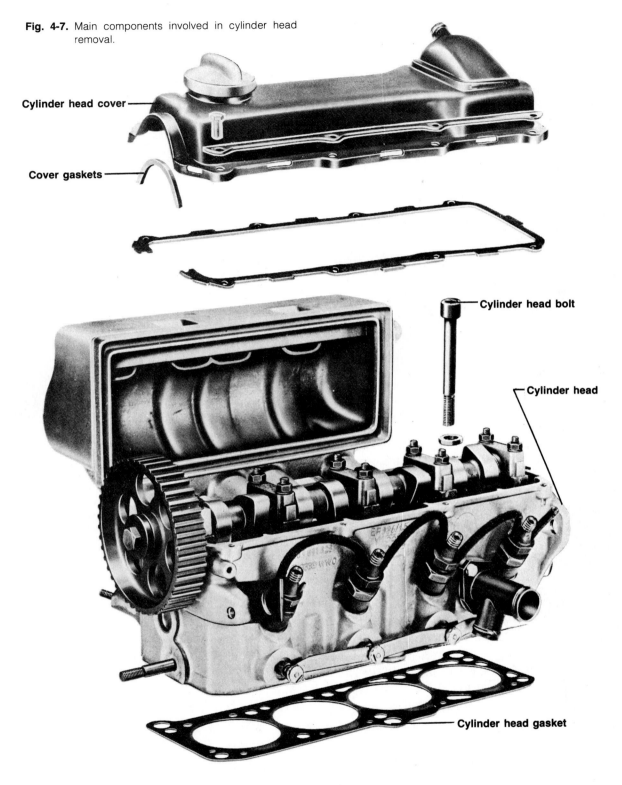

Cylinder head cover

Cover gaskets

Cylinder head bolt

Cylinder head

Cylinder head gasket

3. Disconnect the accelerator cable from the lever of the injection pump. If necessary, consult **10.2 Adjusting Cables.**

4. Disconnect the battery ground strap. Then detach the fuel lines from the injectors by unscrewing the unions. Disconnect the wire from the glow plug bus.

WARNING ——

Fuel will be expelled as you unscrew the unions. Do not smoke or work near heaters or other fire hazards. Have a fire extinguisher handy.

11

5. Disconnect the wire for the temperature gauge sending unit; disconnect any other wires that may be in a position to interfere with removal of the cylinder head.

6. Remove the four nuts that hold the exhaust pipe to the exhaust manifold. Unbolt the exhaust pipe support from the transaxle. See Fig. 4-8.

Fig. 4-8. Exhaust pipe flange (**25**).

7. Working beneath the car, remove the nuts and bolts that hold the exhaust manifold to the cylinder head. Then remove the exhaust manifold from the cylinder head.

8. Disconnect all coolant hoses from the cylinder head; disconnect any other hoses that may be in a position to interfere with cylinder head removal.

9. Remove the eight bolts and cylinder head cover retaining plates. Then carefully lift off the cylinder head cover and its gasket. If the gasket is stuck to the cylinder head, use a dull knife to separate the gasket from the head.

10. Beginning at the outer ends of the cylinder head and working toward the center from both directions, use a hex-shaped driver to remove the eight socket-head cylinder head bolts. (Follow the reverse of the tightening sequence that appears later in Fig. 4-13.)

11. Lift the cylinder head off the engine block. Place it on the workbench, then remove the injectors and the glow plugs before you do any other work on the cylinder head.

To install:

1. Knock out the pre-chamber inserts as shown in Fig. 4-9. Then thoroughly clean the cylinder head.

CAUTION ——

Do not use a metal scraper or a power-driven wire brush to clean the combustion chambers or gasket sealing surface. Doing this can gouge the aluminum, which could cause the head gasket to leak or leave scratches in the combustion chambers. Instead, use solvent to soften combustion chamber deposits, dried sealer, and material torn from the old head gasket. Then remove this foreign matter with a wooden or plastic scraper.

Fig. 4-9. Pre-chamber insert being driven out.

2. Thoroughly clean the gasket sealing surface of the cylinder block, clean the piston crowns, then clean the threads in the head bolt holes.

CAUTION ——

At TDC, the pistons project above the cylinder block, so be careful not to damage the piston head lands when you clean the block. To keep out dirt, stuff clean rags into the cylinder bores and seal all water and oil passages with tape. After you have cleaned the sealing surface of the block, use a thread-cutting tap or thread chaser to clean the bolt holes. It is extremely important that all debris be removed from the bottoms of the bolt holes after you have cleaned the threads.

3. Check the cylinder head for warping. To do this, lay a straightedge lengthwise across the sealing surface of the head as shown in Fig. 4-10. You should not be able to insert a 0.13-mm (.005-in.) feeler gauge between the sealing surface and the straightedge at any point. Repeat the check with the straightedge placed diagonally across the surface in both directions.

Fig. 4-10. A 0.10-mm (.004-in.) feeler gauge inserted between the straightedge and cylinder head sealing surface. 0.10 mm (.004 in.) is the maximum allowable distortion.

NOTE ——

If a 0.13-mm (.005-in.) feeler gauge can be inserted at any point, replace the cylinder head. Resurfacing is not practical because of the pre-chamber inserts.

4. Using the procedure you used for the head, check the engine block for warping. Warped blocks cannot be resurfaced, because of the piston projection, and must therefore be replaced.

5. Using a thread-cutting die, clean the cylinder head bolt threads. Do not use a power-driven wire brush, which could distort the threads. Replace damaged or distorted bolts. Then coat the bolt threads and the head bolt washers with anti-seize compound.

6. If you have replaced the pistons or are installing a short block assembly, you must measure the piston projection as shown in Fig. 4-11 in order to select a new cylinder head gasket from **Table c.** If the pistons and the block are the original components, select a head gasket that has the same identification marks as the original gasket. See Fig. 4-12.

NOTE ——

Piston projection is greater on late engines, beginning with Engine No. CK 024 944. See **8.1 Removing, Checking, and Installing Pistons, Piston Rings, Connecting Rods, and Connecting Rod Bearings.**

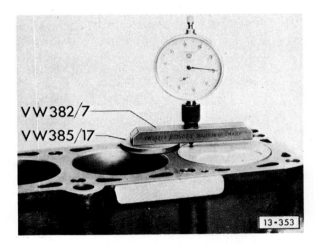

Fig. 4-11. Piston projection at TDC being measured with dial indicator. A depth micrometer can also be used.

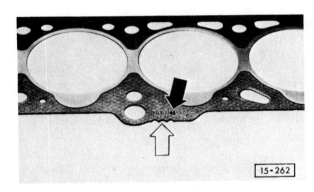

Fig. 4-12. Cylinder head gasket identification. Black arrow indicates Part No., white arrow indicates identification notches.

Table c. Available Cylinder Head Gaskets

Piston projection in mm (in.)	Gasket thickness in mm (in.)	Identification notches	Part No.
0.43–0.63 (.017–.025)	1.30 (.051)	2	068 103 383
0.63–0.82 (.025–.032)	1.40 (.055)	3	068 103 383 C
0.82–0.92 (.032–.036)	1.50 (.059)	4	068 103 383 G
0.92–1.02 (.036–.040)	1.60 (.063)	5	068 103 383 H

11 ■

7. Reinstall the pre-chamber inserts in the cylinder head. Then install a new cylinder head gasket atop the block so that the word OBEN (top) is uppermost. (OBEN is stamped into the gasket near the part number.)

CAUTION ——

Never install a cylinder head gasket that has previously been compressed by tightening the cylinder head bolts. Once compressed, these gaskets lose their resilience and will not produce a reliable seal if reused.

8. Carefully lower the cylinder head onto the gasket, using two of the outermost head bolts and washers to keep the gasket aligned with the cylinder head and to align the head with the block. With the cylinder head thus supported, loosely install the remaining head bolts and washers.

9. Following the sequence given in Fig. 4-13, torque the head bolts to 3.0 mkg (22 ft. lb.). Go over the sequence a second time, torquing the bolts to 6.0 mkg (43 ft. lb.), then a third time, torquing the bolts to 8.5 mkg (61 ft. lb.).

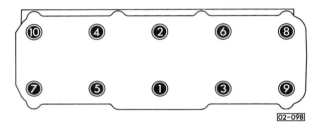

Fig. 4-13. Head bolt tightening sequence.

10. Install the remaining engine parts. See **4.1 Removing, Installing, and Adjusting Camshaft Drive Belt** and **3.1 Replacing Hoses.** Use a new gasket when you install the cylinder head cover and torque the bolts to 1.0 mkg (7 ft. lb.). Install a new gasket for the exhaust manifold. Torque all manifold nuts and bolts to 2.5 mkg (18 ft. lb.). Reconnect the hoses, cables, and wires to the fuel injection system as described in **10. Diesel Engine Fuel Injection.** Fill the cooling system as described in **3. Cooling System.**

NOTE ——

When you install the injectors, always install a new heat shield between the cylinder head and each injector.

11. Reconnect the battery ground strap, then start the engine. When it has warmed up to the specified temperature, adjust the idle speed to 850 to 1000 rpm as described in **10.1 Adjusting Idle and Maximum RPM.**

12. After the car has been driven for approximately 1000 miles (1500 km), remove the cylinder head cover with the engine stopped.

13. Following the reverse of the sequence given earlier in Fig. 4-13, loosen all of the cylinder head bolts by turning each one approximately 30° counterclockwise.

14. Following the sequence given earlier in Fig. 4-13, torque each cylinder head bolt to 8.5 mkg (61 ft. lb.) if the engine is cold or to 9.5 mkg (68 ft. lb.) if the engine is warm (coolant temperature 35°C (95°F) or above).

15. Check the valve clearances and, if necessary, adjust the clearances as described in **4.2 Adjusting Valves.**

16. Install the cylinder head cover. Use a new gasket if the old gasket is hardened or damaged.

4.4 Disassembling and Assembling Cylinder Head

You should not completely disassemble the cylinder head in one continuous operation. Instead, disassemble the head in stages, following the sequence given here, so that you can make various checks and measurements at each stage of disassembly. By doing this, you will be able to determine which parts can be reused and which parts require reconditioning or replacement.

Camshaft and Cam Followers

To check the condition of the camshaft and its bearings, you must first relieve the pressure that is exerted on the cam lobes by the valve springs. Relieving the pressure requires only that the camshaft be removed, the cam followers lifted out, and the camshaft reinstalled. The valves and valve springs need not be removed.

Five bearing caps hold the camshaft to the cylinder head. Each bearing cap is numbered to simplify correct installation, beginning at the camshaft drive end of the head. Because the factory has not always marked the numbers on the same ends of the caps, the numbered ends will not necessarily be toward the manifold side of the head as shown in Fig. 4-14. During bearing cap installation, observe the off center bearing position.

To remove the camshaft, remove the nuts and washers from bearing caps 5, 1, and 3 in that order. Then, loosening each of the four nuts a little at a time so that the valve spring tension is relieved evenly, simultaneously remove bearing caps 2 and 4. If this procedure is not followed, the camshaft may tilt in its bearings, which could damage the bearings or bend the camshaft.

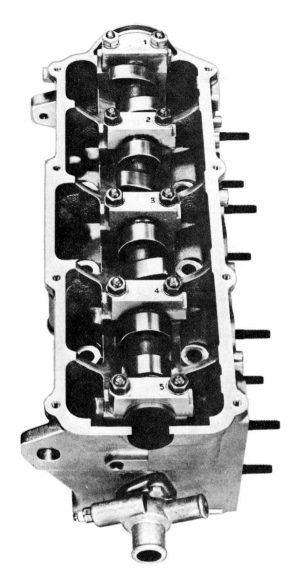

Fig. 4-14. Camshaft bearing caps and bearing cap nuts. There is a flat washer under each nut. It is important that the bearing caps be removed in the correct sequence.

To check camshaft axial play, remove the camshaft and lift out the cam followers. Number each cam follower as you remove it so that the followers can be reinstalled in their original bores. Install the camshaft using only bearing caps 1 and 5. Install a dial indicator as shown in Fig. 4-15. Move the camshaft forward and backward while you observe the dial indicator. Axial play should not exceed 0.15 mm (.006 in.). If the play is greater, the head or the camshaft is worn and must be replaced.

Fig. 4-15. Dial indicator being used to measure camshaft axial play.

To check the camshaft for bending and runout, install the camshaft between centers as shown in Fig. 4-16. Mount a dial indicator so that its gauge pin is against the center bearing journal on the camshaft. Then rotate the camshaft and observe the runout range shown by the dial indicator. If runout exceeds 0.01 mm (.0004 in.), replace the camshaft.

Fig. 4-16. Dial indicator being used to measure camshaft runout.

To measure camshaft bearing clearance, either install one bearing cap at a time and measure the camshaft's radial play with a dial indicator, or use Plastigage®. Plastigage is available from automotive supply stores. Further information on its use can be found in 8.1 Removing, Checking, and Installing Pistons, Piston Rings, Connecting Rods, and Connecting Rod Bearings. Camshaft bearing clearance should be between 0.02 and 0.05 mm (.0008 and .002 in.).

11

Inspect the camshaft lobes for wear (Fig. 4-17). Worn cam lobes are caused by a lack of lubrication. So always lubricate the cam lobes and the adjusting disks on the cam followers during assembly and make certain that the engine's oil passages are clear. Replace worn camshafts and worn adjusting disks.

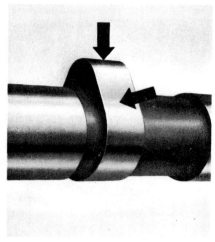

© 1974 VWoA—1242

Fig. 4-17. Cam lobe. Toe of cam (top arrow) should not be scored or worn unevenly. There should be no sign of wear at the second arrow. If there is wear at the second arrow, check for incorrect valve clearances, abrasive substances in the oil, or inadequate lubrication.

Inspect the cam followers for galling and signs of seizure—conditions that indicate a lack of lubrication. If aluminum from the cylinder head is found adhering to a cam follower, replace the cam follower. The cylinder head should be replaced if any of the cam follower bores is rough, gouged, worn, or otherwise damaged.

To install the cam followers and the camshaft, first clean all the parts in order to remove sludge and abrasive dirt. Lightly lubricate the cam follower bores with assembly lubricant (available from automotive supply stores), or with a thin coating of multipurpose grease. Then, with reference to the numbers marked on the cam followers during removal, install each cam follower in its original bore. If undamaged, install the original adjusting disks so that the valve clearance can be measured after you have installed the camshaft.

Coat the tops of the adjusting disks, the camshaft bearing surfaces, and the cam lobes with assembly lubricant or with a thin coating of multipurpose grease, then position the camshaft on the cylinder head. Loosely install bearing caps 2 and 4. Gradually tighten all four bearing cap nuts until the camshaft is drawn down fully and evenly into the bearing saddles. Then install bearing caps 5 and 3. Finally, install bearing cap 1. Torque the bearing cap nuts to 2.0 mkg (14 ft. lb.). Install the end plug at the rear end of the cylinder head. (Obtain a new plug if the original is damaged or does not fit tightly.) Install a new oil seal as shown in Fig. 4-18.

Fig. 4-18. Camshaft oil seal being installed.

If previously removed, install the drive belt sprocket on the camshaft. Then, gripping the sprocket, hand-turn the camshaft to the required positions so that you can adjust the valve clearances as described in **4.2 Adjusting Valves.**

NOTE ——

If the cylinder head is not installed on the engine block, you can delay the valve adjustment until after the cylinder head has been installed. By doing this, your adjustments will take into account minor clearance changes that may result from the torquing of the cylinder head bolts.

Valves and Valve Guides

You must remove the camshaft and the cam followers before you can remove the valves. Do not remove the valve guides unless they are worn badly enough to require replacement. The components of a valve assembly are shown disassembled in Fig. 4-19.

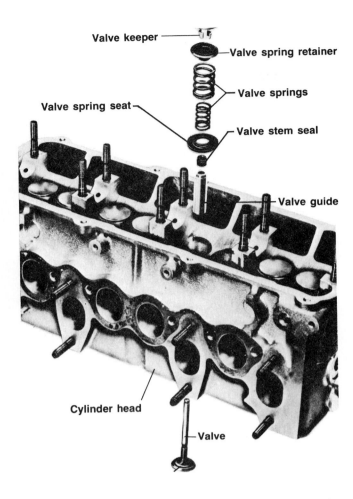

Fig. 4-19. Components of a valve assembly. The valve guides are a press fit in the cylinder head.

To remove valves:

1. With the camshaft and cam followers removed and the cylinder head removed from the engine, compress the valve springs as shown in Fig. 4-20. Doing this should press the valve spring retainer down the valve stem so that the split valve keeper is uncovered.

Fig. 4-20. Lever tool that is used to press down the valve spring retainer and compress the valve springs.

2. Remove the split keeper halves from the valve stem. Release the compressing tool. Then take off the spring retainer and the valve springs.

3. Using long-nose pliers, remove the valve stem seal and the valve spring seat.

4. When all eight valve assemblies have been disassembled, install a dial indicator as shown in Fig. 4-21 so that you can check the valve guides for wear.

CAUTION ——

If the keeper grooves in the valve stems are burred, file them smooth before proceeding. If the burred stems are forced into the valve guides, the guides will be ruined.

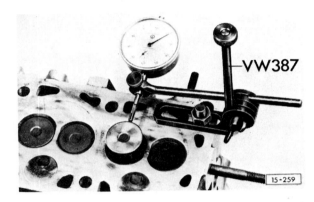

Fig. 4-21. Dial indicator being used to measure the rock of the valves in their guides.

5. One at a time, lift each valve off its seat until the tip of the valve stem is flush with the top of the valve guide. Position the dial indicator's gauge pin against the valve head. Then rock the valve from side to side in its guide while you observe the play range shown by the dial indicator.

NOTE ——

If the rocking play of an intake valve or an exhaust valve exceeds 1.30 mm (.051 in.) when a new valve is used, the guides are excessively worn. The inside diameter of valve guides should be between 8.013 and 8.035 mm (.315 and .316 in.).

CAUTION ——

Before you decide to replace the valve guides, determine whether new guides and the proper installation equipment are available. If guides and tools are unavailable, replace the entire cylinder head. Do not replace the valve guides routinely; replace them only if they are worn. To replace valve guides, follow the procedure given below.

11

6. Remove the dial indicator. Remove the valves, numbering each one so that you can reinstall the valves in their original locations.

7. To determine whether the original valve springs can be reused, check them with a valve spring tester as shown in Fig. 4-22. The outer valve spring should indicate a load of 43.5 to 48.0 kg (96 to 106 lb.) when compressed to a length of 22.3 mm (⅞ in.). The inner valve spring should indicate a load of 21.0 to 23.0 kg (46 to 51 lb.) when compressed to a length of 18.3 mm (²³/₃₂ in.). Replace weak springs.

NOTE ——

If you do not have a spring tester, have the springs tested by your Authorized Dealer or by a qualified automotive machine shop.

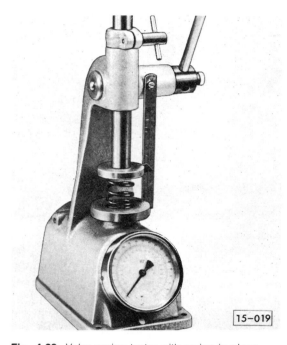

Fig. 4-22. Valve spring tester with spring in place.

8. To check the keepers, oil them and then install them on a removed valve. Hold the keeper valves together while you turn the valve. The valve stem should rotate freely in the assembled keeper. If the keeper is a loose fit, you can grind the mating surfaces to make it a tighter fit.

9. Inspect the valve seats and the valve facings as described in **4.5 Reconditioning Valves and Valve Seats.** If necessary, recondition (grind) the seats and the facings.

CAUTION ——

The exhaust valves must not be machine-ground. If their facing is too deeply worn or pitted to be restored by lapping, replace the valve.

To replace valve guides:

1. Clean and carefully inspect the cylinder head. Do not replace the valve guides in a cylinder head that is cracked or warped. Do not replace the valve guides if the valve seats are too badly worn to be refaced.

2. Using a repair press, press out the worn guides from the combustion chamber side, as shown in Fig. 4-23.

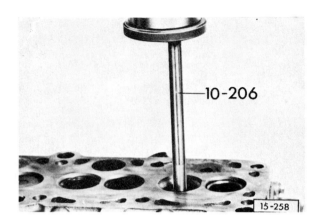

Fig. 4-23. Valve guide being pressed out.

3. Coat the new valve guides with engine oil. Then press the new guides into the cold cylinder head from the camshaft side until the shoulder on the guide firmly contacts the top of the cylinder head.

CAUTION ——

Once the shoulder on the guide is seated against the head, do not use more than 1 ton pressure or the shoulder may break.

4. Ream the guides in order to obtain a uniform inside diameter of from 8.013 to 8.035 mm (.315 to .316 in.). See Fig. 4-24. Lubricate the reamer with cutting oil during the reaming operation.

NOTE ——

The correct tool for checking the guide bore is a "go/no go" bore gauge that has a "go" diameter of 8.013 mm (or .315 in.) and a "no-go" diameter of 8.035 mm (or .316 in.). The 8.013-mm (.315-in.) end of the gauge should enter the guide easily but it should be impossible for the 8.035-mm (.316-in.) part of the gauge to enter the guide bore.

5. To ensure that the valve seats are concentric with the new valve guides, reface the seats as described in **4.5 Reconditioning Valves and Valve Seats.**

Fig. 4-24. New valve guide being reamed.

To install valves:

1. Lubricate the valve stems with engine oil. Then, with reference to the numbers marked on the valves during removal, install the valves in their original locations.

2. Place the cylinder head upright. Install the valve spring seats.

3. Install plastic caps over the valve stem ends (Fig. 4-25).

4. Using the installing tool shown in Fig. 4-25 or a plastic tube of suitable diameter, press the new valve stem seals down over the valve stems and onto the tops of the valve guides.

CAUTION ——

If you do not have the plastic protective cap, wrap the valve stem ends with smooth plastic tape. If you force the new valve stem seals over the bare valve stems, the keeper grooves will damage the seals and the engine will use excessive oil.

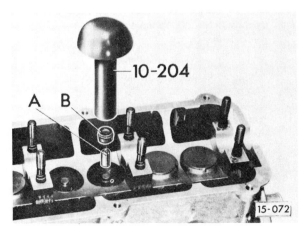

Fig. 4-25. Plastic protective cap (**A**), new valve stem seal (**B**), and installing tool—part 10–204.

5. Install the valve springs so that the closely spaced coils of the outer springs are against the spring seats.

6. Install the spring retainers. Then compress the springs with the valve spring compressing tool and install the keepers.

Removing and Installing Valve Springs and Seals
(cylinder head installed)

A worn valve stem seal, a broken valve spring, a damaged keeper, or a damaged spring retainer can be replaced without removing the cylinder head. To replace these parts, use the procedure that follows.

To remove spring:

1. Remove the cylinder head cover, the camshaft drive belt, the camshaft, and the cam follower.

2. Hand-turn the crankshaft until the piston of the cylinder you are working on is at top dead center (TDC).

3. Using the tool shown in Fig. 4-26, compress the valve spring retainer and the valve springs. Then remove the keeper.

4. Replace the worn or damaged parts. Then reassemble the valve assembly using a reverse of the disassembly procedure.

Fig. 4-26. Valve springs being removed with cylinder head installed.

4.5 Reconditioning Valves and Valve Seats

Carefully inspect used valves in order to determine whether they are suitable for reuse. You can reface intake valves, but not exhaust valves, by machine-grinding. In doing this work, follow a procedure suitable to the valve refacing machine that you have. Alternatively, have worn intake valves refaced by an Authorized Dealer or a qualified automotive machine shop.

11

To inspect and recondition used valves:

1. Discard any valve with damaged keeper grooves or with a stem that has been warped or galled by seizure.

2. Using a motor-driven wire brush, remove the combustion chamber deposits from the valves.

3. Examine the part of the valve facing that contacts the valve seat for pits, burns, and other signs of wear. If the damage to an intake valve is too extensive to be corrected by machine-grinding, replace the valve. Replace any exhaust valve that has pitting or wear that is too extensive to be corrected by lightly hand-lapping the valve into its seat.

> **NOTE** ——
>
> Because of the extreme conditions under which exhaust valves operate, many experienced mechanics routinely replace any exhaust valve that has been in service for 25,000 mi. (40,000 km) or more.

4. After you have refaced the intake valves by machine-grinding, the remaining margin must not be less than the minimum specified in Fig. 4-27. Discard any intake valve that has an irregular margin after machine-grinding—a condition that indicates a warped valve.

> *CAUTION* ——
>
> *Do not machine-grind exhaust valves. Doing this will shorten their service life. Exhaust valves should be hand-lapped only.*

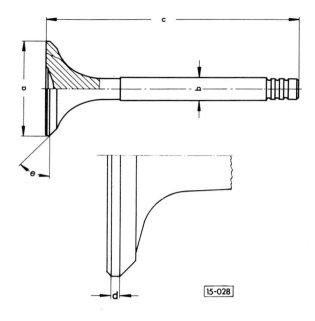

Dimension **a**, valve head diameter	Intake: 34.00 mm (1.338 in.) Exhaust: 31.00 mm (1.220 in.)
Dimension **b**, valve stem diameter	Intake: 7.97 mm (.314 in.) Exhaust: 7.95 mm (.313 in.)
Dimension **c**, valve length	Intake: 104.80 mm (4.126 in.) Exhaust: 104.60 mm (4.118 in.)
Dimension **d**, valve head margin	Intake: 0.50 mm (.020 in.) minimum Exhaust: Do not machine-grind
Dimension **e**, facing angle	Intake: 45° Exhaust: 45°

Fig. 4-27. Dimensions for reusable valves.

To inspect and reface valve seats:

1. If any valve seat is cracked or so badly gas-cut that it cannot be refaced to the specified dimensions, replace the cylinder head.

2. If inspection has shown that the valve guides are no longer serviceable (see **4.4 Disassembling and Assembling Cylinder Head**), either replace the guides or replace the cylinder head. If the correct replacement guides and replacement tools are available, replace the guides before you reface the valve seats.

3. Whether you use a hand-operated seat cutter or a power-driven seat grinder, make sure that the tool pilot fits the valve guides with little or no play.

4. Select a 45° seat cutter or a 45° seat grinding stone. Cutter blades should be straight and not chipped; grinding stones should be freshly dressed to the prescribed 45° angle.

5. Cut or grind to 45° the contact areas of the intake and the exhaust valve seats. See Fig. 4-28 for the finished dimensions of the seats. Remove no more metal than is necessary to erase wear and pitting—the less metal removed the better.

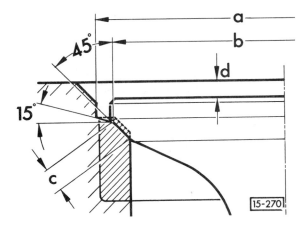

Fig. 4-29. Suction cup tool used to turn valve against seat, as indicated by the curved double arrow.

Dimension **a** seat recess diameter	Intake: 35.20 mm (1.386 in.) Exhaust: 33.20 mm (1.307 in.)
Dimension **b** seat shoulder diameter	Intake: 32.80 mm (1.291 in.) Exhaust: 30.40 mm (1.197 in.)
Dimension **c** contact face width	Intake: 2.00 mm (.079 in.) Exhaust: 2.40 mm (.094 in.)

Fig. 4-28. Dimensions for finished valve seats. Valve seat contact face angle is 45°, correction angle for shoulder is 15°. Dimension **d** must not exceed 1.50 mm (.059 in.).

6. Using a 15° hand seat cutter or a 15° grinding stone, chamfer the seats so that the contact areas are narrowed to the widths specified in Fig. 4-28.

> **CAUTION** ——
>
> *Do not neglect narrowing the valve seats to specifications. Overly wide seats produced by using only a 45° cutter or stone tend to trap carbon particles and other deposits.*

To hand-lap valves and seats:

1. Lubricate the valve stem with engine oil. Coat the valve seat contact area with a small amount of valve grinding compound (available from automotive supply stores).

2. Using a suction cup tool as shown in Fig. 4-29, turn the valve clockwise and counterclockwise against the seat. Lift the valve off the seat every few turns in order to avoid cutting concentric grooves into the seat.

3. Clean away every trace of grinding compound. Inspect the valve and the seat. There should be a uniform dull-gray band completely around the valve facing and the seat contact area.

4. To check the valve seating, lightly coat the valve facing with Prussian blue. Then install the valve. While applying light pressure to the valve, rotate the valve about a quarter turn against its seat.

5. Remove the valve and examine the contact pattern. If the seating is correct, the valve will leave an even coating of Prussian blue on the seat. If it does not, either the valve is warped and must be replaced or the seat must be reconditioned with greater care.

5. LUBRICATION SYSTEM

The lubrication system of the diesel engine operates on exactly the same principles as the lubrication system for the spark-ignition engine. Oil pressure is supplied by a gear-type oil pump that is located inside the engine's crankcase. The oil from the pump passes through a full-flow oil filter before it reaches the moving parts of the engine. A schematic view of the lubrication system can be seen in **ENGINE AND CLUTCH**. Instructions for replacing the oil filter are given in **LUBRICATION AND MAINTENANCE**.

5.1 Testing and Replacing Oil Pressure Switch

The procedure for testing and replacing the oil pressure switch is the same for the diesel as for the spark-ignition engine. Please follow the instructions given under heading 6.1 in **ENGINE AND CLUTCH**.

11

5.2 Removing, Checking, and Installing Oil Pump

The oil pump is housed inside the engine's crankcase. In replacing the oil pump, you must use the correct pump for the Dasher diesel, Part No. 068 115 105 G. You can use neither the oil pump designed for Dashers with spark-ignition engines, nor the oil pumps designed for use in the Rabbit diesel.

To remove and check oil pump:

1. To support the engine while the subframe is off, install a support on the lug at the rear of the cylinder head as shown in Fig. 5-1. Then remove the two nuts that hold the side engine mounts on the subframe and the four bolts that hold the subframe on the body. If necessary, consult **SUSPENSION AND STEERING.**

Fig. 5-1. Support bar installed across engine compartment. A threaded rod attaches the support bar to the lug on the cylinder head.

2. Pull the subframe downward, disengaging it from the side engine mounts and the car body.

   NOTE ——

   The stabilizer bar for the front suspension and the front suspension track control arms remain attached to the subframe and will support the subframe while it is unbolted from the engine and the body.

3. Place a receptacle of at least 1 gallon (or four liters or one Imperial gallon) capacity beneath the engine. Then remove the oil drain plug and allow the engine oil to drain into the receptacle. If necessary, consult **LUBRICATION AND MAINTENANCE.**

4. Using a 5-mm hex driver on a 175- or 200-mm (7- or 8-in.) extension, remove the socket head pan screws and their washers as shown in Fig. 5-2.

Fig. 5-2. Oil pan screws being removed.

5. Remove the oil pan from the engine. If the pan is stuck in place with sealer, tap the sides of the pan with a rubber mallet to break the pan free with a tilting motion.

6. Remove the two socket head pump-mounting bolts. Then remove the oil pump from the engine, leaving the oil pump's pickup tube attached.

7. With the oil pump on the workbench, remove the pickup tube from the pump body.

8. Using feeler gauges of various thicknesses, determine the backlash clearance between the pump gears as shown in Fig. 5-3. The clearance should be between 0.05 and 0.20 mm (.002 and .008 in.). If the clearance is greater, replace the gears or replace the pump.

Fig. 5-3. Feeler gauges being used to determine backlash.

9. Using a machinist's square and feeler gauges of various thicknesses, determine the axial play of the oil pump gears as shown in Fig. 5-4. If the play exceeds 0.15 mm (.006 in.), replace the pump.

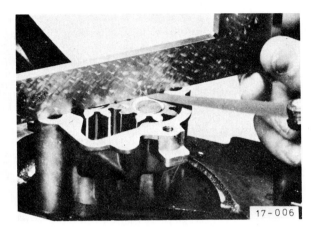

Fig. 5-4. Gear axial play being measured.

To install oil pump:

1. Assemble the pump (Fig. 5-5). Torque the bolts that hold the pickup tube to the housing to 1.0 mkg (7 ft. lb.).

2. Thoroughly clean the mating surfaces of the oil pump and the engine block. Turn the drive gearshaft until it is positioned to engage the vacuum pump drive gear. Then install the pump and torque the socket head mounting bolts to 2.0 mkg (14 ft. lb.).

3. Clean the mating surfaces of the engine block and the oil pan. Then, using a new gasket, install the oil pan on the engine block. Torque the socket head screws to 1.0 mkg (7 ft. lb.). Wait several minutes for the gasket to compress, then re-torque to the same specifications.

4. Install the subframe. Torque the four bolts to 7.0 mkg (50 ft. lb.). Torque the engine mount nuts to 4.0 mkg (29 ft. lb.). Then check and, if necessary, adjust the front wheel alignment as described in **SUSPENSION AND STEERING.**

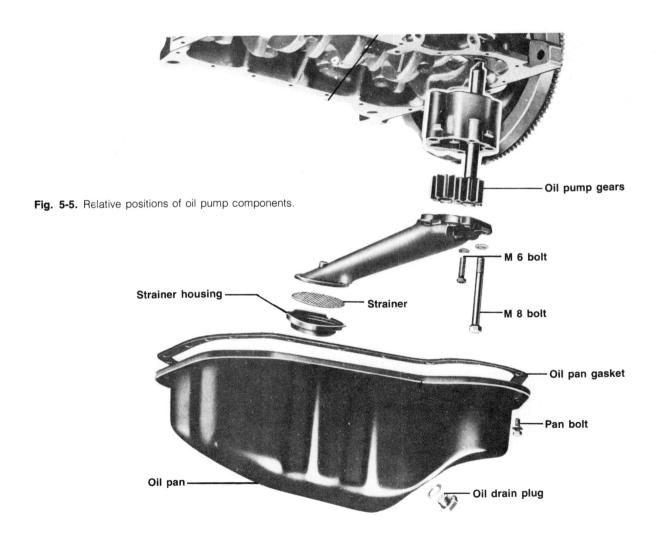

Fig. 5-5. Relative positions of oil pump components.

Oil pump gears

M 6 bolt

M 8 bolt

Strainer housing — Strainer

Oil pan gasket

Pan bolt

Oil pan

Oil drain plug

11

6. REMOVING AND INSTALLING ENGINE

For extensive engine reconditioning you should always remove the engine from the car. Though it is possible to remove the oil pan and the cylinder head so that the pistons and connecting rods can be removed and installed with the engine in the car, more extensive engine reconditioning should be performed only with the engine removed. The engine can be removed separately, as described here, or the engine and the transaxle can be removed as a unit together with the front suspension subframe as described in **SUSPENSION AND STEERING**. The procedure given there, however, is for spark-ignition engines and must be slightly modified using the procedure given here in order to make it applicable to cars with diesel engines.

To remove engine:

1. Disconnect the battery ground strap. Drain the oil.

2. Open the heater valve and remove the radiator cap. Place a receptacle for catching the draining coolant beneath the water pump. If there is a drain plug on the right-hand side of the engine block (some late engines have none), place a second receptacle below the block drain plug. Unbolt the thermostat housing from the water pump and, where applicable, remove the block drain plug. Allow the coolant to drain.

> **CAUTION** ——
>
> *Never drain the coolant while the engine is hot. Doing this could warp the engine block or the cylinder head.*

3. Remove the nut that holds the radiator to its lower support. Disconnect the wires from the thermo switch. See Fig. 6-1.

Fig. 6-1. Under-car radiator disconnecting points. Hose to thermostat housing is at **2**, nut that holds radiator to lower support is at **3**, and thermo switch wiring connector is at **4**.

4. Detach the radiator's air duct by taking off the clips. Disconnect the radiator top hose from the radiator. See Fig. 6-2.

Fig. 6-2. Upper air duct piece (**5**) and top hose connection (**6**). If hose is stuck to connection with sealer, cut hose off; prying can damage radiator.

5. Remove the bolt indicated in Fig. 6-3. Then remove the radiator together with the fan and the air duct.

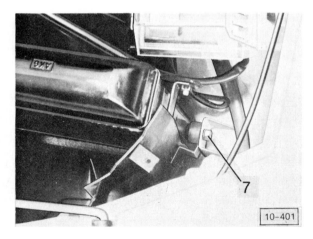

Fig. 6-3. Bolt (**7**) that holds radiator to side support.

6. On cars with air conditioning, unbolt the compressor from its bracket.

7. On cars with air conditioning, unbolt the condenser from the car body. Then place the dismounted

compressor and the dismounted condenser—with their hoses still connected—atop the front of the car or on a stand placed near the right front headlight.

CAUTION ——

Do not loosen or disconnect any of the refrigerant hose connections. If you do, it will make necessary costly and time-consuming air conditioning repairs.

8. On cars with air conditioning, remove the compressor bracket from the engine.

9. Remove the alternator. If necessary, consult **ELECTRICAL SYSTEM.**

10. Detach the fuel supply line, the return line, and the cold-start cable from the injection pump. Disconnect the accelerator cable from the pump lever and detach the cable bracket from the pump, leaving the bracket attached to the cable. Disconnect the electrical wire from the fuel shutoff solenoid. See Fig. 6-4.

WARNING ——

Fuel will be expelled as you disconnect the lines. Do not smoke or work near heaters or other fire hazards. Have a fire extinguisher handy.

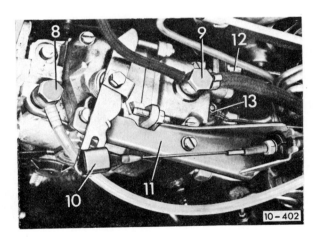

Fig. 6-4. Items to be detached from injection pump. Supply line is at **8**, return line at **9**. Accelerator cable connection is at **10**, cable bracket at **11**, cold-start cable at **12**, and wire for shutoff solenoid at **13**.

11. Disconnect the electrical wires from the oil pressure switch, the coolant temperature sending unit, and the glow plug bus. Disconnect the heater hose from the rear of the cylinder head and disconnect the brake servo's vacuum hose from the vacuum pump. See Fig. 6-5.

Fig. 6-5. Items to be disconnected at rear of cylinder head. Wires are at **14**, **15**, and **16**. Coolant hose is at **17** and vacuum hose at **18**.

12. Loosen the adjusting nut, then detach the clutch cable conduit from its bracket and unhook the cable from the clutch operating lever. See Fig. 6-6.

13. Detach the heater hose from the water pump. Then remove both the top nut and the bottom nut from the rubber part of the left engine mount. See Fig. 6-6.

Fig. 6-6. Items to be disconnected at left side of engine. Clutch cable conduit is at **19**, heater hose from water pump is at **20**, engine mount is at **21**.

11

14. Remove the V-belt(s). Fully remove both parts of the front engine mount. Remove the four nuts that hold the exhaust pipe to the exhaust manifold. Remove the upper nut from the rubber part of the right-hand engine mount. See Fig. 6-7.

Fig. 6-7. Items to be unbolted at right-hand part of engine. First remove V-belt(s) from pulley at **23**. Front engine mount is at **24**, exhaust pipe bolts at **25**, and right-hand engine mount at **26**.

15. Loosen the upper bolts that hold the engine to the transmission. Completely remove the lower bolts that hold the engine to the transmission. Remove the bolts that hold the intermediate plate to the bellhousing.

16. Install a support bar beneath the bellhousing on the transmission case (Fig. 6-8). The transmission must be thus supported when you later remove the upper bolts that hold the engine to the transmission.

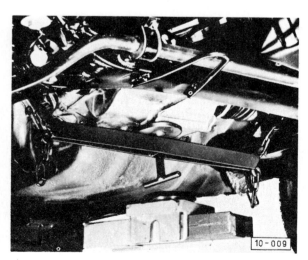

Fig. 6-8. Support bar in place beneath transmission.

17. With the car standing on its wheels, attach an engine hoist as indicated in Fig. 6-9 so that you will be able to lift the engine out of the car.

Fig. 6-9. Engine hoist attached to lugs on head and block.

18. Raise the engine and transmission assembly until the transmission contacts the steering rack housing. Use the threaded adjustment on the support bar to support the transmission in this position. Then remove the upper bolts that hold the engine to the transmission.

19. Carefully pry the engine loose from the transmission. Then remove the intermediate plate.

20. Pull the engine straight forward until the transmission mainshaft is out of the clutch-driven disk.

CAUTION ——

At no time should the weight of either the engine or the transaxle be supported by the transmission mainshaft. If it is, you may damage the clutch or bend the transmission mainshaft.

21. Rotate the front of the engine toward the left side of the car. Then, being careful not to damage any body or mechanical parts, lift out the engine.

Installation is the reverse of removal. Check the dowels that align the engine with the transaxle. Replace damaged dowels. Stick the intermediate plate to the engine with grease so that the plate will not fall off the dowels. Then install the engine, hand-turning the crankshaft to mesh the clutch with the transmission's mainshaft. Torque the bolts that hold the engine to the transmission to 5.5 mkg (40 ft. lb.). For the present, install the engine mounts loosely; after all other components have been installed, align the mountings as described under the next heading. Fig. 6-10 shows the installation of the air conditioning compressor and the correct bolt torques. Fig. 6-11 shows the correct installation of the alternator wiring.

Fig. 6-10. Exploded view of air conditioner compressor installation, giving bolt sizes and tightening torques.

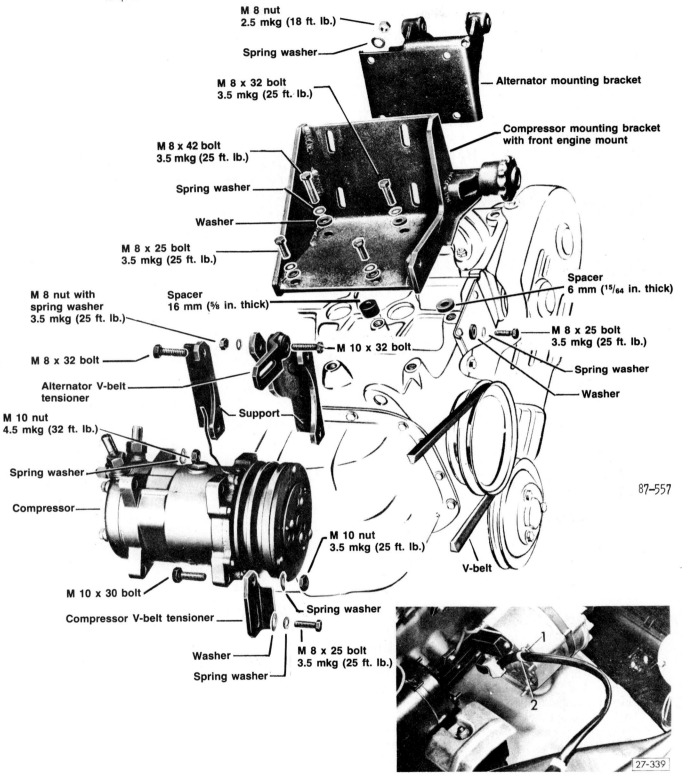

M 8 nut
2.5 mkg (18 ft. lb.)

Spring washer

M 8 x 32 bolt
3.5 mkg (25 ft. lb.)

Alternator mounting bracket

Compressor mounting bracket
with front engine mount

M 8 x 42 bolt
3.5 mkg (25 ft. lb.)

Spring washer

Washer

M 8 x 25 bolt
3.5 mkg (25 ft. lb.)

Spacer
16 mm (⅝ in. thick)

Spacer
6 mm (¹⁵/₆₄ in. thick)

M 8 nut with
spring washer
3.5 mkg (25 ft. lb.)

M 8 x 32 bolt

M 10 x 32 bolt

M 8 x 25 bolt
3.5 mkg (25 ft. lb.)

Spring washer

Washer

Alternator V-belt
tensioner

Support

M 10 nut
4.5 mkg (32 ft. lb.)

Spring washer

Compressor

M 10 nut
3.5 mkg (25 ft. lb.)

V-belt

87-557

M 10 x 30 bolt

Compressor V-belt tensioner

Washer

Spring washer

M 8 x 25 bolt
3.5 mkg (25 ft. lb.)

Spring washer

27-339

Fig. 6-11. Correct installation of wiring harness on Bosch alternator used with VW diesel engine. Clamp is at **1**, plastic clip at **2**.

11

Aligning Engine/Transaxle Assembly Mountings

The engine/transaxle assembly mountings should always be aligned after you have installed the engine, the transaxle, or the engine/transaxle/subframe assembly in the car. The work should also be done to correct certain noises, as described in greater detail at the end of this procedure.

To align engine/transaxle:

1. If not previously loosened during removal and installation of the engine, the transaxle, or the engine/transaxle/subframe assembly, loosen the bolts that hold the front engine mounting to the car body.

2. If not previously loosened during removal and installation of the engine, the transaxle, or the engine/transaxle/subframe assembly, loosen the nuts that hold the bonded rubber parts of the side engine mountings to the subframe and to the engine mountings.

3. Move the engine/transaxle assembly from side to side until the inner core of the transaxle rear mounting is centered in its housing (Fig. 6-12). There should be no twisting or strain in the bonded rubber part. If necessary, reposition the transaxle rear mounting, then torque the nut that holds the bonded rubber mounting to the transaxle carrier to 4.0 mkg (29 ft. lb.).

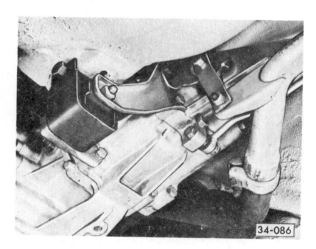

Fig. 6-12. Transaxle rear mounting correctly aligned. Bonded rubber part should be centered in its housing.

4. Move the bonded rubber part of each side engine mounting until it is seated correctly (Fig. 6-13). Torque the nuts to 4.0 mkg (29 ft. lb.). Make sure that neither bonded rubber mounting is twisted or under side-strain.

Fig. 6-13. Bonded rubber part of side engine mounting (**B**) correctly seated and aligned. Triangular metal part at top of bonded rubber mounting part should point to center of hump at bottom, as shown.

5. Align the front engine mount and support (Fig. 6-14) so that the rubber buffer has a clearance of approximately 1 mm (or $1/32$ in.) and does not touch the sides of the housing (**F** in the illustration). Torque the bolts to 2.5 mkg (18 ft. lb.).

Fig. 6-14. Correct installation and alignment of front engine mount and support. Housing for mount is at letter **F**.

Though it is normally necessary to align the engine/transaxle assembly mountings only after the engine, the transaxle, or the engine/transaxle/subframe assembly has been installed in the car, you may also need to carry out the adjustment procedure if there is engine vibration or buzzing noises at certain speeds. If alignment of the mountings fails to help—and whenever you have reinstalled the engine— also check the exhaust system alignment, as described under the next heading.

Checking Exhaust System Alignment

After you have reinstalled the engine—or if there are buzzing noises from beneath the car at certain speeds— check the exhaust system alignment. To do this, loosen all exhaust system clamps. Align the muffler and its pipe so that the rubber rings in front of and behind the muffler are well centered and under uniform tension. You can, if necessary, slightly bend the hooks for the rubber rings. The pipe behind the main muffler should also be aligned so that both the pipe and its mountings are free of uneven tension. With the system correctly aligned and assembled, retighten the clamps.

7. FLYWHEEL AND CLUTCH

Because the flywheel and the clutch (Fig. 7-1) of the diesel engine are similar to those of the spark-ignition engine, the repair and servicing procedures are the same. Please refer to heading 9 of **ENGINE AND CLUTCH** for all work related to the clutch and flywheel.

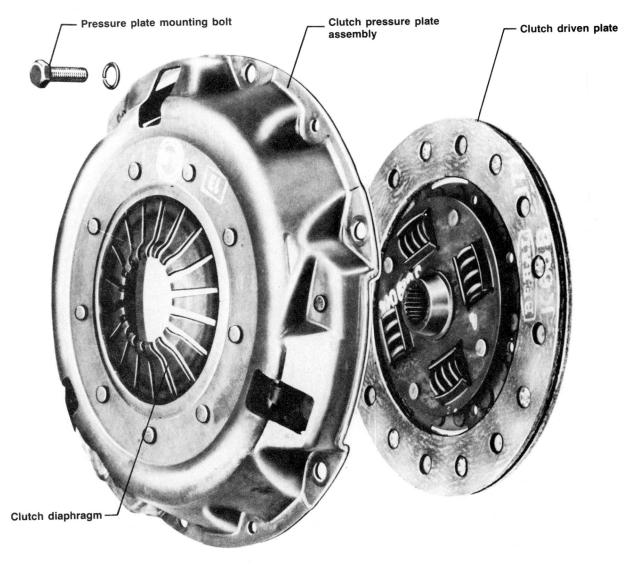

Pressure plate mounting bolt

Clutch pressure plate assembly

Clutch driven plate

Clutch diaphragm

Fig. 7-1. Relative positions of pressure plate assembly and clutch driven plate used with diesel engine.

30-011

11

8. PISTONS, PISTON RINGS, AND CONNECTING RODS

The components of the piston/connecting rod assembly for one cylinder of the engine are shown in Fig. 8-1. Though it is possible to remove the cylinder head and the oil pan so that the connecting rods and pistons can be removed and installed with the engine in the car, that procedure is advisable mainly for the purpose of inspecting the piston rings and the connecting rod bearings.

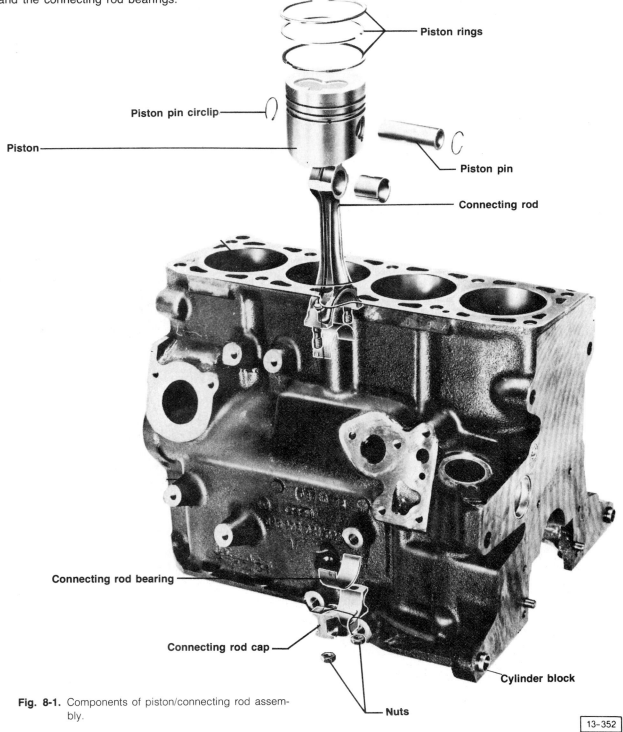

Fig. 8-1. Components of piston/connecting rod assembly.

13-352

Any work that requires grinding or machining, such as removing the top-cylinder ridge or honing the cylinder bores, should be done with the engine removed and disassembled. Otherwise, abrasive dirt and metal particles will remain in the engine, causing bearing damage and rapid wear.

The pistons are completely different from those used in the spark-ignition engine. Though other parts of the piston/ connecting rod assembly may appear identical to those used in spark-ignition watercooled Volkswagen engines, you should always select replacement parts with careful reference to the part numbers in order to make sure that the correct components are obtained for use in your diesel.

8.1 Removing, Checking, and Installing Pistons, Piston Rings, Connecting Rods, and Connecting Rod Bearings

Because the pistons, the connecting rods, and many of their related parts must be reinstalled in their original locations and positions, you should mark the parts as you remove them. Replacement parts should be selected with careful reference to the cylinder bore, the original part, and the other parts in the piston/connecting rod assembly. Because of the special importance of good compression in a diesel engine, it is imperative that new pistons and piston rings be replaced with the greatest possible attention to precision and accuracy.

CAUTION

Precision measurements are required for many of the repair procedures given under this heading. If you lack the skills, tools and equipment, or a clean workshop, we suggest that you leave engine reconditioning to an Authorized Dealer or other qualified shop. We especially urge you to consult your Authorized Dealer before attempting any repairs on a car still covered by the new-car warranty.

To remove, check and install:

1. Unless you are replacing connecting rod bearings only, or are removing the piston and connecting rod for inspection purposes only, remove the engine as described in **6. Removing and Installing Engine.**

2. Remove the cylinder head as described in **4.3 Removing and Installing Cylinder Head and Manifolds.** Remove the oil pan and the oil pump as described in **5.2 Removing, Checking, and Installing Oil Pump.**

3. Mark the cylinder number on the crown of each piston. If necessary, mark arrows on the piston crowns to indicate which side of each piston is toward the camshaft drive end of the engine block. See Fig. 8-2.

Fig. 8-2. Cylinder numbers and arrows marked on piston crowns.

4. Remove the connecting rod nuts. Remove the connecting rod cap from the connecting rod bolts. Then, using a wooden hammer handle, push the piston/ connecting rod assembly away from the crankshaft and out through the top of the cylinder.

CAUTION

If the engine block has pronounced top-cylinder ridges, remove them with a cylinder ridge reamer before you remove the pistons. Otherwise, the piston rings and pistons may be damaged during removal. A top-cylinder ridge is a band of unworn cylinder wall that remains above the part of the cylinder that has been worn to a larger diameter by contact with the piston rings.

11

5. Before you remove each piston/connecting rod assembly, mark the cylinder number on both the rod cap and the connecting rod as shown in Fig. 8-3.

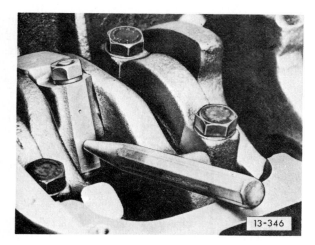

Fig. 8-3. Cylinder number being marked on connecting rod with center punch.

6. Using needle-nosed pliers or a punch, as shown in Fig. 8-4, remove the piston pin circlips from both ends of each piston pin. Then press out the piston pin and remove the piston from the rod.

Fig. 8-4. Circlip being removed. Notice the notch in the piston where the pliers have been inserted.

7. Check each piston for wear as shown in Fig. 8-5. Measure the piston at right angles to the piston pin at a point approximately 15 mm (⅝ in.) from the lower edge of the piston skirt.

8. Compare the measurement obtained in step 7 with the nominal piston diameter that is marked on the piston crown. This comparison will give an indication

of the extent to which the piston is worn. Also, the piston should not be out-of-round by more than 0.04 mm (.0015 in.). However, you can determine whether the piston is suitable for reuse only after measuring the cylinder bore as described in step 9 of this procedure.

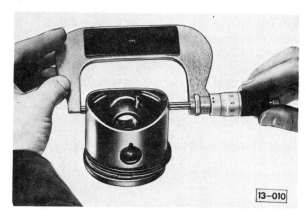

Fig. 8-5. Piston diameter being measured.

9. Using a dial indicator device, as shown in Fig. 8-6, determine the cylinder diameter and the degree of wear.

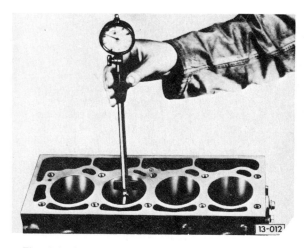

Fig. 8-6. Cylinder bore being measured with a special dial indicator.

NOTE ——

When checking the cylinder bores, make your measurements at three points throughout each cylinder and at right angles to one another (Fig. 8-7). Minor variations in cylinder diameter can be corrected by honing, as described in later steps of this procedure. If, however, there are variations of 0.05 mm (.002 in.) or more among the measurements made in any one cylinder, the cylinder must be rebored to accept an oversize piston.

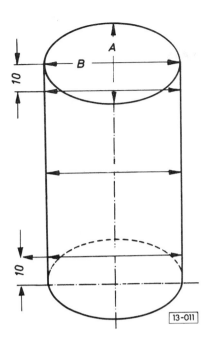

Fig. 8-8. Honing group code stamped on the engine block. This number is derived from the diameter of the original cylinder bore. For example, code 651 indicates that, when manufactured, the cylinders were honed to a diameter of 76.51 mm.

Fig. 8-7. Cylinder bore measuring points. Measurement **1** should be made 10 mm (⅜ in.) from the top of the cylinder, measurement **2** should be made in the middle of the cylinder, and measurement **3** should be made 10 mm (⅜ in.) from the bottom of the cylinder. Make each measurement first in direction **A** and then in direction **B**.

10. Write down the largest bore diameter measurement you obtain for each of the cylinders.

11. Compare the measurements written down in step 10 with the honing group that is marked on the engine block (Fig. 8-8). This comparison will give an indication of the extent to which the cylinder is worn.

NOTE ——

If the measured bore diameter of any cylinder exceeds the largest cylinder diameter listed for the basic dimension or repair stage (as given in **Table d**) by 0.04 mm (.0015 in.) or more, all the cylinders must be rebored and honed to accept new pistons from the next larger repair stage. If the original bore diameter was at the lower limit of the basic dimension or repair group tolerance range, you can hone the cylinders to accept a larger piston from the same basic dimension or repair stage. However, your goal should always be to obtain a clearance of 0.03 mm (.001 in.) between the pistons and the cylinders of a repaired or rebuilt engine.

Table d. Piston and Cylinder Diameters

Repair stage	Piston diameter mm (in.)	Cylinder bore mm (in.)	Honing group
Basic dimension	76.48 (3.0110)	76.51 (3.0122)	651
	76.49 (3.0114)	76.52 (3.0126)	652
	76.50 (3.0118)	76.53 (3.0130)	653
Repair stage 1	76.73 (3.0209)	76.76 (3.0221)	676
	76.74 (3.0213)	76.77 (3.0224)	677
	76.75 (3.0217)	76.78 (3.0228)	678
Repair stage 2	76.98 (3.0307)	77.01 (3.0319)	701
	76.99 (3.0311)	77.02 (3.0323)	702
	77.00 (3.0315)	77.03 (3.0327)	703
Repair stage 3	77.48 (3.0504)	77.51 (3.0516)	751
	77.49 (3.0508)	77.52 (3.0520)	752
	77.50 (3.0512)	77.53 (3.0524)	753

11

12. Compute the clearance between the original pistons and their cylinders. To do this, subtract the measurements obtained in step 7 from the measurements that you obtained in step 9. With new parts, the clearance should be 0.03 mm (.0011 to .0012 in.). The wear limit is 0.07 mm (.0025 in.).

13. If the piston clearance exceeds the wear limit, but the cylinders are not worn to a diameter more than 0.04 mm (.0015 in.) greater than their original honing group, you can correct the clearance by installing new pistons of the original diameter for the cylinder honing group, or by honing the cylinders to the next larger diameter in the same basic dimension or repair stage and then installing new pistons to match the new honing group.

14. If the piston clearance exceeds the wear limit because of cylinder wear, then the cylinders must be rebored and honed to accept new pistons from the next larger repair stage. This work can be done by your Authorized Dealer or by a qualified automotive machine shop.

15. Using feeler gauges of various thicknesses, determine the side clearance of all the piston rings as shown in Fig. 8-9. If the clearances are greater than the wear limits given in **Table e,** replace the pistons and rings. If the clearances are less than the minimum given in **Table e,** either replace the piston or have the grooves reconditioned by your Authorized Dealer or a qualified automotive machine shop.

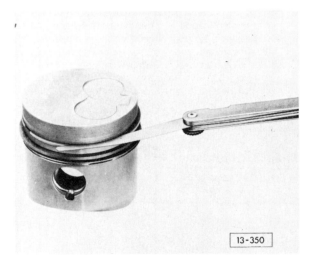

Fig. 8-9. Piston ring side clearance being measured. Insert the feeler gauge between the piston ring and one of the piston lands. Then move the gauge completely around the piston. The clearance must not be outside the specified range at any point.

16. Remove the piston rings from the pistons.

CAUTION——

If you intend to install new rings, it is of no consequence if you break the rings during removal. However, if you intend to reuse the rings, you must work carefully to prevent accidental breakage. It is imperative that used rings be reinstalled in their original grooves and on their original pistons. Otherwise, poor sealing will result—which may cause excessive oil consumption, hard starting, or lost power.

Table e.   Piston Ring Side Clearances

Ring position	Clearance (new parts) mm (in.)	Wear limit mm (in.)
Upper compressor ring	0.06–0.09 (.0024–.0035)	0.20 (.0079)
Lower compressor ring	0.05–0.08 (.0020–.0032)	0.20 (.0079)
Oil scraper ring	0.03–0.06 (.0012–.0024)	0.15 (.0060)

17. Push each ring about 15 mm (⅝ in.) into the bottom of its cylinder. Then measure the ring gap as shown in Fig. 8-10.

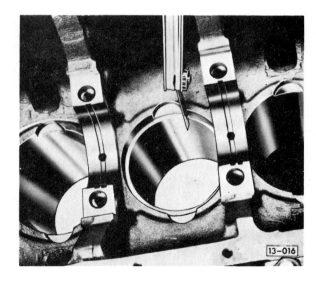

Fig. 8-10. Ring gap being measured with feeler gauge.

NOTE ——

Replacement rings for engines with oversize pistons must be the correct size for the oversize cylinder honing group. If you are checking the end gaps of new rings, which you should always do, the gap should be 0.30 to 0.50 mm (.012 to .020 in.) for the upper and lower compression rings or 0.25 to 0.40 mm (.010 to .016 in.) for the oil scraper ring. If the gap is too narrow, enlarge it with a file or an oil stone. If you are checking used piston rings, the measurement obtained in step 17 must not exceed 1.00 mm (.039 in.)—which is the wear limit. Replace worn-out rings.

18. Check the piston pin fit in each piston. The pin must be a light push fit with the piston heated to approximately 60°C (140°F) in an oil bath. It not, replace both the piston and the pin.

19. Check the piston pin fit in each connecting rod. If the clearance exceeds 0.04 mm (.0015 in.), the wear limit, either replace the rod and pin or fit a new pin and a new rod bushing. Hone the new bushing to obtain a clearance of 0.01 to 0.02 mm (.0004 to .0008 in.), then check the rod's alignment. This work can be done by your Authorized Dealer or by a qualified automotive machine shop.

NOTE ——

If for any reason you replace one or more pistons, all four must be of the same weight class. Unmarked replacement pistons must be within 10 grams of the weight of the other pistons in the engine. Beginning with Engine No. CK 024 944, pistons of greater height are installed in order to increase the piston projection above the engine block. These new pistons (Fig. 8-11) are the only kind used in Dashers with diesel engines. (The old kind are used in early Rabbit diesels.) Replacement connecting rods are available only as sets of four rods of the same weight group.

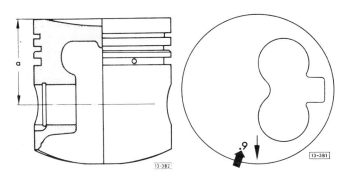

Fig. 8-11. Piston height identification. On early Rabbit diesel engines, dimension **a** is 44.70 mm (1.760 in.) On all Dasher diesel engines, dimension **a** is 44.90 mm (1.768 in.). Arrow indicates identification number near the installation direction arrow of higher late-type pistons.

20. Using the tool shown in Fig. 8-12, install the piston rings. The word TOP, marked on each ring, must be toward the piston crown.

Fig. 8-12. Tool used for installing piston rings on pistons.

21. Install one circlip only in one end of the piston pin bore of each piston. Then heat all of the pistons to approximately 60°C (140°F) in an oil bath.

22. With reference to the cylinder numbers you marked on the pistons and the connecting rods during removal, install the pistons on their original connecting rods so that, when the arrow marked on the piston crown is pointing toward the camshaft drive end of the engine, the marks indicated in Fig. 8-13 will be toward the engine's intermediate shaft.

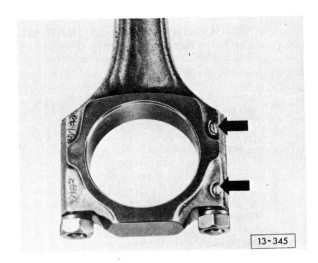

Fig. 8-13. Forged marks (arrows) that must be toward the engine's intermediate shaft with the connecting rod and piston installed in the engine.

11

23. Working quickly, so that the pistons do not have an opportunity to cool, hand-press the piston pins into

position as shown in Fig. 8-14. Seat the pin against the circlip that you have already installed in the piston, then install the other circlip. Make sure that all circlips are firmly engaged in the grooves in the pistons.

Fig. 8-14. Special drift being used to press piston pin into piston and connecting rod.

24. If the cylinders have not been rebored, but you have installed new piston rings, inspect the cylinders to see whether there are top-cylinder ridges. Remove top-cylinder ridges with a cylinder ridge reamer. Then—whether there were ridges or not—lightly hone the cylinder bores with a hone that has fine (220-grit) stones. Move the spinning hone smoothly in and out of the bore to produce a fine cross-hatch pattern on the cylinder walls.

   NOTE ——

   A top-cylinder ridge is a band of unworn cylinder wall that remains above the part of the cylinder that has been worn to a larger diameter by contact with the piston rings. If the ridge is not removed, the new upper compression ring will strike the ridge, breaking the ring and damaging the piston. The object of honing the cylinder is to remove "glaze" that could keep the new rings from seating. In breaking the glaze, remove as little metal as possible.

25. Thoroughly clean the engine block to remove metal particles and abrasive dust. Then install the crankshaft, the intermediate shaft, and their bearings and oil seals (See **9. Crankshaft and Intermediate Shaft.**) Hand-turn the crankshaft to place the connecting rod journal for No. 1 cylinder at bottom dead center (BDC).

26. Thoroughly lubricate the cylinder bores and the piston rings with engine oil only. Stagger the ring gaps so that the oil scraper ring's gap will be toward the left or the right end of the engine and the other two ring's gaps will be offset 120° to each side of the scraper

ring's gap. Then install a piston ring compressor on the piston for the No. 1 cylinder and fully compress the rings (Fig. 8-15).

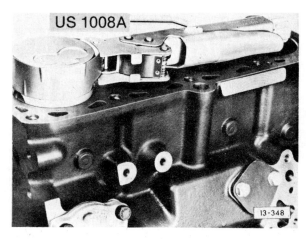

Fig. 8-15. Piston ring compressor installed on piston. Rings must be pressed into their grooves so that piston can be pushed into the cylinder.

27. If previously removed, install the connecting rod bearing shells in the connecting rod and the connecting rod cap. Make sure that the anti-rotation tabs on the bearing shells engage the notches in the rod and the cap. Do not install the cap on the rod.

28. Install the piston/connecting rod assembly in the No. 1 cylinder until the piston ring compressor band contacts the engine block.

29. Being careful to guide the connecting rod bolts over opposite sides of the crankshaft journal, use a wooden hammer handle to tap the piston out of the ring compressor and into the cylinder. Then use the hammer handle to press the piston down in the cylinder until the connecting rod bearing is seated squarely on the crankshaft journal.

   CAUTION ——

   Check the progress of the connecting rod as you press the piston toward the crankshaft. The rod bearing or the crankshaft will be damaged if you drive them together at an angle.

30. Loosely install the connecting rod cap. Using the same procedure you used on the No. 1 cylinder, install the piston/connecting rod assembly of the No. 4 cylinder. Then hand-turn the crankshaft 180° and install the piston/connecting rod assemblies of the No. 2 and No. 3 cylinders.

31. One at a time, remove the connecting rod caps. Then place a piece of Plastigage® (available at automotive supply stores) on the crankshaft journal. Do not lay the Plastigage across the oil hole in the crankshaft journal.

NOTE ——

In checking the clearance, first try red Plastigage, which measures clearances from 0.050 to 0.150 mm (.002 to .006 in.). If red Plastigage is excessively flattened when measured in step 33, repeat the check using green Plastigage, which measures clearances from 0.025 to 0.076 mm (.001 to .003 in.).

32. Install the connecting rod cap. Torque the nuts to 3.5 mkg (25 ft. lb.), then remove the nuts and the connecting rod cap.

NOTE ——

Torquing the nuts will compress and flatten the Plastigage, which you will measure to determine the connecting rod bearing clearance. Do not turn the crankshaft as you compress the Plastigage. Doing this will spread the Plastigage and cause inaccurate measurement.

33. To determine the bearing clearance, compare the flattened Plastigage to the scale that is printed on the edge of the Plastigage package. Read the clearance printed adjacent to the scale band that has the same width as the flattened Plastigage strip (Fig. 8-16).

NOTE ——

Used bearings must be installed in their original positions in their original connecting rods. New bearings must be installed so that their anti-rotation tabs engage the notches in the connecting rod and rod cap. With new parts, the connecting rod bearing clearance should be from 0.028 to 0.088 mm (.0011 to .0035 in.). If clearance is at or near the 0.12-mm (.0047-in.) wear limit, check the crankshaft as described in **9.2 Removing, Checking, and Installing Crankshaft and Main Bearings.** Then replace the bearings.

CAUTION ——

Use solvent to remove the flattened Plastigage. Scraping off the Plastigage could damage the connecting rod bearings.

34. If bearing clearance is correct, lightly coat the connecting rod bearing shells and the crankshaft journals with assembly lubricant.

NOTE ——

If assembly lubricant is not available from your automotive supply store, use a light coating of multipurpose grease instead.

35. Install the connecting rod caps. Torque the connecting rod nuts to 4.5 mkg (32 ft. lb.).

36. Using feeler gauges of various thicknesses, determine the connecting rod bearing axial play. To do this, push each connecting rod as far as possible toward

one side of the crankshaft journal. If you can insert an 0.37-mm (.014-in.) feeler gauge between the opposite side of the journal and the connecting rod (Fig. 8-17), the clearance is excessive. Excessive clearance can be corrected by installing new bearings, a new crankshaft, a new connecting rod, or all three—depending on the extent to which any of these parts is worn.

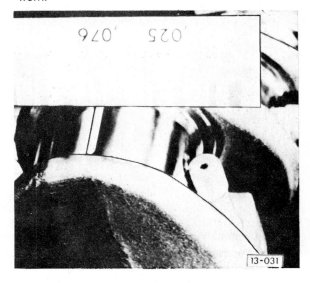

Fig. 8-16. Flattened Plastigage being measured to determine connecting rod bearing clearance.

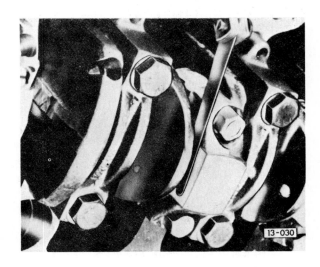

Fig. 8-17. Connecting rod axial play (side clearance) being measured with a feeler gauge.

37. Install the oil pump and the oil pan as described in **5.2 Removing, Checking, and Installing Oil Pump.** Install the cylinder head as described in **4.3 Removing and Installing Cylinder Head and Manifolds.** Then install the engine, if previously removed, as described in **6. Removing and Installing Engine.**

11

9. CRANKSHAFT AND INTERMEDIATE SHAFT

You must remove the engine if you intend to remove the crankshaft or the intermediate shaft from the engine block. The front oil seals for both shafts can be replaced with the engine installed. However, you can replace the crankshaft's rear oil seal only after you have removed the transaxle or the engine/transaxle assembly. See **MANUAL TRANS-MISSION.**

The crankshaft revolves in five split-shell main bearings. The center (No. 3) main bearing shells are flanged. The flanges control crankshaft axial play. The intermediate shaft runs in two ring-type bearings that are driven into bores in the front and the rear of the engine block.

9.1 Replacing Crankshaft and Intermediate Shaft Oil Seals

The oil seals used at the front ends of the crankshaft, the intermediate shaft, and the camshaft have the same diameters. See **4.4 Disassembling and Assembling Cylinder Head** for information on the replacement of the camshaft oil seal.

To replace crankshaft front oil seal:

1. Remove the camshaft drive belt as described in **4.1 Removing, Installing, and Adjusting Camshaft Drive Belt.** Then remove the crankshaft sprocket.

2. Being careful not to damage the light alloy seal carrier, pry out the old oil seal (Fig. 9-1).

3. Using the tool shown in Fig. 9-2, press in the new seal until it is flush with the front of the seal carrier.

4. Remove the seal-installing tool. Then, so that it does not get stuck in the seal recess, remove the steel

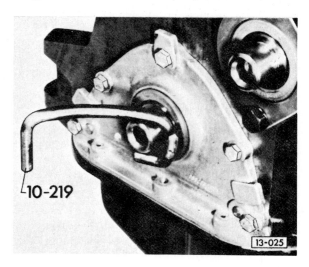

Fig. 9-1. Crankshaft front oil seal being removed. Special tool hooks under inner edge of seal.

driving sleeve from the tool. Using the aluminum part of the tool only, press in the seal until it is recessed 2 mm (.080 in.) from the front of the seal carrier. Then remove the tool and install the sprocket and the camshaft drive belt.

> **NOTE** ——
>
> You can mark the outer surface of the seal-installing tool at a point 2 mm (.080 in.) from the end of the tool that contacts the seal. Press in the seal until the mark on the tool is flush with the seal carrier.

Fig. 9-2. Seal being pressed in. Turn bolt (threaded into crankshaft) as indicated by arrow.

To replace crankshaft rear oil seal:

1. Remove the transmission. Remove the flywheel as described in **ENGINE AND CLUTCH.**

2. Carefully insert a large screwdriver between the crankshaft's flywheel flange and the inner edge of the old oil seal. Then, bracing the screwdriver against the flange, pry out the oil seal. See Fig. 9-3.

Fig. 9-3. Crankshaft rear oil seal being pried out.

3. Start the new seal into the recess using the tool shown in Fig. 9-4.

Fig. 9-4. Crankshaft rear oil seal being started in recess.

4. Remove the starting tool. Then, using the driving plate shown in Fig. 9-5, press in the seal by alternately tightening the two flywheel mounting bolts so that the plate advances evenly toward the seal carrier. When the seal is flush with the carrier, remove the plate and the bolts. Install the flywheel, then install the transaxle.

Fig. 9-5. Seal driving plate and two flywheel mounting bolts being used to press in rear oil seal.

To replace intermediate shaft oil seal:

1. Remove the camshaft drive belt as described in **4.1 Removing, Installing, and Adjusting Camshaft Drive Belt.** Remove the intermediate shaft pulley.

2. Using the tool shown previously in Fig. 9-1, pry out the faulty oil seal. Then install the new seal as shown in Fig. 9-6.

NOTE ——

Because the intermediate shaft of the diesel engine rotates in the direction opposite to that of the spark-ignition engine, the oil seals for the two engines may not be identical. On early parts, the correct application is shown by an arrow on the seal, which indicates the counterclockwise intermediate shaft rotation of the diesel engine. Recently, a new seal (Part No. 056 103 085 B) has been introduced which can be used with shafts that rotate in either direction. It can be identified by its brown inner ring and black outer ring.

Fig. 9-6. Intermediate shaft oil seal being installed.

11

9.2 Removing, Checking, and Installing Crankshaft and Main Bearings

Fig. 9-7 illustrates the removal of the crankshaft, the crankshaft bearings, and the intermediate shaft. In removing the crankshaft, both crankshaft oil seal carriers must be removed from the engine block.

Though the bearing shells for main bearings 1, 2, 4, and 5 are identical, you must always reinstall used bearing shells in their original locations. Similarly, the main bearing caps must always be reinstalled on their original bearing saddles.

To remove, check, and install:

1. Remove the engine. Remove the pistons and connecting rods as described in **8.1 Removing, Checking, and Installing Pistons, Piston Rings, Connecting Rods, and Connecting Rod Bearings.** Remove the flywheel and clutch as described in **ENGINE AND CLUTCH.**

2. With the engine block inverted on an engine repair stand or clamped upside down on a workbench, remove the crankshaft oil seal carriers. Remove the bolts from the main bearing caps, remove the caps and bearings, then lift out the crankshaft.

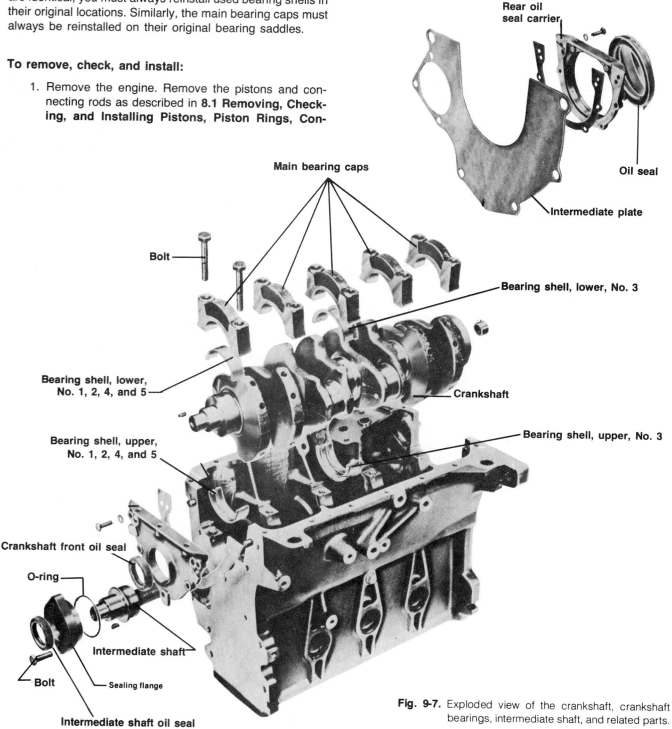

Fig. 9-7. Exploded view of the crankshaft, crankshaft bearings, intermediate shaft, and related parts.

NOTE ——

The main bearing caps are factory-numbered to ensure correct installation. However, if you intend to reuse the bearings, mark the bearing numbers on the backs of the bearing shells as you remove them from the caps and the main bearing saddles.

3. Using a micrometer, measure the crankshaft's main bearing and connecting rod journals. Then compare the measurements with the dimensions given in **Table f.** So that you can be certain the journals are not worn to a taper, duplicate each measurement at opposite sides of each journal. To determine eccentricity, make a second pair of measurements at a point 90° from the initial measurements. Alternatively, check the eccentricity (out-of-round) of the main bearing journals by placing main bearing journals 1 and 5 on V-blocks, and then rotating the crankshaft against a dial indicator positioned, one journal at a time, against main bearing journals 2, 3, and 4.

NOTE ——

If the journals are rough or scored, tapered, exceed the limit for maximum out-of-round, or have worn to such a degree that the connecting rod or the main bearing clearances exceed the wear limit even with new bearings, the crankshaft must be either replaced or reconditioned. You can exchange your worn crankshaft for a new crankshaft or for an undersize reconditioned crankshaft at your Authorized Dealer's parts department. Alternatively, a specialty shop can recondition your worn crankshaft to one of the undersizes listed in **Table f.**

4. Using the original bearings, original-size replacement bearings, or undersize main bearings—depending on the condition of the crankshaft as determined in step 3—install the upper main bearing shells (with oil holes and lubrication grooves) in the bearing saddles of the engine block (Fig. 9-8). Make certain that the bearing saddles are clean and that the antirotation tabs engage the notches in the saddles.

Fig. 9-8. Upper main bearing shells, identified by oil grooves (small arrows). Oil holes (large arrow) must align with oil holes in engine block.

5. Place the crankshaft in the engine block. Install the lower main bearing shells in the bearing caps. Then,

Table f. Crankshaft Journal Sizes

Sizes	Crankshaft main bearing journal		Crankshaft connecting rod journal	
	diameter in mm (in.)	maximum out-of-round mm (in.)	diameter in mm (in.)	maximum out-of-round mm (in.)
Original grade 1 grade 2	54.00–0.04 (2.126–.0015) 54.00–0.06 (2.126–.002)	0.03 (.0012) 0.03 (.0012)	46.00–0.04 (1.811–.0015) 46.00–0.06 (1.811–.002)	0.03 (.0012) 0.03 (.0012)
Undersize I grade1 grade 2	53.75–0.04 (2.1161–.0015) 53.75–0.06 (2.1161–.002)	0.03 (.0012) 0.03 (.0012)	45.75–0.04 (1.8012–.0015) 45.75–0.06 (1.8012–.002)	0.03 (.0012) 0.03 (.0012)
Undersize II grade1 grade 2	53.50–0.04 (2.1063–.0015) 53.50–0.06 (2.1063–.002)	0.03 (.0012) 0.03 (.0012)	45.50–0.04 (1.7913–.0015) 45.50–0.06 (1.7913–.002)	0.03 (.0012) 0.03 (.0012)
Undersize III grade 1 grade 2	53.25–0.04 (2.0965–.0015) 53.25–0.06 (2.0965–.002)	0.03 (.0012) 0.03 (.0012)	45.25–0.04 (1.7815–.0015) 45.25–0.06 (1.7815–.002)	0.03 (.0012) 0.03 (.0012)

11

making sure you install the caps as shown in Fig. 9-9, use Plastigage® to check the bearing clearance with the bolts torqued to 3.5 mkg (25 ft. lb.). Plastigage measurement is described in **8.1 Removing, Checking, and Installing Pistons, Piston Rings, Connecting Rods, and Connecting Rod Bearings.**

6. With new bearings, the bearing clearance (measured with Plastigage) should be between 0.03 and 0.08 mm (.0012 and .003 in.). If the clearance with used bearings exceeds the wear limit—0.17 mm (.007 in.)—replace the bearings. If the clearance exceeds the wear limit even with new bearings, the crankshaft must be replaced or reconditioned to accept bearings for one of the three undersize ranges.

Fig. 9-9. Main bearing cap numbers. Number **1** is at front of engine. All numbers must be toward the right (manifold) side of the engine.

7. Remove the flattened Plastigage strips. Then lift out the crankshaft.

CAUTION —

Use solvent to remove the flattened Plastigage. Scraping off the Plastigage could damage the main bearings.

8. Lightly coat the main bearing shells and the main bearing journals with assembly lubricant.

NOTE —

If assembly lubricant is not available from your automotive supply store, use a light coating of multipurpose grease instead.

9. Place the crankshaft in the engine block, install the bearing caps as shown earlier in Fig. 9-9, then torque the bolts to 6.5 mkg (47 ft. lb.).

10. Using feeler gauges of various thicknesses, determine the crankshaft's axial play. To do this, push the crankshaft as far as it will go toward the rear of the engine. Then insert the feeler gauge between the crank throw for the No. 2 cylinder and the front flange of the No. 3 main bearing, as shown in Fig. 9-10.

NOTE —

With new parts, axial play should be between 0.07 and 0.17 mm (.0025 and .0065 in.). If you can insert a 0.37-mm (.015-in.) feeler gauge between the bearing and the crank throw, the clearance is excessive. Excessive clearance can usually be corrected by replacing the No. 3 main bearing.

Fig. 9-10. Crankshaft axial play being measured.

11. Using new gaskets, install the crankshaft oil seal carriers. Install the flywheel and clutch. Install the pistons and connecting rods as described in **8.1 Removing, Checking, and Installing Pistons, Piston Rings, Connecting Rods, and Connecting Rod Bearings.** Then install the engine.

9.3 Removing and Installing Intermediate Shaft

The intermediate shaft and its bearings are subject to very little wear. Nevertheless, remove the shaft during engine rebuilding so that abrasive particles and other foreign matter can be thoroughly cleaned off the bearings and out of the oil passages.

To remove the intermediate shaft, first remove the engine as described in **6. Removing and Installing Engine.** Then remove the oil pan and the vacuum pump. This is done by taking out the hold-down bolt, the hold-down, and then the vacuum pump. See **5.2 Removing, Checking, and Installing Oil Pump,** and **BRAKES AND WHEELS.**

Remove the camshaft drive belt as described in **4.1 Removing, Installing, and Adjusting Camshaft Drive Belt.**

Remove the two bolts, then remove the intermediate oil seal carrier and the intermediate shaft—being careful not to damage the bearings with the oil pump driving gear on the intermediate shaft.

Installation is the reverse of removal. If the oil seal is cracked or worn, replace it as described in **9.1 Replacing Crankshaft and Intermediate Shaft Oil Seals.** If the bearings are worn so that their copper backing shows through the silvery bearing surfaces, drive out the old bearings. Then, being careful to align the oil holes in the new bearings with the oil holes in the engine block, drive in first the bearing at the flywheel end and then the bearing at the drive belt end. You must use a bearing driver that accurately fits the inside of the bearings and the oil holes must align with the bearings installed.

Coat the bearings with assembly lubricant or multipurpose grease before you install the shaft. Also apply assembly lubricant or multipurpose grease to the oil pump driving gear. Torque the two bolts for the intermediate shaft oil seal carrier to 2.0 mkg (14 ft. lb.). Torque the hold-down bolt for the vacuum pump to 1.5 mkg (11 ft. lb.).

10. DIESEL ENGINE FUEL INJECTION

If the injection pump itself is faulty, it should be replaced. Repairs are not possible without the special test equipment that is available in the pump manufacturer's service facility or in a qualified and properly equipped diesel fuel injection shop. Replacement parts for the pump are not available from Volkswagen.

The injectors can be disassembled, and some parts are available for repairs. However, when working on any part of the injection system, everything must be kept absolutely clean. Wipe clean all pipe unions before you loosen them. Do not use soft, fluffy cloth to dry the injector components, as pieces of lint can partially clog the injectors or cause internal parts to bind.

10.1 Adjusting Idle and Maximum RPM

Because the diesel engine has no ignition system, a special adaptor is necessary before you can check the rpm with a dwell meter/tachometer. These adaptors, US 1324 and VW 1324, are connected to the injection pump so that fuel pressure pulsations are converted into electrical signals. A Bosch EFAW 166C, Sun TDT-12, or similar dwell meter/tachometer can then be attached to the adapter as shown in Fig. 10-1. The correct hook-up is printed on the side of the adaptor itself.

Fig. 10-1. Dwell meter/tachometer connected to diesel rpm adaptor (Rabbit engine shown).

Checking and Adjusting Idle Speed

Warm the engine up to its normal operating temperature, which is indicated by an oil temperature of 50° to 70°C (122° to 158°F). If the idle speed is not between 770 and 870 rpm, loosen the locknut indicated in Fig. 10-2. Then turn the adjusting screw one way or the other until the idle speed is in the correct range. After tightening the locknut, lock it in place with nut-locking sealer.

Fig. 10-2. Locknut (arrow) for idle speed adjusting screw.

11

Checking and Adjusting Maximum RPM

Warm the engine up to its normal operating temperature, which is indicated by an oil temperature of 50° to 70°C (122° to 158°F). With the transmission in neutral and the car stationary, move the lever on the pump until the engine is operating at its maximum speed without load. If the maximum speed is not between 5500 and 5600 rpm, loosen the locknut indicated in Fig. 10-3. Then turn the adjusting screw one way or the other until the maximum rpm is in the correct range. After tightening the locknut, lock it in place with nut-locking sealer.

CAUTION ——

To avoid engine damage, you should at no time allow the engine speed to exceed 5600 rpm.

Fig. 10-3. Locknut (arrow) for maximum rpm adjusting screw.

10.2 Adjusting Cables

Correct operation of the fuel injection system depends on accurate adjustment of the cables. In addition to the accelerator cable, there is the cold starting cable, which is attached to the side of the injection pump that is closest to the engine.

Adjusting Accelerator Cable

If the accelerator cable is not correctly adjusted, it can reduce engine power or place a strain on the cable that may eventually cause the cable to break. New cables bend easily in one direction, and should always be installed in a position that will take advantage of this.

To adjust:

1. If you are installing a new pump, position the ball pin of the governor lever upward and in contact with the end of the elongated hole, as indicated in Fig. 10-4.

2. If you are installing a new cable, loosely install the cable conduit at the upper hole in the bracket.

Fig. 10-4. Ball pin (arrow) end of elongated hole.

3. If necessary, attach the cable end to the ball pin, then install the securing clip.

4. With the engine turned off, have someone hold the accelerator pedal all the way down. By turning the nuts indicated in Fig. 10-5, adjust the cable position until the governor lever just contacts the maximum rpm adjusting screw with no strain on the cable.

5. When the adjustment is correct, tighten the locknuts against the bracket—without overtightening them. Then have your helper release and depress the accelerator pedal several times while you check the cable operation.

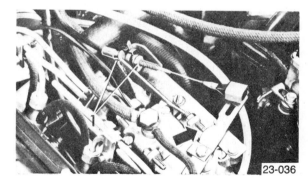

Fig. 10-5. Nuts (**1**) used in making accelerator cable adjustments. Maximum rpm adjusting screw is indicated by arrow.

Adjusting Cold Starting Cable

When the cold starting knob on the dashboard is pulled out, the fuel injection pump's timing is advanced by 2.5°. This earlier introduction of vaporized fuel into the pre-chamber improves starting response.

To adjust cable:

1. If the injection pump or the cable is being installed, insert the washer indicated in Fig. 10-6 onto the cable conduit. Then install the cable conduit in the bracket with the rubber bushing.

2. To attach the cable to the lever, insert the cable into the pivot pin of the lever. Install the locking washer for the conduit. See Fig. 10-6.

3. To adjust, move the lever as far as possible in the direction indicated by the arrow in Fig. 10-6. While holding the lever in this position, pull the cable tight, then secure it in the pivot pin by tightening the pivot pin's clamping screw.

Fig. 10-6. Cold starting cable installation. Washer is at **1**, locking washer for conduit at **2**, and pivot pin at **3**. Arrow indicates "off" position of lever.

11

10.3 Diesel Fuel Injection Troubleshooting

Because the diesel engine's operation and efficiency are highly dependent on cylinder compression, many operating problems that seem to be injection troubles can also be caused by engine mechanical faults. Valves that are badly out of adjustment, valves that are leaking, and a leaking cylinder head gasket are three mechanical faults that can cause poor running, hard starting, or inefficient operation. Worn cylinders or pistons, worn-out or stuck piston rings, and broken pistons can cause similar troubles. Lubricating oil that finds its way past worn piston rings or worn valve stem seals sometimes produces exhaust smoke that is mistaken for the smoke caused by a misadjusted fuel injection system.

It is therefore wise to make certain routine checks of the fuel injection system when operating problems are encountered, but a compression test is an indispensable part of diesel troubleshooting. **Table g** lists six possible problems along with their probable causes and applicable remedies. Check each item in the order that it appears in the table. The numbers in the Remedy column refer to headings in this section of the Manual where the suggested tests and repairs are described.

Table g. Diesel Engine Fuel Injection Troubleshooting

Problem	Probable cause	Remedy
1. Engine does not start	a. Cranking speed too low.	a. Repair starting system or charge or replace battery so that engine cranks at a minimum of 150 rpm. See **ELECTRICAL SYSTEM**.
	b. No voltage at stop solenoid on injection pump	b. Check for voltage with test light. If necessary, replace fuse No. 9 or faulty wires. See **ELECTRICAL SYSTEM**.
	c. Stop solenoid on injection pump loose or faulty	c. Tighten solenoid. Check that solenoid clicks when key is turned off and on. Replace faulty solenoids.
	d. No voltage at glow plug bus	d. If test light shows no voltage at bus with key at "pre-glow" position, test relay and wiring. See **10.8**.
	e. Glow plugs faulty	e. Test and, if necessary, replace glow plugs. See **10.9**.
	f. Air in fuel system	f. Bleed fuel system. See **10.6**.
	g. Injection pump not delivering fuel	g. If no fuel emerges from a loosened injector line during cranking, check camshaft drive belt and fuel supply from filter. See **4.1**.
	h. Injector lines misconnected	h. Connect lines in correct locations. See **10.4**.
	i. Injection timing incorrect	i. Adjust injection timing. See **10.5**.
	j. Faulty injectors	j. Check and, if necessary, repair or replace injectors. See **10.7**.
	k. Engine mechanical faults, as described earlier under this heading	k. Test compression as described in **LUBRICATION AND MAINTENANCE**; if necessary, repair engine. See **4** through **9**.
	l. Faulty injection pump	l. Try to start engine with new pump installed. If necessary, replace pump permanently. See **10.4**.
2. Glow plug warning light not working	Bulb burned out or trouble in glow plug relay circuit	Test and repair as described in **10.8**.
3. Idle speed incorrect or idle rough or irregular	a. Idle speed incorrectly adjusted	a. Check and, if necessary, adjust the idle speed. See **10.1**.
	b. Accelerator control binding	b. Check that governor lever on pump is not loose, then adjust accelerator cable. See **10.2**.
	c. Loose fuel hose between filter and injection pump	c. Replace hose or secure with clamps; bleed air from system. See **10.6**.
	d. Injection pump bracket (rear mounting) cracked or broken	d. Check and, if necessary, replace bracket. See **10.4**.
	e. Air in fuel system	e. Bleed fuel system. See **10.6**.
	f. Inadequate fuel supply owing to clogged fuel filter, or fuel return line and injection pipes leaking, dirty, kinked, or squeezed at connections	f. Inspect and, if necessary, replace lines and hoses; replace fuel filter. See **10.6**.
	g. Faulty injectors	g. Check and, if necessary, repair or replace injectors. See **10.7**.
	h. Injection timing incorrect	h. Adjust injection timing. See **10.5**.
	i. Engine mechanical faults, as described earlier under this heading	i. Test compression as described in **LUBRICATION AND MAINTENANCE**; if necessary, repair engine. See **4** through **9**.
	j. Faulty injection pump	j. Try engine at idle with new pump installed. If necessary, replace pump permanently. See **10.4**.

Table g. Diesel Engine Fuel Injection Troubleshooting (continued)

Problem	Probable cause	Remedy
4. Smoky exhaust (black, blue, or white)	a. Engine lugging in too high a gear b. Engine not reaching correct operating temperature c. Maximum rpm incorrectly adjusted d. Faulty injectors e. Injection timing incorrect f. Restricted exhaust system g. Engine mechanical faults, as described earlier under this heading h. Faulty injection pump	a. Observe correct shift speeds as given in Owner's Manual. b. Check and, if necessary, replace cooling system thermostat. See **ENGINE AND CLUTCH**. c. Check and, if necessary, adjust maximum rpm. See **10.1**. d. Check and, if necessary, repair or replace injectors. See **10.7**. e. Adjust injection timing. See **10.5**. f. Check exhaust system for dents and obstructions. See **FUEL AND EXHAUST SYSTEMS**. g. Test compression as described in **LUBRICATION AND MAINTENANCE**; if necessary, repair engine. See **4** through **9**. h. Observe exhaust with new pump installed. If necessary, replace pump permanently. See **10.4**.
5. Poor power output, slow acceleration or top speed (speedometer accurate, clutch not slipping)	a. Injection pump governor lever loose or not reaching maximum rpm adjusting screw b. Maximum rpm incorrectly adjusted c. Air filter dirty d. Inadequate fuel supply owing to clogged filter; or fuel return line and injection pipes leaking, dirty, kinked, or squeezed at connections e. Air in fuel system f. Ice or solidified wax in fuel lines (wintertime only) g. Faulty injectors h. Injection timing incorrect i. Engine mechanical faults, as described earlier under this heading j. Faulty injection pump	a. Tighten lever, check that accelerator pedal travel is not restricted, then adjust accelerator cable. See **10.2**. b. Check and, if necessary, adjust maximum rpm. See **10.1**. c. Clean or replace air filter. See **LUBRICATION AND MAINTENANCE**. d. Inspect and, if necessary, replace lines and hoses; replace fuel filter. See **10.6**. e. Bleed fuel system. See **10.6**. f. Move car to warm garage until ice or wax has become liquid, then bleed fuel system. See **10.6**. g. Check and, if necessary, repair or replace injectors. See **10.7**. h. Adjust injection timing. See **10.5**. i. Test compression as described in **LUBRICATION AND MAINTENANCE**, if necessary, repair engine. See **4** through **9**. j. Check acceleration and speed with new pump installed. If necessary, replace pump permanently. See **10.4**.
6. Excessive fuel consumption (markedly below 44 mpg in mixed traffic at temperatures above 0°C (32°F))	a. Air filter dirty b. Fuel leaks c. Return pipe blocked d. Idle speed too fast or maximum rpm too high e. Faulty injectors f. Injection timing incorrect g. Engine mechanical faults, as described earlier under this heading h. Faulty injection pump	a. Clean or replace air filter. See **LUBRICATION AND MAINTENANCE**. b. Check and, if necessary, replace or tighten all pipes, hoses and connections. c. Check return line for kinks and dents; replace faulty lines. If line is clogged, blow it out with compressed air, then bleed fuel system. See **10.6**. d. Check and, if necessary, adjust idle speed and maximum rpm. See **10.1**. e. Check and, if necessary, repair or replace injectors. See **10.7**. f. Adjust injection timing. See **10.5**. g. Test compression as described in **LUBRICATION AND MAINTENANCE**; if necessary, repair engine. See **4** through **9**. h. Check fuel consumption with new pump installed. If necessary, replace pump permanently. See **10.4**.

11

10.4 Removing and Installing Injection Pump

The injection pump cannot be serviced or repaired except by its manufacturer, or by a shop that has the correct test equipment and factory specifications on hand. Therefore, faulty pumps should be replaced so that the car can be returned to service immediately.

To remove pump:

1. Remove the camshaft drive belt as described in **4.1 Removing, Installing, and Adjusting Camshaft Drive Belt.**

2. Loosen the nut that holds the pump sprocket to the pump shaft, but for the moment do not fully remove the nut.

3. Using a puller (Fig. 10-7), carefully apply tension to the sprocket. Lightly tap the puller bolt, as indicated by the arrow, until the sprocket comes loose from the tapered pump shaft. Then remove the puller, the nut, the washer, and the sprocket.

Fig. 10-7. Injection pump sprocket being loosened. Notice spacer between nut and center screw of puller. This is to prevent damage to threads on pump shaft.

4. Disconnect the battery ground strap.

5. Detach all fuel pipes and hoses from the injection pump. Cover the unions with a clean, lint-free cloth.

> **WARNING** ——
>
> *Fuel will be expelled when you loosen the unions. Do not smoke or work near heaters or other fire hazards. Have a fire extinguisher handy.*

6. Disconnect the electrical wire from the stop solenoid. Disconnect the accelerator cable and the cold starting cable from the pump levers.

7. Remove the bolts from the injection pump mounting plate and support, then remove the pump.

To install:

1. Loosely install the injection pump on the pump mounting plate and support. Align the marks indicated in Fig. 10-8, then torque the mounting bolts to 2.5 mkg (18 ft. lb.).

Fig. 10-8. Mark on pump aligned with mark on mounting plate (broken line). Fuel supply union bolt is at **A**.

2. Reconnect the fuel pipes and hoses. Torque the fuel pipe connections to 2.5 mkg (18 ft. lb.).

> **NOTE** ——
>
> The injector line connections on the pump are marked **A, B, C, D**. Connect No. 1 cylinder to **A**, No. 3 to **B**, No. 4 to **C**, and No. 2 to **D**. In reconnecting the fuel hoses, be careful not to interchange the fuel supply union bolt, indicated previously in Fig. 10-8, with the return line union bolt, which is marked **OUT** on its head and contains a restrictor.

3. Reconnect the electrical wire to the stop solenoid. Reconnect the cold starting cable and the accelerator cable, adjusting each one as described in **10.2 Adjusting Cables.**

4. Install the sprocket. Torque the nut to 4.5 mkg (32 ft. lb.).

5. Make sure that the crankshaft is still at the TDC position for the No. 1 cylinder. Hand-turn the pump sprocket until the mark on the sprocket is aligned with the mark on the mounting plate, as indicated in Fig. 10-9. Then lock the sprocket in position with special pin 2064.

Fig. 10-9. Mark on pump sprocket aligned with mark on mounting plate (black arrow). White arrow shows installation of pin 2064, used during installation of the camshaft drive belt.

6. Install the camshaft drive belt as described in **4.1 Removing, Installing, and Adjusting Camshaft Drive Belt.** Then adjust the injection timing as described in **10.5 Adjusting Injection Timing.**

Correcting Leaks at Injection Pump

Leaks at the fuel unions or the timing check plug (Fig. 10-10) should be corrected immediately to avoid having diesel fuel be wasted or spray onto the radiator hose. Diesel fuel is damaging to rubber and should be thoroughly cleaned off the hose after the leaks have been corrected.

Fig. 10-10. Fuel unions (small arrows) and timing check plug (large arrow) on injection pump. Radiator hose and pipes to injectors have been removed from engine in illustration.

To correct leaks:

1. Thoroughly clean the fuel pipes, the unions, and the pump head. If the timing check plug is leaking, remove the plug and inspect the sealing washer. Replace the sealing washer if it is faulty, then reinstall the plug.

2. If there are leaks at the unions, detach the fuel pipes from the unions. Then torque the unions, shown previously in Fig. 10-10, to 4.5 mkg (32 ft. lb.).

3. Reinstall the fuel pipes, torquing the connections (union nuts) to 2.5 mkg (18 ft. lb.).

4. Operate the starter in order to determine whether the leaks have been stopped. If there is still leakage, install new union seals on the pipe connections. If this does not stop the leakage, replace the union or unions. See Fig. 10-11.

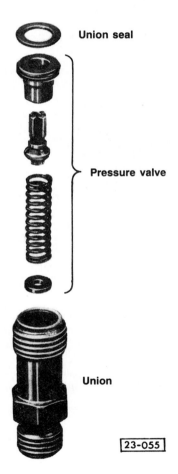

Fig. 10-11. Exploded view of injection pump union, showing union seal and internal parts. Union seal is Part No. 068 130 787; union itself is Part No. 068 130 795.

11

10.5 Adjusting Injection Timing

The injection timing should be adjusted after you have installed the pump or whenever a troubleshooting check shows adjustment to be necessary. The check is carried out with the dial indicator tool, as shown in the following procedure.

To adjust:

1. Hand-turn the crankshaft until the piston for the No.1 cylinder is at TDC on its compression stroke (both valves closed) and the TDC mark on the flywheel is aligned with the pointer as shown in either Fig. 10-12 or Fig. 10-13.

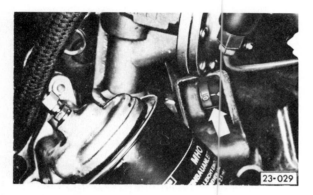

Fig. 10-12. TDC mark on flywheel aligned with pointer in hole in bellhousing (engine installed).

Fig. 10-13. TDC mark on flywheel aligned with special setting bar (engine removed).

2. Remove the timing-check plug from the pump cover, then install a dial indicator with a 3-mm range, as shown in Fig. 10-14. The gauge should be screwed in until it indicates about 2.5 mm with the pump in its No. 1 position.

Fig. 10-14. Dial indicator installed on injection pump.

3. Hand-turn the crankshaft in the direction opposite to normal rotation until the dial indicator stops moving and holds a steady reading. Then readjust the dial indicator so that you can zero it with a 1-mm preload.

4. Hand-turn the crankshaft in its direction of normal rotation back to the TDC point. With the flywheel mark at TDC, the dial indicator should read 0.83 mm. If not, loosen the pump mounting bolts on the mounting plate. Then set the lift to 0.83 mm by turning the pump clockwise or counterclockwise on the mounting plate. Torque the bolts to 2.5 mkg (18 ft. lb.).

NOTE——

If the correct lift cannot be obtained with the flywheel at TDC, the engine's valve timing and injection pump timing are probably incorrect. Check the valve timing/injection pump timing by seeing that the camshaft drive belt is correctly and accurately installed. See **4.1 Removing, Installing, and Adjusting Camshaft Drive Belt.**

10.6 Bleeding Fuel System

When the Volkswagen diesel engine was first introduced in Rabbit models, it was thought that it might be necessary to bleed air from the fuel system after the fuel tank had been allowed to run dry or after fuel system repairs. In practice, bleeding has not proved to be necessary. However, the procedure is given here in the event that bleeding seems advisable on your Dasher diesel owing to unusual circumstances.

It is not necessary to bleed the system after repairs to the injection pump, the injector pipes, or the injectors. However, if the engine will not start you can avoid a long cranking period by loosening the unions on two injectors and then cranking the engine (without using the glow plugs) until fuel appears at the unions. With the unions tightened, the engine can be started.

Though the fuel filters of early-production Rabbit diesels have a priming pump that was to be used in bleeding the fuel system, later Rabbits and all Dasher diesels have a fuel filter assembly that does not include a priming pump. These cars are able to have their fuel systems bled by the procedure given here.

To bleed fuel system:

1. Loosen the fuel line connections at all four injectors.

2. Without using the glow plugs, operate the starter. Continue to crank the engine until fuel emerges from the loosened fuel line connections, then tighten the connections, torquing the unions to 2.5 mkg (18 ft. lb.).

3. Using the glow plugs, start the engine and allow it to run until you are sure that no air remains in the system that could possibly cause stalling.

Draining Water

You should drain the fuel filter between filter changes, whether the fuel is contaminated or not. For example, the filter should be drained at 7500 mi. (12,000 km) and each 15,000 mi. (24,000 km) thereafter, and it should be changed at 15,000 mi. (24,000 km) and at each 15,000 mi. (24,000 km) thereafter.

To drain water:

1. Loosen the vent screw (Fig. 10-15) or, if the filter has no vent screw, disconnect the fuel return hose, which is indicated in Fig. 10-16.

Fig. 10-15. Vent screw (arrow **A**) on filter. Arrow **B** indicates water drain plug, which is found on all filter assemblies whether there is a vent screw or not.

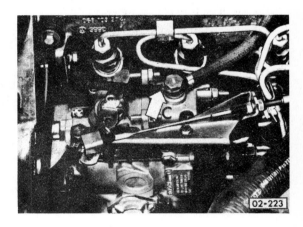

Fig. 10-16. Return line (arrow **C**) that must be removed to vent filter on cars that have filter assemblies with no vent screws (Rabbit engine shown).

11

2. Open the water drain plug (Fig. 10-17) and let fluid run until clean fuel appears. Alternatively, drain out about 100 cm³ of fuel. Then close the water drain plug.

Fig. 10-17. Fluid being drained from filter. Water drain plug is at **B** (Rabbit engine shown).

3. Close the vent screw or reconnect the fuel return hose. Then start the engine and accelerate it a few times to clear the fuel lines of air bubbles.

Replacing Fuel Filter

To replace the fuel filter, loosen it as indicated in Fig. 10-18 and then unscrew it by hand. Alternatively, you can first dismount the filter assembly from the car body and unscrew the filter from the filter flange with an open-end wrench applied to the hexagon into which the water drain plug is screwed. Discard the old filter, then lightly lubricate the seal for the new filter with diesel fuel. Install the new filter using your hand only. If necessary, remount the filter assembly on the car body.

WARNING ——
Fuel will leak out as you remove the filter. Do not smoke or work near heaters or other fire hazards. Have a fire extinguisher handy.

Fig. 10-18. Band-type filter wrench being used to loosen fuel filter (Rabbit engine shown).

10.7 Testing and Repairing Injectors

To remove an injector, first detach the fuel pipe and then unscrew the injector from the cylinder head. Be sure to remove the heat shield from the bottom of the hole and always use a new heat shield during injector installation. (The recess in the heat shield must be upward, towards the injector.) Torque the injector to 7.0 mkg (50 ft. lb.). Bleeding is not necessary.

Injector Troubleshooting

The first signs of injector trouble usually appear as (1) knocking noises from the injectors of one or more cylinders, (2) engine overheating, (3) loss of power, (4) smoky black exhaust, or (5) increased fuel consumption. A faulty injector can be located by loosening the fuel pipe union of each injector in turn with the engine running at a fast idle. If the engine speed remains unchanged after loosening a particular pipe union, the injector for that cylinder is faulty.

WARNING ——

Fuel will be expelled. Do not smoke or work near heaters or other fire hazards. Have a fire extinguisher handy.

Testing Injectors

The injectors can be tested with a special pressure pump. The removed injector can be tested for leakage, spray pattern, noise, and correct breaking pressure. Attach the injector to the test pump as shown in Fig. 10-19.

WARNING ——

When testing the injectors, do not expose your hands or any other parts of your body to the injector spray. Working pressure can cause the fuel oil to penetrate the skin. Do not smoke or work near heaters or other fire hazards. Have a fire extinguisher handy.

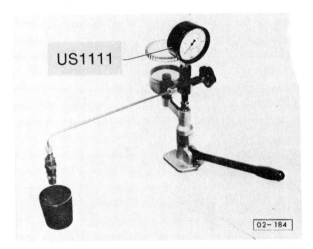

US1111

02-184

Fig. 10-19. Injector installed on special pressure pump. Cup beneath injector catches spray.

Spray Testing

Isolate the gauge from the pressure pump's output. With rapid short strokes of the testing pump lever (4 to 6 strokes per second), the injection sprays should be even and stop cleanly. The injectors must not drip. Repair or replace faulty injectors.

Noise Testing

Isolate the gauge from the pressure pump's output. With long slow strokes of the testing pump lever (1 to 2 strokes per second), the injector is working correctly if it makes a "pinging" sound as fuel emerges. It should not make a heavy "click" or "clack." Replace noisy injectors.

Breaking Pressure Testing

With the gauge working, move the pump lever slowly downward. Observe the pressure at which the injector begins to work, which should be between 120 and 130 ATU (1706 and 1849 psi). If necessary, adjust the pressure by changing the shims, as described under **Repairing Injectors.** A thicker shim will increase the breaking pressure and a thinner shim will reduce it. An increase in shim thickness of 0.05 mm increases the pressure by about 5.0 ATU (71 psi). Shims are available in thicknesses from 1.00 mm to 1.95 mm in 0.05-mm increments.

Leakage Testing

With the gauge working, slowly press down the pump lever and hold it in a position that will maintain a pressure of about 110 ATU (1564 psi) for a period of 10 seconds. During that time, no fuel should leak from the injector nozzle tip.

11

Repairing Injectors

The injectors can be disassembled for cleaning, repair, and adjustment. Clamp the upper part of the injector in a vise as shown in Fig. 10-20. Then loosen—but do not remove—the lower part. Turn the injector over and clamp the lower part in a vise. You can then unscrew the top without the internal parts falling out.

CAUTION ——

If you disassemble more than one injector at a time, keep the parts separate. Interchanging parts from one injector to the other can result in faulty operation or make necessary a lengthy testing and adjustment procedure.

Fig. 10-20. Injector clamped in vise so that lower part can be loosened.

Fig. 10-21 shows the various parts of an injector. The heat shield must always be replaced when you reinstall an injector in the engine. Some replacement parts are available, and the shim determines the injector's breaking pressure (the pressure at which it begins to spray fuel). You can test and adjust the breaking pressure and select new shims using the procedure described earlier under **Breaking Pressure Testing.** During assembly of the injector—which must be done under absolutely clean conditions—torque the upper and lower parts to 7.0 mkg (50 ft. lb.).

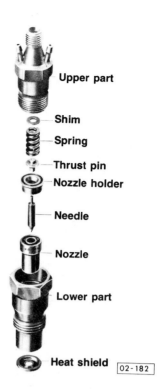

Fig. 10-21. Exploded view of an injector.

10.8 Testing Glow Plug Relay and Warning Light

The glow plug relay is located near the rear end of the cylinder head and receives wires from the glow plug bus, the engine temperature sensor, and the coolant temperature sending unit.

NOTE ——

The following procedure was written for the VW Rabbit diesel, and may not be fully applicable to the Dasher diesel. It is given here because no equivalent procedure or wiring diagram has been issued by the factory.

To test relay:

1. Remove the glow plug relay from its sockets. Test for voltage at terminal 30 of the glow plug relay socket plate (Fig. 10-22). Battery voltage should reach this terminal at all times, regardless of whether the key is on or off. If there is no voltage, either the wire leading to terminal H of the fuse box relay plate is faulty or the fuse box relay plate is faulty.

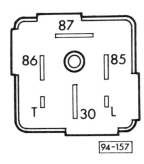

Fig. 10-22. Terminal locations on glow plug relay.

2. If there is voltage at terminal 30, connect the voltmeter or test light to terminal 86 of the glow plug relay socket plate. Voltage should be present with the key turned to the "pre-glow" position. If there is no voltage, check that fuse No. 6 is not blown.

3. If fuse No. 6 is not blown, test the wire that connects terminal 86 with terminal D20 of the fuse box relay plate. If the wire is not faulty, either the fuse box relay plate is faulty or the starting key switch is faulty.

4. If there is voltage reaching terminal 86, test between terminals 30 and 85 (terminal 85 is the ground terminal for the relay). If there is no voltage, the wire that connects terminal 85 to ground is faulty.

5. If voltage is reaching the terminals as it should, but the relay is not sending voltage to the glow plug bus from relay terminal 87, then the relay is faulty and should be replaced.

To test warning light:

1. Remove the glow plug relay from its sockets. Using a jumper wire, connect terminal L of the relay socket plate to ground. If the glow plug warning light does not come on when the key is turned to its "pre-glow" position, the warning light bulb is faulty and should be replaced.

2. If the warning light comes on during the preceding test, check the relay. To do this, disconnect the wire from the engine's coolant temperature sensor. With the key in the "pre-glow" position, allow the warning light to come on for 60 to 80 seconds. The light should go out when you ground the disconnected wire to a clean, unpainted metal part of the engine.

3. If the light functions correctly in the preceding test, the coolant temperature sensor is faulty and should be replaced. If the light does not function as it should in the preceding test, the glow plug relay is faulty and should be replaced.

10.9 Testing and Replacing Glow Plugs

To test whether voltage is reaching the glow plugs, apply a test light to the No. 4 cylinder's glow plug and to ground as indicated in Fig. 10-23. The test light should come on with the key in the "pre-glow" position. If the test light does not come on, test the relay as described in **10.8 Testing Glow Plug Relay and Warning Light.**

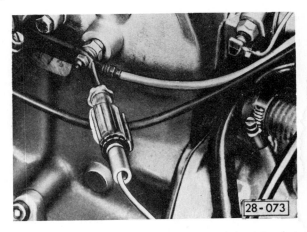

Fig. 10-23. Test light being used to check for voltage at glow plug bus.

If voltage is reaching the glow plug bus, but the engine has starting problems that indicate trouble with the glow plugs, disconnect the wire from the bus and then remove the bus from the glow plug terminals. Connect one lead from the test light to the battery's positive post. Then touch the other test light lead to each of the glow plug terminals, as indicated in Fig. 10-24. If the test light fails to come on when it is touched to the terminal of any glow plug, that glow plug is faulty and should be replaced.

Replacing a glow plug is similar to replacing a spark plug on a spark-ignition engine. Thoroughly clean out the glow plug hole and sealing seat in the cylinder head before you install the new glow plug.

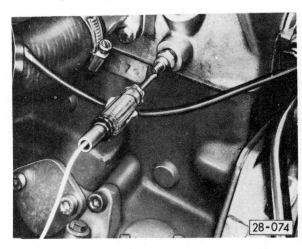

11

Fig. 10-24. Glow plug being tested for continuity.

11. DIESEL ENGINE TECHNICAL DATA

I. General Engine Data

Engine code letter	CK
Number of cylinders	4
Cylinder layout	Inline
Valve operation	Belt-driven single overhead camshaft
Cylinder bore	76.50 mm (3.012 in.)
Piston stroke	80.00 mm (3.150 in.)
Compression ratio	23.5:1
Fuel requirement	Diesel fuel
Horsepower	50 DIN (37 kw) @ 5000 rpm
	48 SAE net @ 5000 rpm
Torque	7.8 mkg DIN @ 3000 rpm
	56.5 ft. lb. SAE @ 3000 rpm

II. Basic Tune-up Specifications

Coolant capacity	5.9 U.S. quarts (5.0 Imperial quarts, 5.6 liters)
Oil capacity	With filter change: 3.7 U.S. quarts (3.2 Imperial quarts, 3.5 liters)
	Without filter change: 3.2 U.S. quarts (2.7 Imperial quarts, 3.0 liters)
Firing order	1–3–4–2
Cylinder location	No. 1 at camshaft drive end of engine, cylinders numbered consecutively from front to rear
Valve clearance	Intake (cold): 0.15–0.25 mm (.006–.010 in.)
	Intake (hot): 0.20–0.30 mm (.008–.012 in.)
	Exhaust (cold): 0.35–0.45 mm (.014–.018 in.)
	Exhaust (hot): 0.40–0.50 mm (.016–.020 in.)
Compression pressure	483 psi (34 atu)
	Wear limit: 398 psi (28 atu)—or a cylinder-to-cylinder difference exceeding 71 psi (5 atu)
Electrical system	12-volt, negative ground
Injection pump timing	0.83 mm (.032 in.) of lift at TDC. See **10.5 Adjusting Injection Timing**
Idle speed	770 to 870 rpm
Maximum rpm (no load)	5600 rpm

III. Tolerances, Wear Limits, and Settings

Designation	New parts on installation mm (in.)	Wear limit mm (in.)
A. Crankshaft		
1. Journal dimensions		
a. Main journals .... grade 1, diameter	54.00–0.04 (2.126–.0015)	—
.... grade 2, diameter	54.00–0.06 (2.126–.002)	—
b. Connecting rod journals .... grade 1, diameter	46.00–0.04 (1.811–.0015)	—
.... grade 2, diameter	46.00–0.06 (1.811–.002)	—
c. Three undersizes of 0.25 mm (.010 in.) each	—	—
2. Main journals .... out-of-round	—	0.03 (.0012)
3. Connecting rod journals .... out-of-round	—	0.03 (.0012)
4. Main bearing/main journal .... clearance	0.03–0.08 (.0012–.003)	0.17 (.007)
5. Connecting rod bearing/rod journal .... clearance	0.028–0.088 (.0011–.0035)	0.12 (.0047)
6. Crankshaft/main bearing No. 3 .... axial play	0.07–0.17 (.0025–.0065)	0.37 (.014)
B. Connecting rods		
a. Piston pin/connecting rod bushing .... clearance	0.01–0.02 (.0004–.0008)	0.25 (.010)
b. Connecting rod/crankshaft .... side clearance	—	0.37 (.014)
C. Pistons and Cylinder		
1. Piston and cylinder sizes		
a. Pistons .... grade 1, diameter	76.48 (3.0110)	—
.... grade 2, diameter	76.49 (3.0114)	—
.... grade 3, diameter	76.50 (3.0118)	—
Three oversizes of 0.25 mm (.010 in.) each		
b. Cylinders .... grade 1, diameter	76.51 (3.0122)	76.55 (3.0138)
.... grade 2, diameter	76.52 (3.0126)	76.56 (3.0141)
.... grade 3, diameter	76.53 (3.0130)	76.57 (3.0146)
Three oversizes of 0.25 mm (.010 in.) each	—	—
2. Cylinders .... maximum taper or out-of-round	—	0.04 (.0015)
3. Piston/cylinder .... clearance	0.03 (.001)	0.07 (.0025)
4. Piston ring/piston .... side clearance	0.02–0.05 (.0008–.002)	—
5. Ring gap (with ring installed in cylinder)		
a. Compression rings .... end gap	0.30–0.45 (.012–.017)	1.00 (.039)
b. Oil scraper rings .... end gap	0.25–0.40 (.010–.016)	1.00 (.039)

III. Tolerances, Wear Limits, and Settings (continued)

Designation	New parts on installation mm (in.)	Wear limit mm (in.)
D. Camshaft, Valves, and Cylinder Head		
1. Camshaft .... axial play	—	0.15 (.006)
2. Camshaft (measured at center bearing, bearings 1 and 5 on V-blocks) .... runout	—	0.01 (.0004)
3. Camshaft/camshaft bearings .... clearance	0.02–0.05 (.0008–.002)	—
4. Valve spring tensions		
a. Outer: spring at loaded length of 22.3 mm (⅞ in.) .... load	43.5–48.0 kg (96–106 lb.)	—
b. Inner spring at loaded length of 18.3 mm (²³/₃₂ in.) .... load	21.0–23.0 kg (46–51 lb.)	—
5. Valve seats		
a. Contact area facing .... angle	45°	—
b. Intake .... width of 45° facing	2.00 (.079)	—
c. Intake .... outside diameter of 45° facing	32.80 (1.291)	—
d. Exhaust .... width of 45° facing	2.40 (.094)	—
e. Exhaust .... outside diameter of 45° facing	30.40 (1.196)	—
f. Seat width correction chamfer .... angle	15°	—
6. Valve guides		
a. Valve guide/intake valve stem .... rock	—	1.30 (.051)
b. Valve guide/exhaust valve stem .... rock	—	1.30 (.051)
c. Valve guide .... inside diameter	8.013–8.035 (.315–.316)	—
d. Tops of valve guides below cover gasket surface on cylinder head .... distance	56.00 ±0.50 (2.204 ±.020)	—
7. Valve stem		
a. Intake .... diameter	7.97 (.314)	—
b. Exhaust .... diameter	7.95 (.313)	—
c. Intake .... overall valve length	104.80 (4.126)	—
d. Exhaust .... overall valve length	104.60 (4.118)	—
8. Valve head		
a. Intake .... diameter	34.00 (1.338)	—
b. Exhaust .... diameter	31.00 (1.220)	—
c. Intake .... margin	—	0.50 (.020) min. Do not machine-grind
d. Exhaust .... margin	—	
9. Valve clearance		
a. Intake (cold) .... setting	0.15–0.25 (.006–.010)	—
b. Intake (hot—coolant temp. approx. 35°C (95°F)) .... setting	0.20–0.30 (.008–.012)	—
c. Exhaust (cold) .... setting	0.35–0.45 (.014–.018)	—
d. Exhaust (hot—coolant temp. approx. 35°C (95°F)) ...... setting	0.40–0.50 (.016–.020)	—
10. Cylinder head		
a. Cylinder head warp .... twist or arch	—	0.10 (.004)
b. Engine block deck warp .... twist or arch	—	0.10 (.004)
E. Cooling System		
1. Radiator cap .... relief pressure	0.88–1.02 ATU (13–15 psi)	—
2. Thermostat		
a. Begins opening .... temperature	80°C (176°F)	—
b. Fully open .... temperature	94°C (201°F)	—
3. Radiator fan thermo switch		
a. Fan goes on .... temperature	90°–95°C (194°–203°F) and above	—
b. Fan goes off .... temperature	85°–90°C (185°–194°F) and below	—
4. V-belt tension—deflection under thumb pressure at a point midway between the driven pulley and the crankshaft pulley	10–15 (⅜–⁹/₁₆)	—
F. Lubrication System		
1. Oil pressure		
a. Warning light goes out .... pressure	0.15–0.45 kg/cm² (2.1–6.4 psi)	—
b. Normal oil pressure @ 2000 rpm with SAE 10 W oil at 60°C (140°F) .... minimum	—	2.0 kg/cm² (28 psi)
2. Oil pump		
a. Oil pump gears .... backlash clearance	0.05–0.20 (.002–.008)	—
b. Oil pump gears .... axial play	—	0.15 (.006)
G. Flywheel and Clutch		
1. Clutch pressure plate .... inward taper of friction surface	—	0.30 (.012)
2. Clutch driven plate ..... runout at a diameter of 175 mm (6⅞ in.)	—	0.40 (.016)
3. Clutch freeplay measured at pedal .... distance	15 (⅝)	—

11

IV. Tightening Torques

Location	Designation	mkg	ft. lb.
Power brake vacuum pump hold-down to engine block	bolt	1.5	11
Temperature gauge sensor in heater hose connection	sensor	0.7	5 (60 in. lb.)
Hose connections to engine block and cylinder head	bolt	2.0	14
Thermostat housing to water pump	bolt	1.0	7
Alternator adjusting bracket to alternator and alternator mounting bracket	bolt/carriage bolt	2.5	18
Alternator to mounting bracket	bolt and nut	2.5	18
Alternator mounting bracket to engine block	bolt	2.0	14
Water pump front part to water pump housing	bolt	1.0	7
Camshaft drive belt tensioner	locknut	4.5	32
Camshaft drive belt cover to engine	bolt or nut	1.0	7
Camshaft drive belt sprocket to camshaft	bolt	4.5	32
Intermediate shaft pulley to intermediate shaft	bolt	4.5	32
Camshaft drive belt sprocket to crankshaft	bolt	8.0	58
Camshaft bearing caps to cylinder head	nut	2.0	14
Cylinder head to engine block (engine cold)	socket-head bolt	8.5	61
Cylinder head to engine block (engine hot)	socket-head bolt	9.5	68
Coolant drain plug in engine block	hex-head plug	3.5	25
Manifolds to cylinder head	nut or bolt	2.5	18
Exhaust pipe to exhaust manifold	nut	2.5	18
Cylinder head cover to cylinder head	bolt	1.0	7
V-belt pulleys to water pump hub or crankshaft sprocket	bolt	2.0	14
Oil filter mounting flange to engine block	socket-head bolt	2.0	14
Oil pressure warning light switch in cylinder head	sensor	1.2	8.5
Oil pickup tube to oil pump housing	M 6 bolt	1.0	7
Oil pump to engine block	M 8 bolt	2.0	14
Oil pan to engine block (retorque after waiting 5 minutes)	special M 6 bolt	2.0	14
Oil drain plug in oil pan	hex-head plug	3.0	22
Engine/transaxle side and rear mountings	bolt or nut	4.0	29
Engine front mounting to body	bolt	2.5	18
Flywheel cover plate to bellhousing	bolt	1.5	11
Engine to transaxle bellhousing	nut	5.5	40
Flywheel to crankshaft (use Loctite® 270 or 271)	bolt	7.5	54
Clutch pressure plate assembly to flywheel	bolt	2.5	18
Connecting rod cap to connecting rod	nut	4.5	32
Crankshaft and intermediate shaft oil seal carriers to engine block	bolt	2.0	14
Main bearing cap to engine block	bolt	6.5	47
Fuel injection pump to mounting plate and support	bolt	2.5	18
Fuel pipe connections to injection pump unions	union nut	2.5	18
Unions in injection pump head	—	4.5	32
Camshaft drive belt sprocket to injection pump	nut	4.5	32
Fuel pipe connections to injectors	union	2.5	18
Injectorrtor in cylinder head (always install with a new heat shield)	injector	7.0	50
Injector upper part to injector lower part	—	7.0	50